The San Juan Islands
Bold numbers indicate chapters from East to West
N
E
Steveston Jetty
Fraser River
VANCOUVER
Nicomekl River
BRITISH
Canoe Passage
Roberts Bank
Mud Bay
Crescent Beach
BOUNDARY BAY
Tsawassen
WHITE RO
CANADA U.S.A.
Pt. Roberts
Seiahmoo Bay
Drayton Harbor
STRAIT OF GEORGIA
Birch Bay
Galiano Island
Active Pass
Mayne I.
Saturna Island
North Pender I.
Plumper Sound
South Pender I.
Bedwell Hbr
Swanson Channel
Patos I.
Sucia I.
Shoal Bay
Echo Bay
Fossil Bay
Matia I.
Lummi Bay
Squalicum Hbr
BELLINGHAM
Hale Passage
Bellingham Bay
Fairhaven
SOUTH BELLINGHAM
Portland I.
Moresby I.
Boundary Pass
Prevost Passage
North Beach
Barnes I.
Clark I.
Portage I.
Waldron I.
EASTSOUND
Lummi I.
Coal I.
Prevost Hbr
Cowlitz Bay
Mt. Constitution
Chuckanut Bay
Pleasant Bay
Domville I.
Stuart I.
Johns Pass
Reid Hbr
President Channel
Orcas
Island
East Sound
Inati Bay
Eliza I.
Gooch I.
Flattop I.
STRAIT
Spieden I.
Cascade Bay
Rosario Resort
Doe I.
DEER HARBOR
WEST SOUND
Spring Passage
Vendovi I.
5
Spieden Channel
Roche Hbr
Jones I.
Deer Hbr
Guthrie Bay
Doe Bay
Sinclair I.
Pelican Beach
Samish Bay
Sidney Channel
HARO
Henry I.
Nelson Bay
West Sound
Grindstone Bay
Buck Bay
Obstruction Pass
James I.
Sidney I.
Westcott Bay
Rocky Bay
Wasp Is.
Pole Pass
Crane I.
3
Obstruction I.
Peavine Pass
Cypress I.
Eagle Harbor
Cordova Channel
Open Bay
Garrison Bay
Mitchell Bay
Mosquito Pass
San Juan Channel
4
Shaw I.
Blind Bay
Indian Bay
Upright Ch
Shoal Bay
Peavine Bay
Blakely I.
Bellingham Channel
Guemes I.
Darcy I.
Smallpox Bay
Odlin Park
Strawberry Bay
Deepwater Bay
Boat Hbr
SIDNEY
FRIDAY HARBOR
Friday Hbr
Parks Bay
Swifts Bay
Saddleback I.
San Juan Island
Turn I.
Frost I.
Cordova Bay
LOPEZ
Thatcher Pass
Guemes Channel
Ship Hbr
ANACORTES
Cap Sante
Padilla Bay
Deadman Bay
North Bay
Lopez Sound
James I.
Decatur Head
2
6
Fisherman Bay
Decatur I.
Flounder Bay
Fidalgo Bay
Vancouver I.
False Bay
Griffin Bay
Center I.
Lopez Pass
Fidalgo Head
Burrows I.
Burrows Bay
Fidalgo Island
1
STRAIT
Kanaka Bay
Lopez Island
Hunter Bay
Mud Bay
ROSARIO
Swinomish Ch.
Eagle Cove
Davis Bay
Chatham I.
Castle Pass
Watmough Bay
Similk Bay
Mackaye Hbr
Discovery I.
Inner Passage
Outer Bay
McArdle Bay
Hughes Bay
Aleck Bay
Flint Beach
Bowman Bay
Deception Pass
Cornet Bay
Hope I.
Shelter Bay
LA CONNER
Middle Channel
CANADA U.S.A.
Goat I.
Skagit River
Skagit Bay
Whidbey Island
STRAIT OF JUAN DE FUCA
Oak Hbr

Anne Vipond

Quiet anchorage in the cruising paradise of the Pacific Northwest

EXPLORING THE SAN JUAN AND GULF ISLANDS

Cruising Paradise of the Pacific Northwest

BY DON DOUGLASS & RÉANNE HEMINGWAY-DOUGLASS

CONTRIBUTIONS BY ANNE VIPOND, PETER FROMM, AND WARREN MILLER

Quotations from *Canadian Sailing Directions*

Quotations from *Canadian Sailing Directions,* Vol. 1 and *Small Craft Guide,* Vol. 1 are used with permission of the Canadian Hydrographic Service. Reproduction of information from Canadian Hydrographic Service Sailing Directions in this publication are for illustrative purposes only, they do not meet the requirements of the Charts and Publication Regulations and are not to be used for navigation. The appropriate Sailing Directions, corrected up-to-date, and the relevant Canadian Hydrographic Service charts required under the Charts and Publications Regulations of the Canada Shipping Act must be used for navigation.

Contact the Canadian Hydrographic Service to obtain information on local dealers and available charts and publications or to order charts and publications directly:

Chart Sales and Distribution Office, Canadian Hydrographic Service
Department of Fisheries and Oceans, P.O. Box 6000
9860 West Saanich Road, Sidney B.C., V8L 4B2
Telephone (604) 363-6358; FAX (250) 363-6841

Legal Disclaimer

This book is designed to provide experienced skippers with cruising information on the San Juan and Gulf Islands. Every effort has been made, within limited resources, to make this book complete and accurate. There may well be mistakes, both typographical and in content; therefore this book should be used only as a general guide, not as the ultimate source of information on the areas covered. Much of what is presented in this book is local knowledge based upon personal observation and is subject to human error.

The authors, publisher, local and governmental authorities, assume no liability for errors or omissions, or for any loss or damages incurred from using this information.

Front cover photo: Anne Vipond
Back cover photos: Tony Fleming and Peter Fromm
Frontispiece photo: Anne Vipond
Text photos as noted
Cover design: Laura Patterson
Book design and production: Melanie Haage
Diagrams: Faith Rumm
Copyediting: Réanne Hemingway-Douglass, Pat Eckart, and Cindy Kamler

Library of Congress Cataloging-in-Publication Data

Douglass, Don
Exploring the San Juan and Gulf Islands : cruising paradise of the Pacific Northwest / by Don Douglass & Réanne Hemingway-Douglass : contributions by Anne Vipond & Peter Fromm ; foreword by Warren Miller.
p. cm.
Includes bibliographical references and index.
ISBN 0-938665-51-0
1. Boats and boating--Washington (State)—San Juan Islands--Guidebooks 2. Boats and boating--British Columbia--Gulf Islands--Guidebooks. 3. San Juan Islands (Wash.)--Guidebooks. 4. Gulf Islands (B.C.)--Guidebooks. I. Hemingway-Douglass, Réanne. II. Title.
GV776.W22S263 1998 98-16845
797.1'09797'74--dc21 CIP

ISBN 0-938665-51-0

Address requests for permission to Fine Edge Productions; Route 2, N. Valley View Dr., Bishop, CA 93514

Contents

Appendices and References

Acknowledgments

We are grateful to our principal contributors—well-known local writers Anne Vipond, Peter Fromm and Warren Miller. In his inimitable style, Warren, who along with his wife Laurie, frequently accompanies us on the Inside Passage to Alaska, has captured the reasons for living on an island in the San Juans. Anne, a Vancouver resident, and Peter, who lives in Friday Harbor, have added color, detail, and depth to this book through their many sidebars and photographs. Without their efforts, it wouldn't be the same book.

We wish to express our gratitude and appreciation to all the others who have helped make this book possible.

To Curtis Adams, Greg Avery, Dan Crookes, Tonnae Hennigan, Colin Jackson, Tom Shardlow, and Duart Snow for sharing their personal experiences and local knowledge by means of their written contributions.

Photos can be worth a thousand words, so thanks to Ian Douglas, Tony Fleming, Peter Fromm, Colin Jackson, William Kelly, Kent and Gina Morrow, Kelly O'Neil, and Anne Vipond for letting us use theirs.

Our appreciation goes to all those whom we meet along the route who share their local knowledge and to Mary Monfort and Zoe Rothchild of the Washington Water Trails Association for permission to use their Cascadia Marine Trail System Site List, and to the staff of the British Columbia Marine Trail Association for their information. We're grateful to the helpful folks at Anacortes Museum, the people at the many marinas and resorts for providing the latest information on their facilities and services, and to the wharfingers and harbormasters who did the same.

To Tom and Gloria Burke, Gary and Jane Gillingham, Herb and Seth Nickles, Kent and Gina Morrow, and Katherine Wells and Lloyd Dennis: thanks, *Baidarka* crew, for keeping watch, pulling up anchor, taking the helm, keeping the galley stove going, and helping to record raw data.

Applause and kudos to our land crew for helping us bring this book from idea to finished volume: Melanie Haage, book design and typesetting; Faith Rumm, computer graphics and diagrams; Laura Patterson, cover design; Pat Eckart, typing and copy editing; Cindy Kamler, research, writing, and copy editing.

Foreword

Warren Miller Tells Why He Lives in These Islands . . .

Why do I live on an island? That's usually the first question I get asked after I meet someone. Why? Let me count the ways:

1. We have one grocery store, half a dozen stop signs, and no traffic signals. Two years ago the population reached the same level it was in 1927.
2. We get an awful lot of rain and fog. In the nearby Olympic Peninsula, they get over three hundred inches a year; south in Seattle, they get over forty inches; we get over twenty inches on our island.
3. I can catch my limit of salmon when I go fishing with someone who knows where they are.
4. Three years ago I bought ten thousand baby oysters for a hundred dollars and I raise them in bags tied under our dock.
5. Depending on which brochure you read in this part of the world, there are between 175 islands or, at low tide, as many as one for every day of the year. If you stood on some of them at low tide, you would be seven feet underwater when the tide came back in.
6. My boating friends can stop by and tie up at my dock, we can go out together and set our crab pots, and after lunch go back and pull up a limit of crabs for dinner.
7. I can enter a fishing tournament and win a prize for the smallest salmon caught in three days.
8. Aside from running aground, there is very little trouble you can get into in a boat. The islands are so close together that even in high winds there's not enough fetch for the waves to get very large or dangerous.
9. Because opposing currents around the islands can run up to six knots or more and most sailboat engines will only go at that rate of speed, you can spend most of your charter boat time just going from *a* to *b*.
10. When the orca whales swim in front of our house, the noise of their spouting sometimes wakes me from my afternoon nap.
11. There is a nearby island I can row my dinghy around in about an hour. En route I can say hello to a seal or two, watch a flock of Canada geese fly overhead honking loudly, see a dozen deer grazing, row through a tangle of seaweed boiling in the outgoing tide (wondering why I went around the island the wrong way once again), wave to the ferryboat passengers who are just up here for a single day in their lives, and I realize that I get to live here. As my wife calls it, a Cosmic Convergence kind of place.
12. A famous man around the turn of the century was told by the doctors that he was going to die in six months. He got on a boat and settled here on my island and lived for thirty-four more years. I plan on doing the same thing and when I'm 107 years old, I will finally know where the salmon are, so I can catch them by myself.
13. In the meantime, I can practice my boating skills, spend more time exploring with my wife and our pets, cruise to Alaska every summer, eat fresh oysters, crabs, and salmon whenever we want them, and never watch Late Breaking News on TV.
14. The islands are a long way from Hollywood, California where I was born—even farther than some of the ski slopes of the world where I spend one-third of my life. The islands are not for everyone, but it is a place for my wife, myself, our two boats, and the remodeled three-car garage we live in most of the time.

In addition to all the above, I have Don and Réanne's books to show me all the good anchor sites in the San Juan and Gulf islands (as well as the Inside Passage), and every day of the year their books keep me from running aground.

Warren Miller, Author and Filmmaker, The San Juan Islands

Peter Fromm

Visitors to the islands come in all sizes

Exploring the San Juan and Gulf Islands

Welcome to the San Juan and Gulf islands, a cruising paradise. This archipelago, stretching from Deception Pass, Anacortes and Bellingham on the southeast to Victoria, Sidney and Nanaimo on the northwest, embraces hundreds of islands in all shapes and sizes, as well as rocky islets and submerged reefs. There are stretches of open water and a few narrows that will challenge your navigational skills. Mostly you will find protected waters, busy harbors, and quiet, intimate coves. Enjoy the solitude of tiny, hidden anchor sites and the natural surroundings and trails of the best marine parks anywhere. Visit busy marinas and resorts featuring fine dining, boutiques, galleries—all the commercial conveniences for nautical travellers. Fishing, beachcombing, whale watching, swimming, hiking, kayaking, day-sailing and people-watching are all world-class here.

You can visit this archipelago by cruising from Seattle or Vancouver; smaller vessels can be trailered to a given destination via the well-developed ferry system. Charter fleets located near popular destinations offer everything from a modest sloop to a large planing cruiser. Excellent float plane service can deliver crew members, friends or family from airport to swim step.

As you travel north, the area becomes less settled and more natural, so you may want to plan your trip from south to north. Many people use the San Juan Islands for a learning, shakedown cruise, then move on to the more remote Gulf

Peter Fromm

Unsurpassed sailing in inland waters

Islands, and finish with a memorable vacation cruise in Princess Louisa Inlet or Desolation Sound if time permits. In this way you gain experience in preparing for the challenges of the more remote areas, and at your own pace. You can linger anywhere among the islands and save the more dramatic environment further north for subsequent trips.

Geological Heritage

The San Juan and Gulf islands share a common geology of uplifted and faulted sandstone extending in a northwest-southeast line for 75 nautical miles from Skagit and Bellingham bays to Departure Bay on Vancouver Island. These formations, known as Chuckanut sandstone, make up the bulk of the seabed of the islands, islets, reefs and anchorages you explore as you travel from one end of the archipelago to the other. By observing the lay of these sandstone ridges you can anticipate where submerged extensions of the land may hide, hazards to be avoided.

Fauna and Flora

The archipelago is rich in wildlife. Marine life is abundant, ranging from orcas and gray whales to the orange sun star and purple urchin. The waters teem with fish; sea and shore birds are plentiful—the islands are situated along a major migratory flyway and almost 300 species can be found here. Land mammals include deer, raccoons and weasels that leave their tracks on mudflats and sandy beaches.

The Vancouver Island shoreline displays a variety of evergreens and deciduous trees; on the islands, Garry oak and arbutus are most common. Lush shrubs and bushes of all kinds, many loaded with berries, account for the presence of so many animals and birds. In season, grassy meadows and hillsides are brilliant with wildflowers.

Nature has been generous to this area, bestowing a multitude of riches for us to enjoy. Please respect and care for all life forms; learn and follow regulations regarding the taking of fish and shellfish, feeding of wildlife, disposal of trash, and other activities that impact the environment.

Peter Fromm

Resident pods are frequently sighted in the San Juan and Gulf islands

Prehistoric and Historic Heritage

The native peoples of these islands and surrounding waters travelled according to seasonal hunter-gatherer patterns, influenced by tribal rituals and customs. The remains of these civilizations have largely been lost, but the alert visitor can find evidence of their presence in the remains of rock fishing weirs and petroglyphs carved into rock faces, especially at the northern end of the island chain. (See Bibliography.) Artifacts are strictly protected by law and must not be disturbed.

With the arrival of European culture came national and geographical divisions (see San Juan Pig War in Chapter 4); the present boundary between Canadian and U.S. waters was established in 1872. The islands along Vancouver Island, west of Haro Strait and north of Boundary Pass, at first were located in British waters that subsequently became the Canadian province of British Columbia. The islands east of Haro Strait and south of Boundary Pass became United States' territory and, eventually, part of the State of Washington.

Today the San Juan and Gulf islands, numbering in the hundreds, span an unarmed international border.

Border Crossings

On either side of the border, there are different jurisdictions and protocols. As you cross back and forth between the Canada-U.S. border in either direction, you need to follow simple customs regulations. A vessel must be cleared by Customs at a designated Port of Entry. Generally this is done by the skipper (or his designate) who reports in person or by telephone. All other crew members must stay aboard (along with baggage or goods) until Customs officials issue a clearance number.

The minimum (and usually sufficient) information required is: the vessel's name, home port and registration number, and the last port of call; Canadian or U.S. clearance number issued (if any), Decal number or Personal Identification Number (PIN), if applicable; names and nationality of crew members; and quantity and description of regulated goods (such as certain fruits and vegetables, pets, firearms, cigarettes, liquor, and other taxed or prohibited goods). The process is quick and straight-forward if the skipper has the required information ready and makes a proper declaration of goods on board. Processing fees are not required in Canada; however, U.S. pleasure craft over 30 feet in length must pay an annual $25 user fee to re-enter the U.S. (A decal can be purchased in advance by mail.) U.S. boats in B.C. should display the cruising permit number on a piece of paper attached to a port-side window.

Customs officials are polite and courteous. They are trained in detecting regulated goods and they take their assignments seriously. Since each country protects its industries differently, get a clarification from the appropriate Customs office prior to crossing the border and try to minimize or eliminate regulated goods. Canadian Customs can be reached from anywhere in the U.S. at 888-226-7277 (toll free). The toll-free number for U.S. Customs is 800-562-5943 for clearance or information. Use these telephone numbers when planning your trip so that later you do not face a delay or an unpleasant experience. Write the Customs clearance numbers in your logbook for future reference. Certain vessels may qualify for CANPASS or telephone pre-crossing clearance. Call Customs for exact qualifications and procedures.

Annual publications such as *Northwest Boat Travel* and *Waggoneer* have useful, fairly-complete lists of current regulations. The actual customs regulations are voluminous; remember, your efficient, correct and courteous dealings will help avoid an occasional border-crossing disaster. Most procedures are over in a few minutes and are not a cause for anxiety.

If a vessel seeking Customs clearance is carrying travellers with other than Canadian or U.S. citizenship, certain additional immigration procedures must be followed. Prior inquiries will ensure that you have the proper documents, are prepared for the clearance procedure, and experience a minimum of delay.

Navigation in the Islands

The island environment has moderately high and low tidal levels, with strong currents occurring in narrow channels and between islands. During fair weather, navigation in the San Juan and Gulf islands is often by visual identification of a destination or a waypoint along the way; be on the alert for vessel traffic and debris in the water, and monitor your progress on a large-scale chart. Because fog or drizzle can reduce visibility in any season or time of day, charting your route ahead of time is a good precaution. Radar and GPS used together provide excellent assistance.

Canadian and U.S. Chart Differences

Measurement and charting systems on either side of the border have a few major, and many minor, differences that can affect your navigation. The U.S. uses the (old) English measurement system: feet, fathoms, pounds and gallons. The Canadians use the metric system: meters, grams and

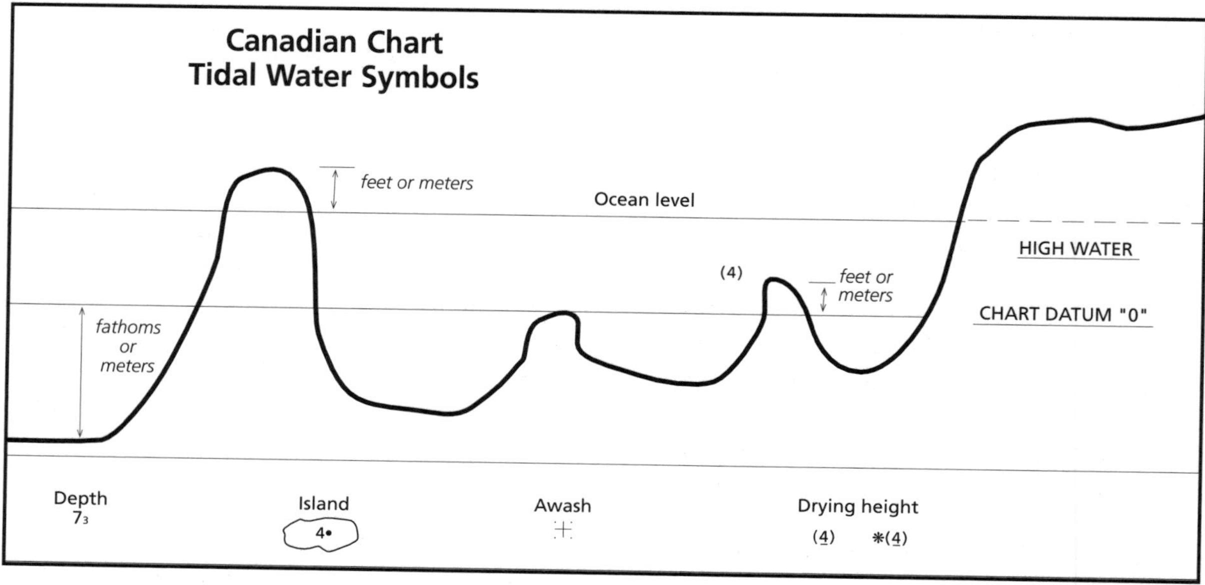

liters. The U.S. has agreed to change to the metric system sometime in the future, but you will find charts published in both systems. Every navigator should carefully verify the system used on a particular chart.

A prudent navigator will carefully check any chart he/she uses in the San Juan or Gulf islands to verify whether numbers are expressed in feet, meters, or fathoms, as well as the different symbol usage. For U.S. charts, consult Chart #1 published by NOAA; for Canadian charts, consult Chart #1 published by the Canadian Hydrographic Service.

A noteworthy difference in Canadian and U.S. charts is zero datum reference used to chart depths. In Canada the chart zero datum is based on the lowest expected tide levels for a particular place. This means that essentially all (except in rare cases) tide levels are expressed as positive numbers above this datum. On U.S. charts the zero datum is MLLW (mean of the lower of low waters) which means that U.S. tide levels at spring tides are frequently minus or below the zero charted value.

Using This Book

Each chapter covers a separate cruising area and generally proceeds from a south to north direction. The San Juan Islands chapters (1-5) proceed from east to west, and the Gulf Islands chapters (6-12) proceed from south to north. The area maps on the inside front and back covers serve as a quick reference for the location of channels, passages and coves found within each chapter text.

Each geographical entry in this book follows a layout as follows (and illustrated below): Place name and island on which it is located, distance to a known point, appropriate chart number(s), position (a site or anchor site we have not personally checked), specific anchor site, midchannel entrance point, buoy, or navigational light.

The first chart listed is always the largest-scale chart available and the one used to determine the latitude and longitude of a place. Additional charts listed are smaller-scale charts covering the area. Latitude and longitude are given to the nearest one-hundredth of a minute. Buoy and light positions are from the latest Canadian Coast Guard *Light List* (1992 edition), with seconds of arc converted to decimal minutes. *Caution:* The lat/long of an anchor site is just that; it is *not* the entrance to a cove. A GPS receiver set to an anchor site—or to any other position—will guide you *directly* there whether there is an intervening land mass or not.

Sample Layout Selection

Indian Cove (Shaw Island)
Indian Cove, on the north side of Upright Channel, is located 0.7 mile northwest of Flat Point.

Chart 18434
Entrance (0.2 mile west of south corner of Canoe Island): 48°33.36′ N, 122°56.00′ W (NAD 83)
Anchor: 48°33.69′ N, 122°56.06′ W (NAD 83)

> *A shoal, covered 7½ fathoms, is 700 yards SSW, and a rock awash is 250 yards SW of the SW end of Canoe Island. Anchorages for small craft may be had in Indian Cove, W of Canoe Island, in 4 to 7 fathoms, soft bottom.* (p. 334, CP)

Because of its convenient location, Indian Cove is a popular anchorage with adequate room for a number of boats over a flat sandy bottom. Canoe Island provides moderate protection from traffic wake, as well as from southeast winds. During north winds, Indian Cove is delightfully calm but driftwood along its north shore attests to the stormy southerly winds that enter the cove.

Shaw Island County Park, the only large piece of public land on the island, has both day-use and camping facilities, fresh water, and a launch ramp with easy dinghy or kayak access. Its beach is one of the nicest in the San Juans.

Anchor in 3 to 4 fathoms over and and mud bottom with good holding.

Place name (island)

Distance from known point

Largest scale chart

Excerpts from official government publications (*CP*-Coast Pilot, *SCG*-Small Craft Guide, *SD*-Sailing Directions)

Our own recorded local knowledge based on personal experience

Describes in fathoms anchor position given above along with holding power

Northwest Anchoring

Northwest cruising is all about anchoring; once you get beyond marinas and fishing resorts, the feeling of being safely anchored in your own secluded cove is unforgettable. Finding an anchorage is one of the challenges and pleasures of Northwest cruising; we hope this book will help you find your *own* special site!

A well-set, over-sized anchor assures a good night's sleep. A conventional cruising anchor (not a lightweight folding version), a boat-length of chain, and good nylon rode are indispensable equipment. We always carry a smaller lunch hook to use during temporary stops or to restrict our swinging room. Sometimes—in close quarters or in deep, steep-to anchorages—we use a stern tie to shore. Although we usually prefer to swing on a single CQR anchor, in marine parks or popular anchorages we try to minimize our impact by matching the mooring technique and swinging radius of other boats. Choosing our site carefully and setting our anchor well assures us that *Baidarka* will rock us to sleep even in occasional downslope winds or williwaws.

Key to Detailed Diagrams

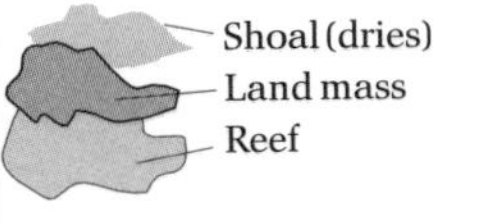

Shoal (dries)
Land mass
Reef

+ + + Rock(s) below or above water; small islet(s)

Anchor site
Mooring buoy
Aid to navigation
Peak or high point
Trails

Anchor check

Don Douglass

Definitions used for holding power

Excellent—very good holding
Anchor digs in deeper as you pull on it—the preferred bottom in a blow, but a rare find—usually thick sticky mud or clay.

Good holding
Generally sufficient for overnight anchorage—anchor digs in but may drag or pull out on strong pull. Common in mud/sand combinations or hard sand.

Fair holding
Adequate for temporary anchorage, but boat should not be left unattended. Bottom of light sand, gravel with some rocks, grass or kelp. Anchor watch desirable.

Poor holding
Can be used for a temporary stop in fair weather only. Bottom is typically rocky with a lot of grass or kelp, or a very thin later of mud and sand—insufficient to properly bury anchor. Anchor watch at all times is recommended.

Steep-to
Depth of water may decrease from 10 fathoms to 1/2 fathom in as little as one boat length! Dead-slow speed approach recommended. Use shore tie to minimize swinging and to keep anchor pulling uphill.

Cruising Ethics

"Leave No Trace" must be the goal of everyone who cruises the San Juan and Gulf islands. Even better, leave a place cleaner than you found it. Take away only great photos and warm memories; leave nothing but echoes of laughter and a fading, gentle wake.

Cruising Etiquette

The Gulf Islands and San Juans are among the busiest cruising areas on our coast. We rub shoulders not only with each other, but with kayakers, campers and a variety of other users. It is critical that, while enjoying the islands, we remember to respect others' rights to enjoy them and that we preserve them for future generations to enjoy as well. A little cruising etiquette is in order:

- Respect the flora, fauna and marine environment of these unique islands, as well as the privacy of the people who live on them.
- Don't discharge raw sewage into bays, harbors, or anchorages. Use shoreside facilities, a holding tank, or an appropriate MSD.
- Manage your trash. Under any circumstances, don't stash it ashore or sink it in the chuck. Sort out recyclables and recycle them. Dispose of the rest at a suitable garbage drop or pack it with you until you find one. Note that fewer and fewer marine parks in the Canadian Gulf Islands have garbage bins these days.
- When choosing a spot to anchor, respect the swinging room and privacy of those who got there before you and leave room for those who may arrive later. Arrange your "swinging circle" to coincide with boats around you. Use a stern line to limit your swing where necessary.
- Remember that most boaters come to the islands for peace and quiet. In anchorages or marinas, keep noise down. If you have a genset or portable generator, use it discreetly. Don't run it during everyone else's cockpit cocktail hour or when people are trying to sleep; don't turn it on and flee in your tender or retreat below because you can't stand the noise. Sailors, tie those halyards away from the mast. Don't "buzz" the anchorage in your tender or PWC, and don't let your crew do it either. If you really want to party, find the nearest pub on shore—there are lots of good ones on the islands.
- Keep your wake down in anchorages, restricted passages and waterways.
- Leave nothing behind but your wake. Your fellow cruisers, both now and in years to come, will thank you for it.

Welcome to the Gulf and San Juan islands!

—Duart Snow, Editor, *Pacific Yachting*

SECTION I

Introduction to the San Juan Islands

Long ago, a mountain range stretched from the North American mainland to what is now Vancouver Island. As the mountains settled and melting glaciers raised the sea level, only the peaks remained above water. Succeeding glaciers covered the sinking mountains, softening their jagged peaks, cutting channels and estuaries, sculpting the granite mountain hearts.

Glacial till, debris left by glacier action, settled in low-lying areas and provided fertile ground for meadows and forests. Wind and water which scoured the miles of coastline, carving coves and bays, cut friezes into rock benches and deposited golden sandspits and beaches.

The San Juans range in size from the larger islands of Orcas, San Juan and Lopez to smaller islands such as Shaw, Blakely, Waldron, Sucia, Matia, and Spieden. Smaller still are Barnes, Clark, Wasp, Jones, and Turn islands.

Much of the land in the San Juans is publicly owned—state and county marine parks, national wildlife refuges, and lighthouse reserves—all of it offers a rich selection of recreational opportunities: fishing, swimming, scuba diving, whale watching, shellfish gathering, camping, hiking, birdwatching, and sightseeing. Wildlife viewing is prime in less-frequented areas. There are historical sites to visit, shedding light on the Salish from Vancouver Island, the original inhabitants, the Lummi people, the waves of explorers, and the early pioneer settlers. Later, smugglers and bootleggers, loggers, miners, and shipbuilders wrote their chapters in the islands' history.

Numerous channels and passes—San Juan, Spieden, Peavine, Upright, President, Obstruction—offer access to nearly every island where quaint towns or villages provide services, shopping, entertainment, galleries, and much more. Fidalgo, Cypress, Guemes, and Lummi islands all have good anchorages—you have a choice of thousands of coves and bays where you can anchor and spend a quiet night—particularly if you explore in the off-season.

Friday Harbor, Bellingham, and Anacortes all have year-round Customs clearance; Roche Harbor has Customs clearance during the summer months. From whatever point you embark, the emerald-green archipelago of the San Juan Islands beckons from the horizon. Whether there are 700 islands in this group, as some references claim, or only 172; whether it's called a reef, a rock or an island—all invite exploration, so come cruise with us through the marine wonderland of the San Juan Islands.

Wind and Weather

Winds funnel and die through the San Juan waterways, making cruising here a challenge. During the summer, when high pressure areas often build, breezes from west-to-southwest or from west-to-northwest bring great sailing weather. When low-pressure systems approach, winds rise from east-to-southeast. Then as the front passes through, winds veer to the southwest or west in Juan de Fuca Strait, and to the northwest in the Strait of Georgia. Gale or storm force winds can occur at any time of the year, although they are more frequent in the spring, fall and winter. Within a week of both the spring and fall equinoxes, March 21 and September 21, gales are common; if you cruise during these times, pay attention to the weather forecasts and plan your anchorages with safety in mind.

During periods of extremely warm weather, mirages sometimes occur and an island's cliffs may seem to tower and large ships rising over the horizon in the distance may appear huge. This phenomenon, which usually happens on clear sunny days, is caused by heat and the curvature of the Earth, but as you approach the object, the distortion disappears.

For marine weather reports, weather radio Channel 02 from Victoria provides the most accurate forecasts because San Juan weather is most like that of Victoria, rather than that of Vancouver or Seattle. Listen to the wind conditions for the entire area. For broadcasts of wind and sea conditions announcements, stations closest to the San Juans are East Point/Saturna Island, Kelp Reef (mid-Haro Strait), Discovery, Trial and Smith islands.—**PF**

Kent Morrow

Cruising toward Deception Pass, the Downeast 32 *and her crew enjoy a warm Sunday afternoon in June*

1

DECEPTION PASS TO BELLINGHAM BAY

Skagit Bay, Swinomish Channel, Fidalgo Island, Anacortes, Guemes Island, Bellingham Harbor, Lummi Island, and Eliza Island

Approaching the San Juan Islands from the south, the principal jumping off ports are Seattle, Anacortes, or Bellingham; along the way you can explore numerous islands, coves, bays and inlets.

From the Seattle area, heading northward toward Rosario Strait, you can sail along the west coast of Whidbey Island and head east through Deception Pass. Don't miss forested Deception Pass State Park in Cornet Bay, where there are camping facilities and hot showers. For a more-sheltered route, you can cruise up Skagit Bay and visit Skagit, Hope and Goat islands. Skagit Island was the hideout for Henry "The Flying Dutchman" Ferguson, a member of Butch Cassidy's Hole in the Wall Gang.

From Skagit Bay you can take the smooth-water, but challenging, Swinomish Channel through Hole in the Wall north to picturesque La Conner, passing first under Rainbow Bridge, then continuing on to Padilla Bay, one of 17 U.S. Natural Estuarine Preserves.

From the Anacortes or Bellingham area, you can explore Guemes, Lummi and Eliza islands and the eastern edge of the Chuckanut sandstone formations that extend 90 nautical miles northwest to Nanaimo on Vancouver Island. Or you can follow the mainland shore, visiting Samish, Chuckanut and Bellingham bays.

Anacortes and Bellingham both offer extensive marine services and facilities, as well as activities and shopping areas for tourists who arrive by land or sea. Bellingham has a major airport, and Anacortes is easily accessible from Seattle by airport limousine.

Skagit Bay

Skagit Bay is located on the east side of Whidbey Island north of Saratoga Passage and south of Deception Pass.

Chart 18427

N part, between the N part of Whidbey Island and the mainland, is entered from the N through Deception Pass and from the S through Saratoga Passage. Skagit River . . . empties into the SE part of the bay.

The greater portion of Skagit Bay is filled with flats, bare at low water. Shoals extend 100 to 300 yards off the Whidbey Island shore.

Along the shore of Whidbey Island, between it and the edge of the flats, is a natural channel varying in width from 0.2 to 0.5 mile, except at

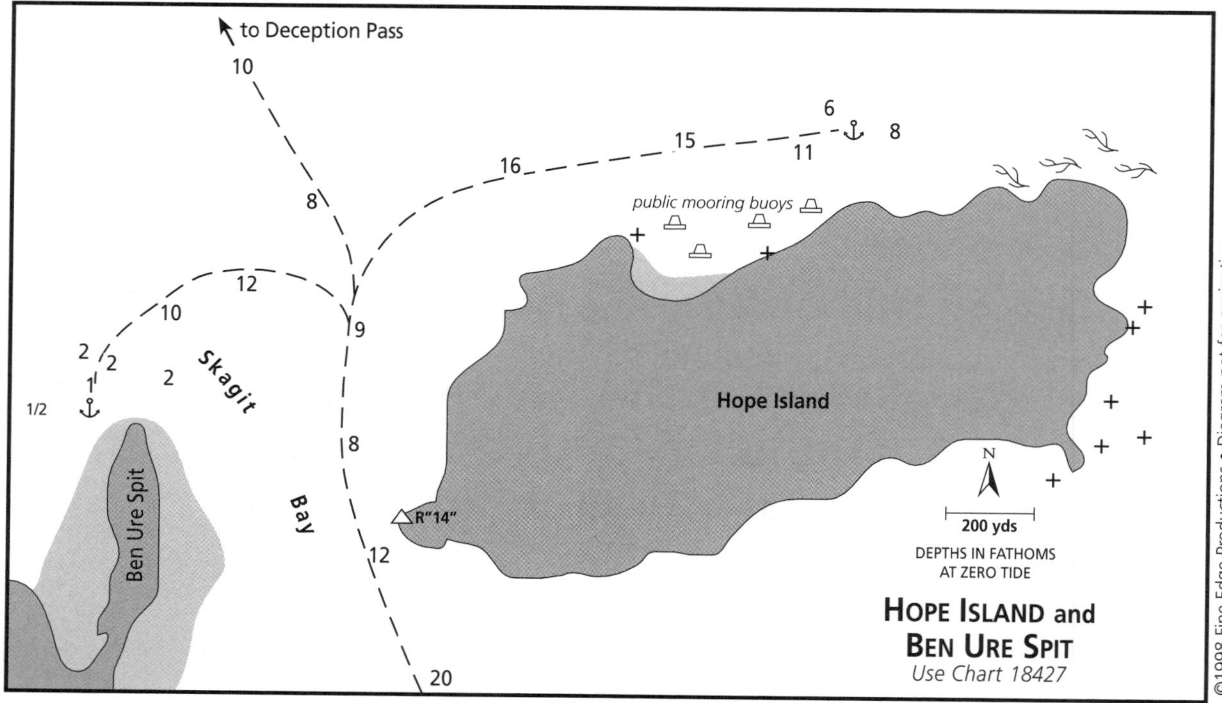

Hope Island, where it narrows to 150 yards. The channel is marked with lights and buoys from Deception Pass to the N entrance of Saratoga Passage. The main channel from Deception Pass S through Skagit Bay has depths of 6 fathoms or more.

Velocity and direction of the current vary throughout this channel. The flood current enters through Deception Pass and sets in a generally S direction. The ebb flows in a general N direction. SW of Hope Island, the velocity is 2.3 knots on the flood and 2.0 knots on the ebb. S of Goat Island the velocity is 1.8 knots on the flood and 1.4 knots on the ebb. N of Rocky Point the velocity is 0.6 knot on the flood and 1.0 knot on the ebb. . . . (p. 339, CP)

Peter Fromm

The Victoria Clipper *crossing Skagit Bay*

Whidbey Island offers protection along its eastern shore for boaters headed north from Puget Sound who want a smooth-water approach to the San Juan Islands. Although the Skagit River which empties into Skagit Bay creates extensive shoaling and drying mud flats, the channel through the bay is well marked and used extensively by pleasure craft that want to avoid the Strait of Juan de Fuca.

From Skagit Bay you can enter Rosario Strait via Deception Pass or take Swinomish Channel north to Anacortes; the latter route, although longer than the one to the west of Fidalgo Island, is more scenic and, in our opinion, more fun.

The channel through Skagit Bay is well marked with buoys and lights; observe these navigational aids with care since the bay has significant currents and you could easily ground on the flats.

Hope Island (Skagit Bay)

Hope Island is 2.8 miles southeast of Deception Pass and 2.2 miles north of the entrance to Swinomish Channel.

Chart 18427
Mid-channel (0.25 mile west of Seal Rocks Light): 48°22.45′ N, 122°34.18′ W (NAD 83)
Mid-channel (0.04 mile west of Hope Island Light "14"): 48°23.75′ N, 122°34.78′ W (NAD 83)
Public mooring buoys: 48°24.10′ N, 122°34.22′ W (NAD 83)
Anchor: 48°24.19′ N, 124°33.97′ W (NAD 83)

> *Hope Island, 1 mile S of Skagit Island, is fringed with rocks off its E side, and marked by a light on its W point.* (p. 339, CP)

Hope Island is a State Marine Park. Its north side offers good protection from southerly weather. You can pick up one of the public mooring buoys or anchor over a large area east of the buoys where swinging room is unlimited.

Anchor in 6 to 10 fathoms over a mud bottom with good holding.

Peter Fromm

Sailing off Snee-oosh Point

Ben Ure Spit (Whidbey Island)

Ben Ure Spit is 0.3 mile west of Hope Island.

Chart 18427
Entrance (0.14 mile north of point): 48°24.00′ N, 122°35.16′ W (NAD 83)
Anchor: 48°23.85′ N, 122°35.22′ W (NAD 83)

> *Ben Ure Spit, across the channel from Hope Island, is a low projecting point within a shoal extending about 350 yards E.* (p. 339, CP)

To the west of Ben Ure Spit is a large mud flat with depths of approximately a half-fathom at zero tide. You can find temporary anchorage over this flat to wait for favorable tides at Deception Pass or to seek protection from southerly winds.

Anchor in 1 1/2 fathoms over gravel and mud with fair holding.

Snee-oosh Point (Fidalgo Island)

Snee-oosh Point is 0.5 mile east of Hope Island.

Chart 18427
Hope Island Channel north entrance (0.25 mile southwest of Lone Tree Point): 48°24.27′ N, 122°33.63′ W (NAD 83)
Hope Island Channel south entrance (0.32 mile west of Snee-oosh Point): 48°23.97′ N, 122°33.34′ W (NAD 83)
Anchor (0.13 mile south of Snee-oosh Point): 48°23.88′ N, 122°32.85′ W (NAD 83)

> *A summer anchorage for pleasure craft is S of Snee-oosh (Hunot) Point. The narrow channel E of Hope Island [called Hope Island Channel above] is used by small craft with local knowledge. This channel, with a controlling depth of 5 fathoms, passes 130 yards off the Hope Island shore. The bottom is rocky and very irregular, and numerous dangers marked by heavy kelp are between the channel and the Fidalgo Island shore.* (p. 339, CP)

If Hope Island is crowded or if you want more protection from westerly weather, you can find anchorage approximately 0.1 mile due south of Snee-oosh Point; this site, however, is exposed to southerly weather. Approach Snee-oosh Point across a 2-fathom shoal south of Hope Island or via Hope Island Channel, a deep-water entrance north and east of Hope Island.

Peter Fromm

Baidarka *at Hope Island*

Anchor in 2 fathoms over a mud and gravel bottom with fair holding.

Kiket Bay (Fidalgo Island)

Kiket Bay is between Hope Island on the south and Kiket Island 1 mile to the north.

Chart 18427
Entrance (0.14 mile south of Skagit Island): 48°24.57′ N, 122°34.77′ W (NAD 83)
Anchor (0.17 mile southeast of Kiket Island): 48°25.00′ N, 122°33.70′ W (NAD 83)

> *Good anchorage may be had in Kiket Bay, N of Hope Island, and vessels at times make use of this anchorage area while waiting for slack water in Deception Pass.* (p. 339, CP)

Good anchorage can be found over a large shoal south and southeast of Kiket Island with unlimited swinging room.

Anchor in 2 fathoms over mud bottom with good holding.

Similk Bay (Fidalgo Island)

Similk Bay is 3 miles northeast of Deception Pass.

Chart 18427
Entrance: 48°25.00′ N, 122°35.00′ W (NAD 83)
Anchor: 48°25.50′ N, 122°34.18′ W (NAD 83)

> *Similk Bay, at the N end of Skagit Bay, is used for log-rafting operations and is unsafe for navigation. Skagit Island and Kiket Island, 111 feet and 194 feet high, respectively, are just S of Similk Bay opposite the E entrance to Deception Pass.* (p. 339, CP)

Kelly O'Neil

Whidbey Island Race in July

Similk Bay is a large bay, shallow throughout. It has been used extensively for logging operations in the past. Despite the *Coast Pilot,* small craft can frequently find temporary anchorage in Similk Bay on the north side of Kiket Island.

Anchor in 2½ fathoms over a mud bottom with good holding.

Dewey Bight (Fidalgo Island)

Dewey Bight is 1.8 miles east of Deception Pass.

Chart 18427
Entrance: 48°25.11′ N, 122°36.43′ W (NAD 83)
Anchor: 48°25.25′ N, 122°36.52′ W (NAD 83)

Dewey Bight provides temporary anchorage in its center, and although exposed to southeast winds, it offers shelter from northwest winds. However, it is subject to wake from passing traffic. When anchoring, avoid approaching the private floats.

Anchor in about 4 fathoms over a mud and rocky bottom with fair holding.

Kent Morrow

Weekenders in their boats are dwarfed by Deception Pass Bridge

Cornet Bay (Whidbey Island)

Cornet Bay is 0.6 mile southeast of Deception Pass.

Chart 18427
Entrance: 48°24.33′ N, 122°37.31′ W (NAD 83)
Anchor: 48°24.12′ N, 122°37.56′ W (NAD 83)

> *Cornet Bay, shallow and suitable for small craft only, indents the N end of Whidbey Island, in Deception Pass. A marina with a privately dredged entrance channel and mooring basin is in the bay; the channel is marked by private daybeacons. The marina has about 85 open and covered berths at the floats, and electricity, water, ice, launching ramp, 4-ton hoist, and marine supplies; hull repairs can be made. A State-maintained small-craft facility is E of the marina; berthing and a launching ramp are available. Overhead power cables with clearances of 56 feet cross the W end of the bay.* (p. 338, CP)

Cornet Bay, a favorite area for small craft and sportfishing boats, is the site of Deception Pass Marina which has a laundry and restrooms (no showers), fuel, propane and provisions. Because moorage is limited, it's a good idea to phone in advance for information (tel: 360-675-5411).

The southern part of Deception Pass State Park, which lies along the shores of Cornet Bay, has five launch ramps with docks and floats, picnic facilities, restrooms and showers; no power. Temporary anchorage can be found between the docks and Ben Ure Island. (You can also find moorage in the northern and more extensive portion of Deception Pass State Park, located along the shores of Bowman Bay, described in Chapter 2; Hope and Skagit islands, also part of the State Park, have mooring buoys but no facilities.)

Anchor in 2 to 4 fathoms, mud bottom with good holding.

Deception Pass

Chart 18427
East entrance: 48°24.36′ N, 122°38.43′ W (NAD 83)
West entrance: 48°24.38′ N, 122°38.77′ W (NAD 83)

> *Deception Pass, the impressive 2-mile passage between Whidbey Island and Fidalgo Island, provides a challenging route that connects the N end of Skagit Bay with the S end of Rosario Strait. Near its middle the width is reduced to 200 yards by Pass Island. A fixed highway bridge over the pass between Pass Island and Whidbey Island has a clearance of 144 feet at the center and 104 feet elsewhere. Overhead telephone and power cables 100 yards and 0.2 mile E of the bridge have a minimum clearance of 150 feet.*
>
> *Deception Pass is used frequently by local boats bound from Seattle to Anacortes, Bellingham, and the San Juan Islands. The pass should be negotiated at the time of slack, since the velocity of the stream at other times makes it prohibitive to some craft. However, many fast boats run it at all stages of the tide. The pass is also used by log tows from the N bound to Everett or Seattle, which prefer this route to avoid the rough weather W of Whidbey Island.*

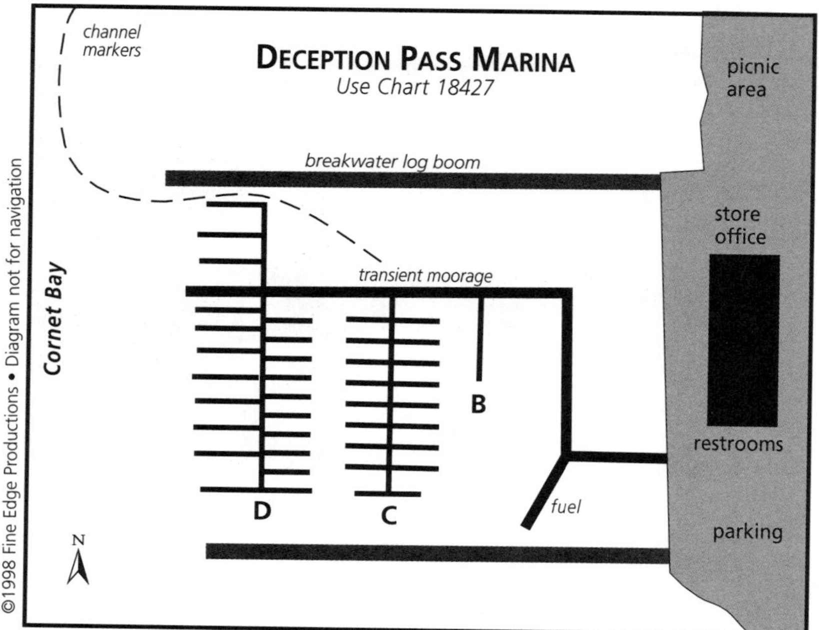

Currents in the narrows of Deception Pass attain velocities in excess of 8 knots at times and cause strong eddies along the shores. With W weather, heavy swells and tide rips form and make passage dangerous to all small craft. (See the Tidal Current Tables for daily predictions.)

From W the best water through Deception Pass will be found 0.3 mile W of Rosario Head, a point 0.5 mile N of Deception Island. Steer a SE course to pass about 100 yards SW of the light on Lighthouse Point; then follow an E course through the middle of the pass, being careful to guard against sets from the current when running partly across it. After passing under the bridge, favor slightly the N shore so as to avoid the pinnacle rocks and ledges making out from the S shore. After leaving Pass Island, steer to pass about midway between Ben Ure and Strawberry Islands. Strawberry Island should not be approached within 125 yards because a reef, marked by kelp, extends S of the island. From a position off Ben Ure Island Light 2, steer a NE course to pass about midway between Hoypus Point and Yokeko Point. The flood current N and W of Strawberry Island sets NE and should be guarded against. (pp. 335, 338, CP)

The main vessel-route through Deception Pass follows the south side of Pass Island. (The north side of Pass Island is known as Canoe Pass.) Boats should time their passage through Deception Pass at or near slack water since the velocity of the stream at other times can be hazardous. At times—on either side of slack water, particularly during neap tides—you may see boats planing through the pass.

Canoe Pass (Fidalgo Island)

Canoe Pass lies on the north side of Deception Pass between Pass and Fidalgo islands.

Chart 18427
East entrance: 48°24.49′ N, 122°38.52′ W (NAD 83)
West entrance: 48°24.51′ N, 122°38.79′ W (NAD 83)

Canoe Pass, N of Pass Island, is not recommended except for small craft with local knowledge. (p. 338, CP)

Canoe Pass from the east

Tiny Canoe Pass should be approached with caution. While it is frequently used by kayakers as a training ground, we do not recommend it as an established route. This narrow, curving passage has restricted visibility, a fairway with minimum depth of 4 fathoms, and strong eddy currents. However, if you have a small boat and want a challenge, Canoe Pass will give you the flavor of some of the narrow, tricky passages between here and Alaska. Check it out first by dinghy or kayak, then try it if you wish, but be sure to blow your horn or make your intentions known on VHF Channel 16. Be prepared to meet other traffic in the very narrow section directly below the bridge.

Kent Morrow

Lottie Bay near Deception Pass is not a recommended anchorage but crabbing can be rewarding

Lottie Bay (Fidalgo Island)

Lottie Bay is 0.23 miles due east of Lighthouse Point.

Chart 18427
Entrance: 48°24.49′ N, 122°39.04′ W (NAD 83)

Lottie Bay—a shallow bay filled largely with drying mud flats and out of the heavy current—is sometimes used by kayaks and other small craft as a temporary place to await slack water in Deception Pass. For larger boats, Bowman Bay, on the north side of Deception Pass, is a better waiting place. (See Chapter 2 for a description of Bowman Bay and the anchorages on the west side of Fidalgo Island.)

Swinomish Channel (South Entrance)

The south entrance to Swinomish Channel is 0.68 mile east of Goat Island and at the north end of Skagit Bay 4.5 miles southeast of Deception Pass.

Chart 18427
South entrance (200 feet southwest of green Buoy "1"): 48°21.68′ N, 122°33.37′ W (NAD 83)

> *Swinomish Channel is a dredged channel that connects the waters of Skagit Bay with those of Padilla Bay, about 10 miles to the N. The entrance channel from Skagit Bay leads ENE between two jetties, thence N of Goat Island . . . thence through Hole in the Wall . . . and thence N to Padilla Bay. The S jetty, submerged except for a small section near Goat Island, extends about 0.6 mile W of Goat Island and is marked by daybeacons; the N jetty, submerged and marked by a light off its W end, extends W about 1.1 miles from the S end of Fidalgo Island. A 072°-252° lighted range marks the entrance channel from Skagit Bay, and other navigational aids mark the channel to Padilla Bay. In February-April 1993, the midchannel controlling depth was 10 feet from Skagit Bay to deep water in Padilla Bay, except for shoaling to 8 feet across the channel just S of the twin fixed highway bridges.*
>
> *Several bridges and overhead power and telephone cables cross Swinomish Channel; minimum clearance of the power cables is 72 feet. Just S of La Conner, the highway fixed bridge has a clearance of 45 feet or 75 feet for a center width of 310 feet. . . .*
>
> *Most of the yachts going between Bellingham and Seattle prefer Swinomish Channel to Deception Pass because of the calmer water and shorter run. The channel is used extensively for towing logs.* (p. 339, CP)

Swinomish Channel can be fun to transit, particularly since it leads to La Conner, one of our favorite towns. However, use caution at the south entrance which is frequently congested with merging traffic where high-speed boats entering and exiting the narrow dredged channel can cause choppy waters. When southbound, as you exit the narrow fairway, use the range marks on Whidbey Island.

While shallow-draft boats can use Swinomish

Peter Fromm

West end Swinomish Channel

Channel at all stages of the tide, boats with deeper draft should time their passage carefully. Avoid the mud flats on either side of the channel by following a midchannel course and observing the turning buoys and range marks shown on Chart 18427.

The flood current enters either end of Swinomish Channel and meets somewhere north of La Conner. Throughout the length of Swinomish Channel, a no-wake speed limit is in effect to prevent damage to homes and boats. *Caution:* Sailing vessels with tall masts should be aware that clearances for the bridges and powerlines in Swinomish Channel are lower than those in Deception Pass.

Goat Island (Skagit Bay)

Goat Island is 2.2 mile southeast of Hope Island.

Chart 18427
Anchor: 48°21.96′ N, 122°33.90′ W (NAD 83)

> *Goat Island . . . is rocky, steep, and timber covered.* (p. 339, CP)

Goat Island was reportedly so named because of a herd of goats brought there by early settlers. On the north side of the island Fort Whitman, a military reservation from 1909-1947, can be visited by finding temporary anchorage on the south side of Swinomish Channel, approachable from the west, except at low tide. This anchorage is subject to heavy wash from passing boats.

Anchor in about 1½ fathoms over an unrecorded bottom.

Hole in the Wall (Swinomish Channel)

Hole in the Wall is 1.9 miles east of the south entrance to Swinomish Channel.

Chart 18427
Midchannel fairway (southeast of Light "13"): 48°22.27′ N, 122°30.62′ W (NAD 83)

> *Hole in the Wall [lies along] the S part of Fidalgo Island . . .* (p. 339, CP)

Hole in the Wall is the narrow passage between Fidalgo Island and McGlinn Island at the point where Swinomish Channel turns northward. Avoid the south side of the channel between Goat Island and Hole in the Wall. This shallow area is used intensively as a logboom storage area.

Shelter Bay (Fidalgo Island)

Shelter Bay is 0.7 mile southwest of La Conner.

Chart 18427
Entrance: 48°22.94′ N, 122°30.51′ W (NAD 83)

Shelter Bay, a private community with an extensive marina and private floats, is—as its name indicates—well sheltered! While no transient

Don Douglass

Pier 7 in picturesque La Conner

moorage is available, the Shelter Bay Yacht Club offers reciprocal moorage for a small number of pleasure craft. Since the bay is home to a sizeable number of cruising boats, use caution when entering or exiting. During freezing weather, an overlay of fresh water creates a thin layer of ice throughout the bay.

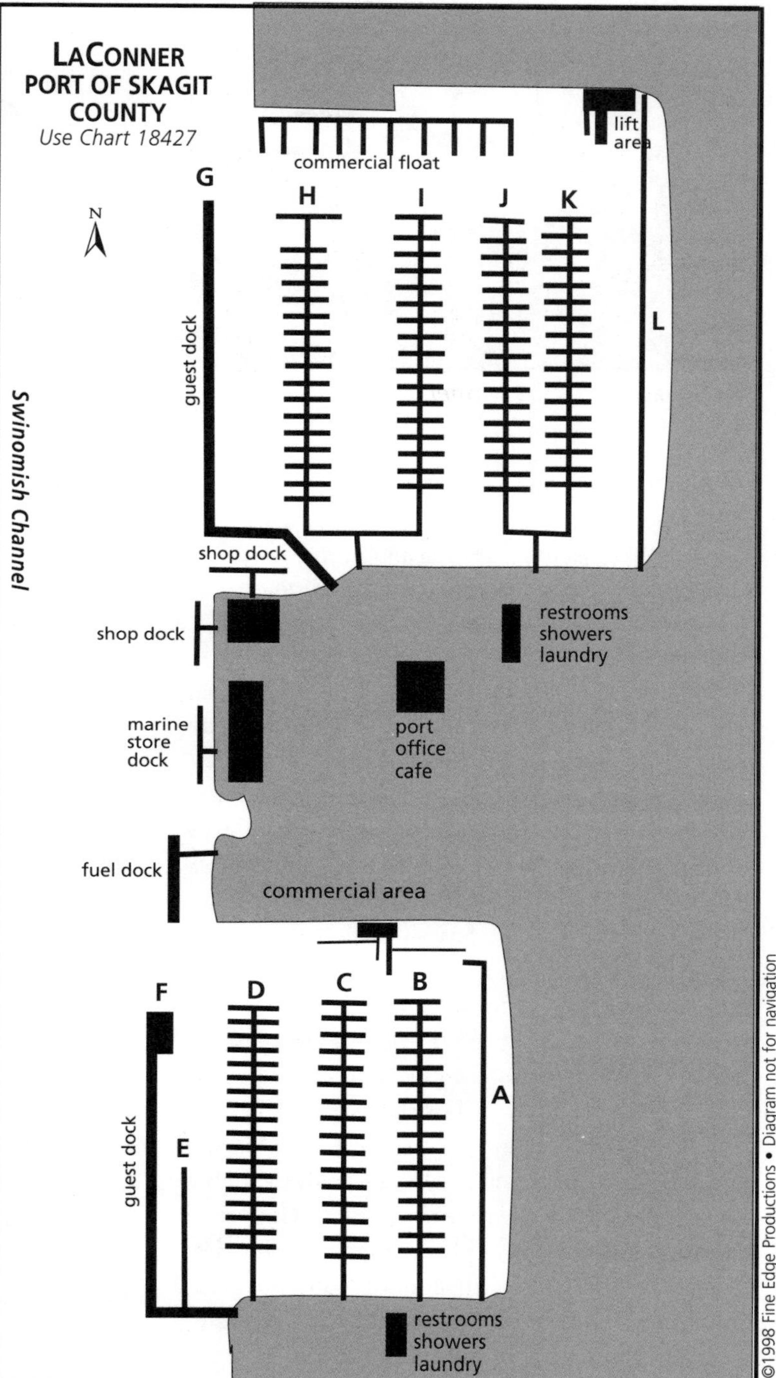

La Conner

La Conner is 3 miles northeast of the south entrance to Swinomish Channel and 7 miles south of the north entrance to Swinomish Channel.

Chart 18427
City floats: 48°23.54′ N, 122°29.82′ W (NAD 83)
South marina entrance: 48°23.79′ N, 122°29.79′ W (NAD 83)
North marina entrance: 48°24.05′ N, 122°29.78′ W (NAD 83)

La Conner, near the S end of Swinomish Channel, is the center of a rich agricultural district, and has several fish canneries. Many commercial fishing boats operate from here. Piers, wharves, and mooring floats are along the entire waterfront, much of which is bulkheaded. There are several marinas along the channel at La Conner. The largest marinas are operated by Skagit County in the county basins on the E side of the channel about 0.6 mile and 0.8 mile N of the highway fixed bridge. The entrance to the S basin is constricted by pilings that extend from the N side. The S basin has over 180 covered and uncovered berths with electricity and water, and a 40-ton mobile hoist at its N end. The hoist is used jointly by the marina and a machine shop on the N side of the S basin. The N basin has over 200 covered and uncovered berths. Complete hull and engine repair facilities are available at the machine shop. Gasoline, diesel fuel, dry storage, launching ramp, and supplies are available in the area. A firm, on the E side of the channel at the S end of town, builds fiberglass boats and

Peter Fromm

Tugs at dock in La Conner

Peter Fromm

Looking east from the south end of Swinomish Channel

does limited hull repair work. A tug company, just N of the S basin, has tugs up to 2,400 hp available. An extensive log storage and sorting yard is on the W side of the channel opposite the tug company. Logs are moored along both sides of the channel near the storage yard. (pp. 339–340, CP)

The picturesque town of La Conner, on the east side of Swinomish Channel, is one of our favorite spots. This pioneer town—the oldest in Skagit County—dates back to the 19th Century. The first settlers arrived in 1864 and a trading post was built in 1867. The town's history is reflected in its many charming old buildings, Victorian houses, and quaint shops. Our favorite cafe—the Calico Cupboard (which also has locations in Anacortes and Mt. Vernon)—is located on First Street, and there are many other good restaurants here, as well as fascinating boutiques and art galleries and, of course, O'Leary's bookstore which carries a great selection of nautical publications. Marine supplies, groceries, and services are all available for visitors. Visit the Skagit County Historical Museum and the 1891 Gaches Mansion. The latter features the Valley Museum of Northwest Art. The south end of town is marked by the graceful, orange-painted arch of Rainbow Bridge.

Dutch settlers created nearby farmland by draining and diking the wetlands. The diversity of crops make the region one of the richest farmlands in the state. Vast fields of tulips and daffodils dazzle springtime visitors with brilliant colors. The Skagit Valley Tulip Festival is held every April. Other festivals include the Smelt Derby in February, La Conner Opening Day Parade in May, Fireworks at Dark on the 4th of July, the Swinomish Blues Festival in August, and a Home Tour and End-of-Season Parade and Sale in September.

Public floats line the business district, so you can sometimes tie up near your favorite restaurant or shop unless you arrive in the busy summer season. Be aware of the strong current along these floats and be particularly cautious when approaching or tying to these floats. (It's easy to misjudge and land in the drink, as one of us knows!)

La Conner Marina (tel: 360-466-3118), located on the east shore just north of downtown, has guest moorage and full facilities. The marina is within easy walking distance of town and maneuvering your boat is a bit easier here.

Swinomish Channel (North Entrance)

Swinomish Channel is 0.7 mile east of the March Point tanker loading terminal.

Chart 18427
North entrance (100 yards north of red Light "2"): 48°30.57′ N, 122°33.29′ W (NAD 83)
Swinging railroad bridge: 48°27.49′ N, 122°30.90′ W (NAD 83)

At Padilla Bay entrance, the railroad swing bridge has a clearance of 5 feet; the span is left in the open position until a train approaches. Twin fixed highway bridges 0.2 mile S of the swing bridge have a clearance of 75 feet.

Two floats and a launching ramp are under the E end of the highway bridge at the N end of Swinomish Channel. (p. 339, CP)

Don Douglass

North Swinomish Channel

Although Swinomish Channel looks rather intimidating on the chart, pleasure craft transit at all tides and in all seasons by carefully staying in the fairway. Deep-draft vessels should consult tide tables and time their passage appropriately. Mud and sand shoals on either side of the narrow channel require careful attention to avoid groundings.

The north entrance to Swinomish Channel is marked by a series of red-lighted markers which define the shallow water along the west side of the channel. Pass close to these markers, particularly near green Marker "7." Be careful to remain in the narrow dredged fairway southbound from Marker "12" to the swinging bridge.

March Point, which separates the north part of Swinomish Channel from Fidalgo Bay, has large oil refining complexes with two tanker-loading facilities off its north end. When entering Fidalgo Bay or Cap Sante, avoid these offshore oil facilities—they are heavily used by large vessels at all hours, day and night.

Fidalgo Bay (Fidalgo Island)

Fidalgo Bay lies between March Point and Anacortes Harbor.

Chart 18427
Anchor (200 yards east of Buoy "C-3"):
48°30.52′ N, 122°35.52′ W

Fidalgo Bay, a shallow arm of Padilla Bay, extends S from the E end of Guemes Channel. (p. 341, CP)

Fidalgo Bay is a shallow bay with dredged Cap Sante Waterway providing access to the marinas on the south side of Anacortes.

Anchorage for small craft is frequently taken off Anacortes Harbor, east of green Buoy "3" in about 3 fathoms. A number of public mooring buoys have been installed east of the kayak/dinghy dock.

Anchor in about 2 fathoms over sticky mud with good holding.

Cap Sante Waterway (Fidalgo Island)

Cap Sante Waterway is 0.17 mile southeast of the southern tip of Cap Sante.

Chart 18427
Red-green entrance buoy (junction lighted Buoy "A"): 48°30.69′ N, 122°35.63′ W (NAD 83)
Cap Sante Boat Haven (described below): entrance to Cap Sante dredged channel (100 yards northeast of green Marker "G1"): 48°30.70′ N, 122°35.88′ W (NAD 83)
Entrance at breakwater: 48°30.71′ N, 122°36.28′ W (NAD 83)
Entrance to the dredged channel leading to Anacortes Industrial Park (200 yards north of green Marker "C3"): 48°30.62′ N, 122°35.68′ W (NAD 83)
Anacortes Marina north breakwater entrance: 48°30.26′ N, 122°36.09′ W (NAD 83)
Anacortes Marina south breakwater entrance: 48°30.13′ N, 122°36.07′ W (NAD 83)

A dredged channel, marked by lights and buoys, extends about 0.7 mile SW from the entrance to Cap Sante Waterway to the waterfront area of Anacortes Industrial Park. In June 1989, the controlling depth was 16 feet. A marina is at the N

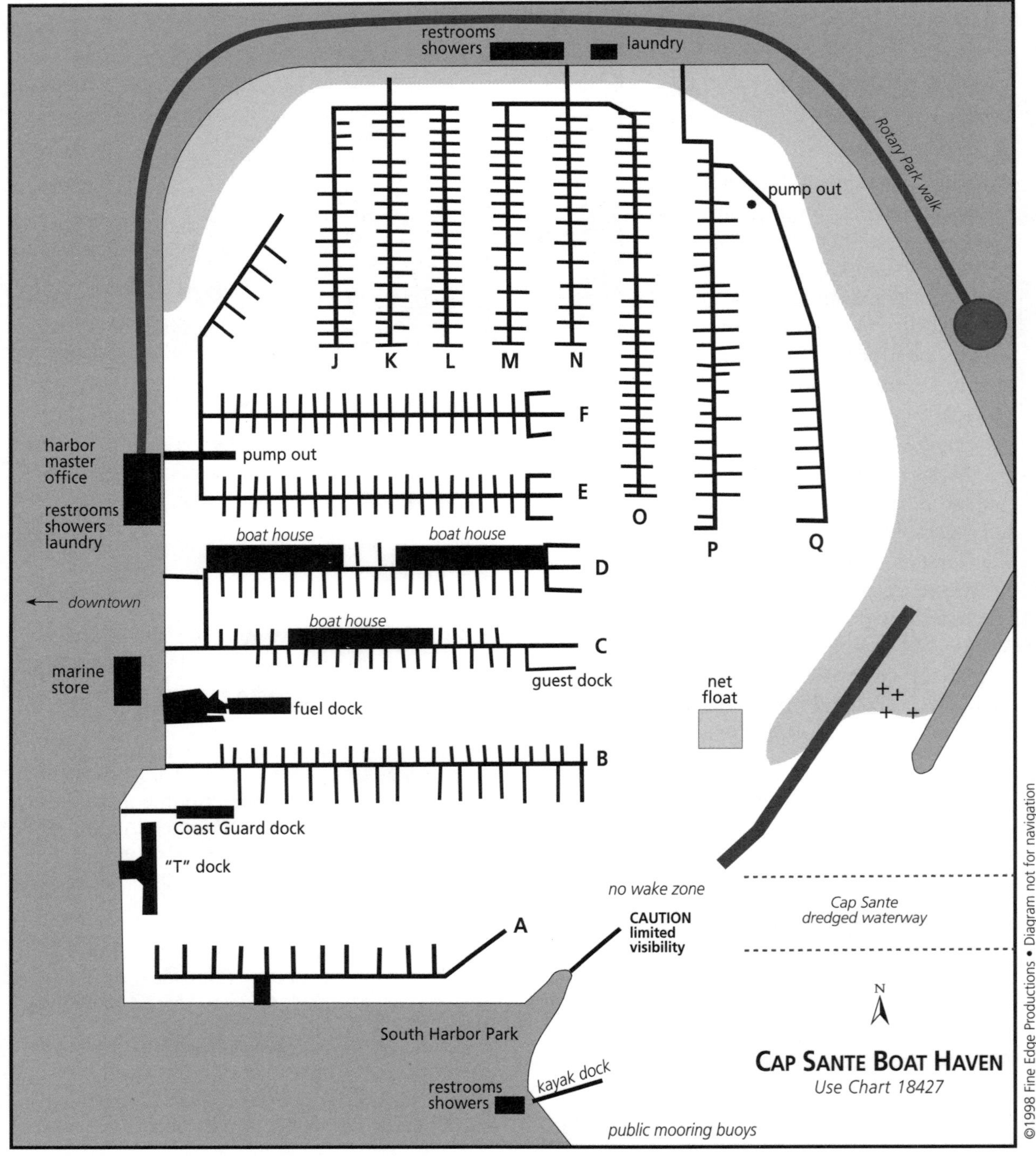

end of the industrial waterfront area. Berthing with water, electricity, storage boxes, and telephone connections are available.

Anchorage is reported available in 8 1/2 to 10 fathoms about 0.8 mile ENE from Cap Sante Waterway Light 2. (p. 340, CP)

Cap Sante Waterway has two dredged channels which converge at red-green Buoy "A." The channel due west from Buoy "A" leads into Cap Sante

Boats entering and leaving Cap Sante Waterway

Approach to Cap Sante Boat Haven

Boat Haven, the large public marina. The dredged channel to the southwest leads to Anacortes Marina and other facilities approximately $^1/_2$ to 1 mile south of Cap Sante Boat Haven.

Cap Sante Boat Haven (Fidalgo Island)

Chart 18427
Breakwater: 48°30.71′ N, 122°36.28′ W (NAD 83)

> *Cap Sante (Capsante) Waterway, a dredged channel leading to the E waterfront of Anacortes, is marked by daybeacons and lights. The ends of the breakwaters forming the boat haven are marked by lights. In April 1993, the controlling depths were 12 feet in the entrance channel and 11 feet in the basin, except for lesser depths along the edges of the basin and in the vicinity of the breakwaters. Vessels should give the S breakwater a berth of at least 40 feet to stay in good water. The Port of Anacortes controls the boat haven. There are berths, with electricity and water, for about 1,100 craft; transient berths and a pump-out station are available. A harbormaster assigns berths. A marina at the basin operates a fuel dock at which gasoline and diesel fuel are available. Water, ice, supplies, a 4-ton lift, and a 30-ton lift that can handle vessels to 55 feet long, are available at the marina. Hull, engine, and electronic repairs can be made at the marina.*
>
> *Gasoline, diesel fuel, and other small-craft supplies may be obtained at the port boat haven. Ice and marine supplies are available in the city.*
>
> *The largest repair facility in the area is the repair yard just W of the port's log handling wharf. The yard has a marine railway which can handle vessels up to 150 feet and has a nominal load rating of 800 tons. . . . A marina on the E waterfront of Anacortes has a mobile lift of 25 tons or 55 feet capacity for complete hull and engine repairs.* (pp. 340–341, CP)

Cap Sante Boat Haven, the marina operated by the Port of Anacortes, is entered 0.4 mile due west of Buoy "A." Transient moorage is available by calling the harbormaster on VHF Channel 66A for a slip assignment (tel: 360-293-0694). The Customs dock is at the east end of C dock.

The marina has clean and extensive facilities which include showers, restrooms and laundries at two locations, power, a pump out station and picnic tables along the walkway. There is a popular deli in the harbormaster complex, and the center of town is just a short walk from the marina.

Anacortes

Anacortes calls itself the "Heart of the Island Empire." Its location, along the northern and western shores of Fidalgo Island, and its abundance of marinas, marine suppliers, and other facilities for boaters, has made it the "Boating Capital of the Northwest." Marinas offering guest moorage include Cap Sante Boat Haven and Skyline Marina in Flounder Bay (see Chapter 2 for details). Privately-owned Anacortes Marina, on the east side of the harbor, has no transient facilities. Cap Sante Marine, in the boat harbor, offers a complete marine repair and maintenance facility.

The town is noted for the many murals that portray its pioneering history. On and near Commercial Avenue, which runs north-south through the city, can be found cafes, restaurants, shops, banks, post office, supermarkets, hardware store, and marine supply stores—everything to fill the needs of a cruising boater or tourist.

G & K Morrow

Tulip Regatta, Padilla Bay

There are many parks in and around Anacortes. Close to Cap Sante Boat Haven is the Seafarer's Memorial, dedicated to mariners who died at sea. Nearby is the W T Preston, an historic steam paddle wheeler, and the restored Railway Depot which houses small gauge train cars, art displays, entertainment, and a Farmers' Market on Saturdays.

Causeland Park, on 8th Street, features native stone mosaics; across the street is the Anacortes Museum.

Popular annual events include the Tulip Festival in March and April, the Waterfront Festival in late May, Shipwreck Days in mid-July, the Pull and Be Damned Rowboat Race in late July, and an arts and crafts festival in early August. Plan to arrive early during such occasions if you want to obtain transient moorage.

Settled in 1860, Anacortes was originally called Ship Harbor. When government surveyor Amos Bowman established a store, wharf, and post office, he dedicated the town to his wife, Anna Curtis, a name which evolved into Anacortes, the Spanish equivalent. Like many frontier towns, Anacortes went through ups and downs—becoming a near-ghost town in the 1890s, saved by lumbering, mills, fish processing, and ship building in the early decades of the 20th century, and bolstered by refineries established in the 1950s, still a major element of the city's economy.

Padilla Bay

Padilla Bay is due east of Anacortes south of Samish Island.

Chart 18427
Position: 48°31.00′ N, 122°33.00′ W (NAD 83)

> *Padilla Bay, between the mainland and the N part of Fidalgo Island, is largely occupied by drying flats, but deep water is E of Anacortes and Guemes Island. Entrance to the bay from Rosario Strait is through Guemes Channel; a passage E of Guemes Island leads into Padilla Bay from the N.* (p. 341, CP)

Like Fidalgo Bay, Padilla Bay is a large, shallow bay with extensive drying mud flats. Both bays

Kent Morrow

A good wind in Padilla Bay

are good places for birdwatching and crabbing. Avoid the crab pot floats which may be hazards along the edge of the bay.

Saddlebag Island (Padilla Bay)

Saddlebag Island is located 0.7 mile northeast of Southeast Point on Guemes Island and 2.4 miles from Cap Sante.

Chart 18427
Saddlebag Island Light "7": 48°32.12′ N, 122°33.55′ W (NAD 83)
South cove entrance: 48°32.04′ N, 122°33.39′ W (NAD 83)
Anchor (south cove): 48°32.08′ N, 122°33.35′ W (NAD 83)
North cove entrance: 48°32.31′ N, 122°33.47′ W (NAD 83)
Anchor (north cove): 48°32.22′ N, 122°33.37′ W (NAD 83)

Saddlebag Island is a marine state park with day use and overnight anchorage. Primitive camping is allowed on shore, but there is no water. It is also an official Cascadia Marine Trail site.

The tiny coves on the north and south side offer some protection depending on the direction of the wind. Space and swinging room are limited; because of their proximity to Anacortes, they are popular destinations in the summer. The coves should be considered fair-weather anchorages only.

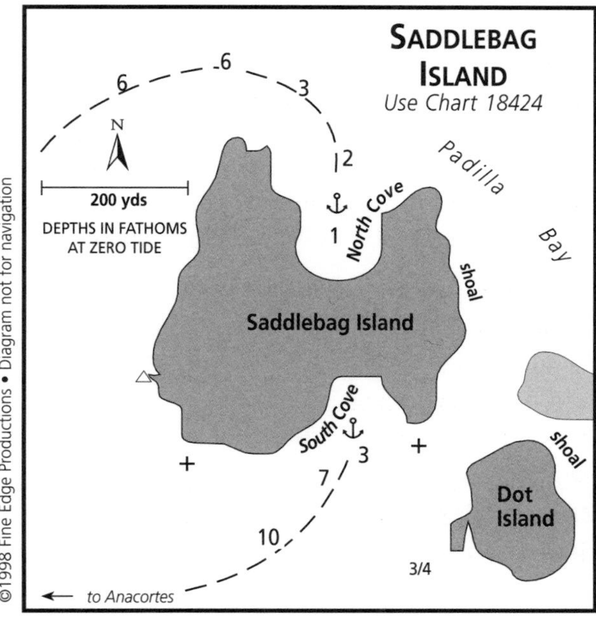

Anchor in either the south or north coves in $1\frac{1}{2}$ to 3 fathoms with fair holding.

A deep-water channel to Bellingham and Vancouver lies between Saddlebag Island and Huckleberry Island east of Guemes Island. The shallow mud flats of Padilla Bay lie east of Saddlebag Island and only kayaks are advised.

Guemes Channel

Charts 18427, 18429, 18423
East entrance (halfway between Cap Sante and Southeast Point): 48°31.38′ N, 122°35.30′ W (NAD 83)
West entrance (half-way between entrance Buoys "G3" and "R4"): 48°31.23′ N, 122°39.29′ W

> *Guemes Channel, between Guemes Island on the N and Fidalgo Island on the S, leads E from Rosario Strait to Padilla Bay. The channel, which is about 3 miles long and 0.5 mile wide at its narrowest point, has depths of 8 to 18 fathoms; the main part of the channel has been wire-dragged to depths of more than 33 feet. Lighted buoys mark the channel at the W end.* (p. 340, CP)

Guemes Channel, the busy channel between Fidalgo and Guemes islands, is fairly well protected from wind-generated chop. However, it has strong currents especially on ebb. Small boats are advised to consult tide and current tables when planning a transit. In fair weather, small craft frequently cross the shoal west of Shannon Point on the northwest corner of Fidalgo Island, but this area can be particularly turbulent and dangerous when a strong ebb is flowing against a southerly wind.

The south shore of Guemes Channel, west of Cap Sante in Anacortes, is developed waterfront with a number of commercial docks and repair facilities, a private marina, and the Guemes ferryboat terminal. The ferryboat terminal for the San Juan Islands is located between Ship Harbor and Shannon Point at the west entrance of the channel.

Cooks Cove (Guemes Island)

Cooks Cove, on the south side of Guemes Island, is 0.4 mile southeast of Deadman's Bay.

Chart 18427
Position: 48°31.92′ N, 122°34.93′ W (NAD 83)

The tiny indentation on the south side of Guemes Island, known as Cooks Cove, is sometimes used as a temporary anchorage for sportfishing boats.

Deadman's Bay (Guemes Island)

Deadman's Bay is 1.4 miles northeast of the Guemes Island ferry terminal.

Chart 18427
Position: 48°32.14′ N, 122°35.50′ W (NAD 83)

Deadman's Bay, an indentation on the south side of Guemes Island, is a shallow bay exposed to southerly weather and the wake from passing vessels. Temporary anchorage can be found here out of the current, with some shelter from northeast winds and good swinging room.

Anchor in $1\frac{1}{2}$ fathoms.

Ship Harbor (Fidalgo Island)

Ship Harbor is located on the south side of Guemes Channel on Fidalgo Island.

Chart 18427
Entrance: 48°30.52′ N, 122°40.33′ W (NAD 83)
Anchor: 48°30.39′ N, 122°40.33′ W (NAD 83)

> *Ship Harbor is a bight close E of Shannon Point, at the west entrance to Guemes Channel. The interisland ferry slips and headquarters are here. Vessels anchoring here in heavy weather should be cautious of dragging anchor because the bottom is not good holding ground.* (p. 340, CP)

Ship Harbor can provide shelter in southeast gales. Avoid the pilings to the southeast of the ferry terminal and mud shoals along shore, as well as the crab pot floats in the area. One of our favorite restaurants, Compass Rose, recently opened above the ferry terminal (tel: 360-293-6600 for hours).

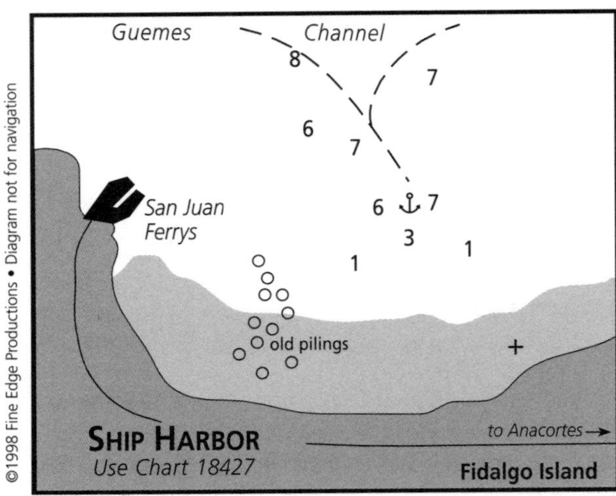

Anchor 0.2 mile east of the San Juan Islands ferry terminal in 5 fathoms over a mud bottom.

Washington Park (Fidalgo Island)

Washington Park is located between Fidalgo Head and Sunset Beach on the northwest tip of Fidalgo Island.

Chart 18427
Position (launching ramp): 48°30.03′ N, 122°41.55′ W (NAD 83)

Washington Park, owned and managed by the City of Anacortes, has a fully-developed campground, picnic area, and small boat launching facilities. A 3.5-mile road, a favorite of bicyclists, hikers, and joggers, loops around Fidalgo Head through a lovely forested area. The views of Rosario Strait and the San Juan Islands from the point are spectacular, particularly at sunset. This is also a popular area for kayaks and sportfishing boats.

Boat Harbor (Guemes Island)

Boat Harbor is 1.0 mile northwest of Saddlebag Island Light.

Charts 18427, 18424
Position: 48°32.87′ N, 122°34.78′ W (NAD 83)

Tiny Boat Harbor, on Guemes Island's east shore, faces Padilla Bay and is exposed to the southeast. It does, however, offer protection from northwest winds for small boats but with limited swinging room.

The schooner Adventuress

Schooners

Several large schooners still sail regularly through the islands in the spring, summer and fall. The *Zodiac* from Bellingham and the *Adventuress* from Port Townsend both offer charters and sail training.

The *Adventuress,* owned by Sound Experience (founded by by Barb Wyatt and Morley Horder), is much like the Hudson River sloop *Clearwater*—a floating environmental education center in New York since 1969. Morley, who was Captain of the *Clearwater* for four years, returned to his native Northwest to create a similar program.

Anyone can be a "volunteer" aboard the *Adventuress* for a week, and many people spend as much as a month aboard as interns. **—PF**

A group of school children on a sail

Samish Island

Samish Island is located between Padilla and Samish bays.

Chart 18427
William Point Light: 48°34.98′ N, 122°33.62′ W (NAD 83)
Anchor Northwest Bight: 48°34.97′ N, 122°32.91′ W (NAD 83)

> *William Point, 100 feet high, is the W point of Samish Island, which forms the N side of Padilla Bay. The point is wooded and, because of the low land E of it, appears as an island although it is connected with the mainland. It is marked by a light.* (p. 341, CP)

Samish Island is a long sandspit that separates Padilla Bay on the south from Samish Bay and Bellingham Bay on the north. A number of houses lie along its north shore.

Anchorage for small craft can be found 0.46 mile east of William Point Light in the northeast bight of the island just outside the line of kelp and east of the piling. Some boats also anchor off a large shoal area 1.3 miles east of William Point Light.

Anchor in 4 to 6 fathoms over a mud and gravel bottom with fair holding.

Peter Fromm

Classic gillnetter in Bellingham Bay

Bellingham Bay

Bellingham Bay is east of Lummi Island and north of Samish Island.

Charts 18424, 18423
Outer entrance (0.4 mile east of Eliza Rock Light): 48°38.59′ N, 122°34.07′ W (NAD 83)
Inner entrance (0.5 mile due west of Post Point red Buoy "2"): 48°42.80′ N, 122°32.50′ W (NAD 83)

> *Bellingham Bay, from William Point to the head, is about 12 miles long and 3 miles wide. Anchorage may be obtained almost anywhere in the bay S of the flats; the depths, over the greater portion, range from 6 to 15 fathoms. Because of the mud bottom, vessels are apt to drag anchor in heavy weather.* (p. 341, CP)

Bellingham Bay, the large indentation along the mainland, has a number of marinas and anchor sites along its shore. While the bay is well protected by the off-lying islands, it develops significant chop during strong winds. Bellingham Bay is a popular area for sailing and kayaking.

Wildcat Cove

Wildcat Cove is located 1.16 nautical miles southeast of Governors Point.

Chart 18424
Position: 48°29.18′ N, 122°29.64′ W (NAD 83)

> *The small-craft launching ramp of Larabee State Park is at Wildcat Cove, 0.6 mile SE of Governors Point at the SW entrance to Chuckanut Bay.* (p. 342, CP)

Wildcat Cove, along Chuckanut Drive, is a small cove where small boats or kayaks can find temporary anchorage off the drying flat. Avoid the rocks off the west corner of the cove.

Chuckanut Bay

Chuckanut Bay is 2.5 miles south of Fair Haven, South Bellingham.

Chart 18424
Anchor (lee of Chuckanut Island): 48°40.60′ N, 122°29.81′ W (NAD 83)
Anchor (north end Chuckanut Bay): 48°41.72′ N, 122°30.17′ W (NAD 83)

> *Chuckanut Bay, which indents the E shore of Bellingham Bay, is a cove affording shelter to small craft. A rock ledge, covered 3 feet is reported just S of Chuckanut Island in about 48°40.5′ N, 122°30.1′ W.* (p. 342, CP)

Peter Fromm

Chuckanut Island

Chuckanut Island and Pleasant Bay

Chuckanut Island, also known as Dot Island, is a delightful place that gives the feeling of being more than just five miles away from the small but growing city of Bellingham. Pleasant Bay, south of Chuckanut Island, was once the winter moorage for large northwest lumber and fishing schooners. In old photos, you can frequently see a dozen of these boats well-secured and rafted together in the bay.—**PF**

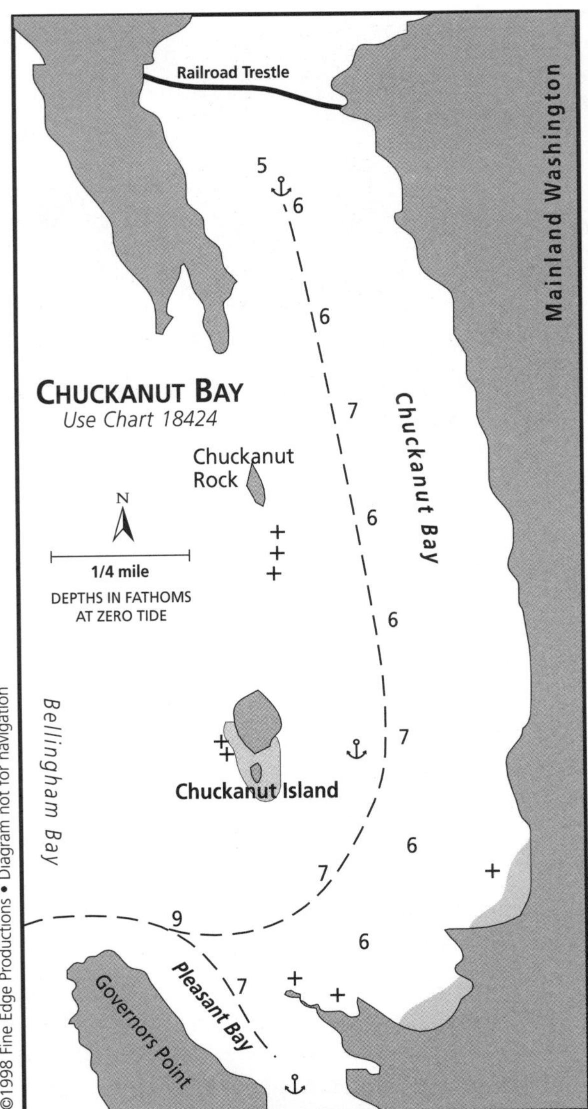

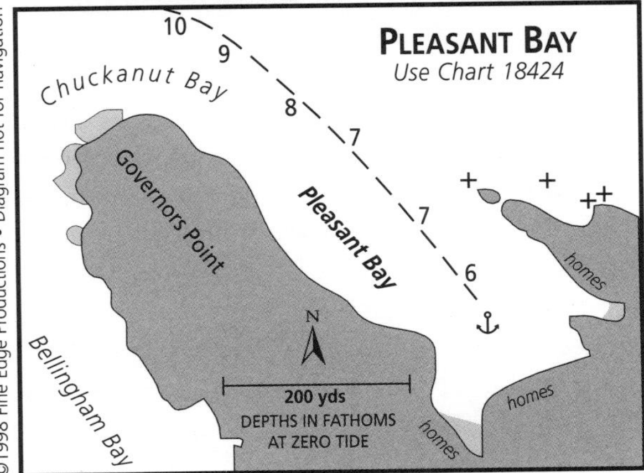

Don Douglass

Pleasant Bay

Chuckanut Bay is the indentation north of Governors Point. In fair weather, you can frequently find anchorage in the lee of Chuckanut Island (known locally as Dot Island) or—for protection from northwest winds—in the north end of Chuckanut Bay, south of the railroad trestle. During southeast weather Pleasant Bay offers good shelter.

Anchor in 6 fathoms over a thin mud, hardpan bottom with fair holding.

Pleasant Bay

Pleasant Bay is located a quarter-mile east of Governors Point.

Chart 18424
Entrance: 48°40.28′ N, 122°30.53′ W (NAD 83)
Anchor: 48°39.89′ N, 122°30.08′ W (NAD 83)

Pleasant Bay, once a popular anchorage for sailing ships, is now lined with beautiful homes. Although you can find good protection from southeast winds at the head of the bay, for safety you may need to tie to shore, much like the old sailing ships did. Avoid a small reef that extends 30 feet from shore in the small notch southeast of Governors Point, as well as private docks and floats.

Anchor in 6 fathoms over thin sand and black mud with stones; poor-to-fair holding.

Don Douglass

Sailboat moored in Pleasant Bay

Bellingham Harbor

Chart 18424

Entrance (0.5 mile north of red bell Buoy "2"): 48°43.31′ N, 122°31.73′ W (NAD 83)

Bellingham is at the head of Bellingham Bay on the E shore. Wood and wood products including pulp, aluminum, chemicals, and general cargo are shipped out; salt, alumina, and general cargo are imported. A large pulpmill is just NE of the port wharves of Bellingham, and an aluminum smelter is at Ferndale. These mills have their own wharves, but use the port facilities to ship and receive some of their material.

Whatcom Creek Waterway at the SE end of Bellingham Harbor, Squalicum Creek Waterway at the NW end of the harbor, and I and J Street Waterway in between, provide dredged channel access to the port facilities at Bellingham. Bellingham Yacht Harbor is adjacent to and SE of Squalicum Creek Waterway . . .

A seafood plant is on the I and J Street Waterway; fishing boats unload at its wharf. The areas on both sides of the waterway channel are used for log storage. There are several other seafood wharves, oil docks, and other commercial facilities round the harbor.

Bellingham Yacht Harbor is adjacent to and SE of Squalicum Creek Waterway . . .

The bottom mud is a thin accumulation over hardpan, and is not good holding ground in heavy weather. (p. 342, CP)

Peter Fromm

Rowers in Bellingham Bay

Bellingham, the closest major U.S. city to the Canadian border and a great starting point for voyages to the San Juan and Gulf Islands, lies 54 miles south of Vancouver and 86 miles north of Seattle. It is also the southern terminus for the Alaskan Marine Highway ferry system. Squalicum Boat Harbor, in the Port of Bellingham, is a customs port-of-entry with plenty of guest moorage. Bellingham Harbor, in the northeast corner of Bellingham Bay, has several marinas where you can obtain transient moorage; you can also anchor at Fair Haven.

Bellingham is a sophisticated city with excellent restaurants, galleries and specialty shops, cafes, hotels, motels, B & Bs, colorful flower vendors, sidewalk food carts, and a European flavor. There are numerous recreational opportunities in the area, including whale watching, fishing, swimming, golf and tennis, hiking, and camping at nearby state parks. May is Maritime Month and features classic boat races, a salmon bake, and arts and crafts exhibits. Boulevard Park in southern Bellingham is a beautiful two-level park

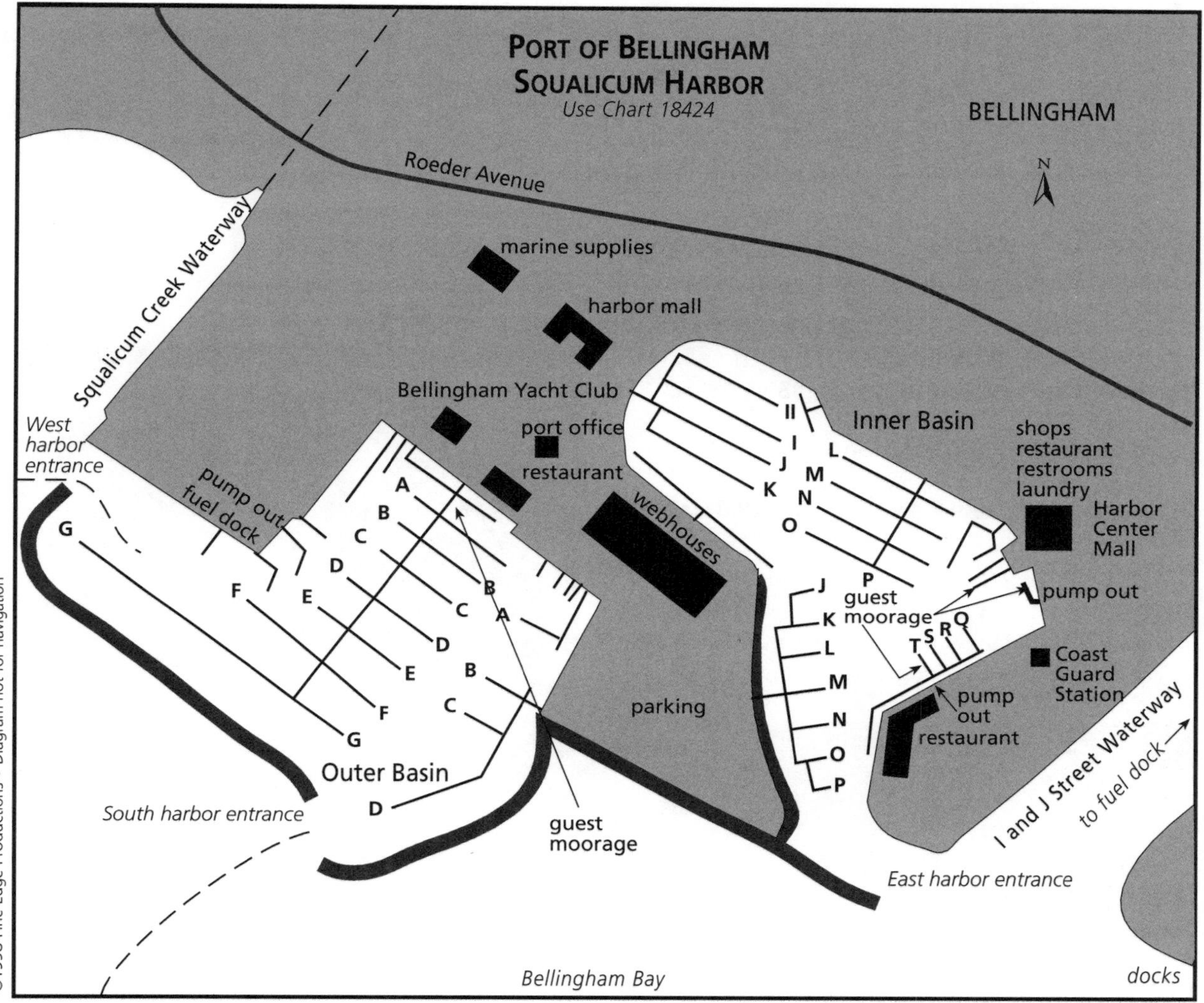

with a pier with floats for day moorage (open to wind and seas), a lookout and gazebo.

Mount Baker Theater is a splendid, historic theater with a Wurlitzer pipe organ. The campus of Western Washington University houses the Western Outdoor Museum, which has art works and sculptures, and a summer stock theater. Close to downtown, on C Street, the Maritime Heritage Center offers fishing for steelhead and trout; at the hatchery you can watch salmon spawn.

In 1792, Captain George Vancouver named Bellingham Bay after Sir William Bellingham. Settlement began in 1852 with the establishment of a lumber mill.

Fair Haven (South Bellingham)

Fair Haven is located in South Bellingham 0.65 mile northeast of Post Point.

Charts 18424, 18427
Entrance: 48°43.55′ N, 122°30.75′ W (NAD 83)
Anchor: 48°43.34′ N, 122°30.69′ W (NAD 83)

> *The S terminal of the Port of Bellingham, a cannery, and a boatbuilding plant are on the N side of Post Point at South Bellingham. The Alaska State Ferries depart from a facility just N of Post Point.* (p. 342, CP)

Fair Haven has linear line public mooring buoys, a system of bow and stern ties which minimizes swinging room. Anchorage can be found east of the Alaska ferry dock and west of the mooring buoys. Fair Haven is a boatbuilding, fishing, and commercial area. Limited facilities are available at Fair Haven Boatworks.

Anchor in 4 to 6 fathoms over a mucky bottom with good holding.

Squalicum Boat Harbor

Chart 18424
Southeast entrance (west basin): 48°45.22′ N, 122°30.44′ W (NAD 83)
Northwest entrance (west basin): 48°45.45′ N, 122°30.68′ W (NAD 83)
I & J Street Waterway position: 48°44.95′ N, 122°30.11′ W (NAD 83)
East basin entrance: 48°45.19′ N, 122°29.81′ W (NAD 83)

Squalicum Boat Harbor, adjacent to and SE of the Squalicum Creek Waterway, is protected by breakwaters on its SE and SW sides. The harbor can be entered from the SE between the two breakwaters,

Don Douglass

Boat harbor, Bellingham

Peter Fromm

Schooner at sail in Bellingham Bay

or from the NW from the Squalicum Creek Waterway. The channelward ends of the breakwaters at the SE entrance are marked by lights; a fog signal is sounded from the southernmost light. The entrance from the Squalicum Creek Waterway is also marked by two lights. Depths inside the harbor are 10 to 15 feet.

Berths for about 2,200 pleasure craft and fishing boats are in the harbor. A guest float is maintained near the harbormaster's office on the NE side of the harbor. Gasoline, diesel fuel, electricity, water, ice, and marine supplies are available. Several marine equipment repair and fishing supply firms are in the area N of the SE entrance to the harbor.

A small-craft basin, protected by a breakwater on its S side, is N of I & J Street Waterway. The basin can be entered from I & J Street Waterway. Depths of 9 to 12 feet are in the basin. (p. 343, CP)

Peter Fromm

Miss Melanie *at Lummi Island*

Squalicum Boat Harbor is divided into two basins; the older basin on the north side is entered via Squalicum Creek or directly through an entrance in the breakwater on the southwest side. The marina has been renovated with complete facilities for guests.

The east basin is known as the I & J Street Waterway Small Craft Basin. A small-craft basin in Squalicum Boat Harbor is on the north side of the I & J Street Waterway. The port office is on the northwest corner of this basin and the harbor mall is located on the east side.

Convenient bus transportation into Bellingham proper can be found on Roeder Avenue.

Lummi Island

Lummi Island is on the west side of Bellingham Bay.

Chart 18424
Position: (ferry dock): 48°43.32′ N, 122°40.86′ W (NAD 83)

Lummi Island, wooded and about 8 miles long, forms the E side of the N end of Rosario Strait, opposite Orcas Island. The N part is low, but in the S part Lummi Peak attains an elevation of over 1,600 feet.

Lummi Island, a village on the W side of Hale Passage, is 1 mile S of Lane Spit. The village and island are linked to the mainland at Gooseberry Point by an automobile ferry. The ferry dock at Lummi Island is marked by a private light and fog signal. (pp. 339, 341, CP)

Lummi Island, whose western shore rises to a 1,600-foot ridge that can be seen from a great distance in fair weather, is a long, thin island. Inati Bay, on its east coast, is a popular anchorage for pleasure craft. Hale Passage, between Lummi Island and the mainland, is used extensively by commercial and small boat traffic.

The western shore of Lummi Island north of the mountains is the site of reef net fishing. See sidebar for a description of this interesting craft.

Inati Bay (Lummi Island)

Inati Bay, on the east side of Lummi Island, is 3.75 miles southeast of the ferry dock.

Chart 18424
Entrance: 48°40.43′ N, 122°37.12′ W (NAD 83)
Anchor: 48°40.31′ N, 122°37.32′ W (NAD 83)

Inati Bay is a small but scenic bay that offers good protection from southeast, south, and northwest winds. It is open to any wind or chop from the northeast. Some wake from passing fishing boats is felt in the bay. As you enter the bay, avoid the rock marked by a buoy 0.17 mile north of the peninsula which forms the east shore of the bay. You can easily land a dinghy at the head of the bay where the Bellingham Yacht Club has some picnic facilities.

Inati Bay

Anchor in 4 fathoms over sand and mud with some kelp; fair-to-good holding.

Reil Harbor (Lummi Island)

Reil Harbor is 0.4 mile southeast of Inati Bay

Chart 18424
Position: 48°39.99′ N, 122°36.99′ W (NAD 83)

Reil Harbor, the small indentation around the "corner" from Inati Bay, offers less shelter, but it can be used as an overflow in fair weather when Inati Bay is full. The harbor has good protection from westerlies but is wide open to southerlies as indicated by driftwood on shore.

Anchor in about 5 fathoms.

Inati Bay

Inati Bay, on the southeast side of Lummi Island, is one of the most beautiful bays in these islands. Thickly-wooded hillsides rise straight up from the water, and the sound of a waterfall on the west side of the anchorage echoes off the cliffs of the eastern point. The Bellingham Yacht Club purchased the land on shore for the use and enjoyment of all boaters.—**PF**

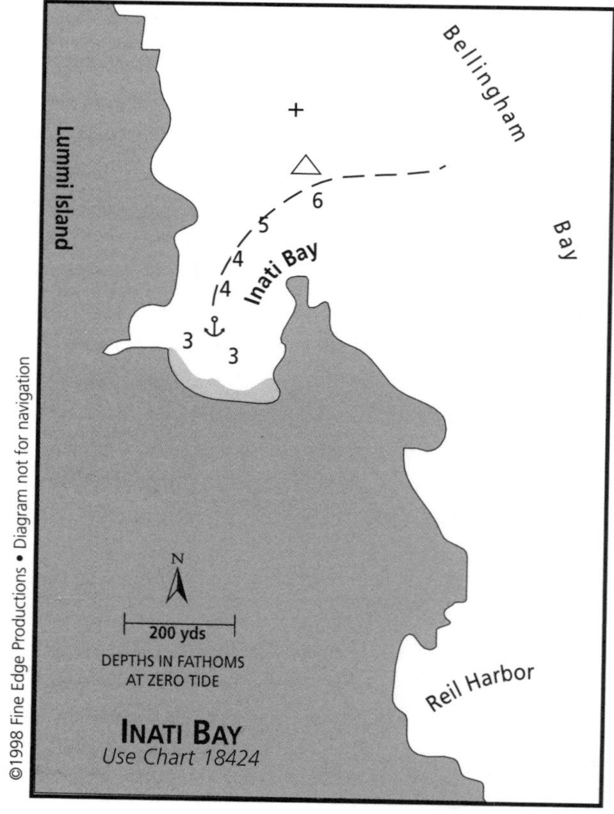

Don Douglass

Bellingham City from harbor

Eliza Island (Bellingham Bay)

Eliza Island is located at the southwest corner of Bellingham Bay.

Chart 18424
Anchor (north bight): 48°39.20′ N, 122°35.53′ W (NAD 83)
Entrance (south cove): 48°38.80′ N, 122°35.30′ W (NAD 83)
Anchor (south cove): 48°38.88′ N, 122°35.00′ W (NAD 83)

> *Eliza Island, low and partly wooded, is 1 mile NE of Carter Point. Shoals fringe most of the island, which should not be approached closer than about 400 yards. A rock covered 1 fathom is some 500 yards N of the W tip of the island.*
>
> *Vessels anchoring between Lummi Island and Eliza Island during heavy weather should be cautious of dragging anchor because of the poor holding ground.* (p. 341, CP)

Eliza Island, which lies 0.6 mile off the southeast tip of Lummi Island, has a number of private homes. You can anchor in the north bight over an irregular bottom, avoiding shoals and kelp patches; the north bight—in the lee of the tree-covered point—offers fair protection from southeasterlies. Better anchorage can be found in the south bight where the bottom is more uniform. Be sure to avoid the numerous private mooring buoys.

Anchor (north bight) in 5 to 6 fathoms over black muck and some grass with good holding.

Anchor (south bight) in $1\frac{1}{2}$ to 3 fathoms over black muck and some grass with very good holding.

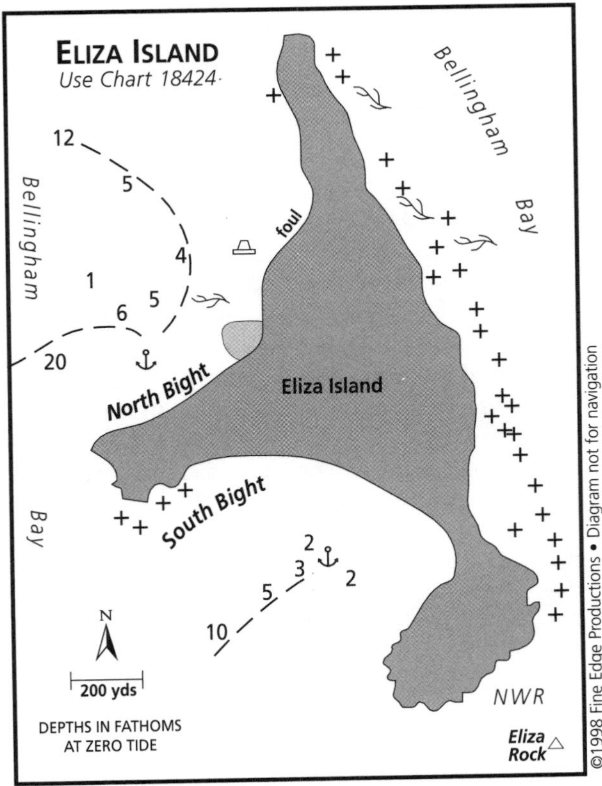

Don Douglass

Fair Haven moorage system

Reef Netting

Historically the commercial salmon fishery in the San Juan Islands employed many people; as fishermen, as aboard-boat buyers, and in canneries. Today this resource has virtually disappeared as a viable industry in which people can earn a living. No fisherman can exist these days solely on income from fishing in these islands.

Although people still fish commercially using many different styles—reef netting, gill netting, and purse seining—everyone involved in this pursuit has other jobs throughout the rest of the year. "Openings"—days when commercial fishermen are permitted to go out and try to catch fish—are severely limited these days.

Reef net fishing, found only in the San Juan Islands, is a relic of the low-tech manner in which Native Americans once caught salmon. Two flat-bottomed, wide boats are anchored in a specific location where schools of salmon swim. Artificial "reefs" of lines with streamers dangling underwater extend outward at angles from the boats, funneling the schools of fish between the boats. A net is suspended between boats and when fish are spotted from a lookout above, the nets are hauled in, often with fish, sometimes without. It takes true patience to wait for the fish to come. Several years ago some of the reef net folks hit it big, catching between three and six thousand salmon! A hundred would be a good day normally.

Gill nets are strung out from a boat and suspended from the surface of the water by a "cork line" of floats; the net may dangle as deep as 60 feet. Different sizes of mesh allow smaller fish to escape through the net. "Keeper-sized" fish get their gills caught in the net and cannot escape. However, this particular kind of net tends to catch surface and diving birds, seals, dolphins and porpoise, killing them indiscriminately.

Purse seining is done from larger vessels with the assistance of a power skiff. When the skipper determines that this is a good spot to try, the skiff motors away from the stern of the seiner, pulling out the net. The skiff driver makes a large circle with the net and returns to the stern of the larger boat. The bottom of the net is then pulled aboard, making a "purse" of the remaining net—hopefully full of salmon.

The numbers of salmon in the San Juan Islands, once the highest on the west coast, have radically decreased due to loss of habitat and may result in the cessation of all commercial salmon fishing. Construction of dams on rivers, clearcutting of forests, and other human development, have caused this massive loss.—**PF**

2

ROSARIO STRAIT

Lopez Island to Thatcher Pass, Blakely Island, Obstruction Pass, Bowman Bay to Bellingham Channel and the Sucia Islands

Rosario Strait, the easternmost of the three main north-south routes between the Strait of Juan de Fuca and the Strait of Georgia, leads eventually to Bellingham and Vancouver. From Deception Pass, you can cruise along the west coast of Fidalgo Island, visiting Burrows Bay with some lovely views; in Flounder Bay, you will find Skyline Marina with its excellent facilities. If you go west across the strait to the southern shore of Lopez, visit Hughes, Aleck and McArdle bays. (The entrance to McArdle is a picturesque cliff-lined passage.) Follow Rosario Strait northward along Decatur and Blakely islands' eastern shores. Blakely Island Marina and General Store has excellent facilities. East of Blakely lies thickly-forested Cypress island where more than 100 species of birds can be seen; there are campsites and great fishing in the various coves.

You can take in Sinclair Island to the northeast of Cypress or head west toward Obstruction Island. Lieber Haven Resort, in the middle of Obstruction Pass, is an unusual spot, with groceries, cabins, kayaks and parrots. Rounding Deer Point, go up the east side of Orcas. Doe Island State Park is relatively secluded and a popular area for scuba diving. You can visit Clark Island State Park, then set off northwestward to Puffin, Matia, Sucia, and Patos islands. Sucia has dramatically-shaped sandstone and a marine park. Patos Island is also a marine park, with relatively primitive facilities.

Rosario Strait

Rosario Strait starts west of Deception Pass at the southeast corner of Lopez Island and runs due north for 21 miles through the San Juan Islands

G & K Morrow

Midchannel buoy, Rosario Strait

to its junction with the Strait of Georgia between Lummi and Matia islands.

Charts 18429, 18430
South entrance (1.9 miles east of Watmough Head at Convergence Zone): 48°25.80′ N, 122°45.50′ W (NAD 83)
North entrance (0.9 mile east of Lawrence Point): 48°39.70′ N, 122°43.20′ W (NAD 83)

> *Rosario Strait, the easternmost of the three main channels leading from the Strait of Juan de Fuca to the Strait of Georgia, is 20 miles long and from 1.5 to 5 miles wide. The water is deep, and the most important dangers are marked.*
>
> *The strait is in constant use by vessels bound to Bellingham, Anacortes, and the San Juan Islands. Vessels bound for British Columbia or Alaska also frequently use it in preference to the passages farther W, when greater advantage can be taken of the tidal currents.*
>
> *For times and velocities of current in Rosario Strait and vicinity, the Tidal Current Tables should be consulted. The currents in Lopez, Thatcher, and Obstruction Passes are reported to attain velocities of 3 to 7 knots. This should be kept in mind when proceeding through Rosario Strait, particularly at night or in thick weather. On the ebb of a large tide off the entrance to the passes, a S wind causes tide rips that are dangerous to small craft.*
>
> *Mariners should give Colville Island and Davidson Rock a good berth. The southbound lane of the Traffic Separation Scheme is close S and E of Davidson Rock.* (p. 335, CP)

Rosario Strait, one of the main north-south routes between Bellingham Bay and the Strait of Georgia, is used extensively by deep-sea ships and barges. Due to its exposure to south winds and strong ebb currents, the strait develops choppy seas in gale or storm conditions. When exiting or entering Thatcher Pass, pleasure vessels should be particularly watchful for large ships steaming in Rosario Strait.

At the south entrance to Rosario Strait there are two traffic separation zones; one for traffic from the Strait of Juan de Fuca, the other for traffic from Puget Sound. Pleasure craft should cross these zones at right angles, keeping a sharp lookout. In restricted visibility, call Vessel Traffic Services on VHF to determine if transit of the strait is safe.

Good shelter can be found along both sides of Rosario Strait.

Northwest Pass

Northwest Pass is the waterway connecting Deception Pass with Rosario Strait.

Chart 18427
Southeast entrance (0.05 mile south of Lighthouse Point): 48°24.43′ N, 122°39.40′ W (NAD 83)
Northwest entrance: (0.22 mile north of Deception Island): 48°24.73′ N, 122°40.35′ W (NAD 83)

> *Foul ground exists between West Point and Deception Island. Vessels should not attempt to pass between them, and should always stay in Northwest Pass. Shoals also extend N of Deception Island with depths of less than 2 fathoms nearly 200 yards offshore.* (p. 338, CP)

Northwest Pass, on the north side of Deception Island, has strong tide rips during spring tides, especially on ebbing currents.

Bowman Bay, also known as Reservation Bay (Fidalgo Island)

Bowman Bay is located 0.7 mile northwest of Deception Pass.

Chart 18427
Entrance: 48°24.70′ N, 122°39.60′ W (NAD 83)
Anchor: 48°24.79′ N, 122°39.23′ W (NAD 83)
Public buoys: 48°24.97′ N, 122°39.27′ W (NAD 83)

Don Douglass

Bowman Bay

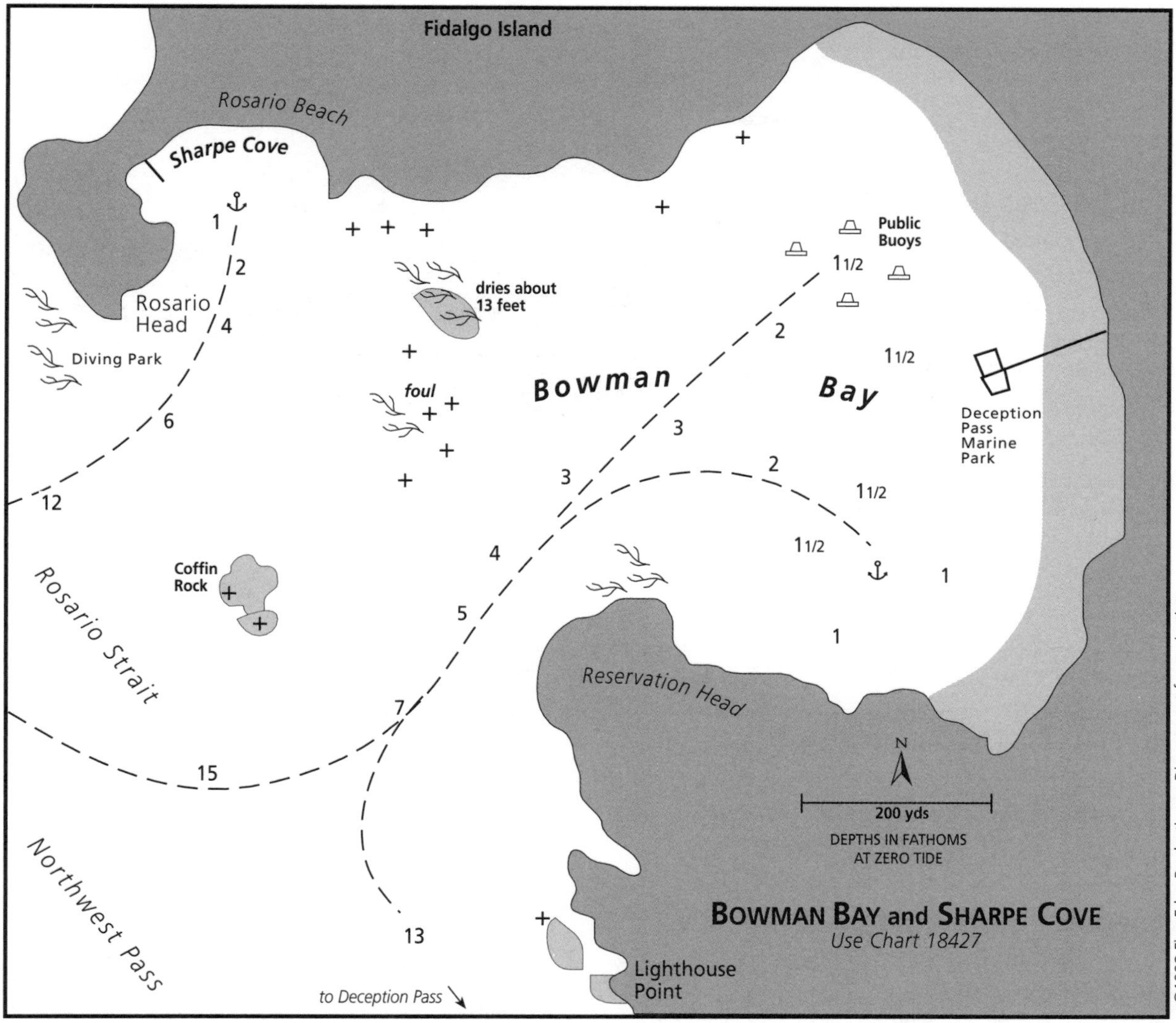

Fidalgo Island
Rosario Beach
Sharpe Cove
Rosario Head
Diving Park
dries about 13 feet
foul
Bowman Bay
Public Buoys
Deception Pass Marine Park
Coffin Rock
Rosario Strait
Reservation Head
Northwest Pass
to Deception Pass
Lighthouse Point
200 yds
DEPTHS IN FATHOMS AT ZERO TIDE

BOWMAN BAY and SHARPE COVE
Use Chart 18427

Bowman (Reservation) Bay, a small bight between Reservation Head and Rosario Head, offers anchorage for small craft in 2 1/4 fathoms, mud bottom. (p. 338, CP)

Bowman Bay, at the southwest tip of Fidalgo Island, offers good shelter throughout the shallow bay. For protection from southeast winds, use the south corner as indicated in the diagram. There are four public mooring buoys in the north end of the bay. The large fishing pier and dinghy dock are convenient for using the park facilities.

Deception Pass State Marine Park is located at two sites within the bay and has picnic and overnight camping and restrooms. Showers and power are not available. An underwater diving park is near Rosario Head on the west side of the bay near Sharpe Cove, and a public pier and float

Don Douglass

Bowman Bay fishing pier

are in front of the large picnic area on the east side of Bowman Bay.

Anchor in 1 to 1 ½ fathoms over a mud bottom with good holding.

Peter Fromm

The vessel Garth Foss *passes through Rosario Strait*

Sharpe Cove (Fidalgo Island)

Sharpe Cove is 0.25 mile northwest of Bowman Bay.

Chart 18427
Entrance (0.1 mile west of Gull Rock):
48°24.86′ N, 122°39.78′ W (NAD 83)
Position: 48°24.98′ N, 122°39.79′ W (NAD 83)

Sharpe Cove is a shallow and scenic area just east of Rosario Head. Small boats in fair weather can find temporary anchorage south of the small islet in the center of the bay. Avoid the reefs between Bowman Bay and Sharpe Cove which extend 0.15 mile from the north shore. Sharpe Cove is also the site of Deception Pass Marine Park and underwater diving park with a public dock on its west side. Anchorage can be found in the cove north of Sharpe Cove; however, it is exposed to westerlies and traffic wake from the strait.

Anchor in 2 to 3 fathoms.

Telegraph Bight (Fidalgo Island)

Telegraph Bight is located 200 yards south of Biz Point.

Chart 18427
Position (0.1 mile south of Biz Point):
48°26.46′ N, 122°40.68′ W (NAD 83)

Telegraph Bight is a tiny bight that provides a temporary stop for kayakers and small boats.

Burrows Bay (Fidalgo Island)

Burrows Bay is on the west side of Fidalgo Island between Langley Bay on the south and Flounder Bay on the north.

Chart 18427
South entrance (0.50 mile west of Biz Point):
48°26.56′ N, 122°41.48′ W (NAD 83)
North entrance (east end of Burrows Pass):
48°29.31′ N, 122°41.00′ W (NAD 83)

> *Burrows Bay indents the W shore of Fidalgo Island between Biz Point and Fidalgo Head. Burrows Bay is a broad open bight affording anchorage in the N part, in 15 to 16 fathoms, soft bottom. Protection from W and N is afforded by Burrows Island and Allan Island, but the bay is exposed to S weather. In the SE part, the depths are less than 6 fathoms, and in places shoals extend almost 0.4 mile off the E and S shores of the bay. E of the passage between Allan and Burrows Islands is a middle ground with a least depth of 5 fathoms. Small craft using Deception Pass, bound to or from points in the islands or from Bellingham Bay, pass through Burrows Bay and the passage N of Burrows Island.* (p. 338, CP)

Burrows Bay is a large bight sheltered from prevailing northwest winds by Fidalgo Head and Burrow and Allan islands. The bay has significant fetch and heavy chop can develop on southeast or southwest winds. High cliffs and large homesites ring the bay.

Langley Bay (Fidalgo Island)

Langley Bay is 2.5 miles northwest of Deception Pass and in the south end of Burrows Bay.

Chart 18427
Position: 48°26.73′ N, 122°40.38′ W (NAD 83)

Langley Bay provides temporary shelter in fair weather or temporary protection in southeast gales. Avoid the reef in the center of the bay and a rock at the north end of the bay and also the reef and kelp off Biz Point.

Anchor in 5 fathoms over a mud bottom with fair-to-good holding.

Burrows Pass

Burrows Pass is located 0.5 mile west of Flounder Bay.

Chart 18427
West entrance: 48°29.32′ N, 122°42.30′ W (NAD 83)
East entrance: 48°29.31′ N, 122°40.96′ W (NAD 83)

Burrows Pass, a busy channel between Fidalgo Head and Burrows Island, is used by pleasure craft headed for Thatcher and Lopez passes. Be on the watch for slow-moving kayaks and canoes.

Burrows Island is a 330-acre undeveloped State Park. Most of the island has steep cliffs. Alice Bight, on the northeast shore, is sometimes used as a temporary anchorage close to shore. Both Alice Bight and Short Bay on the north side of Burrows Island are used as haulouts for kayaks and canoes.

Flounder Bay (Fidalgo Island)

Flounder Bay is 1.0 mile east of Fidalgo Head and 5.2 miles northwest of Deception Pass.

Chart 18427
Entrance (midway private lights): 48°29.35′ N, 122°40.63′ W (NAD 83)

Peter Fromm

Orcas "cruising" the Strait of Juan de Fuca

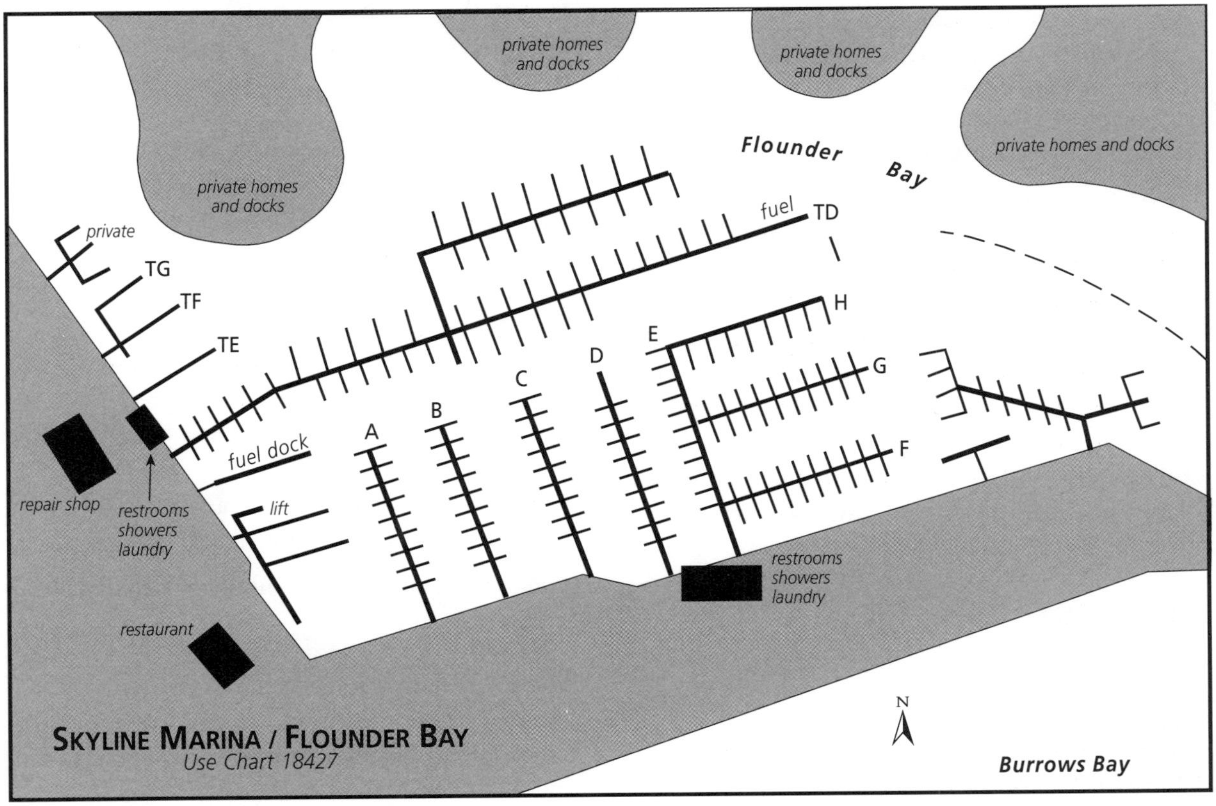

private homes and docks
private homes and docks
private homes and docks
private homes and docks
Flounder Bay
private
TG
TF
TE
fuel
TD
H
E
D
C
B
A
G
F
fuel dock
lift
repair shop
restrooms showers laundry
restrooms showers laundry
restaurant
N
Burrows Bay

SKYLINE MARINA / FLOUNDER BAY
Use Chart 18427

Peter Fromm

Reef netting near Iceberg Point

Peter Fromm

Mackaye Harbor from the air

Flounder Bay, a well-sheltered basin and popular yachting harbor at the N end of Burrows Bay, is the site of a large marina with an airstrip. The entrance channel is protected by jetties and marked by private lights and daybeacons. In 1980, 13 feet was reported in the entrance, thence in 1973, 5 feet was reported in the basin. Gasoline, diesel fuel, water, ice, about 250 berths with electricity, transient berths, dry storage facilities, launching ramp, two 1 1/2-ton hoists, 24-ton lift, and marine supplies are available at the marina. Hull, engine, and electronic repairs can be made. A highway connects the bay with the State ferry terminal in Ship Harbor and with Anacortes. (p. 338, CP)

Flounder Bay is a well-developed pleasure craft and small commercial vessel harbor. The busy entrance is narrow and shallow and exposed to southwest weather, so exercise caution when entering. Larger boats should pay attention to tide levels and the shallow bar in the entrance. There is no public anchoring in Flounder Bay.

Skyline Marina, the large marina at the west end of the bay, has transient moorage with full facilities, a ship store, restaurant, chartering, and fueling (tel: 360-293-5134).

Iceberg Point (Lopez Island)

Iceberg Point is located at the southeast tip of Lopez Island.

Chart 18429
Position (0.25 mile west of light): 48°25.32′ N, 122°54.06′ W (NAD 83)

Iceberg Point, 3.3 miles SE of Cattle Point, is at the W extremity of the S part of Lopez Island. A light and seasonal fog signal are on the point. (p. 331, CP)

Iceberg Point, overlooking the Strait of Juan de Fuca, is surrounded by foul rocks and reefs and should be given a wide berth. Good whale-watching waters are south of the point.

Outer Bay (Lopez Island)

Outer Bay is located 0.65 mile northeast of Iceberg Point.

Chart 18429
Entrance: 48°25.85′ N, 122°53.45′ W (NAD 83)
Position: 48°25.75′ N, 122°53.05′ W (NAD 83)

The south end of Outer Bay offers temporary anchorage in fair weather but is open to northwest winds and chop. During fishing season this quiet bay is used by picturesque reef netters.

Agate Beach County Park is located in the east end of Outer Bay and is undeveloped except for picnic tables, pit toilets, and a good landing beach.

Iceberg Island, 0.25 mile southwest of Outer Bay, is an undeveloped State Park for day use only.

Anchor in about 3 fathoms over a hard bottom with marginal holding.

Mackaye Harbor (Lopez Island)

Mackaye Harbor is located on the southern tip of Lopez Island 1.5 miles northeast of Iceberg Point and 9.2 miles west of Deception Pass.

Sailing into Mackaye Harbor

Chart 18429
Outer entrance (0.38 mile west of Iceberg Point): 48°25.32′ N, 122°54.24′ W (NAD 83)
Inner entrance: 48°26.29′ N, 122°53.74′ W (NAD 83)
Anchor: 48°26.40′ N, 122°52.20′ W (NAD 83)

> *Mackaye Harbor, N of Iceberg Point, has several private piers used by seafood company vessels. The harbor affords good shelter in 5 to 6 fathoms, soft mud. . . . Vessels approaching Mackaye Harbor or Richardson should pass at least 0.3 mile S and E of the off-lying islands and islets. Local vessels, by keeping close to the N shore to avoid rocks near midchannel, use a small passage between Lopez and Charles Islands, but this should not be attempted without local knowledge. Twin Rocks, in midchannel of this small passage, are marked by a daybeacon.* (p. 331, CP)

Anchored in Barlow Bay

Mackaye Harbor offers good protection in bad weather. Larger vessels anchor in the center of Mackaye Harbor where there is plenty of swinging room; smaller boats can head deep into its inner bay, known as Barlow Bay, and anchor between the piers. The boat ramp in the harbor is a popular put-in spot for kayakers and canoeists.

Anchor in 3 fathoms over sand and mud bottom with fair-to-good holding.

Barlow Bay (Lopez Island)

Barlow Bay is located 0.25 mile south of Mackaye Harbor.

Chart 18429
Entrance: 48°26.28′ N, 122°52.31′ W (NAD 83)
Anchor: 48°26.15′ N, 122°52.30′ W (NAD 83)

> *. . . small craft with local knowledge can obtain excellent shelter in Barlow Bay, on the S side of* [Mackaye] *harbor.* (p. 331. CP)

Barlow Bay is a well-sheltered but busy place entered via Mackaye Harbor. You can find anchorage in the center of the small bay, but please do not block any commercial operations in the bay. Due to private piers, floats, and buoys, there is limited swinging room. We have comfortably ridden out a full-blown winter storm here in windy but sheltered waters.

Anchor in 2 fathoms, sticky mud, with very good holding.

Flint Beach (Lopez Island)

Flint Beach is located 1.0 mile east of Iceberg Point.

Chart 18429
Entrance: 48°25.10′ N, 122°52.23′ W (NAD 83)
Anchor: 48°25.20′ N, 122°52.22′ W (NAD 83)

Flint Beach, a tiny, scenic bight on the south end of Lopez Island, has a small rocky beach. Temporary and marginal anchorage can be found on the west side; Aleck Bay, 0.6 mile northeast, is the preferred anchorage. Aleck Rocks in the center of the bight is a National Wildlife Refuge.

Anchor in about 4 fathoms over a mud and rock bottom with poor-to-fair holding.

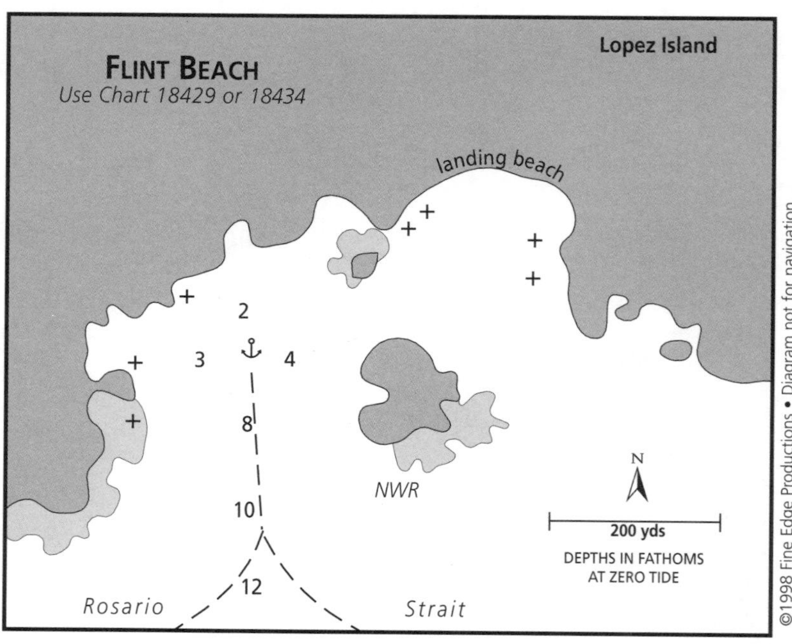

Aleck Bay (Lopez Island)

Aleck Bay is located 1.7 miles east of Iceberg Point and 2.0 mile west of Watmough Head.

Chart 18429
Entrance: 48°25.40′ N, 122°50.70′ W (NAD 83)
Anchor: 48°25.61′ N, 122°51.57′ W (NAD 83)

> *Aleck Bay, the W and largest of three small bays on the S shore of Lopez Island, affords good anchorage except in heavy SE winds for small vessels in 4 to 7 fathoms, mud bottom. Rocks, awash and covered, and reefs abound in these waters, and caution is essential.* (p. 335, CP)

Aleck Bay is a popular summer anchorage with good swinging room over a large flat bottom.

Peter Fromm

Aleck Bay anchorage

Don Douglass

Good swinging room in Aleck Bay

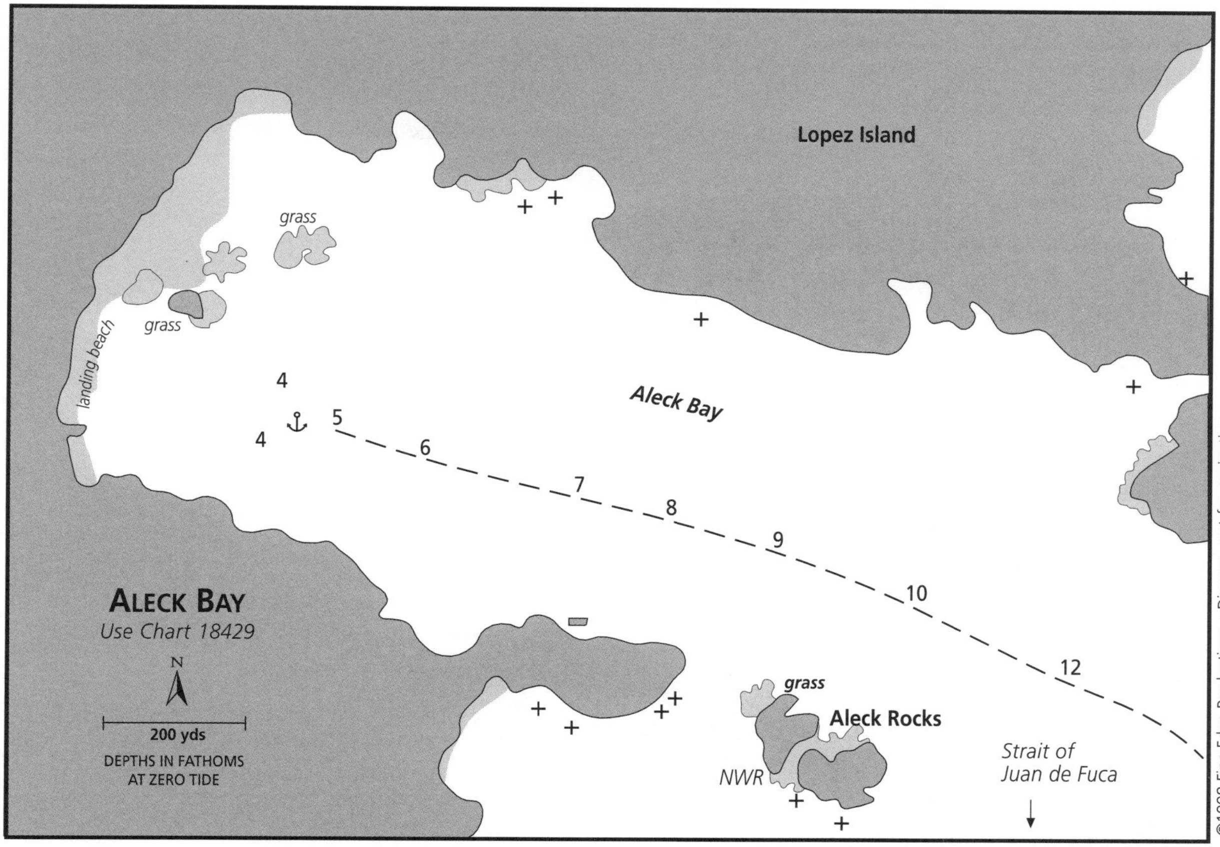

Lopez Island

grass

grass

landing beach

Aleck Bay

4

4

5

6

7

8

9

10

12

ALECK BAY
Use Chart 18429

N

200 yds

DEPTHS IN FATHOMS
AT ZERO TIDE

grass

Aleck Rocks

NWR

Strait of
Juan de Fuca

©1998 Fine Edge Productions • Diagram not for navigation

Good shelter can be found in the southwest corner of the bay. Because it is open to the southeast, the bay is not adequate for anchoring in strong winds from that quarter.

Anchor in 4 fathoms over a mud bottom with good holding.

Hughes Bay (Lopez Island)

Hughes Bay is located 0.5 mile northeast of Aleck Bay.

Chart 18429
Entrance: 48°25.50′ N, 122°50.29′ W (NAD 83)
Anchor: 48°25.84′ N, 122°50.30′ W (NAD 83)

Hughes Bay is exposed to the southeast, but small boats can find temporary anchorage deep in the shallow northeast corner. Avoid submerged rocks found near the south and east shores.

Anchor in 1 to 2 fathoms over a sand and mud bottom with fair-to-good holding.

Don Douglass

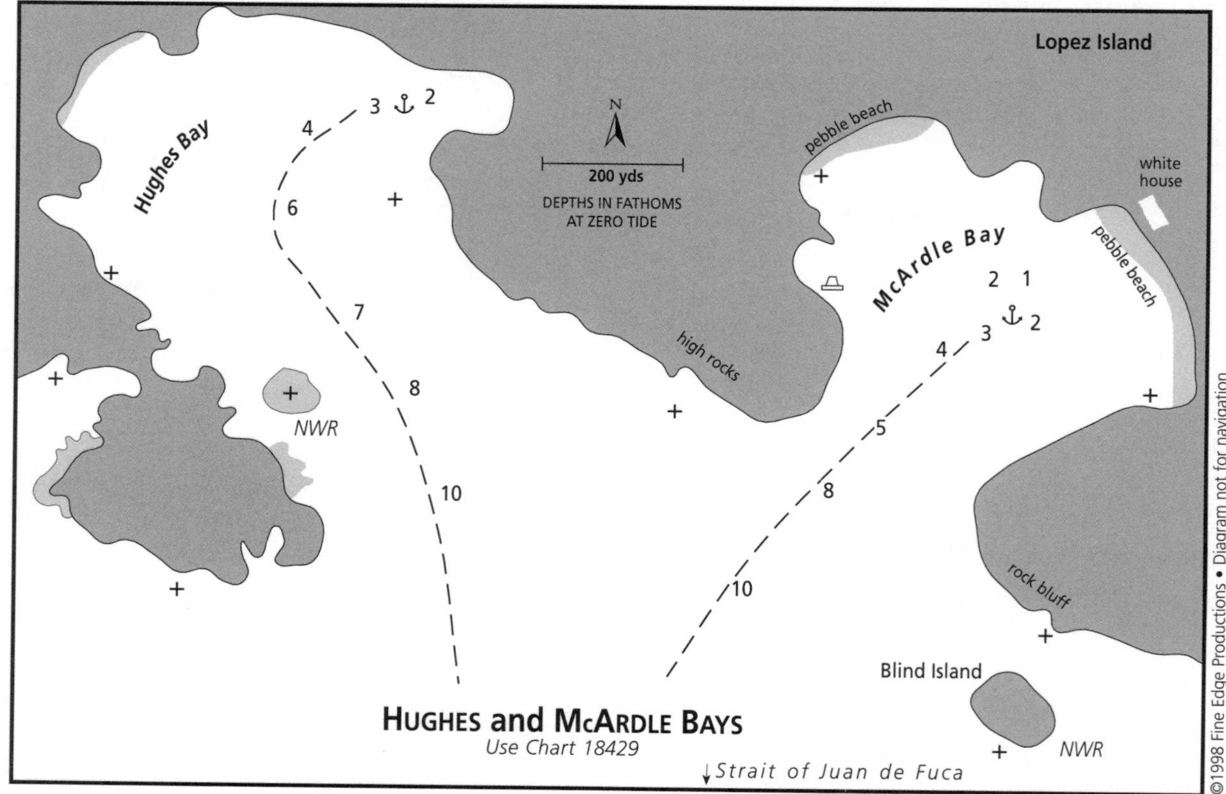

McArdle Bay (Lopez Island)

McArdle Bay is located 1.1 mile east of Aleck Bay and 1.0 mile west of Watmough Head.

Chart 18429
Entrance: 48°25.56′ N, 122°49.81′ W (NAD 83)
Anchor: 48°25.67′ N, 122°49.61′ W (NAD 83)

McArdle Bay is a small, quiet bay with beautiful homes surrounding its shores. Temporary anchorage can be found here, but the bay is open to the south.

Anchor in 1 to 2 fathoms over a sand and mud bottom with fair-to-good holding.

Castle Island (Strait of Juan de Fuca)

Castle Island is located 0.85 mile south of Watmough Head.

Chart 18429
West entrance: 48°25.47′ N, 122°49.71′ W (NAD 83)
East entrance: 48°25.28′ N, 122°49.01′ W (NAD 83)

Castle Island, an undeveloped State Marine Park, is a scenic fishing spot off the south end of Lopez Island. Both Castle and Blind islands are wildlife refuges. A small protected boat passage with an irregular bottom leads inside these islands. Avoid kelp patches which mark rock piles.

"South Watmough Head Bight" (Lopez Island)

South Watmough Head Bight is located 0.25 mile southwest of Watmough Head.

Chart 18429
Entrance: 48°25.48′ N, 122°48.43′ W (NAD 83)
Anchor: 48°25.51′ N, 122°48.49′ W (NAD 83)

Small boats can find temporary anchorage in fair weather in what we call South Watmough Head Bight off its sandy beach. As indicated by the driftwood on shore, this small bight is exposed to southeast seas as well as to the wake of passing traffic. It is a good haulout spot for kayakers.

Anchor in 2 to 3 fathoms over a sand and gravel bottom with fair holding.

Watmough Bay (Lopez Island)

Watmough Bay is located 6.6 miles west of Deception Pass and 2.8 miles south of Lopez Pass.

Chart 18429
Entrance: 48°26.11′ N, 122°24.32′ W (NAD 83)
Anchor: 48°25.92′ N, 122°48.68′ W (NAD 83)

> *Small craft can get good protection from W and S weather by anchoring near the head of Watmough Bay, at the extreme SE end of Lopez Island.* (p. 335, CP)

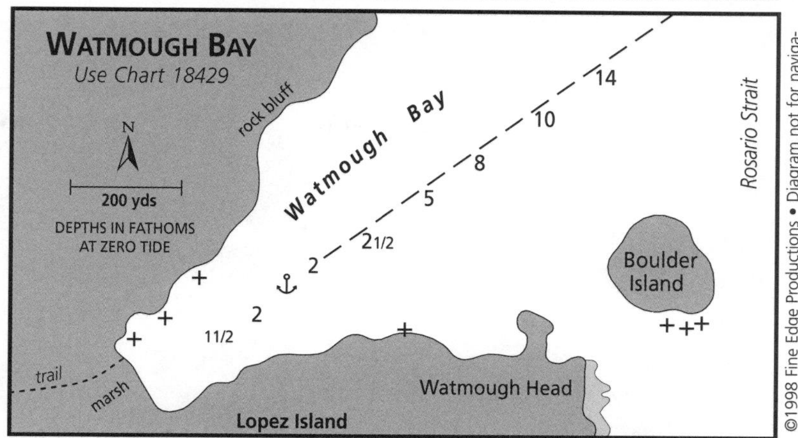

Watmough Bay, immediately north of Watmough Head on the southeast corner of Lopez Island, is a scenic, undeveloped bay surrounded by trees and high rocky bluffs. It is a well-sheltered anchorage for cruising boats, open to infrequent northeast winds. Submerged rocks lie close to the north shore, and rocky patches have been reported in the bay, so set your anchor well. There is a convenient landing beach with a marsh and meadow beyond. A hiking trail leads from the marsh to the peak of Chadwick Hill (500 feet) where you have an excellent view of the entire area.

Peter Fromm

Looking east toward Mt. Baker from Watmough Bay

Peter Fromm

Aerial view of Watmough Bay from the south

Peter Fromm

Sunrise on a foggy morning in Watmough Bay

Anchor in the head of the bay in 2 fathoms over sticky mud with very good holding.

Telegraph Bay (Lopez Island)

Telegraph Bay is located 0.36 mile southwest of Cape St. Mary and 0.5 mile north of Watmough Bay.

Chart 18429
Anchor: 48°26.58′ N, 122°48.43′ W (NAD 83)

Telegraph Bay is a tiny bight with a small beach useful for small craft in settled weather only.

Anchor in 2 to 3 fathoms.

Shoal Bight (Lopez Island)

Shoal Bight is located on the southeast corner of Lopez Island between Cape St. Mary and Lopez Pass.

Chart 18429
Anchor: 48°27.40′ N, 122°48.80′ W (NAD 83)

Shoal Bight, not to be confused with Shoal Bay on the north end of Lopez Island, provides anchorage in fair weather along its mile-long beachfront. Although exposed to southeasterlies, it is useful during prevailing westerly winds. It has plenty of swinging room over a large shallow area. Small boats can anchor close to shore with easy dinghy access to the sand and gravel beach.

Anchor in about 2 fathoms over mud and sand bottom with good holding.

Lopez Pass

Lopez Pass is 8.2 miles northwest of Deception Pass and 4.6 miles southwest of Fidalgo Head.

Chart 18429
East entrance: 48°28.78′ N, 122°48.91′ W (NAD 83)
West entrance (0.12 mile south of red Marker "4"): 48°28.25′ N, 122°50.22′ W (NAD 83)

Lopez Pass, S of Decatur Island, leads from Rosario Strait into Lopez Sound. The pass has depths of 9 to 12 fathoms, but is very narrow and little used. A light is at the S end of Decatur Island. (p. 335, CP)

Pleasure craft wishing to avoid busy Thatcher Pass use Lopez Pass to find the welcome shelter of Lopez Sound. There are good depths of 5 to 15 fathoms in the center of the fairway. You will find significant turbulence in Lopez Pass.

James Island (Rosario Strait)

James Island is located 0.8 mile southeast of Fauntleroy Point.

Chart 18429
Public mooring buoys (east side): 48°30.78′ N, 122°46.41′ W (NAD 83)
Public mooring buoy (west side): 48°30.67′ N, 122°46.65′ W (NAD 83)

Don Douglass

Western cove at James Island

James Island is close off Decatur head, the E end of Decatur Island, and between the two is a deep but narrow passage; on the island are two hills with heights of 260 and 219 feet. (p. 338, CP)

James Island is a popular State Marine Park with two coves, one on the east side and one on the west, with access by trail across the low saddle. The western cove has a small dock with space for about four boats and one mooring buoy. You can take temporary anchorage in the west cove, but heavy current flows between James Island and Decatur Head so maintain a watch since holding is marginal. A designated Cascadia Marine Trail Site, at the south end of the west bay, has a group campground and three tent sites. There are public mooring buoys in the east cove, but it is open to wake from ferries and boats transiting Rosario Strait. The park has hiking trails, picnic tables, and toilets; no water on shore. You can find better anchorage, particularly in southeast weather, 0.6 mile west of Decatur Head.

Decatur Head

Decatur Head is 1.1 mile south of the east entrance to Thatcher Pass.

Chart 18429
Entrance: 48°31.17′ N, 122°47.04′ W (NAD 83)
Anchor: 48°30.70′ N, 122°47.38′ W (NAD 83)

Fair protection in SE weather can be had in the

area W of Decatur Island and N of Center Island in 3 to 5 fathoms, mud bottom. Strong winds blow across the low neck at the S end of Decatur Island and may make the area W uncomfortable for small craft. Good anchorage in W weather can be had in the large bight on the W side of the sound. (p. 335, CP)

Decatur Head, recognizable for its prominent round hill, 123 feet high, is connected to the east end of Lopez Island by a low sandspit. Good shelter can be found from southeast chop and out of the current in the lee of Decatur Head.

Don Douglass

James Island

Anchor in about 2 fathoms over sand, mud and occasional eel grass bottom. Holding is fair to very good.

Thatcher Pass

Lying between Blakely and Decatur islands, Thatcher Pass is the main thoroughfare from Rosario Strait to the San Juan Islands.

Chart 18429
East entrance (half-way between Fauntleroy Point and Lawson Reef): 48°31.68′ N, 122°47.33′ W (NAD 83)
West entrance (0.63 mile southeast of Willow Island): 48°31.75′ N, 122°48.93′ W (NAD 83)

Don Douglass

Anchored near Decatur Head

Thatcher Pass, between Blakely Island and Decatur Island, is about 0.5 mile wide in its narrowest part. The pass is deep and free of danger, except for Lawson Rock, marked by a daybeacon, in midchannel 700 yards N of Fauntleroy Point. The S point of Blakely Island is marked by a light. (p. 335, CP)

Thatcher Pass is used extensively by the San Juan ferry system and pleasure and commercial craft.

Blakely Island

Blakely Island is located to the north of Thatcher Pass.

Charts 18429, 18430
South end light (Thatcher Pass): 48°31.85′ N, 122°48.60′ W (NAD 83)
North end (Peavine Pass): 48°35.31′ N, 122°48.68′ W (NAD 83)

Blakely Island, E of Lopez and Shaw Islands, is privately owned and maintained. . . . At its N end, bordering on Peavine Pass, is a small-craft basin and channel. About 65 berths are at the cove dock and inside the basin. An airplane landing strip and lodging are nearby. Gasoline, diesel fuel, water, ice, and some marine supplies are available.

Blakely Island Shoal, rocky and cov-

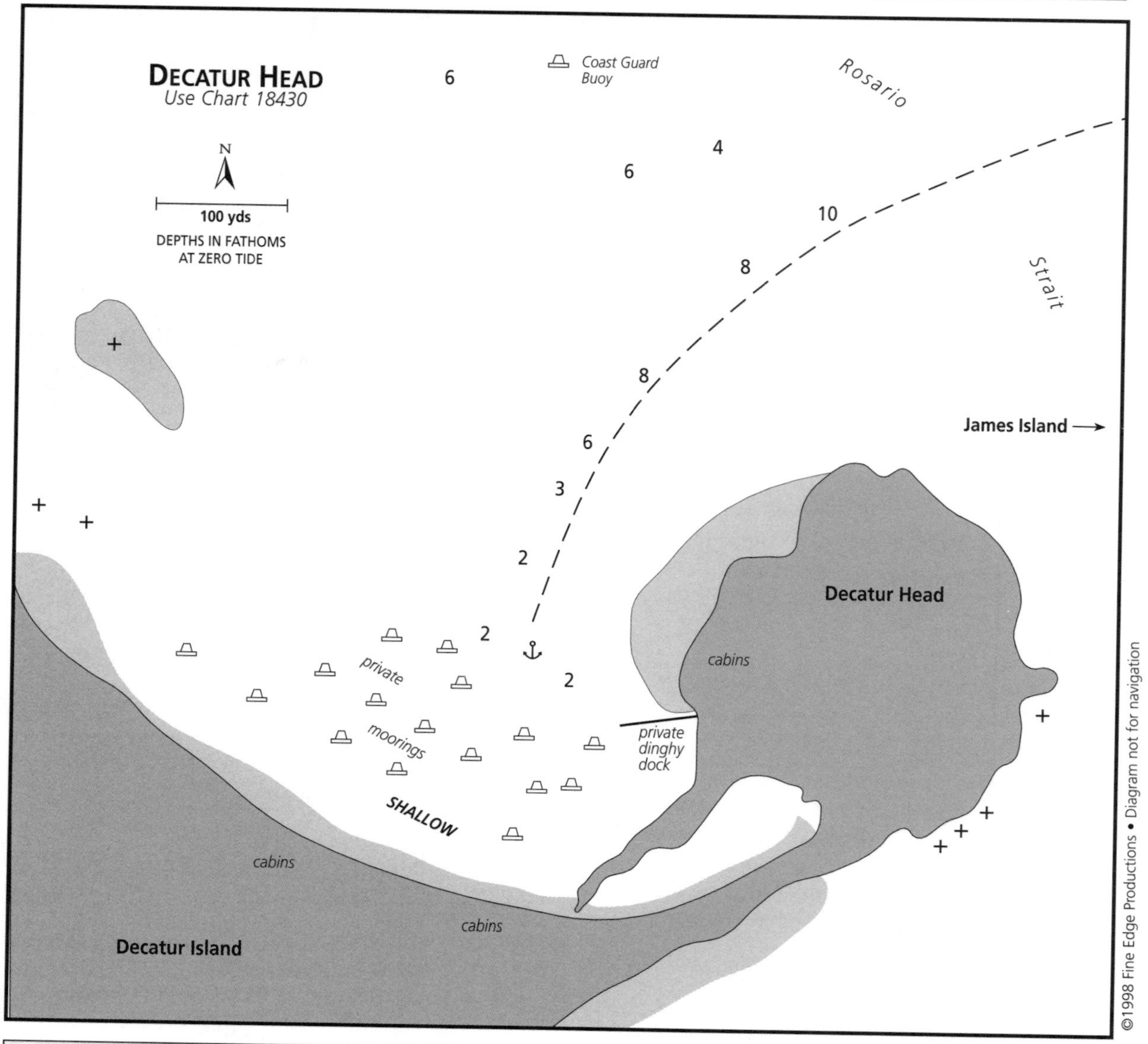
DECATUR HEAD
Use Chart 18430
N
100 yds
DEPTHS IN FATHOMS AT ZERO TIDE
Coast Guard Buoy
Rosario
Strait
6
4
6
10
8
8
6
3
2
2
2
James Island
Decatur Head
cabins
private
moorings
private dinghy dock
SHALLOW
cabins
cabins
Decatur Island
©1998 Fine Edge Productions • Diagram not for navigation

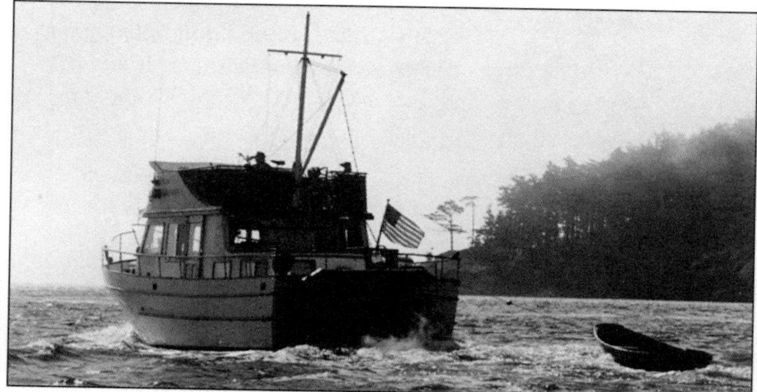

Peter Fromm

Crossing Thatcher Pass

ered 1¾ fathoms, is 0.5 mile off the W side of Blakely Island and is marked on its S side by a lighted buoy. The passage between the shoal and Blakely Island is deep and clear. (p. 335, CP)

Blakely Island's steep and rugged east shore has deep water. Except for the Blakely Island Marina at Obstruction Pass, the island is closed to public entry. Anchorage can be found at Armitage Island Bight and Thatcher Pass.

"Armitage Island Bight" (Blakely Island)

Armitage Island Bight is 0.85 mile northwest of Fauntleroy Point.

Chart 18429
Anchor: 48°32.20′ N, 122°47.88′ W (NAD 83)

Sportfishing boats find temporary anchorage inside Armitage Island on the southeast corner of Blakely Island.

Anchor in 7 fathoms.

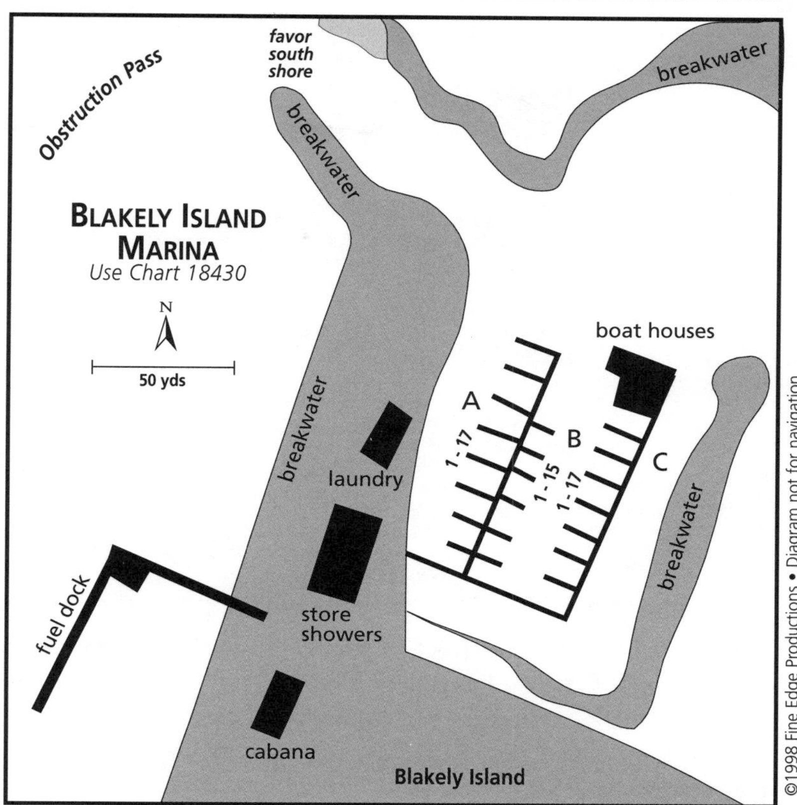

Peavine Pass

(See Blakely Island Marina, Chapter 3.)

Peavine Pass is located between the north end of Blakely Island and Obstruction Island.

Chart 18430
East entrance (0.2 mile north of Spindle Rock): 48°35.52′ N, 122°48.07′ W (NAD 83)
West entrance (0.12 mile southeast of Obstruction Island): 48°35.16′ N, 122°49.42′ W (NAD 83)

> *Peavine Pass, safer and straighter than Obstruction Pass. . . . The pass is a little over 200 yards wide at its narrowest part, and in midchannel the least depth is 6 fathoms. Peavine Pass Light 1, on the SW point of Obstruction Island, marks the W entrance to the pass. In 1973, two submerged rocks were reported in the pass about 0.4 mile E of Peavine Pass Light 1. A group of bare rocks, marked by a daybeacon, lie about 0.2 mile offshore from Blakely Island at the E entrance to Peavine Pass.*
>
> *The currents through Obstruction and Peavine Passes have estimated velocities of 5.5 to 6.5 knots at times. Heavy tide rips occur E of Obstruction Island.* (p. 335, CP)

Both Peavine and Obstruction passes are used by pleasure craft and sportfishing boats. Avoid the unmarked rock on the east side of Obstruction Island as noted on the diagram.

Obstruction Pass

Obstruction Pass is located at the southeast tip of Orcas Island, north of Obstruction Island.

Chart 18430
East entrance: 48°35.94′ N, 122°47.96′ W (NAD 83)
West entrance: 48°35.83′ N, 122°49.55′ W (NAD 83)

> *Obstruction Pass, with a least width of 350 yards, . . . and leads W from Rosario Strait to the inner passages and sounds of the San Juan Islands. A launching ramp and float are on the N side of the pass about 0.6 mile NW of Deer Point; depths alongside the float are about 4 feet. Caution is advised because of the numerous private pilings and moorings in the area. Obstruction Pass is marked by lights on the N side of Obstruction Island.* (p. 335, CP)

Obstruction Pass is used by the San Juans/Bellingham water taxi. Avoid the dangerous unmarked reef which extends out 400 feet east

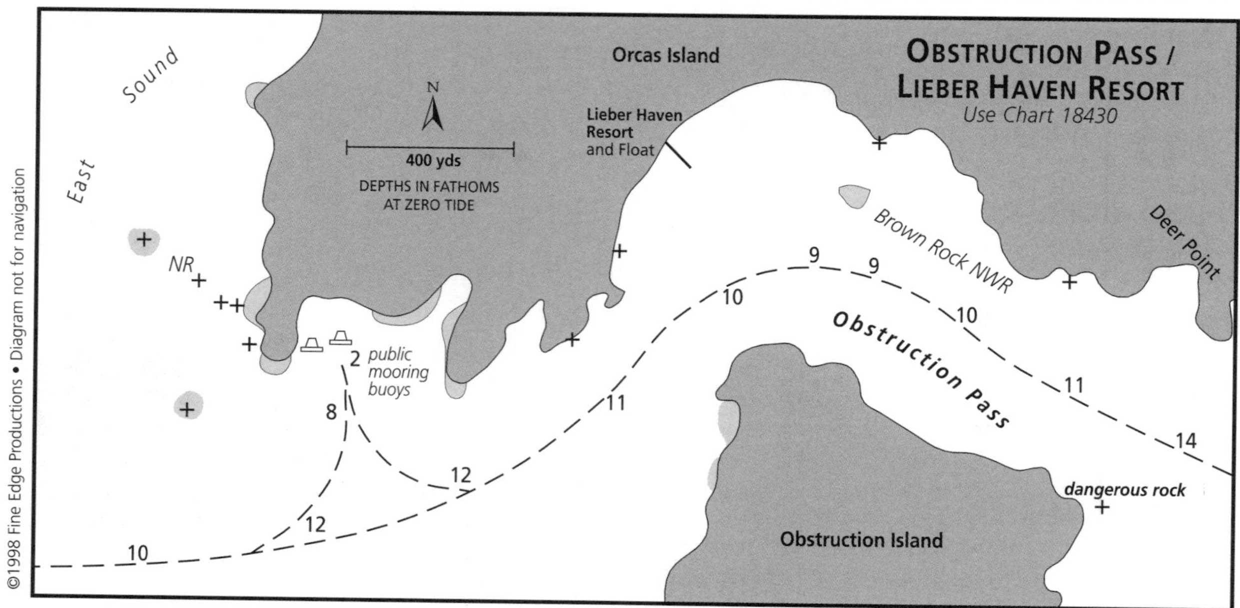

from the east end of Obstruction Island. If you cut the corner between Peavine and Obstruction passes, watch for tide rips and be very careful passing the rock at 48°35.87' N, 122°48.29' W, sometimes marked by kelp.

Obstruction Pass NR (Orcas Island)

Obstruction Pass NR (Natural Resources) is located at the extreme west end of Obstruction Pass.

Chart 18430

West entrance: 48°35.78′ N, 122°49.67′ W (NAD 83)

Buoys: 48°36.04′ N, 122°49.74′ W (NAD 83)

The *Island Transporter*, A Welcome Visitor

For residents of the outlying San Juan archipelago, the *Island Transporter* is a welcome visiter. This Anacortes-based charter landing-craft freight service calls at many islands, including Decatur, Blakely, Obstruction, Sinclair, Eliza, Lopez and San Juan.

The *Island Transporter* was built at the Dakota Creek Shipyard in Anacortes for partners Joe Richter and Dan Crookes. It replaced a 54-foot plywood landing craft that was built in 1968 for the Island Ferry and Barge company. As Dan Crookes tells it, the plywood boat was supposed to last for only 10 years, but it is still in use. "We could write a book on its adventures alone!"

Dan has run the *Island Transporter* since 1989, racking up almost 15,000 hours. His most common route is from Skyline Marina to Friday Harbor, hauling gasoline to islands with ferry stops and live salmon smolt to fish farms. The boat also services the "out" islands carrying supplies and materals. Dan and his partner have hauled logs, sailboats, cement, furniture, and once, a modular home—one half of the house per trip. *Note:* In the late 1800s Dan Crookes' grandfather sailed 'round Cape Horn from England as crew on a coal sailing ship.

Editor's note: In addition to *Island Transporter,* two other privately owned workboats ply these waters. The *Nordland* and the *Pintail* are seen every day of the year, throughout all the islands.

Peter Fromm

Obstruction Pass NR recreation area has two public mooring buoys and campsites with fireplaces and toilets; no drinking water is available. Well-sheltered from prevailing northwest winds, the roadstead is open to southerlies. Its irregular bottom does not provide particularly good anchorage.

Kent Morrow

Campsites fill quickly at little Doe Island State Park

Lieber Haven Resort (Orcas Island)

Lieber Haven Resort is located on the north side of Obstruction Pass on Orcas Island.

Chart 18430
Position: 48°36.30′ N, 122°49.03′ W (NAD 83)

Lieber Haven Resort has a store. The mooring buoys in front of the small resort are private; small craft sometimes anchor on the shoal just to the north. Brown Rock, 0.26 mile east of the resort, is a National Wildlife Refuge.

Buoy Bay (Orcas Island)

Buoy Bay is located 1 mile north of Obstruction Pass on the east side of Orcas Island.

Chart 18430
Position: 48°37.11′ N, 122°48.43′ W (NAD 83)

Buoy Bay, a small bight, is sometimes used as temporary anchorage for sportfishing boats; however, there are a number of submerged rocks in this area and the bay offers shelter only from westerly winds.

Doe Bay (Orcas Island)

Doe Bay is located 2.5 miles north of Obstruction Pass.

Chart 18430
Position: 48°38.35′ N, 122°46.86′ W (NAD 83)

> *Doe Bay indents the SE shore of Orcas Island abreast Peapod Rocks. Doe Bay (Doebay), a village on the bay, has a wharf with 12 feet at its end; during strong S winds the wharf should not be approached. Doe Island, 0.6 mile SSW of Doe Bay, is a State park.* (p. 339, CP)

Doe Bay offers temporary anchorage in the center of the bay in 2 to 4 fathoms. It is exposed to southeast weather.

Pea Pod Rocks, 1.3 miles east of Doe Bay, are a National Wildlife Refuge and offer some fine fishing opportunities.

Doe Island State Marine Park

Doe Island is 0.3 mile southwest of Doe Bay.

Chart 18430
Position: 48°38.04′ N, 122°47.26′ W (NAD 83)

Doe Island has a 6-acre State Park with primitive camping facilities, a dock and a dinghy float (with time limit); no water is available, and you must pack out any garbage. Deep draft boats should anchor in Doe Bay. Anchorage for small craft can be found between Doe and Orcas islands.

Anchor in about 2 fathoms over sand and mud with some rocks; fair holding.

Cypress Island

Cypress Island lies between the main shipping channels of Rosario Strait and Bellingham Channel.

Chart 18424
Extreme north end of island (south side of Towhead Island): 48°36.62′ N, 122°42.78′ W (NAD 83)
South end of island (0.7 mile south of Reef Point): 48°31.98′ N, 122°43.21′ W (NAD 83)

> *Cypress Island, 1,530 feet high, steep on the lower slopes and gently rounding at the top, is on the E side of Rosario Strait and opposite Blakely Island. From S the island appears to lie in the middle of Rosario Strait.*
>
> *A shoal extends about 0.4 mile S from Reef Point, the SW tip of Cypress Island. A lighted buoy is about 0.7 mile S of Reef Point. Vessels rounding the point should not attempt to pass between the buoy and the point as submerged piles and heavy kelp may exist in that area.* (p. 338, CP)

Pleasure craft use the anchor sites found on the Bellingham Channel side.

Peter Fromm

Tide Point, Cypress Island

Strawberry Bay (Cypress Island)

Strawberry Bay is located on the west side of Cypress Island.

Chart 18430
Position: 48°33.70′ N, 122°43.56′ W (NAD 83)

> *An indifferent anchorage may be had in Strawberry Bay in 7 fathoms; it is seldom used.* (p. 338, CP)

Strawberry Bay is a large, open roadstead some-

Cypress Island

Cypress Island was named by Captain George Vancouver, who mistakenly thought the juniper trees growing along the shores were cypress. As on all the other islands, the trees were completely logged—large stumps can be seen all over the island. The State of Washington purchased several scenic areas for parks: Cypress Head and Pelican Beach, the latter named not for the bird but for a unique class of sailboats. The Pelican Club, which made many outings to this location, lobbied the state to buy the land which includes Eagle Cliff. Many Pelican boats have been built by the famed Smith Brothers of Samish Island.

The hike to Eagle Cliff leads through second-growth forest up to a rocky outcropping with a magnificent view. Looking across Rosario Strait to the wooded shores of Orcas and Blakely islands, it is possible to imagine this view as the first explorers saw it. This trail is closed to the public for several months in the spring so that peregrine falcons can raise their young without human interruption,

The scenic beauty and peace of Cypress Island was threatened by plans for large-scale development which included a convention center and marina. Local activists, primarily from Anacortes, fought this development for years and their efforts were eventually successful. The State Parks Department bought out the developer and four-fifths of the island is now public land.

You can anchor in Eagle Harbor; the 10-foot depth continues quite a way into the harbor. Hiking trails begin near the old pier, and there are miles of old logging roads for great mountain biking! With a bicycle you can visit several high lakes, overlooks, and an airport, the only evidence of the former development plans. There are camp sites at both Eagle Harbor and Pelican Beach.

Cypress Head, one of the many tombolos in the San Juan/Gulf Islands, has mooring buoys, campsites, and a small dock.

Deepwater Bay, site of a salmon aquaculture project, is not attractive for pleasure boating. Secret Harbor School, a residential facility for troubled youth, has been in operation here since the late 1940s. —**PF**

times used by commercial fishing boats. Strawberry Island provides some protection from the wake of passing traffic.

Tide Point Bight (Cypress Island)

Tide Point Bight, on the west side of Cypress Island, is 0.4 mile northeast of Tide Point Light and 0.9 mile southwest of Eagle Point.

Chart 18430
Position: 48°35.33′ N, 122°44.13′ W (NAD 83)

> *Tide Point, the W extremity of Cypress Island . . .* (p. 338, CP)

Fishing boats sometimes anchor in the lee of Tide Point on its north side in moderate southerly weather where the bottom is reported to be rocky with kelp.

Bellingham Channel

Bellingham Channel, between Guemes and Vendovi islands on the east and Cypress and Sinclair islands on the west, leads from Rosario Strait to Bellingham Bay.

Charts 18424, 18430
South entrance: 48°32.00′ N, 122°41.25′ W (NAD 83)
North entrance (between Vendovi Island and Viti Rocks): 48°37.50′ N, 122°37.00′ W (NAD 83)

> *Bellingham Channel, deep between Cypress and Guemes Island, is the most direct route to Bellingham Bay from S. Between Cypress, Guemes, and Sinclair Islands, the tidal currents have considerable velocity, but between Sinclair and Vendovi Islands the velocities are considerably less.*
>
> *Deep-draft vessels approaching Bellingham Bay from N use the channel between Lummi and Sinclair Islands. With the exception of Viti Rocks and the dangers N of Sinclair Islands, this channel is free of danger.* (p. 341, CP)

Don Douglass

Cypress Head, north cove

Bellingham Channel is used by large commercial traffic, as well as numerous small craft. It is more protected than Rosario Strait in southerly storms.

Don Douglass

Aquaculture, Deepwater Bay

Deepwater Bay (Cypress Island)

Deepwater Bay lies on the southeast side of Cypress Island.

Charts 18424, 18430
Entrance: 48°33.41′ N, 122°40.54′ W (NAD 83)

The anchor sites in Deepwater Bay are occupied largely by floating aquacultures and their buoys and anchor systems. Large pleasure craft will want to avoid the area. Secret Harbor, in the southwest corner of the bay, is quite shallow but offers marginal anchorage to small craft.

Secret Harbor (Cypress Island)

Secret Harbor is an extension on the southwest corner of Deepwater Bay.

Charts 18424, 18430
Anchor: 48°33.28′ N, 122°41.23′ W (NAD 83)

Secret Harbor is very shallow with large drying mud flats full of eel grass as shown on the diagram. Shallow-draft boats can find sheltered anchor sites on either side of the point on the south side of the harbor.

Anchor in about 1 fathom over sand, mud, and eel grass with fair holding provided you do not foul your anchor.

Cypress Head (Cypress Island)

Cypress Head is located on the extreme east side of Cypress Island and 3.8 miles north of the San Juan Ferry docks at Ship Harbor on Fidalgo Island.

Charts 18424, 18430
Public mooring buoys: 48°34.21′ N, 122°40.24′ W (NAD 83)

Cypress Head is one of the closest scenic anchorages to Anacortes. It is an example of a tombolo, a place where hard rock resisted glacier action and became an islet connected to shore by a sandspit. Tombolos are found throughout the San Juan and Gulf islands.

The picturesque north cove of Cypress Head has public mooring buoys and a park with picnic facilities. While there is good protection from southerly weather, anchorage at the north cove is not recommended due to strong currents and little swinging room. This is a designated Cascadia Marine Trail site. The south cove, which is quite shallow, has little use as an anchorage.

Eagle Harbor (Cypress Island)

Eagle Harbor is located 1.6 miles northwest of Cypress Head on the northeast side of Cypress Island.

Charts 18424, 18430
Entrance: 48°35.27′ N, 122°41.53′ W (NAD 83)
Anchor: 48°35.35′ N, 122°41.77′ W (NAD 83)

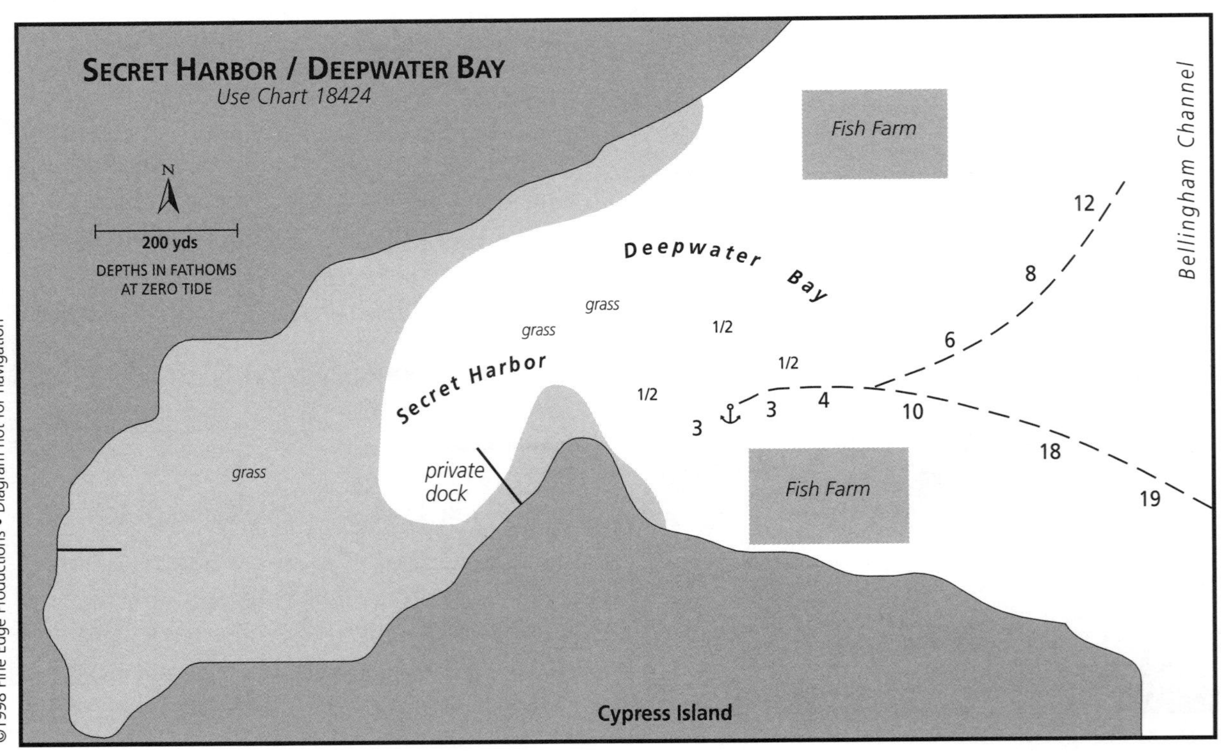

When much of Cypress Island was recently purchased as a State Park, Eagle Harbor became a major access point for the island. It offers good protection from prevailing northwest winds; while it is exposed to the southeast, winds from that quadrant largely blow up Bellingham Channel, as indicated by the moderate driftwood on the beach. You can land a dinghy on the beach and there's a small loading platform on the south side.

Anchor in 1 1/2 to 2 fathoms in the center of the bay with good swinging room.

Eagle Harbor, Cypress Island

Pelican Beach DNR Park (Cypress Island)

Pelican Beach DNR Park is located 0.8 mile north of Eagle Harbor and 0.75 mile southwest of Towhead Island.

Charts 18424, 18430
Mooring buoys: 48°36.12′ N, 122°42.07′ W (NAD 83)

Pelican Beach Park is the shallow bight on the northeast corner of Cypress Island. It is a popular destination point for kayak and small boat groups and a designated Cascadia Marine Trail site. The six public mooring buoys are very close to shore and because of limited swinging room can be used only by small boats. Pelican Beach is an open roadstead that offers fair protection from westerly winds; however, winds from the north through the southeast make this a poor anchorage. In settled weather, however, it is quite a pleasant moorage.

There are four campsites and fire pits just above the gravel beach. A hiking trail that leads west across Cypress Island to Eagle Cliff may be closed during peregrine falcon breeding season.

landing beach
high bluff
Cypress Island
Eagle Harbor
Bellingham Channel
high ridge
200 yds
DEPTHS IN FATHOMS AT ZERO TIDE
EAGLE HARBOR
Use Chart 18424

A Pelican sailboat—source of the name for Pelican Beach

Peter Fromm

Sailboat at anchor in Eagle Harbor

Sinclair Island (Bellingham Channel)

Sinclair Island lies 1 mile northeast of Cypress Island on the north side of Bellingham Channel.

Chart 18424
Position (pier): 48°36.99′ N, 122°41.62′ W (NAD 83)

> *Sinclair Island, N of Cypress Island, is wooded and comparatively low in places; dangerous reefs extend 0.8 mile off the N shore. Portions of Boulder Reef, the outermost danger, uncover at half tide; kelp marking the reef is frequently drawn under by the current. The outer end of the reef is marked by a lighted bell buoy. Urban, a village at the SW end of the island, has a pier with depths of 12 feet at the end.* (p. 339, CP)

Peter Fromm

Wind-blown Pacific madrone, Clark Island

A small breakwater made of pilings protects commuter boats and the water taxi on the south side of the west point on Sinclair Island. Temporary anchorage in fair weather can be found off the breakwater in 4 to 6 fathoms.

The Northern Boundary—Clark, Matia, Sucia, and Patos Islands

Along the northern edge of the San Juan archipelago lies a broken chain of islands. They share a common geological history; glaciers and erosion produced the long parallel ridges that enclose slender bays. The larger islands are thickly covered with trees and brush—one of the most common is the Pacific madrone with its broad evergreen leaves, red bark, and twisted trunks. Eroded sandstone beds reveal fantastic shapes and hide caves once used by smugglers. Sea birds nest in the rocks and seals and sea lions haul out on secluded beaches and reefs.

A few of the larger islands were settled from time to time, but this chain was never officially opened for homesteading. Cobblestones for Seattle streets were once quarried on Sucia, and foxes were farmed on Sucia and Matia.

In the late 1800s, some of these islands were set aside as lighthouse reservations or military reserves; later they were converted to wildlife sanctuaries and State Marine Parks. Sucia was opened for private development in the 1950s. The state purchased part of the land and, in the 1960s, an association of boating clubs purchased 319 acres, entrusting the land to the State for use as a marine park. Sucia Island, Little Sucia, Ewing, and the Cluster islands are now park property.

All or part of Patos, Sucia, Matia, and Clark islands are now State Parks, with mooring and camping facilities, accessible only by boats. Sucia Islands lie 2 nautical miles north of the north shore of Orcas Island. Once you reach Sucia, you can island hop in small boats.

Clark Island (Rosario Strait)

Clark Island lies 3 miles west of Lummi Island on the west side of Rosario Strait, about 2 miles north of the east tip of Orcas Island.

Chart 18430
Mooring buoys (East Cove): 48°41.92′ N, 122°45.73′ W (NAD 83)
Mooring buoys (West Bight): 48°41.87′ N, 122°45.92′ W (NAD 83)

> *Clark Island and Barnes Island, and the several adjacent rocks and islets, lie almost in the middle of Rosario Strait, about 2.5 miles NNW of Lawrence Point on Orcas Island. These islands may be passed on either side, giving them a berth of 0.5 mile.* (p. 338, CP)

Clark Island is a State Marine Park with campsites along the eastern shore. There is a campsite on shore, but no dock and no water. A dangerous rock awash about 4 feet lies on the east side of East Cove. The cove has a slight back eddy current on an ebb tide. There is no camping on the west side.

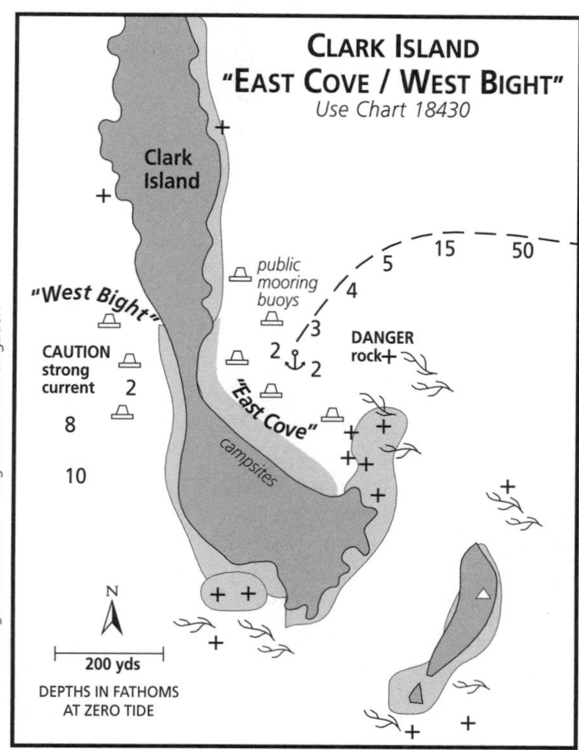

Clark Island State Park

Strong currents reach 3 knots on spring tides. Anchorage can be found near the five public mooring buoys in 3 to 5 fathoms, but it is not recommended due to the current and the nearby rocks. Anchoring is not advised on the west side due to limited swinging room.

Barnes Island, just west of Clark Island, is ringed with rocks and kelp. The island is privately owned.

Matia Island, East End (Rosario Strait)

Matia Island is located 3.5 miles northwest of Clark Island.

Chart 18430
Anchor (west of Puffin Island): 48°44.70′ N, 122°49.60′ W (NAD 83)

> *Matia Island, a wildlife refuge about 4 miles W of Point Migley, is 120 feet high and wooded.*
>
> *Puffin Island, 40 feet high, is about 0.2 mile E of Matia Island. A reef, marked at its SE extremity by a light, extends E from the SE end of Matia Island to a point about 0.2 E of Puffin Island. Mariners should not attempt to pass between the islands.* (p. 339, CP)

Matia Island offers temporary anchorage in a cove on its east end, west of Puffin Island. The cove is protected from northwest winds but open to strong currents and exposed to southeast weather. When approaching from the southeast, favor the Puffin Island shore to avoid the dangerous reef south of Puffin Island that extends southeast from Matia and is marked by kelp.

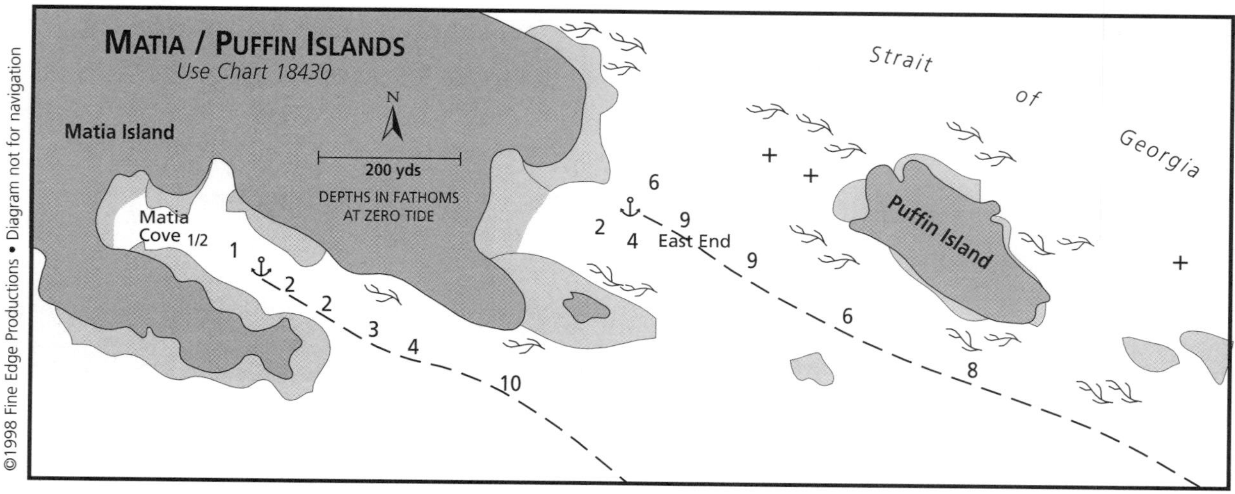

Matia Cove (Matia Island)

Matia Cove is west of the cove described above.

Chart 18430
Entrance: 48°44.57′ N, 122°49.67′ W (NAD 83)
Anchor: 48°44.66′ N, 122°49.93′ W (NAD 83)

Matia Cove, a good fair-weather anchorage for small boats, is exposed to southeast weather. It is short on swinging room.

Anchor in 2 fathoms.

Peter Fromm

Matia Island

Rolfe Cove (Matia Island)

Rolfe Cove, on the northwest corner of Matia Island, is 2.2 miles southeast of Echo Bay on Sucia Island.

Chart 18430
West entrance: 48°44.97′ N, 122°50.81′ W (NAD 83)
North entrance: 48°45.01′ N, 122°50.57′ W (NAD 83)
Anchor: 48°44.91′ N, 122°50.57′ W (NAD 83)

> *The mooring float of a State marine park is in the small cove on the NW side of the island; water is available.* (p. 339, CP)

Rolfe Cove is generally approached from the west but you can also approach through a narrow passage to the east side of a small unnamed island which forms the cove's north shore. This passage carries 2 to 3 fathoms of water. During the summer, there is a small 50-foot float and two mooring buoys here; a 3-mph speed limit is observed in the cove. Rolfe Cove is subject to mod-

Peter Fromm

Hermit's Cove, Matia Island

Don Douglass

Public float, Rolfe Cove

Peter Fromm

Sucia Islands aerial view

erately strong current and there is limited swinging room for anchoring. Due to strong currents and marginal holding, this is not a secure anchorage and you should maintain an anchor watch.

Peter Fromm

Mount Baker seen from Matia Island

Anchor in 2 to 3 fathoms over mixed bottom with fair holding

A tiny cove 0.16 nautical mile southwest of Rolfe Cove offers protection from southeasterlies out of the current, but a stern tie is required since there is little swinging room.

Sucia Islands (Rosario Strait)

Sucia Islands are located 2 miles northwest of Matia Island and 2.5 miles north of Orcas Island.

Chart 18431
East end (North Finger Island):
48°45.05′ N, 122°52.76′ W (NAD 83)
South tip (Fossil Bay): 48°44.75′ N,
122°53.86′ W (NAD 83)
West end (entrance to Shallow Bay):
48°45.76′ N, 122°55.25′ W (NAD 83)

Coast Guard Boardings

A fact of boating life in the Pacific Northwest is the possibility of being stopped and boarded by the U.S. Coast Guard, ostensibly for a "safety inspection" of your vessel's required equipment.

A boarding party of three armed, uniformed young men come aboard from an inflatable. As they approach, they ask how many persons are aboard and if you have any firearms. They are courteous, just doing their jobs, and as interested in getting off your boat as you are in having them leave. They want to know personal identification of the captain, the vessel registration, if there are flotation devices for everyone aboard, and if fire extinguishers were serviced recently. They check engine room ventilation, the flame arrestor on the carburetor of gasoline engines, oil discharge and MARPOL placards, and the holding tank for the boat's head.

If your equipment is up to par, they simply give you a copy of their boarding report. If you have a deficiency, this is noted and you have a limited time to correct the problem.

I have been boarded six times in seventeen years. To me, it is not a big deal, just part of boating at the western edge of the world's longest unguarded border.

—PF

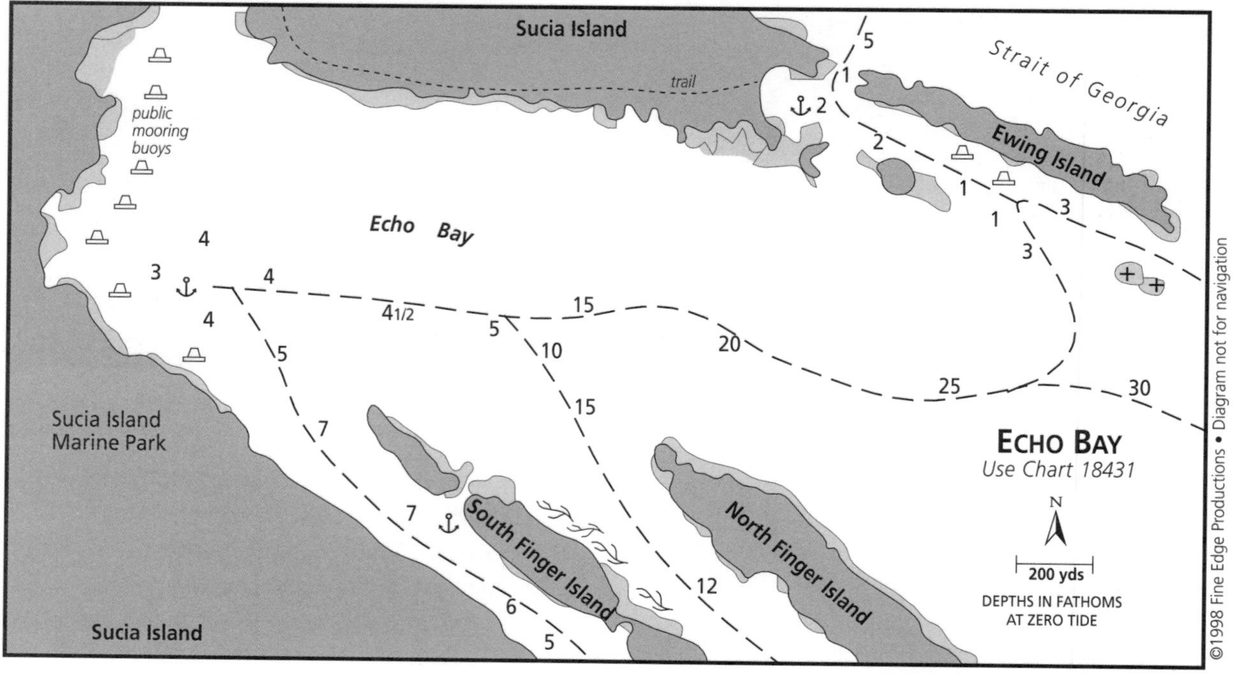

Sucia Islands, consisting of one large and several smaller islands, are SE of Patos Island and 2.5 miles N of Orcas Island. The large island, 200 feet high and heavily wooded, is horseshoe-shaped; its W side is a series of steep, wooded cliffs. It is a state park. (p. 329, CP)

Sucia Island State Marine Park, a favorite destination for pleasure craft in all seasons, offers quiet, picturesque landscape, good anchorages, and several nice, long walking trails. There are 74 buoys in the park.

Don Douglass

Anchored bow and stern, Matia Island, SE Cove

Peter Fromm

Sandstone formations, Sucia Islands

"Ewing Island Cove" (Sucia Islands)

Ewing Island Cove is located 0.8 mile east of Echo Bay.

Chart 18431
Public mooring buoys: 48°45.87′ N, 122°53.03′ W (NAD 83)

Ewing Island Cove is a scenic and quiet anchorage where small boats can find temporary anchorage at its head in about one fathom. This anchorage is subject to moderately strong currents and the bottom has marginal holding, so if you arrive early, you may be lucky enough to pick up one of the three public mooring buoys.

Anchor in 1 fathom over sand bottom with fair-to-poor holding.

Echo Bay (Sucia Islands)

Echo Bay is located 0.7 mile north of Fossil Bay on the east side of Sucia Island.

Chart 18431
Entrance: 48°45.35′ N, 122°52.66′ W (NAD 83)
Anchor: 48°45.76′ N, 122°54.44′ W (NAD 83)

> *Echo Bay indents the E side of the island. In W weather small vessels with local knowledge can find good anchorage in 4 to 5 fathoms near the head of the bay.* (p. 329, CP)

Echo Bay is well sheltered from prevailing westerly summer winds but open to strong southeast weather. The bay has approximately 15 mooring buoys plus enough room for dozens of boats to anchor in the large flat area at the head of the bay.

Don Douglass

Kayakers explore "Ewing Island Cove," Sucia Islands

Peter Fromm

Blue Water, *Sucia Islands*

Anchor in 4 fathoms on the west side of the bay over sand and mud with good holding.

South Finger Island (Sucia Islands)

South Finger Island is located 0.4 mile north of Fossil Bay.

Chart 18431
Anchor: 48°45.23′ N, 122°53.66′ W (NAD 83)

Peter Fromm

Echo Bay, Sucia

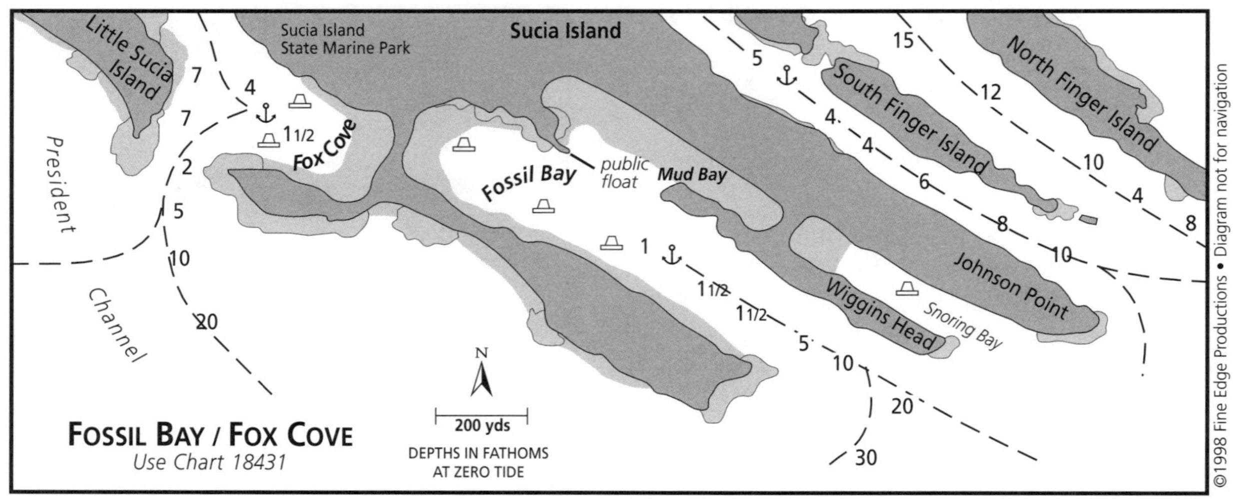

Passages in and out of Echo Bay can be found between North and South Finger islands, as well as between South Finger and Sucia Island. Small boats frequently anchor in the middle of the pass on the south side of South Finger Island.

Anchor in 4 to 5 fathoms over sand and mud bottom with good holding.

Snoring Bay (Sucia Islands)

Snoring Bay is located just east of Fossil Bay separated by Wiggins Head.

Chart 18431
Entrance: 48°44.84′ N, 122°53.22′ W (NAD 83)

Snoring Bay is a tiny, shallow cove with a single mooring buoy in its center. Heavy driftwood at the head of the bay is evidence of strong southeast storms.

Fossil Bay (Sucia Islands)

Fossil Bay is located on the south end of Sucia Island.

Chart 18431
Entrance: 48°44.82′ N, 122°53.56′ W (NAD 83)
Anchor: 48°45.06′ N, 122°54.17′ W (NAD 83)

> *At the head of Fossil Bay, on the S side of Sucia Island, there is a State Parks and Recreation Commission small-craft anchorage and float pier; water is available.* (p. 329, CP)

Fossil Bay is a focus for summer activities. There are about 14 mooring buoys and two public floats at the head of the bay. The main float lies in the shallow passage between Fossil Bay and Mud Bay which largely dries at low water. A large Coast Guard buoy is in the center of Fossil Bay. Anchorage can be found anywhere in the bay by avoiding the public mooring buoys, as well as the shoals on either shore.

You can find good anchorage from prevailing westerlies anywhere in the bay in about 1 fathom; sand, mud and eel grass bottom with good holding, if your anchor doesn't get fouled on the grass.

Don Douglass

Ewing Cove public buoy

Fox Cove (Sucia Island)

Fox Cove is located northwest of Fossil Bay across a narrow sandspit.

Chart 18431
South entrance: 48°45.04′ N, 122°54.93′ W (NAD 83)
Northwest entrance: 48°45.48′ N, 122°55.23′ W (NAD 83)
Anchor: 48°45.20′ N, 122°54.77′ W (NAD 83)

Fox Cove offers good protection from southeast chop. Anchorage can be found off the shoal which fills most of the bay, avoiding the public mooring buoys.

Anchor in about 6 fathoms over a sand and mud bottom with fair-to-good holding.

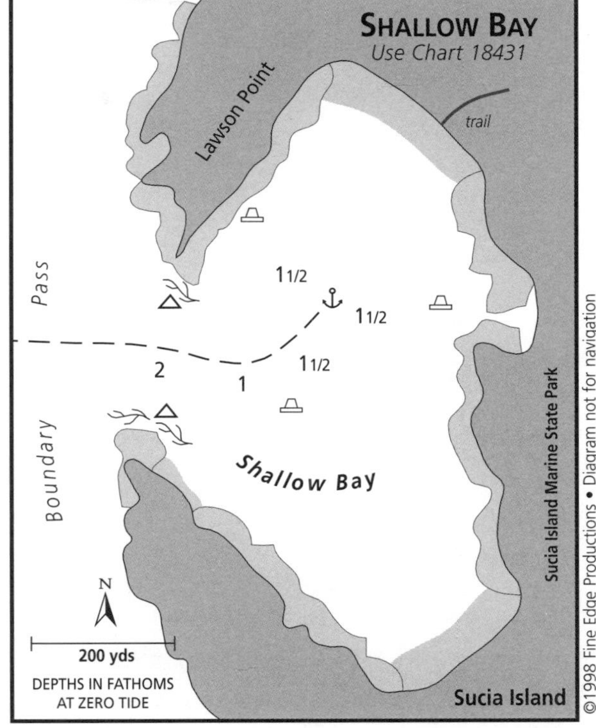

Shallow Bay (Sucia Island)

Shallow Bay is located 0.6 mile northeast of Fox Bay on the west side of Sucia Island.

Chart 18431
Entrance: 48°45.76′ N, 122°55.25′ W (NAD 83)
Anchor: 48°45.77′ N, 122°54.97′ W (NAD 83)

Shallow Bay is just that—shallow—about one fathom over a large area, but the flat bottom has good swinging room. A favorite during all seasons, the bay offers the only good protection in the area from southerly storms. Some good hiking trails lead northeast and southeast from the bay.

Anchor in 1 to 1½ fathoms over sand and mud bottom with good holding.

Peter Fromm

Kayakers in Active Cove, Patos Island

Patos Island (Boundary Pass)

Patos Island is at the extreme northern end of the San Juan Islands, 2.4 miles northwest of Sucia Island, where Boundary Pass meets the Strait of Georgia.

Chart 18431

Patos Island, 4.3 miles NNE of Point Hammond, is 60 feet high and wooded except at its W end toward which it gradually decreases in height. (p. 329, CP)

Peter Fromm

Patos Island lighthouse, Alden Point

Active Cove is the only recommended anchorage on Patos Island.

Active Cove (Patos Island)

Active Cove, on the northwest corner of Patos Island, is located 0.25 mile southeast of Alden Point.

Chart 18431
Entrance: 48°47.22′ N, 122°58.32′ W (NAD 83)
Anchor: 48°47.12′ N, 122°58.03′ W (NAD 83)

> *Active Cove, at the SW extremity of the Island, is reported to be a good anchorage for small vessels with local knowledge.* (p. 329, CP)

Active Cove is well sheltered on its south side by Little Patos Island. On the north side of the cove are the remains of an old pier. Although the cove is small, it is well protected and offers fine anchorage for small boats that need little swinging room or depth; there are also two public mooring buoys. The head of Active Cove is very shallow; currents enter the cove on spring tides. The automated lighthouse has fine views in all directions

Anchor clear of the mooring buoys in 1 to 2 fathoms over sandy bottom with fair holding.

Alden Point Light (Patos Island)

Alden Point marks the south side of Boundary Pass for southbound vessels; it is the northern tip of the San Juan Islands.

Chart 18431
Position: 48°47.34′ N, 122°58.28′ W (NAD 83)

> *Patos Island Light, . . . 52 feet above the water, is shown from a 38-foot white square frame tower on Alden Point, the W point of the island; a fog signal is at the light.* (p. 329, CP)

From the picturesque lighthouse located on Alden Point, it is just 2.9 miles due west to East

Point on Saturna Island (in the Gulf Islands). Beware of strong tide rips off Alden Point.

Toe Point Cove (Patos Island)

Toe Point Cove is located at the east end of Patos Island.

Chart 18431
Entrance: 48°47.20′ N, 122°56.38′ W (NAD 83)
Anchor: 48°47.15′ N, 122°56.50′ W (NAD 83)

Toe Point Cove offers temporary anchorage in fair weather only. Since there is limited swinging room and poor holding, a shore tie may be useful. Avoid the dangerous reef on the northeast tip of Patos Island, 0.25 mile northwest of Toe Point. The cove is not recommended for overnight use.

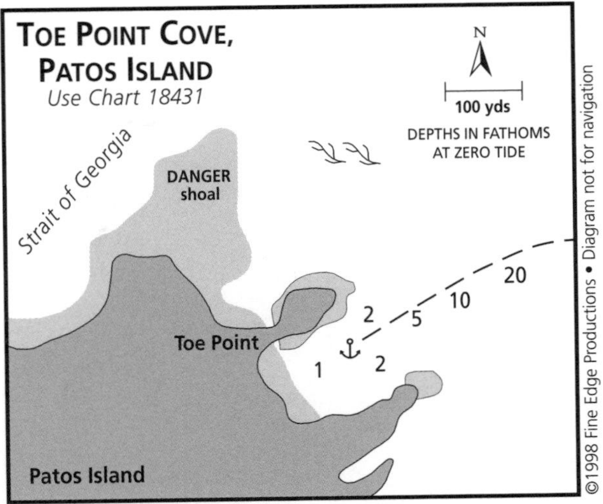

Peter Fromm

"Ruffles" surfacing off Iceberg Point

Peter Fromm

The town of Eastsound, Orcas Island

3

LOPEZ SOUND, HARNEY AND UPRIGHT CHANNELS

Orcas Island, East Sound and West Sound to Pole Pass

The protected waters of Lopez Sound, Harney and Upright channels offer fine sailing and secluded anchorages. Each area has its own microclimate with moderate current, so if you're not satisfied with one area, you can move on to another. Public mooring buoys are located in a number of parks and at Department of Natural Resources (DNR) sites. If you prefer full amenities, you can call at various marinas and resorts that cater to sophisticated needs, such as the beautiful Rosario Resort on Orcas Island.

On a clear day from the San Juans, you can see snowcapped Mt. Baker on the mainland. Closer in, Mt. Constitution (2,400 feet) towers over the eastern side of Orcas Island, providing a convenient landmark. The main east-west ferry route follows the Thatcher Pass and Upright Channel corridor. Local boats, including kayaks, canoes, sailing dinghies, and rowboats use these calm waters, so please watch your speed when transiting the area, especially near docks and anchorages and in posted speed limit areas like Pole Pass.

As an alternative to Thatcher Pass, you can turn east through Lopez Pass into Lopez Sound and explore the southern part of the sound and the west coast of Decatur Island. Continuing northward in the sound, you find Spencer Spit State Park on the northeast tip of Lopez where there is good swimming. Birdwatchers may find great blue herons, Canada geese, kingfishers, and migratory waterfowl in season.

If you continue north, you enter East Sound, Orcas Island, where the small community of Olga is located in Buck Bay. Orcas Island Artworks carries lovely craftwork from the islands; don't miss the Cafe Olga and the Nebula Book Store. From lovely and historic Rosario Resort, you can access Rosario Lagoon and Moran State Park. Check out the head of East Sound and visit the town of Eastsound.

Rounding Upright Head at the north tip of Lopez, you can turn southwest through Upright Channel between Shaw and Lopez islands. Odlin County Park, on the west side of Upright Head, is a favorite of Lopez Islanders with its wide sandy beach, softball field, an old cannon and beached boat, as well as camping, water, phone, and pit toilets. About a mile west is Flat Point, where there is a DNR day park. This long sandspit is a "fragile area."

On Shaw Island, watch for lovely Picnic Cove, a good moorage with sandy beaches nestled along a rocky and thickly-forested shoreline where bald eagles fish. Indian Cove is the site of 30-acre Shaw Island County Park, a great spot for beachcombing that has picnic tables, campsites, and water.

Curving west and north from the top of Lopez Island you can take Harney Channel between Shaw and Orcas islands. Blind Bay on Shaw contains Blind Island, a 6-acre State Marine Park, well worth exploring. Next, sail up into West Sound, home of West Sound Marina, a complete marina with a nearby grocery store and deli. On the eastern shore of Massacre Bay rises 900-foot Ship Peak; at the north end is Skull Island, an undeveloped marine park that offers spectacular views and terrific tidepooling.

Harney Channel is used by pleasure craft heading north via tiny Pole Pass or through winding Wasp Passage. As for all navigation in the San Juan and Gulf islands, a skipper needs to consult large-scale charts for a particular area and pay close attention to progress. Since drift logs and debris circulate slowly within this enclosed body of water, be sure to maintain a sharp lookout at all times.

Lopez Sound (Lopez Island)

Lopez Sound lies between Lopez and Decatur islands.

Chart 18429
North entrance (0.21 mile northwest of Undertakers Reef): 48°31.52′ N, 122°50.02′ W (NAD 83)
East entrance (Lopez Pass): 48°28.78′ N, 122°49.91′ W (NAD 83)

> *Lopez Sound, on the E side of Lopez Island, may be entered from Rosario Strait by Thatcher Pass. The depths in the greater part of the sound are 3 to 5 fathoms, muddy bottom, but a narrow and deeper channel is along the E shore.* (p. 335, CP)

Lopez Sound, entered via Thatcher Pass by larger vessels, has several quiet anchorages which provide good shelter. Smaller craft frequently use narrow Lopez Pass to enter directly from Rosario Strait. (See Chapter 2, Lopez Pass.)

Peter Fromm

Mud Bay, Lopez Sound

Lopez Sound, well protected from serious seas, offers a welcome respite from Rosario Strait. The sound is shallow and its muddy bottom affords good holding over a large area.

"Camp Norwester Cove" (Lopez Island)

Camp Norwester Cove is 0.3 mile northeast of Fortress Island.

Chart 18429
Entrance (0.14 mile northeast of Fortress Island): 48°28.02′ N, 122°50.12′ W (NAD 83)
Anchor: 48°28.01′ N, 122°49.88′ W (NAD 83)

Camp Norwester Cove offers good protection in easterly winds but is open to southwest winds.

Peter Fromm

Kwakiutl long house, Camp Norwester

The remains of Camp Norwester—a famous children's camp for more than 60 years—are evident along the shore. During its operating years, you would see dozens of teepees among the trees. The peninsula has been bought by Microsoft millionaire Paul Allen. Camp Norwester is now located on Cortes Island, British Columbia.

Avoid the submerged rock in the south center part of the bay as shown on the chart; this rock was formerly marked with a pole.

Anchor in about 5 fathoms over a mud bottom with good holding.

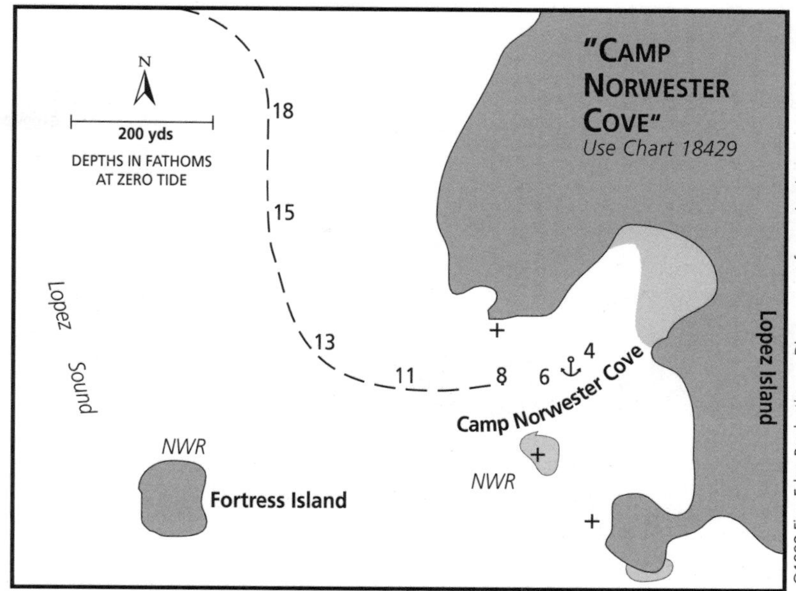

Mud Bay (Lopez Island)

Mud Bay is at the south end of Lopez Sound.

Chart 18429
Entrance (0.17 mile northeast of Crab Island): 48°27.84′ N, 122°50.53′ W (NAD 83)
Anchor: 48°27.30′ N, 122°50.41′ W (NAD 83)

Mud Bay, a large open bay, can be entered between Crab and Fortress islands or between Fortress Island and Camp Norwester Cove. The bay shoals to a drying mud flat in the southwest corner; however, a large area over a 2-fathom flat bottom provides good anchorage with more than ample swinging room. Although Mud Bay is not as snug as Hunter Bay, it provides more convenient anchorage for larger craft. You can dig for clams or just stretch your legs on the beach. *Caution:* Check for red tide alerts before eating any kind of shellfish gathered in the San Juan or Gulf islands.

Anchor in 2 fathoms over a sticky mud bottom with very good holding.

Hunter Bay (Lopez Island)

Hunter Bay is located in the southwest corner of Lopez Sound.

Chart 18429
Entrance: 48°27.89′ N, 122°50.98′ W (NAD 83)
Anchor: 48°27.63′ N, 122°50.22′ W (NAD 83)

Hunter Bay, separated from Mud Bay by a forested peninsula and Crab Island, affords good pro-

Small Town News

Lopez, Orcas and San Juan islands each publish a weekly newspaper. The *Lopez Weekly* is free and the only locally-owned paper. *The Sounder* and *The Journal* can be purchased from vending machines and at markets, pharmacies and other locations. All three papers give news of upcoming events: theater, music, festivals, lectures—community events which visitors are welcome to attend.

Both San Juan and Orcas have wonderful performing arts centers. The Lopez Community Center has a well-established outdoor pavilion, and plans and funds for a new building are well under way.

The local newspapers also keep people in touch with the rumor mills: how the high school sports teams are doing; the latest in San Juan County's battle against jet skis; developers' and environmentalists' latest go-rounds; what interesting things our neighbors are doing with their lives; where the garage sales are; and the sheriff's log.

The islands are "small-town" but their residents have been in every part of the world and are from every walk of life.—**PF**

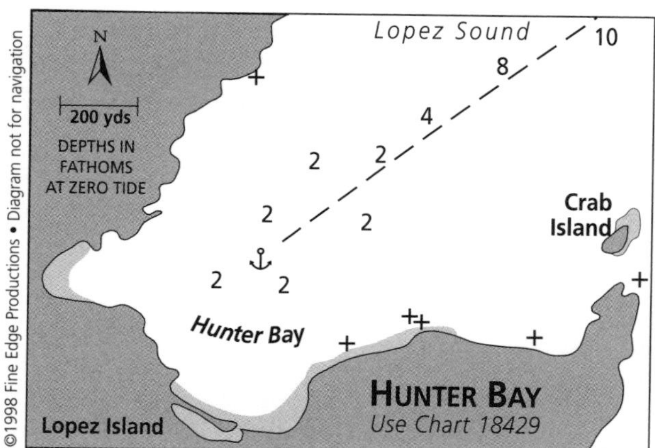

tection in southeast gales over a large flat bottom of about 2 fathoms. Although there is lots of swinging room here, be careful to avoid fouling your anchor on private mooring buoys. Crab Island is a Wildlife Refuge.

Anchor in 2 to 3 fathoms over a sticky mud bottom with very good holding.

Jasper Bay (Lopez Island)

Jasper Bay, on the west side of Lopez Sound, is 0.7 mile north of Hunter Bay.

Chart 18429
Entrance: 48°28.41′ N, 122°51.28′ W (NAD 83)

Jasper Bay is too small and open to provide shelter for anything but sportfishing boats in westerly weather.

Reads Bay (Decatur Island)

Reads Bay is at the southwest corner of Decatur Island.

Chart 18429
South entrance: 48°29.05′ N, 122°49.68′ W (NAD 83)
North entrance: 48°29.82′ N, 122°50.24′ W (NAD 83)
Anchor (large boats): 48°29.84′ N, 122°49.48′ W (NAD 83)
Anchor (south channel): 48°29.26′ N, 122°49.35′ W (NAD 83)

> *Decatur is a small village on the W side of Decatur Island. A wharf with depths of 8 feet at its end is here.* (p. 335, CP)

Hunter Bay

Reads Bay lies between Decatur and Center islands. The village of Decatur, with its piers and floats, is the primary access for residents of Decatur Island. Larger vessels can find good anchorage off the village, anchoring between the two charted cable areas. Smaller vessels can anchor at the south end of the channel, a quarter-mile north of the tombolo (spit) forming the north shore of Lopez Pass. A shoal area due east of Center Island has a 3-foot rock in the center of the channel.

"Lopez Pass Tombolo" (Decatur Island)

Lopez Pass Tombolo anchorage is on the north side of the spit, or tombolo, which forms the north shore of Lopez Pass.

Chart 18429
Entrance (0.25 mile northeast of Rim Island): 48°29.08′ N, 122°49.46′ W (NAD 83)
Anchor: 48°29.09′ N, 122°49.30′ W (NAD 83)

Looking east from Lopez Island toward Decatur Island

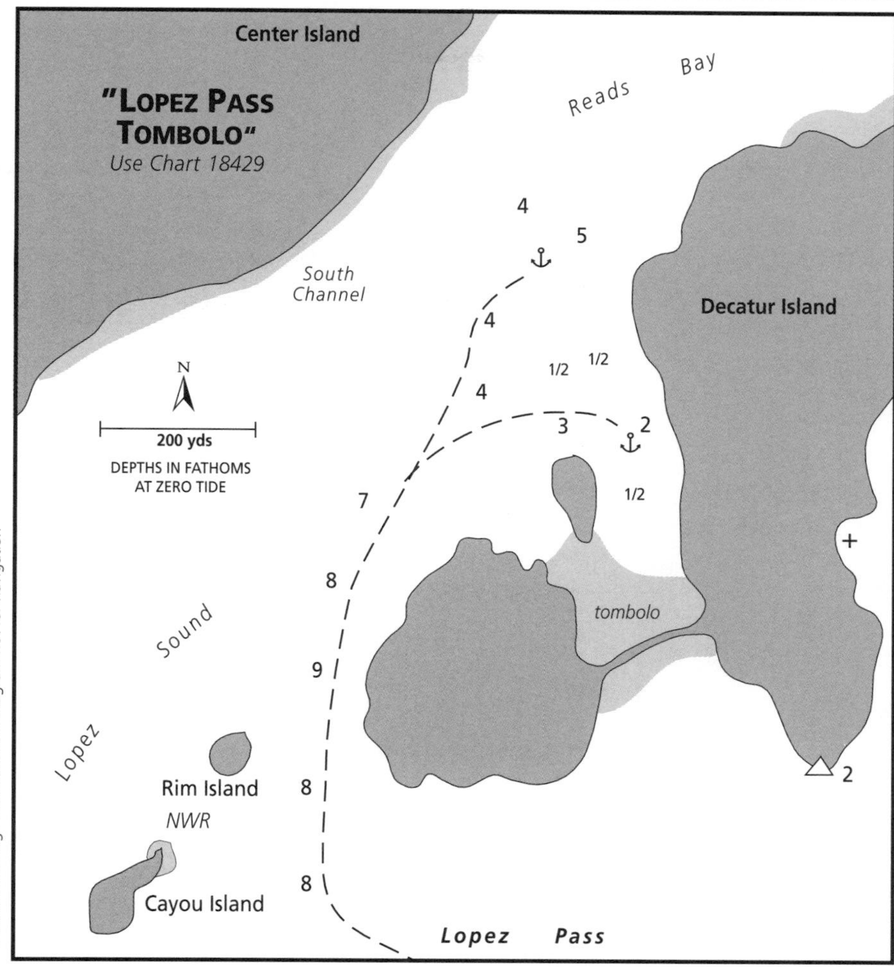

Brigantine Bay (Decatur Island)

Brigantine Bay, on the west side of Decatur Island, is 0.2 mile northeast of Trump Island.

Chart 18429
Northwest entrance (0.17 mile northwest of Trump Island):
48°30.52′ N, 122°50.42′ W (NAD 83)
South entrance (0.19 mile southeast of Trump Island):
48°30.05′ N, 122°50.00′ W (NAD 83)
Anchor: 48°30.51′ N, 122°49.99′ W (NAD 83)

The small bight of Brigantine Bay offers protection from northerly winds for boats nestled close to the head of the bay.

Anchor in 5 to 7 fathoms over a mud bottom with fair-to-good holding.

Lopez Pass Tombolo is what we call the tiny cove where small boats can tuck behind an unnamed islet to the north of the spit. There is room enough for just one or two boats unless a shore tie is used. Shoal water surrounds either side of this anchorage, so larger boats should not attempt to anchor here. The cove, which provides good shelter in all weather, has the added attraction of the spit which is fun to explore, as well as the islet which has a large cement structure on its west face.

Larger boats seeking shelter in this area should head deeper into Reads Bay and anchor between the two charted cable areas.

Anchor in the small 2-fathom hole; very limited swinging room; shore tie recommended.

Sylvan Cove (Decatur Island)

Sylvan Cove is on the west side of Decatur Island.

Charts 18429, 18430
Entrance: 48°31.08′ N, 122°50.06′ W (NAD 83)
Anchor: 48°30.86′ N, 122°49.97′ W (NAD 83)

Sylvan Cove

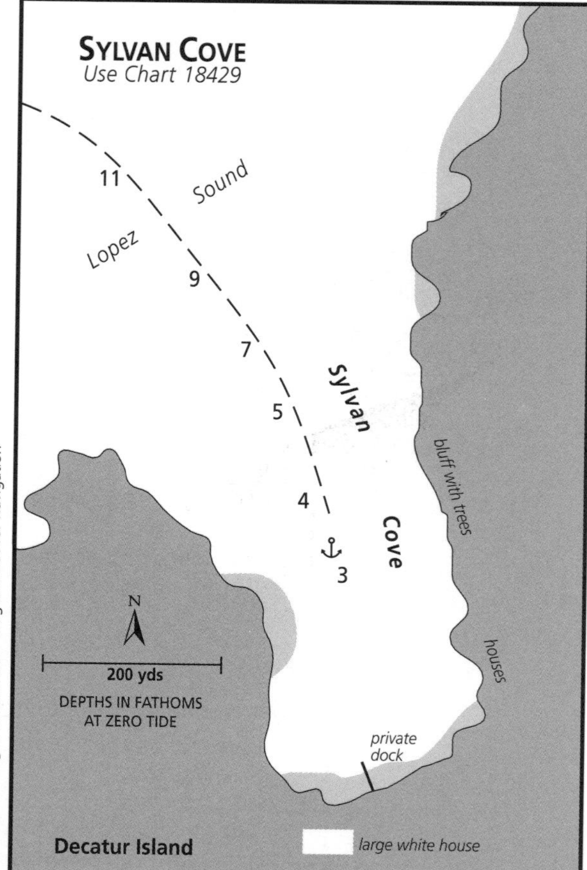

Spencer Spit State Park

Snug little Sylvan Cove is well protected from all winds except those from the northwest. The shores are tree-lined, and a large white house sits at the end of the cove. Avoid the private moorings.

Anchor in 3 fathoms at the head of the bay over sand and mud with fair-to-good holding.

Spencer Spit Anchorage (Lopez Island)

Spencer Spit Anchorage is west of Frost Island.

Charts 18429, 18430
North entrance (0.2 mile southeast of Flower Island): 48°32.65′ N, 122°50.92′ W (NAD 83)
Anchor (1.4 miles due west of Frost Island): 48°32.33′ N, 122°51.18′ W (NAD 83)
South mooring buoys: 48°32.06′ N, 122°51.27′ W (NAD 83)

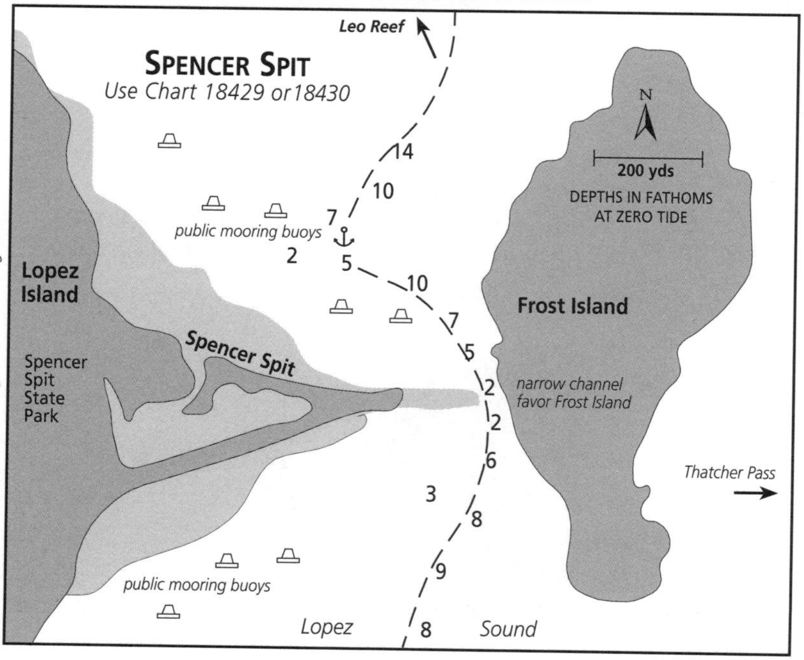

SPENCER SPIT
Use Chart 18429 or 18430
Leo Reef
N
200 yds
DEPTHS IN FATHOMS AT ZERO TIDE
public mooring buoys
Lopez Island
Spencer Spit State Park
Spencer Spit
Frost Island
narrow channel favor Frost Island
Thatcher Pass
public mooring buoys
Lopez Sound
©1998 Fine Edge Productions • Diagram not for navigation

Spencer Spit Anchorage has anchor sites on both the north and south sides of the spit which almost connects to Frost Island. Pleasure craft using the narrow channel between the spit and Frost Island should closely favor the island shore. This anchorage, which is part of Spencer Spit State Park, has a number of public mooring buoys located on either side of the spit. The northern side is more popular because it gives more protection in southerly conditions. When anchoring, avoid these mooring buoys.

Anchor in 3 fathoms over a mud bottom with good holding.

Moored at Spencer Spit State Park

Spencer Spit looking northeast

Leo Reef

Leo Reef is 0.5 mile southeast of Humphrey Head and 0.8 mile northwest of Flower Island.

Charts 18429, 18430
Light: 48°33.19' N, 122°51.26' W (NAD 83)

> *Leo Reef, in the entrance to Swifts Bay on the NE end of Lopez Island, uncovers and is marked by a light.*
>
> *In 1981, a rock covered 3 feet was reported about 350 yards WNW of Leo Reef Light.* (p. 335, CP)

Leo Reef is responsible for frequent groundings in the San Juan Islands, so give this dangerous area a wide berth. A drying reef extends 0.125 nautical mile southwest of the light; a 3-foot shoal is located 0.2 miles northwest of the light on Leo Reef. If you want to explore the reef or fish in its rich environment, do so from a dinghy with your boat safely anchored nearby.

Swifts Bay (Lopez Island)

Swifts Bay, southwest of Leo Reef, is between Frost Island and Humphrey Head.

Charts 18429, 18430
Entrance (0.16 mile southeast of Leo Reef): 48°33.02' N, 122°51.20' W (NAD 83)
Anchor: 48°32.71' N, 122°52.17' W (NAD 83)

> *Port Stanley is a small village on the shores of Swifts Bay.* (p. 335, CP)

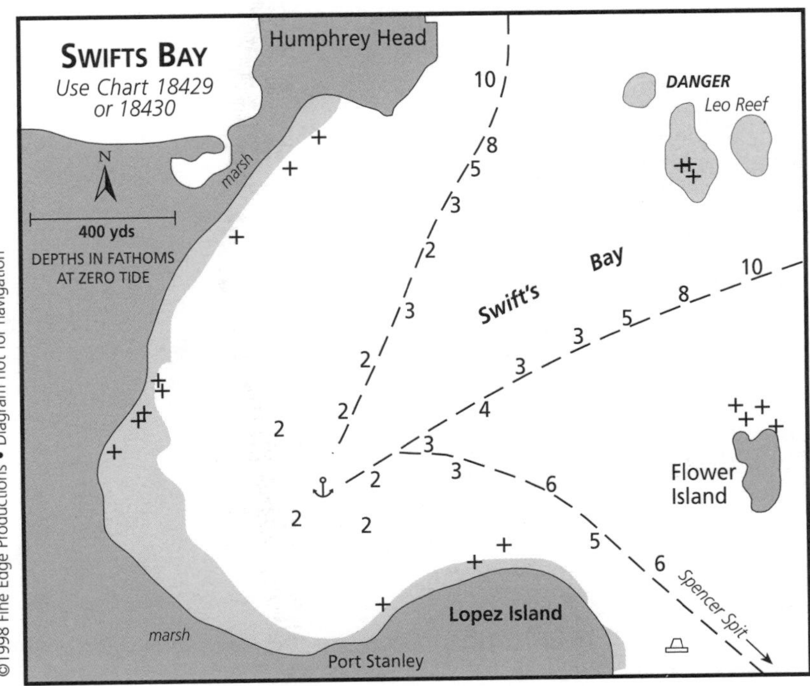

When entering large, shallow Swift's Bay, avoid the extensive rocks around Leo Reef as noted above. The bay has a nearly constant 2- to 3-fathom bottom over a large area, and you can anchor anywhere in the bay avoiding private mooring buoys. There is adequate but indifferent shelter here in most weather. Shoal Bay, directly northwest of Swifts Bay, offers better protection in unsettled weather. The community of homes along the marsh at the head of the bay is known as Port Stanley.

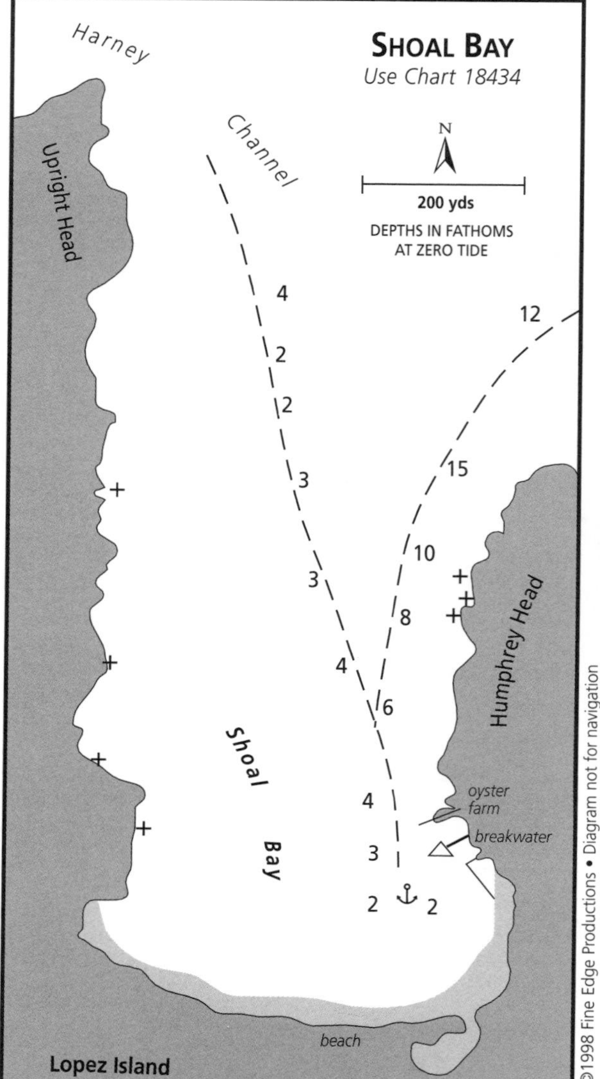

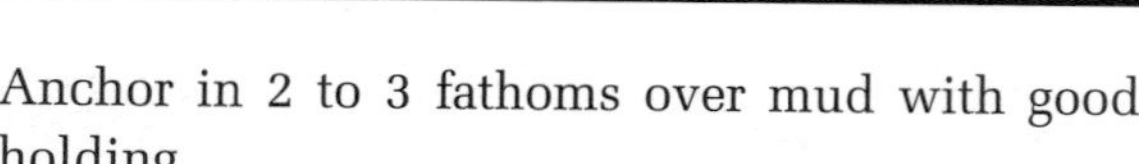
Anchor in 2 to 3 fathoms over mud with good holding.

Shoal Bay (Lopez Island)

Shoal Bay is located at the north tip of Lopez Island between Humphrey Head and Upright Head; the Lopez ferry terminal is at the tip of Upright Head.

Charts 18430, 18434
Entrance: 48°34.00′ N, 122°52.32′ W (NAD 83)
Anchor: 48°33.34′ N,
122°52.42′ W (NAD 83)

Blakely store resident

Shoal Bay offers good shelter in all weather; you can anchor almost anywhere over a large area in 3 to 4 fathoms. The best protection during southeasterlies is in the southeast corner between the small private marina and the private mooring buoys.

Anchor in 2 to 3 fathoms over sand and mud with good holding.

Historic cabin on Spencer Spit

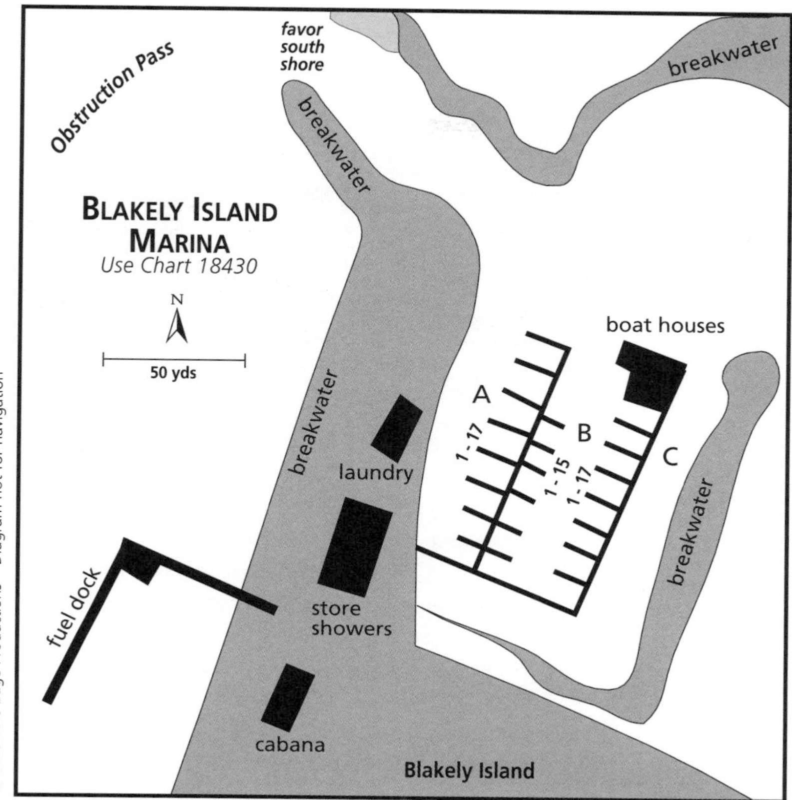

Thatcher Bay (Blakely Island)

Thatcher Bay is located 0.6 mile north of Willow Island on the west side of Blakely Island.

Charts 18429, 18430
Entrance: 48°32.98′ N, 122°49.48′ W (NAD 83)
Anchor: 48°33.10′ N, 122°49.13′ W (NAD 83)

Thatcher Bay offers surprisingly good shelter in most wind conditions and the anchorage is quiet. Open to the southwest, the large bay receives little chop except for ferry wake. The north shore is used as a log booming area; the head of the bay is quite shallow. Its center, however, has a constant 7 feet of water at zero tide over a large area. A small waterfall drops from Spencer Lake into the head of the bay.

Anchor in just over 1 fathom, sticky mud with very good holding.

Blakely Island Marina (Blakely Island)

Blakely Island Marina, at the north end of Blakely Island, is located 2.0 miles north of Thatcher Bay.

Chart 18430
Entrance: 48°35.14′ N, 122°49.04′ W (NAD 83)

Blakely Island Marina (tel: 360-375-6121), open year-round except January, has a fuel dock in its outer bay. The well-sheltered marina is entered via a narrow channel north of the store complex. Full facilities for pleasure boats include two concrete docks, water and power, showers, a laundry, and a well-stocked store. Boaters can use a covered picnic area which has tables and a fireplace. Temporary anchorage can be found off the fuel dock, but

Don Douglass

Blakely Island Marina

Don Douglass

Thatcher Bay log booming area

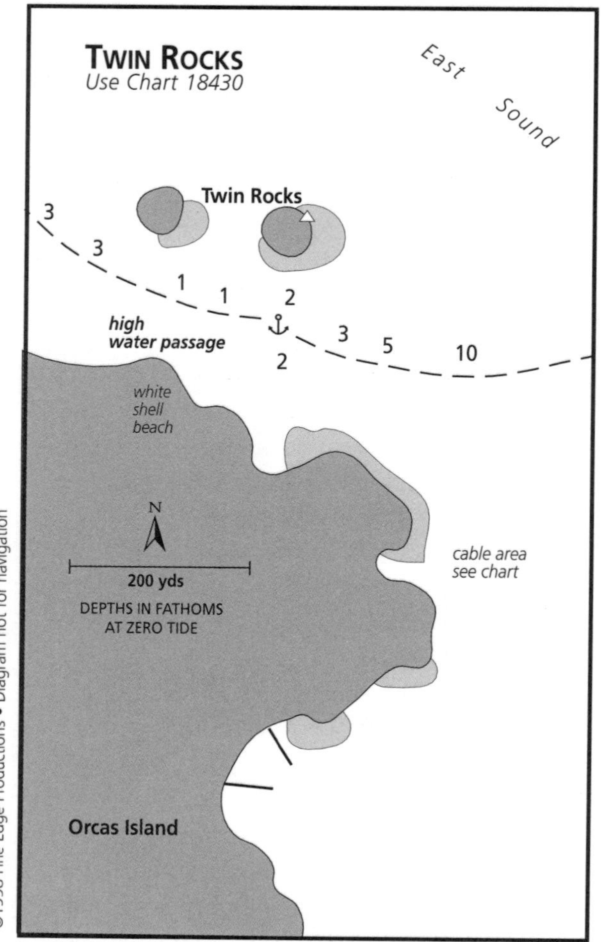

watch for eddy currents from Obstruction Pass.

Anchor in about 4 fathoms over a sand and shell bottom with fair holding.

East Sound (Orcas Island)

East Sound is located in the center of Orcas Island.

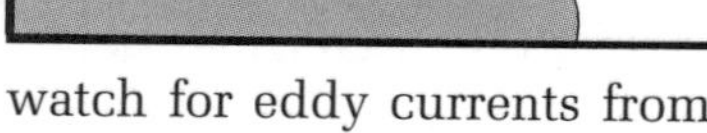

Chart 18430
Entrance (half-way between Diamond Point and Obstruction Pass DNR):
48°36.08′ N,
122°50.83′ W (NAD 83)

East Sound indents Orcas Island NNW for about 6 miles. Depths vary from 15 fathoms at the entrance to 9 fathoms less than 0.2 mile from the head. There are no outlying dangers, and the shores may be approached to within 0.2 mile; however, a shoal covered less than 5 fathoms extends some 700 yards off the W shore, 0.8 mile inside the entrance. Anchorage may be had anywhere in the sound.

Orcas Island is wooded and mountainous. Mount Constitution, in its E part, is marked by a stone lookout tower and a lighted radio tower. Turtleback Mountain (Turtle Back Range) and Orcas Knob, conical, and bare on the summit, in the W part of the island, are prominent and easily recognized. (p. 334, CP)

Don Douglass

Morning's exercise in East Sound

East Sound is marked by 2,400-foot Mount Constitution to its east and Mount Woolard, nearly

Peter Fromm

Peaceful moments near Madrona Point, East Sound

1,200-feet high, to the west. The sound has its own microclimate, often entirely different from that of the outer passages.

White Beach (Orcas Island)

White Beach is located at the southwesternmost corner of East Sound.

Chart 18430
Position (0.3 mile south of Twin Rocks):
48°36.61′ N, 122°51.84′ W (NAD 83)

White Beach is a tiny cove sometimes used as temporary anchorage by sportfishing boats in settled weather. Since it has a cable-crossing area, it is avoided by any but small boats.

Twin Rocks (Orcas Island)

Twin Rocks is 0.3 mile north of White Beach and 1.1 miles west of Olga.

Chart 18430
Anchor: 48°36.88′ N, 122°51.91′ W (NAD 83)

Twin Rocks is an undeveloped State Park for day-use only. If you visit the park and its surrounding reefs, please leave no trace. A shallow passage of about a half-fathom between Twin Rocks and Orcas Island can be used by small boats for temporary anchorage in fair weather only. Larger boats can anchor south of the easternmost rock, avoiding the private mooring buoy.

Anchor in 2 fathoms over a sandy bottom with fair-to-good holding.

Olga (Buck Bay, Orcas Island)

Olga and Buck Bay are located on the east side of East Sound.

Chart 18430
Olga public pier: 48°37.10′ N, 122°50.15′ W (NAD 83)

> *Olga is a summer resort on the W shore of Buck Bay, a small cove on the E shore of the sound just inside the entrance. Gasoline, water, and ice may be obtained. A State-owned pier here has reported depths of 10 feet at its face.* (p. 334, CP)

Olga is a small, easy-going rural community. Due to exposure to southerly winds, the float attached to the State pier is removed during winter. Temporary anchorage can be found off the end of the float in about 4 fathoms, where there is good shelter from northerly winds. Some supplies and tourist amenities are available, including an excellent restaurant 100 yards up the road, but there are no public bathrooms or showers here.

Don Douglass

The small community of Olga

Buck Bay, a small drying mud flat immediately east of Olga, is unsuitable for anchoring.

Dolphin Bay (Orcas Island)

Dolphin Bay is on the west shore of East Sound.

Chart 18430
Position: 48°38.05′ N, 122°52.85′ W (NAD 83)

Dolphin Bay is too small and exposed an anchorage for anything but small sportfishing boats. *Dolphin* refers to the moorage used by the logging industry in prior times.

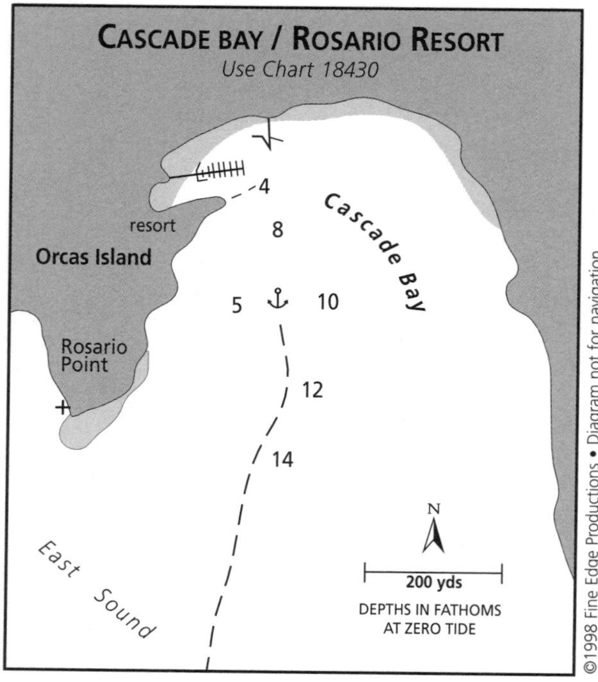

Rosario Resort, Cascade Bay

Cascade Bay (Rosario Resort, Orcas Island)

Cascade Bay, on the east side of East Sound, is 2.1 miles northwest of Olga.

Chart 18430
Entrance: 48°38.54′ N, 122°52.14′ W (NAD 83)
Marina entrance: 48°38.79′ N, 122°52.23′ W (NAD 83)
Anchor: 48°38.73′ N, 122°52.10′ W (NAD 83)

> *Cascade Bay, a small cove on the E side of the sound, about 3 miles N of the entrance, is the site of a large resort with floats having berths with electricity for about 60 craft. Gasoline, diesel fuel, water ice, a launching ramp, and a restaurant are available. Depths of 8 feet are reported alongside the floats. The large white resort hotel on Rosario Point, the W point of the bay, is conspicuous.* (p. 334, CP)

Cascade Bay is home to Rosario Resort, one of the largest resorts in Washington. The resort lies about midway along the east shore of East Sound in a moorage basin created by Rosario Point and a jetty. Open year-round, the resort and marina have deluxe amenities for paying guests that include spa passes, showers, power and water, and use of the resort's swimming pools, tennis courts, and van shuttle service. A gift gallery, cafe, and groceries are available in the complex. Boats wishing to visit the marina for up to two hours may moor at no charge. Past that, you may purchase a landing package. (Please check ahead with the harbormaster on VHF 78). From June through September boats wishing slip moorage are asked to reserve in advance.

Telephone 1-800-562-8820 or visit their Web site: www.rosarioresort.com for up-to-date information on the resort.

Pleasure boats should avoid anchoring in the

Rosario Resort

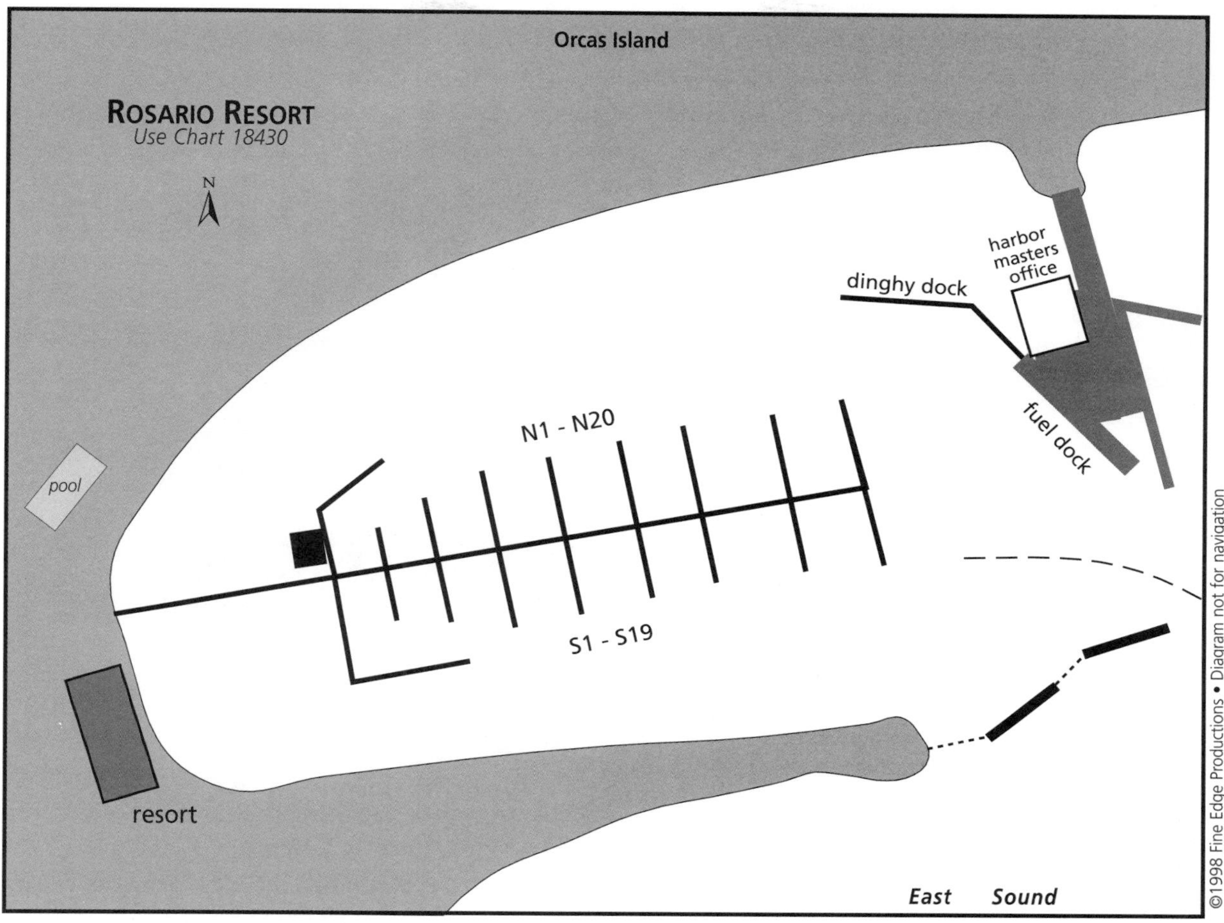

outer bay near private mooring buoys that are used by large vessels requiring ample swinging room. Transient boats may anchor off the Moran mansion or outside the line of mooring buoys.

Anchor in about 10 fathoms.

Rosario Resort (Orcas Island)

Rosario Resort and Convention Center (tel: 800-562-8820 or 360-376-2222) is one of the most outstanding historical landmarks in the San Juan Islands. The original mansion was built in 1904 by Robert Moran, a Seattle shipbuilder and millionaire. Anchored on bedrock, the fifty-four-room main building, which took six years to complete, has concrete walls and inch-thick plate glass windows. The mansion's furnishings were as lavish as the structure itself. Features that remain include an organ with 1,972 pipes, an imported stained glass window, and a figurehead salvaged from a clipper ship wrecked in the islands. There are tennis courts and beautiful walking trails near the resort and around Rosario Lagoon.

Moran purchased large tracts of land on the island; he helped build roads and develop water systems, providing needed jobs during the Depression. Eventually, he donated 3,600 acres of land to the State of Washington, an area which is now Moran State Park.

In 1938, Moran sold Rosario; in 1960, Gilbert Geiser purchased it and turned it into the modern facility it is today. However, the original buildings have been preserved by naming them to the National Register of Historical Places.

Moran State Park (Orcas Island)

For anyone visiting Orcas Island, this park is a must-see. Located in the eastern half of the island, the outstanding feature of the park is the stone lookout tower, built in the 1930s, that stands atop 2,407-foot Mt. Constitution. From this vantage point, there is a spectacular 360-degree view of the San Juan archipelago, Cascades, Olympics, and Vancouver Island. Hiking and camping, bicycling, wildlife viewing and several freshwater lakes for swimming, boating and fishing all make this a place worth visiting.

The park is not accessible from the sea, but from Rosario Resort, a rental car, scooter, or bike can take you the six miles to the park entrance. There is a scenic but somewhat steep hike from the shores of Rosario Lagoon near the resort.

There is an interpretive exhibit of forest recovery near Cascade Lake, where a 1972 storm downed hundreds of trees, some more than 100 years old. Sunrise Rock, a short but steep climb from the Cascade Creek trail, offers views of Cascade Lake and across to the lookout tower. Cascade Creek flows through a chain of waterfalls called Cascade Falls; its shores abound with wildflowers and birdwatching is excellent. Watch for the dipper or water ouzel!

More than 100 species of birds and twenty species of mammals can be found here. For the best wildlife viewing near dusk, take the smaller trails and walk quietly. You may see wild turkeys, raccoons, shy black-tailed deer, muskrat, mink and river otter.

Peter Fromm

View from lookout tower, Mt. Constitution, Moran State Park

Peter Fromm

Sugaree *and power vessel at the head of East Sound*

Coon Hollow (Orcas Island)

Coon Hollow, on the east shore of East Sound, is 2.1 miles north of Rosario Resort.

Chart 18430
Position (0.1 mile north of Griffin Rocks): 48°40.80′ N, 122°53.02′ W (NAD 83)

Coon Hollow, on the north side of Griffin Rocks, has anchoring room for one or two small boats in about 2 fathoms. The hollow was named after raccoons that inhabit the area.

Ship Bay (Crescent Beach, Orcas Island)

Ship Bay is at the head of East Sound just off Crescent Beach.

Chart 18430
Position: 48°41.52′ N, 122°53.73′ W (NAD 83)

The inner part of Ship Bay, along Crescent Beach, has large beds of eel grass where fish spawn, as well as an oyster farm where you can buy fresh oysters. Because of these areas, anchorage in Ship Bay is not recommended. Instead, anchorage can be found in Fishing Bay.

Peter Fromm

County dock, Madrona Point

Fishing Bay (Orcas Island)

Fishing Bay, at the western head of East Sound, is separated from Ship Bay by Madrona Point.

Chart 18430
Anchor: 48°41.50′ N, 122°54.38′ W (NAD 83)

Anchorage can be found south of Indian Island. The head of the bay north of Indian Island is shallow and dries at low water.

The village of Eastsound, at the head of East Sound, has a full assortment of supplies. The county dock provides easy access for your dinghy. You can find good anchorage between tiny Indian Island (known locally as Jap Island) and the dock. At low tide you can walk from shore to Indian Island.

Anchor in 2 to 3 fathoms over sand and mud with fair-to-good holding.

Judd Bay (Orcas Island)

Judd Bay is a half-mile southwest of Fishing Bay.

Chart 18430
Position: 48°41.10′ N, 122°55.17′ W (NAD 83)

Judd Bay is a tiny cove sometimes used by local boats that anchor in about 5 fathoms.

Upright Channel

Upright Channel, between Lopez and Shaw islands, is the main east-west route through the center of the San Juan Islands.

Charts 18434, 18430
East entrance (half-way between Upright Head and Hankin Point): 48°34.59′ N, 122°53.61′ W (NAD 83)
West entrance (0.93 mile southwest of Flat Point): 48°32.51′ N, 122°56.33′ W (NAD 83)

> *Upright Channel, between Lopez Island and Shaw Island, is about 3 miles long. Canoe Island, off Flat Point, constricts the passage to a width of less than 400 yards. Flat Point is marked by a light. General depths in the channel range from 20 to 25 fathoms. A shoal, covered 7 1/2 fathoms, is 700 yards SSW, and a rock awash is 250 yards SW of the SW end of Canoe Island.* (p. 334, CP)

Upright Channel is busy with ferryboat and commercial traffic as well as pleasure craft. If you are proceeding toward Friday Harbor, avoid the kelp and shoal off the south end of Shaw Island. Due to the complicated tidal patterns between San Juan and Harney channels, Upright Channel collects a lot of jetsam and flotsam. Stay alert for logs frequently found in this area.

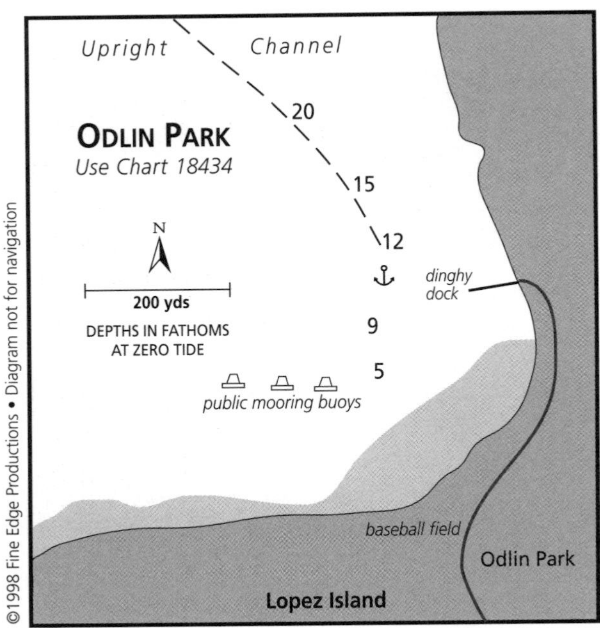

Junk-rigged ketch off Orcas Island

"Odlin Park Bight" (Lopez Island)

Odlin Park, on the south side of Upright Channel, is 0.8 mile southwest of the Lopez Island ferry terminal.

Chart 18434
Mooring buoys (1.12 mile northeast of Flat Point): 48°33.50′ N, 122°53.55′ W (NAD 83)

Odlin Park is a county park offering onshore facilities for picnics and recreation. Several public mooring buoys are close offshore. A convenient dinghy dock is located on the northeast corner of the park. Although the bight is well sheltered from southeast weather, it is subject to channel currents and wake from ferries and other vessels, and its bottom is rather steep-to.

Flat Point (Lopez Island)

Flat Point is the low sandspit to the southwest of Canoe Island in Upright Channel.

Chart 18434
Public mooring buoys (east side of Flat Point): 48°33.06′ N, 122°54.52′ W (NAD 83)

> *Canoe Island, off Flat Point, constricts the passage to a width of less than 400 yards. Flat Point is marked by a light. General depths in the channel range from 20 to 25 fathoms.* (p. 334, CP)

The northeast side of Flat Point offers good shelter from southeast winds but it is in the wake of passing traffic. There are four public mooring buoys near shore off the willow trees, 0.3 mile east of Flat Point. Do not use any private mooring buoys.

Picnic Cove (Shaw Island)

Picnic Cove, on the southeast side of Shaw Island, is immediately east of Indian Cove.

Chart 18434
Entrance (0.28 mile northeast of Canoe Island): 48°33.74′ N, 122°55.15′ W (NAD 83)
Anchor: 48°33.87′ N, 122°55.36′ W (NAD 83)

As its name suggests, tiny Picnic Cove is a good place for a picnic. The head of the cove dries, but good temporary anchorage with limited swinging room can be found in its center. Anchor between the two private mooring buoys in about

Don Douglass

Reef net boats, Shaw Island

3 fathoms. The islet and surrounding reef off Picnic Point becomes a tombolo at low water.

Anchor in 1 to 3 fathoms over clay and soft mud with clumps of grass; good holding if your anchor is well set.

Indian Cove (Shaw Island)

Indian Cove, on the north side of Upright Channel, is located 0.7 mile northwest of Flat Point.

Chart 18434
Entrance (0.2 mile west of south corner of Canoe Island): 48°33.36′ N, 122°56.00′ W (NAD 83)
Anchor: 48°33.69′ N, 122°56.06′ W (NAD 83)

> *A shoal, covered 7 1/2 fathoms, is 700 yards SSW, and a rock awash is 250 yards SW of the SW end of Canoe Island. Anchorages for small craft may be had in Indian Cove, W of Canoe Island, in 4 to 7 fathoms, soft bottom.* (p. 334, CP)

Peter Fromm

Sailboat passenger in Picnic Cove

Because of its convenient location, Indian Cove is a popular anchorage with adequate room for a number of boats over a flat sandy bottom. Canoe Island provides moderate protection from traffic wake, as well as from southeast winds. During north winds, Indian Cove is delightfully calm but driftwood along its north shore attests to the stormy southerly winds that enter the cove.

Marine Life

The San Juan and Gulf islands are in the center of the world's largest estuary. This area, where fresh water mixes with salt, extends from Olympia, Washington to the north end of Vancouver Island. The amount of mixed water entering the Pacific Ocean at the western entrance of Juan de Fuca Strait equals the outflow of the Amazon River. Because the watersheds of the mainland include long stretches of forests and lowlands, huge amounts of nutrients are carried to this inland sea.

Phenomenal numbers of plankton can be seen right under your boat. A small lens and a field guide will enable you to identify what these little floaters will grow up to be—crabs, barnacles, starfish, jellyfish, kelp, or rockweed. Zooplankton are animals and phytoplankton are plants. This microscopic mass of life supports all the other animals that inhabit these waters.

The University of Washington has a well-respected marine science laboratory in Friday Harbor where invertebrates are studied. This area is one of the best places on Earth to find jellyfish, which are free-floating filter feeders.

—**PF**

Shaw Island County Park, the only large piece of public land on the island, has both day-use and camping facilities, fresh water, and a launch ramp with easy dinghy or kayak access. Its beach is one of the nicest in the San Juans.

The small passageway between Indian and Picnic coves on the north side of Canoe Island is constricted by a shoal to the south and a rocky reef to the north. A narrow fairway of 2 to 3 fathoms can be found between the dangers marked by kelp, but it should be used only by small boats; a moderately strong west-flowing ebb current flows through this passage.

Canoe Island is the site of a summer camp that offers intensive study for students of French language and culture. The island is private, so if you're interested in visiting the camp, you must write ahead for permission.

Anchor in 3 to 4 fathoms over sand and mud bottom with good holding.

Squaw Bay (Shaw Island)

Squaw Bay, on the south side of Shaw Island, is 0.4 mile west of Indian Cove.

Chart 18434
Entrance: 48°33.35′ N, 122°56.43′ W (NAD 83)

Although Squaw Bay is largely a drying mud flat, temporary anchorage can be found near its entrance in 4 fathoms, avoiding the rocks and islets on either shore. Indian Cove, immediately northeast, is a better anchorage. A nice sandy beach lies at the head of the bay and is an interesting place to explore by dinghy. Strange-looking reef net rigs, sometimes stored in this area, should be avoided when they are in use, since your presence may disturb the flow of the fish.

Don Douglass

Bellingham ferry, Harney Channel

Harney Channel

Harney Channel lies between Orcas and Shaw islands.

Chart 18434
East entrance (half-way between Hankin Point and Foster Point): 48°35.08′ N, 122°53.63′ W (NAD 83)
West entrance (half-way between Orcas ferry terminal and Broken Point): 48°35.78′ N, 122°57.31′ W (NAD 83)

> *Harney Channel, between Shaw and Orcas Islands, is the approach to West Sound from the E. General depths in the channel range from 11 to 30 fathoms with a 9-fathom shoal 700 yards E of Broken Point, the northernmost extremity of Shaw Island.* (p. 334, CP)

Harney Channel is the busy channel used by vessels heading to Deer Harbor or the west end of Orcas Island via Pole Pass or San Juan Channel, or Friday Harbor via Wasp Passage.

Guthrie Bay (Orcas Island)

Guthrie Bay, on the south shore of Orcas Island, is east of Foster Point and 0.35 mile west of Shag Rock.

Chart 18434
Entrance: 48°35.46′ N, 122°52.97′ W (NAD 83)
Anchor: 48°35.56′ N, 122°53.06′ W (NAD 83)

While scenic Guthrie Bay is exposed to the southeast, moderate winds create little disturbance in the bay. Anchorage can be taken in the center of the bay, avoiding the two or three private mooring buoys. However, use care if you do anchor here. The last time we tested the

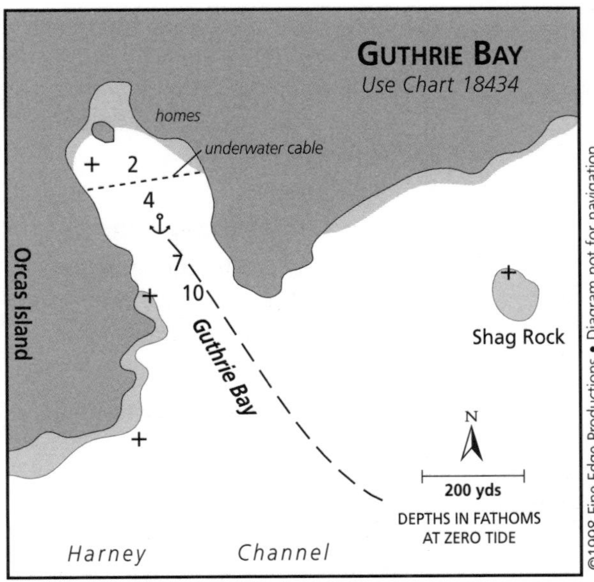

bottom, we hooked our anchor on a large chain running from a line south of the islet toward the house on the east shore. The chain, which was quite heavy, necessitated a dive so we could retrieve our anchor.

Anchor in 5 fathoms or more to avoid the submerged cable near the head of the bay.

Grindstone Harbor (Orcas Island)

Grindstone Harbor is 0.7 mile west of Foster Point.

Chart 18434
Entrance: 48°35.46′ N, 122°54.27′ W (NAD 83)
Anchor: 48°35.75′ N, 122°54.36′ W (NAD 83)

Grindstone Harbor is an attractive, snug anchorage in most weather. The middle of the entrance is marked by two reefs, both of which are marked by kelp during the summer; a narrow fairway can be found along the west shore. While the bay is open to the southeast, its head shows little disturbance from stormy seas. Swinging room, however, is limited by shallow water and a number of private mooring buoys.

Anchor in a $1^1/_2$-fathom hole in the center of the bay over sand and mud with good holding.

Shaw Island (Harney Channel)

Shaw Island lies between Orcas, San Juan, and Lopez islands.

Chart 18434

Shaw Island, a village at the E entrance, is served by the ferry. It has a store, warehouse, and a float landing with berths for about 25 craft. Gasoline, diesel fuel, water, and ice are available. (p. 334, CP)

All land on Shaw Island is private. The island is serviced by a small ferry that lands on the east side of Blind Bay.

Hudson Bay (Shaw Island)

Hudson Bay lies immediately west of Point Hudson.

Chart 18434
Position: 48°35.15′ N, 122°55.41′ W (NAD 83)

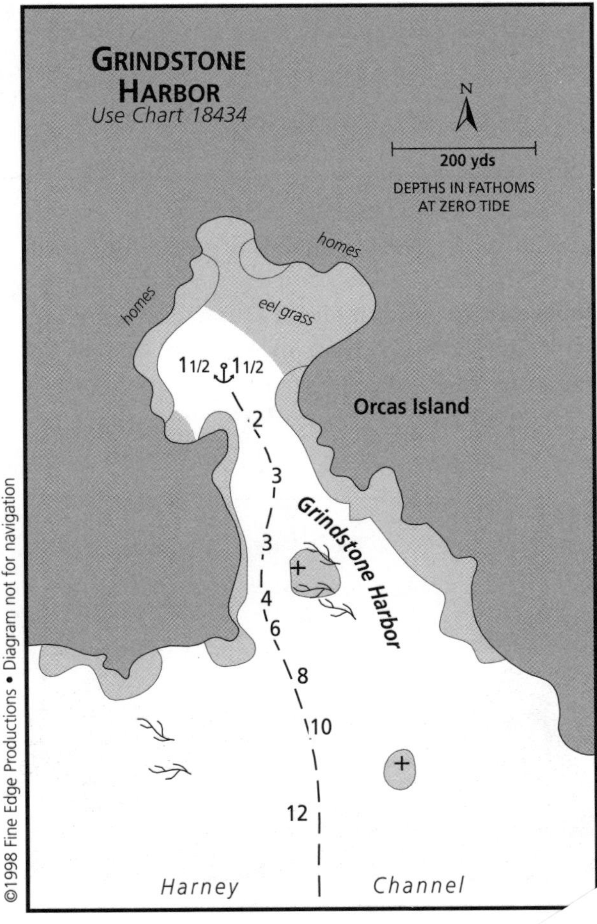

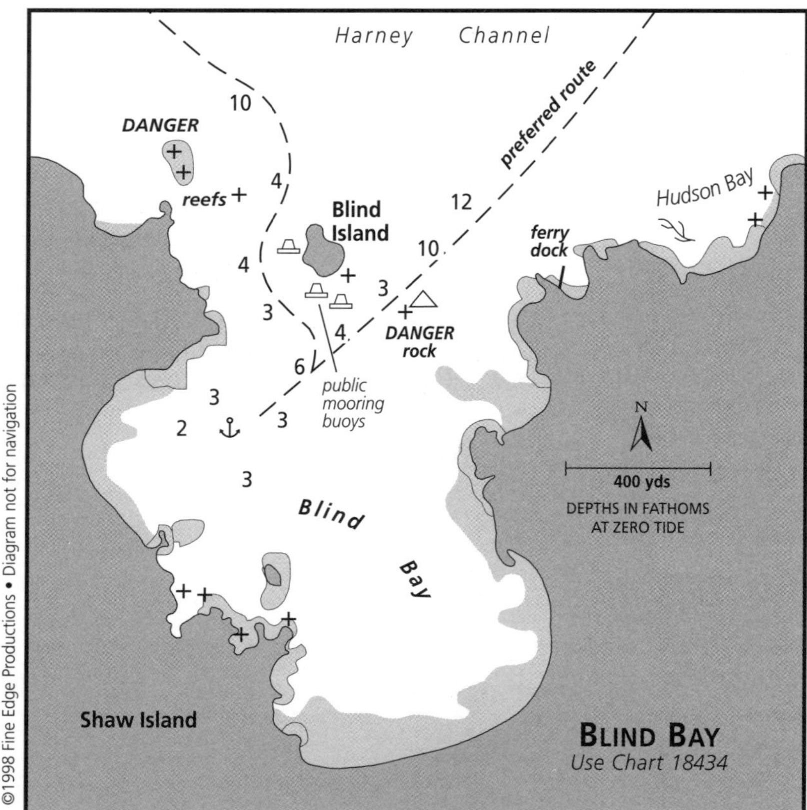

Hudson Bay is too shallow and exposed for good anchorage. However, small craft can find convenient shelter here from southeast winds, saving a long beat to the bottom of Blind Bay. The tiny cove immediately west of Hudson Bay is the ferry landing for Shaw Island.

A small marina adjacent to the ferry dock has limited transient moorage. Little Portion Store, open Monday through Saturday, has seasonal hours. The store, run by Franciscan nuns, is located at the marina. For information call 360-468-2288.

Nisqually *approaching Orcas Landing*

Blind Bay (Shaw Island)

Blind Bay is 0.6 mile southwest of Hudson Point and 1.0 mile south of the Orcas Ferry Terminal.

Chart 18434
Entrance (0.9 mile north of Blind Island): 48°35.20′ N, 122°56.19′ W (NAD 83)
Anchor: 48°34.87′ N, 122°56.38′ W (NAD 83)

Blind Bay, a small cove indenting Shaw Island just opposite Orcas, is shoal and in it there are several reefs. Blind Island is in the entrance. A private daybeacon marks a rock that uncovers 3 feet on the E side of the entrance. (p. 334, CP)

Enter Blind Bay by carefully passing to the east side of Blind Island, favoring the island shore; this preferred route avoids the pole-marked rock 200 yards southeast of Blind Island. Although you can use the west side of Blind Island, shoals and unmarked reefs starting 200 yards northwest of Blind Island make it hazardous.

There are several public mooring buoys on the south side of Blind Island, and anchorage can be found throughout the bay, with good protection from all weather. In strong west winds you can minimize chop by anchoring in the northwest corner of the bay in about 3 fathoms (noted by the anchor position above). In strong southeast weather, anchorage should be taken in the southeast corner of the bay. There is plenty of swinging room and the shallow depths and good-holding mud make this one of the safer San Juan anchorages in stormy weather. Blind Island is a State Marine Park with four mooring buoys. Limited primitive camping, picnic tables and a toilet are available on shore; no water is available, and all garbage must be packed out. Access to the park is by water only; the land above the beach is private.

Anchor in 3 fathoms over sticky mud with very good holding.

West Sound viewed from the southeast

West Sound (Orcas Island)

West Sound, directly north of Shaw Island, is accessible from the east through Harney Channel and from the west via Pole Pass and Wasp Passage.

Chart 18434
Entrance (half-way between Caldwell Point and Orcas ferry): 48°35.89′ N, 122°57.66′ W (NAD 83)

> *West Sound indents the W part of the S shore of Orcas Island for about 2.8 miles.* (p. 334, CP)

The Orcas Island ferry dock is located at the southeast corner of West Sound. The village of West Sound sits on its east shore; Massacre Bay is the large shallow bay at the northwest end of the sound. Moorage and marine services can be found at West Sound Marina or the Orcas Island Yacht Club. A public county dock lies just west of the Orcas Island Yacht Club.

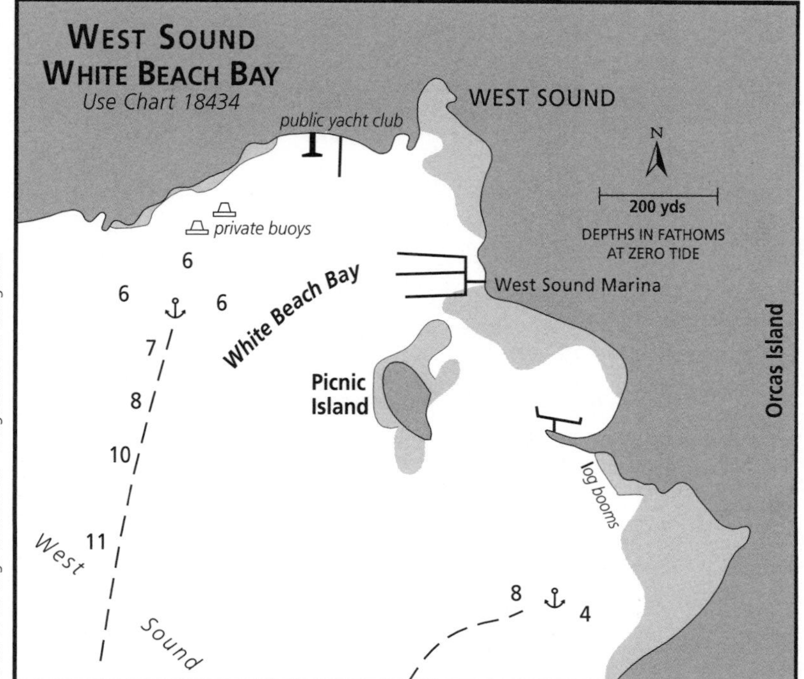

Orcas Landing (Orcas Island)

The Orcas Landing is located 1.9 miles east of Pole Pass and 0.9 mile northwest of Blind Bay.

Chart 18434
Dinghy dock: 48°35.83′ N, 122°56.67′ W (NAD 83)
Anchor: 48°35.69′ N, 122°56.26′ W (NAD 83)

> *Orcas, the settlement on the N shore in a cove at the W end of Harney Channel, is a summer resort. Several stores are at the settlement. An oil company distributor has a wharf with about 10 feet at its face; gasoline and diesel fuel are available. Five white tanks are near the back of the wharf. Water, ice and some marine supplies are available. The ferry slip just E of the wharf serves the interisland ferry that operates from Anacortes. A rock, covered 2 1/2 fathoms, is about 125 yards S of the wharf; deep water is between the rock and the shore.* (p. 334, CP)

Orcas village is a busy summer resort with frequent ferry service. A small dinghy dock, just west of the ferry dock and subject to southerly winds and ferry wake, provides temporary access to the stores and facilities at Orcas. Boats wishing to land here generally anchor about 0.2 mile east of the ferry landing. Orcas Hotel has a bakery, cafe

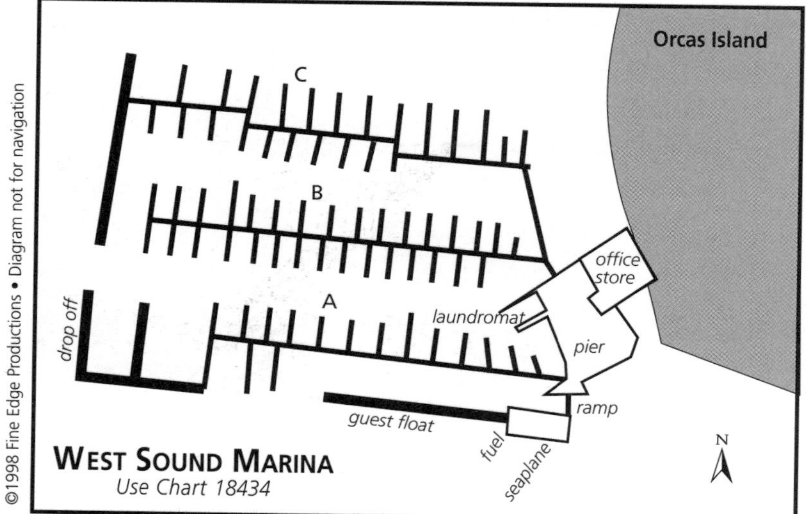

and dining room; the Boardwalk and End of the Line Cafe also have good food.

The two small marinas east of the ferry dock are private with no transient moorage available.

Oak Island (Orcas Island)

Oak Island is 0.8 mile northwest of the Orcas Landing.

Chart 18434
Entrance: 48°36.60′ N,
122°57.38′ W (NAD 83)
Anchor: 48°36.50′ N, 122°57.19′ W (NAD 83)

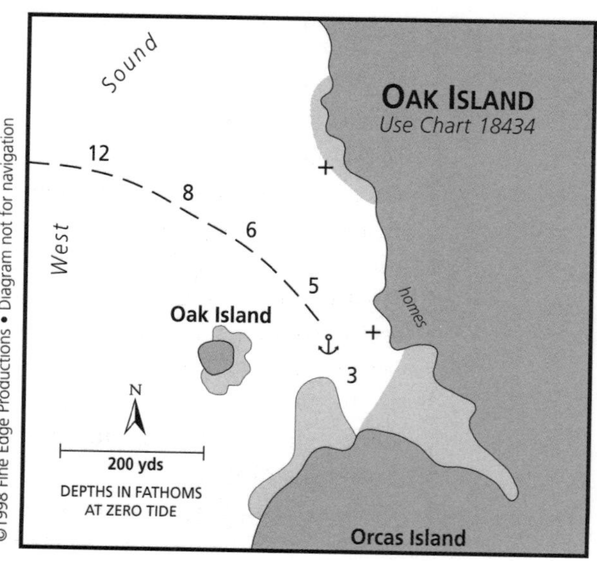

Oak Island, a tiny island with a single oak tree, provides some shelter off its east shore. Temporary anchorage can be found east of the island with limited swinging room.

Anchor in 4 to 6 fathoms.

Evans Cove (Orcas Island)

Evans Cove is on the north side of Caldwell Point.

Chart 18434
Position: 48°36.06′ N,
122°58.63′ W (NAD 83)

Evans Cove is exposed to the southeast and to wake from passing vessels. The area between tiny Evans Cove and Double Island is a cable area with no anchoring allowed.

West Sound totem

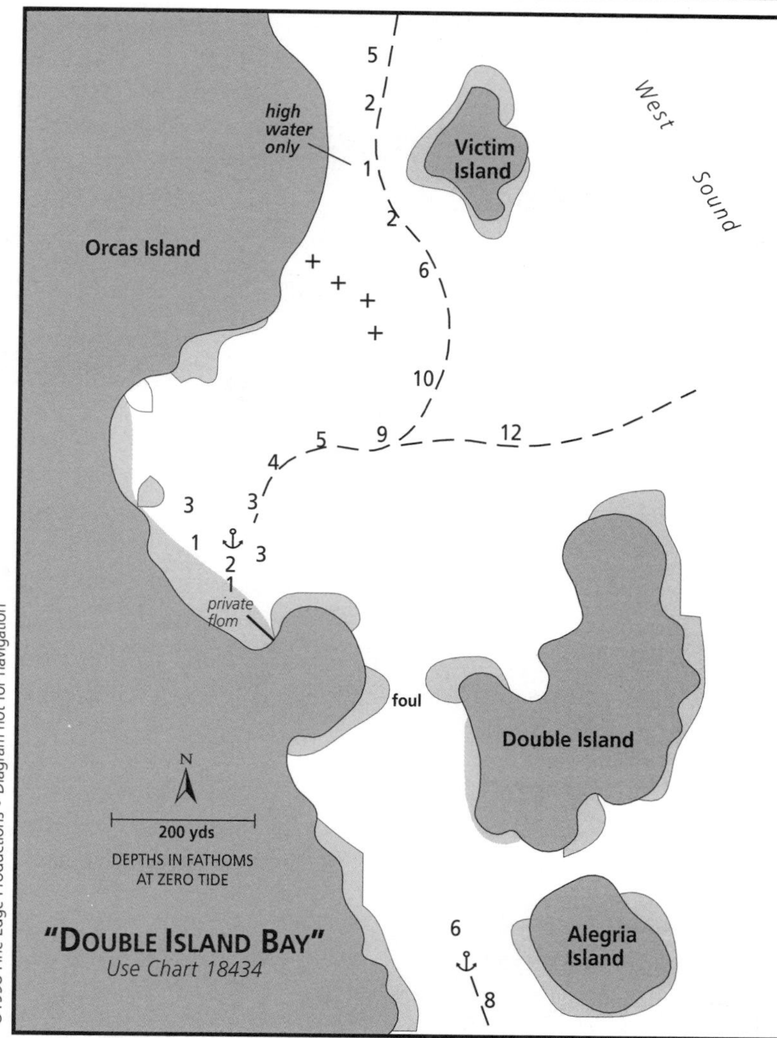

"Double Island Bay" (Orcas Island)

Double Island Bay, on the west shore of West Sound, is 0.6 mile north of Caldwell Point.

Chart 18434
Entrance: 48°36.67′ N, 122°58.38′ W (NAD 83)
Anchor: 48°36.56′ N, 122°58.77′ W (NAD 83)

Anchorage in 7 to 12 fathoms may be had anywhere N of Double Island, which consists of two small islands connected at low water; it is close to the W shore near the entrance [of West Sound] (p. 334, CP)

Double Island Bay is a well-protected, convenient anchorage. The bay is formed by privately-owned Double Island on its southeast, public Victim Island on the north, and a small indentation on Orcas Island. Victim Island is an undeveloped State Park for day-use only with no facilities. It is a good place to explore on foot, but please respect the flora and fauna in this protected area.

Larger vessels can find good anchorage in the middle of the bay in 9 to 12 fathoms; smaller vessels can tuck in close to the southwest corner of the bay. Double Island Bay, one of our favorite anchorages in West Sound, is scenic and generally quiet.

Anchor in 3 to 4 fathoms over a mud bottom with good holding.

Don Douglass

Double Island Bay

"Indian Point Bay" (Orcas Island)

Indian Point Bay, on the south side of Indian Point, is 0.9 mile northwest of Double Island Bay.

Chart 18434
Entrance: 48°37.47′ N, 122°59.08′ W (NAD 83)
Anchor (south end): 48°37.33′ N, 122° 59.20′ W (NAD 83)

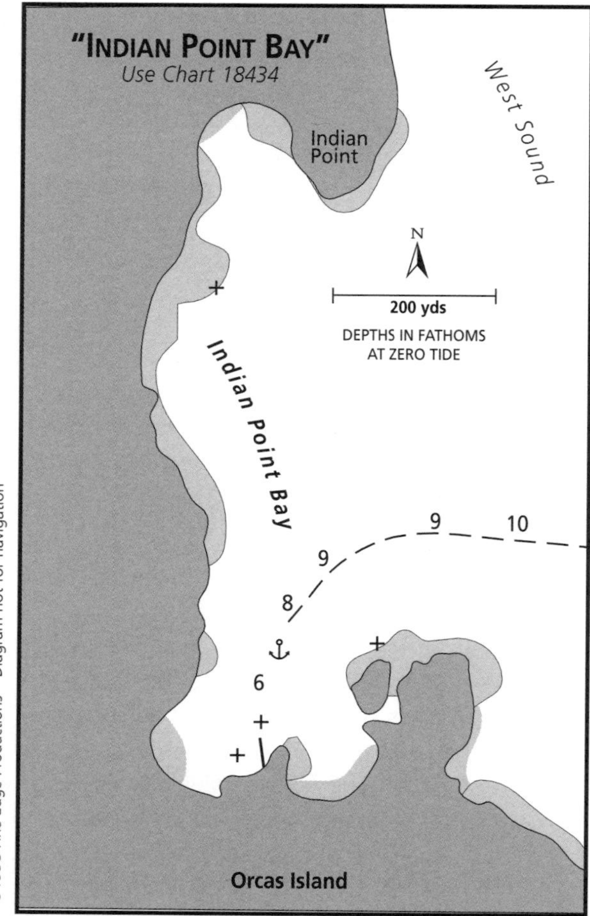

West Sound trawlers

The indentation we call Indian Point Bay provides scenic anchorage for small craft off a private shore; good shelter is provided in the south end of the bay behind the peninsula. Avoid the private floats and rocks marked by kelp.

Anchor in 8 fathoms north of the private dock over gray mud with some rocks; fair-to-good holding.

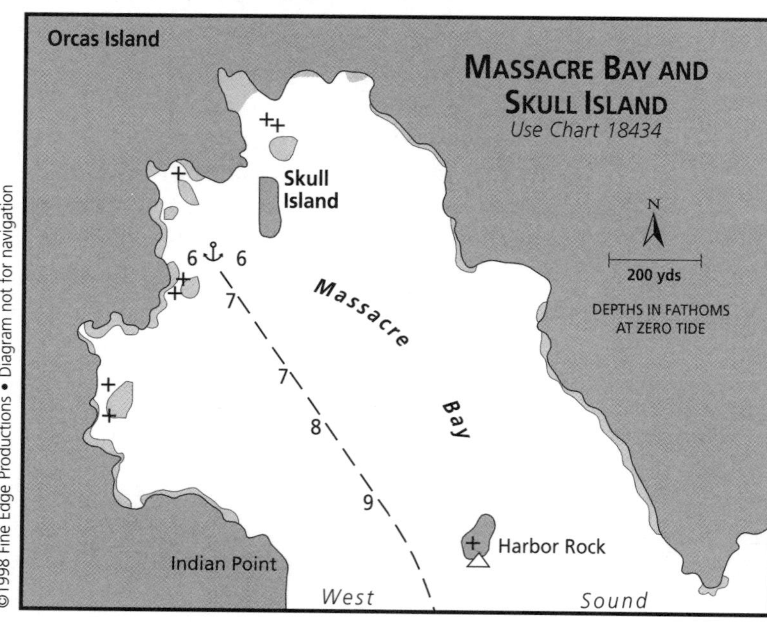

White Beach Bay (Orcas Island)

White Beach Bay, on the east shore of West Sound, is 1.8 miles northwest of the Orcas ferry landing.

Chart 18434
Position: 48°37.51′ N, 122°57.35′ W (NAD 83)

Picnic Island . . . close S from West Sound settlement. A shoal extends about 150 yards W from the island. In the bight E of the island is a marina with berths for about 80 small craft. An 11-ton hoist here can handle craft to 36 feet for hull and engine repairs. Marine supplies and a salvage and retrieval tug are available. In 1969, a channel with a depth of 1 1/2 feet was reported to exist between Picnic Island and Orcas Island; local knowledge is advised. (p. 334, CP)

White Beach Bay has sandy beaches along its private shoreline. Temporary anchorage can be found anywhere in the center of the bay, avoiding the private floats and mooring buoys.

Anchor in 6 to 9 fathoms over a sandy bottom with fair holding.

Village of West Sound (Orcas Island)

The village of West Sound, on the east shore of West Sound, is 2.2 miles north of the Orcas Island ferry landing.

Chart 18434
Entrance: 48°37.54′ N, 122°57.84′ W (NAD 83)
Anchor (0.19 mile east of Haida Point): 48°37.72′ N, 122°57.81′ W (NAD 83)

> *West Sound, a settlement on the E shore about 2 miles inside the entrance, has a wharf with 10 feet off its end. Only a few piling remain of an old sawmill wharf. Care should be taken when leaving the wharf to avoid some submerged piling about 100 feet SW of it. Gasoline, water, and marine supplies are available at West Sound.* (p. 334, CP)

Orcas Island Yacht Club is located north of West Sound Marina (reciprocal privileges only). The small public dock immediately west of the yacht club is for day-use only and is convenient for visiting the grocery store and deli or for stretching your legs. Anchorage can be found off the public dock, avoiding the many private mooring buoys.

West Sound Marina, the large marina north of Picnic Island, has good repair facilities with major renovations currently underway. Transient moorage is limited and by reservations only; the marina is occupied largely by vessels of island residents. Facilities include a travel lift capable of hauling 30 tons, and a fuel dock with gasoline, diesel and propane. Grocery supplies are available nearby. For information on the marina's facilities, call 360-376-2314.

Anchor in 6 to 8 fathoms between the public dock and Haida Point.

Don Douglass

The approach through Pole Pass

Massacre Bay (Orcas Island)

Massacre Bay is located at the north end of West Sound.

Chart 18434
Entrance: 48°37.75′ N, 122°58.85′ W (NAD 83)
Harbor Rock position: 48°37.80′ N, 122°58.67′ W (NAD 83)

> *Massacre Bay is in the N part [of West Sound]. The depths range from 7 to 20 fathoms.* (p. 334, CP)

Massacre Bay is a scenic, quiet anchorage that offers good shelter in prevailing northwest winds. Large vessels can anchor anywhere north of Harbor Rock in 6 to 8 fathoms.

Skull Island (Orcas Island)

Skull Island is located at the head of Massacre Bay.

Chart 18434
Position: 48°38.30′ N, 122°59.18′ W (NAD 83)
Anchor (northeast of Skull Island): 48°38.43′ N, 122°58.97′ W (NAD 83)

Skull Island is a lovely undeveloped State Park for day-use only. Its mixed vegetation, open areas, and excellent views make it a good place to stretch your legs. You can land your dinghy on a small shell beach on its east side and study the tidepools along shore. The route to the north and west side of Skull Island can be transited by cruising vessels only at high tide. Excellent anchorage can be found, 0.12 mile northeast of Skull Island with good swinging room over a flat bottom.

A number of small nooks along the shore of Massacre Bay, north of Harbor Rock, can be used as temporary anchorages; however, there are shoals and rocks in the vicinity, so use caution. The area north and west of Skull Island is shallow with isolated rocks.

Anchor in 6 fathoms over a mud bottom with good holding.

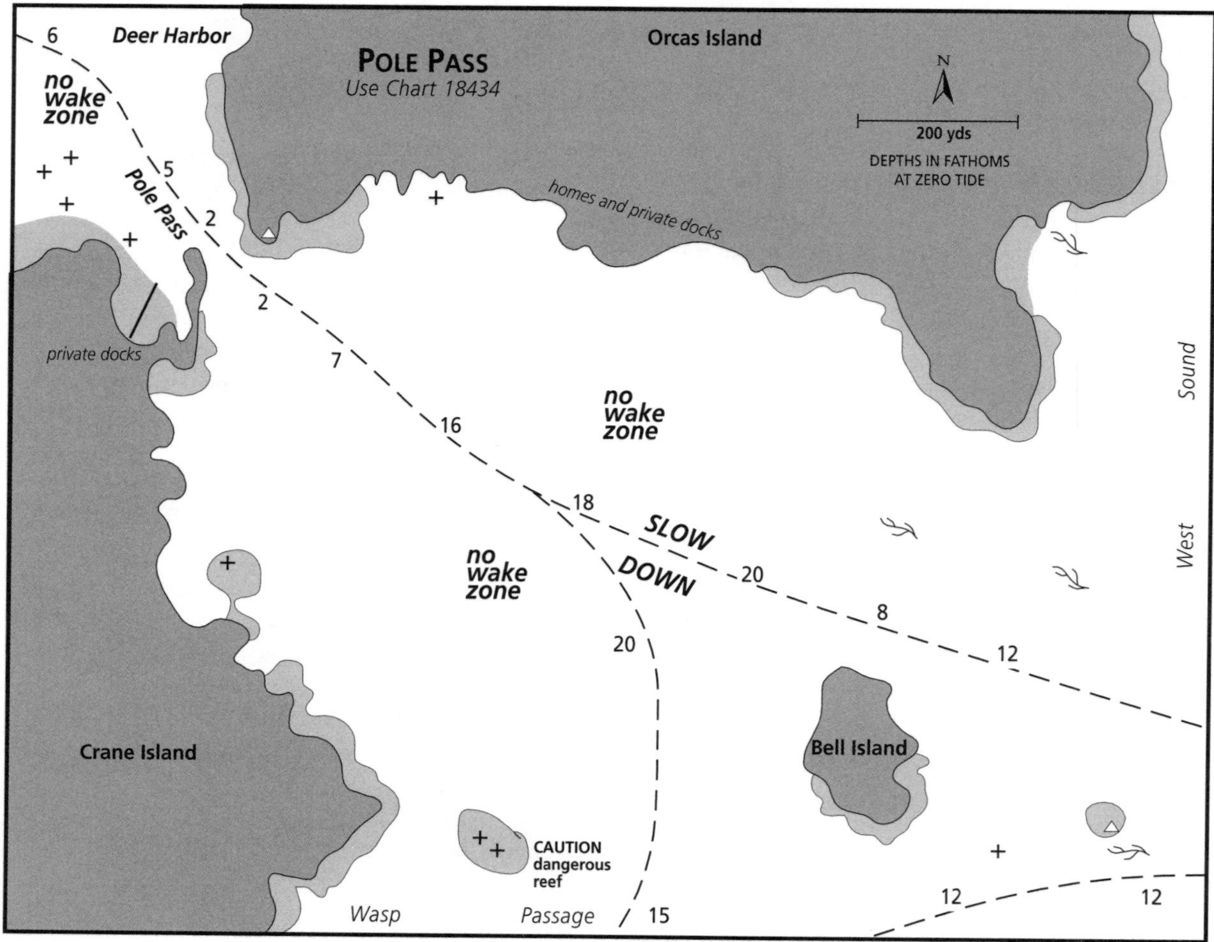

Pole Pass

Pole Pass is at the east end of Crane Island.

Chart 18434
East entrance: 48°36.01′ N, 122°59.38′ W (NAD 83)
West entrance: 48°36.15′ N, 122°59.51 W

> *Pole Pass leads from North Pass to West Sound and separates Crane Island from Orcas Island; the fairway is 75 yards wide in its narrowest part. Pole Pass should not be attempted without local knowledge. A light is on the NE side of the pass at its narrowest part.* (p. 333, CP)

Vessels bound from Harney Channel to Deer Harbor and points west use the S-shaped route through narrow Pole Pass. Approaching from the east, the spits extending from Crane Island make Pole Pass appear to be landlocked. The pass is about 200 feet wide; the fairway, which is much narrower, favors the Orcas Island shore. Avoid all kelp patches and be alert for strong currents and turbulence.

Because of the unique shape of the Pole Pass approaches, major erosion to the shore is being caused by the growing amount of traffic and high-speed boats. Swamping of small boats has become a safety issue for the residents of Crane Island who commute to Orcas Island to catch the ferry.

A 5-mph (no wake) speed limit is now enforced west of Bell Island to well north of Pole Pass. We have witnessed the damage and disturbance caused to property and moored boats—damage which is intensified by strong currents that run in Pole Pass. Please respect this speed limit when you transit the area.

Vessels bound for Friday Harbor normally follow the route south of Crane Island via Wasp Passage.

4

SAN JUAN CHANNEL

Cattle Pass & West Lopez Island to Friday Harbor, Wasp Passage to Deer Harbor and President Channel

San Juan Channel which connects the Strait of Juan de Fuca to Haro Strait and Boundary Pass provides convenient access to any of the San Juan Islands. The channel runs from the extreme southeast tip of San Juan Island to Limestone Point, at the northwestern tip, where it turns into Spieden Channel. Along this route, there are many anchorages with interesting places to explore. Tucking inside Cape San Juan, north of Cattle Point, you can go ashore and visit the old lighthouse, comb the beach for driftwood, and perhaps catch sight of some river otters. From the bluff above the point, you have spectacular views of Lopez Island and the Strait of Juan Fuca.

Several lovely parks lie along the east shore of San Juan Island: Griffin Bay Park is a Department of Natural Resources (DNR) park with a gravel beach, campsites, toilets, and picnic areas. Just south of this park is American Camp Park which offers nice hiking opportunities. There are three lagoons to explore and Mount Finlayson (290 feet high) to climb. Shore and land birds abound, and orcas can sometimes be spotted offshore.

On the west shore of Lopez are Fisherman Bay, site of Islands Marine Center and Lopez Islander Resort. You can walk to Lopez village with its bakery, bookstores, gift shops and art galleries, and visit a farmers' market here in the summer.

Turn Island is a State Marine Park with mooring buoys, beaches, campsites, and primitive toilets—a nice place for picnicking and exploring. Most of the park is a wildlife refuge.

As you round Turn Island on the approach to Hicks Bay, watch for seals off the southwestern shore of Shaw Island.

Peter Fromm

San Juan Channel sailing at its best

Peter Fromm

San Juan Channel

Friday Harbor, on San Juan Island, is San Juan County's government center and the hub for transportation, communication, and outfitting. It is the main terminal for inter-island ferries, as well as for ferries to Anacortes, Port Townsend, and Sidney, B.C.; the Victoria Clipper also makes a stop here. A year-round Customs and Immigration office is located at the head of the public marina in Friday Harbor.

Wasp, Crane, Yellow and Jones islands, which form an intriguing labyrinth on the east of San Juan Channel, are great waters for rowing, canoeing and kayaking, and scuba diving. Yellow Island, owned by the Nature Conservancy, is open to the public—brilliant wildflowers and swift hummingbirds are among its attractions. Isolated reefs and rocks around the Wasp Islands are notorious for causing vessel groundings, especially during poor visibility and strong and irregular currents; be cautious if you take your boat through this area.

The western shore of Orcas Island faces President Channel and Waldron Island to the northwest. To the east, Deer Harbor Resort inside Deer Harbor, offers just about all the amenities, including a swimming pool! As you head northeast along the outer shore, passing West Beach, you'll find Camp Orkila. Freeman Island, just offshore, is ringed with steep cliffs. Waldron is an historic island, mostly private, with only a few places you can access.

Because of its scenic and historic resources, generally moderate weather, and manageable currents, San Juan Channel is a popular destination for charter and whale-watching operations, as well as for vessels crossing the international border.

Cattle Pass

Perhaps the "wildest" spot in the San Juans is Cattle Pass between San Juan and Lopez islands. During periods of large tidal differences of up to 12 feet, the currents sometimes run 8 or 9 knots. When a strong southeast or southwest wind is blowing, large "haystacks" of water can form—towers of water 10-12 feet high. It is a place to treat with respect!

Although Deception Pass, between Fidalgo and Whidbey Islands, has even stronger currents, the waters have never seemed as wild to me as those south of Cattle Pass when the current sets against the wind.—**PF**

Peter Fromm

Seventy-knot gusts, Easter 1997, at Cattle Point lighthouse

San Juan Channel (between San Juan and Orcas Islands to Waldron Island)

Chart 18434

Peter Fromm

Cattle Point lighthouse

San Juan Channel, the middle one of three principal channels leading from the Strait of Juan de Fuca to the Strait of Georgia, separates San Juan Island from the islands E. It is 13 miles long from its S end to its junction with President Channel at the N end. San Juan Channel is deep throughout and, except near its S entrance, has few off-lying dangers.

In the S end of San Juan Channel, between Goose Island and Deadman Island, the average current velocity is 2.6 knots on the flood and ebb, however, maximum flood currents of 5 knots or more cause severe rips and eddies. (p. 331, CP)

San Juan Channel is an alternative to Haro Strait for vessels proceeding to or from either the Strait of Juan de Fuca or the Strait of Georgia. Entering the channel from the south at Cattle Pass can give you a nasty, but short-lived challenge whenever the wind blows against a strong current, so pay particular attention to conditions before you traverse.

Cattle Pass (Middle Channel)

Chart 18434
South entrance: 48°26.00′ N, 122°56.80′ W (NAD 83)
North entrance: 48°28.30′ N, 122°57.30′ W (NAD 83)

Salmon Bank, S of Cattle Point and on the W side of Middle Channel, is an extensive shoal covered 1 1/2 to 3 fathoms; it is marked by a lighted gong buoy. Kelp grows on the rocks. (p. 331, CP)

Cattle Pass, the common name for what is shown as Middle Channel on charts, is the major entrance to the San Juans for boats northbound from the Strait of Juan de Fuca. Small craft should exercise caution any time fresh winds oppose the direction of strong currents flowing in the pass. Between Whale Rocks on the east and Cattle Point on the west, heavy turbulence and tide rips occur during spring tides due to the strong currents and an irregular bottom. Tide rips also occur at the narrows between Goose Island and Deadman Island where San Juan Channel is less than a half-mile wide.

Cattle Point (San Juan Island)

Cattle Point is 0.75 mile east of American Camp boundary.

Chart 18434
Position: 48°27.00′ N, 122°57.75′ W (NAD 83)

Cattle Point, marked by a light and a seasonal fog signal, is the SE extremity of San Juan Island and forms the W point at the S entrance to San Juan Channel. Cattle were once loaded here for shipment to and from Victoria. (p. 331, CP)

Minke Whales

Minke whales can sometimes be sighted in the San Juans. A baleen whale, this sleek, beautiful mammal grows to 30 feet. Its back is black, with a small curved dorsal fin towards its "stern." Minkes are sighted most frequently south of Cattle Pass in San Juan Channel, and around Flattop Island when they surface to breathe. Many boaters, speeding by, never recognize them.—**PF**

Due to the strong tide rips in the area, there is no offshore anchorage at Cattle Point. Although kayaks and beachable boats sometimes use the gravel and driftwood beach to get ashore, pleasure craft should go "around the corner" to the west of Cape San Juan and hike across the peninsula to visit the picnic area. Only strong, experienced kayakers should venture into this area.

Peter Fromm

Orcas off Lopez Island

Inner Passage

Inner Passage lies just south of Cattle Point at the south end of San Juan Island.

Chart 18434
West entrance: 48°26.77′ N, 122°59.47′ W (NAD 83)
East entrance: 48°26.72′ N, 122°57.66′ W (NAD 83)

Inner Passage is a shallow shortcut that passes north of Salmon Bank, paralleling the shore, approximately 1/3 to 1/2 mile off. It is useful for boats headed to or from Victoria or to the west coast of San Juan Island. (Avoid the kelp patches as you pass through!) Salmon Bank is a good place to watch for Minke whales.

Lopez Island (San Juan Channel from the Strait of Juan de Fuca to Rosario Strait)

Lopez Island, east of San Juan Island and south of Orcas Island, is 11 miles west of Anacortes.

Chart 18434

A Sense of Community

A "sense of community" describes people's feelings about their island life. The support of numerous events, programs and buildings are evidence of residents' participation in their community, but no story describes it better to me than the story of Edie's new car.

On Lopez, someone's 50th birthday is a big deal which often involves special ceremonies. A group of friends were returning from a kayaking trip when the topic of a birthday present for their friend Edie came up. Her former husband suggested they stop in Vancouver's Chinatown to look for a gift. An astute friend said, "Edie doesn't need anything from Chinatown. She's recently divorced, starting a new life, and her children are grown and gone. What she needs is a new car."

This simple truth stunned everyone into silence. One of the kids in the group, knowing everyone's economic status, asked, "How will we pay for a new car?"

"We'll just pass the hat," someone said quietly.

And that is just what happened. Everyone who knew and loved Edie saw the wisdom of this gift. Her old Volvo was a good "island car," but not quite right for her new life.

The community pitched in, with more than 200 people contributing $3000. Even the car salesman participated in the giving—when he heard the story he lowered the price by $500!

The best part was that everyone kept the surprise! The new car, wrapped in a big ribbon with a huge bow on its hood, was driven into the middle of Edie's birthday party. The lights were flashing, the horn was honking, and Edie's favorite tape was playing on the stereo. The birthday girl thought her present was in the trunk—until someone handed her the keys and the title to the car! . . . Now that's what I call a sense of community!—**PF**

Lopez Island is the southeasternmost one of the San Juan Islands; Lopez Hill, 488 feet high, is near the S midsection of the island.

Richardson is a village on the N shore of the cove N of Iceberg Point, and close N of Charles Island. Five fuel tanks are prominent from seaward. A wharf directly below the fuel tanks has a face 120 feet long and extends over rocks to a depth of 17 feet. Gasoline, diesel fuel, water, and ice, are available. Outboard engine repairs can be made. Fishing boats operate from here when fishing the Strait of Juan de Fuca. Overhead power cables with clearances of 54 feet are between the mainland and Charles Island. A daybeacon is on a ledge extending from the shore off Richardson. (p. 331, CP)

Jones Bay (Lopez Island)

Jones Bay, on the southwest corner of Lopez Island, is 1 mile northwest of Mackaye Harbor and 2.3 miles southeast of Cattle Pass.

Chart 18429
Entrance: 48°26.74′ N, 122°53.73′ W (NAD 83)

Jones Bay is a shallow circular bay with rocks in its entrance that extend from the west shore. Although this bay can provide protection from northerly winds, it's a rolly anchorage.

The settlement of Richardson in the next cove to the west has a fuel dock only.

Davis Bay (Lopez Island)

Davis Bay is on the southwest corner of Lopez Island.

Chart 18434
Entrance: 48°27.11′ N, 122°55.72′ W (NAD 83)
Position: 48°27.48′ N, 122°55.61′ W (NAD 83)

Davis Bay is a large, open bay exposed to southerly weather with some protection provided by the off-lying islands and rocks. Although it can be a temporary place to wait for favorable tides at Cattle Pass, the bottom is reported to be hard and it is considered a rolly anchorage.

Peter Fromm

Fisherman Bay's narrow entrance

Fisherman Bay (Lopez Island)

Fisherman Bay, on the west side of Lopez Island, is 4 miles north of Cattle Pass and 2 miles south of Flat Point.

Chart 18434
Entrance (0.25 nautical mile west of sector light): 48°31.49′ N, 122°55.53′ W (NAD 83)
Anchor: 48°30.65′ N, 122°55.15′ W (NAD 83)

Fisherman Bay, on the E side of San Juan Channel abreast North Bay, is a shallow lagoon entered by a marked, narrow, and tortuous channel. A rock

Peter Fromm

Davis Bay

awash is on the E side of the channel at the mouth of the bay. Good anchorage with shelter from all winds may be had in 10 to 12 feet, soft bottom, for small craft with local knowledge. The tidal currents have considerable velocity. Lopez is a small village at the entrance. A resort in the bay has a pier and floats with berths for about 45 craft. Electricity, gasoline, water, ice, restaurant, and overnight facilities are available. A marina is adjacent to the resort; water, electricity, marine supplies, and a 15-ton lift is available. (p. 331, CP)

Peter Fromm

Fisherman Bay from the air

Fisherman Bay, a large, shallow bay protected from all seas, is a popular anchorage for vessels that don't mind transiting its rather complex entrance. The numerous facilities on shore make it a popular destination. The bay is a lagoon created by a low man-made spit, so while no seas enter it, the wind can howl in southerly weather. The bay carries less than 2 fathoms over its entire area, so it is easy to get good anchor scope, but you have to be careful to avoid the many private mooring buoys throughout the bay. It is a good place to sail a dinghy and paddle a kayak.

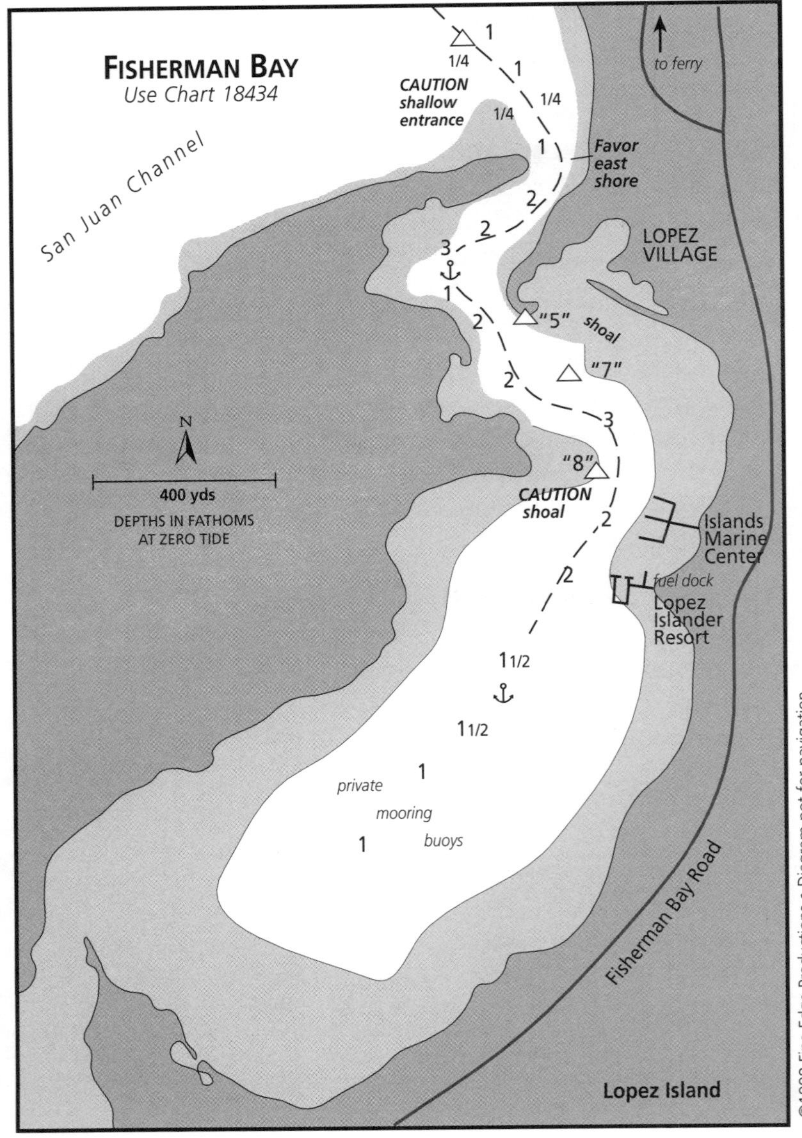

©1998 Fine Edge Productions • Diagram not for navigation

If your boat draws more than a few feet, you should check the tide tables carefully and keep one eye on your echo sounder and one on where you are headed. Spring tides create currents that can easily set an unwary helmsman onto a muddy shoal. Frequent groundings have occurred in the winding channel entrance. Although it is marked by nav-aids, you must pay close attention to Chart 18434, noting that the channel favors the east shore until you have passed green Mark "7." It then follows a mid-channel course to pass red Mark

"8" on your starboard. (Avoid a shoal that extends more than halfway from the western sandspit by favoring the marina complex. See *Entering Tactics* sidebar.)

Upon entering the bay, the first marina to your left is Islands Marine Center which monitors VHF

Peter Fromm

Peter Fromm

Fisherman Bay on the Fourth of July

If your schedule puts you in the San Juan Islands over the July 4th weekend, plan to visit Fisherman Bay.

A wonderful, rural American community parade winds its way all around Fisherman Bay from Legion Hall into Lopez village, and from anywhere along the route you have a great vantage point. After the parade, a salmon bake—one of the most popular events of the year—takes place at the Lopez Community Center. The money raised from the bake goes into a fund for fireworks.

Lopez Island's fireworks display was initiated by Jim Scripps; he loved fireworks so much that he and a friend shot off thousands of dollars' worth of fireworks each year from a rocky islet off the southwest end of Lopez.

After Jim's death, a group of pyro-technicians, known as the "bomb squad," continued setting off fireworks on the Fourth from the spit at the southwest end of Fisherman Bay. Known as the Jim Scripps Memorial Fireworks Show, it is supported by donations from the community.

The Lopez Pyros have become so good at their voluntary skill that they were invited to set off fireworks displays at Grand Coulee Dam. All other sky shows in the islands pale in comparison to the one on Lopez, although in 1997, a lightning and thunderstorm on the morning of July 5 made the previous evening's man-made noises and fireworks seem like kindergarten play.—**PF**

Fisherman Bay: Entering Tactics

Probably the most frequent site for groundings is the entry channel to Fisherman Bay on Lopez Island. I have gone aground there in *Uwila* (which draws 6 feet) seven times! Fortunately, it is all mud and sand and the boat just floats off.

Consult your tide tables before entering or leaving. Rocks on the Lopez shore extend beyond the red Mark "4." Local knowledge says that at zero tide there is just 4 feet of water in the channel. (Note that a minus 2.5-foot tide takes place several times a month!)

I find the following route to have the deepest water: From the outer mark (red and white on a tower) to red Mark "4" at the end of the spit, take a slightly curved course away from the Lopez shore. Pass within 10 feet of red Mark "4." Take a straight line to within 10-15 feet off the dock in front of the houses on the left. Head to mid-channel off green Mark "5" on the tower; it is shallow close to the mark. Stay in midchannel all the way in, past red Mark "8." A large sandbar extends from the wooded point on the right. Do not cut red Mark "8" too closely; it is shallow there at low tide.

Using the above route, I am able to leave Fisherman Bay when the bracket holding the ladder to the outer mark (red and white) is five rungs above the water.

When the current is flooding strongly, quite a back eddy hits the incoming water just inside the red Mark "4." Take your time entering or leaving the bay and give other boats lots of room.—**PF**

Draft horses on Lopez Island

Griffin Bay

San Juan Island, the largest of the group, is about 13 miles long, rugged, and partly wooded. . . . The N end of the island is indented by several small bays that, with the exception of Roche Harbor, are shoal and of no commercial importance.

During the June-October fishing season, many purse seiners operate in this area. At night these vessels anchor close inshore, generally between Cattle Point and Pile Point. (p. 328, CP)

Channel 69 (tel: 360-468-3377). Guest moorage is available, but reservations are advised. The center is open all year and has repairs and marine supplies. Shopping in Lopez village is close at hand.

The second marina is Lopez Islander Resort, which has expanded guest docks, a Chevron fuel dock, and a waterfront restaurant. Reservations are advised (tel: 360-468-2233). The resort monitors Channel 78. Avoid the Kenmore Air Taxi float, since flights arrive at all hours.

Anchor in about 10 feet of water over a sticky mud bottom with good holding.

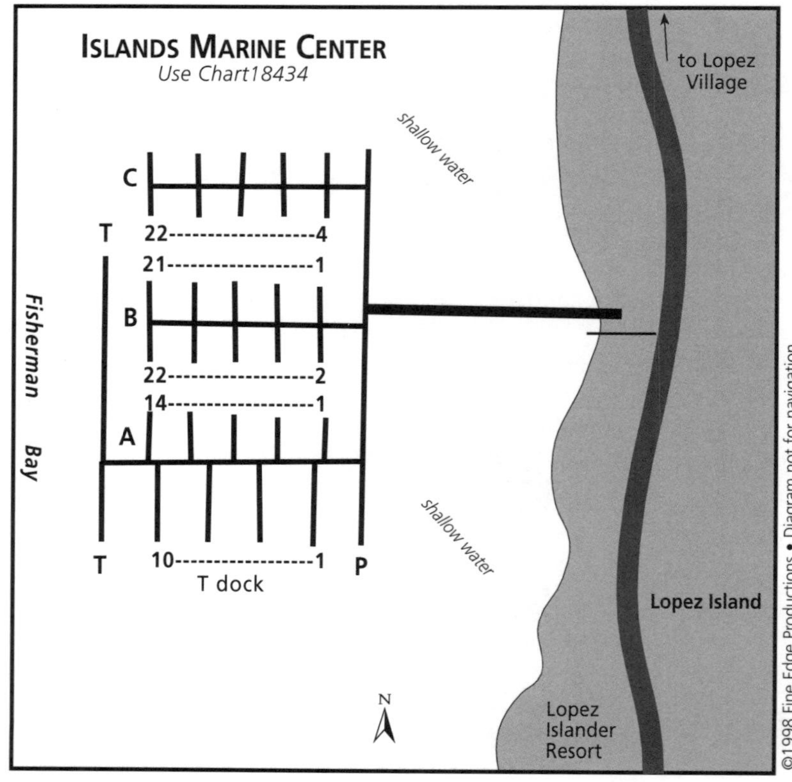

San Juan Island (San Juan Channel/Haro Strait)

San Juan Island is 18 miles west of Anacortes and 15 miles northeast of Victoria.

Charts 18434, 18433

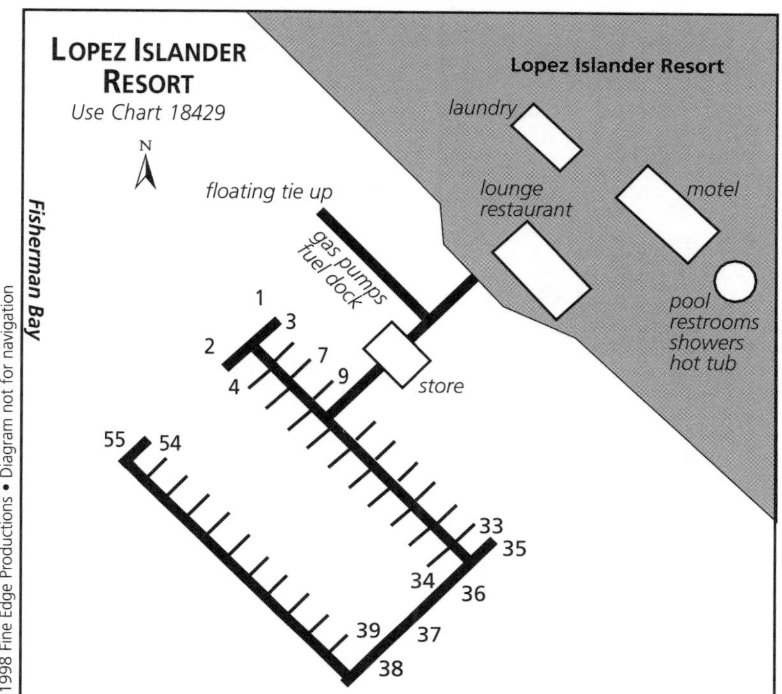

San Juan Island is the most populated of the San Juans. Friday Harbor, on its east shore, is the seat of the county government and the only incorporated community in the San Juans. The town, which is the center of business activity for the islands, has fuel, repair facilities, complete transportation, communications, financial and supply services. Very good shelter in all weather can be found at the Friday Harbor marina or anchored nearby. The northwest corner of the island, which includes Roche Harbor, is a popular destination point for cruising boats. Roche Harbor has summer Customs operation; intricate Mosquito Pass connects to some scenic cruising grounds. [See Chapter 5.]

Gaff-headed sloop in fair winds off San Juan Island

Griffin Bay (San Juan Island)

Griffin Bay, north of Cattle Pass, is the large indentation on the southeast corner of San Juan Island.

Chart 18434
Position: 48°29.60′ N, 122°59.55′ W (NAD 83)

Anchorage can be found in Griffin Bay along shore in the shallow water between Fish Creek at the south and North Bay at the north. The bay is somewhat open to northeast and southeast winds; a number of isolated rocks in the bay and along shore require caution. Good shelter from southerly gales can be found inside the hook of land known as Cape San Juan.

Avoid the following dangers: North Pacific Rock and the shoal 0.22 mile northwest; Half-Tide Rocks and the shoals on its south side; the foul area of old pilings 0.15 mile west of Half-Tide Rocks; the shoals and rocks 0.25 mile northwest of Low Point; the charted rocks and shoals south and east of Dinner Island.

Griffin Bay Park, 0.4 mile south of Low Point, and American Camp, 0.4 mile farther south, are good places for hiking and picnics.

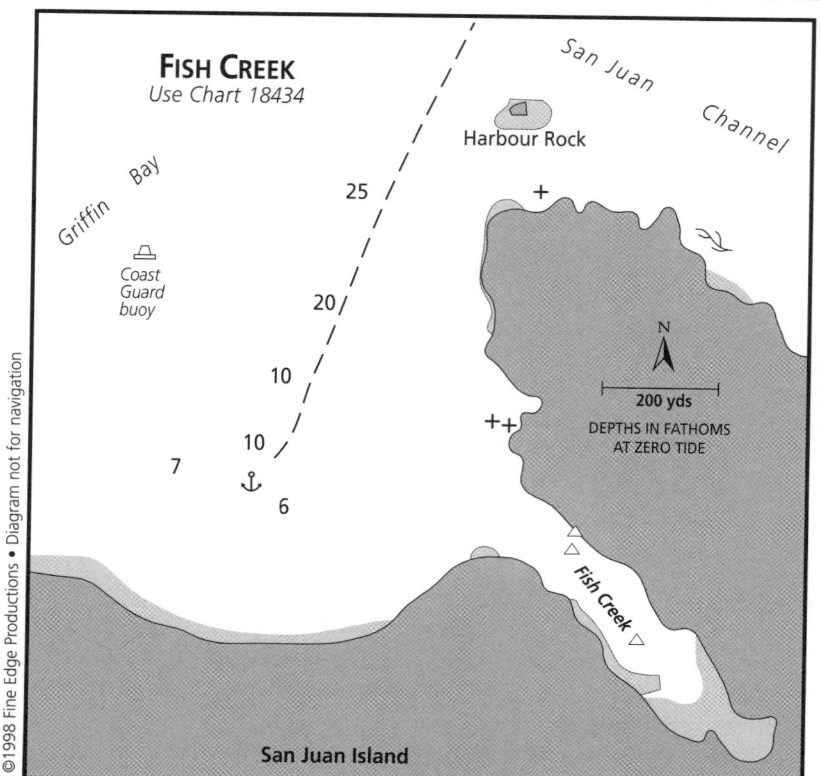

Fish Creek (San Juan Island)

Fish Creek, on the southeast tip of San Juan Island, is 0.9 mile northwest of Cattle Point and 1.2 miles southeast of the American Camp anchorage.

Chart 18434
Entrance: 48°28.25′ N, 122°58.50′ W (NAD 83)
Anchor: 48°27.89′ N, 122°58.61′ W (NAD 83)
Entrance (inner bay): 48°27.85′ N, 122°58.25′ W (NAD 83)

Fish Creek, adjacent to Cape San Juan, is a narrow inlet 0.3 mile long. Numerous homes, private docks, and mooring buoys make it a busy place with little swinging room for even small boats. Anchorage can be found off the entrance to Fish Creek with protection from southeast through southwest winds.

Although local fishing boats pass inside Harbor Rock at the north end of Cape San Juan, the passage can be choked with thick kelp and is not recommended.

Coast Guard Storm Buoy (San Juan Island)

The Coast Guard storm buoy lies 0.3 mile west of the north tip of Cape San Juan.

Chart 18434
Position: 48°28.06′ N, 122°58.72′ W (NAD 83)

Good protection from southeast gales can be found south and southeast of the Coast Guard storm buoy at the end of Griffin Bay. Large vessels can anchor near the buoy, while small craft can anchor 0.17 mile southeast of the buoy.

Anchor in 10 fathoms over mud and sand with good holding. Small craft requiring more scope can anchor closer to shore.

Peter Fromm

Ernest K. Gann's Twilight II *in San Juan Channel*

Peter Fromm

San Juan Island

"American Camp Anchorage" (San Juan Island)

The north end of "American Camp Anchorage" is due west of North Pacific Rock.

Chart 18434
Anchor (0.2 mile west of North Pacific Rock):
48°28.28' N, 123°00.12' W (NAD 83)

American Camp, a national historic site, was used by American soldiers from 1859 until 1872 when the disputed boundary between England and the U.S. was resolved by Kaiser Wilhelm. American Camp has day-use facilities only and is Federal land under the jurisdiction of the National Park Service. The north end of the camp has a picnic ground, toilet facilities and a nice beach. Continuing southeast are three lagoons. You can walk to Cattle Point Lighthouse or along the shore to Fish Creek. You can also follow the trail to 290-foot Mt. Finlayson where you have spectacular views of Mt. Baker and the Olympic Mountains.

Anchor in 2 to 3 fathoms over soft mud with very good holding.

Griffin Bay DNR Park (San Juan Island)

Griffin Bay Park is south of Low Point in Griffin Bay.

Chart 18434
Anchor (0.25 mile west of Half-Tide Rock):
48°28.99' N, 123°00.38' W (NAD 83)

Griffin Bay DNR Park is a 5-acre public park accessible by water only. You can picnic or stretch your legs on its short 300 feet of beach. Above the beach are campsites, pit toilets, and fireplaces. The park is a Cascadia Marine site. Property upland of the park is private; please do not trespass. Three public mooring buoys off the gravel beach are useful for small boats only; they are in shallow water with little swinging room. Avoid the foul area of old pilings 0.15 mile west of Half-Tide Rocks, as well as shoals on the south side of Half-Tide Rocks. Half-Tide Rocks is a National Wildlife Refuge.

Anchor in 2 fathoms over soft mud and sand with very good holding.

The Pig War

Before the boundary between the U.S. and Canada was officially determined, American and British camps were military bases.

The interpretation of where the boundary channel lay between the U.S. mainland and Vancouver Island differed; the Americans felt it should be Haro Strait; the British thought it should be Rosario Strait. Settlers from both countries lived on San Juan Island and each side wanted to possess this archipelago.

The dispute came to a head in 1859 after a pig was shot dead by an American. The pig—a special boar owned by the Hudson Bay Company which had come to the island from England via Cape Horn—had the habit of rooting up the American's potato patch. After repeatedly warning his British neighbors, the American shot and killed the pig. Although he offered to pay for the animal, the fee was $100. More than he could afford!

Tensions and military madness built up until cooler heads prevailed, and for about 13 years, there was peaceful coexistence on the island. In 1872, Kaiser Wilhelm I of Germany determined the present boundary.

Displays at both American and British Camps, the National Historic Park Information Office in Friday Harbor, the San Juan Historical Museum, and the Pig War Museum present information about island life at the time.—**PF**

[*Editor's Note:* See British Camp in Chapter 5.]

Jensen Bay (San Juan Island)

Jensen Bay is located just north of Low Point.

Chart 18434
Position (0.1 mile northwest of Low Point): 48°29.19′ N, 123°00.61′ W (NAD 83)

Temporary anchorage for small boats only can be found northwest of Low Point by avoiding isolated charted rocks; the water in Jensen Bay is too shallow for larger pleasure craft. The foreshore north of Griffin Bay Park is private property all the way to North Bay.

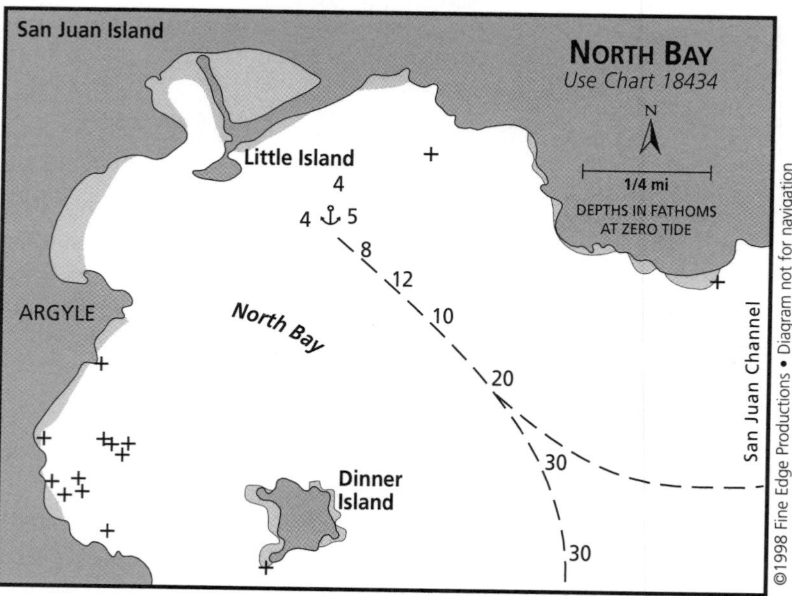

Mulno Cove (San Juan Island)

Mulno Cove is 0.75 mile northwest of Low Point.

Chart 18434
Position: 48°29.66′ N, 123°01.15′ W (NAD 83)

Anchorage for a few small boats can be found in the center of the Mulno Cove, sheltered from prevailing westerlies.

Peter Fromm

Passing Turn Rock nav-aid

Merrifield Cove (San Juan Island)

Merrifield Cove is located 0.45 mile north of Mulno Cove.

Chart 18434
Position: 48°30.10′ N, 123°01.18′ W (NAD 83)

Attractive Merrifield Cove offers some protection from westerlies. Avoid the many rocks in the small cove, especially in the north end.

North Bay (San Juan Island)

North Bay, 1 mile east of Pear Point, is a half-mile north of Dinner Island.

Chart 18434
Entrance: 48°30.30′ N, 122°59.70′ W (NAD 83)
Anchor: 48°31.03′ N, 123°00.39′ W (NAD 83)

> *North Bay is entered between Pear Point and Dinner Island. Gravel is barged from pits on the NW shore of the bay to Vancouver Island. . . . The bay affords fair anchorage in 7 to 10 fathoms, about 800 yards N of Dinner Island. Two dangers are in the approaches to the bay; a rocky shoal covered 3/4 fathom 0.7 mile E of Dinner Island, and another rock shoal covered 3/4 fathom 0.4 mile SE of Dinner Island. The passage W of Dinner Island should not be attempted.* (p. 331, CP)

Good shelter can be found in North Bay in prevailing northwest winds. However, it is open to the southeast and not recommended in unsettled weather due to the fetch. Dinner Island, in the south corner of North Bay, is a National Wildlife Refuge. The area surrounding Dinner Island is foul with an irregular bottom and a number of isolated rocks.

At the north end of North Bay, there is a large loading dock for gravel barges with a submerged off-lying rock in the vicinity. The area south of the dock toward Little Island is Jackson Beach, a public recreation area with easy access for dinghies on its sandy beach. The tidepool west of Little Island is a biological reserve.

Anchor 0.15 mile southeast of Little Island in 4 fathoms over a mixed bottom.

Turn Rock

Turn Rock is the point where San Juan Channel meets Upright Channel.

Chart 18434
Position: 48°32.10′ N, 122°57.87′ W (NAD 83)

> *Turn Rock, about 0.2 mile E of Turn Island, is a ledge bare at half tide; it should be given a berth of at least 100 yards. A light is on the rock.* (p. 331, CP)

Dangerous Turn Rock is marked by a light and large kelp beds. Significant tide rips found in the immediate vicinity should be given a wide berth.

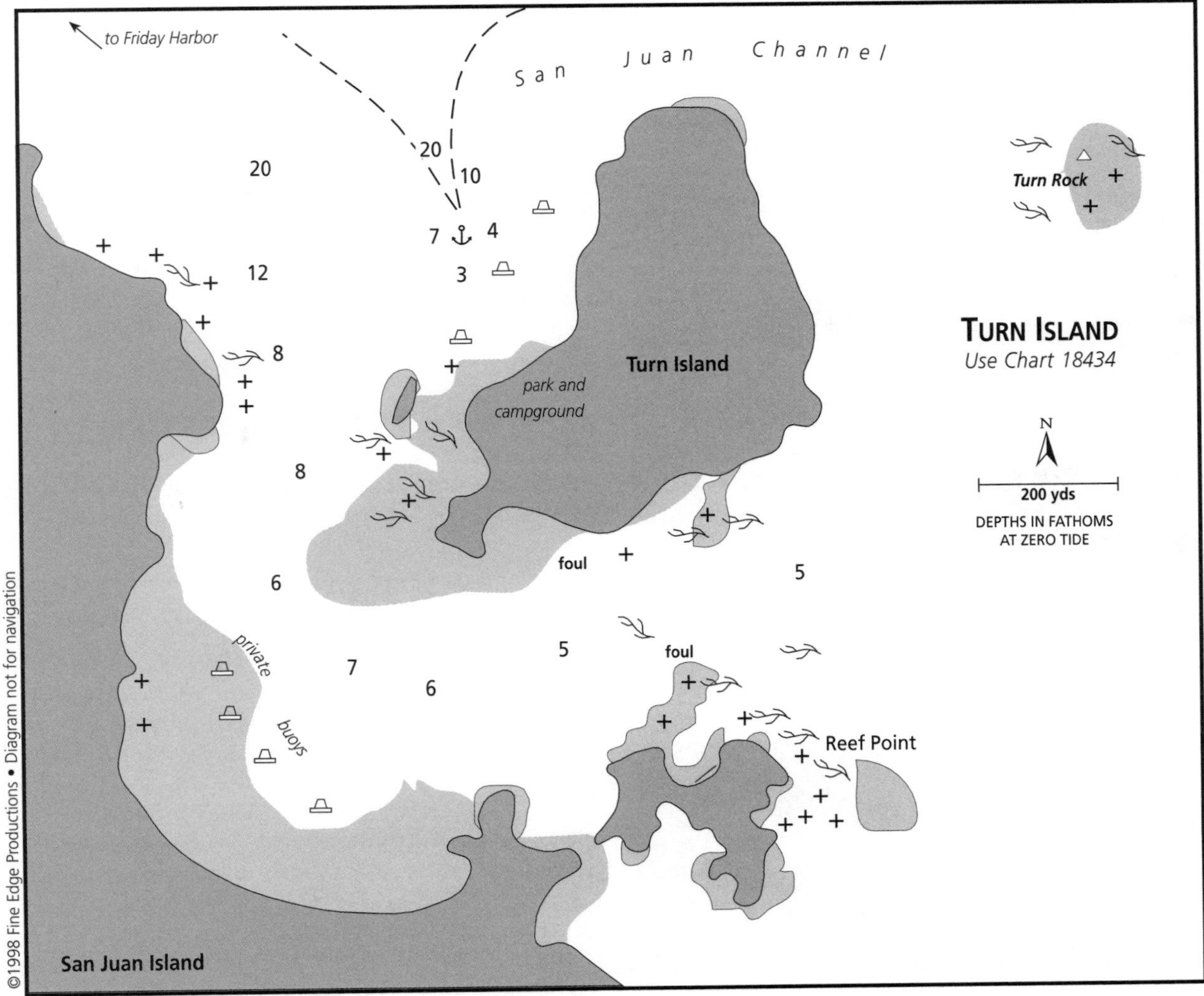

Turn Island (San Juan Channel)

Turn Island is 0.25 mile west of Turn Rock.

Chart 18434
Mooring buoys: 48°32.03′ N, 122°58.44′ W (NAD 83)

> *At Turn Island, off the E side of San Juan Island, San Juan Channel turns NW for about 7.5 miles and connects at its N end with Spieden Channel and President Channel.* (p. 331, CP)

Peter Fromm

Turn Island State Marine Park

Turn Island, a 35-acre State Marine Park, has madrona trees, grassy areas, excellent hiking trails, and a number of campsites. There are public mooring buoys on its northwest side. *Note:* The buoys are less than 2 miles from the Friday Harbor ferry terminal, so you can easily dinghy or kayak over to the town.

Peter Fromm

Baidarka *anchored at Turn Island*

Peter Fromm

Aerial view of Friday Harbor

Anchorage is not recommended on the west or south side of Turn Island due to an irregular bottom with poor holding and strong currents.

Friday Harbor (San Juan Island)

Friday Harbor, on the east side of San Juan Island, is 16 miles west of Anacortes and 16 miles northeast of Victoria.

Chart 18434
North entrance: 48°32.65′ N, 123°00.25′ W (NAD 83)
South entrance: 48°32.19′ N, 122°59.75′ W (NAD 83)
Marina entrance: 48°32.38′ N, 123°00.86′ W (NAD 83)

Emily's Guides

Detailed booklets titled *Emily's Guides* give a lot of information about visiting the San Juans. The three separate guides are published annually for Friday Harbor and San Juan Island; Orcas Island; and Lopez, Shaw and the State Park Islands.

Primarily for visitors, the guides list places to eat, lodging, travel information, art galleries and studios, bookstores, island adventures, farms and gardens to visit, as well as other useful information. The guides are valuable for long-term island residents too!

Emily's Guides can be found in many island stores or ordered by calling 800-448-7782. —**PF**

Friday Harbor, 1.4 miles W of Turn Island, is a small cove about 1 mile long and nearly as wide. Brown Island, locally known as Friday Island because of the housing development here, occupies the middle of the harbor, with shoals nearly 200 yards wide off both its E and S shores. A shoal, covered $3^1/_4$ fathoms and marked by a buoy, extends nearly into midchannel from the W shore of the island. Shoals off the SE end of the island are marked by a daybeacon. The harbor may be entered either E or W of Brown Island. Anchorage may be had off the wharves in 6 to 7 fathoms, and city floats provide berthing space for pleasure craft.

Friday Harbor, the town on the W shore of the cove, is the county seat and the population center of San Juan Island, which has some farming and cattle and sheep raising. It is headquarters for the gill net fishing fleet operating through the W part of the islands.

Friday Harbor is a customs port of entry. The customs office is about 75 yards W of the port's office, at the yacht club building. The customs officer also performs immigration and agricultural quarantine inspections.

The Interisland Medical Center at Friday Harbor is the only complete medical facility in the San Juan Islands. In addition, Orcas and Lopez

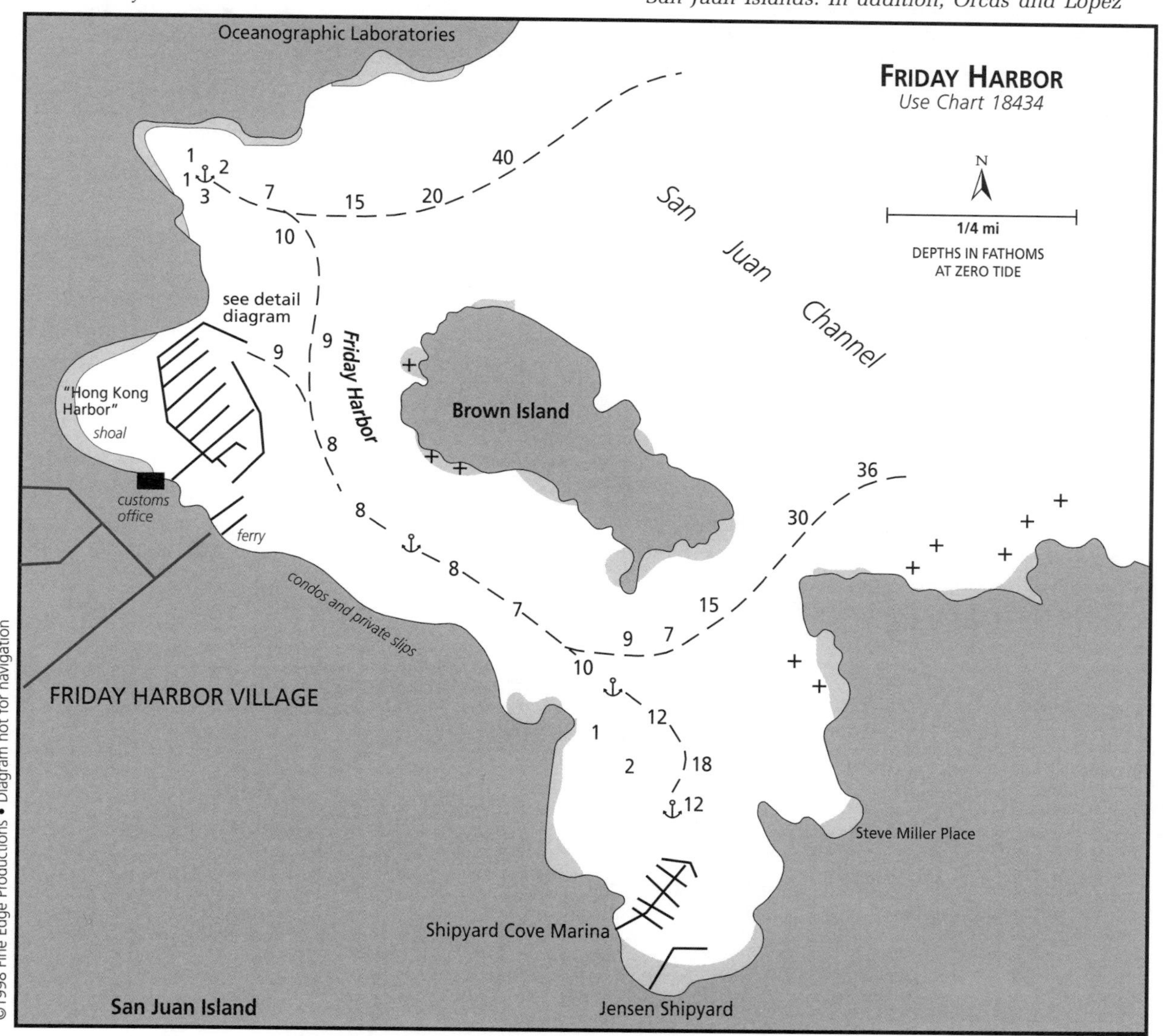

Bounty, *Friday Harbor*

Fishing for crab, Friday Harbor docks

Islands have small clinics with resident physicians and paramedics. Air ambulance service to Seattle, Anacortes, or Bellingham is available on all the larger islands.

Friday Harbor has three wharves. Two are oil wharves with 11 feet reported at their face; they receive petroleum products for the island. Diesel fuel and gasoline are available for small craft at these wharves. The SE oil pier has floats with electricity for about 50 small craft in reported depths of 4 to 9 feet on the S side of the pier. Water and ice are available. Hull repairs can be made. The ferry slip is just SE of these wharves. SE of the ferry slip are condominiums with private docks. The Port of Friday Harbor small-craft harbor, protected on the S and E sides by a long floating breakwater marked at the N end by a light, is just NW of the oil wharves. Berths with electricity for over 460 craft and water are available. At least 150 of this total capacity are used for transient berthing. Note: Vessels should not anchor within 100 yards of the floating breakwater because of the danger of fouling with the breakwater's anchor cables. A seaplane float is near the customs float at the port's small-craft harbor. Water, ice, and some marine supplies are available at Friday Harbor.

A shipyard is at the S end of Friday Harbor. A marine railway that can handle boats to 65 feet long and a 25-ton lift are available. Complete hull and engine repairs can be made.

Freight and passengers reach Friday Harbor by airplane or by State ferry. The town has an airport with surfaced and lighted runways; twin-engine aircraft can be accommodated. Mail is transported by air. (pp. 331, 333, CP)

Friday Harbor, the largest and only incorporated town in the San Juan Islands, is the islands' commercial and government center. It is a Customs port of entry, a fueling stop for vessels northbound into British Columbia, and a focal point for outfitting, repairs and sightseeing. The harbor,

Winter storm, Friday Harbor

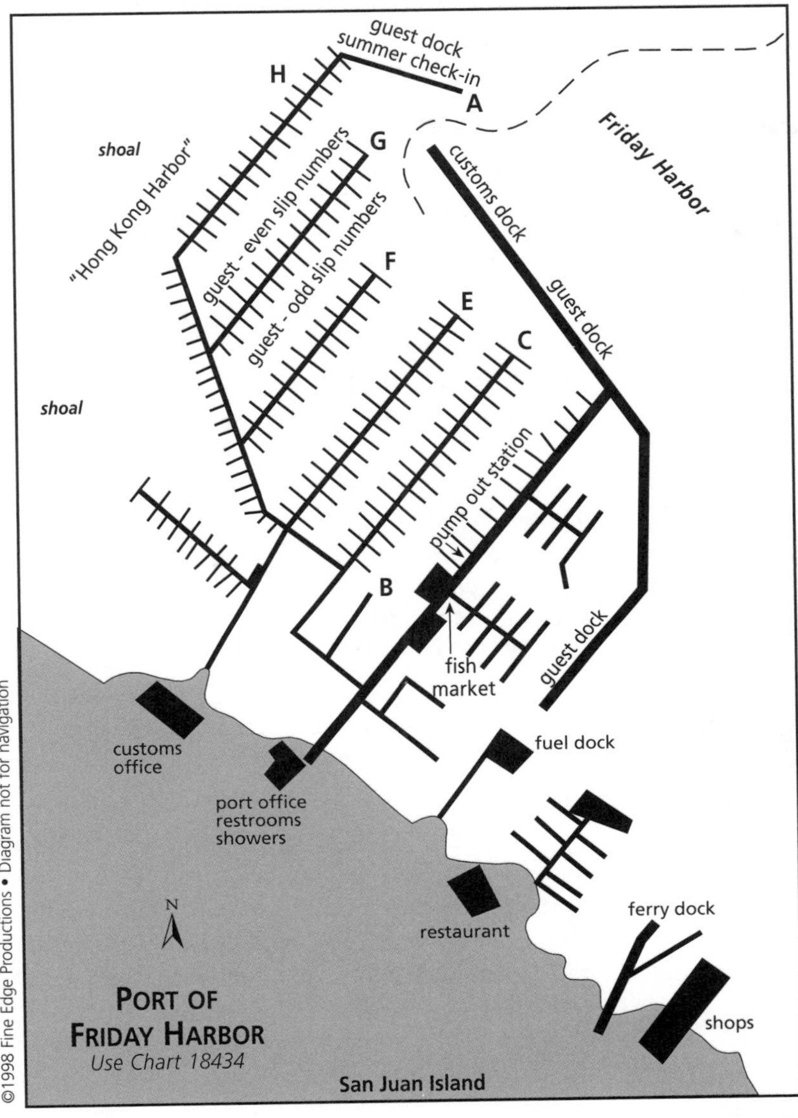

which is well-sheltered on the east by Brown Island, is said to be the busiest transient marina on the West Coast. The south end of Friday Harbor has a marina and a shipyard. Albert Jensen & Son, boat-building and repair since 1910, have a 25-ton travel lift and the only marine railway in the county up to 65 feet (tel: 360-378-4343).

You can enter the harbor by either the north or south end of Brown Island. The larger north entrance is used by commercial traffic. The south entrance which is narrow has a substantial shoal marked by a beacon off the south end of Brown Island. A marked 3-fathom shoal and a half-fathom shoal lie close to the northwest side of Brown Island. The area immediately south of the marina is busy with ferries and air taxi traffic, so be careful when transiting this area.

An anchorage area extends from the south end of Friday Harbor to southeast of the ferry terminal; avoid the cable and pipeline area extending from the southwest side of Brown Island. Transient boats can also find anchorage in the nook between Friday Harbor Marina and the University of Washington Oceanographic Laboratories.

The public marina has guest moorages, harbormaster's office (monitors Channel 66A; tel: 360-378-2688), and restrooms with showers. Half a block west, the yacht club building houses U.S. Customs. You can walk the floats and see boats from ports all over the country and even from abroad. Hundreds of bioluminescent jellyfish float in the waters, and low tide reveals sea anemones, feather duster worms, opalescent nudibranches, and spidery decorator

Peter Fromm

Rafting up in Friday Harbor

Peter Fromm

Jensen & Sons Shipyard, Friday Harbor

crabs on the float pilings.

The town of Friday Harbor mixes historic buildings, some renovated, some not, with new shops and restaurants. The site of the San Juan Island Historical Museum is an historic farmhouse, furnished with antiques, containing memorabilia from the pioneer era and the Pig War. The Whale Museum, the only one in the country devoted exclusively to the study of whales, offers displays, workshops and classes, and conducts cruises. A "Whale Hotline" catalogs sightings of the local orca pods, and there is an Orca Adoption program. You can find art galleries, book, gift and souvenir shops, along with inns, grocery stores, marine suppliers, and other services. King's Market & Deli on Spring Street has as sophisticated a choice of food supplies as you'd find in Seattle. Community theater, movies, tennis and golf, the annual 4th of July jazz festival and county fair round out the recreation and entertainment opportunities. And if you'd like to see the island, there are several businesses where you can rent a bicycle or moped.

San Juan Island from Point Caution to Limestone Point

Chart 18434

The shore of San Juan Island north of Point Caution is precipitous and steep-to. There are several rocks and reefs close to the shore along the way to Limestone Point.

Rocky Bay (San Juan Island)

Rocky Bay is located 0.3 mile southwest of O'Neal Island.

Chart 18434
Entrance: 48°36.00' N, 123°05.40' W (NAD 83)
Anchor: 48°35.97' N, 123°05.95' W (NAD 83)

> *Rocky Bay is an open bight in the E side of San Juan Island. O'Neal Island, surrounded by a shoal, is almost in the middle of the bay.* (p. 333, CP)

Small Rocky Bay is sometimes used as a temporary fair-weather anchorage. Avoid both the submerged rock that extends 0.12 mile east of the north shore and numerous rocks close along shore. Larger boats can sometimes find temporary anchorage due west of O'Neal Island in 15 fathoms over a mud and shell bottom.

Anchor in about 6 fathoms.

Don Douglass

A home with dock and ketch, Friday Harbor

The rebuilding of Timberjack, *a dugout canoe*

Hicks Bay (Shaw Island)

Hicks Bay, immediately southeast of Parks Bay, is 0.9 mile southeast of Point George.

Chart 18434
Position: 48°33.19′ N, 122°58.18′ W (NAD 83)

Hicks Bay offers temporary anchorage in settled weather. Although protected from northwest winds, it is exposed to southwesterlies. Avoid the submerged rocks at the south end of the east

Pintail *making a delivery at Shaw Island*

Shaw Island West Coast

Chart 18434

Shaw Island is a private island. Please respect all posted notices.

Hoffman Cove (Shaw Island)

Hoffman Cove, on the south end of Shaw Island, is 0.95 mile due north of Turn Rock.

Chart 18434
Position: 48°33.02′ N,
122°57.72′ W (NAD 83)

Hoffman Cove has an attractive beach and can offer some protection for small boats in settled weather or northerly winds; however, it is exposed to the south and the full fury of winds blowing up San Juan Channel.

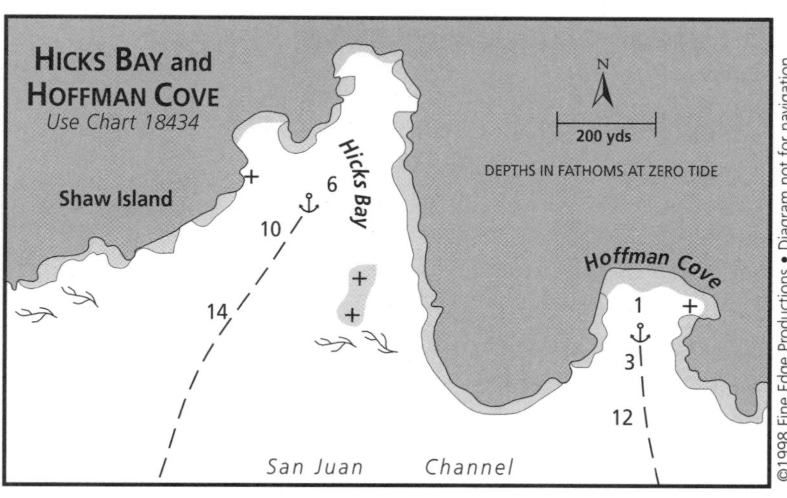

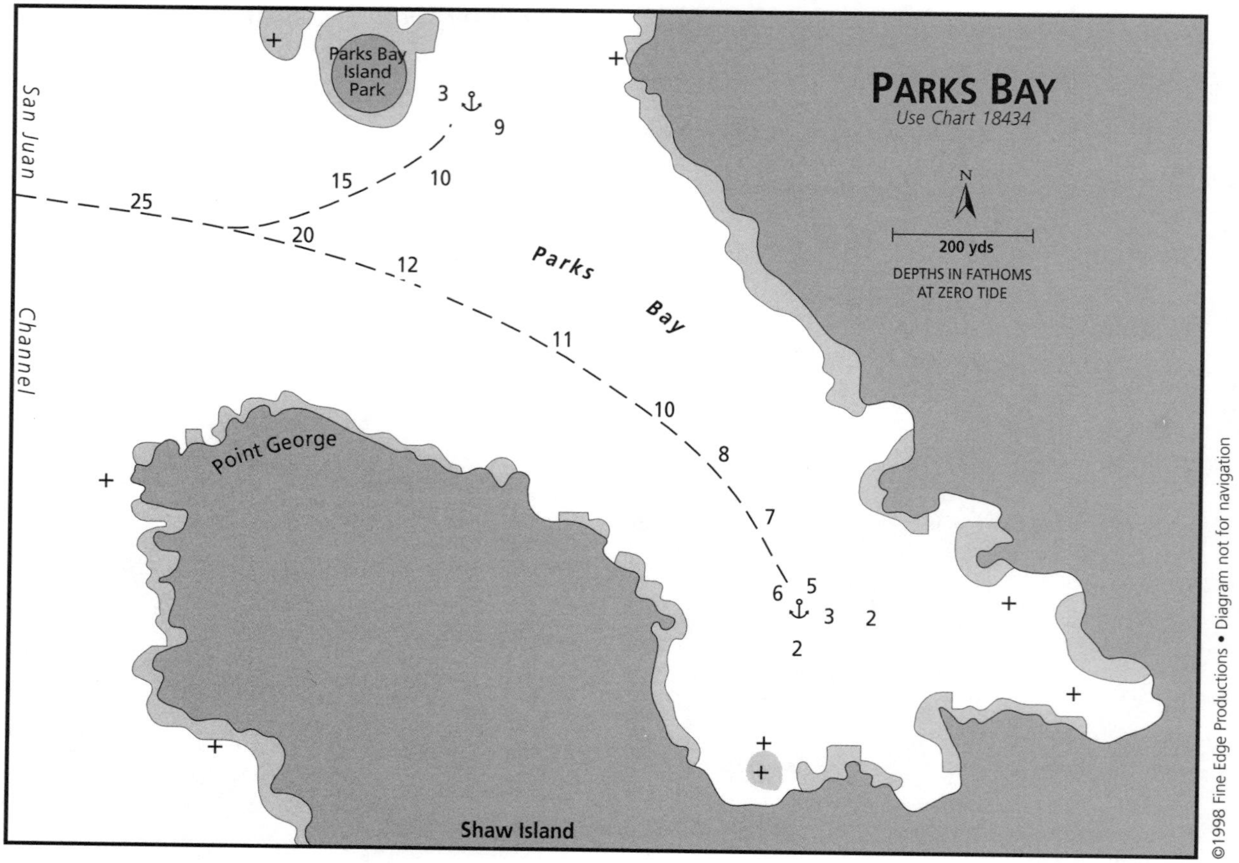

PARKS BAY
Use Chart 18434
200 yds
DEPTHS IN FATHOMS AT ZERO TIDE
Parks Bay Island Park
San Juan Channel
Parks Bay
Point George
Shaw Island

shore. Small boats can tuck deep into the bay and find anchorage in about 7 fathoms. Tide rips are found off the Point George peninsula.

Parks Bay (Shaw Island)

Parks Bay is 1.8 miles northeast of Friday Harbor.

Chart 18434
Entrance: 48°33.88′ N, 122°59.29′ W (NAD 83)
Anchor: 48°33.58′ N, 122°58.63′ W (NAD 83)

> *Point George, the W point at the entrance to Parks Bay, is across the channel from Friday Harbor. Good anchorage for small craft in 6 to 8 fathoms, soft bottom, can be had in this bay. The head of the bay, however, is foul.* (p. 333, CP)

Parks Bay is a favorite anchorage on the west side of Shaw Island. The bay, well sheltered by the Point George peninsula, provides good protection in southeast storms. While the bay is open to the northwest, little westerly winds penetrate to its head. The shore surrounding Parks Bay and Point George is a biological reserve; it is heavily wooded with numerous signs asking visitors not to trespass or build fires. The pilings shown on the chart are no longer visible, but the shallow head of the bay may be foul, so it is best to anchor in 5 fathoms or more.

Peter Fromm

Parks Bay

Anchor in 6 fathoms, mud and shell with sand; very good holding.

Neck Point and Wasp Islands

Neck Point is located on the northwest shore of Shaw Island, at the west end of Wasp Passage.

Chart 18434

> *Wasp Islands are in the W approach to West Sound between Neck Point, the NW tip of Shaw Island, and Steep Point, the SW extremity of Orcas Island. Several narrow channels lead between the islands; the channels in general use are the North and Pole Passes, close under the Orcas Island shore. The tidal currents have considerable velocity in the channels, which should be attempted only by vessels with local knowledge.* (p. 333, CP)

Neck Point is a scenic but rock-infested area. However, it is a great place to explore the many coves, islets and reefs by dinghy. Many of the rocks and islets are National Wildlife Refuges.

Peter Fromm

Wasp Islands

Some local boats use private floats tucked in small nooks; however, local knowledge is required and we do not recommend anchoring in the area.

Caution is advised whenever you navigate in the Wasp Islands due to the numerous submerged rocks and reefs and strong currents which have caused many unfortunate groundings.

Parks Bay Raft-up

by Greg Avery

I work as a marine mechanic in Friday Harbor. My shop is at Shipyard Cove Marina where I keep my 30-foot powerboat. I use the boat a lot—as a diving platform, for fishing, crabbing, and boating with my family.

Some of our most enjoyable outings are quick overnights to Parks Bay on Shaw Island for a raft-up with other boaters from the marina. Maybe four or five times a year, with little or no notice, several of us will decide that it's been too long since we went out. Or someone will say the beautiful weather is about to change, so before northwest rains start again, off we go.

Parks Bay is only three miles from Friday Harbor, but it feels like many of the bays along the Inside Passage: no houses on the shore, cedar trees hanging over the water at high tide—it's beautiful. The view north into San Juan Channel is often spectacular.

Usually we get there by mid-afternoon and raft-up. The first boat to arrive sets anchor to act as "mother ship" for the other boats. We spend the time before sunset sitting on stern decks, eating snacks, drinking wine, heating up our barbeques, and making each other laugh. Our traditional bedtime drink is hot chocolate with rum, making sure to stir the melted chocolate bars in the bottom of the cups.

Early in the morning we down a danish and coffee, then return to the marina and our work day, *almost* on time. It's just a quick overnight from the dock, but one of those bonuses of living here in the San Juans that we don't want to take for granted . . . these raft-ups in Parks Bay with our friends.

Peter Fromm

Parks Bay Raft-up

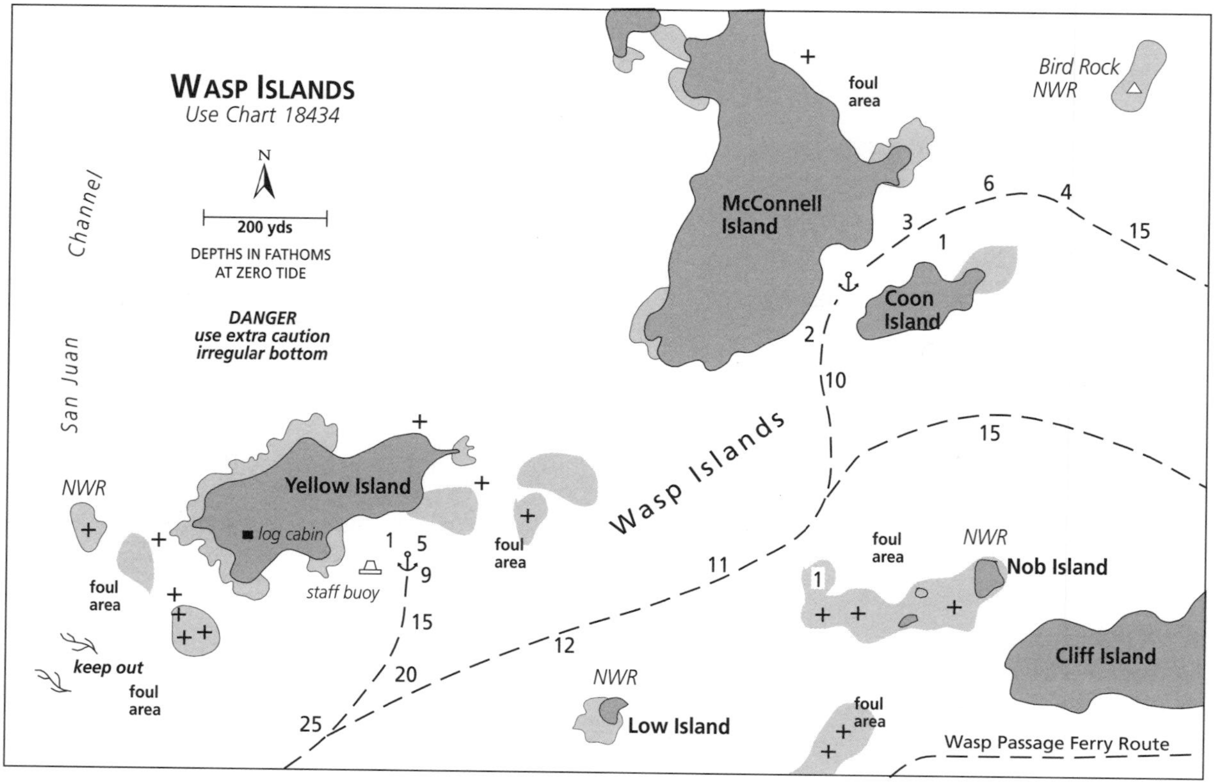

WASP ISLANDS
Use Chart 18434

N
200 yds
DEPTHS IN FATHOMS AT ZERO TIDE

DANGER
use extra caution irregular bottom

San Juan Channel
McConnell Island
Coon Island
Yellow Island
log cabin
staff buoy
Wasp Islands
Nob Island
Cliff Island
Low Island
Bird Rock NWR
NWR
foul area
keep out
Wasp Passage Ferry Route

Wasp Passage

Wasp Passage lies between Shaw and Crane islands.

Chart 18434
East entrance: 48°35.75' N, 122°58.20' W (NAD 83)
West entrance: 48°35.26' N, 123°01.88' W (NAD 83)

> *Wasp Passage leads from San Juan Channel to West Sound and separates Crane Island from the N shore of Shaw Island. A light is on the rock 300 yards E of Bell Island at the E end of the pass, and on Cliff Island and Shirt Tail Reef, at the W end of the pass.* (p. 333, CP)

Wasp Passage is used by ferryboats and high-speed vessels. Cruising boats should pay close attention to Chart 18434 to avoid the dangerous rocks between Crane and Bell islands and the shoals along both shores; the fairway favors the Shaw Island side. During spring tides be particularly alert to strong tides and tide rips. When the inter-island ferry uses Wasp Passage, it generally passes on the south side of Cliff and Bell islands.

Crane Island

Crane Island is southwest of Pole Pass.

Chart 18434
Position (dangerous reef): 48°35.69' N, 122°59.19' W (NAD 83)

> *Crane Island is off the entrance to Deer Harbor and about 1 mile SE of Steep Point. The N shore of the island is foul with bare and covered rocks within 250 yards of it. A shoal covered ½ fathom*

Don Douglass

Anchored temporarily at Yellow Island

is 350 yards N of the center of the N side of the island, and a rock that uncovers 5 feet is 200 yards off the E point, with foul ground between it and the shore. (p. 333, CP)

Crane Island is a private island with isolated rocks and reefs along its shore which invite dinghy exploring. Strong currents and tide rips are found off all sides of the island, especially during spring tides. The dangerous rock off the east point as noted in the *Coast Pilot* quotation above has caused a number of groundings.

Yellow Island, South Bight (Wasp Islands)

Yellow Island is located on the extreme west end of Wasp Passage.

Chart 18434
Anchor: 48°35.46′ N, 123°01.79′ W (NAD 83)

Yellow Island, the westernmost of the Wasp Islands, is about 0.8 mile WNW of Neck Point and about 3.5 miles NNW of Friday Harbor. The island is small, grassy, and nearly bare of trees. A shoal extends 300 yards W of the island and terminates in a rock that uncovers 3 feet and is marked by kelp. This island should be given a berth of not less than 0.5 mile. (p. 333, CP)

Yellow Island is a small, beautiful island surrounded by a number of dangerous reefs, particularly on its west and south sides. These reefs, usually marked by kelp, have been the site of a number of unfortunate groundings. Like all of the Wasp Islands, the irregular bottom provides poor anchorage.

Precarious, temporary anchorage can be found in a small bight on the south side of Yellow Island. The water along shore is shallow and the bottom drops off sharply. The conservancy float is reserved for personnel only.

Anchor in about 5 fathoms over a mud and shell bottom with poor holding.

Yellow Island

Yellow Island is entirely owned by the Nature Conservancy. Visitors are welcome between the hours of 10 a.m. and 4 p.m. Groups of more than six are requested to call ahead to make a reservation. Do not take any food ashore. Land your dinghy at the south-facing beach by the caretaker's cabin and stay on the trails. Yellow Island is renowned for its amazing display of wildflowers; May is the best month for viewing them.—**PF**

Don Douglass

Deer Harbor

"Island Passage Nook" (Wasp Islands)

Island Passage Nook is located between McConnell and Coon islands, 0.275 mile southwest of Bird Rock.

Chart 18434
Anchor: 48°35.71′ N, 123°01.24′ W (NAD 83)

Bird Rock, which uncovers, is between McConnell and Crane Islands, and is marked by a light. (p. 333, CP)

Island Passage Nook is the name we give to the tiny passage where temporary shelter for small boats can be found in 2 fathoms. Swinging room is limited.

North Pass (Orcas Island)

North Pass, north of Reef Island, is the main channel into Deer Harbor from San Juan Channel.

Chart 18434
West entrance: 48°36.02′ N, 123°02.59′ W (NAD 83)
East entrance (0.24 mile southeast of Fawn Island): 48°36.61′ N, 123°00.16′ W (NAD 83)

North Pass, between Steep Point on Orcas Island and the Wasp Islands, leads E from San Juan

Channel to Deer Harbor and into Pole Pass. The pass is about 0.2 mile wide between Steep Point and Reef Island, and is free of outlying dangers, except for a rock covered by $1^3/_4$ fathoms 0.3 mile E of the N end of Reef Island. (p. 333, CP)

Deer Harbor (Orcas Island)

Deer Harbor is the westernmost inlet on the south side of Orcas Island.

Chart 18434
Entrance 0.15 mile east of Fawn Island):
48°36.80′ N, 123°00.15′ W (NAD 83)
Anchor: 48°37.17′ N, 123°00.36′ W (NAD 83)

Deer Harbor, E of Steep Point, has good anchorage in 6 to 7 fathoms about 0.2 mile from the head. Fawn Island is near the entrance of the harbor and about 200 yards from the W shore; vessels may pass on either side. The E shore of Deer harbor should be given a berth of at least 300 yards because of a shoal which in some places extends more than 200 yards off.

Deer Harbor, on the E side of the harbor, is a village with stores, a marina, and an inn. Pleasure boats call here frequently in the summer. Berths, electricity, gasoline, diesel fuel, water, and some marine supplies are available.

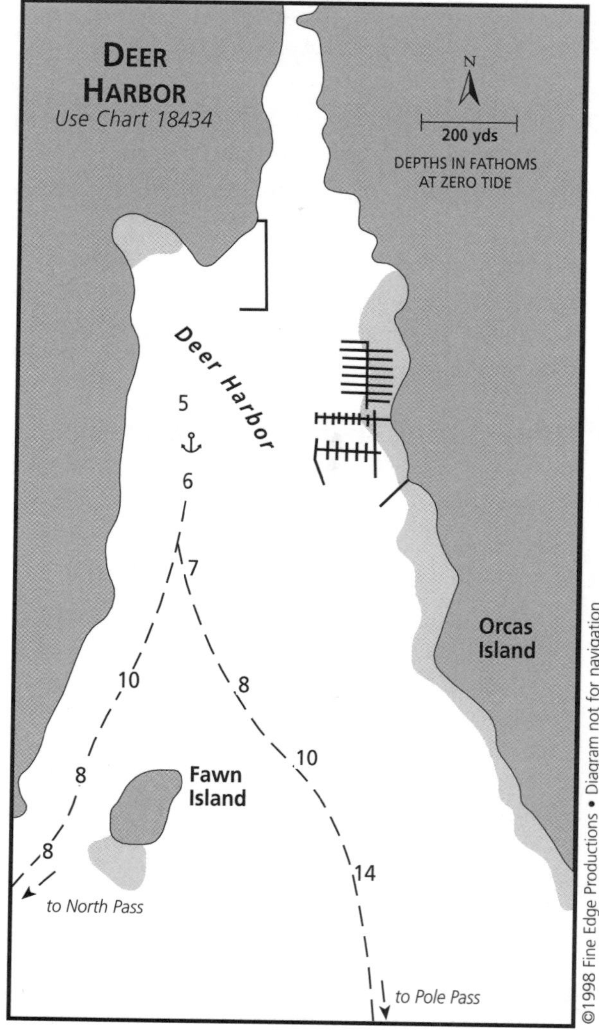

Creative boating in Deer Harbor

Local vessels bound from Friday Harbor to Deer Harbor use a clear deep channel about 70 yards wide through the rocks and shoals lying between Cliff Island and Low Island. (p. 333, CP)

Deer Harbor, a favorite yacht center with excellent marina facilities, is well sheltered in all weather. Adequate space for anchoring can be found 0.14 mile west of Deer Harbor Marina. For a quieter anchorage go behind Fawn Island, avoiding the cable area, and anchor in about 10 fathoms.

Deer Harbor Marina has recently remodeled half of its facility. Plans to remodel the other half, projected for spring 1998, were not definite at press time. Call 360-376-3037 for information.

Anchor in 6 fathoms over mud bottom with good holding.

Peter Fromm

North Bay, Jones Island

Spring Passage

Spring Passage is located on the far west side of Orcas Island.

Chart 18434
South entrance (half-way between Jones Island and Steep Point): 48°36.58′ N, 123°01.90′ W (NAD 83)
North entrance (0.37 mile north of daybeacon): 48°37.57′ N, 123°02.57′ W (NAD 83)

> *Spring Passage separates Jones Island from the SW part of Orcas Island. A daybeacon with the words "Danger-Rocks" is on the NW side of the passage near Jones Island. In general, the passage is free of danger.* (p. 333, CP)

Spring Passage is used by boats headed north from Deer Harbor. Avoid the submerged rock marked by a beacon at the north end of Jones Island.

Jones Island

Jones Island is on the west side of Spring Passage.

Chart 18434
Entrance (north cove): 48°37.28′ N, 123°02.75′ W (NAD 83)
Anchor (south cove): 48°36.66′ N, 123°02.52′ W (NAD 83)
Anchor (north cove): 48°37.11′ N, 123°02.77′ W (NAD 83)

Running Aground

The San Juan Islands are very well charted; detailed NOAA charts are available for the entire archipelago, and navigational markers are found throughout the islands. The many points, headlands, channels and bays can cause people to become disoriented—especially if they lose track of where they started and where they have been. It's a good thing to keep a checklist of the landmarks passed.

It is also a good idea to pay attention to those unmarked rocks and reefs which can be located on the chart and easily avoided with simple, prudent piloting. Every year, however, many boats are damaged by smashing into rocks and reefs.

Larry Hamilton, owner-operator of Vessel Assist San Juan told me, "It is totally random—all the rocks get hit regularly." The area around Yellow Island and Shirt Tail Reef in San Juan Channel top his list. Other commonly hit rocks are: Leo Reef (north of Spencer Spit); around Blind Island (near Shaw); the south end of Henry; the north end of Waldron; around Sucia and Clark; and the west side of Prevost Harbor entrance on Stuart Island.

Larry shared two stories with me. One involved an 80-foot powerboat that piled up at night on Turn Rock in San Juan Channel—the skipper thought the green light was a midchannel marker. Another powerboat with its GPS connected to the autopilot was heading north in the fog in Spring Passage. In trying to avoid a rock on the east side of Jones Island, they ran the boat into Orcas Island! The water is so deep there that they damaged the topsides against the rocky cliffs! Larry contends there are two kinds of boaters—those that *have run* aground and those that are *going to run* aground.

Remember that the tide will most likely float you off again. A large charter sailboat which ran gently onto the Yellow Island reef suffered serious damage when a good Samaritan towed the boat off; the tide would have floated the boat safely had its skipper been patient.—**PF**

Peter Fromm

President Channel, Freeman Island

Jones Island, 2 miles N of Wasp Passage, is on the E side of the N entrance to San Juan Channel; the island is wooded. Small pleasure craft anchor in the bights in the N and S shores. A State marine park in the bight in the N shore has mooring facilities; limited water is available. (p. 333, CP)

Jones Island, a 180-acre island, is a popular State Marine Park with a float, campsites, picnic tables, fireplaces and nice beaches. There are mooring buoys in both the north and south coves. Jones Island is also a designated Cascadia Marine Trail site for kayakers and canoeists.

The south cove, which is less developed than the north cove, is exposed to southerly weather, offering marginal anchorage.

The north cove is well sheltered from southern storms and anchorage can be taken in the center of the cove. Current sometimes enters the cove and the bottom is rocky with fair holding. The north cove is particularly attractive to families because of its easy shore access. A trail leads to the south cove and Spring Passage. The park service recommends not feeding the resident black-tailed deer or any of the animals you see. (Raccoons can be a particular pest.)

The north cove—generally crowded in the summertime—has limited swinging room, so it's a good idea to use a shore tie when you anchor here. There is a pier with a float and seven mooring buoys east of the float.

Anchor (south cove) in about 6 fathoms over mud, shell, sand and grass with fair holding.

Anchor (north cove) in 7 fathoms over mud and gravel with fair holding.

President Channel

Chart 18432
West entrance (1.7 miles south of Point Disney): 48°38.84′ N, 123°02.53′ W (NAD 83)

President Channel, between Waldron and Orcas Islands, is about 5 miles long. Depths are generally great, and the passage is free of dangers. The tidal currents have a velocity of 2 to 5 knots, and heavy swirls and tide rips, especially with an adverse wind, are off the N point of Waldron Island and between Waldron and Patos Islands. The rips are generally heaviest with the ebb current. Rips and swirls are also heavy off Limestone Point and the E end of Spieden Island. (p. 334, CP)

Lovers Cove (Orcas Island)

Lovers Cove, 0.38 mile north of Orcas Knob (the 1,000-foot knob on the west shore of Orcas Island), is 1.7 miles southwest of West Beach.

Chart 18432
Anchor: 48°40.05′ N, 122°59.44′ W (NAD 83)

Don Douglass

Moored for the afternoon

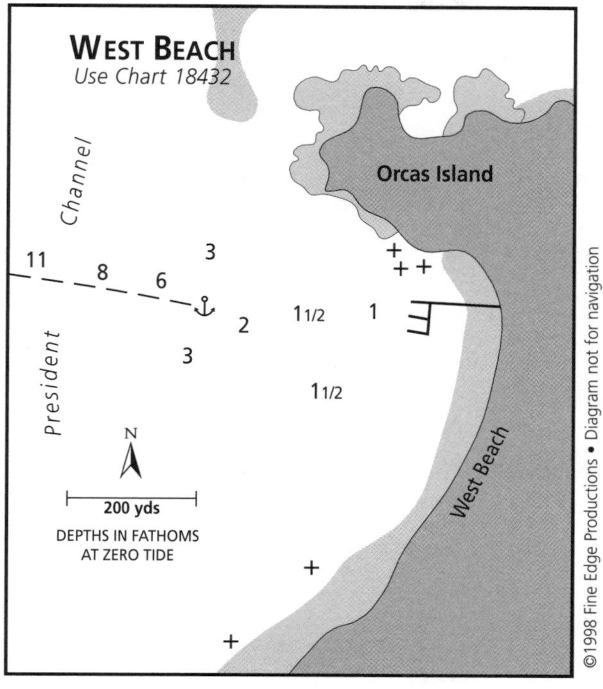

Lovers Cove provides the only convenient temporary anchorage along this western section of Orcas Island. You can land your dinghy on a small beach behind the unnamed islet and sunbathe or picnic. The nearby reefs are a favorite of scuba divers.

Anchor in 5 fathoms due south of the unnamed islet.

West Beach (Orcas Island)

West Beach, on the northwest side of Orcas Island, is 3 miles north of Deer Harbor.

Chart 18432
Entrance: 48°41.30′ N, 122°58.30′ W (NAD 83)
Anchor: 48°41.30′ N, 122°57.80′ W (NAD 83)

> *Point Doughty, the NW tip of Orcas Island, is bare and terminates in a small knob on its outer end. A resort in the bight, 1.5 miles SSW of Point Doughty, has floats with about 40 berths, gasoline, water, ice, a concrete launching ramp, and some marine supplies. In 1973, a depth of 4 feet was reported at the floats.* (p. 334, CP)

West Beach, long and sandy with a few isolated rocks near shore, is a popular fishing resort with cabins, boat ramp, and a small store. It is open all year (tel: 360-376-2240). Anchorage can be found due west of the pier complex.

Anchor in about 3 fathoms over sand, mud and shells with good holding.

Peter Fromm

Lobo del Mar *navigates through fog*

Camp Orkila (Orcas Island)

Camp Orkila, on the west coast of Orcas Island, is 0.7 mile southeast of Point Doughty.

Chart 18432
Entrance (0.2 mile northeast of Freeman Island): 48°42.14' N, 122°57.20' W (NAD 83)
Anchor: 48°42.00' N, 122°56.85' W (NAD 83)

Peter Fromm

Kayak cluster, Camp Orkila

Camp Orkila has a large pier extending from the sandy beach. The bight formed between Point Doughty and Freeman Island provides calm waters during settled weather and offers some protection from easterly winds. Anchorage can be found half-way between the Camp Orkila pier and Freeman Island.

You can carefully pass inside Freeman Island with about 3 fathoms in the fairway. The island is an undeveloped State Park for day-use only. Its shores are rocky and steep with difficult access. To visit the park, you can land a dinghy on the south or west end. "Pack it in; pack it out," if you picnic here. Point Doughty Recreation Site to the north has no access from the water.

Anchor in 3 to 4 fathoms over a mud bottom with good holding.

North Beach (Orcas Island)

North Beach and Terrill Beach lie along the north shore of Orcas Island between Point Doughty and Point Thompson.

Charts 18430, 18432
Position: 48°42.89' N, 122°54.50' W (NAD 83)

Waldron Island

Waldron Island is one of those special rural places found in the San Juans. Like Stuart Island, Waldron has no electricity, telephone or State ferry service, and its residents have steadfastly resisted, as a community, the introduction of such services. Of the approximately 80 residents who live there, many have either gas or wind generators, solar panels or some combination that generates electricity. Cellular phones now enable them to stay in touch with the outside world.

Waldronites are an eclectic mix of northwest islanders—retirees, farmers, fishermen, artists, musicians, herb gatherers, and a variety of others who have chosen to live a remote and rural lifestyle.

A story from the Depression era sums it up. At that time people on Waldron—mostly fishermen and farmers—did not feel the effects of the Great Depression: they were already broke! Gardens were, and still are, an important source of food here, and deer like to feed in these gardens.

Not wanting to build fences around their gardens, the residents continued to lose vegetables to the deer, so they drove them into the water or shot them. To this day, when someone spots deer tracks on shore (deer can easily swim from island to island), they hunt the animal down. No one has a fenced garden.

Waldron, unlike the other islands, lacks a protected harbor. Every year several boats are washed ashore in Cowlitz Bay, which is wide open to both southeast and southwest winds. If you anchor here, pay close attention to the weather forecasts and to what the winds are doing; it can be a bad lee shore.

Living High, a memoir by June and Farrar Burn, recounts the adventures of this unusual couple who homesteaded both Sentinel and Waldron islands. "100 Days in the San Juans," a series of newspaper articles by June Burn, describes their travels through the islands in a sailing dinghy. Their writings give us a good picture of island life in the past.—**PF**

Parker Reef, marked by a light, is about 0.7 mile off the N shore of Orcas Island and uncovers. The rocky reef extends about 110 yards in all directions from the light, except on the E side, where it extends about 160 yards from the light. Kelp covers the reef and the area between it and the shore. (p. 334)

The low, sandy shores of North Beach are prime residential and resort property. You can take temporary anchorage in settled weather against these shores. It is just a short walk to Eastsound but be sure to leave a capable person aboard. The tiny man-made inlet between North Beach and Terrill Beach, referred to as "The Ditch," is private.

Parker Reef, 0.7 mile north of Terrill Beach, is a National Wildlife Refuge; the area has excellent fishing among its shallow kelp beds.

Waldron Island

Waldron Island, on the north side of President Channel, is 2 miles south of Boundary Pass.

Peter Fromm

Waldron Island residents sculling

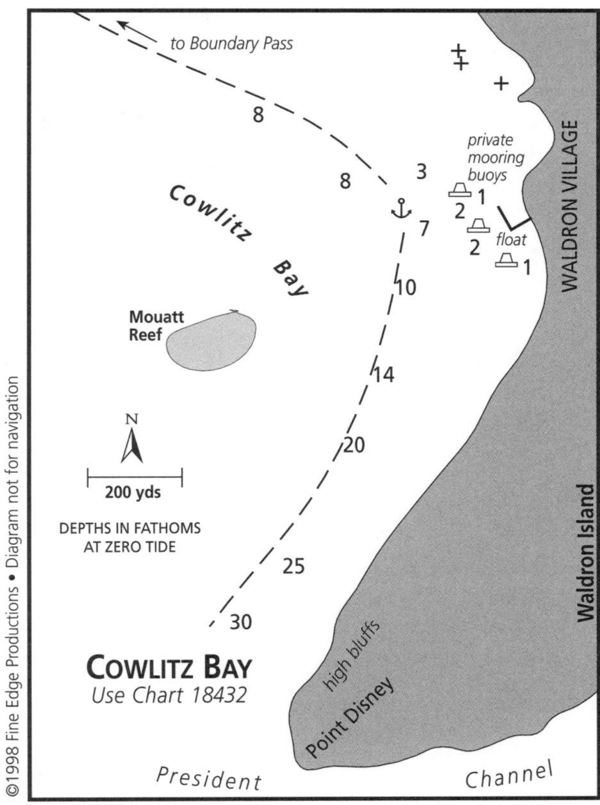

Chart 18432
Position: 48°41.20′ N, 123°02.30′ W (NAD 83)

Waldron Island, 6.5 miles E of Turn Point, is steep and rocky on the E side, but flat with sandy beaches on the N and W sides. It is irregular in shape and 3 miles long. The highest point, 612 feet, is near Point Disney, its S end. (p. 329, CP)

One of the more remote of the San Juan Islands, Waldron Island has no facilities for pleasure boats. Its east shore is composed of interesting conglomerate rock.

Cowlitz Bay (Waldron Island)

Cowlitz Bay, on the southwest corner of Waldron Island, is 6 miles northeast of Roche Harbor.

Chart 18432
South entrance (0.25 mile south Mouatt Reef): 48°40.81′ N, 123°02.77′ W (NAD 83)
Public pier: 48°41.20′ N, 123°02.26′ W (NAD 83)
Anchor: 48°41.12′ N, 123°02.35′ W (NAD 83)

Cowlitz Bay, which indents the SW shore of Waldron Island, is a broad, open bight affording anchorage in fair weather. Shoal water extends 0.5 mile S of Sandy Point, the W end of the island. Mouatt Reef, with a least depth of 1/2 fathom and marked by kelp, is 0.4 mile offshore and 0.5 mile N of Point Disney. A wharf built out to a depth of 7 feet, is on the shore NE of Mouatt Reef. (p. 329, CP)

First mutt

Cowlitz Bay offers fair protection from southeast through northeast winds. Avoid Mouatt Reef at the south end of Cowlitz Bay. The reef is about 3 feet below chart datum and is not marked by kelp.

The village of Waldron, on the east side of Cowlitz Bay, has a small pier surrounded by a number of private floats. Anchorage can be found outside the line of private buoys off the public pier.

Anchor in 2 to 7 fathoms over a mud bottom with fair holding.

Mail Bay (Waldron Island)

Mail Bay is on the east shore of Waldron Island.

Chart 18432
Entrance: 48°42.08′ N, 123°00.25′ W (NAD 83)
Anchor: 48°42.14′ N, 123°00.52′ W (NAD 83)

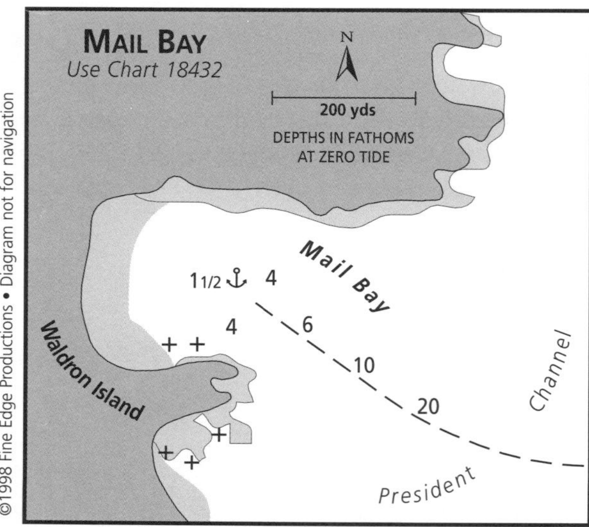

Mail Bay, although protected from westerly winds and from the current in President Channel, is not good in southeast or northeast winds. The head of the bay is shallow and has a number of pilings remaining from logging days.

Anchor in 2 to 4 fathoms over mud and grass with fair holding.

North Bay (Waldron Island)

North Bay is between Sandy Point and Fishery Point on the northwest side of Waldron Island.

Chart 18432
Position: 48°42.50′ N, 123°03.13′ W (NAD 83)

Nature Conservancy

Northwest of the county dock in Cowlitz Bay, there is a 250-acre parcel of land with 4,000 feet of beach owned by the Nature Conservancy. If you go ashore, remain on the beach and do not venture onto private property. The tidelands are protected against removal of any plant or animal life.

The following posted rules apply to Nature Conservancy property:

No hunting, fishing or trapping
No collecting of plants, animals or their remains
No bicycles or off-road vehicles
No pets, with the exception of seeing-eye dogs
Limited hours as posted—**PF**

Cormorants find a convenient perch in Cowlitz Bay

North Bay is not to be confused with the North Bay a mile and a half south of Friday Harbor. This North Bay—a long, shallow bight—offers temporary anchorage in fair weather anywhere 100 yards off its beautiful sandy beach. When crossing Boundary Pass from Plumper Sound, the bay can provide welcome shelter in southeast storms.

Anchor in 2 fathoms over sand, mud, and shells with fair-to-good holding.

Skipjack Island (Boundary Pass)

Skipjack Island is 0.9 mile north of Fishery Point.

Chart 18432
Position: 48°43.95′ N, 123°02.16′ W (NAD 83)

Skipjack Island, along with Bare Island just to the east, is a National Wildlife Refuge closed to the public without special permit. Both islands are just to the north of Waldron Island and 1.5 miles south of the international border. Tide rips occur in this area during spring tides.

Surrounded by a number of reefs and kelp beds rich with sea life, these islands are considered excellent fishing areas. Some of the birds you see around Skipjack Island include black oyster catchers, pigeon guillemots, auklets, glaucous-winged gulls and many other sea birds. To avoid frightening the nesting colonies, do not approach too closely.

The northwest corner of Skipjack Island has a navigation light.

Bare Island (Boundary Pass)

Bare Island is 0.5 mile north of Point Hammond and 0.7 mile east of Skipjack Island.

Chart 18432
Position: 48°43.79′ N, 123°00.87′ W (NAD 83)

Bare Island is a Natural Wildlife Refuge.

Peter Fromm

Orcas glide quietly through Haro Strait

5

SAN JUAN ISLAND WEST COAST TO STUART ISLAND

Haro Strait, Mosquito Pass, Roche Harbor, Spieden Channel, and Boundary Pass

The islands and bays around Mosquito Pass and Roche Harbor at the northwest end of the San Juan Islands include some of the most popular cruising areas of the San Juans.

The west coast of San Juan Island is steep and bold and open to the spacious views of Haro Strait, as well as to its weather. The small beaches filled with driftwood attest to the strength of storm winds along this section of the coast.

Starting at the south end of San Juan Island and heading up its west coast, you pass Eagle Cove, Kanaka Bay, Deadman Bay, and Lime Kiln Point. Who was the dead man of Deadman Bay? There are many stories, but no one knows for certain. Lime Kiln Light marks the site of Lime Kiln State Park, the only official whale-watching park in the United States. Just to the north are the ruins of Cowell's lime kiln, built near the turn of the century.

San Juan County Park at Smallpox Bay has picnic and camping facilities. Andrews Bay was once the site of an extremely productive fish weir and a haven for bootleggers. Mitchell Bay at the south entrance to Mosquito Pass is a welcome refuge from the winds of Haro Strait.

Open Bay on Henry Island is a lovely anchorage in prevailing northwesterly winds. Across the way—along the San Juan Island shore—Garrison and Westcott bays offer year-round shelter. Garrison Bay is the site of British Camp, an historical park and a good area for exploring by foot.

Farther north is historic Roche Harbor with its fabulous old hotel, gardens, and mausoleum. West across the pass is Nelson Bay, home to an outstation of the Seattle Yacht Club. Tiny Posey Island is a State Park, just one acre in size.

As you hopscotch toward Spieden Channel, you pass Battleship and Barren islands and Davison Head, then head north across the channel to Spieden Island. Privately-owned Spieden Island is almost treeless on its southern half, while its northern side is steep and in places deeply forested.

As you continue north, on the way to Stuart Island, study the fascinating rock formations on Johns Island. Both Reid and Prevost harbors offer good anchoring and share State Marine Park lands.

The distance between Prevost and Bedwell harbors is 4 nautical miles, typical of the length of exposed waters a vessel must cross to and from the San Juan and Gulf islands.

Both Haro Strait and Boundary Pass are subject to strong ebb currents with turbulence and

Peter Fromm

The freighter Zircon *passing through Haro Strait*

tide rips, as are the waters off Boiling Reef, Alden Point, and the confluence of Haro Strait and the Strait of Juan de Fuca. When opposed by a fresh wind or southeast gale, these waters can become uncomfortable or dangerous to small craft. Local pods of orcas feed in these turbulent waters. Large and fast-moving commercial traffic makes Haro Strait and Boundary Pass particularly dangerous in times of low visibility; pleasure craft should cross these waters at right angles to minimize exposure to the traffic.

Eagle Cove (San Juan Island)

Eagle Cove, on the south end of San Juan Island, is 0.25 mile north of Eagle Point and 2.7 miles west of Cattle Pass.

Chart 18434
Position: 48°27.55′ N, 123°01.90′ W (NAD 83)

> *From Eagle Point, the W shore of San Juan Island trends NW and forms the E side of Haro Strait. The shore is steep-to and rocky, and beyond 400 yards offshore it is free of danger; however, the depths off this shore are too great for anchoring.* (p. 328, CP)

Eagle Cove, which largely dries at low water and is exposed to southern winds, provides just a temporary stop for small craft in fair weather, avoiding the rocks and kelp on its east side.

The small cove, which has an attractive sandy beach backed by a high bank, is a popular place for swimming, beachcombing and sunbathing. Accessible by land it is also a favorite of scuba divers. At low water only you can walk along shore all the way to Cattle Point.

False Bay (San Juan Island)

False Bay is 1.9 miles northwest of Eagle Point.

Charts 18434, 18433
Entrance: 48°28.64′ N, 123°04.21′ W (NAD 83)

False Bay is a large, circular, drying mud flat with a cluttered entrance. At high water it appears to be a nicely sheltered bay, but it is too shallow for anchoring. Even kayakers may find themselves high and dry and a long way from water.

At low tide, the bay is a nature lover's paradise where you can observe barnacles and rock oysters, purple shore crabs, clams, chitons, cling fish, and worms of various sizes and colors. The University of Washington maintains a biological study area here with a number of ongoing research projects. Do not enter the staked-out areas and do not kill or collect any specimens anywhere in the bay. False Bay is accessible by road.

Kanaka Bay (San Juan Island)

Kanaka Bay, just east of Pile Point, is 0.4 mile west of False Bay.

Charts 18434, 18433
Position: 48°28.92′ N, 123°05.00′ W (NAD 83)

> *Kanaka Bay, a small cove used by fishing boats, is 2.5 miles NW of Eagle Point.* (p. 328 CP)

Kanaka Bay is used by kayakers in fair weather, but it is full of rocks and islets and not recommended for draft boats.

Deadman Bay (San Juan Island)

Deadman Bay is 2.8 miles northwest of Pile Point and 3.8 miles south of Mitchell Bay.

Chart 18433
Position: 48°30.69′ N, 123°08.83′ W (NAD 83)

The shallow bight known as Deadman Bay is a popular scuba diving area. Open to the southwest, it has a number of reefs and rocks on its north shore and is not considered a viable anchorage due to its strong currents and depth. Deadman Bay is sometimes used by kayakers or sportfishing boats as a temporary stop, but the surrounding shores are private, so there is no access for hiking.

Peter Fromm

"Ruffles" surfaces in Kanaka Bay

The navigation light and foghorn on Lime Kiln Point is 0.3 mile to the northwest. Lime Kiln Point State Park, a 39-acre site surrounding the lighthouse, is designated as a whale-watching park, the only such park in the United States. The park has a restroom, picnic tables, interpretive displays, drinking water, and road access.

Smallpox Bay (San Juan Island)

Smallpox Bay is 0.23 mile southeast of Low Islet and 1.5 miles north of Lime Kiln Point.

Chart 18433
Position: 48°32.42′ N, 123°09.68′ W (NAD 83)

Despite its alarming name, Smallpox Bay—a San Juan county park site—is an attractive cove which provides marginal temporary protection for very small boats in shallow water. Frequently used as a kayak stop, the park has a boat launching ramp, picnic facilities, and campsites for kayakers and hikers; there is no water on shore. Low Islet to the northwest is a National Wildlife Refuge.

Andrews Bay (San Juan Island)

Andrews Bay is 0.25 mile north of Low Islet.

Chart 18433
Position: 48°32.88′ N, 123°09.91′ W (NAD 83)

Andrews Bay is an open bight where sports fishermen sometimes find temporary anchorage.

Smugglers Cove (San Juan Island)

Smugglers Cove is a half-mile southwest of the Mitchell Bay marina.

Chart 18433
Position: 48°33.88′ N, 123°10.56′ W (NAD 83)

Smugglers Cove, as the name implies, was once used for clandestine operations. The tiny cove is of interest only to kayakers as a rest stop.

Gray Whales

Gray whales are found here in fairly shallow waters of less than 100 feet. For the past three years, there have been record sightings of these bottom-feeding baleen whales. One of the greatest environmental recoveries has been the growth of the gray whale population which was twice hunted to near extinction. It is estimated that there are around 22,000 gray whales at present.—**PF**

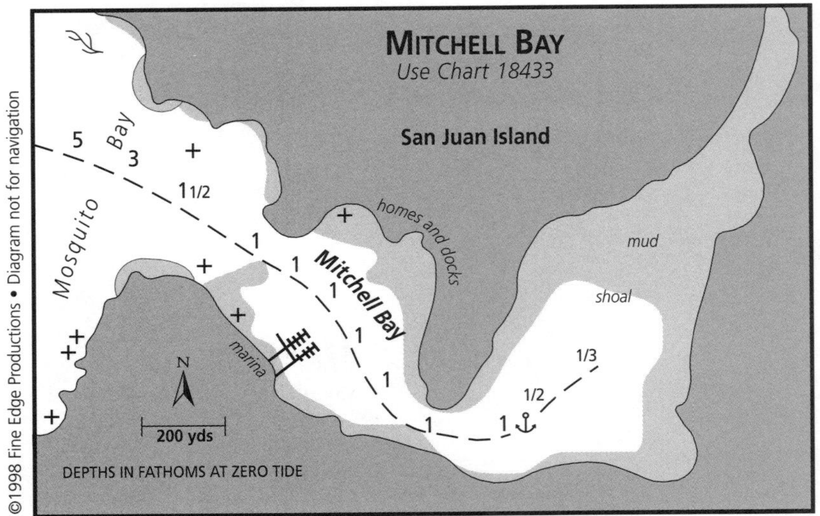

Mosquito Bay (San Juan Island)

Mosquito Bay, southwest of Hanbury Point, is the entrance to Mitchell Bay.

Chart 18433
Position: 48°34.45′ N, 123°10.74′ W (NAD 83)
South entrance to Mosquito Pass (0.09 mile due west of Hanbury Point): 48°34.69′ N, 123°10.56′ W (NAD 83)

Mosquito Bay, the shallow area west of Mitchell Bay, is too exposed for use as an anchorage. Mitchell Bay, immediately east, or Garrison Bay, a mile northwest, are preferred anchorages.

Mitchell Bay (San Juan Island)

Mitchell Bay, due east of Mosquito Bay, is 2.1 miles south of Roche Harbor.

Chart 18433
Entrance: 48°34.45′ N, 123°10.31′ W (NAD 83)
Marina: 48°34.27′ N, 123°10.02′ W (NAD 83)
Anchor: 48°34.16′ N, 123°09.68′ W (NAD 83)

> *Hanbury Point, 3.8 miles N of Lime Kiln Light, is the N entrance point to Mitchell Bay, one of a series of well-sheltered bays on the NW coast of . . .* [San Juan] *island. A small islet 3 feet high is in the center of the bay about 350 yards SE of the entrance. A rock about 100 yards W of the islet uncovers 6 feet. The only safe passage into the bay is N of the islet. Snug Harbor, a resort and yacht haven on the S side of Mitchell Bay, has about 90 berths with electricity, gasoline, water, ice, and limited marine supplies. A launching ramp is available; engine repairs can be made to small craft.* (p. 328, CP)

Mitchell Bay is composed of both an outer and inner bay. The outer bay, located behind a reef that extends most of the way across the entrance from the south shore, has a marina on its south side. Upon entering the bay, favor the north shore to avoid the reef.

A peninsula, with lovely large homes and private docks, extends from the north shore, almost closing off the inner bay which largely dries at low water.

Anchorage may be found almost anywhere in

Schooner under full sail

Peter Fromm

the outer bay where depths are adequate for the tidal conditions. Shallow-draft boats may find some anchorage just east of the peninsula in the inner bay. If you enter, pay careful attention to your echo sounder and to the tide tables. Both the inner and outer bays have limited swinging room and some exposure to west winds. Avoid the moored boats and many private floats in both bays.

Anchor in 1 fathom over black mud with good holding.

Peter Fromm

The halibut schooner Yakutat *off San Juan Island*

Open Bay (Henry Island)

Open Bay, on the south side of Henry Island, is 0.9 mile northwest of the south entrance to Mosquito Pass.

Chart 18433
Entrance: 48°35.07′ N, 123°11.51′ W (NAD 83)
Anchor: 48°35.64′ N, 123°11.28′ W (NAD 83)

> *Henry Island is close W of the N point of San Juan Island, from which it is separated by Mosquito Pass and Roche Harbor.*
>
> *Open Bay, E of Kellett Bluff, offers good holding ground and protection for small boats from N and E weather.* (p. 328, CP)

In fair weather Open Bay is a nice, quiet anchorage. We like its natural and undeveloped setting, yet its closeness to major facilities. Although the bay offers good protection from westerlies, it is open to the south and should be avoided in strong winds from that quadrant.

Anchor in 3 fathoms over a sandy bottom with fair holding.

Mosquito Pass

Mosquito Pass separates the northwest end of San Juan Island from Henry Island.

Chart 18433
North entrance (between Seattle Yacht Club outstation on Henry Island and Bazalgette Point): 48°36.27′ N, 123°10.09′ W (NAD 83)

> *Mosquito Pass, available only to small craft with local knowledge, leads N from Hanbury Point to Garrison Bay, Westcott Bay, and Roche Harbor.* (p. 328, CP)

Mosquito Pass, the narrow, intricate passageway connecting Roche Harbor to Haro Strait, has a lot of traffic during the summer season. Because of its numerous shoals, rocks and strong currents, you should not attempt it without paying close attention to Chart 18433, as well as to your echo sounder and to opposing traffic. The fairway is marked by nav-aids, and it is imperative to pass each buoy on its proper side. On a passage from south to north, pass the red even-numbered nav-aids on your starboard side.

Peter Fromm

At work on a 16-foot Coast Salish canoe

Peter Fromm

Mosquito Pass

The south entrance to Mosquito Pass starts immediately west of Hanbury Point; the Henry Island side of the channel is foul and shallow. From Hanbury Point to Delacombe Point the pass has a shallow, irregular bottom. Nav-aids 2, 3, and 4 help you avoid the shoals on either side of the fairway. Once past red Mark "4," favor the Henry Island shore, then take a midchannel course favoring the San Juan Island shore during the dogleg into Roche Harbor; strong currents run in this dogleg. Be sure to pass west of red Buoy "6," favoring the Henry Island shore to avoid the shoal off White Point. The fairway is east of the midchannel islet, known locally as Pole Island.

Please watch your speed in Mosquito Pass, otherwise your wake can cause major damage to shore facilities or other traffic, particularly during strong currents.

When entering or exiting either Mosquito Pass or Open Bay, give a wide berth to the south point of Henry Island because of the extensive foul area.

Seattle Yacht Club maintains an outstation 0.2 mile west of Bazalgette Point.

Peter Fromm

Youngsters climbing a tree on Mt. Young above British Camp

Garrison Bay (San Juan Island)

Garrison Bay is 0.6 mile east of Mosquito Pass and 1.3 miles south of Roche Harbor.

Chart 18433
Outer entrance: 48°35.38′ N, 123°10.35′ W (NAD 83)
Inner entrance: 48°35.52′ N, 123°09.64′ W (NAD 83)
Anchor: 48°35.19′ N, 123°09.49′ W (NAD 83)

Garrison and Westcott bays are entered via a narrow unnamed channel between Delacombe Point and White Point. Favor the White Point shore to avoid a shoal that extends well out from Delacombe Point. To enter Garrison Bay proper, make your turn south 0.48 mile east of the outer entrance point. The landlocked bay provides good shelter in all seasons and all weather—it is one of our favorite winter anchorages! Its bottom, which is a flat 8 to 12 feet throughout, offers excellent anchorage anywhere northwest of Guss

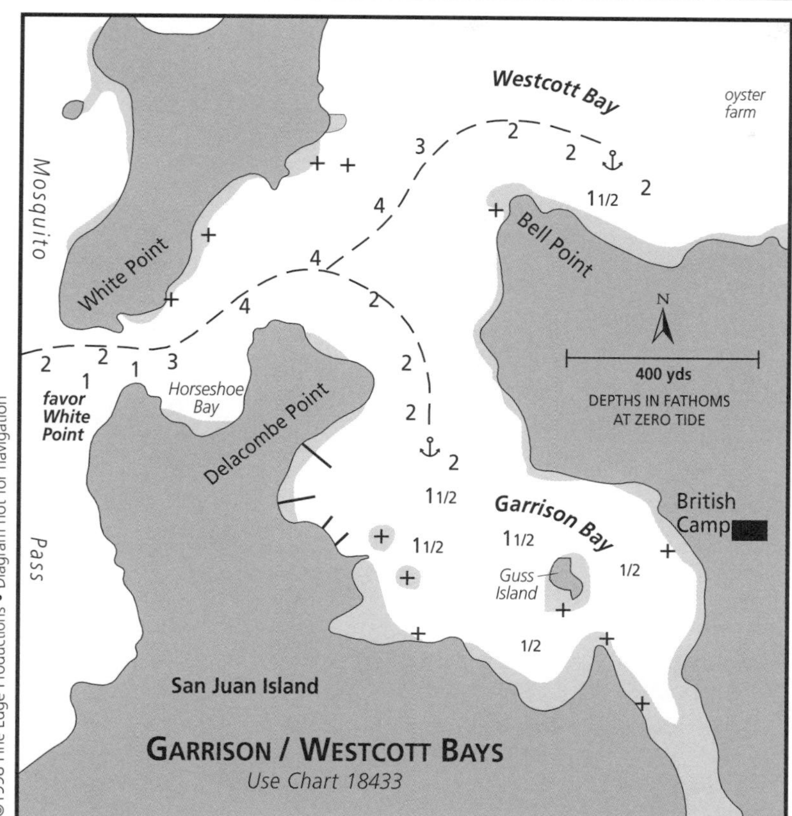

Island—an archaeological preserve closed to the public. Avoid the private docks and two small submerged rocks on the west shore.

The southeast shore of Garrison Bay is the site of British Camp (also known as English Camp) where the British troops were garrisoned during the Pig War. This historical park has renovated buildings and grounds with lovely flower gardens. If you happen to anchor here in the fall when the summer crowds have retreated, you will get a beautiful view of one of the largest maple trees on the West Coast.

The small dock in front of the camp is for dinghies only; the passage between Guss Island and shore is too shallow for other boats—about 2 feet at low water. A steep hiking trail leads to 680-foot Mount Young, the highest point on San Juan Island, which has good views. Another half-mile trail leads to Bell Point on Westcott Bay. British Camp has restrooms but no other facilities.

The narrow drying channel at the bitter end of the bay comes within a hundred yards or so of Mitchell Bay and is fun to explore by dinghy or kayak.

Just east of Delacombe Point, the small bight known as Horseshoe Bay is used principally by local residents.

Anchor in about one and a half fathoms, mud and sand, with very good holding.

Westcott Bay (San Juan Island)

Westcott Bay lies 0.6 mile northeast of Garrison Bay.

Chart 18433
Entrance: 48°35.37′ N, 123°10.34′ W (NAD 83)
Anchor: 48°35.67′ N, 123°09.17′ W (NAD 83)

A large aquaculture facility, covered 3 feet and consisting of clam beds and suspended oyster racks, is in the middle of Westcott Bay about 1

Peter Fromm

Fun for kids in Garrison Bay

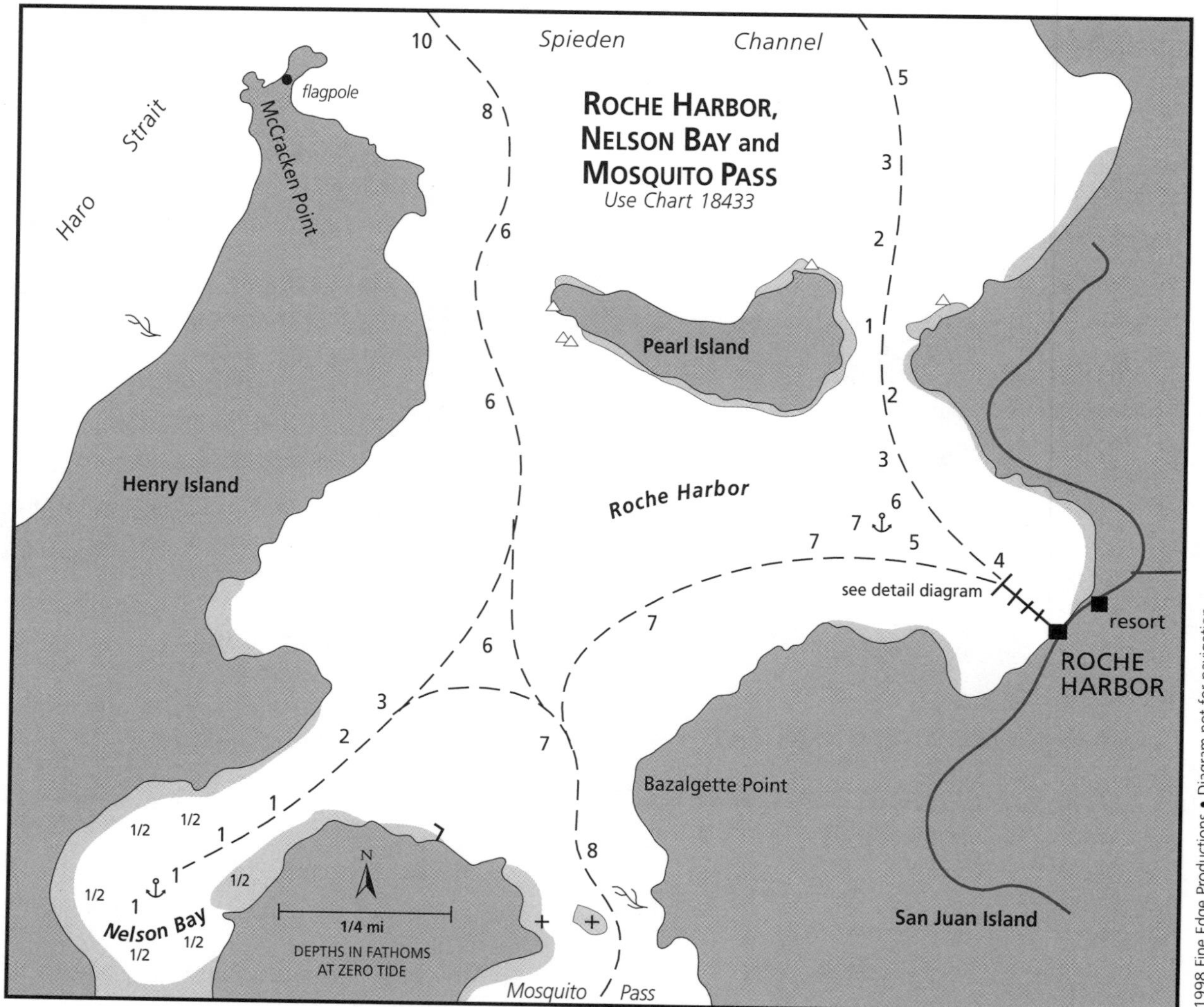

mile above the entrance. Mariners should use caution in the area. (p. 328, CP)

Like Garrison Bay, Westcott Bay is shallow and well protected from all weather. Since its inner part is used principally for aquaculture, most cruising boats prefer to anchor in the outer bay east of Bell Point and west of the oyster farm. There are a number of private mooring buoys in the bay (the best shelter from southeast gales is 0.24 mile east of Bell Point).

Westcott Bay, which is larger and less picturesque than Garrison Bay can serve as an overflow when Garrison is teeming with boats.

Anchor in 2 to 3 fathoms over mud and sand with very good holding.

Nelson Bay (Henry Island)

Nelson Bay is located on the southeast corner of Roche Harbor.

Chart 18433
Entrance: 48°36.33′ N, 123°10.57′ W (NAD 83)
Anchor: 48°36.13′ N, 123°10.96′ W (NAD 83)

Nelson Bay, which nearly communicates with Open Bay at high water, decreases in size by a third at low tide. A narrow channel 6 to 8 feet deep in the center of the bay provides quiet anchorage for a few boats that need only limited swinging room. Take care to avoid the private buoys in the center of the channel, as well as the shoaling mud flats on either side.

Peter Fromm

Westcott Bay, looking toward Roche Harbor

Peter Fromm

A quiet summer moorage near Roche Harbor

Anchor in about 1 fathom over a mud bottom with very good holding.

Roche Harbor (San Juan Island)

Roche Harbor lies at the northern tip of San Juan Island, 7.25 miles northwest of Friday Harbor.

Chart 18433
Outer entrance (halfway between Barren Island and Davison Head): 48°37.36′ N, 123°09.38′ W (NAD 83)
East entrance (pass east of Pearl Island): 48°36.93′ N, 123°09.54′ W (NAD 83)
West entrance (0.21 mile northwest of Pearl Island): 48°37.20′ N, 123°10.30′ W (NAD 83)
Marina: 48°36.57′ N, 123°09.21′ W (NAD 83)
Anchor: 48°36.68′ N, 123°09.55′ W (NAD 83)

Roche Harbor has its main entrance between the N end of Henry Island and the W end of Pearl Island, which is marked by a light. Sandspits covered 17 and 18 feet extend into the channel from the islands on each side of the entrance. The landlocked harbor has depths of 4 to 9 fathoms. It affords good anchorage and in the summer is used extensively by yachts.

A large resort is on the E side of Roche Harbor. The resort operates a wharf with shed, floats with berths for about 250 craft, a hotel, cabins, a general store, and a restaurant. Electricity, gasoline, diesel fuel, water, ice, a launching ramp, and marine supplies are available. A customs office is on the W side of the wharf. A customs officer is here full time in the summer and on call from Friday Harbor in the winter to inspect visiting Canadian yachts. The customs officer also performs immigration and agricultural quarantine inspections. Weekend and after-hours custom service can be obtained from Blaine; a toll-free phone number is posted. Roche Harbor has a paved and lighted airstrip; daily air service is

Peter Fromm

Roche Harbor

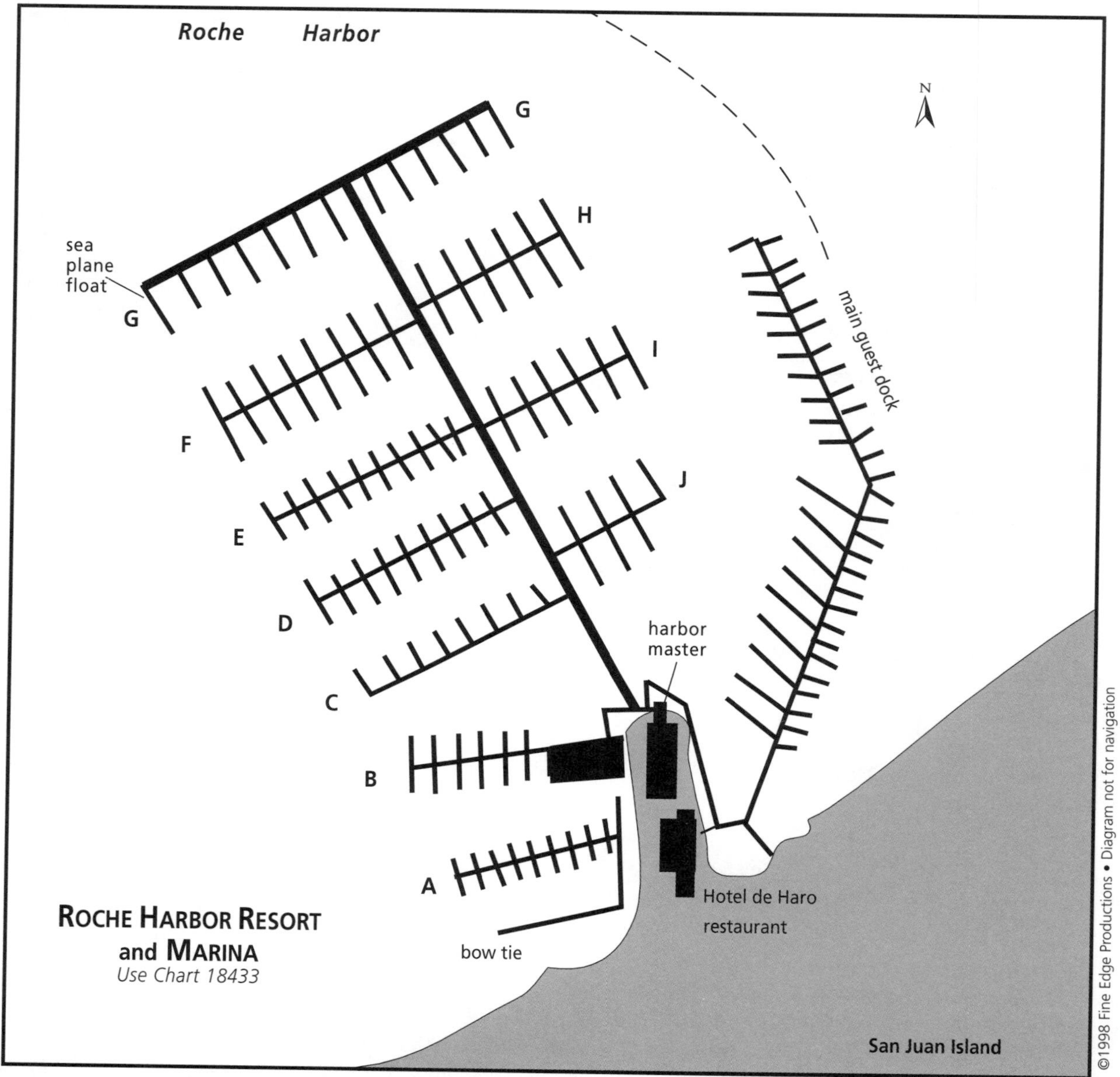

available year-round to Seattle. A paved road leads to Friday Harbor. (p. 328, CP)

Roche Harbor Resort and Marina (tel: 800-451-8910), with more than 100 guest slips, includes the historic Hotel de Haro with an Olympic-size swimming pool, tennis courts and golf course, restaurant, snack bar and more. The hotel, built before the turn of the century around the remains of an 1850s Hudson's Bay trading post, is the center of activity in Roche Harbor. It has a formal flower garden and a display telling of the area's history. Inspection of the register reveals visits by presidents Teddy Roosevelt and William Howard Taft.

Around 1885, a young Indiana lawyer, John Stafford McMillin, came to the island, bought the property, and founded the Tacoma and Roche Harbor Lime Company. If you take the path from the hotel northwest past the church, you will see a one-room log cabin, believed to have belonged to the Scurr brothers who sold the property to McMillin. Continue to Harbor Road and go north past a small cemetery to the gateway arch of the Afterglow Vista Mausoleum. McMillin chose this spot for his tomb because he loved to watch the sunset afterglow on Spieden Channel. Influenced by family history and the Masonic order, the mausoleum design is unusual. An intentionally broken column represents life broken by death, and a table and chairs are placed just as they had been in the family dining room. The bases of the chairs hold ashes of deceased family members. Behind the mausoleum, the trail drops through the woods, past two old log cabins. On the beach are the remains of two ancient boat wrecks.

Peter Fromm

The old classic trawler Westerly *at anchor in Roche Harbor*

To view the abandoned lime kilns, walk southwest along the road from the grocery store. Past the graceful brickwork of the kilns, climb uphill and go left, passing the quarries now slowly being reclaimed by undergrowth. Near the top of the hill there are spectacular views of Roche Harbor, Spieden Channel, Mosquito Pass and Henry Island.

Shallow-draft boats can enter Roche Harbor from Spieden Channel on either side of Pearl Island. Deep-draft boats should enter on the west side. To check on slip availability, call on VHF Channel 78.

Anchor in 6 fathoms over mud and sand with good holding.

Spieden Channel

Spieden Channel is a major route between the San Juan Islands, Sidney, and the Gulf Islands.

Chart 18433
East entrance (half-way between Green Point and Limestone Point): 48°37.70′ N, 123°06.39′ W (NAD 83)
West entrance (0.42 mile southwest of Danger Shoal): 48°38.01′ N, 123°11.42′ W

Danger shoal, with a least depth of 1 fathom, is in the fairway to Spieden Channel about midway between Battleship Island and Spieden Bluff. A lighted horn buoy is close SW of the shoal, which is marked by kelp.

Spieden Channel leads E between Spieden Island on the N and Battleship, Henry, and San Juan Islands on the S; the channel leads from Haro Strait to President Channel and San Juan Channel. The E entrance, the narrowest part, is 0.6 mile wide, and for 2 miles W of it the channel is free of danger. However, in the W entrance, which has an irregular bottom, are several dangers, but the fairway is deep throughout. The meeting of the flood currents, which flow E from Haro Strait and W from San Juan Channel, cause heavy tide rips and eddies. This channel is not recommended for sailing craft. (pp. 328–329, CP)

Spieden Channel is subject to strong currents with accompanying turbulence and chop. The tide rips off Green Point at the east end of Spieden

Don Douglass

Extra security for small craft!

Island, as well as close north of Limestone Point on San Juan Island, can be particularly strong.

Posey Island (Spieden Channel)

Posey Island is 0.1 mile north of Pearl Island.

Chart 18433
Position: 48°37.10′ N, 123°10.10′ W (NAD 83)

Posey Island is easily explored by dinghy, kayak or canoe from Roche Harbor. The park has one campsite, a pit toilet, but no water. It is a popular picnicking area and a Cascadia Marine Trail site.

Don Douglass

Davison Head

Barren Island (Spieden Channel)

Barren Island is 0.36 mile northeast of Posey Island.

Chart 18433
Position: 48°37.36′ N, 123°09.68′ W (NAD 83)

Barren Island is a National Wildlife Refuge. The shoals on the north side of the island are marked with a red and green buoy as well as by kelp.

Battleship Island

Battleship Island is 0.25 mile northwest of McCracken Point on the north tip of Henry Island.

Chart 18433
Position: 48°37.49′ N, 123°11.13′ W (NAD 83)

Battleship Island which, from a distance, looks like a large ship over the horizon, is a National Wildlife Refuge.

Lonesome Cove (San Juan Island)

Lonesome Cove, on the south side of Spieden Channel, is 1.5 miles northeast of Roche Harbor.

Chart 18433
Position: 48°37.33′ N, 123°06.96′ W (NAD 83)

> *Lonesome Cove, 0.2 mile W of Limestone Point, has a resort with cabins. Limited berthage and gasoline are available.* (p. 333, CP)

Lonesome Cove is an open roadstead that offers little shelter except in southerly winds.

Don Douglass

Docked at Neil Bay but prepared for serious anchoring

Neil Bay, Davison Head (San Juan Island)

Davison Head is 1.4 miles west of Limestone Point and 0.8 mile northeast of Roche Harbor.

Chart 18433
Entrance: 48°37.36′ N, 123°08.03′ W (NAD 83)
Anchor: 48°37.30′ N, 123°08.63′ W (NAD 83)

Neil Bay offers very good protection from westerlies and fair-to-good protection in southerlies. Many fine homes and private docks line the shore. In season, the cove is usually filled with many buoys and boats, but you can often find temporary shelter, avoiding the buoys.

Anchor in about 1 fathom.

Spieden Island

Sentinel Island

Sentinel Island is 0.17 mile southwest of Spieden Island.

Chart 18433
Position: 48°38.38′ N, 123°09.06′ W (NAD 83)

Sentinel Island is a National Wildlife Refuge. Sentinel Rock is 0.1 mile west of Sentinel Island; Center Reef, marked by green Buoy "C3," is 0.4 mile southwest of Sentinel Island.

Danger Shoal

Danger Shoal is 0.8 mile north of Battleship Island and 1.1 mile west of Sentinel Island.

Chart 18433
Position: 48°38.34′ N, 123°10.92′ W (NAD 83)

Danger Shoal is marked with a flashing green light and horn.

Spieden Island

Spieden Island is on the north side of Spieden Channel, 1.6 mile northeast of Roche Harbor.

Charts 18433, 18432

Spieden Island lies with Spieden Bluff, its NW end, 1.6 miles NNE of Battleship Island. The island is 2.5 miles long in an E direction with an extreme width of 0.5 mile. Green Point, the E end of which is marked by a light, is low and grassy.

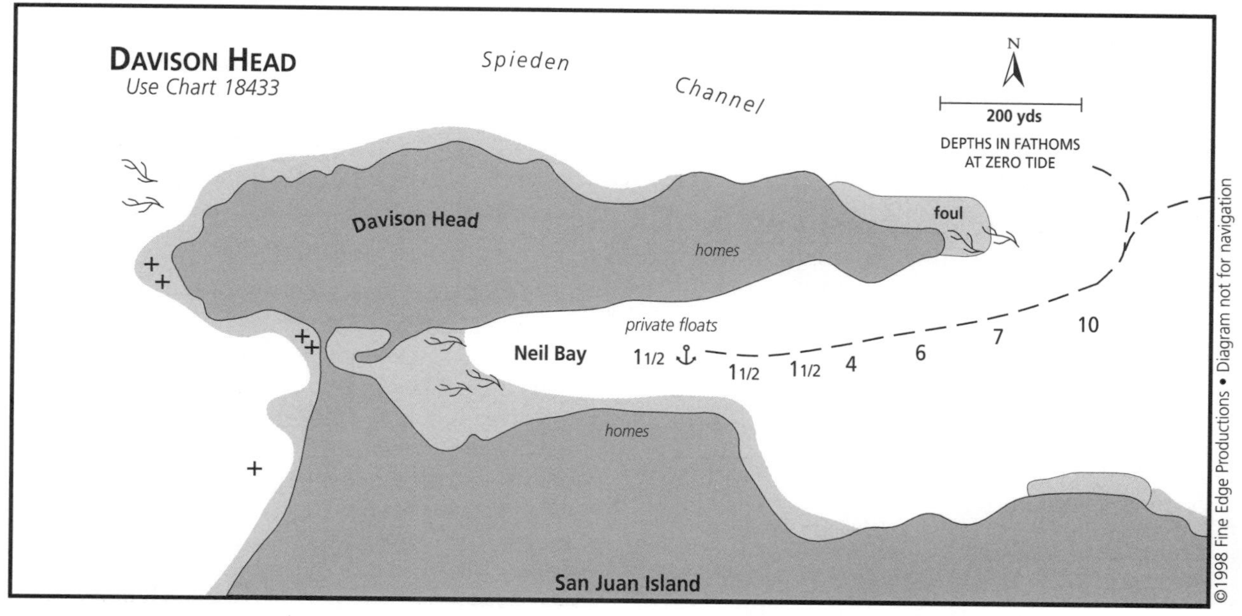

Peter Fromm

The transition zone on Spieden Island

Spieden Island

In the 1960s, two brothers who were taxidermists purchased Spieden Island, renaming it "Safari Island." They imported several species of exotic animals—Mouflon sheep, fallow and Sitka deer—and flew in hunters who paid for the privilege of hunting the animals which were then stuffed and shipped as trophies.

Local outrage at this activity caught the attention of TV newsman Walter Cronkite who produced a nationally-televised program denouncing the brothers and their inhumane treatment of the animals. The brothers subsequently went out of business.

The animals remained and multiplied, overgrazing the vegetation and creating the trails which can be seen on the south side of Spieden. Although most of the animals are now gone, some survivors remain.—**PF**

> *The S side of the island has few trees, but the N face is well wooded.* (p. 329, CP)

Spieden Island is a long, narrow island notable for the grassy, almost treeless slopes of its south side. (See sidebar.) It is a privately-owned island currently undergoing initial development, with no anchorages.

Flattop Island

Flattop Island is 1 mile northeast of Spieden Island's Green Point.

Charts 18433, 18432
Position: 48°38.81′ N, 123°04.99′ W (NAD 83)

Flattop Island, notable for its mesa-like shape, is a National Wildlife Refuge, as is Gull Rock, 0.26 mile northwest of Flattop.

Cactus Islands

Cactus Islands, on the north side of New Channel, are a continuation of a reef that extends from the southeastern tip of Stuart Island.

Charts 18433, 18432
Position: 48°39.00′ N, 123°08.05′ W (NAD 83)

You can carefully pass between the north side of Spieden Island and Cactus Islands, avoiding the shoals as indicated on the chart. All the reefs and islets between Spieden and Johns islands are National Wildlife Refuges.

Johns Pass

Johns Pass separates Johns and Stuart islands.

Chart 18432
North entrance: 48°40.43′ N, 123°09.62′ W (NAD 83)
South entrance: 48°39.83′ N, 123°09.61′ W (NAD 83)

> *Johns Pass, between Stuart Island and Johns Island close E, is much used by fishing vessels and small boats. At the S end of the pass foul ground extends about 0.6 mile SE from Stuart Island.* (p. 329, CP)

Johns Pass is used principally by boats travelling between Prevost and Reid harbors on Stuart

Johns Pass

Johns Pass is the location of one of the most beautiful waterfront farms in San Juan County—a long-established sheep farm. Although real estate people have a list of prospective buyers for the property, it is not for sale.

Other beautiful sites—horizontally-oriented sedimentary rock—can be seen along the northwest shore of Johns Island. On the southeast side of Stuart Island, this same formation has been uplifted and turned 90 degrees vertically. The same formation is also evident in Prevost Harbor.—**PF**

Island. When using this pass, avoid the reefs and a rock ledge that extend off the southeast tip of Stuart Island, 0.6 mile east of Gossip Island. Farther offshore a small-boat passage between reefs and rocks is marked by kelp as indicated on the chart. During spring tides, currents can be strong through Johns Pass. There are private mooring buoys and floats along the Stuart Island side of the channel.

Peter Fromm

Stuart Island—Turn Point Lighthouse looking west

Johns Island Beach (Johns Island)

Johns Island lies immediately east of Stuart Island and north of the Cactus Islands.

Chart 18432
Position (southeast end): 48°39.58′ N, 123°08.67′ W (NAD 83)
Position (northeast side): 48°39.93′ N, 123°08.78′ W (NAD 83)

Johns Island Beach is the small nook on the northeast side of the island. Runabouts and sportfishing boats use the cove as a temporary anchorage to go ashore, but since it is so small and exposed to channel traffic, we do not recommend its use for other pleasure craft.

There are a number of isolated rocks and shoals, particularly off the southeast end of Johns Island.

Stuart Island

Stuart Island is the northernmost of the San Juan Islands, east of the conjunction of Haro Strait and Boundary Pass.

Chart 18432

> *Stuart Island, NW of Spieden Island,* [has] *two prominent hills 640 feet high near the middle.* (p. 329, CP)

More than 80 acres of State Marine Park land lies along the narrow peninsula that separates Reid and Prevost harbors on Stuart Island. Facilities for boaters include mooring buoys, floats, campsites, picnic tables, stoves, drinking water, and pit toilets. A pump-out station is located in Reid Harbor. The park is also a designated Cascadia Marine Trail site.

Both harbors are popular cruising destinations and are conveniently located for boats entering or returning from the Gulf Islands.

Reid Harbor (Stuart Island)

Reid Harbor, on Stuart Island's south shore, is 4.5 miles north of Roche Harbor.

Chart 18432
Entrance (0.16 mile southwest of Gossip Island): 48°39.69′ N, 123°10.59′ W (NAD 83)
Anchor (0.27 mile southeast of the marine park float): 48°40.36′ N, 123°11.67′ W (NAD 83)
Anchor (0.11 mile north of Gossip Island): 48°39.92′ N, 123°10.39′ W (NAD 83)
Public float (north shore): 48°40.52′ N, 123°12.01′ W (NAD 83)

> *Reid Harbor indents the SE shore of Stuart Island and trends NW about 1.5 miles. The harbor, which is landlocked and 400 yards wide, affords good anchorage in 4 to 5 fathoms, soft bottom. The State Parks and Recreation Commission maintains a small-craft pier and floats here. The harbor is free of danger, but from the E entrance point foul ground extends about halfway across*

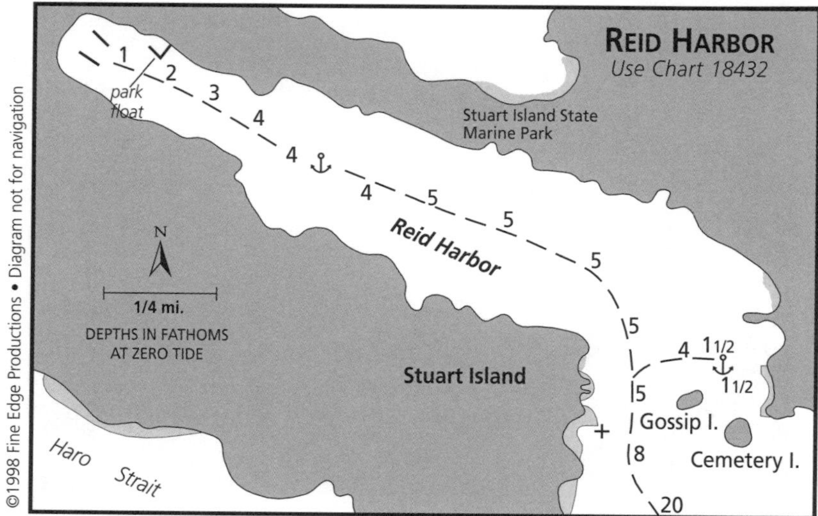

Peter Fromm

Reid Harbor

the entrance. Enter in midchannel and anchor anywhere in the middle of the wider portion of the harbor. (p. 329, CP)

Well-sheltered Reid Harbor has room for a number of boats to anchor anywhere between Gossip Island and the head of the bay. Reid Harbor is somewhat exposed to strong southerly winds; Prevost Harbor, on the north side of the peninsula separating the two harbors, offers better shelter under such conditions.

Small boats can find picturesque anchorage 200 yards north of Gossip Island. Gossip and Cemetery islands, in the entrance to Reid Harbor, are undeveloped State Marine parks for day-use only. The waters surrounding the two islands are a designated Underwater Marine Recreational Area.

The Stuart Island State Marine Park has a pier with a float large enough for several boats; two additional public floats with picnic tables are west of the pier. A hiking trail leads from the pier across the saddle of land to Prevost Harbor. There is a good dinghy-landing beach at the head of the bay.

Anchor (southeast of State Park float) in 4 to 5 fathoms over sand and mud with good holding.

Anchor (Gossip Island) in $1\frac{1}{2}$ fathoms over sand and mud with good holding.

Yangtse Cove (Stuart Island)

Yangtse Cove, on the south shore of Reid Harbor, is 0.4 mile southeast of the Stuart Island State Marine Park float.

Chart 18432
Position: 48°40.20′ N, 123°11.68′ W (NAD 83)

Yangtse Cove, a shallow bight, is the site of an old commune. It was a stop on the "mosquito fleet" circuit when small vessels competed for passengers and freight before the initiation of ferryboats.

Don Douglass

Entering Reid Harbor

Peter Fromm

Public float in Reid Harbor

Turn Point Hike

One of my favorite trails in the islands leads to the Turn Point Lighthouse and back. From either State Park dock on Stuart Island, walk along the ridge trail northwest and down to the beach at the head of Reid Harbor. You can also dinghy to the beach in Reid Harbor. A dirt road at the southwest end of the beach leads uphill and past the historic one-room school. A sign directs the way to the lighthouse.

I find something very special about walking on dirt roads with no electric or phone lines and almost no traffic—the songs of James Taylor and John Denver come to mind.

It is about two and a half miles one way from the dock, so carry drinking water and snacks. Please respect the gardens and orchards you pass along the way—they are all private.

From Prevost Harbor, you can reduce the distance by taking a dinghy to the county dock at the northwest end of the bay. It is a funky landing site, and you must climb a ladder to the pier, but it cuts about a mile off your walk.—**PF**

Prevost Harbor (Stuart Island)

Prevost Harbor faces Boundary Pass and is 0.3 mile north of Reid Harbor.

Chart 18432
North entrance (0.17 mile east of Charles Point): 48°41.17′ N, 123°11.93′ W (NAD 83)
Public float: 48°40.67′ N, 123°11.90′ W (NAD 83)
Anchor (0.15 mile northeast of marine park float): 48°40.72′ N, 123°11.67′ W (NAD 83)

> *Prevost Harbor, on the N shore of Stuart Island about 1.5 miles E of Turn Point, affords good shelter and anchorage. A pier used by the Coast Guard and the county is on the W shore of the harbor. Mail is delivered to the island by air. The States Parks and Recreation Commission maintains a float landing for small boats.* (p. 329, CP)

Except when whipped by strong southeasterly winds, Prevost Harbor offers good shelter. It is entered between Charles Point and Satellite Island. Moorage can be found either in the center of the bay, in "Satellite Island Cove," or at the Marine Park float or public mooring buoys nearby. The State Park maintains a pier and float with 250 feet of dock space; a short trail leads from the pier across the low saddle to Reid Harbor.

Don Douglass

Public dock in Prevost Harbor

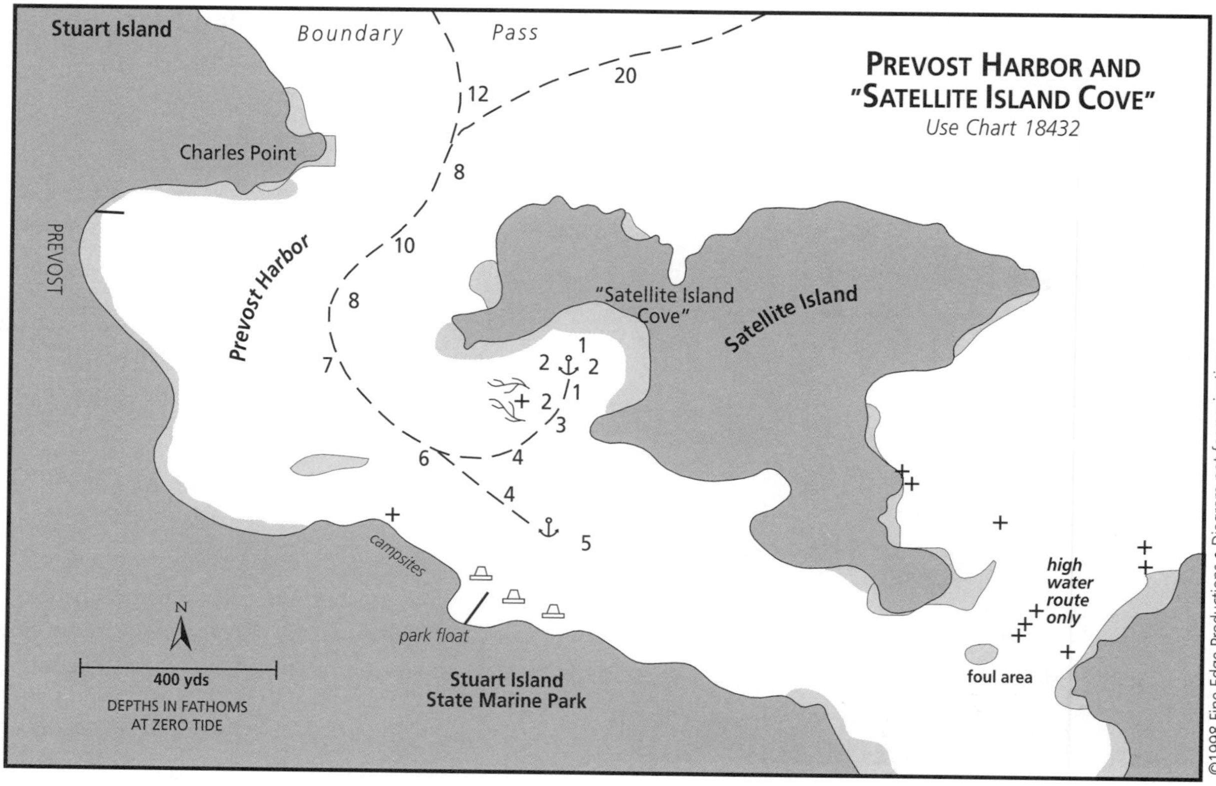

PREVOST HARBOR AND "SATELLITE ISLAND COVE"
Use Chart 18432

Stuart Island
Boundary Pass
Charles Point
PREVOST
Prevost Harbor
"Satellite Island Cove"
Satellite Island
campsites
park float
Stuart Island State Marine Park
high water route only
foul area
400 yds
DEPTHS IN FATHOMS AT ZERO TIDE

A small-craft, high-water route enters Prevost Harbor at the south tip of Satellite Island; however, this foul area with many rocks and reefs is not recommended for transit.

Prevost Harbor is a good jumping-off place for the Gulf Islands and Canadian Customs at Bedwell Harbor, 4.2 miles to the north.

"Satellite Island Cove" (Stuart Island)

Satellite Island Cove is 0.27 mile north of the State Park pier.

Chart 18432
Anchor: 48°40.92′ N, 123°11.75′ W (NAD 83)

Satellite Island lies within Prevost Harbor, with reefs and shoals extending off its SE extremity. Vessels should not pass E of the island. Enter in mid-channel W of Satellite Island and anchor in 6 to 7 fathoms, muddy bottom, in the middle of the wider portion just within the entrance, keeping clear of a rock that uncovers 6 feet, 200 yards off the S shore. (p. 329, CP)

Peter Fromm

Prevost Harbor is a good jumping-off place for the Gulf Islands

We have found good, quiet anchorage in the nook we call Satellite Island Cove. This anchorage has the advantage of a small window-like opening to the north in Satellite Island that allows you to check sea conditions in Boundary Pass. Avoid the large reef in the west section of the cove.

Anchor in about 2 fathoms over mud and sand with good holding.

Boundary Pass

Boundary Pass joins Haro Strait with the Strait of Georgia. (The international border is 1.5 miles north of Prevost Harbor.)

Chart 18432

Haro Strait and Boundary Pass form the westernmost of the three main channels leading from the Strait of Juan de Fuca to the SE end of the Strait of Georgia; it is the one most generally used. Vessels bound from the W to ports in Alaska or British Columbia should use Haro Strait and

Peter Fromm

Be on the alert for commercial traffic in Boundary Pass

Orcas (Killer Whales)

The west side of San Juan Island, past Turn Point on Stuart Island and East Point on Saturna Island, is the most common route for orcas that often spend an entire week along this stretch looking for salmon. Orcas can cover a lot of territory, up to 100 miles a day.

Resident orcas differ from *transient* orcas in several ways: The size of a resident pod—20-50 animals—is much larger than transients, which tends to travel in pods of two to six. Residents have a shorter range of travel, from Tacoma to mid-Vancouver Island, compared with the transients that travel from Northern California to Alaska. Their vocalizations include many more squeaks, clicks, and whistles than transients which are quiet most of the time. Residents primarily eat fish; transients—top predators in the ocean—eat marine mammals such as seals, sea lions, or great whales.

Both of these groups are found in every ocean on the planet; it is believed that killer whales have been divided into these two distinct groups for over 10,000 years. Second only to humans, orcas are the most widely-dispersed mammal on Earth. Although transient orcas swim through this area at any time of the year, they are found most frequently in August and September, a time when harbor seal pups—one of their favorite food sources—are being weaned.

Resident killer whales stay here because the area is a good source of salmon that swim in island waters before heading upstream to spawn and die. While one resident pod lives in the area all year, two others probably spend winter and spring in the North Pacific Ocean.

Researchers have determined that the life span of killer whales in the wild is 70 to 80 years for females, 50 to 60 years for males; in captivity, the average is less than 15 years. No killer whales have been captured in the Pacific Northwest since 1976.

If you are lucky enough to sight an orca's tall dorsal fin or its breath spouts, please respect Federal guidelines by staying at least 100 yards away when your engine is in gear. Should the whales surface close to you, put your engine in neutral and watch the show. Never follow closely behind them.

Whale watching is a big business in the San Juan and Gulf islands. Observe the behavior of commercial operators as they maneuver their boats. Many belong to the Whale Watching Association and can act as role models for other boaters.—**PF**

Peter Fromm

Peter Fromm

Turn Point Lighthouse, looking east toward Mt. Baker

> *Boundary Pass, as it is the widest channel and is well marked. Vessels bound N from Puget Sound may use Rosario Strait or Haro Strait; the use of San Juan Channel by deep-draft vessels is not recommended.*
>
> *From off the S part of San Juan Island, Haro Strait extends N for about 16 miles to Turn Point Light on Stuart Island, thence Boundary Pass leads NE for 11 miles to its junction with the Strait of Georgia between East Point, the E end of Saturna Island, B.C. and Patos Island, the small United States island; both of which are marked by lights. These waterways have widths from 2 to 6 miles and the depths are generally great.* (p. 326, CP)

Boundary Pass, known for its choppy seas when strong currents and southeast winds are blowing, is notorious in a storm. Due to heavy international traffic using Haro Strait and Boundary Pass, in foggy weather you must pay particular attention to the commercial traffic transiting Boundary Pass.

In stormy conditions we have encountered "square" waves which make travel extremely uncomfortable and even dangerous. In December 1961, a small vessel carrying the entire school population of Stuart Island foundered and sank with the loss of all the school children on board. The school did not resume operation for 16 years.

SECTION II
Introduction to the Gulf Islands

Northwest of the San Juans, you enter Canada and head toward the Gulf Islands and some of the most popular cruising destinations in British Columbia. Stretching along Vancouver Island's southeast coast and lying in the island's rain shadow, these islands are protected from the winds and rains of the west coast and the seas of the Pacific. The Gulf Islands and the adjacent shores of Vancouver Island give the boater a varied choice of places to visit. However, people and boats multiply in the summer months, so plan accordingly.

Eons ago, these islands were probably part of Vancouver Island, then rising water and glacier action formed myriad islands. Consisting primarily of sedimentary rock—sandstone, shale or conglomerate—they lie in a roughly northwest/southeast direction; ridges and valleys run in the same direction.

Summer temperatures usually range from 50 to 70 degrees F, earning the islands the name, "Canada's Hawaii." Moderate temperatures and rainfall have created dry woodlands on the islands. Douglas firs dominate, along with coppery-barked, gnarled, evergreen arbutus (madrone); prickly pears can even be found on some of the southernmost islands!

The waters are rich with colorful marine life: spiny red urchins, green anemones, ochre stars, and blue mussels. Orcas are frequently spotted here. Along the shores and rocks, harbor seals and Steller sea lions feed and bask, while otters, mink and raccoons forage along shores and streams. Thousands of migratory seabirds fill the sky with sound and grace; cormorants, and gulls nest in the wave- and wind-carved sandstone cliffs; great blue herons and bald eagles nest in the islands.

Marine parks, provincial parks, ecological reserves, and Indian reserves are scattered throughout the area. Access to all or parts of some lands may be restricted, and regulations apply to camping, fires, and gathering shellfish. Please respect these regulations and help to protect these fragile areas for future generations.

Currents in the Gulf Island

The tidal currents of the Gulf Islands, as well as the entire Strait of Georgia to Desolation Sound, ebb and flood through the Strait of Juan de Fuca. These currents are felt most strongly near headlands and in narrow channels and passages. Favorable currents can be used to advantage up to the point where their speed becomes excessive or turbulence becomes threatening. It's always prudent to wait for slack water in narrow passages or off headlands where the currents react strongly with opposing winds.

Peter Fromm

Wooden Boat Festival draws sailboats from both sides of the border

Summer weather usually brings mornings with gentle winds and calm seas. By late afternoon, however, brisk westerly winds and chop usually develop. If you plan a crossing, start early in the morning to avoid these uncomfortable conditions. Southeast gales occasionally blow through the area, but you can find many good places to shelter until the front passes.

Charming towns and the lovely city of Victoria are filled with good restaurants and cafes, museums and art galleries, gift shops, boutiques, marine suppliers, services—everything the visiting boater may want or need. Whale watching, diving, fishing, beachcombing, birdwatching, tidepooling, golfing, canoeing, kayaking, hiking, and camping are available for recreation.

The larger islands have substantial populations while many of the smaller islands are uninhabited. A multitude of bays, coves, and inlets invite you to enter and explore, to stay the night lulled to sleep by gentle winds and the cries of seabirds. The history of the native Indian bands, explorers, early pioneers, miners, loggers, and fishermen is written in decaying cabins, rotting wrecks, and ancient petroglyphs.

The population of the Gulf Islands increases nearly two-fold in the summer, and the number of visiting pleasure craft increases many times that,

B.C. Marine Trails

The British Columbia Marine Trail Association was established to preserve recreational access to the coast from the water. Using advocacy, education, and stewardship the BCMTA will facilitate the creation and maintenance of a water trail from the 49th parallel to Canada's border with Alaska in the north. Every 8 to 10 miles, wherever possible, will be a site accessible to the public for landing and/or camping. These sites, not solely restricted to human-powered craft, cater to all types of small craft exploring B.C.'s rugged coast. Some sites are already established in the form of existing Marine Parks under various government organizations. Other sites have been licensed to the BCMTA by the private landowners. Depending upon the usage of the site, the BCMTA uses the volunteer initiative of its members to clean up and build any appropriate facilities such as a composting toilet at Blackberry Point on Valdes Island (Gulf Islands).

For a small fee/donation the public can now enjoy this site and all its amenities. It is the long-term goal to have the trail completed by the year 2005. We encourage everyone to participate by joining the Association and volunteering to help out. The recent publication "Kayak Routes of the Pacific Northwest" outlines roughly the current trail and is available from the BCMTA. You can contact the BCMTA by writing to 1668 Duranleau Street, Vancouver, B.C. V6H 3S4. Being a member allows you to participate in this ambitious project plus the newsletters will inform you of new sites being developed. Come to B.C. and enjoy the beauty of our coast.

so you can expect congestion in the more popular anchorages. However, if you want to find solitude, plan your itineraries around some of the lesser-used anchorages; or better yet—if you don't mind cooler temperatures—try to schedule a cruise in the off-season. [See sidebar.] You may find yourself alone in an anchorage, or sharing it with just one or two other boats, and we can guarantee you'll get hooked!

All this and the natural beauty of the Gulf Islands and Vancouver Island coast make this a region to be visited, explored and cherished.

Peter Fromm

The J boat Endeavor *heads north*

An Off-Season Cruise of the Gulf Islands

by Tonnae K. Hennigan

After one too many Christmas parties in Vancouver, a winter cruise in the Gulf Islands—far from the madding crowd—looked like a dream vacation, the nearest thing to heaven.

On January 2nd we had crossed the Strait of Georgia from Vancouver and found shelter from southeast winds between the Secretary Islands. This was our first night on the water since the Christmas fever, and it was bliss to be rocked to sleep on our modest, though well-found, 25-foot sailboat.

Since purchasing our first boat, *Wave Dancer,* a Northern 25, three years before, we had discovered the unbelievable, enchanted Gulf Islands. Experiencing these islands on a boat is far different than in a car. Most of the smaller islands are not on the ferry route, and it's always a voyage of discovery: countless protected nooks and crannies make perfect anchorages, all of enormous beauty. The arbutus tree proliferates in the area, its red bark and gnarly branches framing views of ferries plying blue, blue channels dotted with deep green islands.

On that first morning, we awoke late to the high, chirping call of the bald eagle. We grabbed our binocs and received our last gift of the Season—the sight of a pair of these majestic creatures high in the branches of a tree, sharing our shelter. We were to see many more during our trip, and each sighting was magical.

The biggest surprise of all was the weather. The Gulf Islands get half the precipitation of the Lower Mainland (Vancouver and its suburbs), approximately 30–35 inches annually. And here we were, accustomed to mild, wet winters, blessed with sunshine on all but two of the 16 days. Added to that was the wonderful solitude of the season. Fact is, most boaters are proverbial "fair weather sailors" and do not venture beyond hearth and home when they expect wet, cold weather. That was fine with us. We enjoyed each anchorage, walked or ran the trails, and played on the beaches—all the while restoring harmony and inner peace.

Montague Harbour, at Galiano Island, with its near-perfect circle of protection—white sand beaches formed by ancient middens—has a shoreline trail with wonderful views. The regular blasts of the ferries churning through nearby Active Pass were pleasant background drones, like haunting train whistles. Ganges, on Saltspring Island, is an art-lover's paradise. With its well-tended trails Princess Margaret Marine Park, Portland Island, was truly a jewel bequeathed by a princess, again offering views of the channels beyond.

Sidney felt like Hawaii! Port Sidney Marina offers a no-nonsense breakwater and substantial, well-serviced docks within walking distance to Waikiki-like shops and restaurants, along with a "tropical" view of crescent-shaped Sidney Island. That island, a lovely, thin stretch of sand, is a beachcomber's paradise, even in cold weather, with 15–20 mooring buoys to make things easy. At Chatham Islands we tromped the trails, enjoying the arbutus trees and views uncluttered by other boats. Next stop was Victoria, for two nights at the Coast Hotel on the Inner Harbour where there is a convenient marina for visiting boats. Surprisingly, two nights in a hotel just didn't cut it! We enjoyed the quaint, picturesque city, but were anxious to get back to our own wee, floating hotel and the freedom from plastic people and their media-driven judgements.

The route back took us to Oak Bay Marina, still in Victoria, and a short walk to Sealand and many quaint shops and teahouses. When we left Sidney the following day, an ebb tide running in Baynes Channel against a southeast gale made for mountainous waves and a very sick first mate. I worked it off with a walk around Isle de Lis Marine Park on our way to Bedwell Harbour, South Pender Island—an attractive spot when it isn't humming with Customs clearance and resort traffic.

The next day a whale surfaced in the strait as we were rounding the south side of Saturna Island en route to Reef Harbour between Tumbo and Cabbage islands. That night we were entertained with the vigorous smacking of seals working parasites off their pelts.

Then it was off to Winter Cove at Saturna Island where we loosened our limbs on another winding trail and were entertained by seals and otters before retiring to play Scrabble. The next day from shore we checked out Boat Passage, a tiny shortcut to the strait, navigable only at high tide and in daylight. We overnighted at Port Browning on North Pender Island, after a fishburger and a wonderful shower, and we discovered another family of cheeky otters under the docks. Doubling back now, we sailed up Trincomali Channel for Wallace Island, where we enjoyed the Wallace Island Marine Park, several pairs of bald eagles, and flocks of squawking cormorants whose nesting ground is on a nearby islet. To clear Gabriola Passage before ebb tide, we left early, making for Silva Bay at Gabriola Island, where we always enjoy a long, hilly run topped off by a luxurious, hot shower.

A vigorous beam reach with 10-15 knot northwest winds across the Strait of Georgia took us to Plumper Cove at Keats Island.

A final night in our own "stomping grounds" at Snug Cove, Bowen Island—a quick jaunt from Vancouver—eased us back into city living.

A Caribbean cruise may be warm, but it pales in comparison with the serenity and beauty of our Gulf Islands cruise. I'd recommend it any day as a post-Christmas excursion. It's a great way to start the New Year!

Don Douglass

Approaching Victoria Outer Harbour

6

VICTORIA TO SAANICH INLET

Although not actually part of the Gulf Islands, a visit to the eastern coast of Vancouver Island is a must for boaters cruising the area. Victoria, British Columbia's capital, sometimes called the "City of Gardens," is historic and lovely with an old-world charm. First settled in 1843, the original Hudson's Bay fort has become a sophisticated city, home to the Provincial Legislature, the famous Empress Hotel, and the Maritime and Royal British Columbia museums. With its Thunderbird Park totems, Chinatown, rose gardens and horse-drawn buggies, Victoria captivates all her visitors.

Marine parks are scattered throughout the islands lying to the east of Vancouver Island. Discovery Island is almost due east of Oak Bay, while D'Arcy Island is to the north as you cruise along the Saanich Peninsula. Still further north is Sidney Island and Sidney Spit Marine Park. This picturesque park, with its white sand beach and lagoon, is popular for wildlife viewing. Don't miss the great blue herons and fallow deer. A well-developed park, Sidney Spit has campsites, picnic areas, and a float.

The town and port of Sidney lie north of Victoria on Vancouver Island. There are many excellent marinas in Tsehum Harbour, Sidney, and Canoe Bay. Sidney offers the traveller all amenities, including the Sidney Museum with its wonderful whale murals, a racetrack, golf course, restaurants and shops. For adventurous small boats, Rum Island—the tiny site of Isle-de-Lis Marine Park six miles northeast of Sidney Spit—makes a nice picnic stop. As you can guess, the island was named for rum runners who once frequented this coast.

Rounding the northern tip of the Saanich Peninsula to the west, you head into the famous fishing grounds of Saanich Inlet which has numerous coves and bays to explore. Don't miss magnificent Butchart Gardens near Brentwood Bay where Saturday evenings in summer you can view fireworks after touring the lighted gardens.

Please note: The metric Chart Book 3313 (NAD 83) replaces 3310 (NAD 27). The coordinates listed in this chapter are based on NAD 83.

Approaches to Victoria Outer Harbour (Vancouver Island)

Charts 3415 metric, 3440 metric, 3313 metric
Entrance (200 yards west of breakwater light): 48°24.81′ N, 123°23.78′ W (NAD 83)
Entrance (100 yards west of Shoal Point Light): 48°25.41′ N, 123°23.41′ W (NAD 83)

Victoria Harbour is entered between Macaulay Point and the Ogden Point breakwater. East of a line joining Colvile Island and Shoal Point up to the Johnson Street Bridge is known as Inner Harbour.

The harbour entrance is easily recognized by the breakwater, Ogden Point light and a long, low grey building close north on the east side of the entrance.

Peter Fromm

The yawl Zulu *enjoys summer in the islands*

> *The special regulations for Victoria Harbour affecting pleasure craft . . .* [include:] *no vessel shall anchor in that part of the Harbour of Victoria situated between the railway bridge and the shore of James Bay except as a temporary expedient, and the harbour master may order the immediate removal of any vessel so anchored.*
>
> *The Harbour Master for Victoria . . . monitor*[s] *Channel 73 Monday to Friday from 0800 to 1630 hours.*
>
> *Proceeding under sail in Victoria Harbour, north of a line drawn between Shoal Point and Berens Island lights, is prohibited.*
>
> *Do not anchor in Victoria Harbour except as directed by the Harbour Master.* (pp. 111, 113, SCG, Vol. 1)

Cruising vessels approaching Victoria from the north generally use Baynes and Mayor channels. Boats approaching from Cattle Pass and Rosario Strait pass either north or south of Trial Islands. Boats leaving from the west or from Port Townsend can take a tack directly for the harbor entrance.

Warning: Be on the alert for seaplanes. There has been an increase in the number of aircraft that land in Victoria Harbour waters. Two major traffic areas or runways lie east-west and north-south of Shoal Point in the Fisherman Bay area. Contact the Victoria Harbour Office at 250-363-3273 for information on docking.

Fleming Bay (Vancouver Island)

Fleming Bay is located 0.25 mile northwest of Macaulay Point and 0.8 mile northwest of the Victoria Harbour breakwater.

Charts 3415 metric, 3440 metric, 3313 metric
Outer entrance (0.1 mile northwest of Macaulay Point): 48°25.08′ N, 123°24.84′ W (NAD 83)
Breakwater entrance: 48°25.19′ N, 123°24.82′ W (NAD 83)

Fleming Bay, a tiny bay west of the entrance to Victoria Harbour, is strategically located to provide shelter for small craft that may have difficulty entering Victoria Harbour. Shelter can be found in the lee of Gillingham Islands or behind the breakwater. Swinging room is tight, so if you need to anchor temporarily, it's a good idea to use a stern tie to the breakwater. In an emergency, shallow-draft boats can tie to the launch ramp float. When entering, avoid the Gillingham Islands, many of which are underwater reefs marked by substantial kelp beds.

There are picnic facilities along shore and you can walk to Saxe Point Park and English village on Lampson Street where you can visit a replica of Anne Hathaway's cottage.

Anchor in 2 to 3 fathoms.

Rose Bay (Vancouver Island)

Rose Bay is 0.28 mile northeast of McLoughlin Point.

Charts 3415 metric, 3440 metric, 3313 metric
Entrance: 48°25.32′ N, 123°23.73′ W (NAD 83)

> *Rose Bay, between McLoughlin Point and Work Point, 0.3 mile NE, is a booming ground. Two rocks awash lie in the centre part of the bay.*
>
> *The Work Point Boat Club floats, protected by a rockfill breakwater, are at the head of Rose Bay.* (p. 114, SCG, Vol. 1)

Rose Bay is a shallow bay on the west side of

Victoria Harbour. Work Point Boat Club behind a breakwater may offer emergency shelter for small craft.

Haulout time for a Pinkeye schooner

West Bay (Vancouver Island)

The entrance to West Bay, on the north side of Berens Island, is 0.1 mile northeast of Work Point.

Charts 3415 metric, 3440 metric, 3313 metric
Entrance to dredged channel: 48°25.48′ N, 123°23.53′ W (NAD 83)

> *West Bay, between Work Point and Coffin Island Point, is a booming ground. A channel, dredged to a depth of 5 feet (1.5 m), leads NW to the marina on the west side of the bay. The outer end of the channel is marked by a port hand buoy, identified "V23", and the north side is marked by dolphins.* (p. 114, SCG, Vol. 1)

West Bay is entered through a dredged channel on its southwest side, avoiding a shallow booming area to the north of the channel. West Bay Marina (tel: 250-385-1831), on the inner bay, has moorage for small craft. Just west of the marina there is a marine ways, with a store and pub nearby. West Bay has been newly developed with high-rise apartments and walkways that connect several parks along the north shore of the bay.

Lime Bay (Vancouver Island)

Lime Bay is 0.25 mile north of Shoal Point.

Charts 3415 metric, 3440 metric, 3313 metric
Entrance: 48°25.57′ N, 123°23.21′ W (NAD 83)

> *Lime Bay, filled with a mud flat, is a booming ground.* (p. 114, SCG, Vol. 1)

Spinnakers, which lies at the head of Lime Bay, is a popular gathering place for meals and beer. For reservations telephone 250-384-2112.

Erie Street Government Wharf, known locally as Fishermen's Wharf (Victoria Harbour)

Erie Street Government Wharf, on the south side of the Victoria Harbour, is 0.1 mile east of Shoal Point.

Charts 3415 metric, 3440 metric, 3313 metric
Fuel dock: 48°25.44′ N, 123°23.11′ W (NAD 83)
Wharf Street public floats: 48°25.43′ N, 123°23.06′ W (NAD 83)

> *The fisherman's floats with ten finger floats, close east of Shoal Point, are generally used by the fishing fleet. Between May 30 and August 31, when the fishing fleet is at sea, they are used by pleasure craft.* (p. 115, SCG, Vol. 1)

Fishermen's Wharf—the public floats just east of the fuel dock—may offer transient moorage for pleasure craft, depending on commercial fishing activities. The floats are usually quite crowded and rafting may be required. Power, water, and shower facilities are available. Call on VHF channel 73 for space availability. A second fuel dock is at the east end of the floats at Raymur Point.

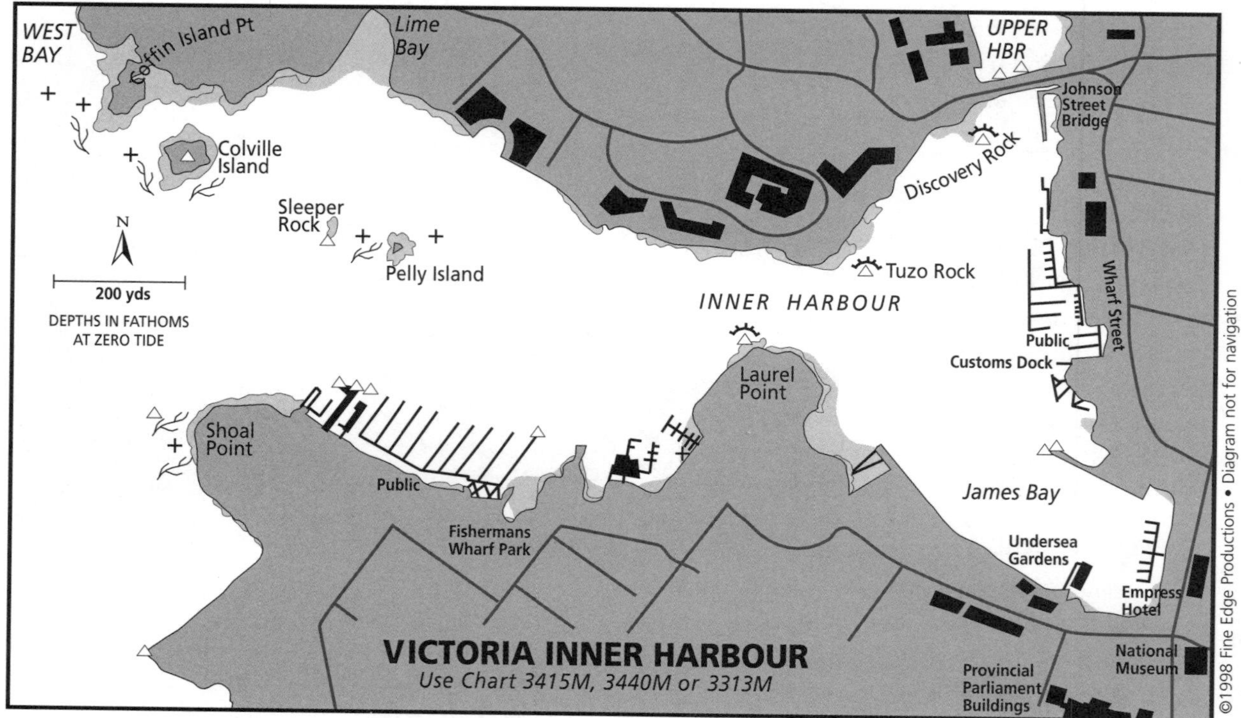

Victoria Inner Harbour

Charts 3415 metric, 3440 metric, 3313 metric
Entrance (Inner Harbour between Laurel and Songhees points): 48°25.50′ N, 123°22.61′ W (NAD 83)

Victoria Harbour is a water aerodrome. The normal landing and taking off area is between Shoal and Laurel Points. A seaplane taxying area has been established for that portion of Victoria Harbour bounded on the west by a line between Laurel and Songhees Points and on the north by Johnson Street Bridge.

Large freighters and cruise ships use the outer part of the harbour and berth at Ogden Point wharves. The Inner Harbour is used by large ferries, tugs towing logbooms or barges, fishing vessels and, during summer months, by numerous pleasure craft.

Tidal streams of 2 kn can be encountered flowing across the entrance to the harbour, between Macaulay Point and Brotchie Ledge; the flood sets SE and the ebb NW. In the Inner Harbour tidal streams do not present any difficulties. (pp. 111, 113, SCG, Vol. 1)

Passenger ferry, Victoria Inner Harbour

Victoria, one of the most beautiful and welcoming cities accessible by pleasure craft, has all the charm of an English town. (Residents have even told us that it's *more* British than England!) The public floats in James Bay offer some of the finest city-docking anywhere in North America. From the Inner Harbour everything is within easy walking distance—restaurants, art galleries, gift shops, museums, marine supply stores, and markets.

Anne Vipond

Parliament Building seen from Victoria Inner Harbour

James Bay (Victoria Inner Harbour)

Charts 3415 metric, 3440 metric, 3313 metric
Entrance James Bay: 48°25.40′ N, 123°22.36′ W (NAD 83)
Public docks (Empress Hotel): 48°25.31′ N, 123°22.17′ W (NAD 83)

> *Victoria is a Port of Entry. A telephone reporting system is available in Victoria for pleasure boaters entering Canada from the United States. A Customs Officer may issue verbal clearance or if documentation is required an Officer will go to the Customs Dock, on the east side of Inner Harbour close SW of the foot of Fort Street. The Customs office is nearby at the corner of Government and Wharf Streets.* (p. 113, SCG, Vol. 1)

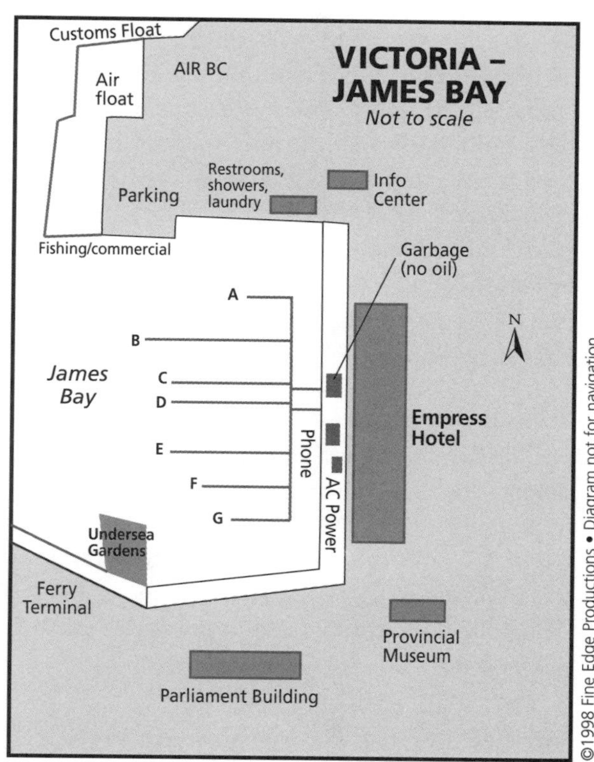

The public dock just below the Empress Hotel in James Bay is our favorite urban port of call. Moorage is usually limited to two days and a nominal fee is charged. Water and power (15 amp) are available; restrooms, showers, and laundry facilities (open during summer season only) are located below the InfoCentre on the lower quay.

Food provisions can be purchased at Thrifty Foods, 475 Simcoe, three blocks from the harbor; open seven days a week from 0800 to 2100 hours, the supermarket includes an in-house bakery and deli (tel: 250-544-1234). Thrifty offers free delivery to your boat.

Although we leave it to you to scout out your own favorites among Victoria's many fine restaurants, shops, boutiques and art galleries in the city, we list a few of our favorites: Murchies' for cappuccino, teas, coffees, sandwiches and pastries, 1110 Government Street. (We've been mail-ordering their products for over twenty years!) Munro's Books, right next door, has a terrific selection of books on British Columbia. Wells Book Group at 832 Fort Street has one of the best selections of used nautical books we've run across in the Northwest. The Provincial Museum across from the Parliament House is well worth a visit. And don't miss the Maritime Museum at 28 Bastion Square where you can see Captain Voss' *Tilikum* [see sidebar] and John Guzzwell's 20-foot *Trekka* which was once the smallest sailboat to circumnavigate the world. For additional information, visit the InfoCentre at the north end of the quay.

The Customs wharf in Victoria is located north of Ship Point Wharf on the left of the Inner Harbour, just before you enter James Bay. If you have your ship's identification papers, and information on your crew available, you can clear quickly and easily. It's a good idea to overstate your planned length of stay in Canada by a week or two to allow for contingencies. Your clearance number must be displayed from a dockside port light or window.

Note: Many of the telephone numbers listed *in Sailing Directions* and *Small Craft Guide* are outdated. The toll-free number for Canadian Customs is 888-226-7277 (for boats with or without CANPASS). Since most of the telephone numbers for government agencies are in the process of being changed, you may need to check with B.C. Tel information.

Wharf Street Government Public Floats (Victoria Inner Harbour)

Wharf Street Government Public Floats are 0.2 mile northwest of the James Bay floats.

Anne Vipond

Wharf Street Government Public Floats

Charts 3415 metric, 3440 metric, 3313 metric
Position: 48°25.48' N, 123°22.30' W (NAD 83)
Customs dock: 48°25.46' N, 123°22.27' W (NAD 83)

> *Public floats, close north of the Customs wharf, consist of a large T-shaped float with numerous finger floats extending from it. Power and water are available on some of these floats and garbage disposal facilities are available at the head of the rampway. Another set of public floats are on the east side of the channel, close south of the Johnson Street bridge.* (p. 115, SCG, Vol. 1)

The Wharf Street Government Public Floats provide convenient transient and long-term moorage for visiting pleasure boats. Showers, electricity, and garbage collection are available near the wharf (showers and laundry are closed during winter season). All amenities are within walking distance, and Bastion Square, the home of the B.C. Maritime Museum, lies just east of these floats.

Victoria

Rudyard Kipling once commented that a visit to Victoria was "worth a very long journey" and boaters who moor in Victoria's Inner Harbour are sure to agree. The capital of British Columbia, Victoria began as a fur trading post when the Hudson's Bay Company built a fort here in 1843. Bastion Square is the site of the original fort and, like many of Victoria's attractions, is located an easy walk from James Bay where the public docks are part of an imperial setting of lawns and lamp posts overseen by The Empress, a grand hotel built by the Canadian Pacific Railway in the early 1900s. Designed by the flamboyant British architect Francis Rattenbury and named for Queen Victoria, Empress of India, the hotel has been restored to its original Edwardian opulence and afternoon tea in the elegant tea lobby is a long-standing tradition.

Equally imperious and also designed by Rattenbury are the adjacent Legislative Buildings, completed in 1898. Their design incorporates Roman, Italian, Renaissance and Victorian styles, described as "free classical" by Rattenbury, and at night the structures' many lines, arches and domes are outlined with thousands of white lights. Other Rattenbury designs include the Crystal Garden (behind The Empress) and the former CPR steamship terminal, on the south harbour front, now housing the Royal London Wax Museum.

Anne Vipond

Victoria's Maritime Museum on Bastion Square

Other museums worth visiting include the Royal British Columbia Museum, just south of The Empress, with its impressive exhibits on the region's natural and human history. Nearby is Helmcken House, built by a pioneer doctor in 1852. An island in Johnstone Strait was named for Dr. Helmcken in 1850 when he was a passenger on board a steamer heading up the coast. As the ship struggled against a contrary current off the island which splits the channel, Dr. Helmcken asked Captain Dodd the name of it. The captain said, "It has no name, but I will call it after you, doctor, for it is like you, always in opposition."

The Maritime Museum in Bastion Square is popular with mariners. The museum is housed in the city's original courthouse where visitors can ride an ornate elevator built in 1900 for an elderly judge. Exhibits include John Guzzwell's ketch *Trekka* and Captain Voss's dugout canoe *Tilikum* which he sailed from Victoria to England. Just down the street is the Nautical Mind bookstore and close by is the Garrick's Head Pub, which opened for business in 1867.

For shoppers, some of the best browsing can be done on Government Street where the late Victorian era is architecturally preserved in chocolate shops, bookstores, tobacconists and tea merchants. Munro's Books, housed in a restored heritage building, has been called the most magnificent bookstore in Canada. Market Square on Johnson Street contains offbeat shops housed in restored heritage buildings that front an open-air square, formerly the Olde Town's hotel and saloon district. A narrow street called Fan Tan Alley leads from Market Square to colorful Chinatown and is lined with interesting shops, as is Fort Street's "Antique Row."

Famous for its flower gardens, such as the one at Government House, Victoria can be explored by taking various city and garden tours—including those on double-decker buses and by horse-drawn carriage. Information on these and the city's many attractions can be obtained at the Visitor's Bureau, located on the north side of the harbour at Government and Wharf streets.

—AV

Peter Fromm

Glaucous-winged gull, a Vancouver Island resident

Broughton Street Customs Float (Victoria Inner Harbour)

The Broughton Street Float is immediately south of the Wharf Street Government Public Floats, north of the seaplane terminal.

Chart 3415
Position: 48°25.46′ N, 123°22.27′ W (NAD 83)

The Broughton Street Float is reserved for vessels clearing customs.

Johnson Street Bridge (Victoria Inner Harbour)

Johnson Street Drawbridge is 0.38 mile northwest of the Empress Hotel floats.

Charts 3415 metric, 3440 metric, 3313 metric
Position: 48°25.68′ N, 123°22.32′ W (NAD 83)
Upper Harbour position: 48°25.94′ N, 123°22.4′ W (NAD 83)

> *Johnson Street Bridge, at the NE extremity of Inner Harbour, consists of separate road and rail spans. Radio communications with the bridge must be made on Channel 12. The signal for opening the bridge is three blasts on a ships horn.*
>
> *A flashing amber light, at the top of the bridge structure, indicates that the operator has received the signal. Should he be unable to lift the bridge, due to some obstruction, the amber light will be switched to flashing red.*
>
> *The vertical clearance under the Johnson Street Bridge at HW is 19 feet (5.9 m) and the width of the channel between fender pilings is 122 feet (37 m).*
>
> *Selkirk Water extends from the Point Ellice Bridge to Chapman Point; it is used mainly by tugs and log rafts.*
>
> *The C.N. Railway Bridge crosses Selkirk Water and has a vertical clearance of 1.8 m (6 ft).*
>
> *Banfield Park, on the south shore of Selkirk Water, has a small public float.* (pp. 116–117, SCG, Vol. 1; see also SD, p. 81)

The Johnson Street drawbridge leads to Upper Harbour, Rock Bay, Selkirk Water, Gorge Water, Gorge Park, and Portage Inlet. Ebb currents reach 2 knots at Johnson Street Bridge. Upper Harbour is a busy industrial area. North of Upper Harbour, where the water becomes shallow and there are a number of bridges, the inlet is used for recreation only.

Ross Bay (Vancouver Island)

Ross Bay is 2 miles east of Ogden Point breakwater.

Charts 3424 metric, 3440 metric, 3313 metric
Position: 48°24.40′ N, 123°20.60′ W (NAD 83)

> *Ross Bay, east of Clover Point, can be identified by the cemetery near its north end. It is not recommended as an anchorage because of its exposed position.* (p. 117, SCG, Vol. 1; see also SD, p. 82)

Ross Bay, which has Clover Point to its west and Gonzales Bay to its east, is directly open to southeast weather. Between Ogden Point and Holland Point, on the south side of Beacon Hill, there is a nice walkway where you can watch colonies of seals playing in the water and hauling out on the rocks.

Gonzales Bay (Vancouver Island)

Gonzales Bay, immediately west of Harling Point, is east of Ross Bay.

Charts 3424 metric, 3440 metric, 3313 metric
Entrance (.075 mile northwest of Templar Rock): 48°24.43′ N, 123°19.79′ W (NAD 83)

> *Gonzales Bay, formerly known as Foul Bay, lies close east of Ross Bay and is encumbered with rocks. Templar Rock, in the entrance, is awash.* (p. 117, SCG, Vol. 1; see also SD, p. 82)

The eastern part of tiny Gonzales Bay is filled with rocks. An observatory open to the public is located on Gonzales Hill, 0.2 mile northeast of the bay.

McNeill Bay (Vancouver Island)

McNeill Bay is 0.9 mile northwest of Trial Island Light at the west end of Enterprise Channel.

Charts 3424 metric, 3440 metric, 3313 metric
Position: 48°24.63′ N, 123°18.74′ W (NAD 83)

> *McNeill Bay, between Harling Point and McMicking Point, 0.8 mile ENE, has several drying rocks on its east side. Kitty Islet, 7 feet (2 m) high, lies on the east side of the bay.* (p. 117, SCG, Vol. 1)

McNeill Bay is open to the full force of southerlies. The area immediately to the southeast, around the Trial Islands (an Ecological Reserve), has strong tide rips. While we don't recommend McNeill Bay for anchoring, kayaks can haul out on several beaches in the vicinity.

Enterprise Channel (Strait of Juan de Fuca)

Charts 3424 metric, 3440 metric, 3313 metric
West entrance: 48°24.19′ N, 123°19.04′ W (NAD 83)
Center of narrows: 48°24.53′ N, 123°18.43′ W (NAD 83)
East entrance: 48°24.36′ N, 123°17.86′ W (NAD 83)

> *Enterprise Channel, known locally as Trial Island Pass, separates Trial Islands from Vancouver Island; it should not be attempted without local knowledge. The fairway is tortuous and less than 0.1 mile wide in its narrowest part; tidal streams run at 3 kn. A considerable amount of kelp grows in the channel.*
>
> *Mouat Reef, which dries 3 feet (0.9 m), lies on the north side of the east entrance to the channel and a depth of 5 feet (1.5 m) lies about 0.1 mile SW of it. Kelp grows in this vicinity in summer and autumn. Brodie Rock, 0.6 mile SE of Mouat Reef, is a pinnacle with 18 feet (5.5 m) over it.*
>
> *A south cardinal buoy, identified "VE", lies south of Mouat Reef.* (p. 118, SCG, Vol. 1; see also SD, p. 82)

Enterprise Channel is a short passage on the north side of Trial Islands along the Victoria shore. At spring tides currents run up to 3 knots in Enterprise Channel; off the south end of Trial Islands, they run 6 knots or more. Whenever strong currents oppose local winds, the Trial Islands are known for turbulent waters and rough seas. Standing and breaking waves have been observed close to the Trial Islands.

Enterprise Channel is used by small craft and kayakers under favorable current and sea conditions.

Mayor Channel

Mayor Channel, entered 0.6 mile northeast of Gonzales Point, is the south entrance to Oak Bay.

Charts 3424 metric, 3440 metric, 3313 metric
South entrance: 48°24.81′ N, 123°17.00′ W (NAD 83)
North entrance (0.20 mile east of Fiddle Reef): 48°25.78′ N, 123°16.80′ W (NAD 83)

> *Mayor Channel is the passage generally used by coastal vessels. It is entered south between Thames Shoal and the reefs extending south from Great Chain Island; the north entrance is between Lewis and Fiddle Reefs.*
>
> *Tidal streams follow the fairway of Mayor Channel at 2 and 3 kn. The flood sets north and the ebb south.*
>
> *Lee Rock, which dries 3 feet (0.9 m), lies 0.15 mile NW of Thames Shoal.*
>
> *Chain Islets, on the east side of Mayor*

The schooner Trader *profits from good weather*

Oak Bay

Oak Bay is one of Victoria's most established and exclusive neighborhoods, many of its turn-of-the-century mansions designed by the British architect Francis Rattenbury. When entering Oak Bay, visitors are said to be going "behind the Tweed Curtain," for the area's British traditions of cricket, golf, and afternoon tea are as solid as the stately homes built on granite and volcanic bedrock.

The historic Oak Bay Beach Hotel, a short walk from the Oak Bay Marina along Beach Drive, contains Victoria's oldest English pub called The Snug, as well as a formal dining room. The Marina Restaurant, overlooking the Oak Bay Marina, is another popular dining spot with views of Haro Strait, an elegant atmosphere and a menu featuring fresh seafood, including a sushi bar. A few blocks inland the local shops are located on Oak Bay Avenue. Lit with replica gas lanterns, this shopping district is reminiscent of an English village's high street, its Tudor-style buildings housing tea rooms and boutiques.

There is regular bus service from Oak Bay to downtown Victoria, including double-decker buses. —**AV**

Channel, are a group of scattered rocks and islets on an extensive shoal area.

No attempt should be made to pass between any of the Chain Islets; the passages are tortuous and strong tidal streams run through them. (p. 120, SCG, Vol. 1; see also SD, p. 82)

Mayor Channel, which lies to the west of Chain Islands and Oak Bay, leads eventually to Baynes Channel and then into Haro Strait.

Oak Bay (Vancouver Island)

Oak Bay is on the east side of Victoria, 0.87 mile northwest of Gonzales Point.

Charts 3424 metric, 3440 metric, 3313 metric
Mary Tod Island entrance light: 48°25.55′ N; 123°17.92′ W (NAD 83)
Marina: 48°25.55′ N, 123°18.05′ W (NAD 83)

Oak Bay is entered between the breakwater at Turkey Head and the breakwater projecting south from Mary Tod Island.

Willows Beach, at the north end of Oak Bay, is an area reserved for bathers; power boating is prohibited unless under special authority. (pp. 118, 120, SCG, Vol. 1)

The preferred entrance to Oak Bay is on the south side of Mary Tod Island; the entrance northwest of Mary Tod Island is not recommended due to shallow depths. Cruising vessels from the Gulf and San Juan islands that want to avoid entering the Strait of Juan de Fuca can take moorage in Oak Bay; downtown Victoria is just a twenty-minute bus ride.

Oak Bay Marina, open year-round, has full facilities for pleasure boaters that include fuel, power, showers and laundry, a repair shop and a small chandlery; there is a Customs telephone at the dock. During summer season it's a good idea to phone ahead for availability of slips (tel: 250-598-3366). There are also launching ramps, restaurants, and fishing supplies. The marina is within walking distance of Oak Bay Village and convenient bus service to downtown Victoria.

Willows Beach, 0.7 mile due north of the marina, has restricted boating.

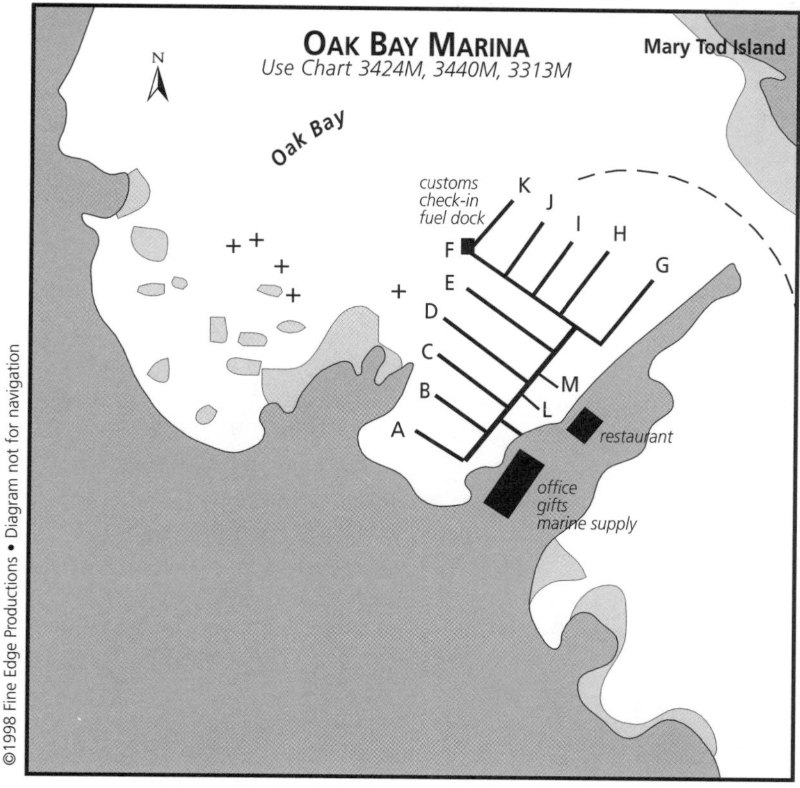

Due to the numerous rocks and reefs surrounding Chain Islets, Discovery Island, and Chatham Islands, the area is best explored by small boat. The Chathams, which are low-lying with grassy areas and arbutus trees, are Indian reserves, as is the northern part of Discovery Island; please respect these reserves and do not go ashore. The southern part of Discovery Island is a Marine Park with shore access.

In settled weather, small craft can find temporary anchorage in Puget Cove in 1 to 2 fathoms in the northeast corner of the largest of the Chatham Islands; in "Alpha Islet Cove" between Discovery Island and Alpha Islet; at the west end of "Alpha Islet Cove," due south of Griffin Island; or in a larger 6-meter hole south of Alpha Islet.

Chatham Islands

Puget Cove is 1.2 miles northwest of the Sea Bird Point Lighthouse.

Chart 3424 metric
Position (Puget Cove): 48°26.38′ N, 123°14.66′ W (NAD 83)
Position: ("Alpha Islet Cove"): 48°25.90′ N, 123°13.83′ W (NAD 83)

> *Chatham Islands, on the east side of Baynes Channel, are a compact group of islands and rocks and rocks.*
>
> *The largest of the Chatham Islands is an Indian Reserve. Puget Cove penetrates the NW part of this island; local knowledge is required to enter the cove.* (p. 122, SCG, Vol. 1)
>
> [*Editor's note:* Puget Cove is incorrectly located in SCG; its entrance is on the northeast part of the island.]

A favorite destination of kayakers and other small boats, the Chain Islets and Chatham Islands lie at the convergence of Juan de Fuca and Haro straits.

Discovery Island Marine Park, Rudlin Bay (Strait of Juan de Fuca)

Rudlin Bay is 2.7 miles west of Oak Bay.

Charts 3424 metric, 3440 metric, 3313 metric
Position: 48°25.15′ N, 123°13.77′ W (NAD 83)

> *Discovery Island . . . is wooded, rises to a height of 125 feet (38 m) at Pandora Hill, and the shores are fringed with rocks. Foul ground extends 0.3 mile south and SW from Commodore Point, the south extremity of the island; the point should be given a wide berth.*
>
> *Heavy rip-tides, often dangerous to small craft, are formed in the vicinity of Discovery Island, particularly near Sea Bird Point.*
>
> *Discovery Island Marine Park, which consists of the south half of the island, offers no sheltered anchorage and is undeveloped. The north half of the island is an Indian Reserve.* (p. 121, SCG, Vol. 1; see also SD, p. 82.)

Peter Fromm

Folk Song *in a calm Strait of Juan de Fuca*

Discovery Island Marine Park, the southern two-thirds of the island, is maintained in its relatively wild and natural condition with a few primitive campsites; fires are forbidden. The park is a good place from which to visit the rocky shores and reefs, home to many shore birds.

The bottom in Rudlin Bay and around the island is uneven with many rocks and reefs, some of which are marked by kelp in summer. Exposed to the south, the bay is not recommended as an overnight anchorage. Although there is no all-weather protection from winds that sometimes whip through the area, temporary anchorage in fair weather can be found 0.3 southwest of Seabird Point. For more protection from southwest winds, Alpha Islet Cove, on the north side of Discovery Island, may be a better choice. Be careful to avoid the turbulent waters off Sea Bird Point.

Anchor in 1 to 3 fathoms over an irregular and rocky bottom with kelp.

Cadboro Bay, Royal Victoria Yacht Club (Vancouver Island)

Cadboro Bay is located 1.1 miles west of Cadboro Point.

Charts 3424 metric, 3313 metric, 3440 metric
Bay entrance: 48°26.67′ N, 123°17.01′ W (NAD 83)
RVYC entrance: 48°27.19′ N, 123°17.66′ W (NAD 83)
Anchor: 48°27.37′ N, 123°17.66′ W (NAD 83)

> *Though open to the SE, Cadboro Bay is not subject to heavy seas. The shores are fringed with rocks and shoals; on the east side of the bay are Staines Island and Flower Island.*
>
> *A rock breakwater, on the west side of the bay, shelters the Royal Victoria Yacht Club.*
>
> *Tugs with logbooms frequently shelter in Cadboro Bay.* [The bay and] *its approach are often used for yacht races, therefore, various buoys and markers used for these races are likely to be encountered. Numerous private mooring buoys lie in the bay.*
>
> *Cadboro Bay is a public bathing area.*
>
> *Anchorage can be obtained at the head of the bay, mud bottom . . . the approach from north or east should be south of Jemmy Jones Island because of the shoal areas and concentrations of heavy kelp found in the passage between it and the shore to the north.* (pp. 121–122, SCG, Vol. 1, see also SD, p. 84)

Cadboro Bay is a very good place to anchor if you need to wait for fog to dissipate or for an unfavorable current to change. There is ample room for anchoring north of the Royal Victoria Yacht Club. The yacht club itself has reciprocal moorage and Customs clearance.

Anchor in 3 fathoms, mud and sand bottom with good holding.

Baynes Channel

Baynes Channel is south of Cadboro Point, north of the Chatham Islands.

Charts 3424 metric, 3440 metric, 3313 metric
Southwest entrance: 48°26.31′ N, 123°16.00′ W (NAD 83)
Northeast entrance: 48°26.90′ N, 123°15.22′ W (NAD 83)

Tidal streams set along the axis of Baynes Channel at 4 to 6 kn at the north entrance and between Strongtide Islet and Cadboro Point, and at 2 to 3 kn at its south entrance . . . The flood sets NE and the ebb SW. The winds can be very changeable in Baynes Channel; a strong wind opposing the tide will cause heavy tide-rips with short, steep seas. (p. 122, SCG, Vol. 1; see also SD, p. 84)

Baynes Channel is commonly used as a shortcut for boaters wishing to avoid a passage outside Discovery Island. The waters in the channel can be turbulent and a wind shift is frequently experienced in the transition from Juan de Fuca Strait to Haro Strait.

Maynard Cove (Vancouver Island)

Maynard Cove is located just north of Cadboro Point.

Charts 3424 metric, 3440 metric, 3313 metric
Position: 48°27.11′ N, 123°15.93′ W (NAD 83)

Maynard Cove has a submarine cable laid down its centre. (p. 125, SCG)

Small craft should not anchor in tiny Maynard Cove because of a submarine cable.

Haro Strait

Located between Vancouver Island and San Juan Island, Haro Strait connects the Strait of Juan de Fuca to Boundary Pass.

Charts 3440 metric, 3313 metric
South entrance (2 miles east of Discovery Island): 48°25.00′ N, 123°10.00′ W (NAD 83)
North entrance: 48°41.63′ N, 123°16.05′ W (NAD 83)

Haro Strait lies between Juan de Fuca Strait and Boundary Pass, encompassing the waters between San Juan Island and Vancouver Island. The southern limit is between Sea Bird Point (Discovery Island) and Cattle Point (San Juan Island).

Shortcutting through Baynes Channel

Don Douglass

Attention is drawn to the Traffic Separation Scheme as shown on Chart 3462.

The main shipping route connecting Juan de Fuca Strait to the Strait of Georgia is by way of Haro Strait and Boundary Pass. Sidney Channel and its continuation Moresby Passage, are the most frequented channels leading north for pleasure craft and small coasters.

A ferry crosses the north end of Haro Strait running between Sidney and Anacortes, Washington. Small craft navigators are advised to keep clear of the ferry. (p. 123, SCG, Vol. 1)

The Canada-U.S. border runs through Haro Strait, separating Vancouver Island from San Juan Island. Since Haro Strait is the main north-south shipping lane for large vessels, use caution when crossing this body of water, particularly in low visibility.

For information on tidal streams in Haro Strait and the *huge gyre* spiral east of Discovery Island, see SCG, Vol. 1, p. 123 and diagram, p. 124.

Telegraph Cove (Vancouver Island)

Telegraph Cove is 0.84 mile north of Ten Mile Point.

Charts 3440 metric, 3313 metric
Position: 48°27.98′ N, 123°16.76′ W (NAD 83)

Telegraph Cove, 0.8 mile NW of Ten Mile Point, has a rock, which dries 3 feet (0.9 m), in its entrance. The cove affords limited anchorage because of a submarine cable laid down the length of it. (p. 125, SCG, Vol. 1, see also SD, p. 88)

Telegraph Cove is a tiny cove with the above-mentioned rock in the center of its entrance.

Finnerty Cove (Vancouver Island)

Finnerty Cove is 0.87 mile northwest of Telegraph Cove.

Charts 3440 metric, 3313 metric
Position: 48°28.44′ N, 123°17.87′ W (NAD 83)

Finnerty Cove and Arbutus Cove, 0.8 mile NW of Telegraph Cove, are used by small craft. (p. 125, SCG, Vol. 1, see also SD, p. 88)

Temporary anchorage with marginal protection can be found in fair weather in tiny Finnerty and Arbutus coves.

Arbutus Cove (Vancouver Island)

Arbutus Cove is 1.4 mile south of Gordon Head and 0.25 mile north of Finnerty Cove.

Charts 3440 metric, 3313 metric
Position: 48°27.68′ N, 123°18.03′ W (NAD 83)

Arbutus Cove is shallow and exposed to southeast weather.

Peter Fromm

Pride in seamanship: a Flemish coil dock line

Margaret Bay (Vancouver Island)

Margaret Bay is located at the south end of Cordova Bay, immediately west of Cormorant Point.

Charts 3440 metric, 3313 metric
Entrance: 48°30.01′ N, 123°18.58′ W (NAD 83)
Anchor: 48°29.83′ N, 123°18.69′ W (NAD 83)

Margaret Bay, between Gordon Head and Cormorant Point, provides shelter in westerly weather, as does the area close west of Cormorant Point. A rock, which dries 1 foot (0.3 m), lies close off Cormorant Point. (p. 125, SCG, Vol. 1)

Margaret Bay has easy access to Haro Strait in case you need to wait for fog to lift. Anchorage can be found 0.15 mile west of Gordon Rock. Avoid kelp patches, the charted Gordon Rock, and the foul east end of the bay.

Anchor in 1 to 2 fathoms.

Cordova Bay (Vancouver Island)

Cordova Bay is 5 miles northwest of Ten Mile Point and 2.5 miles southeast of Cowichan Head.

Charts 3440 metric, 3313 metric
Entrance: 48°30.21′ N, 123°19.28′ W (NAD 83)
Anchor: 48°29.77′ N, 123°19.12′ W (NAD 83)

Cordova Bay . . . is fringed in its north part by drying and sunken boulders extending 0.4 mile offshore. Kelp fringes the shore during summer months. Cordova is a popular bathing area.

Anchorage can be obtained in the south part of Cordova Bay inside Cormorant Point; the holding ground is good.

A torpedo firing area is located in the north end of Cordova Bay and extends north to Cordova Spit. (pp. 125–126, SCG, Vol. 1; see also SD, p. 88)

Cordova Bay is a large bight which, at its southeast end inside Cormorant Point, is fairly well sheltered from westerlies as well as southerlies. If you happen to get caught in the vicinity in fog and your experience using radar is not strong, this is a good place to head for shelter. Anchorage can be found 0.25 mile southwest of Cormorant Point. Avoid the kelp beds near shore. During settled weather, the sand and gravel beach affords good access.

Mount Douglas Park, on the south shore of Cordova Bay, is named for the first governor of the colony of Vancouver Island. Mount Douglas (740 feet) has trails and good views of the San Juan Islands to the east, Victoria to the south, and the Gulf Islands to the north.

Anchor in 2 fathoms over sand with fair-to-good holding.

Peter Fromm

Checking out favorite places

Zero Rock

Zero Rock is 2.5 miles east of Cordova Bay.

Charts 3440 metric, 3313 metric
Position (half-way between Zero and Little Zero Rocks): 48°31.59' N, 123°18.11' W (NAD 83)

Zero Rock, 1.8 miles NNE of Gordon Head, dries 10 feet (3 m); it lies in the south approach to Cordova and Sidney Channels. Shoal pinnacles lie within 0.5 mile north of Zero Rock.

Little Zero Rock, 1 mile WNW of Zero Rock, dries 8 feet (2.4 m) and is steep-to on its east side. Shoal pinnacles extend 0.6 mile WNW from Little Zero Rock. (p. 125, SCG, Vol. 1)

When heading north from Victoria toward Sidney, avoid the complex of rocks and reefs off Cordova Bay in the vicinity of Zero Rock and Little Zero Rock.

D'Arcy Island Marine Park (Sidney Channel)

D'Arcy Island Marine Park lies 1 mile southeast of Sidney Island.

Charts 3441 metric, 3313 metric
Anchor (west side): 48°33.80' N, 123°17.00' W (NAD 83)
Anchor (east side): 48°34.00' N, 123°16.21' W (NAD 83)

D'Arcy Island and Little D'Arcy Island are wooded and have foul ground between them.

D'Arcy Island Marine Park is undeveloped, surrounded by numerous reefs and shoals, and offers no sheltered anchorages. (p. 126, SCG, Vol. 1; see also SD, p. 90)

D'Arcy Island, now a provincial park, was a small leper colony until 1924. The wooded island has no overnight shelter and the undeveloped park has a few walk-in campsites. Numerous rocks and shoals (many of which are marked by kelp in summer) surround the island creating an irregular bottom. To explore by dinghy or kayak you can anchor temporarily in the southwest bight if the weather is fair and stable. Some small craft can anchor in stable weather on the east side of D'Arcy Island; however, the entrance is narrow and the bottom is rocky and uneven.

Anchor in 2 to 5 fathoms.

Hughes Passage

Hughes Passage lies between Sidney and D'Arcy Island.

Charts 3441 metric, 3313 metric
East entrance: 48°34.88' N, 123°15.93' W (NAD 83)
West entrance: 48°34.55' N, 123°17.93' W (NAD 83)

Hughes Passage separates D'Arcy and Sidney Islands. Its south side is encumbered by drying

> *and above- and below-water rocks.* (p. 126, SCG, Vol. 1; see also SD, p. 88)

Hughes Passage, 2 miles due west of the south entrance to Mosquito Pass on San Juan Island, is used by many boats headed for Port Sidney. Small craft may find temporary anchorage in fair weather close to shore on either side of Hughes Passage avoiding the rocks and reefs.

Cordova Channel

Cordova Channel lies between Vancouver Island and James Island.

Charts 3441 metric, 3313 metric
South entrance: 48°35.10′ N, 123°21.49′ W (NAD 83)
North entrance: 48°37.00′ N, 123°23.14′ W (NAD 83)

> *Cordova Channel separates James Island from Saanich Peninsula. Tidal streams in Cordova Channel, though weak, have a variable rate and direction.* (p. 127, SCG, Vol. 1; see also SD, p. 90)

In southeast weather, with an option of good anchorage in Saanichton Bay, Cordova Channel offers slightly more protection than Sidney Channel.

Don Douglass

Cordova Channel

Sidney Spit

Sidney Island is part of an interesting collection of small islands strung along Haro Strait. Some are privately owned, others are marine parks, and their shorelines range from rocky bluffs to sandy beaches. Worth millions of dollars in today's recreational real estate market, they were not always so highly prized. Back in 1860, when the Hudson's Bay Company held an auction in Victoria for lots on Sidney Island, there were few takers and, as recounted in Walbran's *British Columbia Coast Names*, one skeptical settler remarked that "he would not give six-pence an acre let alone six shillings."

Sidney Island has since become the "Pearl of the Gulf Islands," enjoyed each summer by hundreds of boaters and by visitors from Sidney who arrive by passenger ferry. A long spit of soft sand extends from the island's northern tip where a marine park with on-shore trails, picnic facilities and campsites is located.

The sandy beaches of Sidney Island and neighboring James Island are drift deposits left behind by retreating glaciers some 10,000 years ago. These land forms of ground-up sand, gravel and clay are subject to erosion with coastlines that are shallow and constantly shifting, but they provide beautiful beaches such as the one at Sidney Spit which is ideal for sunbathing and swimming in the warm water.

In the early 1900s, before Sidney Island became a vacation playground, the island's clay was scraped from the ground and turned into bricks at a local mill, its ruins located in the meadow that borders a saltwater lagoon at the south end of the park. The rest of Sidney Island is in private hands, as is James Island where an explosives plant once operated. Currently owned by a Seattle billionaire, James Island has become a multi-million-dollar retreat with sandy beaches, a golf course and other amenities.

—**AV**

Anne Vipond

Sidney Spit Marine Park

Saanichton Bay (Vancouver Island)

Saanichton Bay is 3.3 miles south of Sidney Harbour.

Charts 3441 metric, 3313 metric
Entrance: 48°36.00′ N, 123°22.81′ W (NAD 83)
Anchor: 48°35.70′ N, 123°22.80′ W (NAD 83)

> *Saanichton Bay, entered between Cordova Spit and Turgoose Point, affords a good anchorage with protection from all winds. The holding ground is good and tidal streams are not significant.*
>
> *Privately owned mooring buoys lie in Saanichton Bay. The two charted buoys are for securing logbooms.* (p. 127, SCG, Vol. 1; see also SD, p. 90)

Saanichton Bay affords good shelter from southeast winds and currents in Cordova and Sidney channels. Anchorage can be found 0.4 mile southwest of Cordova Spit, avoiding private buoys.

Anchor in about 4 fathoms over sand, mud and gravel with good holding.

Ferguson Cove (Vancouver Island)

Ferguson Cove, just north of Saanichton Bay, is 0.8 mile northwest of Cordova Spit.

Charts 3441 metric, 3313 metric
Position: 48°36.08′ N, 123°23.45′ W (NAD 83)

> *Ferguson Cove, on the north side of Turgoose Point, is filled with a drying flat.* (p. 127, SCG, Vol. 1)

Ferguson Cove is a cable crossing area. There is a small public dock on the south side of the cove at Turgoose Point.

Bazan Bay (Vancouver Island)

Bazan Bay is 0.8 mile southwest of the Washington State ferry dock at Sydney.

Charts 3441 metric, 3313 metric
Position: 48°37.83′ N, 123°24.31′ W (NAD 83)

> *The west shore of Cordova Channel, from Turgoose Point to Bazan Bay, 1.8 miles NNW, is free of off-lying dangers. On the east side of the channel, an island and shoal water extend west from the south end of James Island.* (p. 127, SCG, Vol. 1; see also SD, p. 90)

Bazan Bay is a shallow, open bight useful as a temporary anchorage in settled weather only.

Sidney Channel

Sidney Channel lies between James and Sidney islands.

Charts 3441 metric, 3313 metric
South entrance: 48°34.91′ N, 123°18.68′ W (NAD 83)
North entrance: 48°37.75′ N, 123°21.42′ W (NAD 83)

> *Sidney Channel is entered from the south between James Spit and D'Arcy Island; its north entrance is between the north extremities of James and Sidney Islands.* (p. 126, SCG, Vol. 1; see also SD, p. 90)

Peter Fromm

Beachcombing reveals nature's art

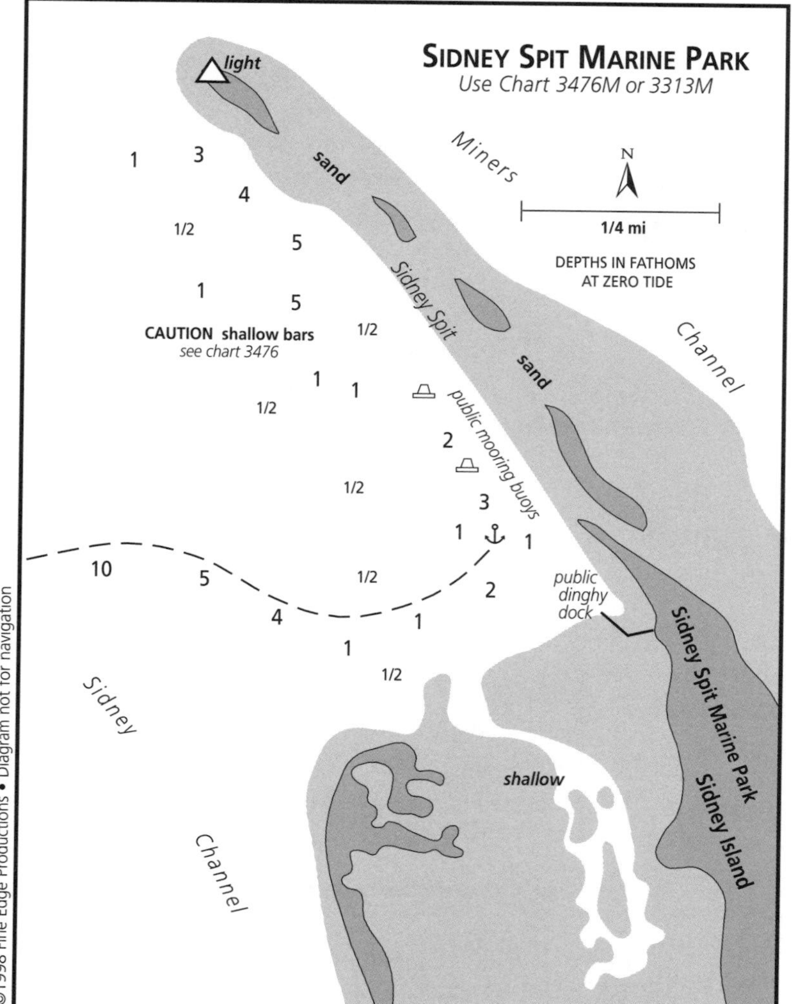

Strong ebb currents may be experienced in Sidney Channel, as well as choppy waters when a southeast wind is blowing.

Sidney Spit Marine Park (Sidney Island)

Sidney Spit Marine Park is 2.3 miles southeast of Sidney Harbour breakwater.

Charts 3441 metric, 3313 metric
Entrance: 48°38.47′ N, 123°20.87′ W (NAD 83)
Float: 48°38.50′ N, 123°19.93′ W (NAD 83)
Anchor: 48°38.58′ N, 123°20.16′ W (NAD 83)

Sidney Spit Marine Park is at the north end of Sidney Island. There are plastic donut mooring buoys and a landing float for small craft. Craft can anchor on a sand bottom or moor on the west side of the spit; the minimum depth in the anchorage is about 3 feet (0.9 m). Entry is made between the shoal areas which are covered by eel grass. Camping and picnic facilities and drinking water are available.
(p. 127, SCG, Vol. 1)

Sidney Spit Marine Park is located on a low, sandy spit about a mile long with a sand, grass and gravel beach. Douglas fir and arbutus grow at its grassy south end. The bottom is shallow and flat over a large area. In summer, you may be able to pick up one of the 35 mooring buoys or tie to a small craft landing float. Although the park is open all year, in winter, with the passage of fronts, strong northwest winds can create an uncomfortable chop. A hiking trail loops around the park and out to the north end of the spit. You can easily land a dinghy inside the spit, comb the outer beach for driftwood, or use the excellent facilities that include picnic tables, toilets, a campfire ring, and play areas. During summer months, a passenger ferry connects to Sidney.

Anchorage can be found on the west side of Sidney Spit in the small 3-fathom hole northwest of the dinghy float, or farther west in the channel between the two shoal areas extending south from Sidney Spit light.

Anchor in 2 to 3 fathoms over a sandy bottom with good holding.

Isle-de-Lis Marine Park (Rum Island)

Isle-de-Lis Marine Park is 2.8 miles northeast of Sydney Spit immediately east of Gooch Island.

Charts 3441 metric, 3313 metric
Anchor: 48°39.83′ N, 123°16.85′ W (NAD 83)

> *Isle-de-Lis Marine Park, on Rum Island, is undeveloped and camping is not permitted. It is reported that anchorage can be obtained on the north shore of the island.* (p. 129, SCG, Vol. 1)

Undeveloped Isle-de-Lis Marine Park makes a good picnic stop in fair weather. Temporary anchorage can be found along the steep-to shoreline.

Anchor in about 5 fathoms.

Sidney (Vancouver Island)

Sidney, 2.3 miles south of the Swartz Bay ferry terminal, is 14 miles north of Victoria.

Charts 3476 metric, 3441 metric, 3313 metric
Entrance (0.067 mile north of green Buoy "U-5"): 48°38.89′ N, 123°23.31′ W (NAD 83)
Public pier: 48°38.96′ N, 123°23.56′ W (NAD 83)
Temporary anchorage: 48°39.02′ N, 123°23.54′ W (NAD 83)
Breakwater light to Port Sidney: 48°39.15′ N, 123°23.52′ W (NAD 83)

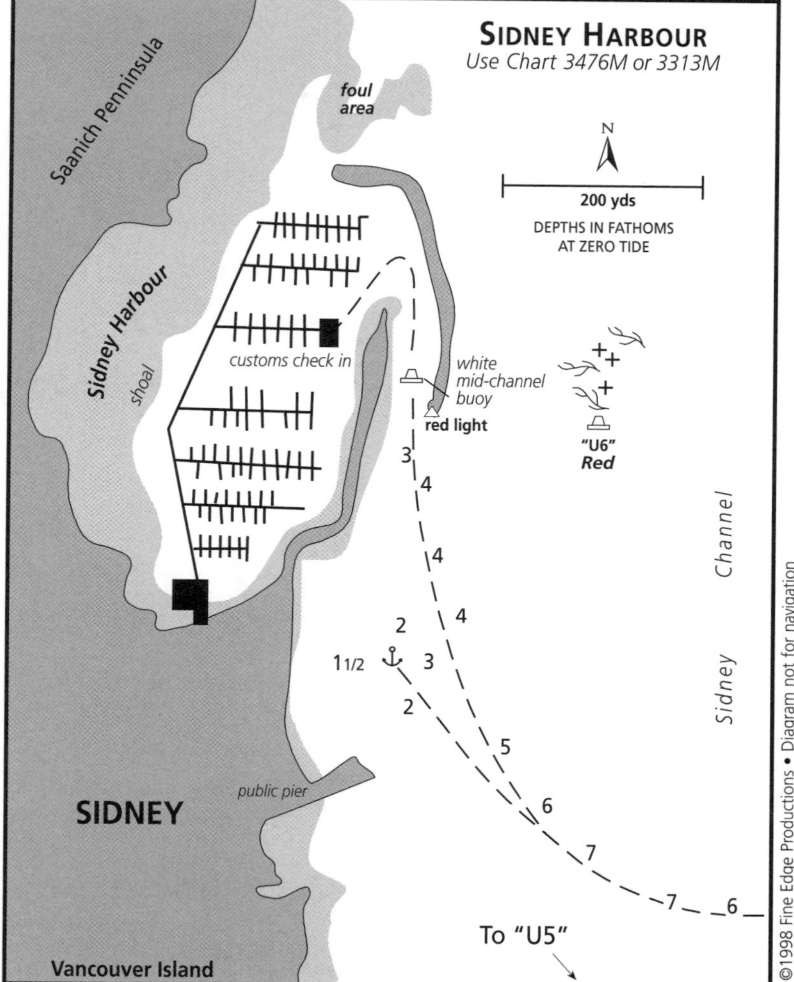

Islands disappearing into the sunset

> *Sidney . . . is a terminus of the Washington State Ferry which runs to Anacortes; the Victoria International Airport is close west of the town site.*
>
> *A marina, protected by a rock breakwater extending 250 m (810 ft) north from a point close north of the public wharf and a second rock breakwater extending south from drying ledges 0.3 mile north of the public wharf, has a drying rock 90 m (295 ft) west of the north end of the south breakwater. The entrance between the breakwaters is about 30 m (98 ft) wide with depths of about 2 m (7 ft) alongside the floats.*

The Washington State Ferry landing is 0.4 mile south of the public wharf. (p. 92, SD)

Sidney, whose origins date back to the late nineteenth century, has become a major seaside resort. The public pier is used by commercial fishing boats only; there is no sheltered anchorage at Sidney, except for temporary anchorage just north of the pier in 1 to 3 fathoms as noted in the Sidney Harbour diagram.

Located behind the rock breakwater, Port Sidney Marina is the lovely, large marina entered between green Buoy "U-5" and red Buoy "U-6." Reefs that extend between the north breakwater and shore are not visible at high tides, so do not attempt to enter from the north in anything larger than a kayak. You can clear Customs by phone from the outer dock; there is a fee for overnight moorage and facilities are excellent.

The town of 11,000, just a few blocks from the marina, has full services with many fine stores, restaurants, and bakeries. Tanner's Bookstore has a good selection of books and charts.

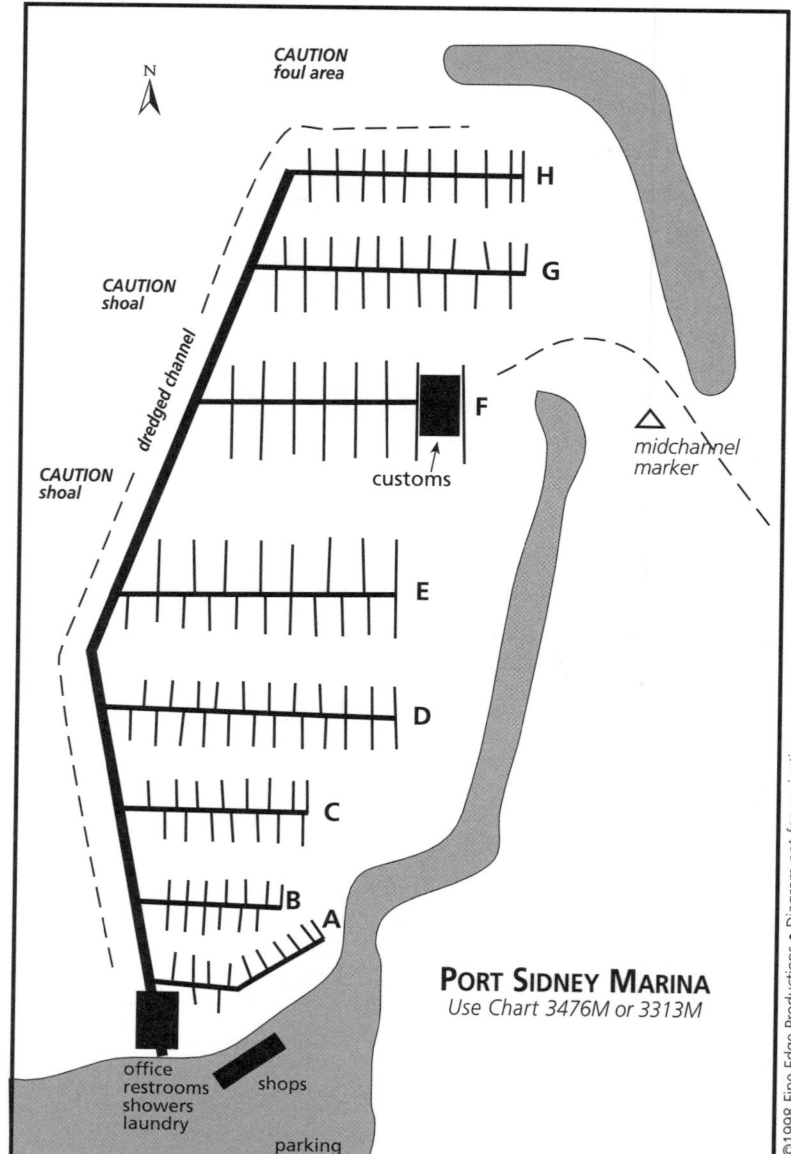

Sidney

Sidney by the Sea has retained its small town charm while providing visiting boaters with modern facilities at the Port Sidney Marina. Customs can be cleared here, and the marina provides a courtesy shuttle bus to Victoria and the Butchart Gardens. Other waterfront attractions include a seafront walkway and shoreside restaurants, including the Hotel Sidney with its coffee shop and sea view dining room. Beacon Avenue leads from the waterfront into the heart of town. The street which is lined with specialty shops and other services leads to a grocery and liquor store.

At the foot of Beacon Avenue is the Sidney Museum with two distinct collections. One consists of historical photographs and artifacts portraying the lives of the area's Coast Salish natives and early settlers. The other exhibit traces the biology and evolution of whales with models, skeletons and murals. Admission is by donation and whale watching tours are available—three resident pods of killer whale frequent the waters off Sidney.

—**AV**

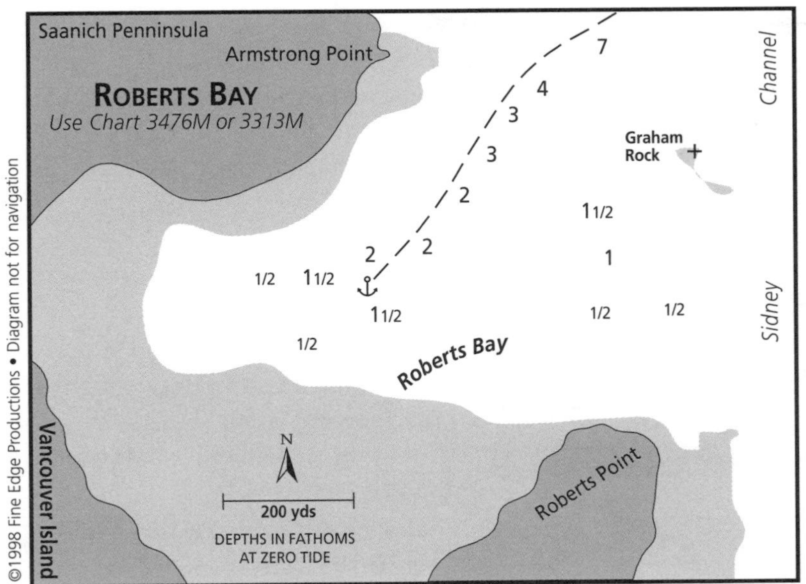

Roberts Bay (Vancouver Island)

Roberts Bay is 0.75 mile north of Sidney Marina.

Charts 3476 metric, 3441 metric, 3313 metric
Entrance: 48°40.02′ N, 123°23.64′ W (NAD 83)
Anchor: 48°39.86′ N, 123°23.87′ W (NAD 83)

> *Roberts Bay, entered between Roberts Point and Armstrong Point, is filled with an extensive mud flat. It is used by small craft and there is a launching ramp.* (p. 132, SCG, Vol. 1)

If you need to wait for proper tide or current conditions in the area, shallow Roberts Bay, bordered by lovely homes, offers temporary anchorage. Avoid Graham Rock at the entrance and drying mud flats and shoals inside the 1-fathom curve.

Anchor in 2 fathoms over mud and sand with good holding.

Anne Vipond

The commercial pier, Sidney Harbour

Tsehum Harbour (Vancouver Island)

Tsehum Harbour is 1.25 miles northwest of Sidney Marina.

Charts 3476 metric, 3441 metric, 3313 metric
Outer entrance: 48°40.25′ N, 123°23.85′ W (NAD 83)
Entrance (0.04 mile northeast of Thumb Point breakwater light): 48°40.29′ N, 123°24.24′ W (NAD 83)
Anchor: 48°40.32′ N, 123°24.78′ W (NAD 83)

> *Tsehum Harbour . . . is entered between Armstrong Point and Curteis Point, 0.45 mile north. The harbour, extensively used by small craft, is well marked by lights, daybeacons and buoys.* (p. 132, SCG, Vol. 1)

Tsehum (pronounced "see-'em" from the Cowichan word for "clay") Harbour, an inlet known locally as Shoal Harbour for its shallow depths, has a number of public and private marinas and yacht clubs that cater to pleasure craft. Van Isle Marina in All Bay, the first marina at the south end, has Customs check-in by telephone, a fuel dock, laundry, showers and electricity. This is a busy marina, so it's a good idea to call ahead for availability (tel: 250-656-1138).

Blue Heron Basin lies in the western end of the harbor; the north channel has several marinas and an outstation of the Royal Victoria Yacht Club. There are additional marinas within Tsehum Harbour.

Anchorage can be found 0.1 mile southeast of Mill Point in the

Anne Vipond

Boathouses in Tsehum Harbour

west end of Tsehum Harbour avoiding the rocky shoals.

Anchor in about 1 fathom over mud with good holding.

Van Isle Marina (Vancouver Island)

Van Isle Marina, on the south shore of Tsehum Harbor, is just inside the breakwater.

Charts 3476 metric, 3441 metric, 3313 metric
Fuel dock: 48°40.25′ N, 123°24.41′ W (NAD 83)

> *. . . customs clearance can be obtained at Van Isle Marina by calling the Customs House at Sidney.* (p. 132, SCG, Vol. 1)

Newly enlarged Van Isle Marina has a fuel dock and full marine facilities. Transient as well as long-term moorage is available, but they recommend phoning ahead for availability (tel: 250-656-1138).

Tsehum Harbour Authority Wharf (All Bay Public Floats)

The Tsehum Small Craft Government Wharf, on the south shore known as All Bay, is immediately southwest of Van Isle Marina.

Charts 3476 metric, 3441 metric, 3313 metric
Entrance: 48°40.23′ N, 123°24.48′ W (NAD 83)
Floats: 48°40.10′ N, 123°24.47′ W (NAD 83)

> *All Bay, on the south side of Tsehum Harbour, is entered between Thumb Point and a small island about 0.2 mile west; this island is connected to shore by a bridge.*
>
> *The bay between All Bay and Mill Point has numerous rocks in its entrance and extensive drying flats along its shores. A channel, boat basin and marina in this bay was dredged to a depth of 6 feet (1.8 m) in 1972.* (p. 132, SCG, Vol. 1)

Transient moorage is available at the Tsehum Harbour Authority Wharf in July and August.

Tsehum Harbour

This marina-packed harbour with its numerous sailing schools, charter operators and boat yards is the boating hub of the southern Gulf Islands. Van Isle Marina provides guest moorage (and Customs clearance) and a coffee shop on shore. Waterfront dining can be enjoyed next door at the Blue Peter Pub & Restaurant where guest moorage is usually available right in front of the restaurant. A short walk down Harbour Road toward Armstrong Point will take you to the Latch Restaurant, a timbered building with a huge stone fireplace, set among manicured gardens. Built in 1920 as a summer retreat for a former Lieutenant-Governor, it is now a restaurant open daily for dinner and lunch on Sundays.

Curteis Point marks the north entrance to Tsehum Harbour and it was there that Muriel Wylie Blanchett, author of *The Curve of Time,* lived with her children on seven wooded acres when they weren't exploring the coast in their cabin cruiser during the summers of the 1930s. Directly north is Canoe Bay (locally known as Canoe Cove) which is a good spot to tie up when meeting passengers arriving by ferry at Swartz Bay. The marina facilities here are excellent for doing maintenance or repairs, and just up the hill on the edge of the forest is the Stonehouse Pub where you can enjoy lunch, dinner or snacks with your pint of beer.

—AV

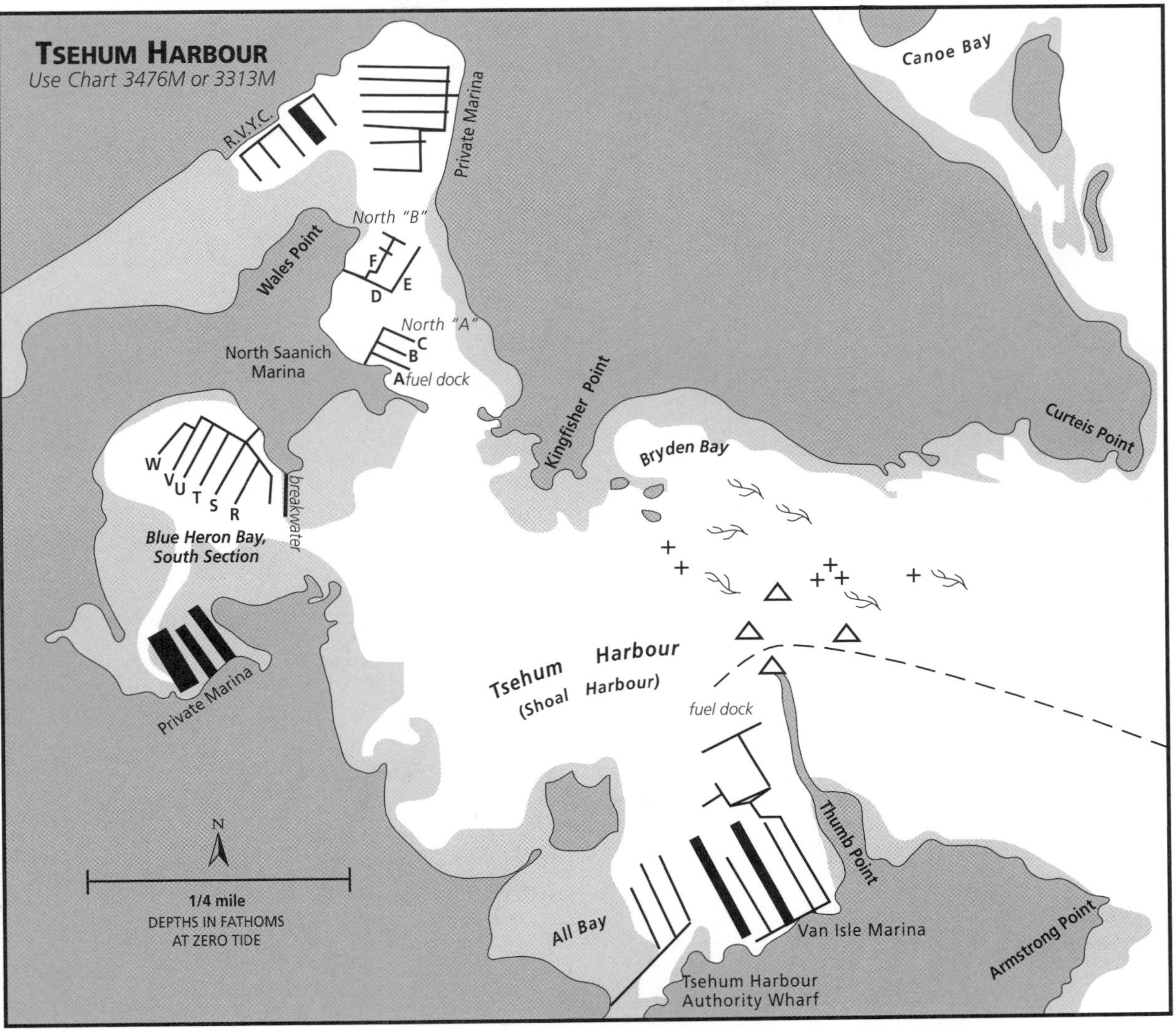

TSEHUM HARBOUR
Use Chart 3476M or 3313M

R.V.Y.C.
Private Marina
North "B"
Wales Point
F
D
E
North "A"
C
B
A fuel dock
North Saanich Marina
Canoe Bay
Kingfisher Point
Curteis Point
Bryden Bay
W
V
U
T
S
R
breakwater
Blue Heron Bay, South Section
Private Marina
Tsehum Harbour (Shoal Harbour)
fuel dock
Thumb Point
N
1/4 mile
DEPTHS IN FATHOMS AT ZERO TIDE
All Bay
Van Isle Marina
Armstrong Point
Tsehum Harbour Authority Wharf

Anne Vipond

Shore scene at Tsehum Harbour

Water, power, and phones are available; showers are located nearby (tel: 250-655-4496).

Blue Heron Basin (Tsehum Harbour)

Blue Heron Basin is west of Mill Point.

Charts 3476 metric, 3441 metric, 3313 metric
Entrance: 48°40.40′ N, 123°24.84′ W (NAD 83)

Blue Heron Basin, 0.2 mile west of Kingfisher Point, is entered between Mill Point and Nymph Point. A narrow channel leads

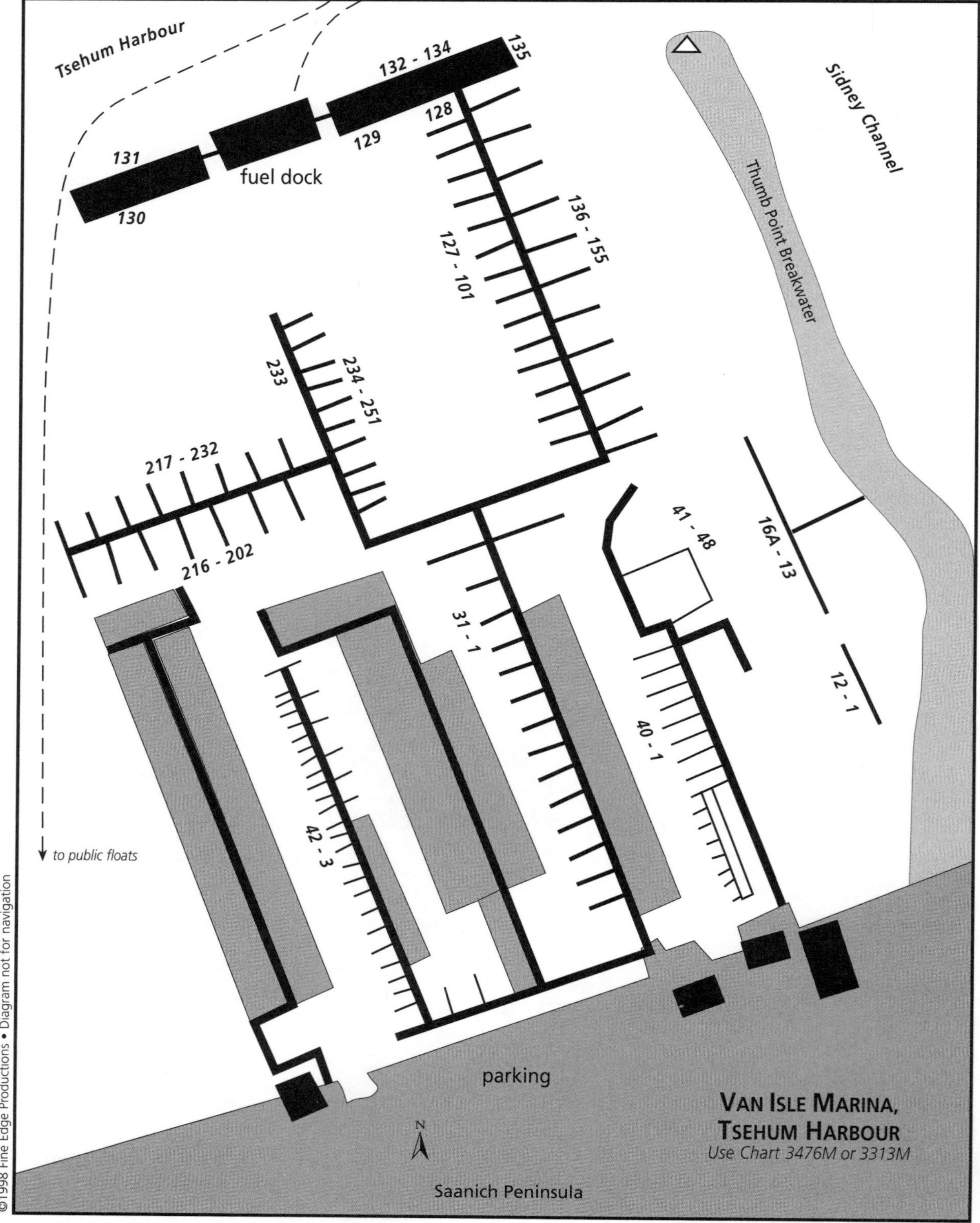

VAN ISLE MARINA, TSEHUM HARBOUR
Use Chart 3476M or 3313M

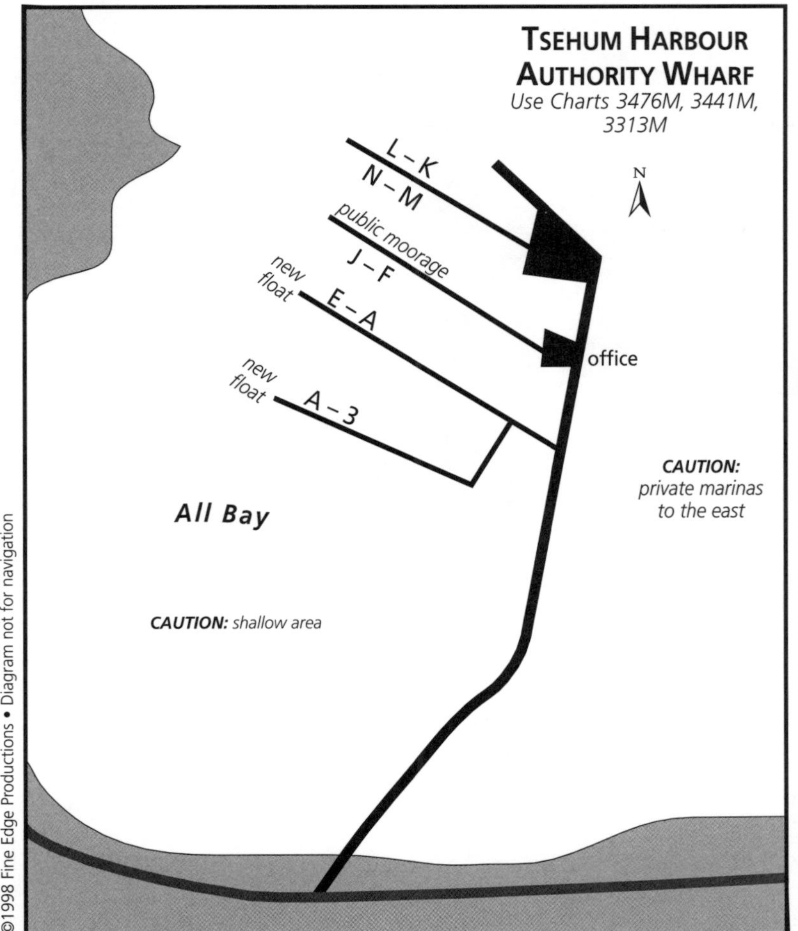

through the bay to two boat basins. The boat basin in the north corner of Blue Heron Basin is protected by a floating concrete breakwater. (p. 132, SCG, Vol. 1)

The marina complex at the north side of Blue Heron Basin is known as North Saanich Marina, Blue Heron Bay, south section.

North Saanich Marina (Tsehum Harbour)

North Saanich Marina is 0.15 mile northwest of Kingfisher Point.

Charts 3476 metric, 3441 metric, 3313 metric
Entrance: 48°40.42′ N, 123°24.74′ W
Fuel dock: 48°40.55′ N, 123°24.79′ W (NAD 83)

North Saanich Marina has a fuel dock and some transient moorage. The entrance to the marina is narrow and intricate, requiring close attention to the buoys and any opposing traffic.

Bryden Bay (Tsehum Harbour)

Bryden Bay is 0.13 mile east of Kingfisher Point.

Charts 3476 metric, 3441 metric, 3313 metric
Position: 48°40.47′ N, 123°24.43′ W (NAD 83)

Bryden Bay, close east of Kingfisher Point, has numerous drying rocks in it. (p. 132, SCG, Vol. 1)

Bryden Bay, located on the north side of Tsehum Harbour, has a shallow irregular bottom with many rocks and reefs, some of which are marked by kelp.

Page Passage

Page Passage, between Fernie Island and Harlock Islet, is south of Iroquois Passage.

Charts 3476 metric, 3441 metric, 3313 metric
South entrance: 48°40.61′ N, 123°23.67′ W (NAD 83)
North entrance: 48°40.94′ N, 123°23.76′ W (NAD 83)

Page Passage is entered from the south between Curteis Point and Kamaree Point. Fernie Island and Johnson Islet lie on the east side of the passage and Kolb Island, with Harlock Islet close SE, form its west side.

A speed limit of 8 km/h (4.3 kn) is prescribed.

Rose Rock, 4 feet (1 m) high, lies in mid-channel at the north end of Page Passage. Two rocks, with less than 6 feet (2 m) over them, lie in or near mid-channel.

A port hand buoy, identified "U7", marks a rock with 2 feet (0.7 m) over it lying in mid-channel between Kolb Island and Johnson Islet. (pp. 135, 137, SCG, Vol. 1)

Anne Vipond

Canoe Cove Marina

Secure anchorage can be obtained in Canoe Bay between the marina and Kolb Island. This is one of the few all weather anchorages between Oak Bay and Fulford Harbour. Numerous private mooring buoys lie in the bay. (p. 137, SCG, Vol. 1)

Page Passage is frequently used by small boats headed for Canoe Bay. The passage is narrow and has several shoals; caution is advised because of strong currents. Refer to chart 3476. Vessels headed for Colburne Passage can use the less intricate John Passage 0.4 mile to the northeast.

A small canoe passage west of Harlock Islet should be used only by kayaks and canoes; it is clogged with rocks and reefs, and its shallow waters are subject to strong currents and turbulent water.

Canoe Bay ("Canoe Cove," Vancouver Island)

Canoe Bay is 0.4 mile southeast of Swartz Bay and 0.7 mile northeast of Tsehum Harbour.

Charts 3476 metric, 3441 metric, 3313 metric
Entrance (from Iroquois Passage): 48°40.98′ N, 123°23.82′ W (NAD 83)
Outer float: 48°40.95′ N, 123°24.03′ W (NAD 83)
Anchor: 48°40.91′ N, 123°24.04′ W (NAD 83)

Canoe Bay, locally known as Canoe Cove, is approached from Iroquois Passage between Musclow Islet and Kolb Island. Numerous drying and below-water rocks lie north and west of Musclow Islet.

Well-sheltered Canoe Cove can be entered from either Iroquois Passage on the east or Page Passage on the south. Both have a number of unmarked rocks and shoals and reference should be made to the large-scale chart (1:10,000) 3313, page 7, or 3476 (same scale). During spring tides swift currents are encountered in the area. Since the cove is small, turning room is limited and a sharp lookout is advised.

Canoe Cove contains large Canoe Cove Marina (tel: 250-656-5566) complete with repair facilities and 24-hour customs check-in by telephone. From here, it's a half-mile walk to Swartz Bay ferry terminal. You can find temporary anchorage on the south side of the long marina floats where space is available.

Anchor in 3 fathoms over sand and mud with good holding.

Anne Vipond

Canoe Cove offers all-weather protection

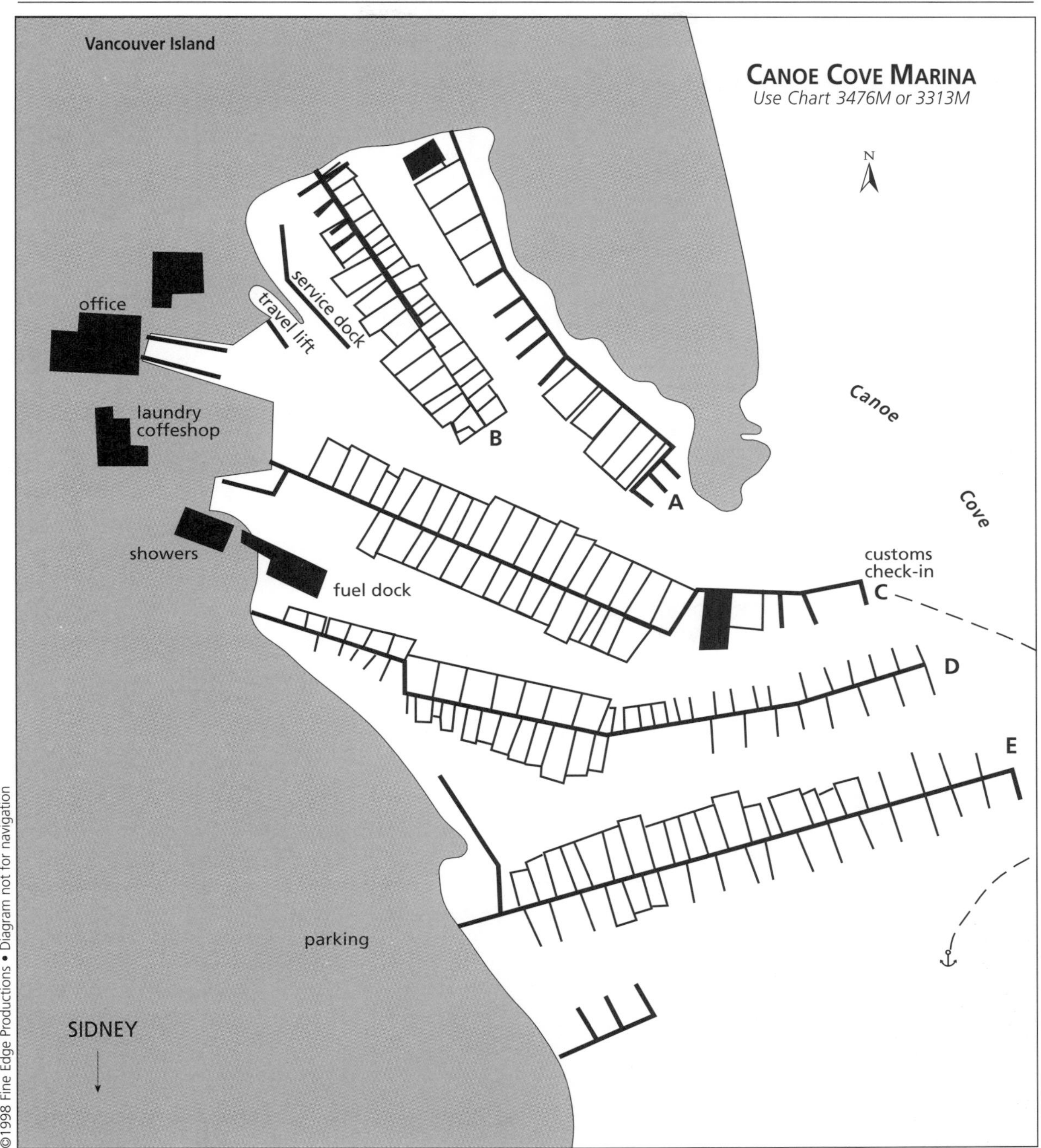

Iroquois Passage

Iroquois Passage, west of Goudge Island, is 0.5 mile southeast of Swartz Bay.

Charts 3476 metric, 3441 metric, 3313 metric
South entrance: 48°40.81′ N, 123°23.45′ W (NAD 83)
North entrance: 48°41.36′ N, 123°23.92′ W (NAD 83)

Iroquois Passage, entered from the south between Goudge Island and Fernie Island, leads NW passing east of Musclow Islet; it enters Colburne

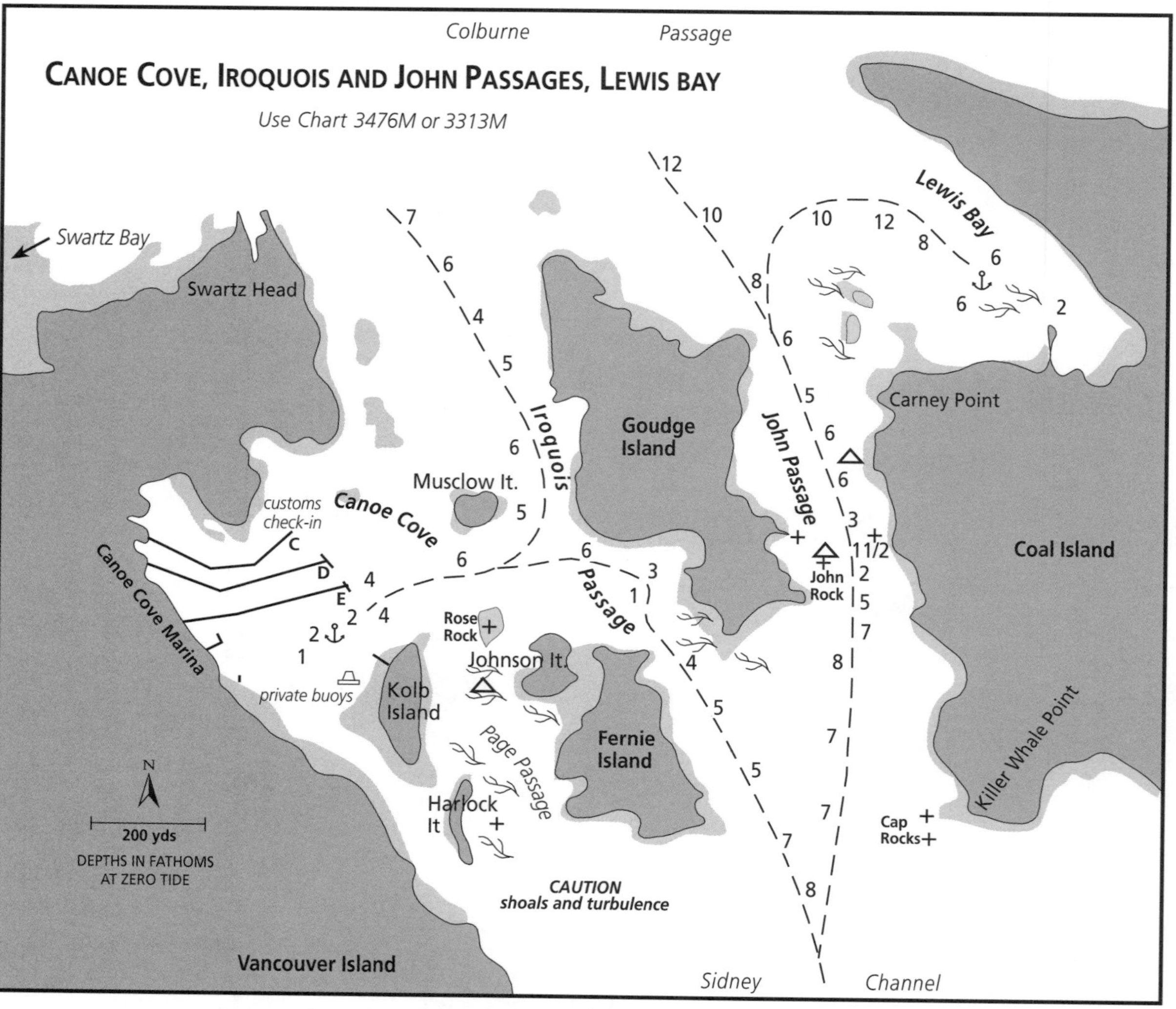

Canoe Cove, Iroquois and John Passages, Lewis Bay

Use Chart 3476M or 3313M

Colburne Passage
Swartz Bay
Swartz Head
Lewis Bay
Carney Point
Goudge Island
Iroquois Passage
John Passage
Musclow It.
customs check-in
Canoe Cove
Canoe Cove Marina
C
D
E
John Rock
Coal Island
Rose Rock
Johnson It.
private buoys
Kolb Island
Page Passage
Fernie Island
Killer Whale Point
Harlock It
Cap Rocks
N
200 yds
DEPTHS IN FATHOMS AT ZERO TIDE
CAUTION *shoals and turbulence*
Vancouver Island
Sidney Channel

Peter Fromm

A peaceful island sunset

Passage between Swartz Head and Goudge Island light. [A] *reef of above-water and drying rocks extends NNW from Musclow Islet to Swartz Head.* (p. 135, SCG, Vol. 1; see also SD, p. 93)

Iroquois Passage is used by pleasure craft for entering Canoe Cove or as a shortcut between Tsehum Harbour and Swartz Bay. As you enter the passage, favor the southwest side of Goudge Island to avoid the submerged mid-channel rock shown on chart 3476.

Minimizing Piloting Risks in Hazardous Areas

by Colin Jackson

Crunch! The boat comes to a sudden stop and the crew members are thrown forward against bulkheads and fittings. The 35-foot sailing yacht *Granite Seeker* has hit a rock at full speed. The boat is severely damaged and the crew bruised and sore, their holiday over.

Each year, many boaters find themselves in trouble because of the underwater features of this coastline. Accidents range from a light touch on the hull when attempting to enter a shallow anchorage or plowing into an underwater rock at full speed as described above.

Unfortunately, many boaters are unaware of the dangers and the potential severity of this type of accident. The first step to avoiding the rocks in B.C. is to have a healthy fear. Not to say that fear of rocks should prevent cruising, but at all times *any* sailor should fear an unexpected "landfall" in potentially dangerous areas.

A second step to avoiding rocks is preparation time with charts. I have interviewed many people who had accidents and it is surprising how many spent time studying the charts before setting out without ever looking for potential problems. In planning their passages, some actually drew lines over major hazards and during their trip proceeded to follow their plotted track, colliding with a charted obstacle. When looking through the charts and planning your routes, remember that identifying hazards near your intended course is as important as the actual bearings to steer!

Clear instructions for people on the helm is another important step to avoiding rocks. No one can steer to within one degree of a compass course, so instructions should include an ideal bearing for a lead mark, along with an acceptable range of variance, calculated in advance. As an example, a good set of instructions might read: "Steer for the light with a red band on top directly ahead of us. The course should be 250 degrees on the compass, but it may safely range from 240 to 255 without any problem." This kind of information is useful to the helmsman who would then know to alert the navigator if the bearing starts reaching the edge of the "safe range."

By establishing clearing bearings in advance, the helmsman knows when to alert the skipper. (Many accidents have occurred when the navigator was not on deck.) The only time a navigator should go below deck is in the middle of open water, when the helmsman needs only to maintain a course bearing and keep an eye out for traffic and debris in the water.

Navigators should avoid entering areas with unmarked hazards. The B.C. coastline is littered with so many rocks and hazards that it would be impossible to mark them all with navigational aids. However, where navigational aids do exist, it is a good idea to give them a wide berth, as they often mark one end of a hazard or the centre of a reef that extends several hundred yards. This is especially important with fluctuating tides: the potential for danger increases with a low tide, and the chance of disaster comes with a falling tide. Some sailors, with each successful trip, come incrementally closer to danger as their confidence increases. Their comment, "But I've been there many times before without a problem," demonstrates that an accident victim probably used progressively less care with each trip.

The final piece of advice is to *slow down*. When entering an area of potential danger, slow to a crawl and remember: when you are unsure, stop the boat, get a fix, then continue on a safe course. Speed increases damage from minor to major and exponentially adds to the problems created by underwater collisions. A tap at a half-knot can probably be fixed with a paintbrush. One knot means a bit of putty and an extra day out of the water for the annual haul out. But five or six knots could put a modern production boat out of commission for three weeks or more, with repair costs ranging from $5,000 to $30,000 and beyond.

There is nothing that adds misery to a holiday faster than an accident. In my mind, hitting a partially submerged log is an accident. Logs don't appear on the charts, but rocks do. Hitting a rock demonstrates poor piloting skills or carelessness on the part of the navigator. When I hear about a boat running aground at full speed, although I may ask *Where?* or *When?*, my only real question is *Why?*

Don Douglass

A motor sailor heads down Saanich Inlet

John Passage

John Passage, 0.8 mile southeast of Swartz Bay, lies between Goudge and Coal islands.

Charts 3476 metric, 3441 metric, 3313 metric
South entrance: 48°40.85′ N, 123°23.29′ W (NAD 83)
North entrance: 48°41.31′ N, 123°23.43′ W (NAD 83)

> *John Passage separates Coal Island from Goudge Island and is entered from south between Killer Whale Point and Fernie Island. Numerous drying and below-water rocks lie in the fairway.* (p. 135, SCG, Vol. 1)

If you're north- or southbound, John Passage is somewhat easier than Page and Iroquois passages, but it still requires careful piloting.

Lewis Bay (Coal Island)

Lewis Bay, at the north end of John Passage, is on the northwest side of Coal Island.

Charts 3476 metric, 3441 metric, 3313 metric
Entrance: 48°41.35′ N, 123°23.31′ W (NAD 83)
Anchor: 48°41.27′ N, 123°23.12′ W (NAD 83)

> *Lewis Bay, in the NW part of Coal Island, is entered between Carney Point and Fir Cone Point 0.3 mile north. A reef of drying rocks extends 0.1 mile NW from Carney Point. A rock, with 4 feet (1.3 m) over it, lies in the centre of the bay. A breakwater with privately owned floats close east of it are at the head of the bay.* (p. 135, SCG, Vol. 1)

Lewis Bay provides temporary shelter from southeast weather. Be careful to avoid the cable crossing on the north side of the bay.

Anchor in 7 fathoms.

Colburne Passage

Colburne Passage connects Haro Strait with Satellite Channel.

Charts 3476 metric, 3441 metric, 3313 metric
East entrance: 48°41.58′ N, 123°23.08′ W (NAD 83)
Narrows (midchannel southwest of Piers Island): 48°41.87′ N, 123°25.48′ W (NAD 83)
West entrance (0.24 mile southwest of Arbutus Islet): 48°42.22′ N, 123°26.43′ W (NAD 83)

> *Colburne Passage is entered from the east between Fir Cone Point, the NW extremity of Coal Island, and Pym Island. It leads west to Satellite Channel between Coal Island, Goudge Island and Saanich Peninsula on the south and Pym, Knapp and Piers Islands on the north.* (p. 137, SCG, Vol. 1)

Swartz Bay (Vancouver Island)

Swartz Bay, at the northeast end of Saanich Peninsula, is 2.2 miles northwest of Sidney Marina.

Charts 3476 metric, 3441 metric, 3313 metric
Entrance: 48°41.36′ N, 123°24.32′ W (NAD 83)
Public wharf: 48°41.25′ N, 123°24.44′ W (NAD 83)
Anchor: 48°41.29′ N, 123°24.38′ W (NAD 83)

> *Five ferry landings and one layover berth are in Swartz Bay. These ferries provide frequent service, carrying passengers and automobiles to Tsawwassen on the mainland, and to various places in the Gulf Islands.*
>
> *Small craft should, at all times, keep well clear of the ferry landings in order to give the ferries the maximum possible space in which to manoeuvre.* (p. 137, SCG, Vol. 1)

The public wharf, just east of the ferry terminal and north of Dolphin Road, is useful for dropping off or picking up crew who use the Inter-island or Tsawwassen ferries.

Satellite Channel

Satellite Channel is the main east-west route between Saanich Peninsula and Saltspring Island.

Charts 3441 metric, 3313 metric
East entrance: 48°45.56′ N, 123°21.67′ W (NAD 83)
West entrance: 48°44.71′ N, 123°33.57′ W (NAD 83)

> *Satellite Channel is entered from Swanson Channel at its east end; Shute and Colburne Passages enter its south side. It leads round the south end of Saltspring Island to Fulford Harbour, Saanich Inlet, Cowichan Bay and the south end of Sansum Narrows.*
>
> *The east end of Satellite Channel is frequently (twice an hour) used by large ferries going between Saanich Peninsula, and Tsawwassen on*

the mainland; these ferries use Active Pass. Smaller ferries cross Satellite Channel running between Swartz Bay and Fulford Harbour.

Tidal streams attain 1 to 2 kn in Satellite Channel. The flood sets NW and the ebb SE in the vicinity of Cape Keppel, the SW corner of Saltspring Island. (p. 140, SCG, Vol. 1)

Satellite Channel is used by vessels bound for Saanich Inlet or those northbound via Sansum Narrows.

Saanich Inlet (Vancouver Island)

Saanich Inlet is west of Saanich Peninsula and south of Satellite Channel.

Charts 3441 metric, 3462 metric, 3313 metric
North entrance: 48°41.52′ N, 123°30.35′ W (NAD 83)

Twelve-mile-long Saanich Inlet is known chiefly for its upscale settlement of Brentwood Bay and—for cruising boats—as the gateway to Butchart Gardens. Most boaters planning to visit the gardens moor at one of the marinas in Brentwood Bay and either walk from the docks or take their dinghy to the dinghy dock in Butchart Cove. Brentwood Inn Resort (tel: 250-652-3151) and Angler's Anchorage Marina (tel: 250-652-3531) both have full amenities. The public dock in Brentwood Bay has no amenities. The main street of the village directly above the ferry dock is lined with small shops and a good ice cream parlor. The ferry here runs between Brentwood Bay and Mill Bay.

Deep Cove (Vancouver Island)

Deep Cove, immediately south of Moses Point, is 6.6 miles north of Brentwood Bay.

Charts 3441 metric, 3313 metric
Position: 48°41.02′ N, 123°28.63′ W (NAD 83)

Deep Cove lies between Moses Point and Coal Point, 0.7 mile south. Several pilings and a rubble breakwater are at the head of the cove.

The remains of a public wharf lie in the south part of Deep Cove. The float was removed (1978) and only the pier remains. Numerous private floats and mooring buoys are in Deep Cove.

The marina, adjacent to the public wharf pier, has berthing, fuel, garbage disposal and sewage pumpout. (p. 144, SCG, Vol. 1)

Deep Cove can be entered on either side of Wain Rock. The cove is generally too deep and exposed for convenient anchorage. Avoid the rocks and shoals in the southeast portion of the bay by

Brentwood Bay and Butchart Gardens

The village of Brentwood Bay, with marina facilities, several stores and restaurants, is a popular sportfishing resort. Nearby are the world famous Butchart Gardens and any boater with a green thumb is sure to visit this dazzling display of flowers and fountains. Boats can anchor close by in Tod Inlet or in a cove at the inlet's entrance where a dinghy dock provides access to a path leading to the Gardens' back entrance, open during the summer.

Jennie Butchart began cultivating these magnificent gardens in 1904 after her husband's cement company had excavated a limestone quarry on their property. She transformed an eyesore into what is now called the Sunken Garden. A spectacular fountain was added in 1964 by her grandson Robert Ian Ross, who was given the gardens for his twenty-first birthday. Neglected during the war years, Ross set about restoring them in the late 1940s, hiring top gardeners and adding night illumination in 1953. In keeping with his grandmother's original vision, Ross maintained the grounds as a gracious private garden and left the plants unlabelled. He was known to stroll among the visitors, listening to their comments. Shortly before his death in early 1997, at the age of 78, Ross was still working at the gardens, parking cars and making sure the grounds were kept in immaculate condition.

In addition to the Rose, Italian and Japanese gardens, other attractions include a concert lawn, horticultural center, show greenhouse, restaurant and gift shop. At night the gardens are transformed by concealed lights, and visiting boaters often stay for the summer fireworks on Saturday evenings before heading back to their bunks. —**AV**

Peter Fromm

Finding a good place to beach a dinghy

paying close attention to the buoys. The Deep Cove Marina, which has limited moorage for visiting boats, is on the south shore of the cove (tel. 250-656-0060).

Towner Bay (Vancouver Island)

Towner Bay, 0.8 mile southeast of Coal Point, is 1 mile northwest of Patricia Bay.

Charts 3441 metric, 3313 metric
Position: 48°40.04′ N, 123°28.53′ W (NAD 83)

> *Towner Bay, north of Warrior Point, is fringed by a drying flat with numerous drying rocks on it.* (p. 144, SCG, Vol. 1)

Towner Bay is a tiny, shallow bight, too small to be of much use as an anchorage.

Patricia Bay (Vancouver Island)

Patricia Bay is 5 miles north of Brentwood Bay.

Charts 3441 metric, 3313 metric
Position: 48°39.43′ N, 123°27.31′ W (NAD 83)

> *Patricia Bay, known locally as Pat Bay, 1.5 miles south of Deep Cove, is fringed by drying flats. The Institute of Ocean Sciences is on the SE side of the bay and the Victoria International Airport is east of the bay.* (p. 144, SCG, Vol. 1)

Patricia Bay is the home of the Institute of Ocean Sciences and the Pacific Geoscience Centre. Temporary anchorage can be found in the north part of the bay, avoiding the government docks and buoys.

Mill Bay (Vancouver Island)

Mill Bay is 5.7 miles northwest of Brentwood Bay.

Charts 3441 metric, 3313 metric
Public wharf: 48°38.82′ N, 123°33.02′ W (NAD 83)
Anchor: 48°38.95′ N, 123°32.91′ W (NAD 83)

> *Mill Bay, on the west side of Saanich Inlet opposite Patricia Bay, is entered south of Whiskey Point. A rock, with 14 feet (4.4 m) over it, lies near the middle of the bay, just within the entrance.*
>
> *Mill Bay is a good anchorage. During winter months, or low pressure periods, Mill Bay is open to weather from the SE. Numerous mooring buoys lie between the marina and public wharf.*
>
> *The public wharf and float, in Mill Bay, provide 100 feet (30 m) of berthing with depths of 4 to 10 feet (1.2 to 3 m) alongside. A launching ramp is adjacent to the marina.* (p. 145, SCG, Vol. 1)

Mill Bay offers very good protection from prevailing summer northwesterlies but it is open to southeasterlies. The Mill Bay Marina (tel. 250-743-4112) is located behind the small breakwater on the west side of the bay. It has fuel, marine supplies, boat ramp, and laundry facilities. The public wharf and float, just south of the marina, are used by fishing boats. Anchorage can be taken over a large part of the bay, avoiding private mooring buoys.

Anchor in 5 to 7 fathoms over sand and mud with good holding.

Coles Bay (Vancouver Island)

Coles Bay is 2 miles south of Patricia Bay, east of Yarrow Point.

Charts 3441 metric, 3313 metric
North entrance: 48°37.59′ N, 123°29.08′ W (NAD 83)
South entrance: 48°36.93′ N, 123°29.07′ W (NAD 83)
Anchor: 48°37.66′ N, 123°28.15′ W (NAD 83)

> *Coles Bay, east of Yarrow Point, offers good temporary anchorage and has a pebble beach and small park. Larger vessels can anchor in 10 to 15 fathoms (18 to 27 m) in the middle of the bay with Dyer Rocks bearing 290°. Approaching Coles Bay*

from north give Dyer a berth of at least 0.5 mile to avoid the shoals extending south from them. (p. 145, SCG, Vol. 1)

Coles Bay offers fair-to-good protection in all but stormy weather. By avoiding Dyer Rocks, access is easy. There is a small park ashore with picnic sites and trails.

Anchor in 5 fathoms over a sandy bottom.

Anne Vipond

Tod Inlet

Thomson Cove (Vancouver Island)

Thomson Cove is 1.5 miles north of Brentwood Bay.

Charts 3441 metric, 3313 metric
Position: 48°35.96′ N, 123°28.63′ W (NAD 83)

Thomson Cove, 1.5 miles south of Dyer Rocks, lies north of Henderson Point and offers limited anchorage. Private floats line the shores of the cove. A large flagpole is on Henderson Point

A private warning buoy marked "Electric Cables—No Anchoring within 50 feet" is moored at the head of Thomson Cove. (p. 145, SCG, Vol. 1)

Thomson Cove, the small indentation on the north side of Henderson Point, has good protection from southeast weather. However, due to its depths and limited swinging room, Brentwood Bay or Tod Inlet are better choices for anchorage.

Brentwood Bay (Vancouver Island)

Brentwood Bay is 7 miles south of Satellite Channel.

Charts 3441 metric, 3313 metric
North entrance (0.19 mile northeast of Senanus Island): 48°35.71′ N, 123°28.99′ W (NAD 83)
South entrance: 48°34.99′ N, 123°29.22′ W (NAD 83)
Public float: 48°34.35′ N, 123°27.86′ W (NAD 83)

Brentwood Bay is entered between Senanus Island and Willis Point, 0.8 mile south.

Do not approach the Brentwood Inn Marina between the above-mentioned buoy and daybeacon, several vessels have grounded on the rocks lying between the buoy and shore.

The public float, 0.3 mile SE of the ferry landing, has 164 feet (50 m) of berthing space with a depth of 14 feet (4.2 m) alongside.

Medical, dental and hospital facilities are available at Victoria and Sidney. Retail stores, including a pharmacy and a post office (V0S 1A0) are close by.

Diesel fuel, gasoline, lubricants, provisions, ice and fresh water are obtainable.

A boat slip and hoists, with a 2 ton capacity, are available. Small craft hull and engine repairs can be carried out.

Regular bus service operates to Sidney and Victoria. (p. 145–146, SCG, Vol. 1)

Brentwood Bay with its entry to Butchart Gardens is a major boating destination. The bay can be entered from either side of Senanus Island. The south portion of Brentwood Bay has transient moorage available for boaters wishing to visit Butchart Gardens. The world-class gardens include over 25 acres of international floral exhibits, changed according to the season, and well-lighted for nighttime viewing.

Both Anglers Anchorage Marina (tel: 250-652-3531) and the Brentwood Inn Resort (tel: 250-652-3151) are open all year with full facilities. Anglers has Customs clearance; Brentwood Inn monitors VHF channel 68. The public wharf has no facilities.

Boaters may also anchor in the small cove in Tod Inlet 0.35 mile southwest of the marinas.

Tod Inlet (Vancouver Island)

Tod Inlet extends 0.8 mile south from Brentwood Bay.

Charts 3441 metric, 3313 metric
Entrance: 48°34.35′ N, 123°28.30′ W (NAD 83)
Anchor: 48°33.60′ N, 123°28.24′ W (NAD 83)

> *Tod Inlet, at the south end of Brentwood Bay, is less than 0.1 mile wide but depths in the fairway are not less than 30 feet (9 m) for 0.5 mile, whence it trends SE and shoals gradually to the head. The inlet provides excellent anchorage and shelter for small craft. Between Brentwood Bay and Tod Inlet in a small indentation on the east shore there is a float and two large yellow mooring buoys for the use of tourists visiting Butchart Gardens. Overnight mooring at this float is discouraged. Private boat houses, floats and a marine railway are at the head of Tod Inlet.*
>
> *A port hand buoy, identified "U21", on the east side of Tod Inlet, marks a rock on the outer edge of a small gravel spit.* (p. 146, SCG, Vol. 1; see also SD, p. 98)

Tod Inlet provides excellent shelter from all weather near its bitter end. The narrow, steep sides of the inlet create a sense of isolation from the bustling tourist center nearby.

Anchor in 2 to 3 fathoms over mud bottom with very good holding.

Butchart Cove (Vancouver Island)

Butchart Cove, on the east side of Tod Inlet, is 0.35 mile southwest of the Brentwood marinas.

Charts 3441 metric, 3313 metric
Position: 48°34.11′ N, 123°28.24′ W (NAD 83)
Butchart Cove dinghy dock: 48°34.07′ N, 123°28.21′ W (NAD 83)

You can take your boat into tiny Butchart Cove and anchor or pick up one of the four or five mooring buoys provided for visitors (limit one night). In summer months, however, when it tends to be congested, Tod Inlet is a better alternate anchorage. If you enter Butchart Gardens gate from above the dinghy dock, you must return via the same gate.

Butchart Cove may freeze over completely in a severe winter due to the fresh water on its surface. However, we spent one cold New Year's eve here without any signs of ice.

Temporary anchorage can be taken just north of the dinghy dock in 2 fathoms, sand, gravel and mud bottom with fair holding and limited swinging room.

Finlayson Arm (Vancouver Island)

Finlayson Arm, at the south end of Saanich Inlet, is 12 miles from Satellite Channel.

Charts 3441 metric, 3313 metric
Marina: 48°29.85′ N, 123°33.10′ W (NAD 83)

> *Finlayson Arm extends 3.5 miles south from Elbow Point and forms the south end of Saanich Inlet.*
>
> *A marina is on the west side of Finlayson Arm at the edge of the drying flat. . . .* (p. 148, SCG, Vol. 1)

Finlayson Arm, which extends deep into Vancouver Island, is a beautiful fjord. The mud flats and delta of the Goldstream River lie at the head of the arm. The river has a major salmon run in the fall and is a great place to explore by dinghy or kayak. Goldstream Provincial Park has campsites and trails, including a trail to the top of Mount Finlayson (1,365 feet).

Goldstream Boathouse (tel: 250-478-4407), at the edge of the drying flats, has moorage for just four to six boats. Facilities include water, toilets, a boat ramp and picnic area.

Misery Bay, the small bay 0.9 mile north of Goldstream Boathouse is too deep for convenient anchoring.

Peter Fromm

Island sunrise

7

BOUNDARY PASS TO ACTIVE PASS

Plumper Sound and Swanson Channel

The Gulf Islands surrounding Plumper Sound are sometimes referred to as the lower outer islands; to some boaters, they are the most remote and scenic in the cruising paradise of the Gulf and San Juan islands. Life is slow and quiet here, but serious currents and turbulent waters are found in the surrounding waters of Boundary Pass, Active Pass, and the Strait of Georgia. Safe inside Plumper Sound and Swanson Channel, the islands and sheltered coves take on an added charm. When gales are predicted in the area of Boundary Pass, you can head to Bedwell Harbour, Boot Cove or Hyashi Cove.

The northeast end of Boundary Pass brings you to Saturna Island, one of the largest of the Gulf Islands, but relatively undeveloped, with a permanent population of less than 300. There are many coves and bays to explore along the shores of Saturna and the smaller nearby islands of Cabbage and Tumbo. Cabbage Island Marine Park is a pretty spot with good crabbing in Reef Harbour which lies between Cabbage and Tumbo.

Sailing southwest, visit Bedwell Harbour, a customs port-of-entry, and take the Pender Canal toward Port Browning and Plumper Sound, or cruise up Plumper Sound, visiting the west side of Saturna and the eastern shores of South and North Pender islands. Beaumont Marine Park, on South Pender, is a popular park with a beach, drinking water, hiking trails, and campsites. There is a Public Market in Port Browning every Saturday morning from mid-June through October. Come early!

Hopscotching back and forth, visit North Pender, Mayne, and Prevost islands, then sail through Active Pass to the southeastern end of Galiano Island. Winter Cove Marine Park, Saturna Island, is a well-protected anchorage with good hiking trails and a great picnic area. Mayne Island is a quiet place of farms and orchards, with historic sites such as the Mayne Museum, Church of St. Mary Magdalene, and the Active Pass light Station.

Anne Vipond

East Point, Saturna Island, looking out on Boundary Pass

Boundary Pass

Boundary Pass connects Haro Strait with the Strait of Georgia.

Charts 3441 metric, 3462 metric
West entrance: 48°41.63′ N, 123°16.05′ W (NAD 83)
East entrance (1.6 miles northwest of Alden Point and 1.8 miles northeast of East Point): 48°48.00′ N, 123°00.50′ W (NAD 83)

> *Boundary Pass lies between Haro Strait and the Strait of Georgia, encompassing the area from Stuart Island to Patos Island.*
>
> *Boundary Pass is the channel most frequently used by large freighters. Operators of pleasure craft are reminded that for large vessels this is a narrow channel and their ability to manoeuvre is limited; it is advisable to give them a wide berth.*
>
> *Caution: Between Saturna Island and Patos Island the tidal streams are strong and somewhat erratic, with tide-rips and eddies; care should be observed when navigating this area.* (p. 180, SCG, Vol. 1)

Don Douglass

East Point light, Saturna Island

Don Douglass

Driftwood on the Tumbo Island reef

The international boundary runs down the center of 11-mile Boundary Pass in a northeast-southwest direction and the distances between the Gulf and San Juan islands vary between 2 and 6 miles. Boundary Pass is known for its strong currents, particularly ebb flows which include the outflow of the Fraser River. Tide rips, standing waves, and turbulent waters can be found during spring tides or when strong winds blow against the currents.

Prevost Harbour on Stuart Island and Bedwell Harbour on South Pender Island offer the best shelter on either side of the pass.

In restricted visibility it is particularly important to cross the shipping channels at right angles and to watch for high-speed vessels.

East Point Light, Saturna Island (Boundary Pass)

East Point is 2.9 miles west of Alden Point on Patos Island and 8.6 miles northeast of Prevost Harbour on Stuart Island.

Charts 3441 metric, 3462 metric
Position: 48°46.99′ N, 123°02.76′ W (NAD 83)

> *Boiling Reef extends 0.4 mile NE from East Point; a rock, 6 feet (2 m) high, stands on the centre of the reef. The area near this reef has heavy tide-rips and overfalls, which can be dangerous to small craft, and should be given a wide berth.* (p. 181, SCG, Vol. 1)

Tide rips, standing waves, and turbulent waters are found in the vicinity of East Point. This area is particularly dangerous on strong spring ebb tides when the Strait of Georgia empties its pent-up waters, including the outflow of the Fraser River. Boiling Reef offers good sportfishing in settled weather during neap tides.

East Point is considered one of the better places for sighting orcas.

Tumbo Channel (Strait of Georgia)

Tumbo Channel lies between Tumbo and Saturna islands west of East Point.

Charts 3441 metric, 3462 metric
East entrance (0.39 mile northeast of Boiling Reef): 48°47.66′ N, 123°02.22′ W (NAD 83)
West entrance (1.0 mile west of Tumbo Island): 48°48.09′ N, 123°07.54′ W (NAD 83)

> *Tumbo Channel, between Tumbo Island and the north coast of Saturna Island, is deep but has dangers in both entrances. A small cove on Saturna Island, at the east end of Tumbo Channel, offers shelter from west and NW winds.* (p. 213, SCG, Vol. 1)

Tumbo Channel, a deep-water route along the north shore of Saturna Island, is largely protected from the Strait of Georgia seas. The currents in the channel flow easterly during both falling tides and rising tides due to the back eddy formed off Boiling Reef. The private mooring buoys found along the Saturna shore, west of East Point, indicate fair shelter during summer weather. The west entrance to Tumbo Channel leads into Reef Harbour.

The south side of Tumbo Island, which is steep-to, can be approached closely to study the interesting sandstone cliffs. This same Chuckanut sandstone is found in Bellingham Bay and extends across the Sucia Islands and northwest along the south side of the Strait of Georgia. The tilted sandstone layers form many of the rocks and reefs which become hazards for boaters; the Belle Chain Islets to the northwest of Saturna Island are an example of this.

Reef Harbour (Tumbo Island)

Reef Harbour, 1.9 miles northwest of East Point.

Charts 3441 metric, 3462 metric
West entrance: 48°48.13′ N, 123°06.57′ W (NAD 83)
Anchor: 48°47.81′ N, 123°05.36′ W (NAD 83)

> *Reef Harbour, between Cabbage Island and the west end of Tumbo Island, can be used as a temporary anchorage for small craft; local knowledge is required.* (p. 213, SCG, Vol. 1)

Reef Harbour is a favorite anchor site for boaters who want a centrally-positioned overnight anchorage at the confluence of the Strait of Georgia and Boundary Pass. Approach Reef Harbour carefully from the northwest, avoiding the rocks and reefs off Tumbo Island. The east end of the harbor is quite shallow with a number of submerged rocks. Do not attempt to enter the harbor without carefully consulting chart 3441 and posting alert lookouts; not all rocks are marked by kelp.

Although Tumbo Island protects the harbor from southeast seas, the low profile of this island, as well as Cabbage Island, allows the wind to whip through the anchorage. Due to exposure to wind and the limited swinging room, Reef

Anne Vipond

Low tide on Cabbage Island, Reef Harbour

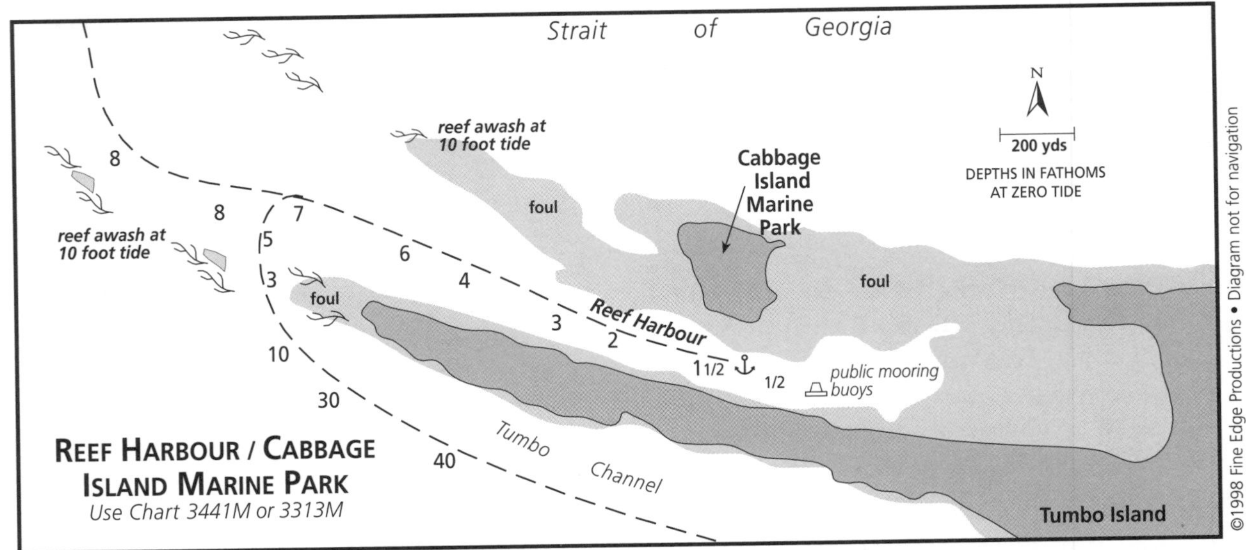

Harbour should be used only in settled weather.

There are several public mooring buoys in Reef Harbour.

Anchor in 2 fathoms over mud and sand with good holding. Be sure to check your anchor set.

Cabbage Island Marine Park (Reef Harbour)

Cabbage Island lies on the north side of Reef Harbour.

Charts 3441 metric, 3462 metric, 3313 metric
Anchor: 48°47.81′ N, 123°05.36′ W (NAD 83)

> *Cabbage Island Marine Park encompasses Cabbage Island; it is undeveloped.* (p. 213; SCG, Vol. 1)

Anne Vipond

Beach and anchorage at Cabbage Island

Don Douglass

Cabbage Island

When pioneer Isaac Tatton bought 11-acre Cabbage Island in 1888, he paid $1 an acre. When the provincial government and various non-profit organizations made a group purchase of the island in 1977, the price was $100,000. A year later, Cabbage Island became a provincial marine park, and the tiny island has been left in its natural state with few park facilities. Its main appeal is the lovely beach that lies along the island's southern shore. Mooring buoys have been installed in Reef Harbour and the beach is ideal for landing a dinghy. A leisurely hike around Cabbage Island takes about half an hour, and the cod fishing is good along the reefs and islets to the west. —**AV**

Exposed and windswept, undeveloped Cabbage Island Marine Park is surrounded by a large sandy beach with good picnic sites on its south shore. The shoals to the east of Cabbage Island have tide pools that provide fascinating exploration. The trees in the center marsh on the island were either killed by saltwater intrusion or blown down during a winter storm in the last decade. Driftwood on the island indicates its exposure to Fraser River outflow winds as well as to southeast storms, giving it a sense of isolation and vulnerability.

Don Douglass

Cabbage Island is exposed and windswept

Fiddlers Cove (Saturna Island/Boundary Pass)

Fiddlers Cove is 1.45 miles southwest of East Point Light.

Charts 3441 metric, 3462 metric, 3313 metric
Position: 48°46.82′ N, 123°04.93′ W (NAD 83)

Fiddlers Cove is too small for anything but temporary anchorage for sportfishing boats during prevailing northwest weather.

Narvaez Bay (Saturna Island/Boundary Pass)

Narvaez Bay is 2.2 miles southwest of East Point.

Charts 3441 metric, 3462 metric, 3313 metric
Entrance: 48°46.49′ N, 123°05.16′ W (NAD 83)
Anchor: 48°46.48′ N, 123°06.04′ W (NAD 83)

> *Narvaez Bay, entered east of Monarch Head, is free of dangers. It is not recommended as an anchorage, except in fine weather, as it is exposed to the east; with strong winds from that direction a heavy sea rolls in.* (p. 181, SCG, Vol. 1)

Narvaez Bay provides temporary shelter when seas in Boundary Pass are kicking up or a convenient overnight anchorage in fair weather.

Small boats find anchorage off the tiny cove on the south side of the bay with a modicum of protection from southeast winds. Avoid the several private mooring buoys in the cove. Larger

Don Douglass

Narvaez Bay, a fair-weather anchorage

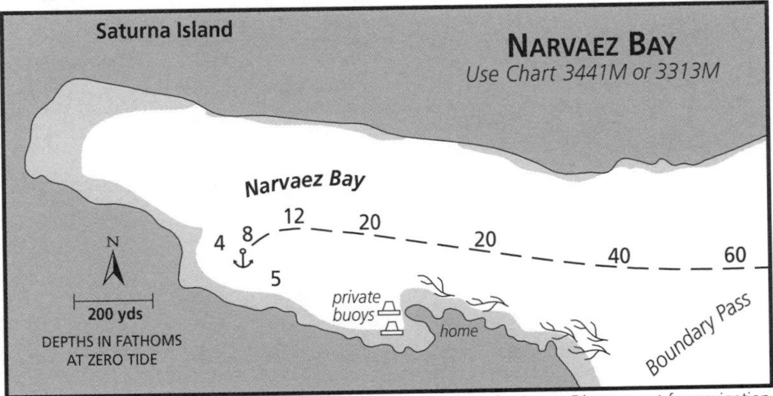

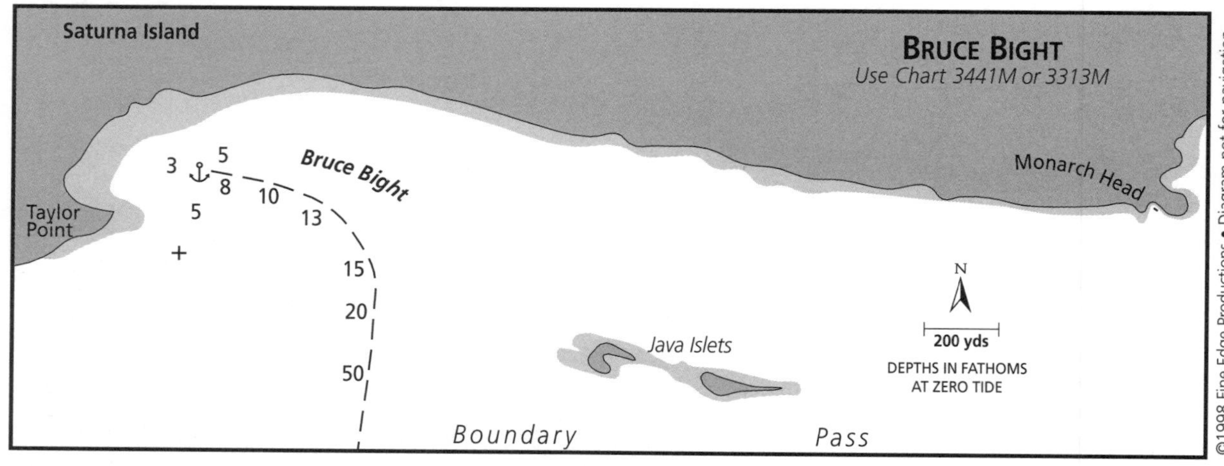

boats anchor off the head of Narvaez Bay.

Anchor in 2 fathoms over a mud bottom with good holding.

Statue of Washington Grimmer, early Pender settler

Bruce Bight (Saturna Island/ Boundary Pass)

Bruce Bight, immediately east of Taylor Point, is 1.4 miles west of Monarch Head and 1.2 miles southwest of Narvaez Bay.

Charts 3441 metric, 3462 metric, 3313 metric
East entrance (0.3 mile southwest Monarch Head): 48°45.70′ N, 123°06.02′ W (NAD 83)
South entrance: 48°45.66′ N, 123°07.39′ W (NAD 83)
Anchor: 48°45.90′ N, 123°07.71′ W (NAD 83)

> *Bruce Bight, close east of Taylor Point, affords shelter from north and NW winds.* (p. 181, SCG, Vol. 1)

Shelter from westerly winds is reported deep in Bruce Bight. Avoid a submerged rock 0.11 mile southeast of Taylor Point.

Anchor in 5 fathoms over a mixed bottom, fair holding.

Camp Bay (South Pender Island/Boundary Pass)

Camp Bay, 6.0 miles southwest of East Point, is 1.9 miles east of Bedwell Harbour.

Charts 3441 metric, 3462 metric, 3313 metric
Entrance: 48°44.43′ N, 123°10.64′ W (NAD 83)
Anchor: 48°44.66′ N, 123°11.03′ W (NAD 83)

> *Camp Bay, between Higgs Point and Teece Point, 0.3 mile NE, has drying ledges at its head.* (p. 181, SCG, Vol. 1)

Camp Bay is open to the southeast but provides shelter from westerly winds. The passage between Teece Point and Blunden Islet is clear for small craft, 6 fathoms minimum in fairway. Anchorage can be found at the north side of the bay.

Anchor in about 3 fathoms over mud, gravel and sand with fair holding.

Canned Cod Bay (South Pender Island/Boundary Pass)

Canned Cod Bay, immediately south of Camp Bay, lies 0.22 mile north of Gowlland Point.

Charts 3477 metric, 3441 metric, 3313 metric
Position: 48°44.35′ N, 123°11.00′ W (NAD 83)

> *Canned Cod Bay is a small cove, 0.2 mile north of Gowlland Point, on the south side of Higgs Point. A private mooring buoy is in the cove.* (p. 181, SCG, Vol. 1)

Canned Cod Bay, a tiny bay in the lee of Higgs Point, is used as a temporary anchorage by sportfishing boats. It is exposed to southeast weather and has limited swinging room.

Drummond Bay (South Pender Island/Boundary Pass)

Drummond Bay is 0.3 mile southwest of Gowlland Point.

Charts 3477 metric, 3441 metric, 3313 metric
Position: 48°44.03′ N, 123°11.44′ W (NAD 83)

Drummond Bay is a shallow bight that offers little shelter. It has a foul bottom.

Peter Cove (North Pender Island/Boundary Pass)

Peter Cove, 0.6 mile southeast of Bedwell Harbour, is 1.9 miles west of Gowlland Point.

Charts 3477 metric, 3441 metric, 3313 metric
Entrance: 48°44.32′ N, 123°13.83′ W (NAD 83)
Anchor: 48°44.32′ N, 123°14.00′ W (NAD 83)

> *Peter Cove, close north of Wallace Point, is a small, shallow bay, with a 7 foot (2.1 m) high rock in its entrance. The foreshore of Peter Cove is a park reserve. Several privately owned mooring buoys lie in Peter Cove and in the bay north of it.* (p. 183, SCG, Vol. 1)

Anne Vipond

Bedwell Harbour in autumn

Peter Cove, at the south tip of North Pender Island, has a good view of Boundary Pass to the southeast that can be used to advantage while waiting for conditions to improve before crossing Boundary Pass to the San Juans. It should be used as a temporary anchorage in settled weather only. The small cove is crowded with limited swinging room and private mooring buoys to avoid. *Caution:* The bottom is irregular and there are several unmarked submerged rocks, including a large uncharted rock in the southwest corner of the cove.

Anchor in 2 to 3 fathoms over sand, mud and rock with poor-to-fair holding.

Bedwell Harbour (North Pender/South Pender Islands)

Bedwell Harbour lies 4.2 miles north of Stuart Island's Prevost Harbour.

Charts 3477 metric, 3441 metric, 3313 metric
Entrance: 48°44.09′ N, 123°13.32′ W (NAD 83)
Customs float: 48°44.83′ N, 123°13.69′ W (NAD 83)
Anchor: 48°45.11′ N, 123°14.05′ W (NAD 83)

> *Bedwell Harbour, entered between Tilly Point and Wallace Point, 1 mile WNW, is formed by the overlap of North Pender Island and South Pender Island. Strong south winds funnel through the harbour, but no heavy sea is raised. Pender Canal connects the NW end of Bedwell Harbour with Port Browning.*
>
> *Anchorage, with the exception of in the vicinity*

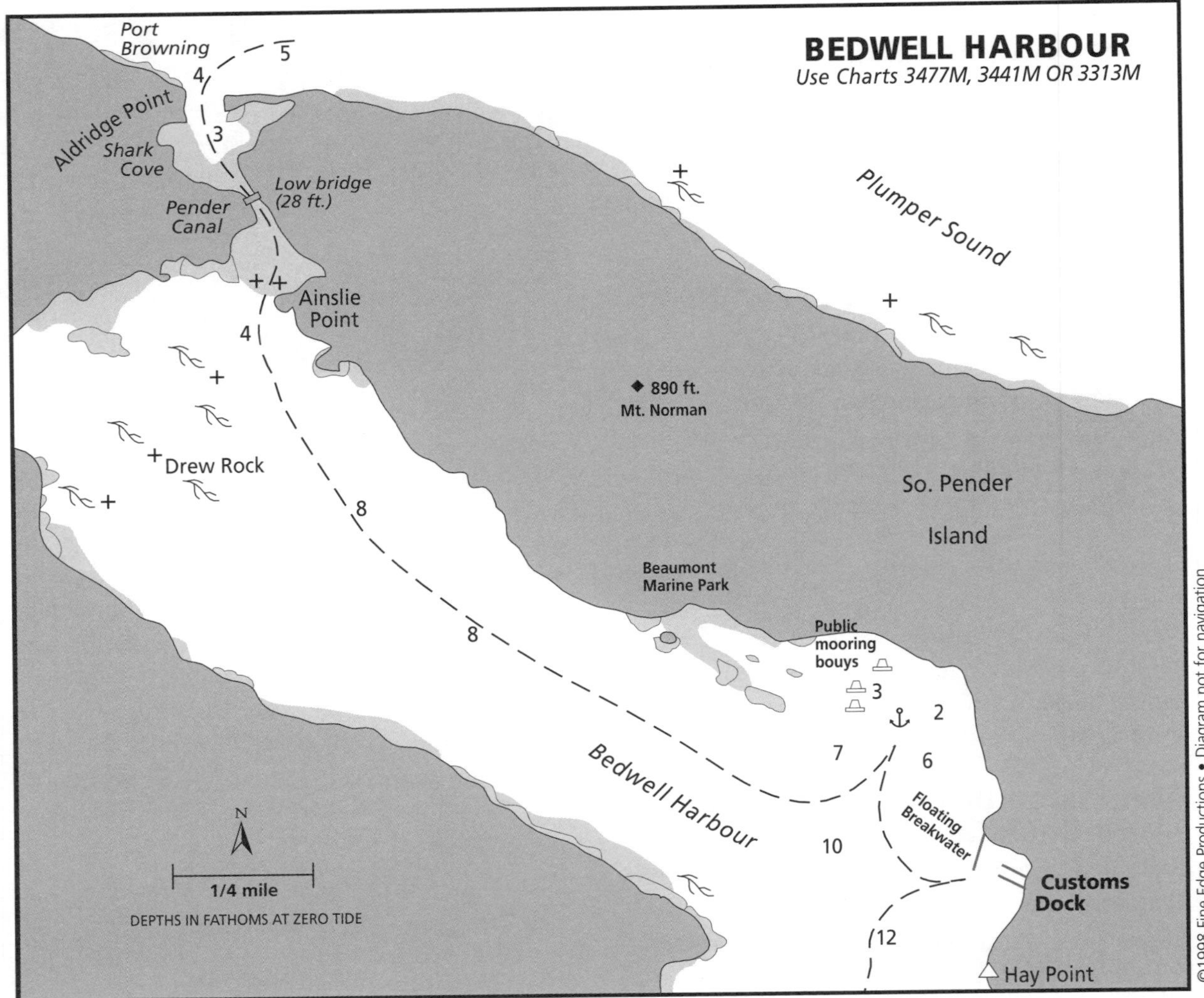

of the submarine cable, can be obtained almost anywhere in Bedwell Harbour. The best position is 0.2 mile SE of Skull Islet; in this position there is some shelter from strong SE winds on a good holding ground of stiff mud.

Four public floats, attached to the south side of the main public float, are reserved for vessels entering and clearing customs. They are 40 to 160 feet (12 to 49 m) long, in a T-formation, with 15 to 25 feet (4.6 and 7.6 m) alongside. (p. 183, SCG, Vol. 1; see also SD, p. 105)

Bedwell Harbour, at the south end of North Pender Island and the west side of South Pender Island, is the site of Beaumont Marine Park. The southeast corner of the harbor is known as Egeria Bay. Behind the breakwater is the Bedwell Harbour Resort and Marina which has a heavily-used Customs dock in the summer season. Bedwell Harbour Resort (tel: 800-663-2899, website: www.islandnet.com), monitors VHF Channel 68.

The most popular entry point for U.S. boats heading into Canadian waters is the efficient and courteous Bedwell Harbour Customs office—open May 1 to September 30, 0800 to 2000 daily. Since their customs operation is computerized, they frequently have your boat's information on the screen by the time you reach their office; they

Anne Vipond

Heading to the restaurant at Bedwell Harbour

can be called into service at other hours with an overtime fee required.

Good anchorage can be found to the southeast of the public mooring buoys.

Anchor in 5 fathoms over a mud bottom with good holding.

Beaumont Marine Park (South Pender Island)

Beaumont Marine Park, on the north side of Skull Islet, is 0.5 mile northwest of Bedwell Harbour Resort.

Charts 3477 metric, 3441 metric, 3313 metric
Anchor: 48°45.14′ N, 123°14.09′ W (NAD 83)

Beaumont Provincial Park, open all year, has fresh water, walk-in camping, picnic sites, and fresh water. The 143-acre park was once the site of an Indian camp. There are 15 mooring buoys, and well-sheltered anchorage can be found east of the mooring buoys. The bottom north of Skull Islet is shallow and foul.

Anchor in 4 to 5 fathoms over sand, mud and gravel with fair holding.

Bedwell Harbour

The ridges that run in a northwest-southeast direction on the Gulf Islands, formed by upthrusting of the earth's crust, now shelter such bays as Bedwell Harbour on South Pender Island. At its head is a large gravel beach backed by a brackish marsh used by a variety of birds. In an effort to protect these wetlands, the Pender Island Conservancy Association acquired Medicine Beach Marsh which is now a nature sanctuary. The bird life seen here includes great blue herons and ospreys.

Beaumont Marine Park, on the east side of Bedwell Harbour, provides mooring buoys, a beach and beautiful wooded trails. Picnic tables are stationed along the shoreside trail and serious hikers will want to follow the trail to the summit of Mount Norman where a viewing deck provides a panorama of distant islands and mainland mountains. Beaumont Park, established in 1962, occupies land that was donated by philanthropist Captain Ernest Godfrey Beaumont and by the Crown Zellerbach logging company.

Resort facilities are found at Bedwell Harbour Marina which is open throughout the summer, from Easter until the end of September. (Moorage with power is available over the winter.) Reservations are recommended, as the marina docks and government float are busy places at the height of summer when Bedwell Harbour is a popular port of entry for boats clearing Canadian Customs. The resort has a dining room and marine pub with an outdoor viewing deck as well as a swimming pool, tennis courts and art gallery.

The resort's site was once occupied by a tiny shack of a post office, built as a guard house by the crew H.M.S. *Egeria* in 1902, and four boathouses made of rough-hewn cedar and shakes. At the end of the First World War, a huge picnic was held here to celebrate the return of local men by troopship in 1919. "Boat days" were another island event, occurring once or twice a week when the coal-fired S.S. *Otter* would dock in Bedwell Harbour. In winter, when the ship was late due to fog, those waiting on the wharf would help guide the vessel in by their waving lanterns.—**AV**

Pender Canal (North Pender/ South Pender Island)

Pender Canal, dividing North and South Pender islands, is 1.4 miles northwest of Bedwell Harbour Resort.

Charts 3477 metric, 3441, metric, 3442 metric, 3313 metric
North entrance: 48°46.06′ N, 123°15.54′ W (NAD 83)
South entrance: 48°45.74′ N, 123°15.44′ W (NAD 83)

> *Pender Canal leads north from the head of Bedwell Harbour into Shark Cove and Port Browning. It has about 75 feet (23 m) wide with a least depth of 7 feet (2.1 m) and is fringed on both sides by drying ledges and kelp extends across the channel in places.*
>
> *At the south entrance to Pender Canal, a fairway is between two rocks; the east rock, close north of Ainslie Point, dries 4 feet (1.3 m) and the west rock has a depth of 0.1 m (awash).*
>
> *Starboard hand buoy "U54" marks the rock on the east side of the entrance and port hand buoy "U53" marks the rock awash. Passage into Pender Canal is made between these buoys.*
>
> *A highway bridge, with a vertical clearance of 28 feet (8.5 m) and a horizontal clearance of 40 feet (12 m), crosses Pender Canal near its north end.*
>
> *Overhead cables, close north of the bridge, have a vertical clearance of 37 feet (11.4 m).*
>
> *Tidal streams in Pender Canal attain 3 to 4 kn at springs; the flood sets north and the ebb south.* (p. 184, SCG, Vol. 1; see also SD, p. 105)

Don Douglass

Tight clearance under the bridge in Pender Canal

The route north from Bedwell Harbour through Pender Canal to Port Browning is scenic and interesting but suitable only for small craft. Boaters are asked to slow down and watch their wake through the canal especially when powering against the current.

The canal, 0.3 mile long, reaches its narrowest point (40 feet at high water) at the bridge joining the two islands. Since clearance under the bridge is just 28 feet, larger yachts and sailboats must use Swanson Channel to the west or Plumper Sound to the east when heading for Port Browning or points north.

Plumper Sound

Plumper Sound lies between Boundary Pass on the south and Navy and Trincomali channels on the north.

Charts 3441 metric, 3477 metric, 3313 metric
Southeast entrance: 48°45.10′ N, 123°09.25′ W (NAD 83)
Northwest entrance (0.5 mile north of Fane Island): 48°48.94′ N, 123°16.13′ W (NAD 83)

> *Plumper Sound . . . between Saturna Island, Samuel Island and Mayne Island on the east, and North and South Pender Islands on the west, is entered from Boundary Pass between Blunden Islet and Taylor Point, and leads NW to Navy Channel which in turn leads to the junction of Swanson and Trincomali Channels.*
>
> *Georgeson Passage and Winter Cove, on the NW and SE sides, respectively, of Samuel Island, lead into the Strait of Georgia. Port Browning and*

Anne Vipond

Port Browning

Pender Canal, between South and North Pender Islands, lead into Bedwell Harbour and Swanson Channel.

Merchant vessels use Plumper Sound as an anchorage. Several coves within the sound offer anchorage to small craft. (p. 190, SCG, Vol. 1)

Plumper Sound is a large body of water sometimes used as temporary anchorage for ships waiting to cross over to Vancouver Harbour. A 3-knot ebb current flows southbound in Plumper Sound on spring tides or during heavy runoffs in the Fraser River. Large northbound boats clearing customs in Bedwell Harbour frequently use Plumper Sound and Swanson Channel as alternatives to Pender Canal.

Port Browning (North Pender Island)

Port Browning, 2.2 miles northwest of Bedwell Harbour Resort, is 3.8 miles southwest of Winter Cove.

Charts 3477 metric, 3441 metric, 3442 metric, 3313 metric
East entrance: 48°46.06′ N, 123°14.08′ W (NAD 83)
Public float: 48°46.65′ N, 123°16.12′ W (NAD 83)
Anchor: 48°46.60′ N, 123°16.08′ W (NAD 83)

[Port Browning] *affords convenient anchorage, depths gradually decrease from 33 feet (10 m) at*

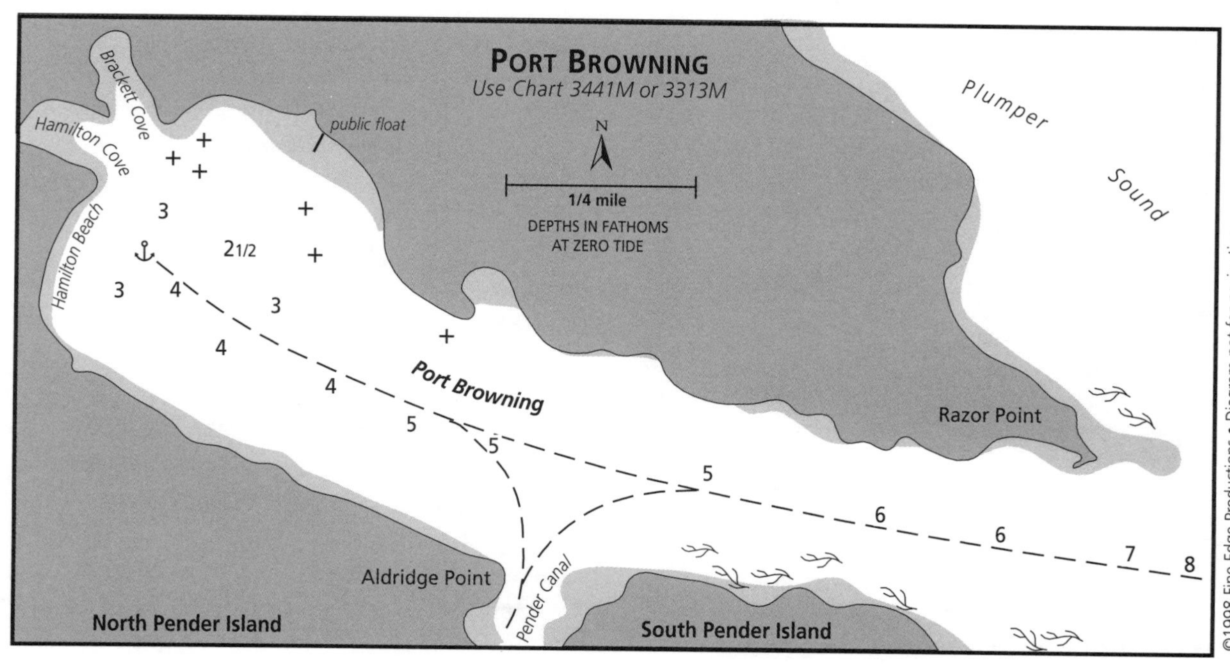

the entrance to 24 feet (7.3 m) at the head; the bottom is mud. (p. 194, SCG, Vol. 1)

For a quiet anchorage with easy access, Port Browning has lots of good swinging room in shallow water. A number of submerged rocks at the head of the bay are marked by the red Buoy "U52." Anchorage can be found southeast of the public wharf and float; take care to avoid the private buoys in the vicinity. For those who want less crowded surroundings, anchorage can be taken almost anywhere along the periphery of the bay. Because of the long fetch in Port Browning, the anchorage can be choppy in southeast weather; Port Browning Marina behind the breakwater in Brackett Cove offers protection in such conditions.

Anne Vipond

Shark Cove

Port Browning

Port Browning offers both a full-service marina and easy access to the Driftwood Centre, commercial hub of North Pender. Marina facilities at the head of Port Browning include a pub, restaurant, cold beer and wine store, tennis courts and swimming pool. Nearby is the Driftwood Centre with a grocery store, liquor store, post office, bank and bakery which serves soup and sandwiches. From May to October, the shopping center bustles with its Saturday morning Farmer's Market. An annual Fall Fair is held on a Saturday in late August at Hastings Field next to the Driftwood Centre.

The Penders were once one island, joined by a neck of land over which the natives would portage their canoes. In 1903, a short canal was dredged to accommodate small passenger steamships, and the islands were rejoined by the construction of a bridge in 1957. Thirty years later an archaeological dig revealed evidence of native occupation at this site which dates back several thousand years. Some of the artifacts found here are on display at the Pender Library, located about 2 ½ miles north of Port Browning on Bedwell Harbour Road.

The canal, which connects Port Browning with Bedwell Harbour, has a least depth of 7 feet and a vertical clearance of about 26 feet at high water. Explore by dinghy the "canal zone" if you are moored in Port Browning. The Helisen Archeological Site lies on the North Pender side of the bridge where roadside plaques recount the history of the area. On the South Pender shore is Mortimer Spit, its shell beach ideal for picnics while watching boat traffic in the canal. —**AV**

Anchor in 3 to 5 fathoms over a mud bottom with good holding.

Shark Cove (Port Browning/North Pender Island)

Shark Cove lies immediately north of the Pender Canal Bridge.

Charts 3477 metric, 3441 metric, 3442 metric, 3313 metric
Position: 48°45.95′ N, 123°15.55′ W (NAD 83)

Shark Cove, on the south side of Port Browning, is sheltered by Mortimer Spit . . . The cove affords very good shelter for small craft. (p. 194, SCG, Vol. 1)

Shark Cove offers excellent emergency shelter for small boats, but with very limited swinging room.

Pollard Cove (Port Browning/North Pender Island)

Pollard Cove is 0.4 mile southeast of the Port Browning public wharf and 0.5 mile north of the Pender Canal Bridge.

Charts 3477 metric, 3441 metric, 3442 metric, 3313 metric
Position: 48°46.38′ N, 123°15.61′ W (NAD 83)

Brackett Cove (Port Browning/ North Pender Island)

Brackett Cove is 0.2 mile west of the Port Browning public wharf.

Charts 3477 metric, 3441 metric, 3442 metric, 3313 metric
Entrance (breakwater) : 48°46.61′ N, 123°16.31′ W (NAD 83)

Brackett Cove, at the head of Port Browning, has a shopping mall including a liquor store, a neighbourhood pub and restaurant. Pender Island Post Office, the only post office on the Pender Islands is within walking distance of Port Browning.

A public float, 50 feet (15.2 m) long with 8 feet (2.4 m) alongside, is close NE of Brackett Cove.

A marina, protected by a floating breakwater, is on the south shore of Brackett Cove. When approaching the marina pass close to the end of the breakwater to avoid the rocks on the east side of the entrance. (pp. 194–195, SCG, Vol. 1)

Brackett Cove, at the bitter end of Port Browning, is the home of Port Browning Marina (tel: 250-629-3493). The marina, which monitors VHF channel 68, is protected by a floating breakwater. Fuel, repairs, and shopping, nice accommodations and full services are available. The marina is a half-mile walk from a shopping center.

Hope Bay (North Pender Island, Plumper Sound)

Hope Bay, on the northeast corner of North Pender Island, lies 3.2 miles west of Winter Cove.

Charts 3477 metric, 3442 metric, 3313 metric
Entrance: 48°48.24′ N, 123°15.95′ W (NAD 83)
Public float: 48°48.20′ N, 123°16.50′ W (NAD 83)

Hope Bay, 2.5 miles NW of Razor Point, is entered between Auchterlonie Point . . . and Fane Island. The settlement is on the main road system.

The public wharf is on the south side of Hope Bay.

Anchorage can be obtained in Hope Bay, about 0.2 mile south of Fane Island, in 43 to 52 feet (13 to 16 m), mud bottom. (p. 194, SCG, Vol. 1)

Hope Bay provides shelter in westerly weather; it is out of the strong current occurring along the east side of Fane Island that exceeds 3 knots during spring tides. Its bottom has irregular depths with a 25-fathom hole halfway between the public float and Fane Island. Anchorage can be found north of the public float avoiding private mooring buoys.

Anne Vipond

A calm and peaceful sunset, Plumper Sound

Welcome Cove (North Pender Island)

Welcome Cove, immediately north of Hope Bay, is 0.22 miles west of Fane Island.

Charts 3477 metric, 3442 metric, 3313 metric
Position: 48°48.41′ N, 123°16.57′ W (NAD 83)

Welcome Cove lies between Hope Bay and Colston Cove. It is reported that temporary anchorage can be obtained in Welcome and Colston Coves. (p. 194, SCG, Vol. 1)

Welcome Cove is a tiny, shallow indentation that offers temporary shelter to sportfishing boats. Avoid the reef 0.13 mile west of Fane Island.

Colston Cove (North Pender Island)

Colston Cove, on the northeast side of North Pender Island, is 0.4 mile northwest of Hope Bay.

Charts 3442 metric, 3313 metric
Position: 48°48.61′ N, 123°16.66′ W (NAD 83)

Between Fane Island and Colston Cove, 0.4 mile NW, two islets lie close offshore. (p. 194, SCG, Vol. 1)

Colston Cove, a tiny cove somewhat out of the current of Navy Channel, provides moderate shelter for sportfishing boats in fair weather. Avoid a rock and reef off its entrance.

Navy Channel

Navy Channel lies 2 miles southeast of Active Pass and 3 miles west of Winter Cove.

Charts 3442 metric, 3313 metric
East entrance: 48°48.94′ N, 123°16.13′ W (NAD 83)
West entrance: 48°49.63′ N, 123°19.64′ W (NAD 83)

> *Navy Channel leads WNW between Mayne and North Pender Islands and connects Plumper Sound to the north end of Swanson Channel and the south end of Trincomali Channel.* (p. 194, SCG, Vol. 1)

Navy Channel has strong currents during spring tides and can be choppy when strong southeast winds occur on an ebb current. Avoid the foul area behind Conconi Reef on the north shore.

Davidson Bay (North Pender Island)

Davidson Bay, on the north shore of North Pender Island, is 1.4 miles northwest of Hope Bay.

Charts 3442 metric, 3313 metric
Position: 48°49.11′ N, 123°17.97′ W (NAD 83)

> *Davidson Bay lies on the south side of Navy Channel, opposite Conconi Reef.* (p. 196, SCG, Vol. 1)

Davidson Bay, an open bight in Navy Channel, affords temporary anchorage to sportfishing boats in fair weather. Although it is exposed to the wake of passing vessels, it is somewhat protected from prevailing winds.

Gallagher Bay (Mayne Island)

Gallagher Bay, on the south side of Mayne Island, is 1.7 miles southeast of Dinner Point.

Charts 3442 metric, 3313 metric
Position (0.16 mile east of Conconi Reef): 48°49.45′ N, 123°17.30′ W (NAD 83)

Gallagher Bay, on the north shore of Navy Channel, is a small development in the bight behind Conconi Reef. It is useful only as a temporary anchorage for sportfishing boats in fair weather. *Caution:* North and east of Conconi Reef, Gallagher Bay has a number of isolated rocks.

Anne Vipond

Lyall Harbour, Saturna Island

Trueworthy Bight (Saturna Island)

Trueworthy Bight is 0.6 mile southeast of Croker Point.

Charts 3477 metric, 3442 metric, 3313 metric
Position: 48°46.27′ N, 123°11.34′ W (NAD 83)

> *Drying and below-water rocks lie about 300 feet (912 m) offshore on the west side of Trueworthy Bight.* (p. 191, SCG, Vol. 1)

Saturna Beach (Saturna Island)

Saturna Beach, on the south side of Breezy Bay, is on the north side of Croker Point.

Charts 3477 metric, 3442 metric, 3313 metric
Position: 48°46.66′ N, 123°12.16′ W (NAD 83)

Saturna Beach lies at the south end of Breezy Bay, an open roadstead on the west end of Saturna Island. The water off the beach is shallow, and the land behind is a bench leading southward below nearly-vertical Brown Ridge. Mount Warburton Pike (1,607 feet) is 1.2 miles east of Saturna Beach. The flashing red lights of TV towers on the peak can be seen for many miles in the Gulf and San Juan islands.

Breezy Bay (Saturna Island)

Breezy Bay is 0.4 mile north of Croker Point.

Charts 3477 metric, 3441 metric
Position: 48°46.90′ N, 123°12.23′ W (NAD 83)

> *Breezy Bay, between Croker Point and Elliot Bluff, is shallow; the deepest part of the bay has 8 feet (2.4 m) of water.* (p. 191, SCG, Vol. 1)

Small craft can sometimes find shelter from easterly winds over the large 1-fathom flat in Breezy Bay. The south end of Breezy Bay, which has private floats and mooring buoys, is known as Saturna Beach. Scuba diving is popular at the north end of Breezy Bay and along Elliot Bluff to the north.

BOOT COVE
Use Charts 3477M, 3441M or 3313M

Saturna Point (Saturna Island)

Saturna Point is 0.5 mile east of Payne Point and 0.8 mile south of Winter Cove.

Charts 3477 metric, 3441 metric, 3313 metric
Public wharf: 48°47.89′ N, 123°12.03′ W (NAD 83)

> *Saturna, close east of Saturna Point, is a landing for B.C. Ferries. A general store, post office (V0N 2V0) and pub are in the community.*
>
> *The public wharf, with a depth of 26 feet (7.8 m) alongside, is on Saturna Point. A float, 100 feet (30 m) long with a depth of 18 feet (5.5 m) alongside, is attached to the east end of the wharf.*
>
> *The ferry wharf lies close west of the public wharf.* (p. 191, SCG, Vol. 1)

Saturna Point has a small public wharf and a fuel dock just east of the ferry dock; a small village lies east of the point.

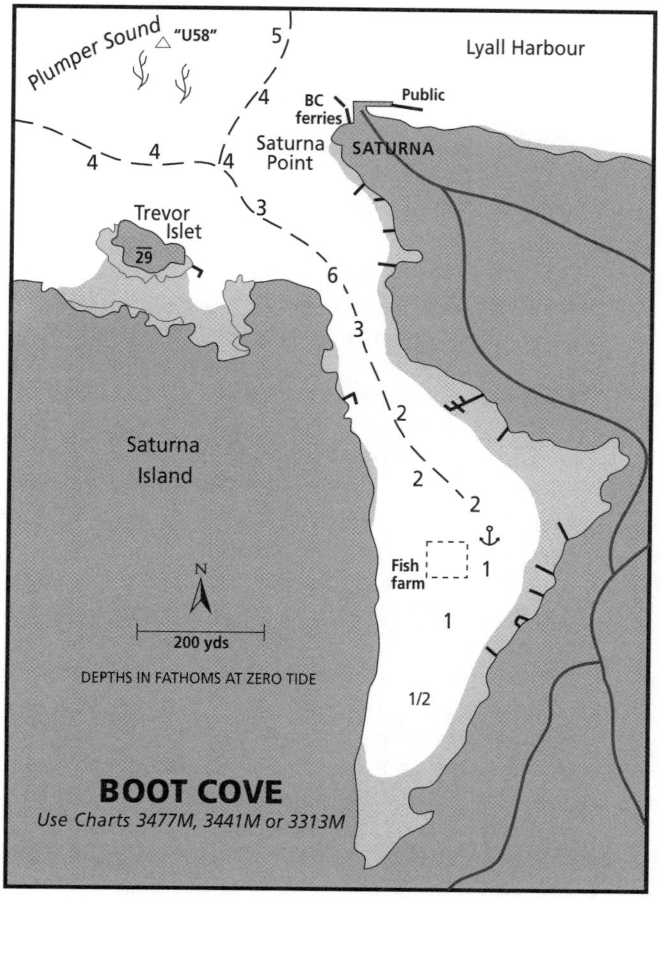

Boot Cove (Saturna Island)

Boot Cove is entered 0.1 mile south of Saturna Point.

Charts 3477 metric, 3441 metric, 3313 metric
Entrance (0.1 mile northeast of Trevor Islet): 48°47.82′ N, 123°12.19′ W (NAD 83)
Anchor: 48°47.57′ N, 123°11.91′ W (NAD 83)

> *Boot Cove entered between Trevor Islet and Saturna Point affords anchorage for small craft on a mud bottom. Favour the starboard side when entering to avoid the rock with 2 feet (0.6 m) over it.* (p. 192, SCG, Vol. 1)

Boot Cove is a narrow, landlocked inlet with very good protection from all quarters. The wind may gust here but there is little fetch. During southerly storms, the cove is subject to strong williwaws that descend from Brown Ridge. Anchorage can be found in the northeast corner avoiding the aquaculture, private docks, and mooring buoys all of which restrict swinging room.

Anchor in 1 fathom over a mud bottom with good holding.

Lyall Harbour (Saturna Island)

Lyall Harbour, immediately east of Saturna Point, is 0.7 mile south of Winter Cove.

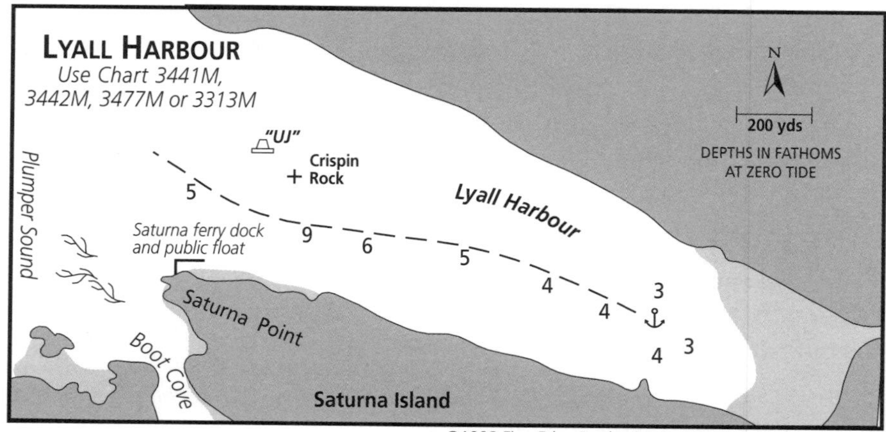

©1998 Fine Edge Productions • Diagram not for navigation

Charts 3477 metric, 3441 metric, 3313 metric
Entrance: 48°48.09′ N, 123°12.38′ W (NAD 83)
Anchor: 48°47.81′ N, 123°10.98′ W (NAD 83)

> *Anchorage in Lyall Harbour is sheltered from all but west winds and can be obtained, clear of the submarine cable area, in depths of 43 feet (13 m) in the entrance decreasing to 16 feet (5 m) about 0.1 mile from the mud flat at the head.* (p. 191, SCG, Vol. 1)

Lyall Harbour is easy to enter; anchorage can be found at the head of the bay off a drying mud flat with lots of swinging room. Some southeast gusts enter the harbor from the low pass along Lyall Creek. The public wharf just east of the ferry dock caters mostly to fishing vessels. There are no pleasure craft facilities other than the fuel dock.

Anchor in 3 fathoms over a mud bottom with good holding.

Lyall Harbour

Steep slopes line both sides of Lyall Harbour where hillside homes sit nestled among the trees. A small valley at the head holds a village with a schoolhouse, playground and two tennis courts for public use. A pair of rubber boots is recommended for hauling your dinghy across the muddy foreshore at low water. Sunset Boulevard leads through the center of the village to East Point Road. If you turn right and follow this road along the harbor's south shore you will soon reach the island's general store which sells groceries and liquor, as well as freshly baked cookies and bread from the local Haggis Farm Bakery. Heading in the opposite direction, you can take a scenic, two-to-three mile hike over fairly steep terrain to Winter Cove. For the longer trek to East Point, along the island's north coast, a bicycle is recommended.

The ferry docks at the entrance to Lyall Harbour where a pub/restaurant and store are located just a few steps from the government wharf. From here it's a pleasant walk along the road that rings Boot Cove. Serious hikers will want to tackle Mt. Warburton Pike, Saturna's highest mountain. It's reached by tracing East Point Road to the Narvaez Bay Road junction (location of the general store); there you take nearby Harris Road which veers to the right. Follow Harris for about half a mile, then turn left onto Staples Road, a packed dirt road that leads through a forest reserve to the mountain summit. Warburton Pike was named for an Oxford-educated and widely-traveled Englishman who arrived on Saturna Island in 1884 to take up sheep farming. Both an adventurer and businessman, he soon owned much of Saturna Island from Breezy Bay to East Point.

The first light at East Point was constructed in 1888, on land acquired from Warburton Pike. It was built following the 1886 grounding of the barque *Rosenfeld* when the tug towing her ventured too close to East Point. Boiling Reef extends about half a mile northeast of the point; before a fog horn was installed in 1939, East Point was widely considered the most dangerous point on the route between Vancouver and Victoria. The original lighthouse was replaced in 1967 with a modern house and skeleton tower. Natural attractions at East Point include the eroded sandstone formations, a protected beach and sweeping views across the water where it's not unusual to see a pod of killer whales rounding the point.

—**AV**

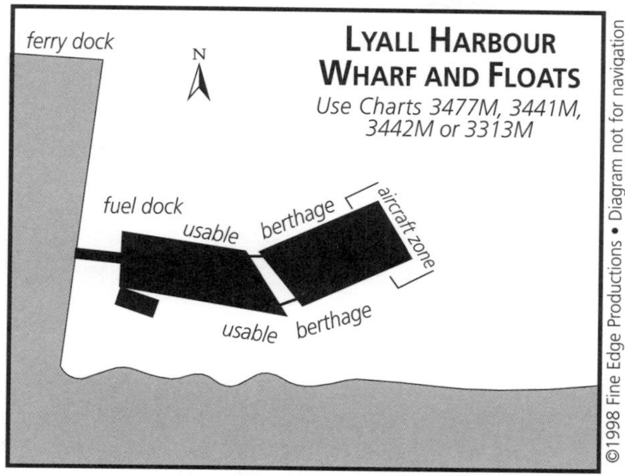

Anne Vipond

Who checked the tide tables yesterday?

Veruna Bay (Saturna Island)

Veruna Bay is north of King Islets between Digby and Mikuni points.

Charts 3477 metric, 3441 metric, 3313 metric
Position: 48°48.57′ N, 123°12.23′ W (NAD 83)

> *Veruna Bay, north of Digby Point, is not recommended for anchorage because of the submarine cable area.* (p. 192, SCG, Vol. 1)

Winter Cove (Saturna/ Samuel Islands)

Winter Cove is 5.9 miles southeast of Active Pass and 4.1 miles northeast of Bedwell Harbour.

Charts 3477 metric, 3441 metric, 3313 metric
Outer entrance (0.08 mile north of Minx Reef): 48°48.91′ N, 123°12.60′ W (NAD 83)
Inner entrance (0.14 mile east of Mikuni Point): 48°48.66′ N, 123°11.98′ W (NAD 83)
Winter Cove Yacht Club float: 48°48.50′ N, 123°11.69′ W (NAD 83)

> *Winter Cove, between the NW side of Saturna Island and the SE side of Samuel Island, is shallow and has several drying reefs, below-water rocks and some piles lying off its shores. It affords shelter for small craft and a route from Plumper Sound to the Strait of Georgia.* (p. 192, SCG, Vol. 1)

Winter Cove is a popular boating area with its sand and mud beaches and its waters protected from all but northwest winds. When you enter from Plumper Sound, avoid the widespread shoals and isolated rocks inside the cove, especially Minx Reef. Photos of up-ended sailboats, high and dry in Winter Cove, are legendary, so be sure to check your tide tables and monitor your echo sounder. Because of its proximity to the silt effluent of Fraser River, the water in the cove is opaque and its isolated rocks difficult to see. Mooring buoys along the southwest shore are private.

Anne Vipond

Floats, Lyall Harbour

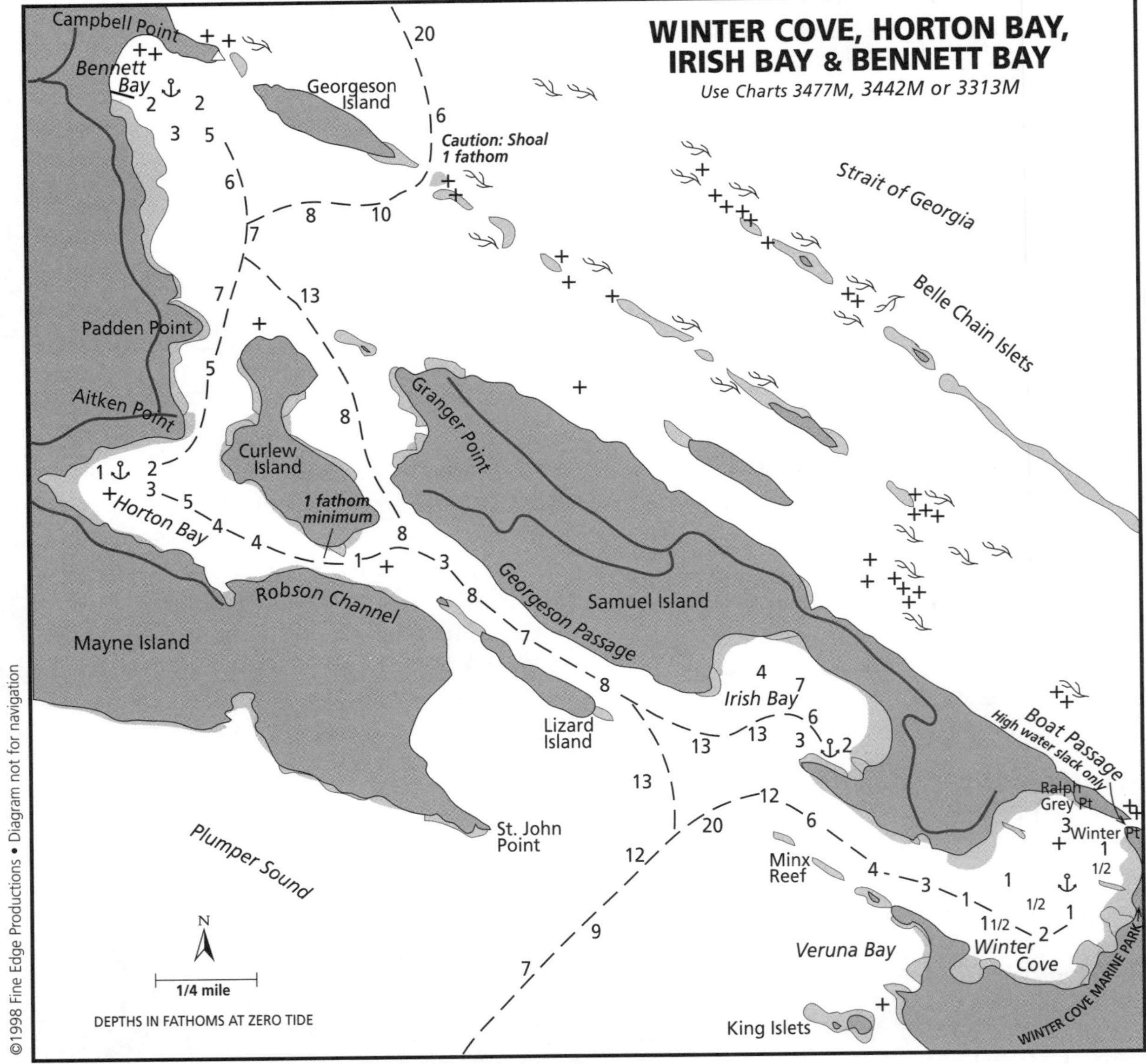

Winter Cove Marine Park (Saturna Island)

Winter Cove Marine Park is on the southeast shore of Winter Cove.

Charts 3477 metric, 3441 metric, 3313 metric
Anchor: 48°48.68′ N, 123°11.56′ W (NAD 83)

> *Winter Cove Marine Park, on the SE shore of Winter Cove, has picnic facilities.* (p. 192, SCG, Vol. 1)

Winter Cove Marine Park is a good place to limber up and roam around on shore. Anchoring in Winter Cove is the butt of cruising jokes. The east shore is quite shallow and there is a sandbar with 4 feet over it in the center of the cove. Sailboats frequently find themselves listing at odd angles on low water. Using chart 3477 and an echo sounder will prevent these problems.

The 228-acre marine park has a picnic area, launching ramp, and delightful hiking trails.

Anchor in about 1 1/2 fathoms, over sand and mud with fair-to-good holding.

Boat Passage

Boat Passage lies between Winter Point on Saturna Island and Ralph Grey Point on Samuel Island.

Charts 3477 metric, 3442 metric, 3313 metric
Position: 48°48.85′ N, 123°11.33′ W (NAD 83)

> *Boat Passage, at the north end of Winter Cove . . . has a least depth of 7 feet (2.1 m) and leads into the Strait of Georgia. This passage is narrow with tidal rapids occurring on large tides and should only be used by small craft at or near slack water; local knowledge is necessary.* (p. 192, SCG, Vol. 1)

William Kelly

Boat Passage viewed from Winter Point

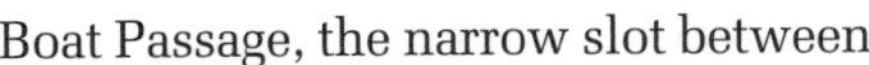

Boat Passage, the narrow slot between Winter Point and Ralph Grey Point, is best observed from land because of the rocks and very strong currents that menace this passage during spring tides with flows up to 7 knots. This creates 2-foot high "rooster tails" for 50 yards. Boat Passage is not recommended for anything other than a dinghy or kayak at slack water. When the current is flowing through the passage, there is

Winter Cove

Winter Cove Marine Park, established in 1979, is a great place for walks ashore or for embarking on bicycle rides along the quiet roads of sparsely-populated Saturna Island. Most boaters land their dinghies on the broad sand-and-mud beach beside the boat launch. Nearby lies an open area of lawn with picnic tables overlooking the cove. A trail leads from the edge of the grassy clearing into the forest where it loops around Winter Point with views overlooking the Strait of Georgia. Offshore lie Anniversary Island and the Belle Chain Islets.

At Winter Point you can take a close look at Boat Passage, a narrow gap between Saturna and Samuel islands. This is a tricky pass with reefs on either side and currents reaching 6 knots. During prohibition it was used by rumrunners dodging government revenue boats in the Strait of Georgia.

Samuel Island has been owned by a succession of prominent people since the early 1900s, including Ralph Grey, a relative of Earl Grey who was governor-general of Canada from 1904 to 1911. The island was purchased in the 1930s by the engineer A.J.T. Taylor, builder of Vancouver's Lions Gate Bridge, who leased the island to a resident caretaker named George McRae Thompson and his family.

Taylor had a lodge built overlooking Winter Cove to serve as a private residence whenever he and his friends visited the island, and in summer they often anchored their luxury yachts in Irish Bay. Meanwhile, Thompson raised Jersey cows on Samuel Island and worked at odd jobs on Saturna Island.

The Belle Chain Islets were used for target practice at the beginning of World War II, and all day long fighters and bombers would fly over Samuel Island dropping cartridge cases and, in one instance, mistakenly firing at the lodge. When an officer came to investigate Thompson's complaint, he was shown five paint drums filled with spent shells and clips, as well as the path a bullet had taken through the lodge, narrowly missing one of Thompson's daughters and killing three sheep. Damages were paid and the training pilots became more careful about hitting the correct target base.

Saturna Island's July 1st Lamb Barbecue is one of the Gulf Islands' most popular annual events. Formerly held in Breezy Bay, it now attracts dozens of boaters to Winter Cove on the Canada Day holiday. —**AV**

danger that your boat could be swept through. Although at high-water slack it is sometimes used by local sportfishing boats that cross to the outer coast of Saturna Island or fish the Belle Chain Islets, it is safer to use Georgeson Passage.

Church Cove (Winter Cove)

Church Cove is at the south end of Winter Cove.

Charts 3477 metric, 3442 metric, 3313 metric
Position: 48°48.53′ N, 123°11.90′ W (NAD 83)

> *Church Cove is a small indentation on the south side of Winter Cove.* (p. 192, SCG, Vol. 1)

Church Cove has a sandy flat which dries at low water. It is sometimes used by local boats.

Irish Bay (Samuel Island)

Irish Bay, on the south side of Samuel Island, is 0.8 mile northwest of Winter Cove.

Charts 3477 metric, 3442 metric, 3313 metric
Entrance: 48°49.09′ N, 123°12.71′ W (NAD 83)
Anchor: 48°49.05′ N, 123°12.42′ W (NAD 83)

> *Irish Bay, on the south side of Samuel Island provides good anchorage and is well sheltered at each end.* (p. 192, SCG, Vol. 1)

Undeveloped Irish Bay offers good protection just inside its east bight.

Georgeson Passage

Georgeson Passage, along the southwest side of Samuel Island, leads from Plumper Sound to the Strait of Georgia.

Charts 3477 metric, 3442 metric, 3313 metric
South entrance: 48°49.15′ N, 123°13.10′ W (NAD 83)
North entrance (0.20 mile northwest of Grainger Point): 48°50.11′ N, 123°14.26′ W (NAD 83)

> *Georgeson Passage, entered from Plumper Sound between the SE extremity of Lizard Island and the SW side of Samuel Island, leads NW then north between Curlew and Samuel Islands into the Strait of Georgia. The least depth through the fairway is 34 feet (10.4 m) but dangerous shoals and rocks lie in the north entrance. Two small islets, joined by a drying ledge, also lie in the north entrance to Georgeson Passage, close off Grainger Point.*
>
> *The flood sets NW and the ebb SE through Georgeson Passage.* (p. 192, SCG, Vol. 1)

Georgeson Passage provides access to Horton, Bennett, and Campbell bays and the fishing grounds of Belle Chain Islets. The passage is used by small vessels as an alternative to Active Pass. Avoid the shoals and reefs indicated on the charts. While currents on spring tides are strong, they run about half those in Active Pass. The bottom is irregular and turbulence can be encountered.

Robson Channel

Robson Channel, between Mayne Island and the south shore of Curlew Island, is the south entrance to Horton Bay.

Charts 3477 metric, 3442 metric, 3313 metric
East entrance: 48°49.57′ N, 123°14.04′ W (NAD 83)
West entrance: 48°49.57′ N, 123°14.41′ W (NAD 83)

> *Robson Channel, between the south end of Curlew Island and Mayne Island, leads into the*

Don Douglass

Heading carefully through Robson Channel

south part of Horton Bay. A rock, with less than 6 feet (1.8 m) over it, lies in the east entrance to Robson Channel. (p. 192, SCG, Vol. 1)

Robson Channel, the narrow entrance to Horton Bay, is subject to strong ebb currents. The channel is shallow and has about 1 fathom minimum in the fairway. Avoid the submerged rock south of the entrance point by favoring the north shore but remain alert to the small reef extending south from Curlew Island. The bottom of Robson Channel is rocky and irregular.

Horton Bay (Mayne Island)

Horton Bay, on the southeast corner of Mayne Island, lies 2.3 miles northwest of Winter Cove.

Charts 3477 metric, 3442 metric, 3313 metric
East entrance: 48°49.57′ N, 123°14.41′ W (NAD 83)
North entrance (0.05 mile east of Paddon Point): 48°50.10′ N, 123°14.62′ W (NAD 83)
Public floats: 48°49.52′ N, 123°14.66′ W (NAD 83)
Anchor: 48°49.75′ N, 123°15.00′ W (NAD 83)

Horton Bay affords snug anchorage for small craft; it should be entered at or near slack water. Entering Horton Bay from the north Paddon Point can be passed reasonably close-to but Aitken Point should be given a wide berth in order to avoid the piles extending south from it. A rock, with less than 6 feet (2 m) over it, lies 0.1 mile off the head of the bay.

The public float, 80 feet (24 m) long with depths of 6 to 12 feet (1.8 to 3.7 m) alongside, is on the south shore of Horton Bay. (pp. 192, 194, SCG, Vol. 1)

Horton Bay provides good shelter for small craft either at the public dock on the south shore or along the north shore. Strong and unrelenting currents, particularly on spring tides, make anchoring or docking difficult. The public dock is subject to strong currents alongside and is often crowded. The bay should be entered during daylight hours only.

Good anchorage can be found in the northwest corner of the bay, out of the current except for some weak eddies. Avoid the private moorings and drying mud flats.

Anchor in 2 fathoms, over sand and mud with good holding.

Bennett Bay (Mayne Island)

Bennett Bay, on the east side of Mayne Island, is 1 mile north of Horton Bay.

Charts 3477 metric, 3442 metric, 3313 metric
Anchor: 48°50.72′ N, 123°14.84′ W (NAD 83)

Bennett Bay, south of Campbell Point, affords good anchorage but is exposed to SE winds. (p. 213, SCG, Vol. 1)

Bennett Bay, with its flat, shallow bottom, provides good protection from northwest winds. However, we do not recommended it in southeast gales. (Notice the piles of driftwood on shore!)

Anchor in 1 to 2 fathoms over mud with good holding.

"Georgeson Island Pass"

Georgeson Island Pass, 1 mile northeast of Horton Bay, is 3.9 miles southeast of Active Pass.

Charts 3477 metric, 3442 metric, 3313 metric
Position: 48°50.49′ N, 123°13.89′ W (NAD 83)

Georgeson Island Pass is what we call the small-boat passage clear of kelp at the southeast end of Georgeson Island. The narrow passage lies between the reef and kelp beds that extend 0.06 mile southeast of Georgeson Island and the chain of reefs that begin 0.12 mile from Georgeson Island. Use charts 3477 or 3313 as your guide. The fairway is difficult to gauge during foul weather, limited visibility, or strong currents. The fairway which carries between 1 and 2 fathoms should be attempted only in fair weather.

At the west end of Georgeson Island, a small-boat passage with about 1 foot of water at zero tide is frequently used by sportfishing boats at adequate tide levels. Larger boats entering or exiting the Strait of Georgia will find a deep-water route 1.9 miles to the southeast of Georgeson Island along the south side of Belle Chain Islets.

Campbell Bay (Mayne Island)

Campbell Bay, on the northeast corner of Mayne Island, is 2 miles southeast of Active Pass.

Charts 3477 metric, 3442 metric, 3313 metric
Entrance: 48°51.08′ N, 123°14.64′ W (NAD 83)
Anchor: 48°51.53′ N, 123°16.20′ W (NAD 83)

> *Campbell Bay, entered between Campbell Point and Edith Point, affords temporary anchorage, mud bottom; it is exposed to the SE. Foul ground extends SE of Edith Point. Private floats and mooring buoys are in the bay.* (p. 213, SCG, Vol. 1; see also SD, p. 125)

Campbell Bay offers quiet moorage in fair weather at its head. A number of fine homes with summer docks sit along its south shore. While the bay is open to southeast storms, it does offer protection from prevailing northwest winds. Light southeast winds peter out before reaching the head of the bay.

Anchor in 4 fathoms over sand and mud with good holding.

David Cove, Mayne Island (Strait of Georgia)

David Cove, on the north coast of Mayne Island, is 0.8 mile southeast of Georgina Point.

Charts 3442 metric, 3313 metric
Position: 48°52.00′ N, 123°16.54′ W (NAD 83)

> *David Cove . . . is fringed by drying ledges and kelp and has depths of 7 to 9 feet (2.1 to 2.7 m) near its head. Anchoring is not recommended because of the submarine cables running through it.* (p. 214, SCG, Vol. 1)

David Cove is a small indentation on the outer coast of Mayne Island. Although it is full of mooring buoys, it can be used as a temporary stop to wait for favorable conditions in Active Pass. Avoid the cable crossing area at the north end of the cove.

Swanson Channel

Swanson Channel, on North Pender Island's west side, connects Active Pass to Boundary Pass and Satellite Channel.

Charts 3441 metric, 3442 metric, 3313 metric
South entrance: 48°43.33′ N, 123°15.63′ W (NAD 83)
North entrance: 48°49.45′ N, 123°20.43′ W (NAD 83)

> *Swanson Channel, entered between Pelorus Point and Tilly Point at its south end, leads north to Trincomali Channel, Active Pass and Navy Channel; its north end lies between Portlock and Stanley Points. North Pender Island forms the east side of Swanson Channel; Moresby, Saltspring and Prevost Islands form its west side. Satellite Channel leads west between Moresby and Saltspring Islands. Captain Passage . . . offers no saving in distance to vessels proceeding up Swanson Channel for the upper reaches of Trincomali Channel but by taking this passage the ferry traffic entering and leaving Active Pass is avoided.*
>
> *Tidal streams flood NW and north through Swanson Channel, but a branch flows into Navy Channel; the ebb flows SE. At the north end of Swanson Channel, there is another division of the flood stream, one part going through Active Pass, and the other through Trincomali Channel. Toward Enterprise Reef there is a significant increase in the velocity of the flood stream, and, at the entrance to Active Pass 5 to 7 kn can be expected with large tides; 3 to 5 kn on smaller tides.*
>
> *The north part of Swanson Channel is used by ferries operating between Swartz Bay and Tsawwassen, and the Gulf Islands. The tracks are usually mid-channel, however, inter-island ferries cross Swanson Channel between Captain Passage and Otter Bay. Small craft navigators are advised to keep clear of the ferries.* (pp. 182–183, SCG, Vol. 1)

Swanson Channel is the main north/south route in the southern Gulf Islands. It is used by boats that are too large to squeeze through Pender Canal. Because the northern section is a main ferry route and fast-moving ferries leave large wakes, use caution throughout the area.

Smugglers Nook (North Pender Island/Swanson Channel)

Smugglers Nook, on the south tip of North Pender Island, is 0.27 mile northwest of Wallace Point

Charts 3477 metric, 3441 metric, 3313 metric
Position: 48°44.29′ N, 123°14.26′ W (NAD 83)

> *Smugglers Nook . . . has a rock, which dries 8 feet (2.4 m), in its central part.* (p. 186, SCG, Vol. 1)

Smugglers Nook, a tiny indentation, is used only by small sportfishing boats.

Boat Nook (North Pender Island)

Boot Nook is 3.1 miles northwest of Bedwell Harbour.

Charts 3441 metric, 3442 metric, 3313 metric
Entrance: 48°45.84′ N, 123°18.19′ W (NAD 83)
Anchor: 48°45.93′ N, 123°18.18′ W (NAD 83)

> *Beddis Rock dries 12 feet (3.7 m) and lies in the entrance to Boat Nook. Between Beddis Rock and the shore to the north there are other drying and sunken rocks.* (p. 186, SCG, Vol. 1)

Boat Nook is a tiny cove used by sportfishing boats. Open to the south, it provides temporary anchorage in fair weather. Upon entering, avoid the mooring buoys and Beddis Rock and anchor to the west side of the cement piling. Kelp north of Beddis Rock keeps chop to a minimum.

Anchor in 1 to 2 fathoms over sand, mud and shells with good holding.

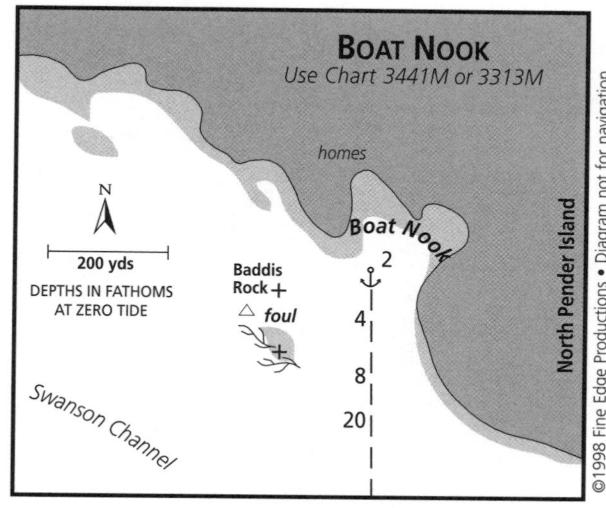

Thieves Bay (North Pender Island)

Thieves Bay, a half-mile southeast of Mouat Point, is 3.6 miles northwest of Bedwell Harbour.

Charts 3441 metric, 3442 metric, 3313 metric
Entrance: 48°46.30′ N, 123°18.95′ W (NAD 83)
Position: 48°46.26′ N, 123°18.79′ W (NAD 83)

> *Thieves Bay, 0.5 mile NW of Beddis Rock, is shallow with 2 foot (0.6 m) depths. A pinnacle rock lies off the south entrance point.* (p. 186, SCG, Vol. 1)

Thieves Bay is filled largely by a private marina (members only). Avoid the kelp, rock and reef off the point when entering. Since the small bay has no swinging room, it is useful only in an emergency.

Shingle Bay (North Pender Island)

Shingle Bay is 0.38 mile northeast of Mouat Point and 4.8 miles southeast of Active Pass.

Charts 3441 metric, 3442 metric, 3313 metric
Entrance: 48°47.00′ N, 123°19.13′ W (NAD 83)
Anchor: 48°46.88′ N, 123°18.64′ W (NAD 83)

> *Shingle Bay, NW of Mouat Point, has a drying ledge, with a rock 6 feet (1.8 m) high on it, lying close off the east shore.*
>
> *Anchorage can be obtained in Shingle Bay but it is exposed to west winds.* (p. 186, SCG, Vol. 1)

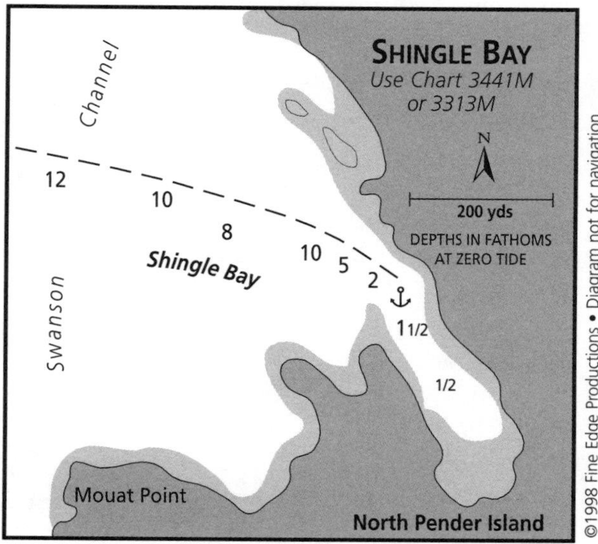

Anne Vipond

Otter Bay Marina, North Pender Island

Shingle Bay is a scenic, shallow bay offering good protection from southerly weather off its drying flat. Before you anchor, check the tide tables carefully. The small bay has limited swinging room. Avoid the four rocks off the south entrance point.

Anchor in 1 to 2 fathoms over mud with good holding.

Ella Bay (North Pender Island)

Ella Bay is immediately south of Otter Bay on the south side of Roe Islet.

Charts 3441 metric, 3442 metric, 3313 metric
Position: 48°47.67′ N, 123°18.81′ W (NAD 83)

Ella Bay offers good shelter in its center to small craft in fair weather. Avoid the rocks off the south entrance.

Otter Bay (North Pender Island)

Otter Bay is 4.0 miles southeast of Active Pass and 4.4 miles northwest of Bedwell Harbour.

Charts 3441 metric, 3442 metric, 3313 metric
Entrance: 48°47.88′ N, 123°19.04′ W (NAD 83)

Anne Vipond

Otter Bay homes

Anchor: 48°47.82′ N, 123°18.43′ W (NAD 83)

Otter Bay, north of Shingle Bay, has a ferry landing on its north shore from which regular ferry service operates to Swartz Bay.

Anchorage for small vessels can be obtained in Otter Bay in 43 to 56 feet (13 to 17 m), mud bottom. The anchorage is exposed to west winds but offers a good sheltered anchorage out of the swells from passing ferries. (p. 186, SCG, Vol. 1)

Otter Bay is a large bay that offers good protection from southeast weather. The head of Otter Bay or small Ella Bay to the south behind the small islet are popular spots to anchor and have a number of private mooring buoys. Ferry wash is minimal but some afternoon westerly chop is common. Hyashi Cove on the north side of Otter Bay is the site of Otter Bay Marina.

Anchor in 2 to 4 fathoms over a mud bottom with good holding.

Hyashi Cove

Hyashi Cove is in the northwest corner of Otter Bay.

Charts 3441 metric, 3442 metric, 3313 metric
Marina: 48°47.96′ N, 123°18.59′ W (NAD 83)

Otter Bay

Around the corner from the B.C. Ferries dock, tucked behind a breakwater in Hyashi Cove, is the Otter Bay Marina—its grounds containing an outdoor swimming pool, small playground, kayak rentals, store and laundromat. Bicycles can be hired at the marina for a tour of North Pender, its hilly and winding roads leading past leafy lanes and country craft shops. A number of shops are located on or near Port Washington Road which leads to Hope Bay where additional studios and craft stores are located.

At the junction of Port Washington Road and Otter Bay Road is Old Orchard Farm, its Victorian farmhouse begun in 1882 by Washington Grimmer, one of Pender's first settlers. Born in London, England, Grimmer married a young local woman named Elizabeth Auchterlonie in 1885. Their second child was delivered in the middle of Navy Channel while Grimmer was rowing Elizabeth to the midwife on Mayne Island. They named the boy Neptune in honor of his waterborne birth and he lived well into his nineties.

Washington Grimmer was the island's first postmaster and once a week he would row the seven miles to Mayne Island to collect the mail. After a government wharf was built at Port Washington in 1890, mail and other goods arrived by steamer. However, the steamer captains disliked the tiny dock and in bad seas they would often signal for Washington to row out and retrieve passengers or supplies.

A short walk north from Otter Bay Marina is the island's nine-hole golf course where you can rent clubs and carts. The course was built in the late 1930s when George Grimmer, a son of Washington, agreed to sell his sheep pasture in Grimmer Valley. The clubhouse serves lunches, snacks and dinner which can be enjoyed outside on the verandah in sunny weather. A bronze sculpture of Washington Grimmer on horseback stands on the edge of the golf course. The Stand at the Otter Bay ferry dock, just down the hill from the marina, is popular for take-out food and provides a small outdoor garden in which to enjoy your milk shakes and seafood burgers.

A Visitor Information Centre is located on Otter Bay Road about a quarter-mile east of the marina. With a map in hand, you could follow South Otter Bay Road to the Malahat Properties park land. Purchased in 1996 by the Pacific Marine Heritage Legacy, this 215-hectare parcel of mostly second-growth forest is, overall, in a natural state with numerous trails, a small lake and some water frontage bordering the northeast shores of Shingle Bay. —**AV**

Anne Vipond

Otter Bay pumpkin time

Anne Vipond

B.C. ferry entering Active Pass

Hyashi Cove, on the north side of Otter Bay, has a boat launching ramp. The point south of the marina is fringed with rocks and kelp. (p. 186, SCG, Vol. 1)

Otter Bay Marina is fast becoming one of the most popular destinations in the Gulf Islands. Open twelve months, it has power, laundry, showers, and a heated pool. Access to the B.C. ferry is just a short walk. The marina monitors VHF Channel 68; reservations are recommended (tel: 250-629-3579).

Grimmer Bay / Port Washington (North Pender Island)

Grimmer Bay is 1 mile northwest of Otter Bay.

Charts 3442 metric, 3313 metric
Entrance: 48°48.75′ N, 123°19.67′ W (NAD 83)
Public float: 48°48.78′ N, 123°19.26′ W (NAD 83)
Anchor (north): 48°48.72′ N, 123°19.24′ W (NAD 83)

From the middle of the bay, a chain of above-water and drying rocks extends 0.25 mile WNW terminating in Boat Islet.

The public wharf is 150 feet (46 m) long with depths of 15 to 19 feet (4.6 to 5.8 m) alongside; floats for small craft, about 65 feet (19 m) long, are attached to the east and west sides.

Danger.—A rock, with less than 6 feet (1.8 m) over it, lies about 150 feet (46 m) south of the SE end of the public wharf. (p. 186, SCG, Vol. 1)

Grimmer Bay is divided into north and south sections by a reef that extends 0.2 mile offshore and is marked by a flashing red light. Quiet anchorage can be found in either the north or south sections of the bay, with the north part providing more protection. There is a lot of swinging room and the bottom is fairly flat. Other than the public wharf and small float on the north shore, there are no facilities here. Port Washington is the small development at the public wharf on the north shore of Grimmer Bay.

Anchor southeast of the public float in 3 fathoms.

Ellen Bay (Prevost Island)

Ellen Bay is on the south side of Prevost Island.

Charts 3442 metric, 3313 metric
Entrance: 48°48.71′ N, 123°21.50′ W (NAD 83)
Anchor: 48°49.18′ N, 123°22.60′ W (NAD 83)

Ellen Bay, on the north side of Point Liddell, affords fair anchorage about 0.1 mile from the head of the bay in 60 feet (18 m), mud bottom. (p. 184, SCG, Vol. 1)

Although open to southeast winds, Ellen Bay provides good anchorage with protection from prevailing northwest winds. A shallow 1- to 2-fathom shelf at the isthmus to Annette Inlet can be used as a scenic anchor site (private property, no fires). From your boat at high water you can look into Annette Inlet. Boats wishing more swinging room can anchor farther out in 7 to 8 fathoms. Moderate southerly swell and chop die off along the southern shore before reaching the head of the bay. This can be considered a fair-weather anchorage only—driftwood on the beach indicates this is no place to be caught in a southeast storm.

Anchor in 2 fathoms over a mixed bottom (mud with rocky spots). Holding is fair-to-good if you set your anchor well.

Diver Bay (Prevost Island)

Diver Bay, immediately north of Ellen Bay on the southeast shore of Prevost Island, is 0.5 mile southwest of Portlock Point.

Charts 3442 metric, 3313 metric
Entrance: 48°49.06′ N, 123°21.17′ W (NAD 83)
Anchor: 48°49.48′ N, 123°21.85′ W (NAD 83)

> *Diver Bay, north of Ellen Bay, is entered between Red Islets and Bright Islet.*
>
> *Anchorage for small craft in 30 to 42 feet (9 to 13 m), sand and mud, is obtainable in Diver Bay; it is exposed to the SE.* (p. 184, SCG, Vol. 1)

Looking down on Active Pass from Galiano Island

Diver Bay, like Ellen Bay, offers protection in prevailing westerlies, but it is exposed to the southeast and can be considered a fair-weather anchorage only. Anchorage can be found off the small brown house in the north corner at the head of the bay.

Anchor in 4 to 5 fathoms over sand, mud and some rocks.

Richardson Bay (Prevost Island)

Richardson Bay, on the east end of Prevost Island, lies 1.9 miles south of Active Pass.

Chart 3313 metric
Entrance: 48°49.57′ N, 123°21.05′ W (NAD 83)
Anchor: 48°49.63′ N, 123°21.19′ W (NAD 83)

> *Richardson Bay is a small, shallow indentation 0.4 mile north of Bright Islet.*
>
> *Note: Ellen Bay, Diver Bay and Richardson Bay are exposed to swells from passing ferries.* (p. 184, SCG, Vol. 1)

Richardson Bay, a tiny nook 0.5 mile north of Diver Bay, offers shelter to one or two boats in the lee of a small, unmanned lighthouse on Portlock Point. Rocks and reefs extend 100 yards or more from Portlock Point and an islet with three trees is off the south shore. Ferry wake, southeast exposure, and the occasional bellowing foghorn are the only concerns in this otherwise natural and quiet place.

Since swinging room is limited, it's a good idea to use a second anchor or a stern tie to shore. Note the rebar stakes and old chain on the north wall.

Anchor in 1 to 3 fathoms over brown sand, mud and sea lettuce with fair holding.

Active Pass

Active Pass, between Mayne and Galiano islands, joins the Strait of Georgia with Swanson and Trincomali channels.

Charts 3473 metric, 3442 metric, 3313 metric
South entrance (0.6 mile northwest of Enterprise Reef): 48°51.21′ N, 123°21.31′ W (NAD 83)
North entrance: 48°52.91′ N, 123°17.76′ W (NAD 83)
Georgina Point light: 48°52.40′ N, 123°17.49′ W (NAD 83)
Helen Point light: 48°51.46′ N, 123°20.70′ W (NAD 83)

> *Active Pass . . . is a deep but tortuous channel leading from Swanson and Trincomali Channels into the Strait of Georgia. The fairway is about 0.2 mile wide in its narrowest parts, and there are*

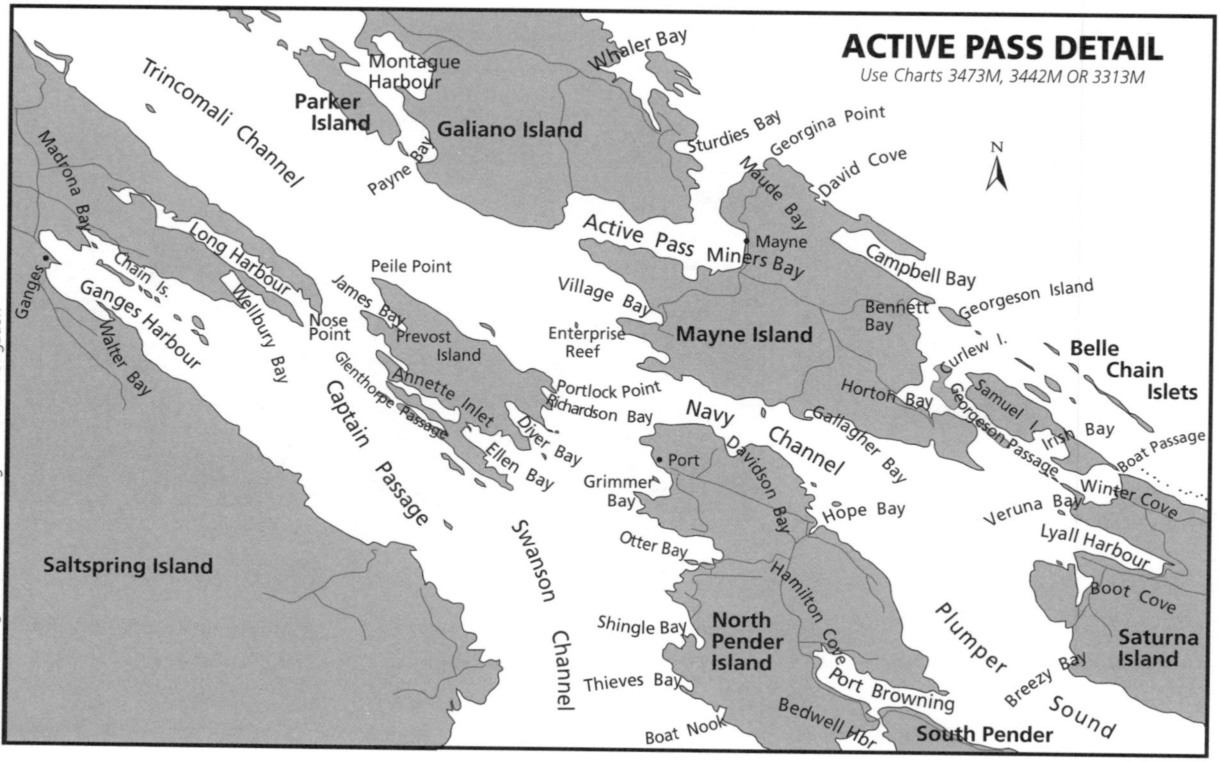

ACTIVE PASS DETAIL

Use Charts 3473M, 3442M OR 3313M

no dangers at a greater distance than 0.1 mile from either shore, with the exception of a group of rocks, with less than 6 feet (2 m) over them, 0.4 mile NNE of Collinson Point in Georgeson Bay.

Within Active Pass all small craft must comply strictly with Rule 9(b) of the Collision Regulations which states "A vessel of less than 20 metres in length or a sailing vessel shall not impede the passage of a vessel which can safely navigate only within a narrow channel or fairway".

Predictions for the times and rates of maximum current and the time of slack water when the direction of the current turns are given in the Tide Tables, Volume 5.

On the north-going (flood) tidal stream there is a strong set into Miners Bay along its north shore and on the south-going (ebb) tidal stream there is a corresponding set into the bay along its south shore.

On strong flood tides violent rips, dangerous to small craft, occur over an area extending from mid-channel south of Mary Anne Point to Laura Point. Strong rips also occur near Fairway Bank and are increased in violence during strong winds from the north quadrant.

Caution. On the Strait of Georgia side of Active Pass heavy tide-rips

Anne Vipond

A passing wake becomes a standing wave in Active Pass

occur in the vicinity of Gossip Island, Lion Islets and Salamanca Point, particularly with the flood tidal stream and strong NW winds. (pp. 205–208, SCG, Vol. 1)

Active Pass is known for its turbulent waters and strong currents which often reach several knots with breaking waves. Please see the full descriptions in *Coast Pilot*. It is not recommended that sailboats or low-powered pleasure craft use Active Pass since they cannot maintain normal speeds in the turbulence of spring tides.

The pass carries all ferry and commercial traffic between the Strait of Georgia and the ferry terminal in Swartz Bay. Ferry boats and other large ships announce their pending transit through Active Pass with a security call on VHF Channel 16. If you have restricted maneuverability, respond to their announcement on Channel 16 before they come roaring around the bend.

Within Active Pass, Sturdies Bay and Miners Bay have major facilities in case you need to stop.

Enterprise Reef

Enterprise Reef lies at the southern entrance to Active Pass at the confluence of Trincomali, Swanson, and Navy channels.

Charts 3473 metric, 3442 metric, 3313 metric
Enterprise Reef light: 48°50.70′ N, 123°20.90′ W (NAD 83)

Enterprise Reef . . . consists of two rocky heads, 0.25 mile apart; the west head dries 3 feet (0.9 m) and the other has 1 foot (0.3 m) over it.

A deep passage, 0.3 mile wide, between the east end of Enterprise Reef and Crane Point is available to small vessels and used by the ferries serving Village Bay.

Enterprise Reef lights (L.L. No. 271), on the west rock, are shown from a white circular tower with a red band at the top. The upper light, exhibited at an elevation of 21 feet (6.4 m), is visible all round the horizon and fitted with a radar reflector. (p. 197, SCG, Vol. 1)

Just west of Enterprise Reef the area is very busy with high-speed ferry traffic that requires alert helmsmanship.

Don Douglass

Enterprise Reef light

Village Bay (Mayne Island)

Village Bay, on the west coast of Mayne Island, lies 0.9 mile east of Enterprise Reef.

Charts 3473 metric, 3442 metric, 3313 metric
Entrance: 48°50.81′ N, 123°20.08′ W (NAD 83)
Anchor: 48°50.59′ N, 123°19.53′ W (NAD 83)

Village Bay is entered between Crane Point, 0.55 mile NW of Dinner Point, and Helen Point, 1 mile farther NW. The floats and mooring buoys in the bay are private. A ferry landing is on the north shore of Village Bay. Regular ferry service is maintained to Swartz Bay and Tsawwassen (reservation only). Small craft navigators are advised to keep clear of the ferry landing.

Anchorage.—Village Bay affords good anchorage, mud bottom. This anchorage is subject to the effects from the ferry wash and NW winds. (p. 197, SCG, Vol. 1)

Village Bay, the site of the Mayne Island ferry terminal, offers good protection from southeast winds; however, it is subject to ferry wake and open to the northwest. Anchorage can be found in the south side of the bay avoiding the numerous private mooring buoys.

Anchor in 5 fathoms over a mud bottom.

Georgeson Bay (Galiano Island)

Georgeson Bay, 1.25 miles north of Enterprise Reef, lies 1.9 miles northwest of Miners Bay.

Charts 3473 metric, 3442 metric, 3313 metric
Position: 48°51.95′ N, 123°20.83′ W (NAD 83)

> *Georgeson Bay, on the north side of the channel, lies between Collinson Point and Matthews Point. Off the west shore is a drying ledge, and further north are several shoals and rocks with less than 6 feet (2 m) over them.* (p. 208, SCG, Vol. 1)

Small craft wanting to get out of the way of ferryboat traffic can anchor temporarily on the 3-fathom shallow north of the submerged rocks.

Naylor Bay (Mayne Island)

Naylor Bay is 0.5 mile west of Miners Bay.

Charts 3473 metric, 3442 metric, 3313 metric
Position: 48°51.10′ N, 123°18.80′ W (NAD 83)

> *Naylor Bay, south of Mary Anne Point, lies between Lord Point and Reserve Point. Because of the submarine cable area, anchorage is prohibited in the bay.* (p. 208, SCG, Vol. 1)

Miners Bay (Mayne Island)

Miners Bay lies in the center of Active Pass on the northwest side of Mayne Island.

Charts 3473 metric, 3442 metric, 3313 metric
Entrance: 48°51.33′ N, 123°18.24′ W (NAD 83)
Public float: 48°51.13′ N, 123°18.12′ W (NAD 83)
Anchor: 48°51.24′ N, 123°18.04′ W (NAD 83)

> *Miners Bay between Reserve Point and Laura Point, 0.75 mile NNE, is deep and anchorage can be found only close inshore. Even there a vessel will be barely clear of the whirl of the tidal streams; caution is necessary because of the strong eddies which set into the bay. Numerous private mooring buoys lie close offshore.*
>
> *Anchorage is prohibited in the submarine cable area, west of the public wharf.*
>
> *Mayne, a small settlement in the SE corner of Miners Bay, has a general store, post office (V0N 2J0) and a lodge.* (p. 208, SCG, Vol. 1)

Miners Bay, on the east shore of Active Pass, is off to the side of traffic and turbulence found in Active Pass; however, a moderately strong countercurrent to Active Pass circulates inside the bay. It is also subject to frequent ferry wake.

The public wharf and fuel dock have limited moorage. Temporary anchorage can be taken north of the public wharf and fuel dock, avoiding private mooring buoys.

Miners Bay gets its name from a local campsite once used by gold miners travelling to the Fraser River from Victoria.

Anchor in 4 fathoms over sand and gravel with fair holding.

Bellhouse Bay (Galiano Island)

Bellhouse Bay, on the east end of Galiano Island, lies 0.35 mile south of Sturdies Bay.

Charts 3473 metric, 3442 metric, 3313 metric
Position: 48°52.25′ N, 123°18.69′ W (NAD 83)

> *Bellhouse Bay, on the west side of Active Pass, lies between Scoones Point and Burrill Point. The bay is foul with several drying heads.* (p. 209, SCG, Vol. 1)

Bellhouse Bay is too shallow for convenient anchorage.

Sturdies Bay (Galiano Island)

Sturdies Bay lies at the north end of Active Pass on the east end of Galiano Island.

Charts 3473 metric, 3442 metric; 3313 metric
Entrance: 48°52.53′ N, 123°18.65′ W (NAD 83)
Public float: 48°52.59′ N, 123°18.93′ W (NAD 83)

> *Sturdies Bay . . . is shallow and has foul ground extending 0.1 mile from the head.*
>
> *Sturdies Bay community, at the head of the bay, has stores, including a liquor store, a lodge and public telephones.*
>
> *The combined public wharf and ferry landing has a depth of 16 feet (4.9 m) alongside its head.* (p. 209, SCG, Vol. 1)

Sturdies Bay, one of the two ferry landings for Galiano Island (the other being Montague), serves the residents of Cain Peninsula and Whaler Bay. The bay offers moderate and temporary shelter.

A public float is located on the west side of the ferry complex. Beware of strong ferry wake and shallow waters at this float. It is a short walk up the ferry ramp to the Sturdies Bay community. Bellhouse Park, on the south shore of Sturdies Bay, is a good place to picnic and observe the ferryboats plowing through Active Pass.

Temporary anchorage may be found south of the ferry terminal in 1 to 2 fathoms.

Don Douglass

Sturdies Bay cormorants

Maude Bay (Mayne Island)

Maude Bay lies in the north of Mayne Island at the north end of Active Pass.

Charts 3473 metric, 3442 metric, 3313 metric
Position: 48°52.33' N, 123°17.60' W (NAD 83)

> *Maude Bay lies south of Georgina Point.* (p. 209, SCG, Vol. 1)

Maude Bay is a small, shallow indentation on Lighthouse Point 0.1 mile southwest of Georgina Point Light.

Whaler Bay (Galiano Island, Strait of Georgia)

Whaler Bay is 0.7 mile northwest of Sturdies Bay.

Charts 3473 metric, 3442 metric, 3313 metric
Southeast entrance: 48°53.08' N, 123°18.88' W (NAD 83)
North entrance: 48°53.87' N, 123°19.83' W (NAD 83)
Small craft public float: 48°53.02' N, 123°19.57' W (NAD 83)
Position (Murchison Cove): 48°53.40' N, 123°20.11' W (NAD 83)

> *The passage between Gossip Island . . . and Cain Peninsula leads to Whaler Bay; it has rocks and shoals in its SE entrance and a least depth of 29 feet (8.8 m).*
>
> *The south arm of Whaler Bay is shallow; its central part is obstructed by drying reefs, covered by kelp, west of Cain Point.*
>
> *The public wharf and float are in the south arm of Whaler Bay, 0.25 mile south of Cain Point. Depths of as little as 1 foot (0.3 m) are found in the vicinity of this wharf.*
>
> *There are numerous private wharves and floats in Whaler Bay.* (p. 214, SCG, Vol. 1)

Whaler Bay, sheltered by Gossip Island on the east and Galiano Island on its south and west, is very shallow with a number of reefs and submerged rocks. Shelter can be found off the coves along the west side of Whaler Bay. Murchison Cove, at the southwest corner of Whaler Bay, dries completely at low water.

The bay, while exposed to winds from the north and northeast, is generally a good place to await favorable conditions in Active Pass. The public float located in the shallow waters of the south arm of Whaler Bay can be used only with careful reference to tide tables.

Peter Fromm

Elea in light winds

8

CAPTAIN PASSAGE TO SANSUM NARROWS

Saltspring and Prevost Islands, Portland Island, and Satellite Channel

Introduction

From the southern end of Galiano Island, it's just a short hop southwest across Trincomali Channel to Prevost Island. Ringed by small inlets offering scenic beauty in intimate settings, Prevost Island is one of the more isolated islands in terms of access and development. It is a beautiful place, a quiet pastoral countryside that has been farmed by the family of Hussey de Burgh since 1924. The seven large indentations in Prevost's shoreline, including James Bay, Selby Cove, Annette Inlet, and Glenthorne Passage, offer isolated anchorages far from the bustle of busier islands.

Saltspring Island, which lies across Captain Passage from Prevost, is the largest and most populous of the Gulf Islands and the center of island enterprise. Known originally by the native peoples as Klaathem, it received its current name from officers of the Hudson's Bay company because of its brine pools—14 in all—that lie inland. The first permanent settlers were freed black slaves seeking to avoid the prejudice they encountered in the U.S. With its 77 miles of shoreline, Saltspring offers numerous harbors, bays and coves to entice the cruising visitor. Ganges Harbour—a major tourist attraction—is a busy place with several marinas, shops, boutiques, galleries, and restaurants.

Portland Island, site of Princess Margaret Marine Park, and nearby Brackman Island Ecological Reserve are just a short distance south across Satellite Channel.

Portland Island was given to Princess Margaret on her visit to Victoria in 1958, and she in turn gave the island to British Columbia. The Marine Park encompasses the entire island, offering a unique opportunity to explore a complete island in its natural setting. The island is heavily wooded with many hiking trails along its slopes. Portland Island can be easily circumnavigated by dinghy or kayak to observe the tide zone. The east side of the island is a paradise for scuba divers. Off the southwest shore, a sunken freighter serves as an artificial reef for divers.

From Portland Island, take Satellite Channel south to Fulford Harbour or the southernmost shores of Saltspring and over to Vancouver Island for a visit to Cowichan and Genoa bays. Cowichan is a picturesque, bustling village with some marvelous inns, restaurants, a great deli, and several marinas and marine supply stores. Genoa Bay is the site of Genoa Bay Marina, with excellent facilities for transients, including showers, cafe, crafts, and a friendly atmosphere. There are some good hikes from Genoa Bay, especially up to Mount Tzuhalem for terrific views down Satellite

Anne Vipond

Good holding over sticky bottom can be found in James Bay

Channel to the Saanich Peninsula.

Sansum Narrows runs almost due north-south between Vancouver and Saltspring islands. This winding channel is well sheltered and the shortest route between Saanich Peninsula and Dodd Narrows at the north end of the Gulf Islands.

On the Saltspring side of the narrows, Musgrave Landing offers some enticing hikes; beautiful Burgoyne Bay is a good place to swim and nearby Mount Maxwell Provincial Park offers hiking, picnicking, hidden caves, and spectacular views. Adjoining the park is an ecological reserve—a great spot for watching the dynamic flights of turkey vultures, peregrine falcons, and bald eagles. On the Vancouver side are Maple Bay and Birds Eye Cove. Popular Maple Bay Marina has showers, laundry, gift shop, groceries, and a restaurant; the beautiful grounds entice most visitors to stroll the garden. At Birds Eye Cove Marina, look for their new mural.

Captain Passage

Captain Passage leads from Swanson Channel to Trincomali Channel.

Out of the main ferry traffic lanes, Captain Passage is frequently used by pleasure craft as an alternative to Active Pass. Numerous rocks and reefs in the passage are well marked and charted.

When following the center of Captain Passage avoid Horda Shoals marked by green-red-green Buoy "UD" on the west the shoal marked by red Buoy "U62" on the east; both are off the entrance to Glenthorne Passage.

Prevost Island (Captain Passage)

Prevost Island is 2 miles southwest of Active Pass, between Captain Passage, Trincomali Channel, and Swanson Channel.

Charts 3478 metric, 3442 metric, 3313 metric

> *Prevost Island is moderately high and thickly wooded; its SE and NW shores are deeply indented.* (p. 184, SCG, Vol. 1)
>
> *Captain Passage, entered from Swanson Channel between Beaver Point and Point Liddell, leads NW between Prevost and Saltspring Islands, to Ganges Harbour and Trincomali Channel.* (p. 187, SCG, Vol. 1)

Prevost Island is privately owned and has no regular ferry service. It has several deep coves which afford some good anchor sites, as well as opportunities for fishing and recreation.

For anchor sites on the east side of Prevost Island facing Swanson Channel, please see Chapter 7.

James Bay (Prevost Island)

James Bay, at the northwest end of Prevost Island, is 3.8 miles east of Ganges Harbour.

Charts 3478 metric, 3442 metric, 3313 metric
Entrance: 48°50.78′ N, 123°24.39′ W (NAD 83)
Anchor: 48°50.48′ N, 123°23.89′ W (NAD 83)

> *James Bay . . . has O'Reilly Beach at its head. A rock ledge, with a below-water rock close off it, extends 0.1 mile NW from the south side of the head of the bay. Small craft can obtain good shelter from south winds near the head of James Bay, about 0.1 mile NW of the rock ledge.* (p. 188, SCG, Vol. 1)

James Bay offers very good protection from southeast storms with lots of swinging room over a rare sticky bottom; a number of boats can crowd

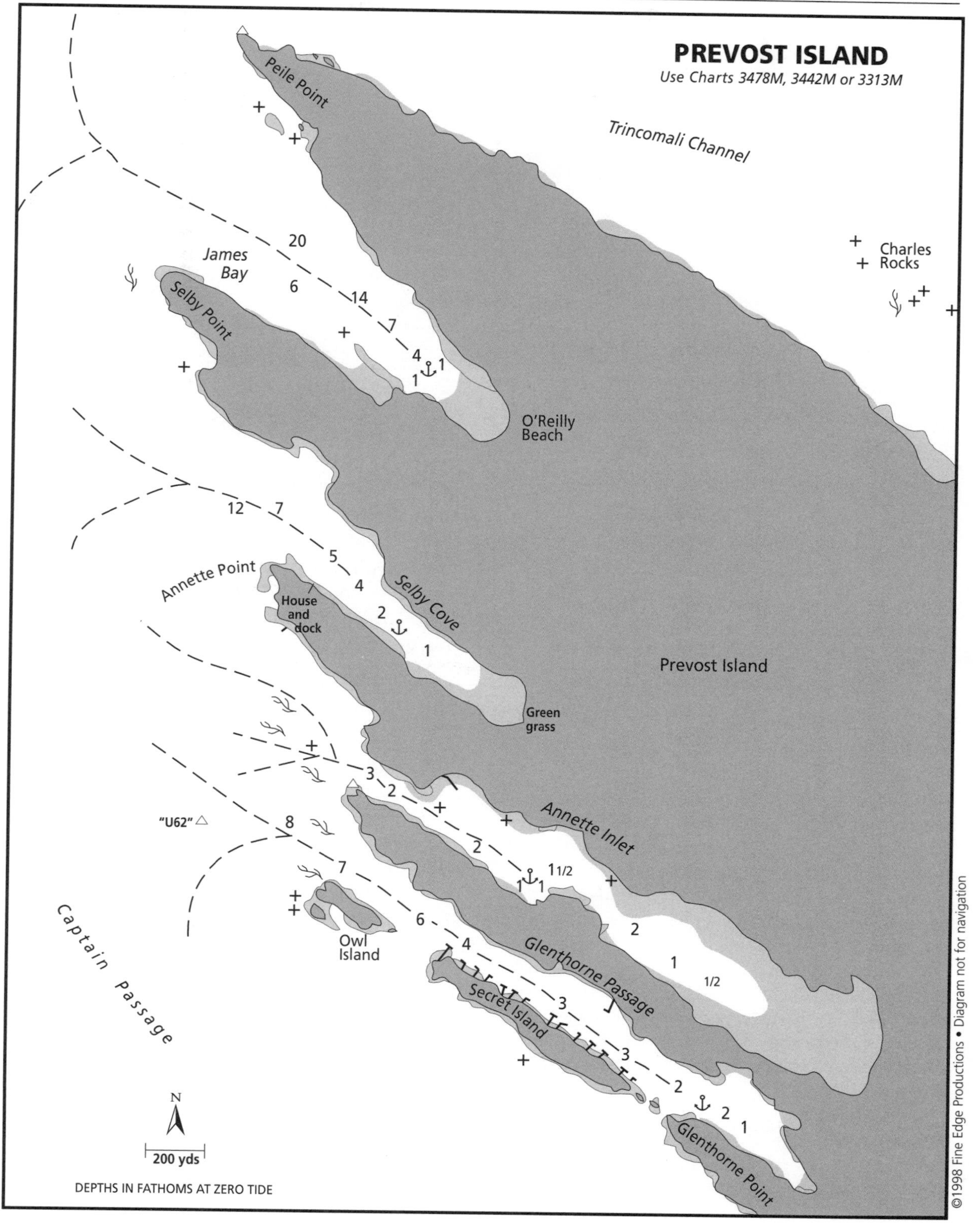
PREVOST ISLAND
Use Charts 3478M, 3442M or 3313M
Peile Point
Trincomali Channel
Charles Rocks
James Bay
Selby Point
O'Reilly Beach
Annette Point
House and dock
Selby Cove
Prevost Island
Green grass
Annette Inlet
"U62"
Captain Passage
Owl Island
Glenthorne Passage
Secret Island
Glenthorne Point
200 yds
DEPTHS IN FATHOMS AT ZERO TIDE
©1998 Fine Edge Productions • Diagram not for navigation

in here. Although it is open to the northwest, afternoon chop usually dies off before reaching the head of the bay. However, when strong northwesterlies blow through Trincomali Channel, James Bay can become uncomfortable. In settled weather, it is a quiet anchorage and a favorite of cruising boats.

Avoid the foul ground just south of Peile Point light and the long reef along the south shore. The beach at the head of the drying flat is known as O'Reilly Beach.

Anne Vipond

James Bay's broad gravel beach

Anchor in 4 to 6 fathoms over thick black mud with very good holding.

Selby Cove (Prevost Island)

Selby Cove, on the northwest side of Prevost Island, is 0.8 mile south of Peile Point.

Charts 3478 metric, 3442 metric, 3313 metric
Entrance: 48°50.27′ N, 123°24.38′ W (NAD 83)
Anchor: 48°50.05′ N, 123°23.96′ W (NAD 83)

> *Selby Cove, on the NW side of Prevost Island* [is] *narrow and shallow but afford*[s] *sheltered anchorage to small craft.* (p. 188, SCG, Vol. 1)

Selby Cove, separated from James Bay by the long peninsula of Selby Point, is protected on its south side by Annette Point. Entered between Annette and Selby points, the cove offers snug anchorage at its head off the drying flat. Avoid the rock at Annette Point and the large private dock just to

James Bay and Selby Cove

Prevost Island, accessible only by private craft, is one of the least developed of the Gulf Islands, much of it remaining pastoral farmland. To preserve some of this island's pristine scenery, the Pacific Marine Heritage Legacy—a federal-provincial partnership—acquired waterfront property on James Bay and adjacent Selby Cove in 1996.

James Bay is now almost completely surrounded by park land, from its northeast entrance point to its head and halfway along its southwest shoreline where a small orchard has always been an attraction with its springtime apple blossoms. Boaters can go ashore on the broad gravel beach at the bay's head where a cleared valley leads inland and a sheep trail can be hiked to Peile Point. The entire Peile Point peninsula, with views overlooking Trincomali Channel, is part of the park.

About half of Selby Cove's northeast shoreline, opposite the Annette Point peninsula, is now park. Any park services on Prevost will be minimal since it's the natural scenery of this island that the Legacy is striving to preserve. Forest trails and grassy bluffs make these Prevost anchorages ideal for hikes and picnics.

Prevost Island, along with James Bay, was named by Captain Richards in 1859 for Captain James Prevost, commander of the HMS *Satellite*. Captain Prevost, the British commissioner appointed to settle the San Juan boundary dispute between British Columbia and the United States, was a key witness in the arbitration hearings. He died, an admiral, in 1891.

Prevost Island was acquired by Digby Hussey de Burgh in the 1920s. An Irishman of noble lineage whose family owned an estate in County Limerick, de Burgh raised sheep, goats and cattle on Prevost's pastures. His son Hubert took over the island property in 1938. His four daughters grew up on this isolated island—one becoming a concert pianist. Upon Hubert's death, his widow Jean, two of their daughters and a son-in-law continued living on Prevost and much of the island remains in the family's hands. —**AV**

Looking north from the hilltop at James Bay

the southeast. Night or radar approaches to Selby Cove are the easiest of any on Prevost Island.

Selby Cove, although more intimate and scenic than James Bay, has more limited swinging room.

Anchor in 1 to 2 fathoms over a sand bottom with fair-to-good holding.

Annette Inlet (Prevost Island)

Annette Inlet, on Prevost Island's west shore, is 1.2 miles south of Peile Point.

Charts 3478 metric, 3442 metric, 3313 metric
Entrance: 48°49.94′ N, 123°24.21′ W (NAD 83)
Anchor: 48°49.63′ N, 123°23.61′ W (NAD 83)

Annette Inlet has a drying rock in its approach and shoal depths on the north side of the entrance. (p. 188, SCG, Vol. 1)

Landlocked Annette Inlet is a quiet and picturesque place to get away from it all. Avoid the dangerous rock and shoal 200 yards off the center of the entrance by favoring either the Annette Point side or the Glenthorne Passage side. There is another submerged rock 250 yards inside the inlet, south of a private dock.

The head of the inlet dries and is shallow throughout—a good environment for birds. You can anchor mid-channel off the flat or, for protection from southeast gusts, in the little nook on the south shore. Although Annette Inlet provides very good shelter it has limited swinging room. At high tide you can see across the head of the inlet into Ellen Bay.

Anchor in 1/2 to 1 fathom over soft mud with very good holding.

Glenthorne Passage

Glenthorne Passage is southwest of Prevost Island and northeast of Secret Island.

Charts 3478 metric, 3442 metric, 3313 metric
Entrance: 48°49.70′ N, 123°24.13′ W (NAD 83)
Anchor: 48°49.28′ N, 123°23.22′ W (NAD 83)

Several private floats and mooring buoys lie along the shores of Glenthorne Passage. (p. 188, SCG, Vol. 1)

Stern-tied to shore in Selby Cove

Nestled in a scenic setting, Glenthorne Passage is a cruising favorite that gives very good protection in all weather. It is entered at its northwest opening by passing on either side of Owl Island. The north shore of Secret Island has many private homes and docks. Anchorage can be taken anywhere along the narrow channel. The southeast entrance, a window off Glenthorne Point, is only 10 yards wide with a half-fathom in the fairway at low water; it is used as a dinghy passage.

Anchor in 2 to 3 fathoms over mud with good holding.

Saltspring Island

Twenty miles long and eight miles wide, Saltspring Island is the largest of the southern Gulf Islands. Explored by the Spanish and English in the 1700s, and first settled in the 1850s, the island became a major sheep-farming area in the 1900s.

Lying in the rain shadow of Vancouver Island, Saltspring Island has cool, dry summers with lots of sunshine. There are quiet beaches, acres of forest with miles of trails, and an abundance of wildlife. It is a wonderful place for hiking, camping, cycling, riding, diving and kayaking.

Many well-known artists live on Saltspring, and the island has become a center for arts and crafts. There are galleries, inns, pubs, restaurants, and shopping to suit everyone. (Please see Anne Vipond's Sidebar under Ganges.)

Long Harbour (Saltspring Island)

Long Harbour is 1.3 miles northeast of Ganges Harbour.

Charts 3478 metric, 3442 metric, 3313 metric
Entrance: 48°50.48′ N, 123°25.30′ W (NAD 83)
Anchor (Nose Point Islets): 48°50.83′ N, 123°25.69′ W (NAD 83)
Anchor (in nook 0.27 mile northwest of Clamshell Islet): 48°51.39′ N, 123°26.64′ W (NAD 83)
Anchor (head of the harbor): 48°51.64′ N, 123°27.90′ W (NAD 83)

Anne Vipond

Tucked behind the spit in Long Harbour

Anne Vipond

Gulf Island hideaway

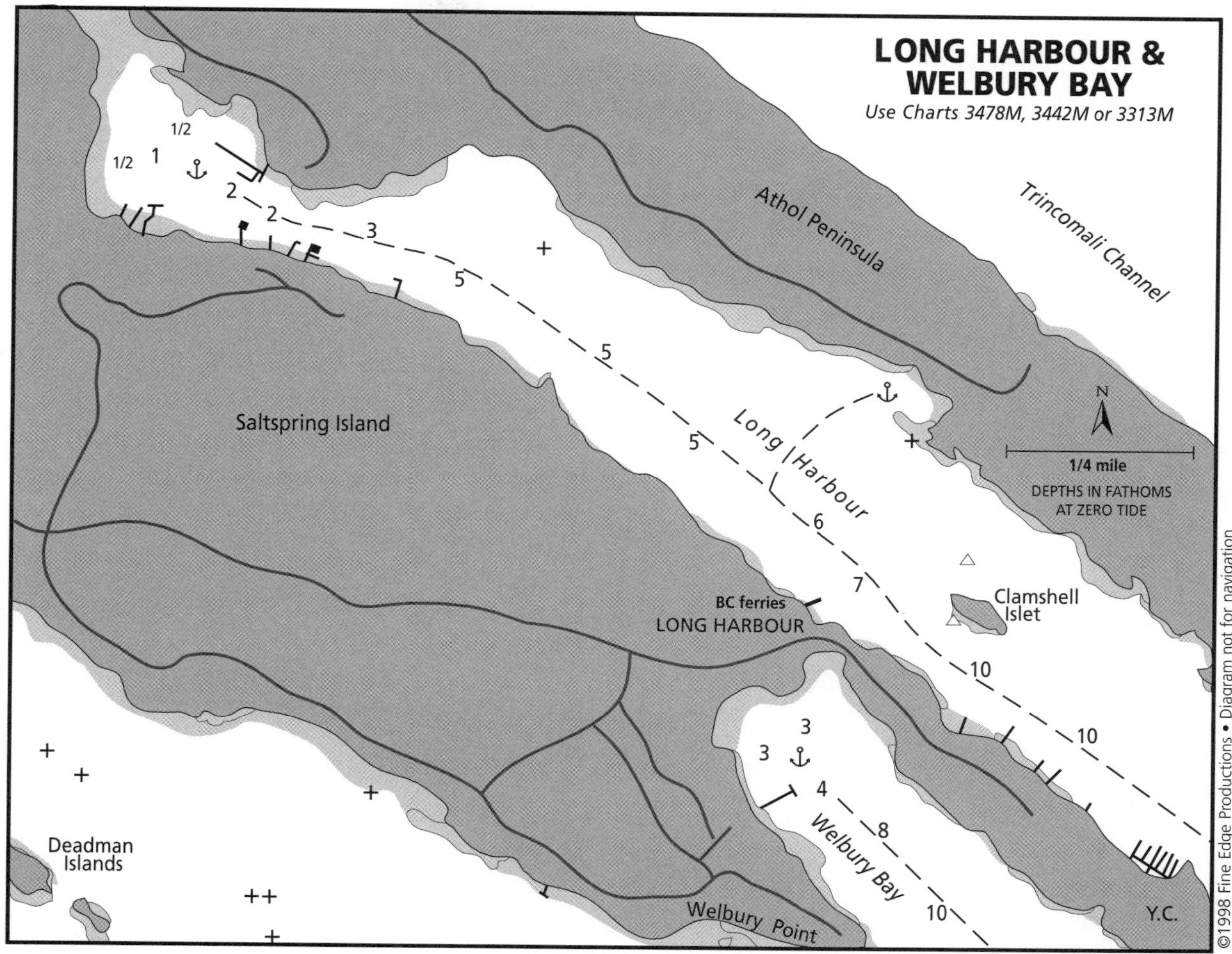

Long Harbour, entered between Scott Point and Nose Point, extends 2 miles NW and terminates in a drying mud flat.

A portage for canoes and small boats, near the ferry landing, connects with Welbury Bay.

Anchorage can be obtained in Long Harbour behind the islets NW of Nose Point or at the head of the harbour, clear of the submarine cable, in 10 to 15 feet (3 to 4.6 m), mud bottom. (pp. 189–190, SCG, Vol. 1)

Long Harbour, on the south side of Athol Peninsula, extends 2.2 miles deep into Saltspring Island. This long, scenic inlet becomes quiet past the area of local traffic between the Royal Vancouver Yacht Club outstation and the ferry terminal.

Along with beautiful private homes along the shore, you may frequently see classic wooden schooners moored at the head of Long Harbour. Good protection is afforded in most weather as southeast chop tends to die off the deeper you go into the harbor. The head has numerous private docks and mooring buoys. Avoid anchoring near the cable crossing 0.45 mile northwest of the ferry dock.

Anchor (head of the harbor) in 1 to 2 fathoms over sticky gray mud with very good holding.

Welbury Bay (Saltspring Island)

Welbury Bay, on the northeast corner of Saltspring Island, lies between Long and Ganges harbors.

Charts 3478 metric, 3442 metric, 3313 metric
Entrance: 48°50.31′ N, 123°25.64′ W (NAD 83)
Anchor: 48°50.94′ N, 123°26.21′ W (NAD 83)

Welbury Bay, NW of Welbury Point, is a narrow inlet with shallow depths at its head. (p. 189, SCG, Vol. 1)

Welbury Bay is well placed on Captain Passage to offer shelter from north and west winds; it is open to the southeast. Except for the rocky patch northwest of Buoy "U49," it has easy access. The northeast corner of the bay is just a few yards from the Long Harbour B.C. ferry dock.

Welbury Bay is surrounded by fine homes along the tree-covered shore and does not have the local and commercial traffic found in Long Harbour and Ganges Harbour.

Anchor in 3 to 4 fathoms over mud with good holding.

Madrona Bay (Saltspring Island)

Madrona Bay is 0.5 mile northeast of Ganges, inside the Chain Islets.

Charts 3478 metric, 3442 metric, 3313 metric
East entrance: 48°50.49′ N, 123°26.91′ W (NAD 83)
South entrance: 48°51.19′ N, 123°29.11′ W (NAD 83)
Anchor: 48°51.46′ N, 123°29.17′ W (NAD 83)

Madrona Bay is the small bay protected by and separated from Ganges Harbour by the Chain Islets. Away from the bustle of Ganges Harbour, Madrona Bay offers a quieter anchorage for cruising boats with a view of attractive homes among the trees.

The deep-water channel to Madrona Bay starts 0.23 mile southwest of Welbury Point and 0.38 mile northeast of Second Sister Island. Stay north of the reefs and rocks and favor the Saltspring Island shore until you have passed Money Maker Reef and the reef north of Deadman Islands. Once past these reefs, favor the north shore of Goat Island to avoid two rocks near the center of the channel.

Anne Vipond

Nose Point

Anne Vipond

Peile Point, Prevost Island

The south entrance between Powder Islet and the west corner of Goat Island is marked with a navigational aid; however, use caution in transiting this narrow passage—the fairway carries just 2 fathoms and has reefs on either side.

Anchor in 2 to 3 fathoms over grey mud with very good holding.

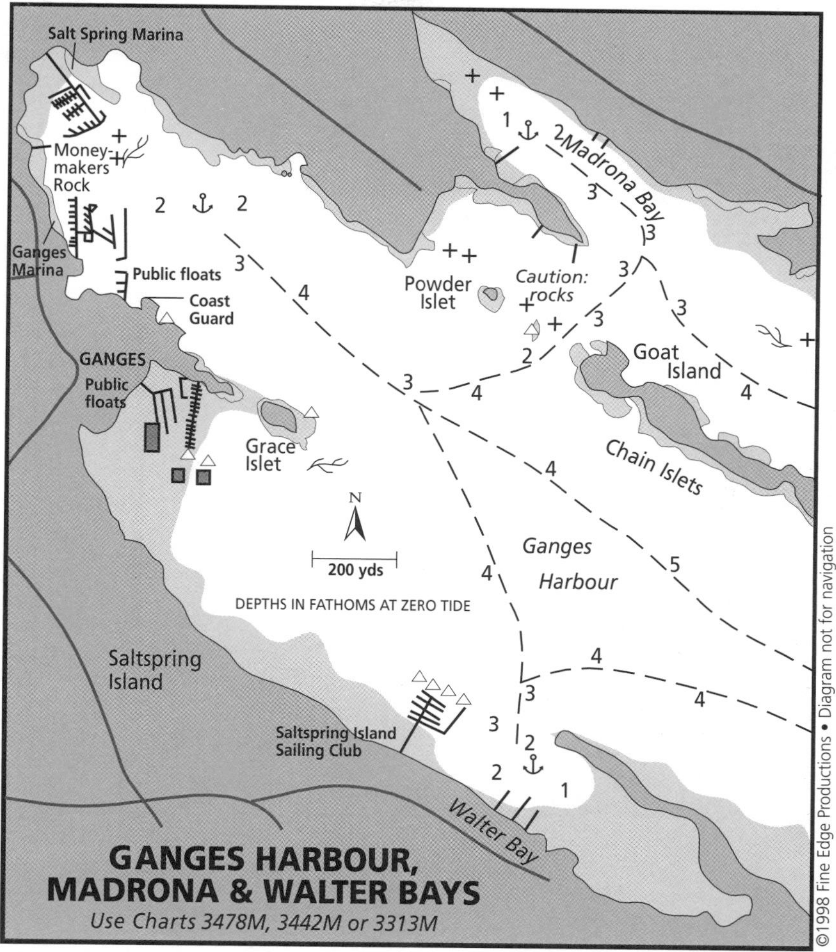

GANGES HARBOUR, MADRONA & WALTER BAYS

Use Charts 3478M, 3442M or 3313M

Ganges Harbour (Saltspring Island)

Ganges Harbour, on the east side of Saltspring Island, is 5.9 miles west of Active Pass, 12.4 miles northwest of Bedwell Harbour, and 5.4 miles north of Fulford Harbour.

Charts 3478 metric, 3442 metric, 3313 metric
Entrance (0.15 mile southeast of Second Sister Island light and 0.12 mile northeast of Ganges Shoal): 48°50.10′ N, 123°27.32′ W (NAD 83)
Government boat basin entrance (0.13 mile southwest of Grace Islet light): 48°51.04′ N, 123°29.76′ W (NAD 83)
Public floats (immediately northwest of the Coast Guard wharf): 48°51.27′ W, 123°29.91′ W (NAD 83)
Anchor (0.14 mile northeast of the Coast Guard wharf): 48°51.36′ N, 123°29.75′ W (NAD 83)
Ganges Marina (north end of breakwater): 48°51.36′ N, 123°29.92′ W (NAD 83)
Saltspring Marina (harbor's end): 48°51.45′ N, 123°30.03′ W (NAD 83)

Ganges Harbour, entered from Captain Passage, is free of dangers in the fairway with the exception of Ganges Shoal, which has 13 feet (4 m) over it.

Numerous small floats attached to fishing gear can be encountered in Ganges Harbour.

The public wharf, 0.2 mile NW of Grace Islet light, has a berthing length of 180-feet (55 m) with 17 to 23 feet (5.2 to 7 m) alongside.

A float, connected to the shore, for small craft is about 150 feet (46 m) NW of the public wharf.

The boat basin, west of Grace Islet and south of the small peninsula, is protected on its east side by a breakwater. Three public floats with a common connection to shore are at the north end of this boat basin . . . Power is available on the floats; garbage and used oil disposal facilities are at the head of the floats.

Numerous private floats and mooring buoys lie along the shores in Ganges Harbour.

On approaching the marina at the head of the harbour take extra caution to avoid Money Makers Rock, which has less than 6 feet (1.8 m) over it.

The approach to Ganges is without danger or difficulty provided it is made south and west of the Chain Islands; but a good lookout should be

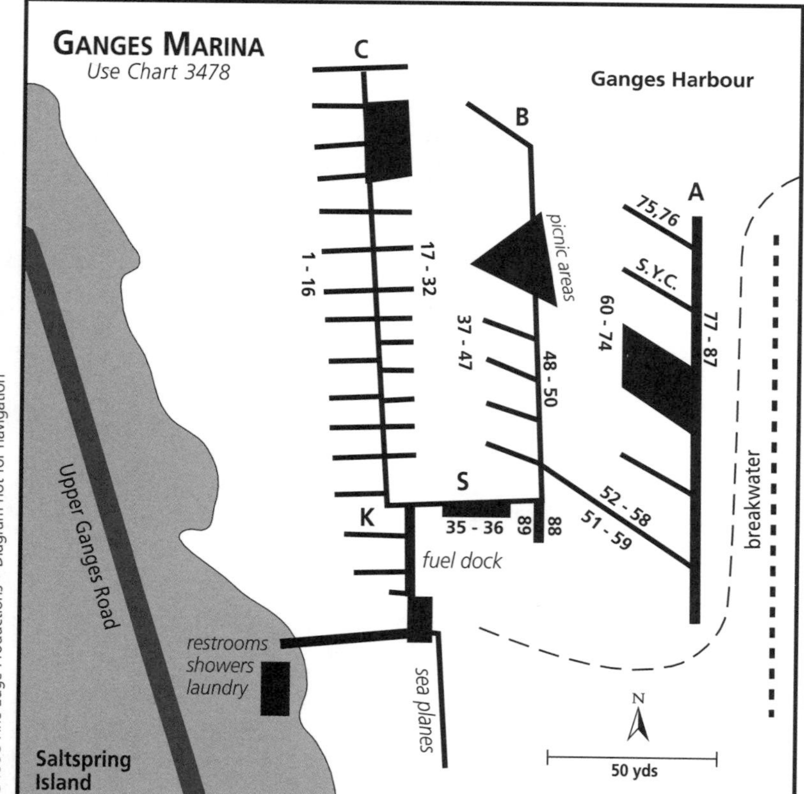

kept for seaplanes landing and taking off in the harbour. (pp. 188–189, SCG, Vol. 1)

Ganges Harbour, the largest of the settlements on Saltspring Island, is a quaint town with a variety of gift shops, restaurants, galleries and a market, all within a short walking distance of the boat harbor.

The public Ganges Boat Harbour Wharf has power, showers, garbage and waste disposal, launch ramp, and telephone; transients are welcome; they monitor VHF Channel 69 (tel: Harbour Authority of Salt Spring Island, 250-537-5711). Two private marinas include Salt Spring Marina at the head of the bay (tel: 250-537-5810) and Ganges Marina, just north of the public floats next to the Coast Guard pier (tel: 250-537-5242). Both marinas offer full amenities and monitor VHF Channel 68.

For reading matter and charts, we like to head to Volume II Bookstore in Mouat's Mall near the public dock (open seven days a week in summer).

Ganges Harbour can be very busy in the summer, but you can usually find fair-weather anchorage across the bay off the northeast shore. Walter Bay, 0.85 mile southeast of Ganges, provides shelter from southeast winds; Madrona Bay, 0.5 mile northeast of Ganges, offers a quiet escape from the traffic and bustle of Ganges.

Money Makers Rock (mentioned above in the quotation from *SCG*) is sometimes marked by kelp; it lies 400 feet north of the Ganges breakwater and 300 feet southeast of Saltspring Marina.

Walter Bay (Ganges Harbour)

Walter Bay is 0.55 miles southeast of the Ganges public wharf.

Charts 3478 metric, 3442 metric, 3313 metric
Entrance: 48°50.77′ N, 123°29.22′ W (NAD 83)
Anchor: 48°50.66′ N, 123°29.15′ W (NAD 83)

Anne Vipond

Anchorage in Ganges Harbour, northeast of Chain Islets

Ganges

The pretty seaside village of Ganges is the commercial hub of Saltspring Island. It is the largest and most populated of the Gulf Islands with about 10,000 residents, including a number of talented artists such as Robert Bateman.

Ganges is a delight to stroll, especially in summer when flowers spill from hanging baskets. Its pedestrian boardwalks lead past waterfront parks, restaurants and art galleries featuring fine art and local crafts. A summer-long fair called ArtCraft is held at Mahon Hall, a heritage building standing opposite the Ganges Marina, where you can shop for locally hand-crafted jewelry, folk art and other items.

For more details on local fairs and galleries, pop into the Chamber of Commerce building beside the Fire Hall, where walking maps and visitor information are provided. Local services include two banks and a credit union (all with bank machines), a post office, liquor store and two supermarkets. Each Saturday throughout the summer a food-and-crafts market is held at Centennial Park where a playground and picnic overlook the harbor.

A few miles north of town, the Lower Ganges Road intersects with other island roads at a spot called Central, the location of Portlock Park—site of an outdoor swimming pool, tennis courts, playground and golf course. Scooters and bikes can be rented at Ganges Marina and a free shuttle runs to the local golf course.

Saltspring Island was given its name by Hudson's Bay Company officers after they found springs of brine on the island. In 1859, Captain Richards changed the name to Admiral Island in honor of Rear Admiral Baynes who was Pacific Commander at the time. However, the former name remained in common use and in 1905 the Geographic Board of Canada adopted "Saltspring" as the island's official name. Ganges was named for the HMS *Ganges*, flagship of Rear Admiral Baynes and a line-of-battle ship which served in local waters from 1857 to 1860.

Saltspring's first house was erected by a handful of settlers on the shores of Ganges Harbour in 1859, near the site of the present Harbour House Hotel. The early settlers, who hailed from such diverse places as Scotland, Australia, and the West Indies, all came to Saltspring to forge a new life farming the land. Many were discouraged by various setbacks, including cattle rustling and wolf attacks on their farm animals. Winters could be lonely with no mail service, and the winter of 1861-62 was particularly severe, with dozens of cattle lost due to heavy snowfall and a lack of hay. In addition to these hardships was the fear of raids by local Cowichans, not all of whom took kindly to the newcomers. The Cowichans also had a long-simmering dispute with the northern tribe of Bella Bella natives, a number of which they massacred in July 1860 at Ganges Harbour.

Civility soon prevailed, however. More settlers arrived, fruit orchards flourished, and in 1892 a wealthy young Englishman named Henry Wright Bullock moved to Saltspring and built a country estate just outside Ganges where he held lavish balls and seven-course dinner parties. The good life continues today in Ganges, especially at the award-winning Hastings House—a gracious country inn and member of the internationally-renowned Relais et Chateaux. This luxury inn, set amid manicured grounds, is a short walk east of Salt Spring Marina along Upper Ganges Road. The cuisine, which has been featured in Gourmet Magazine, often serves local produce. Reservations are a must for both dinner (served each evening at 7:30 p.m.) and Sunday brunch. —**AV**

Anne Vipond

Ganges village

Ganges—a delight to stroll

Walter Bay, on the SE shore of Ganges Harbour, offers sheltered anchorage from SE weather. (p. 188, SCG, Vol. 1)

Walter Bay offers good shelter east of the Saltspring Island Sailing Club facilities and west of the drying mud flat, avoiding the private mooring buoys.

Anchor in 1 to 2 fathoms over mud with good holding.

Satellite Channel

Satellite Channel, on the south side of Saltspring Island, joins Swanson Channel and Sansum Narrows.

Charts 3441 metric, 3313 metric

Satellite Channel is entered from Swanson Channel at its east end; Shute and Colburne Passages enter its south side. It leads round the south end of Saltspring Island to Fulford Harbour, Saanich Inlet, Cowichan Bay and the south end of Sansum Narrows.

The east end of Satellite Channel is frequently (twice an hour) used by large ferries going between Swartz Bay, at the north end of Saanich Peninsula, and Tsawwassen on the mainland; these ferries use Active Pass. Smaller ferries cross Satellite Channel running between Swartz Bay and Fulford Harbour. Small craft navigators are advised to keep clear of the ferries. Most of the shorelines and coves along this stretch of the coast are exposed to the wash of these ferries.

Tidal streams attain 1 to 2 kn in Satellite Channel. The flood sets NW and the ebb SE in the vicinity of Cape Keppel, the SW corner of Saltspring Island. (p. 140, SCG, Vol. 1)

Satellite Channel and Sansum Narrows provide the fastest route to Nanaimo from Saanich Peninsula; northbound vessels can use a favorable flood current all the way through Stuart Channel to Dodd Narrows.

Princess Margaret Marine Park, Portland Island

Portland Island, on the south side of Satellite Channel between Saltspring and Moresby islands, is 4 miles north of Sidney Marina.

Charts 3476 metric, 3441 metric, 3313 metric
Entrance (Princess Bay): 48°43.03' N, 123°22.00' W (NAD 83)

Princess Margaret Marine Park, which encompasses the whole of Portland Island, has minimal development; drinking water is obtainable . . . Because of the dangers around it, Portland Island must be approached with extreme caution. (p. 130, SCG, Vol. 1)

Anchor sites can be found on Portland Island in Royal Cove, Princess Bay, Pellow Islets, and in the channel adjacent to Brackman Island. An arti-

Walter Bay offers shelter from southeast weather

Don Douglass

Looking for friends, Satellite Channel

ficial reef used by scuba divers lies on the east side of Portland Island.

Originally given to Princess Margaret Windsor to commemorate her visit to British Columbia during the province's Centennial in 1958, Portland Island was returned to the province to be designated as a marine park. The 450-acre island has drinking water, camping and toilet facilities, and a nice trail that leads through an abandoned apple orchard.

In fair weather, you can anchor in Royal Cove behind Chad Island and in Princess Bay near Tortoise Island, at the southeast side of the island. Chad and Tortoise islands are privately owned; Brackman Island is an ecological reserve. *Caution:* Drying and below-water rocks extend a half-mile offshore to the north, east, and south sides of the islands.

Royal Cove (Portland Island)

Royal Cove, on the northeast tip of Portland Island, is 3.8 miles southeast of Fulford Harbour.

Charts 3476 metric, 3441 metric, 3313 metric
Entrance (0.06 mile east of Chads Island): 48°44.16′ N, 123°22.33′ W (NAD 83)
Anchor: 48°44.07′ N, 123°22.26′ W (NAD 83)

Royal Cove is a well-sheltered, all-year anchorage, and a nice base from which to picnic and

Portland Island

Portland Island is not only a beautiful marine park, but its history is unique. The island's earliest inhabitants were Coast Salish natives, as evidenced by the shell middens. Then, in the mid-1800s, a few hundred Hawaiians were brought to local waters under contract by the Hudson's Bay Company. They were hired to work the Company's land and, because of their facility with the natives' languages, acted as interpreters for the fur traders. When their contracts expired, a number of these Hawaiians (known as "Kanakas") decided to stay and settle on Portland Island which had been given to them by the Hudson's Bay Company.

In the 1930s a colorful character named Major General Frank (One-Arm) Sutton lived on the island. After losing an arm at Gallipoli, for which he received the military cross, Sutton pursued various exploits which included golf championships and gold prospecting in Siberia. After working for a Manchurian warlord during the Chinese civil war, Sutton retired a millionaire in Victoria. Upon buying Portland Island, he stocked it with pheasants and built a stable for his race horses in a pasture near the island's southern anchorage; nearby is the fruit orchard he planted. The Crash of '29 brought an end to Sutton's lavish lifestyle, but Portland Island remained in private hands until the province acquired it in 1958, then gave it to Britain's Princess Margaret who later returned it so the island could become a marine park in 1967.

A cross-island trail connects the two main anchorages and a shoreside trail loops around the island, taking hikers past shell beaches—perfect for picnics—such as the one overlooking Brackman Island. Most of the islets surrounding Portland are privately owned with the exception of Brackman Island which is a nature reserve created by The Nature Conservancy of Canada.

Sheep once roamed Portland Island and a springtime visit was rewarded with the sight of newborn lambs. The wild sheep were apparently destroying the island's grassland and wild flowers, so they were rounded up in 1989, leaving the island to river otters and other indigenous animals. —**AV**

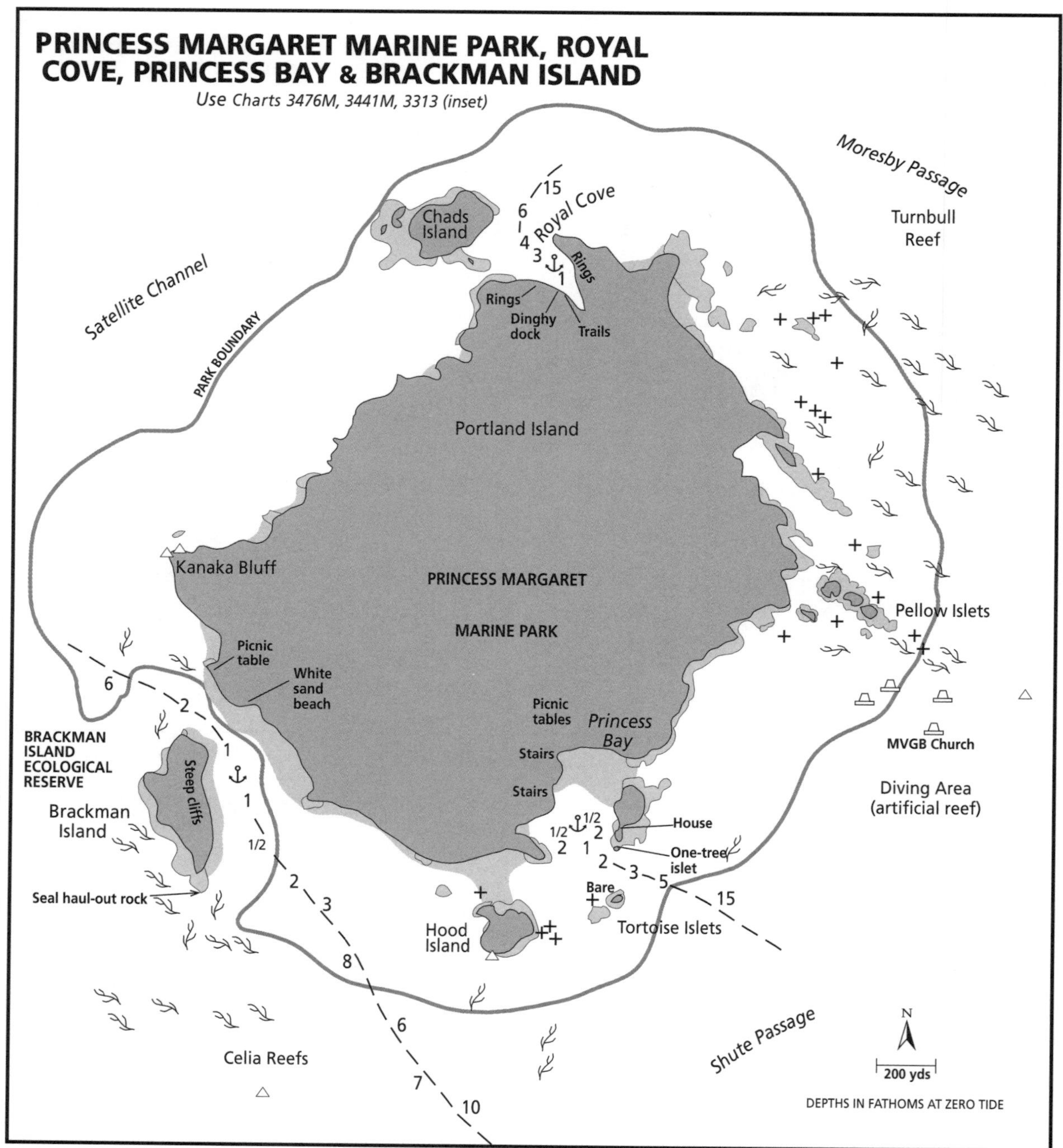

hike on Portland Island. Moderate ferry-wash enters this cove.

During the busy summer season, many boaters use a stern shore tie, made easier by use of steel rings secured to the rock along shore (7 on the north, 9 on the south).

Royal Cove has a dinghy dock, picnic and toilet facilities, and trails that lead to the other side of the island through the old orchard.

Anchor in 2 to 3 fathoms over sand, mud and small grasses with good holding.

Princess Bay or "Tortoise Bay" (Portland Island)

Princess Bay, on the southeast tip of Portland Island, is 4.0 miles northeast of Sidney Marina.

Charts 3476 metric, 3441 metric, 3313 metric
Entrance: 48°43.03′ N, 123°22.00′ W (NAD 83)
Anchor 48°43.09′ N, 123°22.20′ W (NAD 83)

> *Anchorage can be obtained at the south end of Portland Island in Princess Bay locally known as Princess Margaret Bay or Tortoise Bay. When entering the bay, enter north of and close to Tortoise Islets.* (p. 130, SCG, Vol. 1)

Royal Cove, Portland Island

Popular Princess Bay, also known as Tortoise Bay, offers fair-weather anchorage for small boats in summer. It is sheltered from northwest winds but exposed to strong southerlies.

Enter the bay via the deep-water route north of Tortoise Islets. Because its depths are shallow, watch tide levels.

Anchor in 1 fathom, soft mud and shell with eel grass; fair-to-good holding.

Pellow Islets

Pellow Islets, on the east side of Portland Island, are 0.7 mile northeast of Princess Bay.

Charts 3476 metric, 3441 metric, 3313 metric
Position: 48°43.60′ N, 123°21.54′ W (NAD 83)
Southernmost diving buoy: 48°43.31′ N, 123°21.36′ W (NAD 83)

> *Pellow Islets lie on a drying reef extending from the east extremity of Portland Island.* (p. 130, SCG, Vol. 1)

Pellow Islets are a popular stop for scuba divers. Small boats with local knowledge can anchor temporarily north of the Pellow Islets. Since the bottom in this area is quite irregular with many rocks, reefs and kelp, caution is required.

The sunken M/V *G.B. Church,* located 350 yards west of green Buoy "U-15," creates an artificial reef that makes diving attractive. The three mooring buoys here are designated exclusively for dive boats. Buoys mark the bow and stern of the sunken vessel. To keep it safe for divers, motor vessels should avoid the vicinity of the artificial reef.

The area between Pellow Islets and Turnbull Reef is a great place to kayak, and haulout spots can be found on small, sandy beaches.

Pellow Islets make great scuba diving and kayaking

Anne Vipond

The lovely forest trails on Portland Island

River otters, mink, and harbor seals can frequently be sighted along the shoreline. Bird life includes songbirds, bald eagles, oystercatchers, great blue herons, and cormorants. The reserve is closed to the public but, on the southwest side of Portland Island, there's a grassy knoll with a picnic table where you can view the animal and bird life without disturbing it.

The narrow channel between Portland Island and Brackman Island can be used as an anchorage in fair weather, but it is subject to moderate ferry wake and exposed to southeast weather.

Anchor in 1 to 2 fathoms over sand, white shell and grass; fair-to-good holding if your anchor is well set.

Brackman Island Ecological Reserve (Portland Island)

Brackman Island, on the southwest tip of Portland Island, is 0.5 mile west of Princess Bay and 1 mile southeast of Royal Cove.

Charts 3476 metric, 3441 metric, 3313 metric
South entrance: 48°43.03′ N, 123°22.89′ W (NAD 83)
North entrance: 48°43.34′ N, 123°23.27′ W (NAD 83)
Anchor: 48°43.19′ N, 123°23.03′ W (NAD 83)

> *Brackman Island, off the SW side of Portland Island, is wooded and cliffy on its east side. It is reported that temporary anchorage can be obtained between Brackman and Portland Islands.* (p. 131, SCG, Vol. 1)

Small Brackman Island was set aside as a reserve in 1989 to protect the outstanding plant, animal, and bird life representative of the dry Gulf Islands. Old-growth Douglas fir, arbutus trees, Garry oaks, white fawn lily, sea blush, chocolate lily and camas are among the eighty species of plant life found on the island.

Fulford Harbour (Saltspring Island)

Fulford Harbour, on the north side of Satellite Channel, is 5.5 miles southeast of Ganges and 3.8 miles northwest of Portland Island.

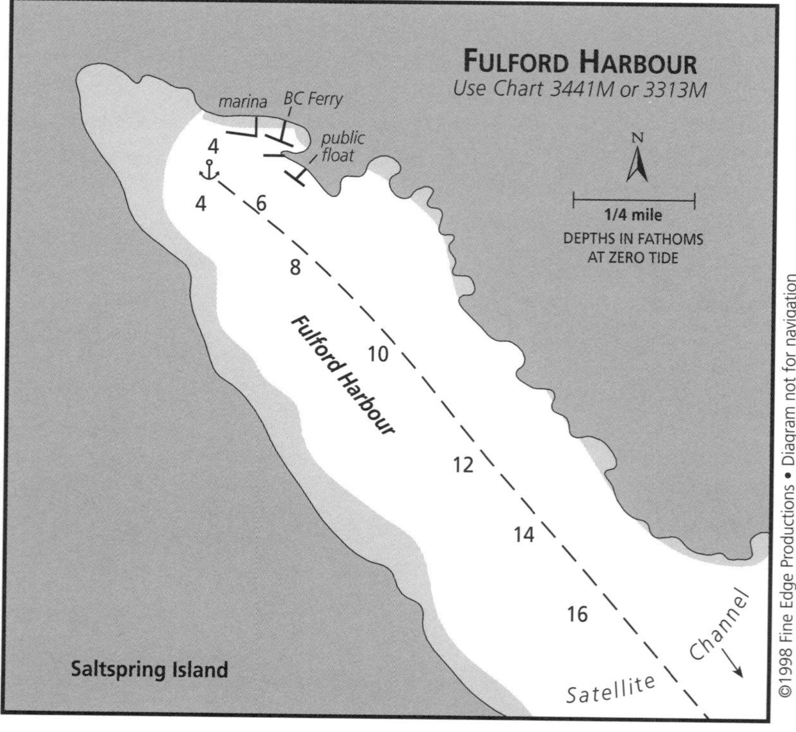

Charts 3478 metric, 3441 metric, 3313 metric
Entrance (0.18 mile southwest of Jackson Rock): 48°45.10′ N, 123°25.88′ W (NAD 83)
Ferry landing light: 48°46.18′ N, 123°27.10′ W (NAD 83)
Anchor (0.17 mile southwest of ferry landing): 48°46.12′ N, 123°27.30′ W (NAD 83)

Fulford Harbour, which penetrates the south shore of Saltspring Island, is entered between Jackson Rock and Isabella Point. Numerous private floats and moorings are in Fulford Harbour.

Anchorage can be obtained as convenient in the centre of Fulford Harbour in 59 to 85 feet (18 to 26 m); keep clear of the ferry route.

Fulford Harbour village, at the head of the inlet, has a post office (V0S 1C0), store, restaurant and a public telephone. (p. 141, SCG, Vol. 1)

Brackman Island Ecological Reserve

Anne Vipond

Fulford Harbour

Fulford Harbour is one of the oldest communities on Saltspring Island, its settlers first arriving in the Burgoyne Valley in 1862. Bob Akerman, a descendant of these early settlers, operates a museum near Fulford at 2501 Fulford-Ganges Road. Housed in a hand-crafted log building, the museum was built as a tribute to Akerman's maternal grandmother who was the daughter of a hereditary chief of the Cowichan. Exhibits include a collection of her woven baskets as well as native arrowheads, fish net weights, and canoe anchors. The museum has no set hours but visitors can phone 250-653-4228 to arrange a viewing or drop by on the chance Akerman is home and free to give a tour.

Inter-island ferry, Fulford Harbour

Don Douglass

Also of historical interest are Fulford's St. Paul's Catholic Church, built in 1880, and St. Mary's Anglican Church, built in 1894. The village, which is clustered around the ferry dock, contains several stores, eateries, galleries, and gift shops. Fulford Marina has a grocery store and deli as well as tennis courts. The Fulford Inn, an easy walk from the Fulford Marina, stands on the site of two previous inns. Lunch and dinner can be enjoyed outside on the patio or in the pub with its open fireplace. On summer weekends, an outdoor market is held beside the Fulford Inn.

Drummond Park, on the west side of the harbor, is the site of a Sea Capers festival in June and Fulford Days in August. The park is bordered by a long, partly sandy beach and contains a playground, picnic tables, and sheltered cooking area. Further afield, about 5 1/2 miles from the Fulford Harbour ferry dock, is Ruckle Park. Located at Beaver Point, this beautiful park is over a thousand acres with plenty of forest and beachside trails. Lying between Fulford Harbour and Ruckle Park, along Beaver Point Road, are Stowell and Weston lakes, both popular swimming holes.

—AV

Fulford Harbour is a large bay open to the southeast which offers surprisingly good shelter in summer weather. It has easy access from Satellite Channel and is connected by road to Ganges. There are two small marinas at the head of the bay behind the ferry dock. A small public wharf and float are adjacent to the ferry dock.

Anchorage can be taken anywhere in the center of the bay off the large drying flat, staying clear of the ferry route and public floats.

Anchor in 5 fathoms, over sand and gravel with fair holding.

Beach rocks

Cowichan Bay (Vancouver Island)

Cowichan Bay, on the west side of Satellite Channel, is 8.8 miles northwest of Swartz Bay and 4.5 miles south of Maple Bay.

Charts 3478 metric, 3441 metric, 3313 metric
Entrance (0.29 mile southwest of Separation Point): 48°44.32′ N, 123°34.42′ W (NAD 83)
Public float: 48°44.49′ N, 123°37.07′ W (NAD 83)

> *Cowichan Bay, entered south of Separation Point, extends 3 miles west and terminates in a large drying mud flat . . .*
>
> *Cowichan Bay settlement, on the south shore, is a resort for sportsmen who take part in the fishing for which the bay has achieved a wide reputation.* (p. 142, SCG, Vol. 1)

Cowichan Bay, open to southeast winds, is a large, deep-water commercial port fringed with shallow mud flats used for log storage. The attractive village of Cowichan Bay on the south side of the bay is geared to the sportfishing industry.

A small and crowded public float (Cowichan Bay Harbour Authority Wharf, tel: 250-746-5911) lies behind a substantial wooden breakwater. Visiting boats generally raft alongside local boats. West of the public float are several private marinas and the Cowichan Bay Yacht Club. Bluenose Marina (tel: 250-748-2222), offers full facilities. Cowichan Bay is too deep and exposed for convenient anchorage.

Genoa Bay, on the north shore of Cowichan Bay, offers good anchorage as well as marina facilities.

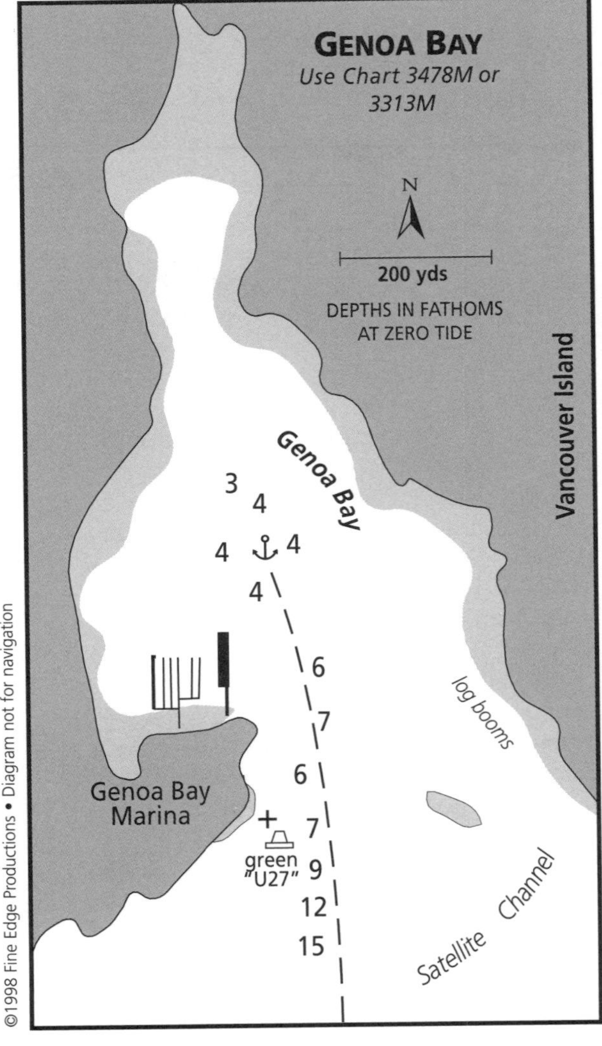

Genoa Bay (Vancouver Island)

Genoa Bay, indenting the north shore of Cowichan Bay, is 1.4 miles northeast of the village of Cowichan Bay and 3.3 miles south of Maple Bay.

Charts 3478 metric, 3441 metric, 3313 metric
Entrance: 48°45.42′ N, 123°35.72′ N (NAD 83)
Anchor: 48°45.72′ N, 123°35.88′ W (NAD 83)

> *Genoa Bay, on the north side of Cowichan Bay, is used by small craft . . . The central portion is exposed to SE winds and sea.*
>
> *Marine farm facilities and a wharf . . . are on the west side of Genoa Bay, a short distance inside the entrance.*
>
> *A store and restaurant are open during summer months.*
>
> *The east side of Genoa Bay is a logboom storage area.* (p. 143, SCG, Vol. 1; see also SD, p. 96)

Genoa Bay is a good place to anchor to wait for a change of current in Sansum Narrows or to seek protection from northerly and westerly winds. Avoid the private floats and logbooms.

The Genoa Bay Marina (tel: 250-746-7621), located on the southwest corner of the bay, provides a full range of services on a seasonal basis. Fuel, moorage, and groceries are available.

Genoa Bay is used as a center for the excellent sportfishing found in the area.

Anchor in 2 to 3 fathoms, sand and mud with reported good holding.

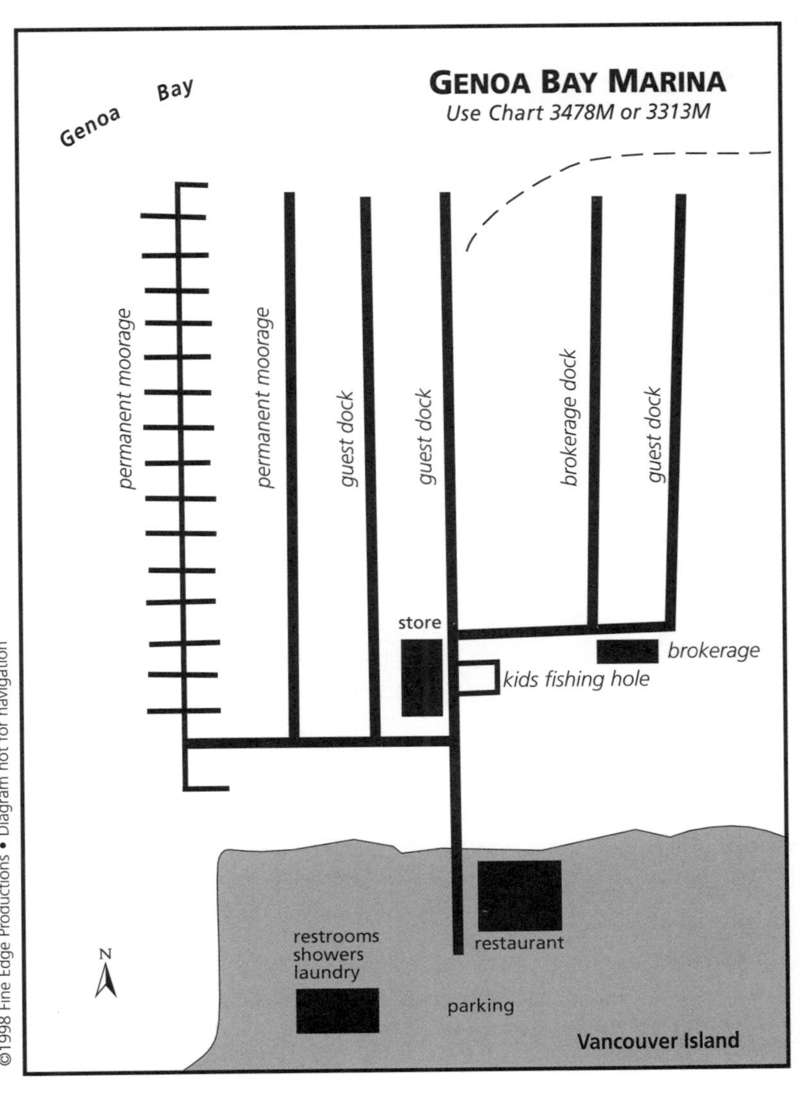

Sansum Narrows

Sansum Narrows lies between Vancouver Island and the west coast of Saltspring Island.

Charts 3478 metric, 3441 metric, 3442 metric, 3313 metric
South entrance (0.45 mile east of Separation Point): 48°44.58′ N, 123°33.53′ W (NAD 83)
North entrance (0.42 mile east of Grave Point light): 48°50.90′ N, 123°34.92′ W (NAD 83)

> *Sansum Narrows . . . leads from the west end of Satellite Channel to the south end of Stuart Channel; its narrowest part is 0.3 mile wide.*
>
> *The wind tends to funnel along the axis of the narrows and down the valleys leading into it; for this reason the wind is inclined to be directionally erratic.*
>
> *Tidal streams flood north and ebb south through Sansum Narrows. In the narrower parts of the fairway the tidal stream seldom exceeds 3 kn, being usually much less; in the wider portions 1 to 2 kn can be expected.*
>
> *Whirlpools and tide-rips occur around Burial Islet, also between*

Anne Vipond

Northwest solitude at its best

> *Sansum Point and Bold Bluff Point; under some conditions of wind and tide these can be hazardous to small craft.* (p. 149, SCG, Vol. 1; see also SD, p. 98)

In fair weather, Sansum Narrows seldom presents a problem for cruising boats; on the north-flowing flood current you get a welcome boost. Musgrave Rock, marked by red Buoy "U26," can be passed on either side.

Both Maple Bay on Vancouver Island and Burgoyne Bay on Saltspring offer good shelter toward the north end of the narrows.

Musgrave Landing (Saltspring Island)

Musgrave Landing, at the south end of Sansum Narrows, is on the west side of Saltspring Island.

Charts 3478 metric, 3441 metric, 3313 metric
Public dock: 48°44.95′ N, 123°33.00′ W (NAD 83)

> *Musgrave landing . . . on the north side of Musgrave Point, has a 40 foot (12 m) public float extending west from an approach ramp; depths alongside range from 6 to 22 feet (1.8 to 6.7 m).*
>
> *Several drying and below-water rocks lie within 0.1 mile offshore between 0.3 and 0.8 mile NW of Musgrave Point.* (p. 149, SCG, Vol. 1)

Cowichan Bay and Genoa Bay

Cowichan Bay was named for a large tribe of natives that once inhabited the sheltered bays of Vancouver Island's east coast. The tribe, which consisted of various small bands such as the Saanich and Chemainus, thrived on the area's abundance of fresh water, wood and seafood. The name Cowichan means "between streams" and two rivers form a delta at the head of Cowichan Bay where tidal flats lead to a fertile valley now filled with farms and vineyards.

White settlers moved into the area in the mid-1800s and the South Cowichan Lawn Tennis Club was established in 1887, making it the world's oldest lawn tennis club after Wimbledon. The club's early members included Robert Service, who would sit in the shade of a maple tree penning his poems. Back then, the seven grass courts were leveled by roller, pulled by a horse wearing leather boots to protect the lawns. Today the club's international tournament, held each summer, attracts seeded players and former champions from across North America. They come not only to play on grass but to enjoy the club's beautiful setting and genteel atmosphere where traditions include afternoon tea and old-fashioned sportsmanship.

The village of Cowichan also features art galleries and restaurants serving local seafood. Several marinas line the bay's south shore. Lying opposite is Genoa Bay, named for the Italian birthplace of an early settler who built the first hotel in Cowichan Bay. Genoa Bay is a beautiful inlet with Mount Tzuhalem rising above its shores. The mountain is named for a Cowichan war chief and fierce murderer who lived there in a cave after being banished by his own tribe. From the Genoa Bay Marina you can hike up Skinner Bluff to Mount Tzuhalem for spectacular views. The marina has a store and licensed restaurant. —**AV**

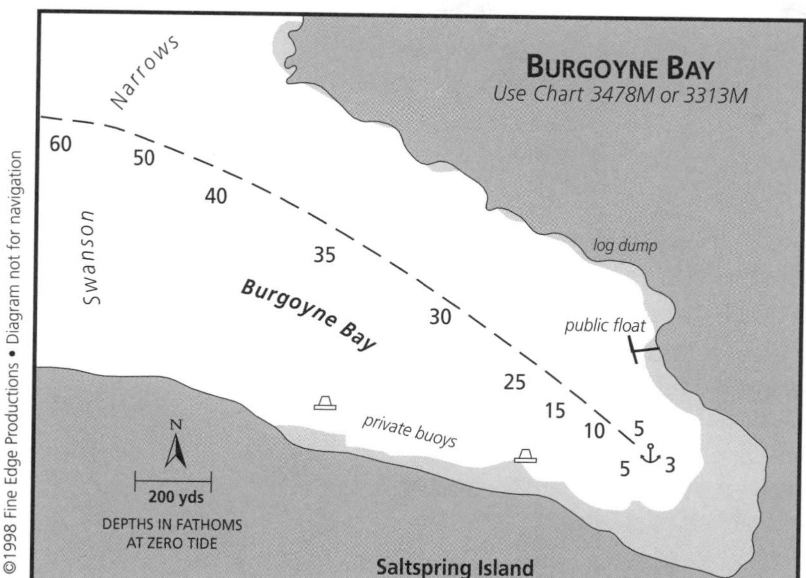

Musgrave Landing, the tiny cove immediately north of Musgrave Point, has a small public float; you can find temporary protection from southeast weather here.

Burgoyne Bay (Saltspring Island)

Burgoyne Bay, on the north end of Sansum Narrows, is 3.75 miles southeast of Maple Bay.

Charts 3478 metric, 3442 metric, 3313 metric
Entrance: 48°47.84′ N, 123°32.45′ W (NAD 83)
Public float: 48°47.57′ N, 123°31.31′ W (NAD 83)
Anchor: 48°47.41′ N, 123°31.29′ W (NAD 83)

> *Burgoyne Bay, entered north of Bold Bluff Point, extends 1.25 miles ESE and terminates in a drying flat of mud and sand. A sandy beach is on the south side near the head. Small craft can obtain anchorage near the head of the bay, in 24 feet (7.3 m) or more, mud bottom.* (p. 150, SCG, Vol. 1)

Burgoyne Bay, on the west side of Saltspring Island, provides good shelter in southeast storms, but it is open to northwesterlies. Anchorage can be found deep in the center of the bay off the drying flat, avoiding the private floats. The small public float is used for loading or emergency mooring only.

Anchor in 5 fathoms over mud and sand.

Maple Bay (Vancouver Island)

Maple Bay, near the north end of Sansum Narrows, is 3.3 miles north of Genoa Bay and 3.5 miles southeast of Crofton.

Charts 3478 metric, 3442 metric, 3313 metric
Entrance (0.33 mile south of Arbutus Point): 48°48.92′ N, 123°35.25′ W (NAD 83)
Public wharf: 48°48.89′ N, 123°36.55′ W (NAD 83)

> *Maple Bay is entered between Paddy Mile Stone and Arbutus Point, 0.75 mile north. The community of Maple Bay is on the west side of the bay . . . Numerous private floats lie along the shores of Maple Bay and Birds Eye Cove.*
>
> *Two public floats, in the west part of the bay, have depths of 15 to 27 feet (4.6 to 8.2 m) alongside.*

Don Douglass

Time to fish or cut bait

Caution: A rock, with less than 6 feet (2 m) over it, and a shoal with 7 feet (2.1 m) over it, lie close SE of the public floats. (p. 150, SCG, Vol. 1)

Maple Bay has a public dock with floats which can be used by cruising boats while visiting the community of Maple Bay.

Birds Eye Cove (Vancouver Island)

Birds Eye Cove is 0.9 mile south of Maple Bay public float.

Charts 3478 metric, 3442 metric, 3313 metric
Entrance: 48°48.30′ N, 123°36.00′ W (NAD 83)
Anchor: 48°47.85′ N, 123°35.99′ W (NAD 83)

Birds Eye Cove is the south arm of Maple Bay. Small craft can obtain anchorage in 24 to 36 feet (7.2 to 11 m), mud, near the head of the cove. (p. 150, SCG, Vol. 1)

Maple Bay and Birds Eye Cove have facilities for pleasure craft, among which are Maple Bay Marina (tel: 250-746-8482), Maple Bay Yacht Club (tel: 250-746-5421), and Birds Eye Cove Marina (tel: 250-748-4255). Maple Bay Marina has fuel and full amenities for cruising boats, in addition to a store and pub. Birds Eye Cove Marina, in the south end of Maple Bay, has fuel, limited guest moorage and no showers.

The western half of the cove is taken up with floats, but well-sheltered anchorage can be found along the east shore. There are reports of a sunken fishing boat having fouled anchors; the boat lies 100 feet off the Birds Eye Cove dock.

Anchor in 4 to 6 fathoms, over sand and mud with good holding.

Maple Bay

Maple Bay is one of the finest natural harbors found in the Gulf Islands area and it contains full-service marinas, a yacht club and government dock. The beach beside the public wharf is popular for swimming; the community of Maple Bay stretches up the hill behind it. Marina facilities are located in Birds Eye Cove at the head of the bay, and there are stores, restaurants and a pub housed in a former shipyard.

The fishing is good both in the bay and in nearby Sansum Narrows, as is wildlife watching. Maple Bay is also the closest tie-up to Duncan where the Native Heritage Centre is well worth a visit. Situated on the Cowichan River, it features totem poles, a magnificent Big House and a gallery that displays genuine Cowichan sweaters, carvings, masks, prints and jewelry. At the center you can watch totem poles being carved and the traditional weaving, beading, spinning and knitting of native crafts. —**AV**

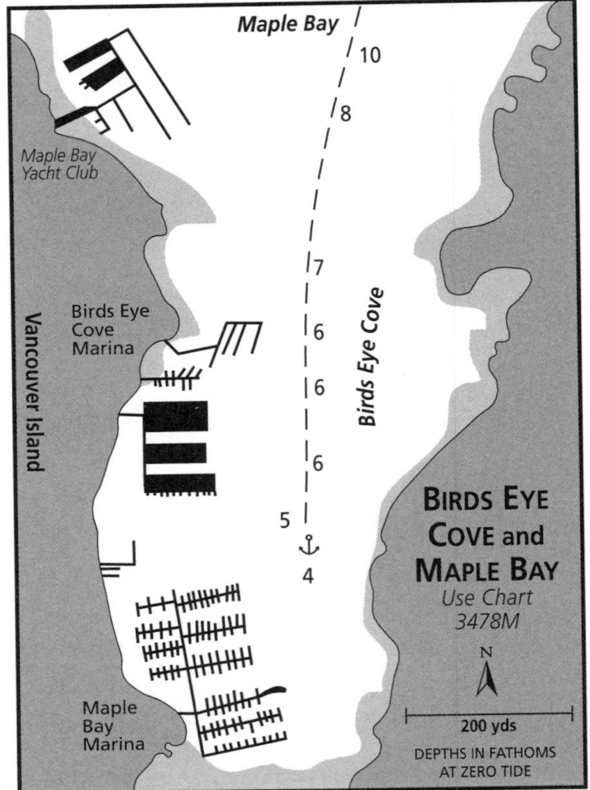

Don Douglass

Classic Woody, Birds Eye Cove

9

TRINCOMALI CHANNEL

Montague Harbour, Galiano Island, East shore of Saltspring, Kuper and Thetis Islands, Houstoun Passage (Wallace Island), Porlier Pass, to Valdes Island

Introduction

Trincomali Channel lies between Galiano Island, to the northeast, and Thetis, Kuper, and Saltspring islands to the southwest. Reid, Hall, Secretary, and Wallace islands lie in the channel itself. Along Trincomali Channel excellent anchorages can be found in Montague Harbor—a favorite Gulf Islands destination—and at Wallace Island Marine Park. Numerous small bights and coves along the sides of the channel offer quiet and attractive anchor sites in fair weather.

Long and narrow, Galiano is one of the driest of the Gulf Islands and a good spot for hiking and biking. Bluff Park is a long, hilly hike from beautiful Montague Harbour, but its panoramic views make it worthwhile. Montague Harbour Marine Park has a white shell beach, picnic and campsites, and water.

On the northeast side of Saltspring lies Fernwood Point with a public pier and mooring float. There's a store, and Salty Springs spa is nearby. A one-mile walk takes you to St. Mary Lake where there is swimming and fishing.

Almost all of Wallace Island is a Provincial Marine Park, well worth a stop on your cruising itinerary. The waters around the various anchorages—"Panther Point Cove," Conover Cove, and Princess Bay—can be tricky, so keep a sharp lookout.

Kuper Island is a native reserve that is thickly forested and relatively pristine. The Cut is a drying channel between Thetis and Kuper islands, with Telegraph Harbour at its west end and Clam Bay on its east.

Back along the Galiano shoreline, Spotlight and "Flagpole" coves invite exploration, as do Baines and Lighthouse bays. Cruise through Porlier Pass between Galiano and Valdes and around the northernmost tip of Galiano to Dionisio Point Park, with its lovely sandy beaches, comfortable swimming waters and tidepools to explore. There are unusual sandstone formations or ledges, and arbutus, oak and juniper can be found upland of the shores.

Cardale Point, on Valdes, has a beautiful beach. Nearby Strawberry Point is the site of native burial grounds. Please honor all such archaeological features and leave them as you found them.

Trincomali Channel

Trincomali Channel extends northward from Active Pass to Porlier Pass and Stuart and Pylades channels.

Charts 3442 metric, 3313 metric
South entrance (0.35 mile west of Enterprise Reef): 48°50.71′ N, 123°21.42′ W (NAD 83)
Northwest entrance (at Stuart Channel between Danger Reefs and Tree Island): 49°03.45′ N, 123°42.30′ W (NAD 83)
North entrance (at Pylades Channel): 49°03.60′ N, 123°40.20′ W (NAD 83)
Ben Mohr Rock light: 48°51.63′ N, 123°23.38′ W (NAD 83)

> *Trincomali Channel leads NW from Navy Channel, Swanson Channel and Active Pass to Pylades and Stuart Channels . . . At the NW end of Trincomali Channel, Stuart Channel is entered between Thetis and Pylades Islands.*
>
> *The NE side of Trincomali Channel is formed by Galiano Island and Valdes Island; Prevost, Saltspring and Thetis Islands form its SW side.*
>
> *Tidal streams in the SE and wider part of Trincomali Channel attain 1.5 kn, but north of Wallace Island there is an increase in velocity and up to 3 kn can be expected.* (p. 196, SCG, Vol. 1)

Trincomali Channel, the most direct route for boats heading north from the San Juan Islands in the direction of Nanaimo, is well protected by Galiano, Valdes and Saltspring islands. While open to southeast winds, it can be used by small boats in stormy weather when the Strait of Georgia is impassable.

Con Douglass

Sun time, Trincomali Channel

Don Douglass

Fog in Trincomali Channel

Galiano Island

Galiano Island, between Trincomali Channel and the Strait of Georgia, is northwest of Mayne Island and southeast of Valdes Island,.

Charts 3442 metric, 3313 metric

> *Galiano Island, with Porlier Pass at its north end and Active Pass at its south end, is 14 miles long in a NW/SE direction. The island has a population of 754 (1986).* (p. 114, SD)

Galiano Island, one of the chain of islands stretching from Saturna Island to Gabriola Island, provides separation and protection from the Strait of

Georgia. The island, with its hills, helps create a smooth-water route in Trincomali Channel.

Montague Harbour is among the most protected and most popular small-craft destinations in the Gulf Islands.

Don Douglass

Payne Bay

Payne Bay (Galiano Island)

Payne Bay is 1 mile southeast of the Montague Marine Park float.

Charts 3442 metric, 3473 metric, 3313 metric
South entrance (0.1 mile west of Phillimore Point): 48°52.30′ N, 123°23.67′ W (NAD 83)

Learning About the Venturi Effect

by Tom Shardlow

I learned firsthand about the Venturi effect when I was a student biologist conducting research in the Gulf Islands. It happened many years ago during a wonderful summer I spent aboard a 22-foot Lynwood. My work involved towing an underwater video camera with a lure attached. I watched the video monitor on top of the small galley table and was fascinated by the fish that appeared on the flickering screen. I marveled at the power and precision of coho as they torpedoed unerringly toward the bait. I watched dogfish make awkward attempts at capturing my slow-moving lure and wondered how they could make a living trying to catch live prey. These observations, along with a paper printout from the echo sounder, told me how many and what kinds of fish lurked beneath as I weaved my little boat through a fleet of anglers. My research involved correlating the fish population with the fishermen's catch and to do this I also needed a catch survey.

The survey was simple enough—just a few questions on a sheet of paper asking how long the fishermen had been fishing and how many fish they had caught. The difficult part was to get the questionnaire to the anglers and recover it without bumping into their boat or making them reel in their lines.

I devised a long pole made from a 14-foot length of 2-inch doweling and affixed a clip to the end. To prevent damage when I stretched the pole between my boat and the fishermen's, I added a soft rubber ball to the end.

Things went well on the first field trial. After a few careful maneuvers I was able to hold the pole under one arm while I steered with the other. The fishermen would unclip the envelope containing the form and, later when I returned, they would reclip the completed form to the pole.

I had just completed the survey, but there was one last boat. He was fishing in the swift current of Porlier Pass. Eager to get every last data point, and having gained confidence in the form-transfer maneuver, I sped toward him with the pole tucked under my arm, like a knight in a jousting tournament. I smiled inwardly at his look of concern as I approached.

Then the Venturi effect came into play. A fluid flowing between two objects produces a force that pulls the objects together. The Venturi effect can occur with surprising suddenness, and our boats were sucked together by the fast-moving current. The pole found the centre of the fisherman's chest as he reached for the form, knocking him to the deck of his boat. Thinking my steering or his was at fault, I pulled away and reined my boat into a 360-degree turn to make ready for the second pass. If he had looked concerned on my first approach, he now looked downright alarmed as he ducked to avoid being impaled a second time. He had, however, managed to get possession of the envelope. Deciding against a third attempt, I shouted that he could post the self-addressed stamped envelope when he got to shore. His hand gestures, however, left no doubt that this was one data point science was going to have to do without.

[*Editor's note:* Tom is an author and marine biologist who also holds a 40-ton vessel masters ticket. He has cruised extensively on the coast of B.C.]

North entrance (0.18 mile south of Winstanley Point): 48°53.07′ N, 123°23.97′ W (NAD 83)
Anchor: 48°52.42′ N, 123°23.29′ W (NAD 83)

> *Payne Bay . . . offers temporary anchorage, mud and sand bottom.* (p. 198, SCG, Vol. 1)

Payne Bay offers shelter along its south shore east of Phillimore Point. Anchor in its southeast corner where there's good protection from all weather. Avoid the private mooring buoys.

Anchor in 4 to 6 fathoms over mud and sand with good holding.

Montague Harbour (Galiano Island)

Montague Harbour, between Parker Island and the southwest side of Galiano Island, is 2.8 miles northwest of the southwest entrance to Active Pass.

Charts 3473 metric, 3442 metric, 3313 metric
South entrance (0.18 mile south of Winstanley Point): 48°53.07′ N, 123°23.97′ W (NAD 83)
North entrance (0.23 mile west of Gray Peninsula): 48°53.83′ N, 123°24.97′ W (NAD 83)
Float: 48°53.83′ N, 123°24.16′ W (NAD 83)

Montague Harbour Marine Park

Montague Harbour is the location of British Columbia's first marine park, established in 1959. Situated at the northwest end of the harbor, this popular park provides mooring buoys and an extensive wharf where small runabouts and tenders can dock. Other park facilities include a campground, picnic shelter and pay phones.

A lovely trail leads through the campground to Gray Peninsula and loops around the shoreline past beautiful beaches of crushed clamshell which are popular with sunbathers and swimmers in summer. Such beaches are ancient kitchen middens of the Coast Salish natives, a large settlement having thrived at Montague Harbour for several thousand years. Middens were formed from empty clam and mussel shells tossed into heaps which, over time, were crushed and compressed into beaches several yards deep. These white beaches were easily spotted by villagers returning after dark in their canoes. From an archaeologist's point of view, they have preserved ancient artifacts such as antler carvings and stone bowls thanks to the shells neutralizing the acid in the soil. An archaeological dig that took place in Montague Harbour just east of the park wharf in the mid-1960s unearthed hundreds of stone and bone implements, some dating back 3,000 years.

From mid-May to the end of September, a shuttle bus runs between Montague Harbour and the Hummingbird Pub. The bus picks up at both the marine park and the marina located near the opposite end of the harbour beside the public docks and old ferry wharf where there is a store and phone booth. Should you feel like taking a hike, Bluffs Park overlooking Active Pass is worth the four-mile trek up Montague Harbour Road to Georgeson Bay Road where you turn right and continue to Bluff Drive which leads to the park entrance. A path will take you to the edge of a bluff overlooking Georgeson Bay and the western entrance to Active Pass. From this lofty vantage you can watch the vessel traffic in Active Pass below while eagles soar overhead. The park is situated on land donated by the late Max and Marion Enke, a newly-married couple when they settled on Galiano in 1907. Their daughter was the first white child born on the island; in 1913 the family moved to a large home in Victoria's Oak Bay neighborhood. —**AV**

William Kelly

Unwinding at Montague Harbour

Anchor (0.1 mile southeast of park float): 48°53.75′ N, 123°24.00′ W (NAD 83)
South anchorage (0.22 mile southwest of ferry dock): 48°53.30′ N, 123°23.56′ W (NAD 83)

Montague Harbour, on the SW side of Galiano Island, is sheltered by Parker Island and affords a good anchorage. Its south entrance, between Phillimore Point and Julia Island, is easy of access. The north entrance, between Gray Peninsula and the peninsula on the NE side of Parker Island, has a depth of 17 feet (5.2 m) through the centre of its fairway.

Anchorage: Good anchorage, mud bottom, can be found on the NE side of Montague Harbour; care should be taken to avoid anchoring in the approach to the ferry wharf. (p. 198, SCG, Vol. 1)

MONTAGUE HARBOUR AND MARINE PARK
Use Charts 3473M, 3442M, 3313M

©1998 Fine Edge Productions • Diagram not for navigation

Montague Harbour, one of the most protected and well-used shelters in the Gulf Islands, is a primary destination for cruising boats. Montague Harbour Marine Park, the first of such British Columbia marine parks, lies in the northwest corner of the harbor. The park includes a dinghy and mooring dock (length limit 30 feet), 25 mooring buoys (fees collected), picnic tables, toilets and several pay telephones. The park has excellent trails and beaches, with swimming off the north beach of Gray Peninsula spit where the water warms to comfortable temperatures in summer due to the shallow depths. Montague Harbour Marine Park is a very good place to kayak or sail a dinghy.

Excellent moorage can be found anywhere outside the line of mooring buoys; some shallow-draft boats anchor inside the line of mooring buoys. Boats wishing more isolation can find anchorage in the isthmus coves of Parker Island, as noted below. Anchorage can also be found off the beach north of Gray Peninsula.

The southeast corner of the harbor offers very good shelter during southeast gales and provides overflow anchorage for the marine park or for those not interested in using the park facilities.

Anne Vipond

Montague Harbour Marine Park in autumn

Anne Vipond

Montague Harbour

The north entrance to Montague Harbour is shallow (3 fathoms minimum) but with a clear fairway. In addition to the mooring buoys and public wharf which are frequently filled during the summer, there are other alternatives, as indicated on the diagram. In southerly winds, well-sheltered anchorage can be found in the south quadrant of Montague Harbour.

Anchor (0.1 mile southeast of park float) in 4 fathoms over mud and shells with very good holding.

Anchor (0.22 mile southwest of ferry dock) in 3 to 5 fathoms over mud, sand and shells with good holding.

"Isthmus Coves" (Parker Island)

Isthmus Coves are 0.6 mile southwest of the Montague Marine Park float.

Charts 3473 metric, 3442 metric, 3313 metric
Anchor (south isthmus cove): 48°53.42′ N, 123°24.72′ W (NAD 83)
Anchor (north isthmus cove): 48°53.70′ N, 123°25.21′ W (NAD 83)

> *Parker Island, 0.4 mile NW of Phillimore Point, lies across the entrance to Montague Harbour and has steep cliffs on its SW side. Julia Island lies close off its SE extremity; the channel between these islands is usable by small craft.* (p. 198 SCG, Vol. 1)

Isthmus Coves are the two coves—one on each side of the isthmus—formed by the mushroom-shaped peninsula on the northeast side of Parker Island. Avoid private mooring buoys in both coves.

Anchor in 3 to 5 fathoms over sand and gravel with fair-to-good holding.

Gray Peninsula Anchorage (Galiano Island)

Gray Peninsula Anchorage is 0.35 miles northwest of the Montague Harbour Marine Park float.

Charts 3473 metric, 3442 metric, 3313 metric
West entrance (between Parker and Sphinx islands): 48°43.66′ N, 123°25.77′ W (NAD 83)
Anchor: 48°53.96′ N, 123°24.64′ W (NAD 83)

> *A hydro tower on Gray Peninsula is conspicuous from seaward and a useful landmark when making for Montague Harbour.* (p. 198, SCG, Vol. 1)

Gray Peninsula can be entered from Trincomali Channel on either side of Sphinx Island. A pleasant anchorage—with good beach access to marine park facilities, beautiful sunsets and less commotion—can be found on the west side of the peninsula. Avoid the rocks off the northwest corner of Gray Peninsula that are marked by kelp in the summer; anchor in front of the long sandy beach. Although this site is open to westerly chop, it is otherwise well sheltered.

Anchor in 3 to 4 fathoms over mud, sand and gravel with fair-to-good holding.

Taylor Cove/Cook Cove (Galiano Island, Strait of Georgia)

Cook Cove is 1.4 miles north of Montague Harbour; Taylor Cove is 1.7 miles northeast of Montague Harbour.

Charts 3442 metric, 3473 metric, 3313 metric
Position (Taylor Cove): 48°54.43′ N, 123°21.68′ W (NAD 83)
Position (Cook Cove): 48°55.23′ N, 123°24.35′ W (NAD 83)

Taylor Cove and Cook Cove, 0.6 and 2.6 miles west of Salamanca Point, are not recommended for anchoring because of the submarine cable area. (p. 214, SCG, Vol. 1)

Cook and Taylor coves, on the north side of Galiano Island, are the only *named* coves on the Strait of Georgia side of the island. They may provide temporary emergency shelter for small craft in southerly weather.

Don Douglass

Retreat Cove public floats

Ballingall Islets Park (Trincomali Channel)

Ballingall Islets are 2.3 miles northwest of Montague Harbour.

Charts 3473 metric, 3442 metric, 3313 metric
Position: 48°54.40′ N, 123°27.48′ W (NAD 83)

Ballingall Islets, NW of Wise Island, are low and covered with stunted shrubs. Drying and sunken rocks, extend 0.2 mile NW from Ballingall Islets. Ballingall Islets are a Provincial Nature Park. (p. 200, SCG, Vol. 1)

Strangely-shaped trees and abundant wildlife make this islet park a good place for some great nature shots with a telephoto lens.

Retreat Cove (Galiano Island)

Retreat Cove is 4.7 miles northwest of Montague Harbour and 5.5 miles southeast of Porlier Pass.

Charts 3473 metric, 3442 metric, 3313 metric
Entrance: 48°56.33′ N, 123°30.13′ W (NAD 83)
Anchor: 48°56.41′ N, 123°30.10′ W (NAD 83)

Retreat Cove, 1 mile NNW of Walker Rock, affords good shelter in its SE corner in depths of 6 to 27 feet (1.8 to 8.2 m).

The public wharf, with a float attached to its outer end, is in the SE part of Retreat Cove; the float is 100 feet (30 m) long with 13 feet (4 m) alongside. (p. 201, SCG, Vol. 1)

Retreat Cove, a small nook with temporary shelter available at the public float or immediately north, should be entered on the southeast side of Retreat Island. It's interesting to compare the two charts that show Retreat Cove; the differences in horizontal datum can clearly be seen. (See sidebar below.)

Anchor in 1 fathom over mud with good holding and limited swinging room.

Fernwood Point (Saltspring Island)

Fernwood Point, on the northeast side of Saltspring Island, is 1.87 miles southwest of Retreat Cove and 3.1 miles southeast of Southey Point.

Horizontal Datum Makes a Difference!

Comparing the two existing charts of Retreat Cove on Galiano Island is a graphic way to see the differences in horizontal chart datum.

On Chart 3442 metric (NAD 27), the longitude line for 123°30.00′ W runs through the very tip of the south entrance to Retreat Cove, i.e., west of the public wharf.

On Chart 3313 metric, p. 17 (NAD 83), the same longitude line (123°30.00′ W) lies entirely *over land* and *east* of the public wharf on the south side of Retreat Cove! The horizontal datum on Chart 3313 metric (NAD 83) is roughly 100 yards east of the position taken from chart 3442 (NAD 27). This difference in the two datums varies as the latitude varies and needs to be carefully noted if you switch between charts drawn to different datums.

Don Douglass

Fernwood Point public float

Charts 3442 metric, 3313 metric
Public float: 48°54.98′ N, 123°31.94′ W (NAD 83)

> *Fernwood Point is the SE entrance point to Houstoun Passage.*
>
> *A public pier with a float attached to its outer end, extends over the tidal flats at Fernwood Point; the float has 100 feet (30 m) of berthing space with a depth of 10 feet (3 m) alongside.* (p. 166, SCG, Vol. 1)

The public dock on the north side of Fernwood Point is used as a dinghy dock for commuters going to Galiano Island. A small store is located 50 yards above the dock on the left side of Fernwood Road. The store has a deli with produce, dairy, some staples, gasoline and very good homemade pizza. Boats from Wallace Island Marine Park can place their orders by cell phone and make a dinghy run for pickup!

Houstoun Passage

Houstoun Passage wraps around the north tip of Saltspring Island. [*Note:* Houstoun is spelled "Houston" on chart 3313 but "Houstoun" elsewhere.]

Charts 3442 metric, 3313 metric
East entrance (0.44 mile south of Panther Point light): 48°55.39′ N, 123°31.96′ W (NAD 83)
West entrance (0.98 mile southeast of North Reef and 0.66 mile northwest of Parminter Point): 48°54.30′ N, 123°36.40′ W (NAD 83)

> *Houstoun Passage connects Stuart Channel to Trincomali Channel.*
>
> *Merchant vessels awaiting berths in Crofton or Chemainus often anchor in the western portion of Houstoun Passage.*
>
> *Tidal streams within Houstoun Passage are generally weak. The flood sets NW and the ebb SE.* (p. 165, SCG, Vol. 1)

Houstoun Passage affords convenient passage to Wallace Island Marine Park and to Telegraph Harbour and Chemainus. Avoid North Reef at the west entrance, the reefs on the south side of Wallace Island, and the rocks in Trincomali Channel east of Fernwood Point.

Wallace Island Marine Park (Wallace Island)

Wallace Island, between Trincomali Channel and Houstoun Passage, is 1.5 miles east of the north tip of Saltspring Island.

Charts 3442 metric, 3313 metric
Southeast end (Panther Point light): 48°55.82′ N, 123°31.98′ W (NAD 83)
Northwest end (Chivers Point): 48°57.40′ N, 123°34.46′ W (NAD 83)

> *Wallace Island is separated from Secretary Islands by a narrow channel which has a drying reef and below-water rocks in mid-channel . . . A narrow chain of rocky islets, drying rocks and shoals lie parallel with, and 0.2 mile from the SW shore of Wallace Island.* (p. 166, SCG, Vol. 1; see also SD, p. 105)

Wallace Island Marine Park, open all year, is one our favorite off-season anchorages. It is tree-covered and has toilets, campsites, picnic areas and hiking trails. While the most popular anchorages are Conover and Princess coves, anchor sites can be found in many nooks and crannies including the window between the Secretary Islands. The Chuckanut sandstone formations of the San Juan and Gulf islands are clearly visible as narrow seams in a northwest-southeast orientation. When these seams reach the surface, they create many reefs and rocks which, in Houstoun Passage, are not marked by navigation aids and must be carefully avoided, particularly on the southeast side of Wallace Island.

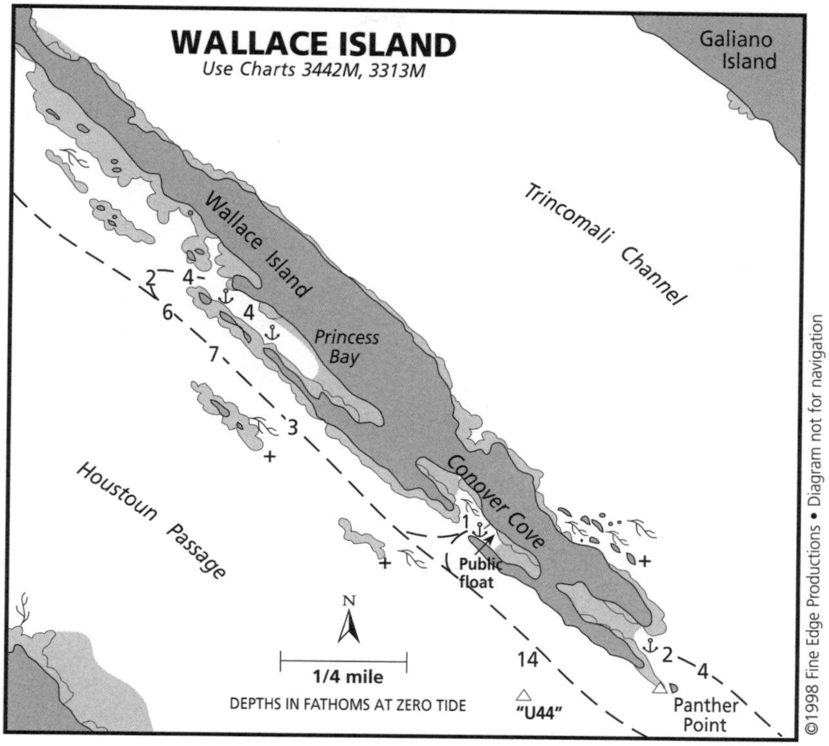

"Panther Point Cove" (Wallace Island)

Panther Point Cove, on the southeast tip of Wallace Island, is 1.0 mile north of Fernwood Point.

Charts 3442 metric, 3313 metric
Entrance: 48°55.88′ N, 123°31.81′ W (NAD 83)
Anchor: 48°55.96′ N, 123°32.13′ W (NAD 83)

> *Panther Point, the SE extremity of Wallace Island, has a drying ledge extending 0.2 mile SE from it.* (p. 166, SCG, Vol. 1)

Panther Point Cove, our favorite small nook on the south end of Wallace Island, is scenic and well sheltered from all winds but those which blow up Trincomali Channel from the southeast. It makes a wonderful lunch stop or overnighter in fair weather. The bottom shoals gradually to the drying flat so, as you choose your spot, keep a lookout over your bow.

Wallace Island

In the early 1980s, when Wallace Island belonged to a consortium of property owners, Princess Cove offered good shelter from winter winds but little in the form of shoreside activity. The island is now a marine park (except for two private properties at the mouth of Princess Cove), and a trail runs the length of the island, joining its two anchorages. Originally called "Narrow Island," Wallace was the site of a boys camp when it first attracted the attention of David Conover, a young man living in Los Angeles who spotted a newspaper ad seeking youth counselors for an island retreat in the Canadian wilderness.

Conover and his wife Jeanne eventually purchased the island in 1946 and, with little experience but plenty of enthusiasm for the pioneering life, they packed up a trailer and moved from Los Angeles to Wallace Island. After a series of setbacks and hardships, they developed a summer resort at Conover Cove which they operated for 20 years before selling most of the island to a group of private investors and moving into a house they had built at Princess Cove. David also wrote two books—*Once Upon an Island* and *One Man's Island*—about their life on Wallace Island.

Three of the island resort cabins remain and are part of a tour offered on summer weekends by Cees and Ellen den Holder, the park's first Facility Operators. Semi-retired residents of Galiano Island, the den Holders spend over a hundred hours each month maintaining the park. They also taxi Galiano residents—seniors and those with disabilities—to Wallace Island for afternoons of picnicking and exploring the island's trails.

—**AV**

Avoid crossing the reef that extends from Panther Point to the daymark. The waters around this reef and the submerged rocks a quarter-mile north are good for snorkeling or kayaking. Starfish and other sea life are clearly visible in these waters.

Anchor in 1 to 2 fathoms midchannel over sand and mud with good holding.

Don Douglass

Réanne at work in Conover Cove

Conover Cove (Wallace Island)

Conover Cove, on the south side of Wallace Island, is 1.3 miles northwest of Fernwood Point.

Charts 3442 metric, 3313 metric
Entrance: 48°56.15′ N, 123°32.71′ W (NAD 83)
Anchor: 48°56.18′ N, 123°32.64′ W (NAD 83)

> *Conover Cove, on the SW side of Wallace Island, affords good shelter for small craft.* (p. 166, SCG, Vol. 1)

Conover Cove, the focal point of the popular Wallace Island Marine Park, is a small, well-sheltered cove.

The entrance bar is quite shallow (less than a fathom at zero tide) and should be approached cautiously. The deepest water appears to favor the south shore. Conover Cove largely dries, but several small craft can find room to anchor with limited swinging room on either side of the public float. Avoid impeding access to the float. Any anchoring here should be done in concert with prior arrivals who sometimes use a stern shore tie or a very short scope. Nice hiking and nature trails lead from the head of the float gangway.

Anchor in 1 fathom south of the float and off two pilings; sand and mud with fair holding.

Anne Vipond

Princess Bay, Wallace Island Marine Park

Princess Bay (Wallace Island)

Princess Bay, a mile north of Conover Cove, is 1.8 miles northwest of Fernwood Point.

Charts 3442 metric, 3313 metric
Entrance: 48°56.64′ N, 123°33.58′ W (NAD 83)
Anchor: 48°56.56′ N, 123°33.28′ W (NAD 83)

> *A long, narrow, sheltered bay, close NW of Conover Cove, is known locally as Princess Bay; it affords good anchorage.* (p. 166, SCG, Vol. 1)

Princess Bay offers good anchorage with more swinging room than Conover Cove. Shore ties are helpful—onshore rings at the head of the cove facilitate tying. Dinghies can be landed at the head of the bay, avoiding the private inholdings on the north shore. Princess Bay provides snug protection from southeast winds and very pleasant anchorage in anything but a strong northwester.

On low tides, it's fun to watch the mud flats at "South Window" erupt with clams squirting water 2 to 3 feet high like a programmed fountain.

Caution: The submerged ridges on the south side of the bay and farther offshore are hazardous and should be avoided.

Anchor in 4 fathoms deep in the bay opposite "South Window" over mud with good holding.

"Secretary Islands Window" (Secretary Islands)

Secretary Islands Window is immediately northwest of Wallace Island, 1.6 miles northwest of Princess Bay.

Charts 3442 metric, 3313 metric
Anchor: 48°57.68' N, 123°35.23' W (NAD 83)

> *Secretary Islands, two in number, are wooded and lie close SE of Mowgli Island. The islands are connected to one another by a drying ridge of sand and gravel.* (p. 166, SCG, Vol. 1)
>
> *Good anchorage can be obtained in the bight between the Secretary Islands in about 12 feet (3.7 m).* (p. 200, SCG, Vol. 1)

In fair weather, small craft find temporary anchorage in the window between the Secretary Islands or in the shoals between Secretary and Mowgli islands. Use care in navigating these waters since a number of parallel ridges just below the surface or awash in this area make travel hazardous. "Secretary Islands Window," entered from Trincomali Channel, has room for two or three boats.

Anne Vipond

Sunset at Mowgli Island near Porlier Pass

There is room for just one boat between Mowgli Island and north Secretary Island. We have also seen a boat anchored between south Secretary Island and Chivers Point on Wallace Island, but this area may be foul and careful reconnoitering is advised. From Secretary Islands, the closest protection in southeast weather is Princess Bay (Wallace Island) to the southeast or Clam Bay to the northwest.

Anchor in about 2 fathoms over sand and gravel with fair holding.

Anne Vipond

Mowgli Island, Secretary Islands

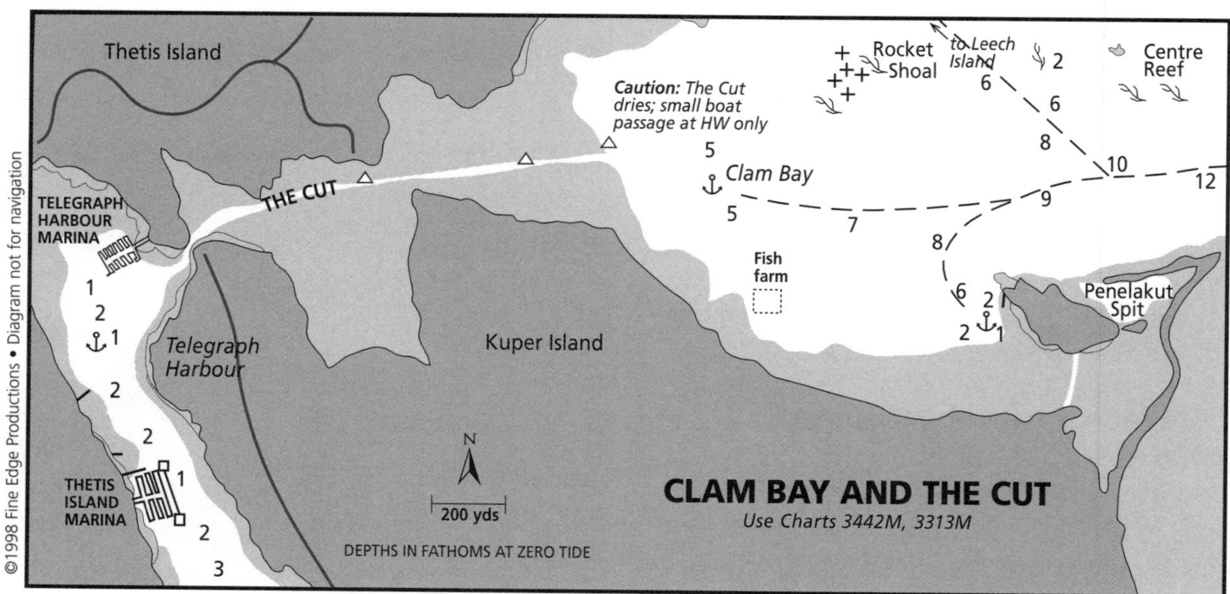

Clam Bay (Kuper and Thetis Islands)

Clam Bay, on the north side of Kuper Island, is 1 mile east of Telegraph Harbour and 2.5 miles southwest of Porlier Pass.

Charts 3477 metric, 3442 metric, 3443 metric, 3313 metric
East entrance (0.13 mile west of Centre Reef Buoy): 48°59.17′ N, 123°38.01′ W (NAD 83)
North entrance (0.18 mile southeast of Leech Island): 48°59.41′ N, 123°38.61′ W (NAD 83)
Anchor (west of Penelakut Spit and Island 27): 48°58.90′ N, 123°38.55′ W (NAD 83)
Anchor (off the Cut): 48°59.10′ N, 123°39.08′ W (NAD 83)
Anchor (west of Leech Island): 48°59.46′ N, 123°39.04′ W (NAD 83)

> *Clam Bay, between the north end of Kuper Island and the SE part of Thetis Island, is entered between Penelakut Spit and Leech Island; it has a drying bank at its head through which The Gut [sic], a narrow, dredged boat passage leads into the head of Telegraph Harbour.*
>
> *Anchorage, well sheltered, in 30 feet (9.1 m), mud bottom, can be obtained south of Rocket Shoal and along the SE shore of Clam Bay.* (p. 200, SCG, Vol. 1)

Clam Bay offers calm anchorage behind the spit just west of Island (27). In northwest weather, you can anchor in 4 fathoms in the cove west of Leech Island, or west of Rocket Shoal in 5 fathoms near the entrance to "The Cut." (See Telegraph Harbour, Chapter 10, for a description of The Cut.) We prefer the south anchorage west of Penelakut Spit, particularly when the wind howls from the southeast. From this site you can comfortably watch all the action since Penelakut Spit breaks the seas.

Clam Bay, however, is open to the north and only partially protected by Centre Reef and Rocket Shoal. Depths along its flat bottom are 5 to 8 fathoms. You can anchor close to shore west of Penelakut Spit, avoiding the small, private float attached to Island (27).

Anchor (west of Penelakut Spit and Island 27) in 4 to 6 fathoms over sand, mud and shells with very good holding.

Hall Island (Trincomali Channel)

Hall Island is 1.6 miles south of Porlier Pass and 1.4 miles east of Penelakut Spit.

Charts 3442 metric, 3443 metric, 3313 metric
Entrance: 48°58.94′ N, 123°35.82′ W (NAD 83)
Anchor: 48°58.90′ N, 123°36.01′ W (NAD 83)

> *Hall Island . . . in mid-channel between Kuper and Galiano Islands, is wooded and an islet lies close off its south end.* (p. 201, SCG, Vol. 1)

Good shelter from prevailing northwesterlies can be found on the southeast corner of Hall Island. Anchor off the small gravel beach, avoiding the rock in the inner bay to the west.

Anchor in about 3 fathoms.

The Cut, looking east toward Clam Bay

Reid Island (Trincomali Channel)

Reid Island is 1.6 miles west of Porlier Pass and 1.4 miles north of Penelakut Spit.

Charts 3442 metric, 3443 metric, 3313 metric
Position (south end): 48°59.45′ N, 123°36.85′ W (NAD 83)
Position (north end): 49°00.42′ N, 123°37.98′ W (NAD 83)

> *Reid Island, 0.5 mile NW of Hall Island, is 23 feet (7 m) high and grassy.*
>
> *Anchorage, in 18 feet (5.5 m), is obtainable inside the ring of drying rocks off the south end of Reid Island.* (p. 201, SCG, Vol. 1)

Temporary anchorage can be found along the perimeter of Reid Island in fair weather avoiding private mooring buoys along shore and the reefs and rocks associated with Rose Islets. There is limited swinging room since the water is largely steep-to with the exception of the south and north ends of Reid Island. Local boats anchor off the northwest side of Reid Island with fair protection from southerly chop, but the area is entirely exposed to the northwest.

Clam Bay

A striking natural feature of Clam Bay is Penelakut Spit—a natural jetty of clamshell beach named for the natives whose original village stood nearby. They were members of the powerful Cowichan tribe which once thrived along the east coast of Vancouver Island and in the Gulf Islands. When white colonists began settling the area, clashes ensued between the Cowichans and the newcomers. Disease killed many of these natives, and today their reserves are located on several of the Gulf Islands, including Kuper Island. Reserve land is private but the foreshore, up to the high tide mark, is public.

Kuper Island originally was joined to Thetis by a narrow strip of land until a canal was dug in 1905 to allow the passage of small boats. A bridge was built, only to be knocked down in 1946. However, livestock owned by the natives on Kuper Island continued to cross over to Thetis at low tide and help themselves to the farmers' crops—a source of grievance on both sides whenever an animal got shot.

The first white settler arrived on Kuper in 1870, before the island was designated a reserve. Two bands of Cowichan natives—the Penelakut and Lamalchi—lived on the island at the time. In 1882, an Anglican missionary named Reverend Roberts moved his family to Kuper Island where he ran a mission and residential school at Lamalchi Bay. In summer, the native students would join their parents fishing or working in canneries on the Fraser River. In 1890, the government built a school on the west side of the island; administered by the Roman Catholic Church it was closed in 1975 forcing students to commute by ferry to the school in Chemainus.

—AV

Spotlight Cove (Galiano Island)

Spotlight Cove is 3.6 miles northwest of Retreat Cove and 2 miles south of Porlier Pass.

Charts 3442 metric, 3473 metric, 3313 metric
Entrance: 48°58.71′ N, 123°34.16′ W (NAD 83)

> *Spotlight Cove . . . is a booming ground. Private moorings lie in the cove and the main road passes close by.* (p. 201, SCG, Vol. 1)

Spotlight Cove, a tiny, shallow, and largely foul cove, has an irregular bottom and large amounts of kelp. Some private residents find shelter in the narrow channels in the north end, but expert local knowledge is required.

"Flagpole Cove" (Galiano Island)

Flagpole Cove is 1.6 miles southeast of Porlier Pass.

Charts 3442 metric, 3473 metric, 3313 metric
Entrance: 48°59.12′ N, 123°34.61′ W (NAD 83)

> *An unnamed bay lies 0.6 mile NNW of Spotlight Cove. The south end is open to the west with some shelter spots; near the centre are piles and ruins, the north end is foul. The floats are private.* (p. 201, SCG, Vol. 1)

We call this Flagpole Cove because of the conspicuous flagpole on the south peninsula. Temporary shelter from southeast winds can be found just east of the flagpole.

North Galiano (Galiano Island)

North Galiano, on the northwest tip of Galiano Island, is 0.96 mile south of Porlier Pass.

Charts 3442 metric, 3313 metric
Public float: 48°59.69′ N, 123°35.09′ W (NAD 83)

> *North Galiano, 1.1 miles NNW of Spotlight Cove, has the Galiano Post Office (V0N 1P0), a general store and a marine service station. A weekly freight service operates to and from Chemainus.*
>
> *The public wharf in North Galiano has a depth of 10 feet (3 m) alongside the wharf face; a float on the north side of the wharf has 8 feet (2.4 m) alongside.* (p. 201, SCG, Vol. 1)

North Galiano, a shallow bight, offers limited protection in fair weather only. It is exposed to westerlies and traffic in Trincomali Channel. The public float is used by sportfishing boats and dinghies. The small community is on the road to Porlier Pass.

Porlier Pass ("Cowichan Gap")

Porlier Pass, between Galiano and Valdes islands, is 11 miles southeast of Dodd Narrows and 10 miles northwest of Montague Harbour.

Charts 3473 metric, 3442 metric, 3313 metric
South entrance: 49°00.32′ N, 123°35.57′ W (NAD 83)
North entrance: 49°01.28′ N, 123°34.74′ W (NAD 83)
Mid-pass position (0.14 mile northwest of Race Point): 49°00.90′ N, 123°35.24′ W (NAD 83)

> *Porlier Pass . . . is known locally as Cowichan Gap.*
>
> *The maximum flood is 9 kn and the ebb is 8 kn; it sets from Trincomali Channel into the Strait of Georgia on the flood and in the reverse direction on the ebb.*
>
> *On the Strait of Georgia side of Porlier Pass, during summer months, the effects of the freshet from the Fraser River combined with NW winds*

Peter Fromm

Catching the wind in Cowichan Gap

which blow strongly nearly every afternoon, cause rough conditions along the west side of the Strait of Georgia. Crossings to the mainland or travel along the east shores of Valdes and Gabriola Islands should be carried out early in the morning, but the most preferred time is late afternoon or early evening when the winds die away. Radio weather reports should be monitored. (p. 210, SCG, Vol. 1)

Skin diver in Baines Bay

Porlier Pass is known for its excellent fishing due to upwellings caused by its highly irregular bottom. This irregular bottom and numerous rocks on both sides of the pass create turbulence and hazardous eddies, especially at spring tides when current in the pass can reach 9 knots. It is best to transit Porlier Pass at slack water.

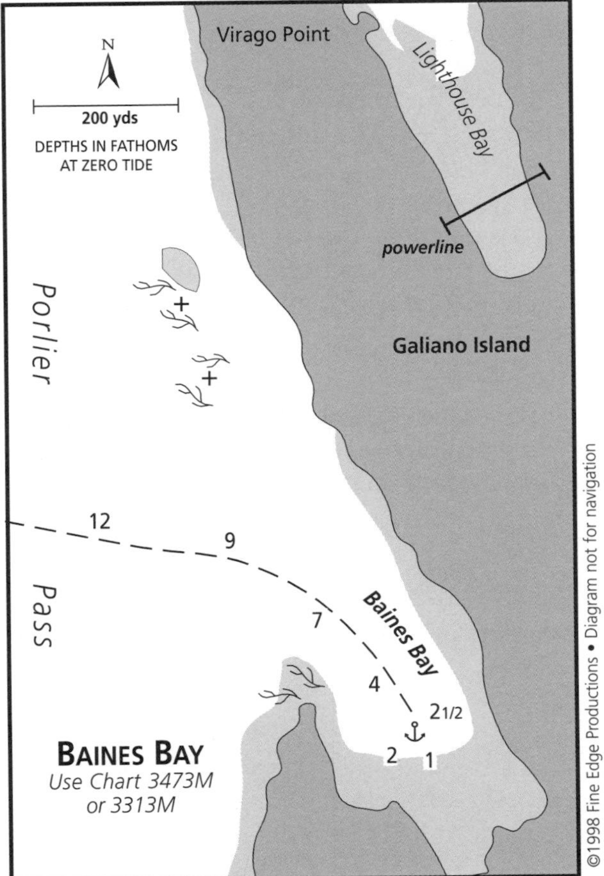

The safest passage through Porlier Pass favors the Galiano Island shore. Remain about 200 yards west of both Virago and Race points, avoiding Boscowitz Rock, Virago Rock, Black Rock and the shoals northwest of Dionisio Point. When you approach from the Strait of Georgia, the two lights on Race Point and Virago Point make a range bearing 196° true or the reciprocal, 016° true. This course will take you 175 yards east of bell Buoy "U41" on the east side of Canoe Islets, and you can guide west as you cross midchannel in order to remain about 200 yards west of both lights.

Baines Bay (Galiano Island)

Baines Bay is in Porlier Pass, 0.23 mile southeast of Virago Point.

Charts 3473 metric, 3442 metric, 3313 metric
Entrance: 49°00.35′ N, 123°35.23′ W (NAD 83)
Anchor: 49°00.33′ N, 123°35.17′ W (NAD 83)

Baines Bay offers temporary shelter with limited swinging room in southeast weather or from the strong currents of Porlier Pass. Avoid the rocks and kelp patches along the east shore of Baines Bay and the kelp patches off the west entrance. There is a deadhead on the east side of the bay and an old mooring on the west side. The bay is a favorite area for dive boats.

Anchor in 4 to 5 fathoms over sand and mud with good holding.

Don Douglass

Old cannery ruins at Lighthouse Bay

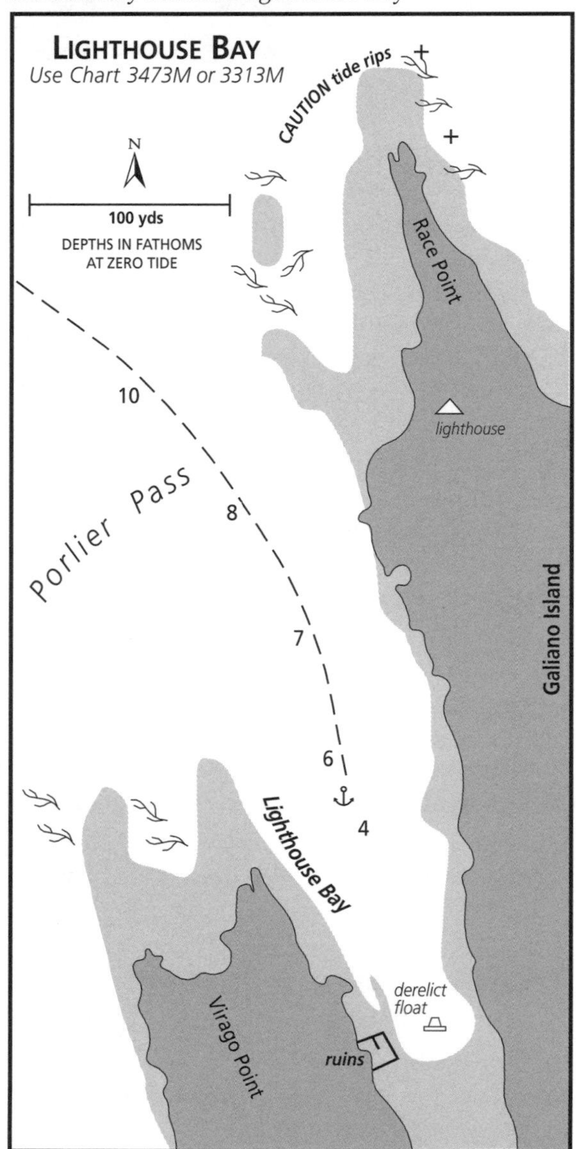

Lighthouse Bay (Galiano Island)

Lighthouse Bay is in the center of Porlier Pass, 0.24 mile north of Baines Bay.

Charts 3473 metric, 3442 metric, 3313 metric
Entrance: 49°00.69′ N, 123°35.24′ W (NAD 83)
Anchor: 49°00.58′ N, 123°35.16′ W (NAD 83)

> *Anchorage can be obtained in Lighthouse Bay, south of the submarine cable.* (p. 212, SCG, Vol. 1)

Lighthouse Bay, which is out of the main current, provides good protection in most weather. The inner bay does not get much sunlight and is rather dark and dank.

Anchorage can be taken anywhere south of the submarine cable that crosses the entrance to Lighthouse Cove. Swinging room is limited. Avoid the derelict float in the middle of the bay off the old cannery ruins. *Caution*: The bottom may contain old cables.

Anchor in about 4 fathoms over mud and sand with rocks; fair holding.

"Cove 0.25 Mile NW of Virago Rock" (Valdes Island)

Cove 0.25 Mile NW of Virago Rock is half-way between Cayetano Point and Vernaci Point on the north side of Porlier Pass.

Charts 3473 metric, 3442 metric, 3313 metric
Anchor: 49°01.00′ N, 123°35.73′ W (NAD 83)

Cove 0.25 Mile NW of Virago Rock—the unimaginative name we have given to this small unnamed cove—offers good temporary shelter from strong currents and from west through northeast winds. On the north shore of the cove is a small, private float. Temporary anchorage can be taken due south of this float. A house on the beach with the letters RUS on its roof serves as a landmark.

When transiting Porlier Pass to reach this cove during a south-flowing ebb current, low-powered boats stay north of Black and Virago rocks and favor the Valdes Island shore. When conditions are favorable, you can power across Porlier Pass, passing 200 yards off Race Point. Avoid the unmarked rocks off the cove.

Anchor in 3 to 4 fathoms south of the pilings over

gray mud with shells, isolated gravel and kelp with fair-to-good holding.

Dionisio Point Park (Galiano Island)

Dionisio Point Park, on the southeast shore of Porlier Pass, is 0.44 mile east of Race Point light.

Charts 3473 metric, 3442 metric, 3313 metric
Entrance: 49°01.10′ N, 123°34.66′ W (NAD 83)
Anchor: 49°00.85′ N, 123°34.48′ W (NAD 83)

> *Dionisio Point, the NE corner of Galiano Island, is a small, rocky peninsula connected to the island by a narrow ridge of sand. Two narrow reefs extend 0.3 mile NNW from Dionisio Point.*
>
> *Good anchorage is afforded just within Dionisio Point or in the bay to the west.* (p. 212, SCG, Vol. 1)

Dionisio Point, one of the more recently designated provincial parks, becomes an island at high tide. The lovely bay, immediately west of the point, has a nice sandy beach with weathered drift logs. Although open to the Strait of Georgia, the bay is fine as a temporary anchorage in fair weather; it does, however, receive sizeable chop during strong northwesterlies. The next bay to the west, 0.3 mile southeast of Race Point, offers somewhat better shelter.

Don Douglass

Anchor check

The eroded sandstone formations on shore are the largest examples of such rocks in the Gulf Islands. Some of the hollows make wonderful tidepools, and cormorants have even been known to use them for nesting. In summer, the shallow waters of the bay heat up enough for pleasant swimming. Diving is also reported to be good in this area.

Small boats can pass carefully between the two coves at the north end of Galiano Island by staying south of the large kelp bed.

Anchor immediately west of Dionisio Point in $1^1/_2$ fathoms over sand and kelp with poor-to fair-holding.

DIONISIO POINT PARK
Use Chart 3473M or 3313M

N
200 yds
DEPTHS IN FATHOMS AT ZERO TIDE
Porlier Pass
Strait of Georgia
foul
foul
second bay west of Dionisio Point
Dionisio Point
Dionisio Point Park
Galiano Island

Don Douglass
Canoe Islet

"Second Bay West of Dionisio Point" (Galiano Island)

Second Bay West of Dionisio Point is 0.3 mile southeast of Race Point.

Charts 3473 metric, 3442 metric, 3313 metric
Entrance: 49°00.91′ N, 123°34.85′ W (NAD 83)
Anchor: 49°00.70′ N, 123°34.70′ W (NAD 83)

The second bay west of Dionisio Point offers better protection under most conditions than the bay directly off the park's sandy beach. It is a good place to wait for slack water in Porlier Pass.

Anchor in about 3 fathoms over a sandy, rocky bottom with shells; poor-to-fair holding.

Cardale Point (Valdes Island)

Cardale Point is 0.7 mile northwest of Porlier Pass.

Charts 3473 metric, 3442 metric, 3313 metric
Position: 49°00.92′ N, 123°36.65′ W (NAD 83)

> *Cardale Point is a low, sandy projection at the SW end of Valdes Island.* (p. 202, SCG, Vol. 1)

On the south side of Cardale Point is a particularly beautiful white shell beach with a warm southern exposure. The drying flat off the beach is foul with rocks. However, temporary anchorage in fair weather can be obtained just off the drying flat, allowing exploration on shore. Nice beaches and temporary anchorage can also be found at Shingle Point, 2.0 mile northwest of Porlier Pass and Blackberry Point, 3.0 mile northwest of Porlier Pass.

Caution: You should always leave a responsible crew member aboard your vessel here, because wind or current off the point can easily cause an anchor to drag.

Noel Bay (Valdes Island)

Noel Bay, on the southeast coast of Valdes Island, is 1 mile southeast of Detwiller Point and 1.5 miles north of Cardale Point.

Charts 3473 metric, 3442 metric, 3313 metric
Position: 49°02.49′ N, 123°36.45′ W (NAD 83)

Although Noel Bay is found on the charts, it is not mentioned in the *Coast Pilot* and we have no local knowledge to add.

Canoe Islet (Valdes Island)

Canoe Islet, at the north entrance to Porlier Pass, is 0.9 mile north of Race Point.

Charts 3473 metric, 3442 metric, 3313 metric
Position (diver information buoy, 0.95 mile northwest of Dionisio Point): 49°01.60′ N, 123°35.30′ W (NAD 83)

> *Canoe Islet, 0.25 mile east of Shah Point, is 10 feet (3 m) high. Drying reefs extend 0.2 mile SSE from the islet. An information/mooring buoy lies close west of the reef SSE of Canoe Islet. Its purpose is to prevent diving vessels visiting the site of the sidewheel steamer Del Norte from damaging the remains by anchoring in its vicinity.* (p. 212, SCG, Vol. 1)

Canoe Islet Ecological Reserve is known to scuba divers because of the nearby remains of the sidewheel steamer *Del Norte*. Located on the Strait of Georgia, the islet is exposed to the wind and currents found off the entrance to Porlier Pass.

10

STUART CHANNEL FROM SANSUM NARROWS TO DODD NARROWS

Introduction

Heading north through Sansum Narrows takes you into Stuart Channel, the "pathway" to Dodd Narrows. Along the northern part of Saltspring Island you pass Booth and Vesuvius bays and Vancouver Island. Booth is an open roadstead that has little appeal for pleasure boaters. Vesuvius Bay has a small public dock with a pub at its head. In nearby Duck Bay, north of Vesuvius, cruising boats can find good anchorage and enjoy lovely sunsets. Osborn Bay, on the Vancouver Island shore across from Booth Bay, is a commercial center with little interest for cruising boats. Tent Island, off the south entrance to Houstoun Passage, is an Indian reserve with no public access.

Running northward along the east side of Vancouver Island, well-protected Stuart Channel has generally light winds, gentle currents and warm waters. Cruising boats can find a number of rarely-visited small coves that provide quiet anchorage. Telegraph Harbour is one of the major attractions for yachts. There are two marinas in Telegraph Harbour, both of which offer just about everything you need in the way of food, supplies, showers, laundry, and more. Thetis Island Marina has a restaurant and pub, Telegraph Harbour Marina has a coffee shop and great ice cream concoctions.

Chemainus and Ladysmith, on the Vancouver Island side of the channel, are commercial centers. The lovely town of Chemainus—one of the oldest European settlements—is renowned for its numerous murals. In June, the Festival of Murals begins, continuing throughout the summer; there are parades, entertainment, artists in action, and much more.

Ladysmith is a charming place with historic buildings, shops, restaurants, and services of every kind. The Black Nugget Museum, Community Center Pool, and Transfer Beach Park are some of the attractions. Ladysmith Celebration

Don Douglass

Far from the madding crowd

Days are held in August, and there are fireworks, parades, and a soap box derby.

Following the Vancouver Island shore, you transit Dodd Narrows in the direction of Nanaimo. The current in the narrows is swift and there is strong turbulence on spring tides so passage should be timed near slack water.

Stuart Channel

Stuart Channel, east of Vancouver Island, runs north of Maple Bay to Northumberland Channel.

Charts 3442 metric, 3443 metric, 3475 metric (inset), 3313 metric
South entrance (0.42 mile east of Grave Point light): 48°50.90′ N, 123°34.92′ W (NAD 83)
North entrance (0.34 mile north of Round Island): 49°07.40′ N, 123°47.75′ W (NAD 83)

> *Stuart Channel . . . leads from the north end of Sansum Narrows to Dodd Narrows and is bounded on its east side by Saltspring, Kuper, Thetis, Ruxton and De Courcy Islands. On the west side of the channel are the harbour facilities of Crofton, Chemainus and Ladysmith.*
>
> *Tidal streams in Stuart Channel ebb in a general south direction, following the contour of the channel; a velocity of 1 kn can be expected. The flood stream is weak and variable. At the north end of Stuart Channel, in the approach to Dodd Narrows, both the flood and ebb attain 3 kn.* (p. 152, SCG, Vol. 1)

Stuart Channel, a major north-south route along the western edge of the Gulf Islands, is the direct route from Saanich Inlet to Nanaimo. The channel is well sheltered and a smooth-water route in most weather.

Osborn Bay, Crofton (Vancouver Island)

Osborn Bay is 3.3 miles northwest of Maple Bay.

Charts 3475 metric (inset), 3442 metric, 3313 metric
Entrance: 48°52.27′ N, 123°37.16′ W (NAD 83)
Entrance (small craft basin): 48°51.91′ N, 123°38.23′ W (NAD 83)

> *Crofton, in the SW part of Osborn Bay, is a community and port engaged almost exclusively in processing and shipping forest products.*
>
> *The small craft basin, close south of the public wharf, is sheltered by a breakwater and was dredged to a depth of 7 feet (2 m) (1976).* (p. 153, SCG, Vol. 1)

Osborn Bay, with the town of Crofton on its south quarter, is a giant logging complex with limited facilities or appeal for cruising boats. A small public wharf and float and a small craft basin principally serving locals can be used in case of emergency.

Booth Bay (Saltspring Island)

Booth Bay, on the northwest side of Saltspring Island, is 3.8 miles northeast of Maple Bay.

Charts 3442 metric, 3313 metric
Position: 48°52.00′ N, 123°33.26′ W (NAD 83)

> *Booth Bay has shoals near its head extending 0.1 mile offshore. Temporary anchorage, mud bottom, can be obtained near the head of the bay but being exposed to the prevailing wind is not recommended*
>
> *Booth Inlet leads SE from the head of Booth Bay; it can be entered in a dinghy on a rising tide over the entrance bar. Depths are less than 2 feet (0.6 m) in the inlet at LW.* (p. 154, SCG, Vol. 1)

Booth Bay is suitable for anchorage in fair weather only.

Vesuvius Bay (Saltspring Island)

Vesuvius Bay, on the northwest side of Saltspring Island, is 4.3 miles northeast of Maple Bay.

Charts 3442 metric, 3313 metric
Entrance: 48°52.89′ N, 123°34.63′ W (NAD 83)
Public dock in Vesuvius: 48°52.85′ N, 123°34.40′ W (NAD 83)

> *Vesuvius Bay lies close north of Booth Bay and is separated from it by a drying reef. An islet at the extremity of the reef is 10 feet (3 m) high. Two drying rocks lie inside the bay, close off the sandy beach at its head.*
>
> *Vesuvius settlement, on the north shore of Vesuvius Bay, has a hotel, restaurant and store . . . Regular ferry service is maintained with Crofton and a taxi is available at the settlement.*
>
> *The public wharf, with a depth of 8 feet (2.4 m)*

Réanne Hemingway- Douglass

Native arbutus tree

alongside, is at the settlement.

Several small coves between Vesuvius Bay and the north end of Saltspring Island offer limited anchorage and shelter from SE weather. (p. 154, SCG, Vol. 1)

Vesuvius Bay, a tiny bay with a small public dock and a few facilities, has ferry service to Crofton on Vancouver Island. Between Vesuvius Bay and Houstoun Passage, you can find several small coves that offer limited anchorage and shelter from southeast weather. The first of these is Duck Bay.

Duck Bay (Saltspring Island)

Duck Bay, on the northwest corner of Saltspring Island, is 0.5 mile northwest of Vesuvius Bay.

Charts 3442 metric, 3313 metric
Entrance: 48°53.43′ N, 123°35.09′ W (NAD 83)
Anchor: 48°53.29′ N, 123°34.70′ W (NAD 83)

Duck Bay is separated from Vesuvius Bay by Dock Point. Steep wooded cliffs rise from the east shore and it affords good shelter from east winds for small craft.

The drying ridge and rocks, extending 0.1 mile NW from Dock Point, should be given a wide berth; small craft have had difficulties in them when proceeding between Duck Cove and Vesuvius Bay. (p. 155, SCG, Vol. 1)

Duck Bay, a half-mile northwest of Vesuvius Bay, is reported to offer emergency protection from southerlies. Anchor well inside the bay, close in to the drying flat which is steep-to; avoid Duck Point Reef.

Anchor in 6 to 7 fathoms.

Idol Island (Houstoun Passage)

Idol Island, off the northwest tip of Saltspring Island, is 1.6 mile south of Southey Point.

Charts 3442 metric, 3313 metric
South entrance: 48°54.93′ N, 123°35.67′ W (NAD 83)
North entrance: 48°55.26′ N, 123°35.74′ W (NAD 83)
Anchor: 48°55.19′ N, 123°35.39′ W (NAD 83)

Idol Island, 1 mile east of Sandstone Rocks, lies in a bight on the NW side of Saltspring Island; drying rock ledges extend south from it. (p. 165, SCG, Vol. 1)

Idol Island, once an Indian ceremonial burial ground, is now a park reserve. Protection from easterly weather may be found 0.2 mile east of the island.

Anchor in 6 to 10 fathoms.

Stone Cutters Bay (Saltspring Island, Houstoun Passage)

Stone Cutters Bay, indenting the northwest tip of Saltspring Island, is 1.1 mile south of Southey Point.

Charts 3442 metric, 3313 metric
Entrance: 48°55.76′ N, 123°35.84′ W (NAD 83)
Anchor: 48°55.68′ N, 123°35.64′ W (NAD 83)

Stone Cutters Bay, 0.5 mile north of Idol Island, is the site of a log dump. Houses surround the bay. (p. 165, SCG, Vol. 1)

Stone Cutters Bay, a small indentation in Saltspring Island, provides some protection from easterly and southerly weather. Anchor off the private breakwater extending from the west point, but be careful to avoid the private buoys along the stone bluff. In 1998, there were no longer log booms stored in the bay. Swinging room is limited and larger boats will find more acceptable anchorage east of Idol Island.

Anchor in about 7 fathoms.

Southey Bay (Saltspring Island, Houstoun Passage)

Southey Bay, immediately west of Point Southey, is 2.1 miles northwest of Conover Cove and 4.8 miles east of Chemainus.

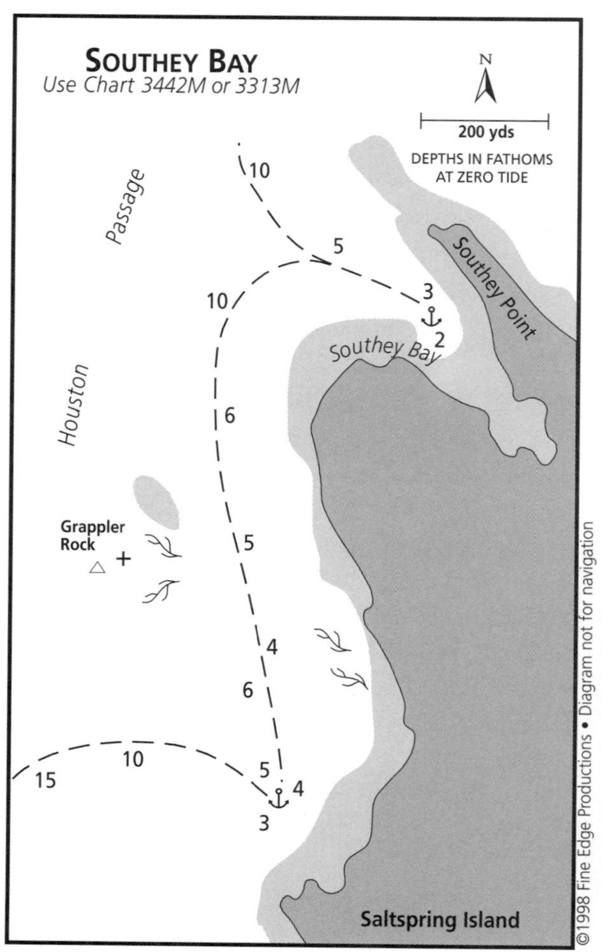

Charts 3442 metric, 3313 metric
Entrance: 48°56.69′ N, 123°35.85′ W (NAD 83)
Anchor: 48°56.61′ N, 123°35.71′ W (NAD 83)

> *Southey Point . . . is the north extremity of Saltspring Island. A drying ledge extends 0.1 mile NW from the point. The cove SW of Southey Point, known locally as Southey Bay, offers shelter from all points except north. The mooring buoys and floats in the bay are private.* (p. 165, SCG, Vol. 1)

Southey Bay, the tiny indentation on the south side of Southey Point, affords good protection from southeast storms when anchored close to the beach behind the shoal projecting out from the north shore. Avoid the private mooring buoys.

Another anchorage with more swinging room can also be found off a sandy beach, 0.28 mile southeast of Grappler Rock in about 5 fathoms.

Anchor in 4 fathoms.

Light winds! Time for the spinnaker

Tent Island (Stuart Channel)

Tent Island is 3.3 miles east of Chemainus and 3.3 miles southeast of Telegraph Harbour.

Charts 3442 metric, 3313 metric
Position: 48°55.66' N, 123°37.88' W (NAD 83)

> *Tent Island, 1.8 miles NW of Parminter Point, is an Indian Reserve. It is separated from North Reef to the south by a deep channel; the north end of the island is separated from Josling Point by a drying passage which can be traversed at HW.*
>
> *Rocks and islets extend 0.2 mile SE and east from Tent Island, terminating in Sandstone Rocks.* (p. 165, SCG, Vol. 1)

Temporary anchorage can be found off the drying flat in the west indentation of Tent Island in fair weather only or sometimes off the northern tip of the island. Both locations are completely exposed to westerlies. Camping is not allowed on shore without prior permission from the Indian Reserve. Interesting sandstone formations are found at the south end of Tent Island, including a formation that resembles a large throne.

Anchor in about 2 fathoms off the drying mud flat.

Lamalchi Bay (Kuper Island)

Lamalchi Bay is 2.3 miles southeast of Telegraph Harbour.

Charts 3442 metric, 3313 metric
Anchor: 48°56.42' N, 123°38.44' W (NAD 83)

> *Lamalchi Bay, at the SW extremity of Kuper Island, is filled by mud and sand flats.* (p. 155, SCG, Vol. 1)

Don Douglass

Chemainus Ferry

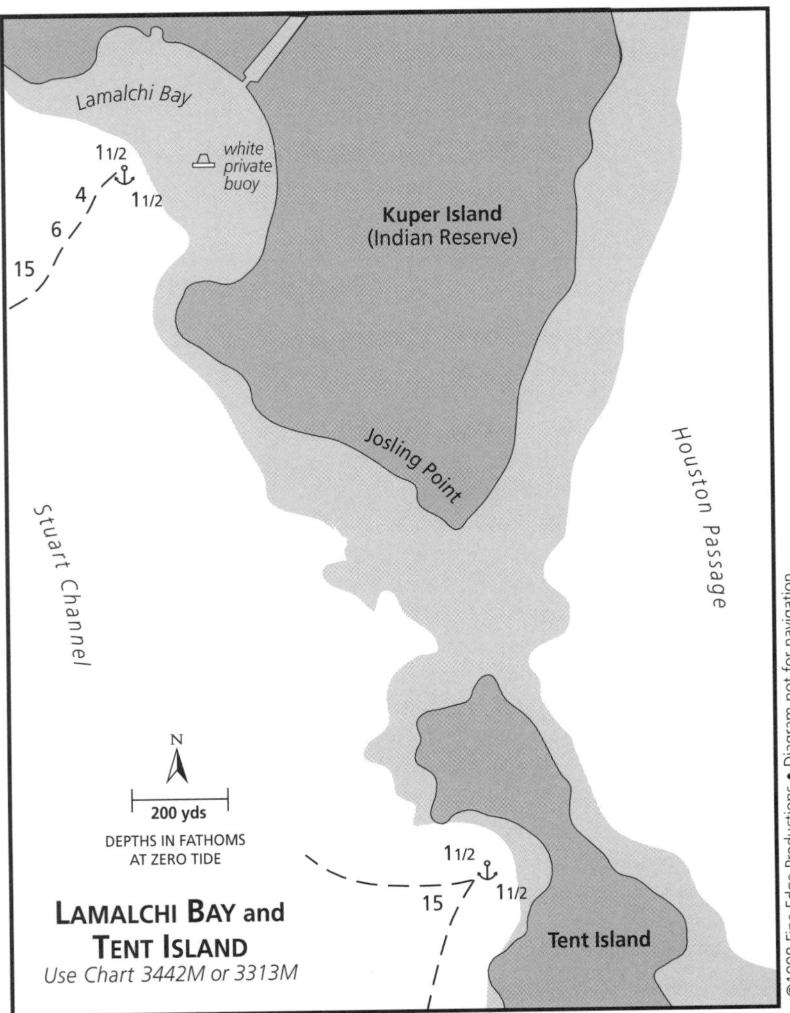

LAMALCHI BAY and TENT ISLAND
Use Chart 3442M or 3313M

Don Douglass

Thetis Island Marina

Anchor in 1 $^1/_2$ fathoms, sandy bottom with some grass; fair holding.

Telegraph Harbour (Kuper/Thetis Islands)

Telegraph Harbour, between Kuper and Thetis islands, is 3.7 miles northeast of Chemainus and 3.4 miles southwest of Porlier Pass.

Charts 3477 metric, 3442 metric, 3443 metric, 3313 metric
Outer entrance: 48°57.46′ N, 123°40.12′ W (NAD 83)
Inner entrance: 48°58.25′ N, 123°39.86′ W (NAD 83)
Anchor: 48°58.91′ N, 123°40.26′ W (NAD 83)
Public dock (Kuper Island): 48°58.19′ N, 123°39.58′ W (NAD 83)
Thetis Island Marina: 48°58.61′ N, 123°40.09′ W (NAD 83)
Telegraph Harbour Marina: 48°58.94′ N, 123°40.20′ W (NAD 83)

The entire Kuper Island is an Indian Reserve and permission is required to go ashore. (The painted sign on a building warns *Salish Nation Penelakut Band, Stay Off.*)

Anchorage is available in fair weather only. The inner bay, which is quite shallow, should be used only when tide tables indicate adequate depth.

Telegraph Harbour

This popular harbour offers plenty of shoreside diversions with two full-service marinas and numerous crafts shops and studios within walking distance of the waterfront. Thetis Island Marina offers patio dining at its fully licensed restaurant and pub. Telegraph Harbour Marina is ideal for families with its spacious grounds and freshly-baked homemade pies. Both marinas are a 10-minute walk to the ferry terminal at Preedy Harbour where the Chemainus ferry docks ten times a day.

A pleasant day-excursion from Telegraph Harbour is the 30-minute ferry trip across Stuart Channel to Chemainus, a former logging town now famous for its colorful street murals which depict the local history and have transformed a small mill town into the world's largest outdoor art gallery. Sidewalk cafes, ice cream parlors and tea rooms line the charming streets as do art galleries, antique shops and a museum. A pleasant stroll can be enjoyed in Waterwheel Park, taking the Gateway to Old Town where Heritage Path leads to more murals and shops.

Telegraph Harbour has its own share of artisans, and a walk along the road that joins the two marinas will take you past a few crafts shops and studios. The island's three Bible camps attract student visitors, a tradition that began back in 1904 when a retired British major and his spinster sister established an Anglican retreat on Thetis. The island had already become known as an English col-ony through the efforts of Mr. and Mrs. Henry Burchell who trained young bachelors from England in the rudiments of farming. These men lived in a dormitory building behind Preedy Hall, a spacious home the energetic Burchells built using lumber they cut at their own sawmill.

The Burchells had lost most of their life savings in a business venture when they settled at Preedy Harbour in 1892, working diligently to establish a new life on Thetis where they operated a store, farm and orchard. Each Christmas they held a children's party; in the fall, on the night of the first full moon after haying, a dance complete with oysters and sparkling white wine was attended by guests who would sail or row from the other Gulf Islands. The original Preedy Hall burned down in the 1920s, after the widowed Mrs. Burchell sold it, and a new Preedy Hall was built around 1930. —**AV**

Telegraph Harbour lies between the NW side of Kuper Island and the SE extremity of Thetis Island. It is used exclusively by small craft. Regular ferry service is maintained between Kuper Island and Chemainus.

Anchorage can be obtained NW of the public wharf; be sure to clear the submarine cable. The upper reaches of the harbour, beyond Foster Point, offers snug anchorage for small craft. (p. 156, SCG, Vol. 1; see also SD, p. 103)

Don Douglass

Preedy Harbour public float

Telegraph Harbour, which is a major cruising destination for pleasure craft, contains two popular marinas. The marinas lie at the north end of the harbor in the narrow channel between Kuper and Thetis islands, 0.75 mile northwest of the B.C. ferry dock. Shallow water between the two marinas offers anchorage for several small- to medium-sized boats among the many private mooring buoys found there. Large vessels can anchor in deeper water off Foster Point and have more swinging room. A small, drying canal known as "The Cut" leads through the mud flats to the east, allowing small boats to enter Clam Bay at high water. From the marinas, it's just a half-mile walk to the ferry in Preedy Harbour on Thetis Island. There is also ferry service to Chemainus from Telegraph Harbour on Kuper Island.

Both Thetis Island Marina (tel: 250-246-3464) on the west shore, and Telegraph Harbour Marina (tel: 250-246-9511) at the northeast head of the bay are popular stops that offer warm, friendly facilities for cruising boats. (Reservations recommended during summer.)

Please respect the no-wake speed limit in the upper reaches of Telegraph Harbour, and watch for small float planes which use the channel.

Anchor in 1 to 2 fathoms over mud and sand with good holding.

Don Douglass

Classic "old world" style architecture at Preedy Harbour

Preedy Harbour (Thetis Island)

Preedy Harbour is 0.5 mile west of Telegraph Harbour.

Charts 3477 metric, 3442 metric, 3443 metric, 3313 metric
Southwest entrance (0.17 mile south of Dayman Island): 48°58.11′ N, 123°41.26′ W (NAD 83)
West entrance (0.19 mile southwest of Crescent Point): 48°58.83′ N, 123°41.72′ W (NAD 83)
Public float: 48°58.79′ N, 123°40.70′ W (NAD 83)
Anchor: 48°58.76′ N, 123°40.87′ W (NAD 83)

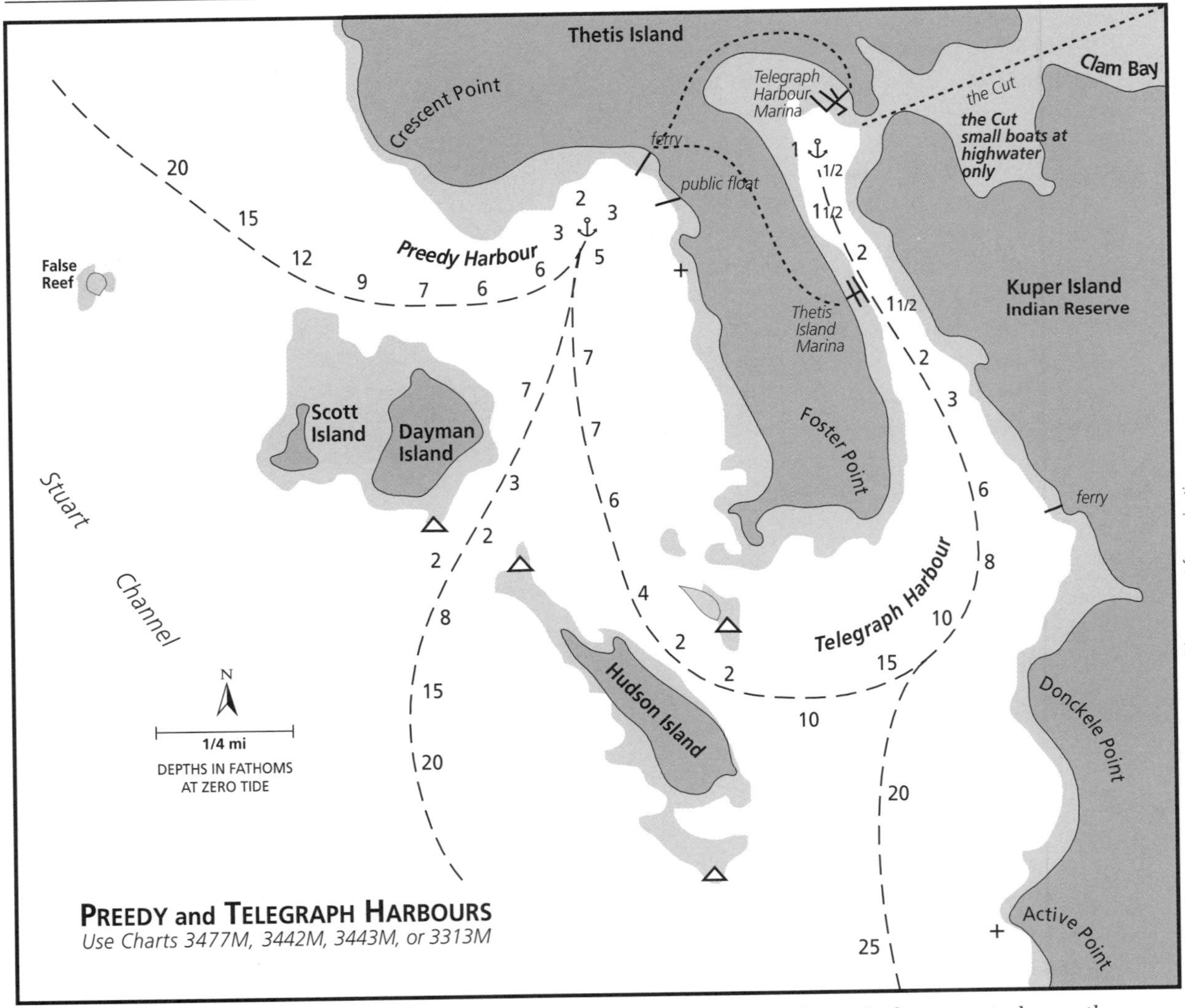

PREEDY and TELEGRAPH HARBOURS

Use Charts 3477M, 3442M, 3443M, or 3313M

1/4 mi

DEPTHS IN FATHOMS AT ZERO TIDE

Preedy Harbour, fronted by Dayman Island and Hudson Island, has three entrances.

The entrance from Telegraph Harbour, between Hudson Island and Foster Point, has drying reefs along its centre line, and the fairway, which lies between the drying reefs and Hudson Island, has a least depth of 10 feet (3 m).

Light.—Hudson Island North light (L.L. No. 294.5) at the south extremity of the above-mentioned drying reefs, is exhibited at an elevation of 17 feet (5.2 m) from a white circular tower with a red band at the top.

Beacons.—Telegraph Harbour daybeacon, 0.1 mile north of the above-mentioned light, consists of a concrete base surmounted by a mast displaying a starboard hand daymark.

Preedy Harbour daybeacon, at the north extremity of the drying reefs, consists of a concrete base surmounted by a mast displaying a starboard

Don Douglass

Float plane mooring at Telegraph Harbour

hand daymark; it is fitted with a radar reflector.

The entrance channel between Hudson and Dayman Islands has a least depth of 14 feet (4.3 m) between the drying ledges extending from both island.

Anchorage.—Good anchorage, mud bottom, can be found on the north side of Preedy Harbour; keep well clear of the submarine cables.

Thetis Island settlement is at the NE end of Preedy Harbour, near the public wharf.

Wharf.—Ferry landing.—The public wharf, in the NE corner of Preedy Harbour, has a depth of 18 feet (5.5 m) alongside. A float, attached to the north side of the wharf, is 80 feet (24 m) long with a depth of 8 feet (2.4 m) alongside.

Caution.—A rock, with 1 foot (0.3 m) over it, lies about 148 feet (45 m) due south of the head of the public wharf. (pp. 156, 158, SCG, Vol. 1)

Preedy Harbour is less protected than Telegraph Harbour but pleasant anchorage in fair weather can be found either in its extreme northern or southern ends. It is far less crowded than Telegraph Harbour and provides more swinging room. Good anchorage can be found about 250 yards west of the public float.

Anchor in 3 fathoms over mud and sand with good holding.

Don Douglass

Chemainus Bay public floats

Chemainus Bay (Vancouver Island)

Chemainus Bay is 8.42 miles northwest of Maple Bay and 3.7 miles southwest of Telegraph Harbour.

Charts 3475 metric (inset), 3442 metric, 3313 metric
Entrance: 48°55.81′ N, 123°42.57′ W (NAD 83)
Public docks: 48°55.53′ N, 123°42.83′ W (NAD 83)
Anchor (west of Bird Rock light): 48°55.87′ N, 123°43.23′ W (NAD 83)

Anchorage in Chemainus Bay is not advisable because of the extensive booming grounds and congestion inside the bay. The best anchorage can be obtained on the east side of Stuart Channel, either in Telegraph Harbour or Preedy Harbour. (p. 159, SCG, Vol. 1)

Chemainus has undergone a metamorphosis from a logging and mill town to an attractive town that lures tourists to its many shops and galleries. Since anchoring is not convenient in the bay, you may wish instead to anchor in Telegraph Harbour and take the Thetis Island ferry to Chemainus for a day of shopping and eating.

A small public boat harbor, generally crowded with commercial fishing boats, lies immediately south of the Chemainus ferry terminal.

A temporary and somewhat exposed anchorage can be found on the northwest side of Chemainus Bay 0.1

Don Douglass

One of the many Chemainus murals

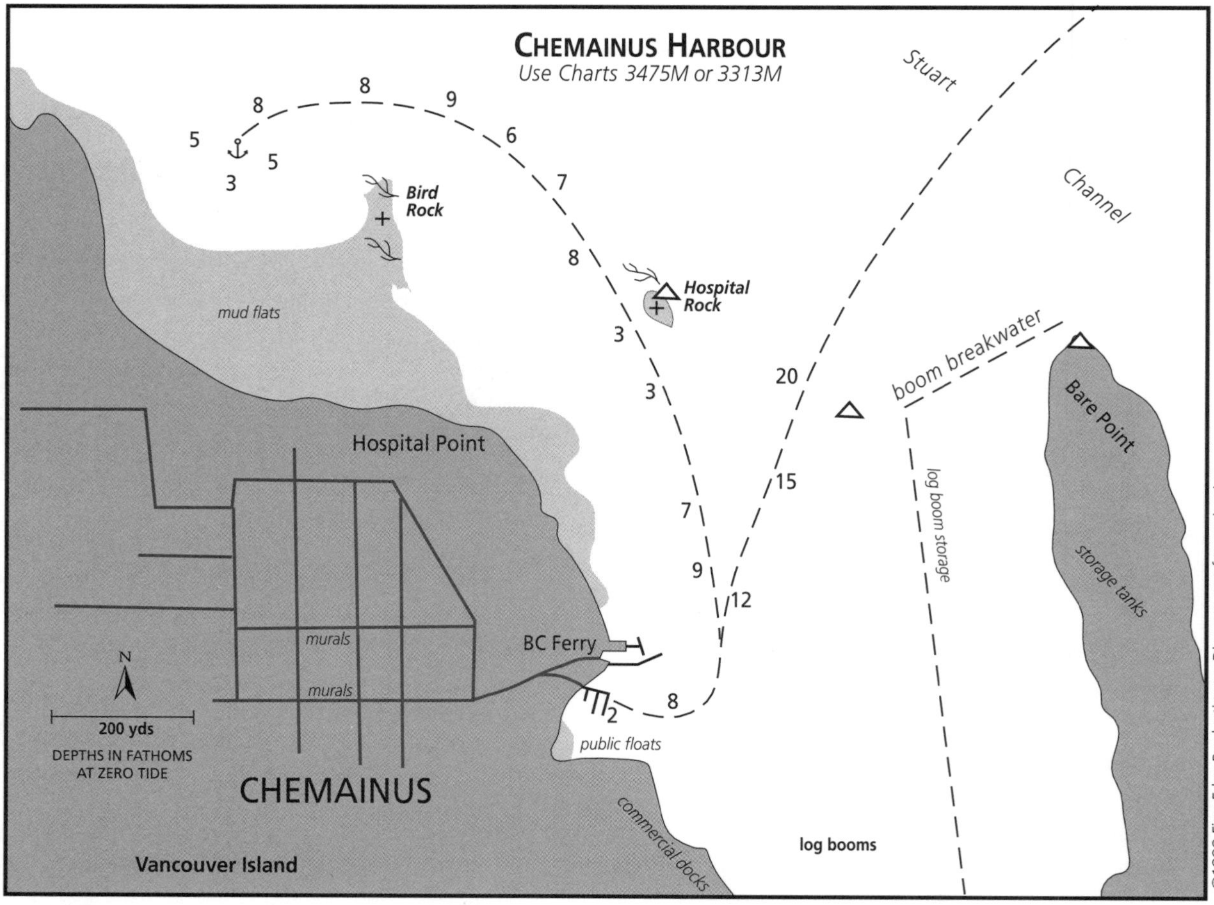

CHEMAINUS HARBOUR
Use Charts 3475M or 3313M

Stuart Channel
Bird Rock
Hospital Rock
mud flats
Hospital Point
boom breakwater
Bare Point
log boom storage
storage tanks
murals
murals
BC Ferry
public floats
commercial docks
log booms
CHEMAINUS
Vancouver Island
N
200 yds
DEPTHS IN FATHOMS AT ZERO TIDE

Don Douglass

Ladysmith Harbour entrance

mile west of Bird Rock light. The head of this small bay has a park and launching ramp, but it largely dries at low water.

Anchor in 3 to 5 fathoms off the drying mud flat, over sand and mud with fair-to-good holding.

Ladysmith Harbour (Vancouver Island)

Ladysmith Harbour is 6 miles northwest of Chemainus and 5.5 miles west of Preedy Harbour.

Charts 3475 metric (inset), 3443 metric, 3313 metric
Entrance: 48°58.50′ N, 123°46.25′ W (NAD 83)
Ladysmith Maritime Society floats: 48°59.72′ N, 123°48.70′ W (NAD 83)
Public docks: 48°59.98′ N, 123°48.86′ W (NAD 83)
Ladysmith Yacht Club: 49°00.39′ N, 123°49.61′ W (NAD 83)
Anchor (deep in harbor): 49°00.74′ N, 123°49.78′ W (NAD 83)
Mañana Lodge mooring: 49°00.68′ N, 123°49.37′ W (NAD 83)

> *Ladysmith Harbour* [is] *also known as Oyster Harbour . . . the SW shore is boulder strewn and in some areas there are oyster beds marked only by thin stakes. When entering Ladysmith Harbour a*

large blue crane NW of Slag Point and a large white conveyor near Williams Point are conspicuous landmarks.

. . . Small vessels can anchor in the upper reaches of the harbour, in the bays east and west of Dunsmuir Islands, or along the west shore clear of the wharves. (p. 160, SCG, Vol. 1)

Ladysmith Harbour

Don Douglass

Although the town of Ladysmith has undergone extensive renovations, the waterfront is still largely industrial and offers little in the way of facilities for cruising vessels; local and commercial fishing boats have priority. Temporary anchorage can be taken beyond the log-boom areas, deep in Ladysmith Harbour, 0.3 mile west of Page Point, or preferably in Sibell Bay between Dunsmuir Islands and Hunter Point on the north side of Ovens Island.

Temporary moorage may be available at the Ladysmith Marine Society floats, the first float complex located approximately 0.4 mile north-west of Slag Point.

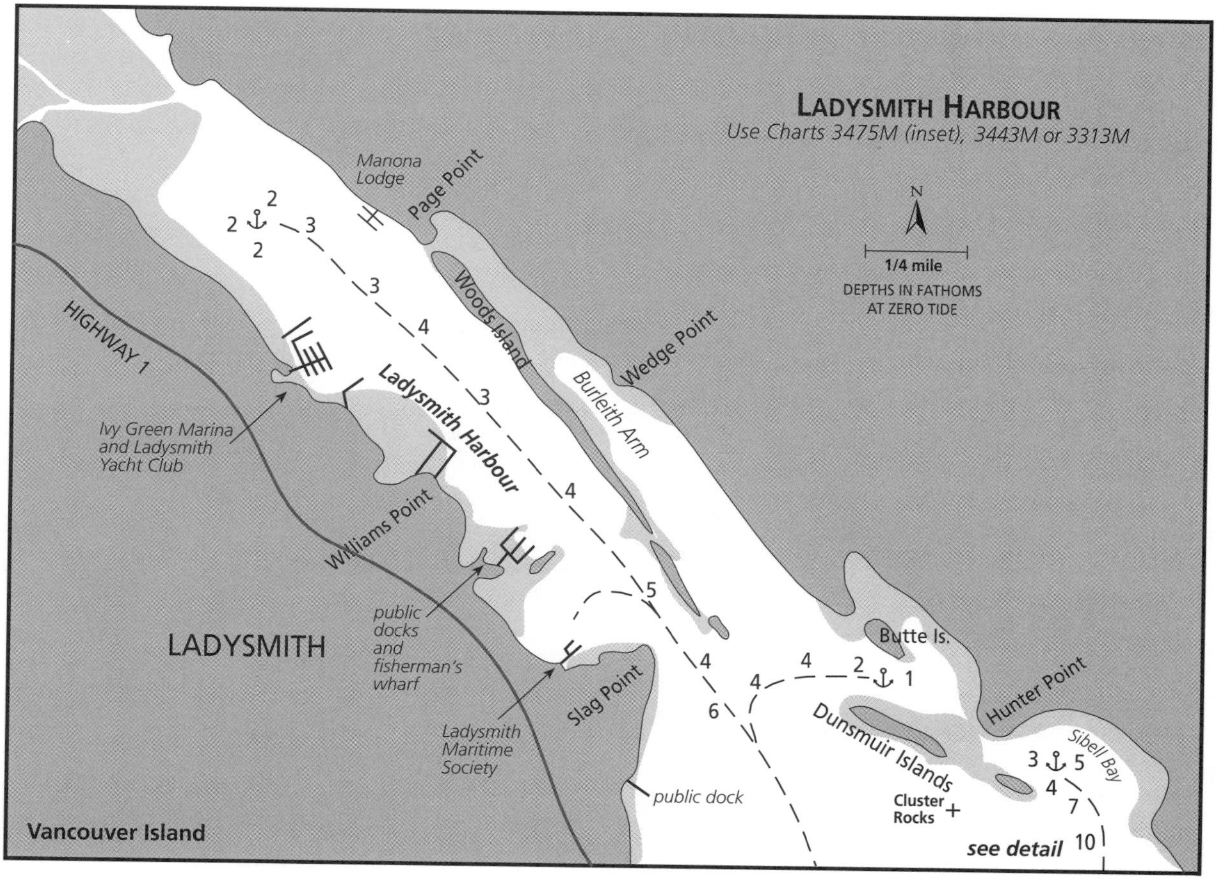

Ladysmith Harbour

Ladysmith Harbour was first called Oyster Bay in 1859 when extensive oyster beds were found along its south shore. The town of Ladysmith was founded in 1900 as a shipping port by the powerful coal baron James Dunsmuir. He chose the name upon receiving news that Ladysmith in South Africa, under siege by the Boers, had been relieved by British troops. The woman who originally inspired this place name was a descendant of a noble Spanish family. A beautiful 14-year-old maiden in 1812, she was brought by her older sister to a British military camp for protection. There she met Sir Harry Smith, a young captain who soon became her husband. He pursued a successful military career, accompanied by Lady Smith, and eventually retired a major-general.

The town of Ladysmith is pleasant for strolling, with its award-winning collection of restored heritage buildings such as those lining First Avenue. Shoppers can browse the antique shops and craft stores, and those seeking outdoor recreation can visit Transfer Beach Park where there is a playground, picnic shelters and horseshoe pitch. The town holds a Maritime Festival the first weekend in June and Ladysmith Days are held on the August long weekend.

Times were once a lot tougher for the town that recently won a provincial award as the most beautiful community on Vancouver Island. When James Dunsmuir operated mines in the area, conditions were less than ideal for the men working in them. On October 5th, 1901—the "Day of Horror"—an underground explosion killed 32 miners at the Extension Mine, which continued operations until the 1930s. Dunsmuir, who was appointed lieutenant governor of British Columbia in 1906, was the eldest son of Robert Dunsmuir who immigrated from Scotland in 1851 and built a family fortune in coal mining on Vancouver Island. James was born at Fort Vancouver on the Columbia River while his parents were en route to their new country, arriving at Victoria a few months later on board a brigantine. —**AV**

Sibell Bay and Dunsmuir Islands (Vancouver Island)

Sibell Bay, on the north shore of Ladysmith Harbour, is 0.8 mile northwest of Sharpe Point and 1.0 mile southeast of Slag Point.

Charts 3475 metric (inset), 3443 metric, 3313 metric
Entrance: 48°59.32′ N, 123°46.90′ W (NAD 83)
Anchor (Sibell Bay): 48°59.47′ N, 123°47.09′ W (NAD 83)
Anchor (north side Dunsmuir Islands, 0.17 mile northwest of Hunter Point): 48°59.64′ N, 123°47.42′ W (NAD 83)

> *Dunsmuir Islands lie on the north side of the* [Ladysmith] *harbour, off Hunter Point, from which they are separated by a narrow, shallow channel. The SE island of this group, known locally as Ovens Island, has a float belonging to a yacht club on its NE side.*
>
> *Sibell Bay, east of Dunsmuir Islands, and the bay to the north with Bute Island in it, have marine farm facilities in them.* (p. 162, SCG, Vol. 1)

Sibell Bay provides shelter from prevailing northwest winds in a quiet setting. Shallow-draft boats can find good shelter north of Dunsmuir Islands, south of Bute Island, avoiding the shoal areas and mud flats. Deeper draft boats can anchor 100 yards northeast of the Seattle Yacht Club outstation located on Ovens Island (the southernmost Dunsmuir Island).

Anchor (Sibell Bay) in 2 to 3 fathoms over mud with good holding.

Anchor (north side Dunsmuir Islands) in 1 fathom over mud with good holding.

Don Douglass

Seattle Yacht Club Outstation in Sibell Bay

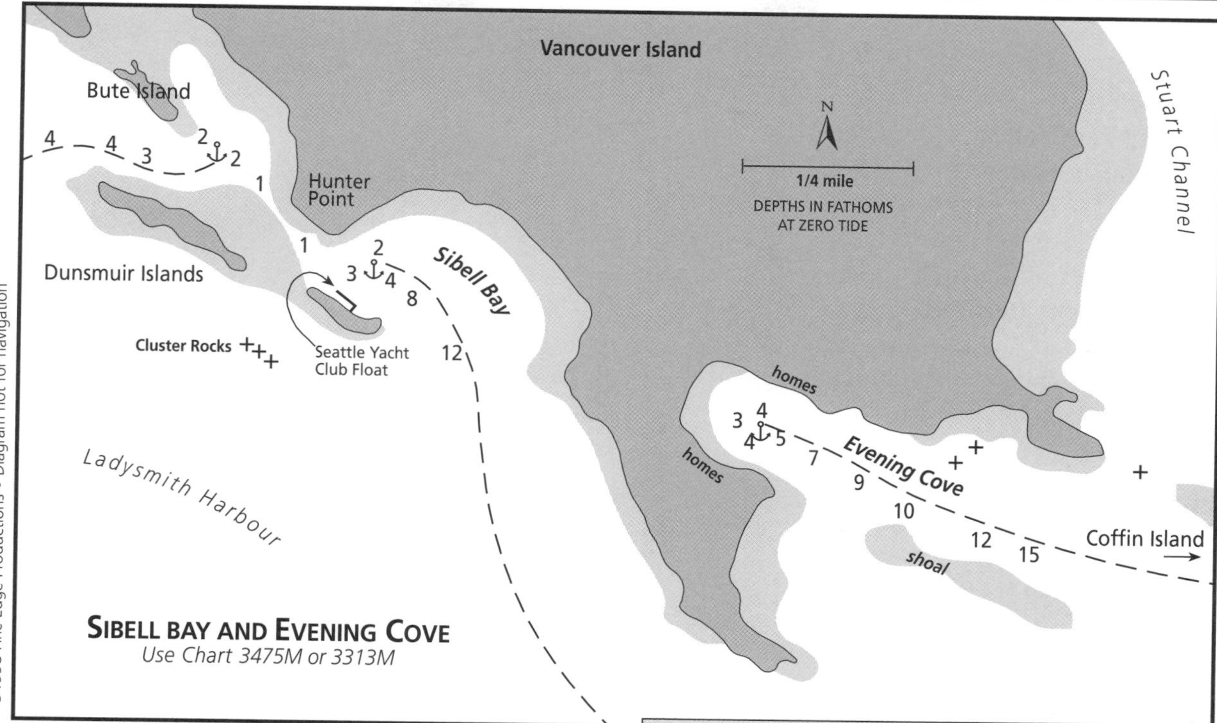

SIBELL BAY AND EVENING COVE
Use Chart 3475M or 3313M

Evening Cove (Vancouver Island)

Evening Cove is 0.6 mile southeast of Sibell Bay and 3.5 miles west of Preedy Harbour.

Charts 3475 metric (inset), 3443 metric, 3313 metric
Entrance: 48°58.93′ N, 123°45.08′ W (NAD 83)
Anchor: 48°59.25′ N, 123°46.20′ W (NAD 83)

> *Evening Cove, between Sharpe Point and Coffin Point, has Collins Shoal in the centre of its entrance. Small craft can obtain anchorage near*

Anne Vipond

Weather-worn rocks along the Vancouver Island shore

Don Douglass

Entering Evening Cove in the morning

the head of the cove but it is exposed to SE winds. (p. 160, SCG, Vol. 1)

Evening Cove offers easy access and good protection from northwest winds with moderate exposure to southeast winds. Avoid the private buoys off the homes along shore. When transiting Stuart Channel, avoid Collins Shoal in the center of the entrance south of Coffin Point.

Anchor in 4 fathoms over mud and gravel with fair-to-good holding.

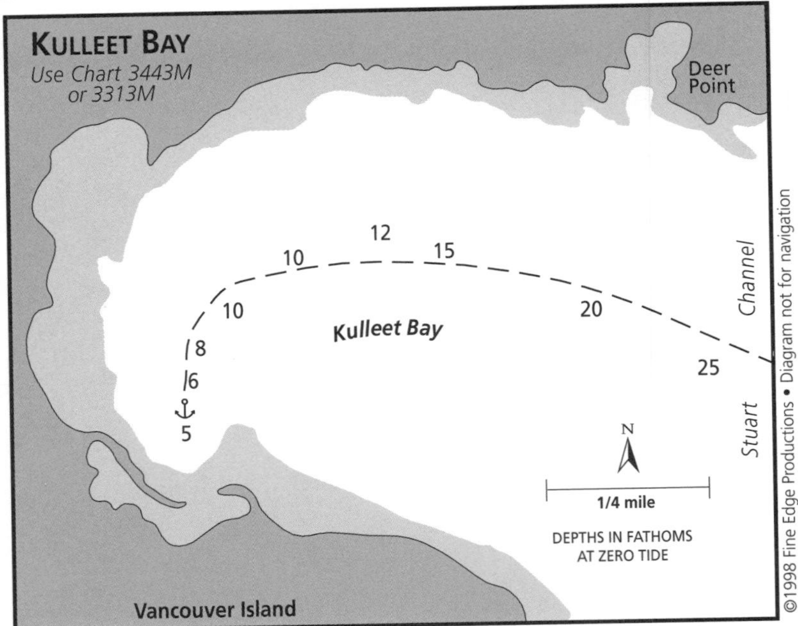

Kulleet Bay (Vancouver Island)

Kulleet Bay is 2.2 miles northeast of Evening Cove.

Charts 3443 metric or 3313
Entrance: 49°01.31′ N, 123°45.83′ W (NAD 83)
Anchor: 49°01.23′ N, 123°47.15′ W (NAD 83)

Kulleet Bay is a designated anchorage for merchant vessels awaiting a berth at Ladysmith. Small craft can also find anchorage, on a bottom of sand and shells, on the shoal area extending north from the south side of the bay; it is exposed to east winds. This area is narrow and falls off sharply into relatively deep water The land surrounding Kulleet Bay is an Indian Reserve. (p. 163, SCG, Vol. 1)

Kulleet Bay, a large bay fringed with rocks and reefs, provides temporary anchorage in the southwest corner behind the reef to the east and off the front of a muddy lagoon.

Anchor in 6 to 8 fathoms over sand and shells with fair holding.

Anchor check—good mud bottom

North Cove (Thetis Island)

North Cove is 2.5 miles north of Preedy Harbour and 3.9 miles west of Porlier Pass.

Charts 3442 metric, 3443 metric, 3313 metric
Entrance: 49°01.53′ N, 123°42.08′ W (NAD 83)
Anchor: 49°00.88′ N, 123°41.72′ W (NAD 83)

North Cove, at the north end of Thetis Island, is

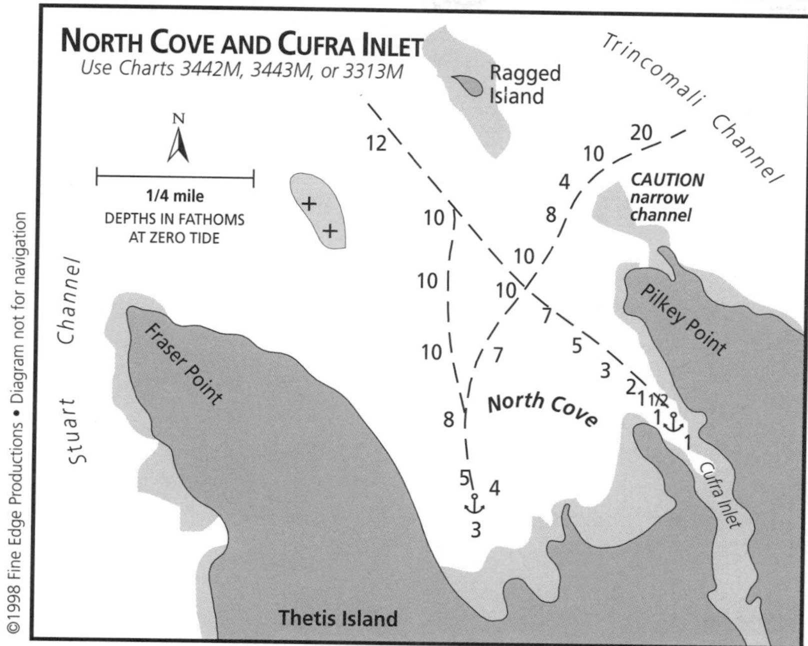

entered between Fraser Point and Pilkey Point. A reef, with less than 6 feet (1.8 m) over it, lies 0.3 mile east of Fraser Point.

Anchorage in 43 feet (13 m), mud, can be obtained in the middle of North Cove; the cove affords shelter from south winds. (p. 163, SCG, Vol. 1)

North Cove offers two anchor sites: North Cove, the broader of the two anchorages, is the more accessible, but it is open to northwest winds; the smaller and more protected anchorage can be found in Cufra Inlet, but with space limited to about two boats.

Anchor in about 4 fathoms (off the small sandy beach in the southeast corner of North Cove) over sand and mud with good holding.

Cufra Inlet (Thetis Island)

Cufra Inlet is the narrow, shallow indentation at the southeast end of North Cove.

Charts 3442 metric, 2443 metric, 3313 metric
Entrance (0.61 mile north of Pilkey Point): 49°01.46′ N, 123°41.42′ W (NAD 83)
Anchor: 49°01.01′ N, 123°41.22′ W (NAD 83)

Cufra Inlet . . . is a narrow arm which affords shelter for small craft; the major portion of the inlet dries.

A breakwater, near the mouth of Cufra Inlet, extends from the east shore about half the distance to the west side of the arm, providing shelter in the inner anchorage. (p. 164, SCG, Vol. 1)

You can explore Cufra Inlet by dinghy for quite a distance at high water by carefully watching your echo sounder or by watching the bottom. Be sure to consult the tide tables ahead of time.

When entering the cove, avoid the rocks off the northwest entrance, and the rocks and shoals northwest of Pilkey Point and Ragged Islets. Anchor inside the old stone breakwater (space permitting) near the drying flat, with limited swinging room.

Anchor in about 1 fathom over sand and grass with fair holding.

Anne Vipond

Private moorage in Kenary Cove Marina

Nicholson Cove (Vancouver Island)

Nicholson Cove is 0.7 mile northwest of Yellow Point and 1.8 miles northeast of Kulleet Bay.

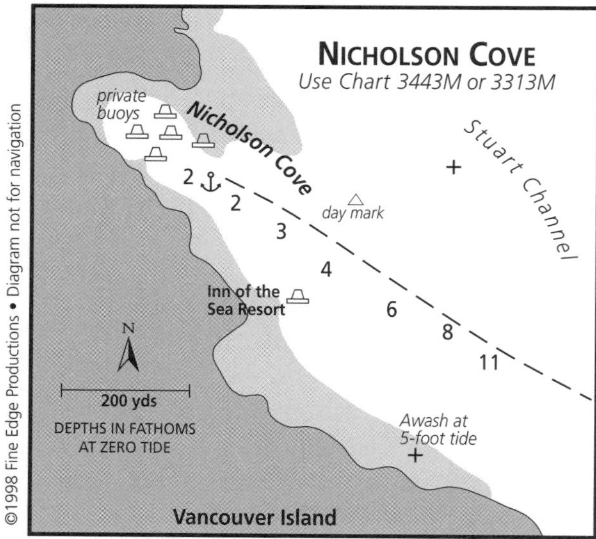

Charts 3443 metric, 3313 metric
Entrance: 49°02.72′ N, 123°44.94′ W (NAD 83)
Anchor: 49°02.87′ N, 123°45.40′ W (NAD 83)
Inn of the Sea dock: 49°02.77′ N, 123°45.28′ W (NAD 83)

> *Nicholson Cove . . . provides shelter for small craft from north winds. A drying ledge and a chain of drying rocks extend from the north entrance of the cove.* (p. 163, SCG, Vol. 1)

Nicholson Cove can be used as a temporary anchorage with shelter from westerly winds. There are rocks along both shores which must be avoided and the inner bay is full of private mooring floats. A starboard daymark is located on one of the drying rocks and caution is advised upon entering the small cove. Anchor just outside the line of mooring buoys.

Inn of the Sea Resort has a restaurant and a private dock with moorage for guests only. For information, tel: 250-245-2211.

Anchor in 1 to 2 fathoms over sand and gravel and some rocks with fair holding.

Boat Harbour

A visit to Boat Harbour is an opportunity to hike into beautiful Hemer Provincial Park where wide, groomed trails lead past the pristine shores of Holden Lake. The park, a gift to the province from John and Violet Hemer, can be reached by a trail that starts on the peninsula near the head of Boat Harbour. This peninsula is where a marine engineer named Flewett used to load coal onto a steam launch in the 1870s, and the narrow neck of land was once a rail embankment. The foreshore is also fascinating to explore, where low banks of sandstone have been eroded over time into smooth and unusual shapes.—**AV**

Boat Harbour/Kenary Cove (Vancouver Island)

Boat Harbour is 4.4 miles north of Kulleet Bay and 2.6 miles south of Dodd Narrows.

Charts 3443 metric, 3313 metric
Entrance: 49°05.70′ N, 123°47.69′ W (NAD 83)
Anchor: 49°05.65′ N, 123°48.00′ W (NAD 83)

> *Boat Harbour . . . is often used as a temporary anchorage for vessels awaiting slack water in Dodd Narrows. The cove in the south part of Boat Harbour, west of Flewett Point, is known locally as Kenary Cove. The floats in Boat Harbour are private.*
>
> *Anchorage can be obtained in the entrance of Boat Harbour in 49 feet (15 m), mud bottom. Well sheltered anchorage for small craft can be obtained in Kenary Cove in 10 to 16 feet (3 to 5 m), mud bottom.* (p. 163, SCG, Vol. 1)

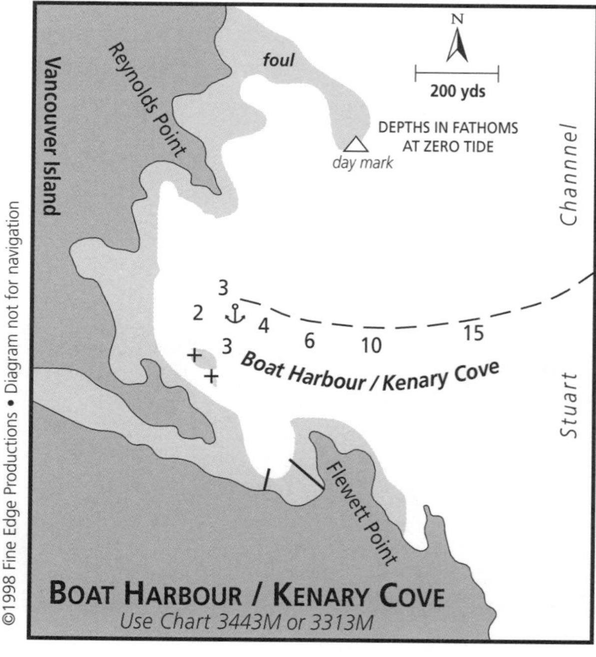

Boat Harbour, another lovely anchor site

Boat Harbour (Kenary Cove) offers temporary anchorage for boats awaiting slack water at Dodd Narrows.

Boat Harbour anchor site

The marina at the south end of Boat Harbour has private moorage only. Temporary anchorage may be found on the west side of the bay.

Anchor in about 3 fathoms over mud and gravel with fair holding.

Dodd Narrows

Dodd Narrows is 21 miles north of Maple Bay and 5 miles southeast of Nanaimo Harbour.

Charts 3443 metric, 3313 metric
South entrance: 49°08.00′ N, 123°48.90′ W (NAD 83)
North entrance: 49°08.28′ N, 123°49.09′ W (NAD 83)

Dodd Narrows connects Stuart Channel with Northumberland Channel and is separated from False Narrows by Mudge Island.

Dodd Narrows is used mainly by tugs, barges and logbooms. It is not a recommended passage for much larger craft, however, vessels up to 230 feet (70 m) have passed through at slack water without undue difficulty.

Predictions for the times and rates of maximum current and the time of slack water when the direction of the current turns are given for Dodd Narrows in the Tide Tables, Volume 5.

The maximum flood is 9 kn and the ebb is 8 kn; it sets north on the flood and south on the ebb.

When the tidal stream is running at strength tide-rips, formed by the stream and its counterflow, occur off the north entrance on the flood and in the vicinity of the overhead cable on the ebb. No attempt should be made to alter course out of the main stream until clear of this turbulence. The gradual disappearance of these tide-rips is an indication of the slackening in the tidal stream.

Dodd Narrows is more difficult to pass through when entering from north than from south, for in the former case, the slight alteration of course, necessary when passing through, has to be made immediately on entering the narrow part; in addition the entrance to Dodd Narrows is difficult to see when approaching from Northumberland Channel.

It is recommended that passage through Dodd Narrows be made at slack water. Before passing through Dodd Narrows other than at slack water be sure the vessel has the ability to proceed against the tidal stream; if there is any doubt, passage should be delayed until slack water.

Care should be taken not to hinder tugs with barges or logbooms passing through the narrows and attention should be given to the sound and radio signals for narrow channels. (p. 167, SCG, Vol. 1; see also SD, pp. 157, 159)

Don Douglass

Turbulence at flood, Dodd Narrows

Dodd Narrows is one of the many fast-moving saltwater rapids along the south coast of British Columbia. Transiting is not particularly difficult at or near slack water, especially during neap tides—the window of passable times is usually quite wide. Consult the current tables in Volume 5; if you're in doubt about entering the Narrows, follow the lead of experienced boats your size. Boats passing through Dodd Narrows against the current should be especially careful with their wake to avoid swamping small boats heading in the opposite direction.

If you wish to avoid Dodd Narrows on your way to Nanaimo, you can use Gabriola Passage (moderate rapids and tide rips), passing north of Gabriola Island. Or you can transit False Narrows (an alternative route for intrepid skippers) on the north side of Mudge Island, very narrow and encumbered with reefs. False Narrows has less current than Dodd, but the fairway is very shallow and choked with kelp. (See False Narrows, Chapter 11.)

11

PYLADES CHANNEL, GABRIOLA PASSAGE TO SILVA BAY

The northwestern section of the Gulf Islands, centered around Pylades Channel and Gabriola Passage, has a charm of its own with well-sheltered nooks and crannies that allow explorers to get off by themselves, particularly during off-season. Pirates Cove and Whaleboat Island—both small Marine Parks in the De Courcy Group—are popular cruising destinations; Pirates has a lovely hiking trail, picnic tables, well water, and walk-in campsites. Throughout this area, there are striking examples of the wind- and wave-sculpted sandstone for which the Gulf and San Juan islands are so well known.

If you are heading for Dodd Narrows from Pylades Channel, Ruxton Passage—which dissects the De Courcy Group—provides easy access to Stuart Channel.

False Narrows is an interesting pass used by locals as a short cut between Degnen Bay, Northumberland Channel and Nanaimo. However, it is a difficult passage that only experienced and adventurous sailors should attempt. Be sure to consult a detailed chart and note the serious cautions for transiting this area.

Valdes Island is notable for its steep cliffs which can be seen from Trincomali Channel. As you approach the island, you may imagine that you see "carvings" of people's faces in the unusual rock formations.

Gabriola Passage is a major route to the Strait of Georgia, as well as to Degnen and Silva bays on Gabriola Island and Dogfish Bay at the north end of Valdes Island. Be sure to note the listed cautions on the charts before transiting Gabriola Passage. Degnen Bay has a public wharf; from there you can walk southeast to Drumbeg Provincial Park for swimming, fishing or hiking. At the head of the bay is a petroglyph of a killer whale. Silva Bay, surrounded by the Flat Top Islands off the east side of Gabriola Island, is a favorite stop for pleasure boats wishing a few more amenities. It has marinas, stores, laundry facilities and a pub.

Pylades Channel

Pylades Channel leads from Trincomali Channel to Gabriola Passage at its northeast end and to False Narrows at its northwest end.

Charts 3443 metric, 3475 metric, 3313 metric
South entrance: 0.65 mile southeast of Pylades Island): 49°03.60′ N, 123°40.20′ W (NAD 83)
Northwest entrance (False Narrows): 49°07.43′ N, 123°45.58′ W (NAD 83)
Northeast entrance (Gabriola Passage): 49°07.60′ N, 123°43.22′ W (NAD 83)

> *Pylades Channel leads NW from Trincomali Channel between the west side of Valdes Island and the De Courcy Group to the SE. From the NW end of Pylades Channel, Gabriola Passage leads east into the Strait of Georgia and False Narrows . . . leads NW into Northumberland Channel.*
>
> *Whaleboat Passage and Ruxton Passage lead west through the De Courcy Group to Stuart Channel. . . .*
>
> *Tidal streams in Pylades Channel attain 2 kn*

Don Douglass

Pylades Channel

at times; the flood sets NW and the ebb SE. (p. 202, SCG, Vol. 1)

Pylades Channel is sheltered by Gabriola Island on the north, Valdes Island on the east, and the De Courcy Group on the west. False Narrows is the shallow, kelp-infested alternative route to and from Nanaimo on Vancouver Island. (See False Narrows below.)

Don Douglass

Good News *on moorings*

Pylades Island (Pylades Channel)

Pylades Island, between Stuart and Pylades channels at the south end of the De Courcy islands, is 3.7 miles southeast of Gabriola Passage and 6.4 miles southeast of Dodd Narrows.

Charts 3443 metric, 3313 metric
Anchor (south side): 49°03.78′ N, 123°41.27′ W (NAD 83)

> *Pylades Island, 1 mile NE of Danger Reefs on the NE side of Stuart Channel, has some broken cliffs, about 80 feet (24 m) high, on its west side.* (p. 164, SCG, Vol. 1)

Small craft can find anchorage in calm weather along the south and east shores of Pylades Island. Avoid the rocks and shoal areas on the east side of Pylades Island. This area, exposed to southerly weather up Trincomali Channel, should be used in stable conditions only.

Whaleboat Passage

Whaleboat Passage is located between Pylades Island on the south and Ruxton and Whaleboat islands on the north.

Charts 3443 metric, 3313 metric
West entrance: 49°04.20′ N, 123°42.04′ W (NAD 83)
East entrance: 49°04.35′ N, 123°41.34′ W (NAD 83)

> *Whaleboat Passage . . . has a least depth of 7 feet (2.1 m) in mid-channel and is only suitable for small craft.* (p. 164, SCG, Vol. 1)

Whaleboat Passage leads from Stuart Channel to Whaleboat Island Marine Park on the east side of Ruxton Island. Avoid the rock and shoal off the north end of Pylades Island.

Whaleboat Island Marine Park

Whaleboat Island Marine Park, on the east side of Ruxton Island, is 2.0 miles southeast of Pirates Cove Marine Park.

Charts 3443 metric, 3313 metric
Position: 49°04.50′ N, 123°41.60′ W (NAD 83)

> *Whaleboat Island lies in the NE approach to Whaleboat Passage, close off the SE side of Ruxton Island. Whaleboat Island Marine Park is*

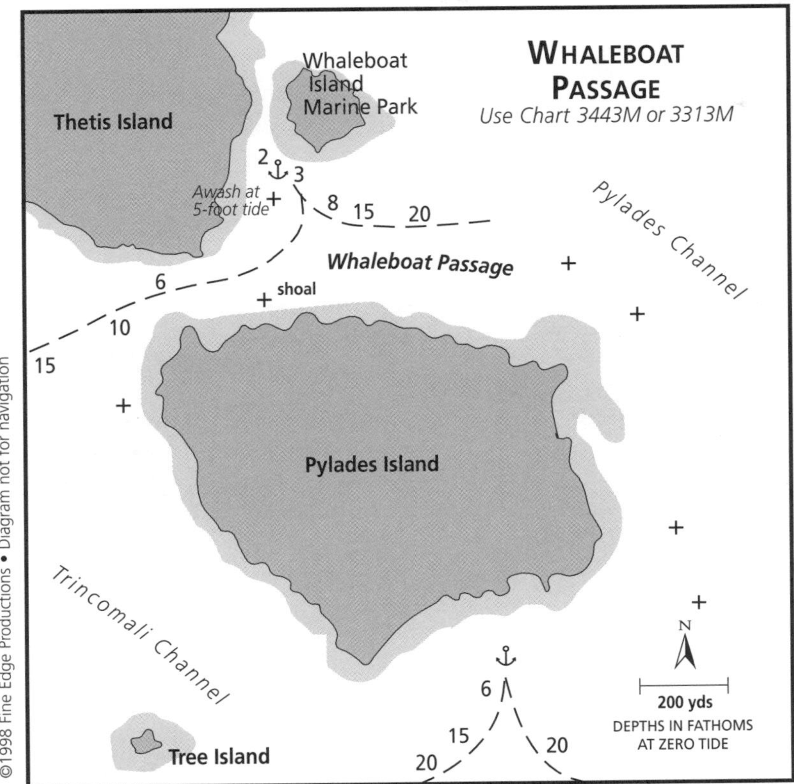

undeveloped; several private mooring buoys lie close to shore. (p. 164, SCG, Vol. 1)

Whaleboat Island Marine Park is a small, undeveloped area. Anchorage can be found on the north side of the 5-foot rock between Ruxton and Whaleboat islands. We have also seen boats anchored on the south side of Whaleboat Island; however, the bottom along this south shore of the De Courcy Group is irregular and likely to be rocky or foul. Avoid the rocks and shoals off the east side of Pylades Island north to Ruxton Passage. The small passage between Whaleboat and Ruxton islands is primarily a dinghy passage and choked with kelp. This is a fair-weather anchorage only and swinging room is limited.

Anne Vipond

Thar she blows!

Anchor between 3 and 6 fathoms over rock and sand with poor-to-fair holding.

West Bay (Ruxton Island)

West Bay, on the west shore of Ruxton Island, is 1.4 miles south of Pirates Cove Marine Park.

Charts 3343 metric, 3313 metric
Entrance: 49°04.65′ N, 123°42.56′ W (NAD 83)
Anchor: 49°04.70′ N, 123°42.48′ W (NAD 83)

Ruxton Island is high and wooded near its south end. West Bay, near the middle of the west side of the island, is suitable only for small craft; it has a depth of 9 feet (2.7 m) in its central part but is nearly closed at LW. (p. 164, SCG, Vol. 1)

West Bay is full of mooring buoys; the shore is lined with homes. The tiny bay, open to southwest weather, is useful mainly for sportfishing skiffs.

Herring Bay (Ruxton Island)

Herring Bay, at the northwest end of Ruxton Island, is 1.0 mile southeast of Pirates Cove Marine Park.

Charts 3475 metric, 3343 metric, 3313 metric
North entrance: 49°05.28′ N, 123°43.20′ W (NAD 83)
West entrance: 49°05.06′ N, 123°43.13′ W (NAD 83)
Anchor: 49°05.00′ N, 123°42.88′ W (NAD 83)

Herring Bay, at the NW end of Ruxton Island, offers good anchorage, sand bottom. (p. 164, SCG, Vol. 1)

Herring Bay, on the south side of Ruxton Passage, is a lovely cove with white shell beaches and interesting sandstone formations. It has become an alternative to popular Pirates Cove. A daymark identifies the tip of the reef off the north entrance—the preferred way to enter is by taking the daymark to starboard. Entrance can be made from the west through a break in the reef and the peninsula. However, the reef is unmarked at its south end and the fairway difficult to locate at high water.

Don Douglass

Gillcrest *in Herring Bay*

Swinging room is limited, and the cove is unsafe in strong northerly winds, but in fair weather or moderate southerlies this can be a delightful anchor site. The sandstone islets and reefs of Herring Bay are fun to explore by dinghy.

Anchor northwest of the seven private mooring buoys at the south end of Herring Bay with good protection from the southeast.

Anchor in 3 to 4 fathoms over sand and shells with fair-to-good holding.

Ruxton Passage

Ruxton Passage joins Pylades and Stuart channels at the north end of Ruxton Island.

Charts 3375 metric, 3443 metric, 3313 metric
West entrance: 49°05.26′ N, 123°43.66′ W (NAD 83)
East entrance: 49°05.43′ N, 123°42.88′ W (NAD 83)

> *Ruxton Passage between Ruxton and De Courcy Islands connects Stuart Channel to Pylades Channel. A shoal, with 25 feet (7.6 m) over it, lies in the east entrance, otherwise the fairway is deep and can be navigated on a mid-channel course.* (p. 164, SCG, Vol. 1)

Ruxton Passage connects Stuart Channel to Pylades Channel south of De Courcy Island and north of Ruxton Island. The center of the passage is deep, presenting little difficulty. Avoid the shoal off the southeast point of De Courcy Island.

Don Douglass

Anchored off the driftwood beach, Ruxton Passage Cove

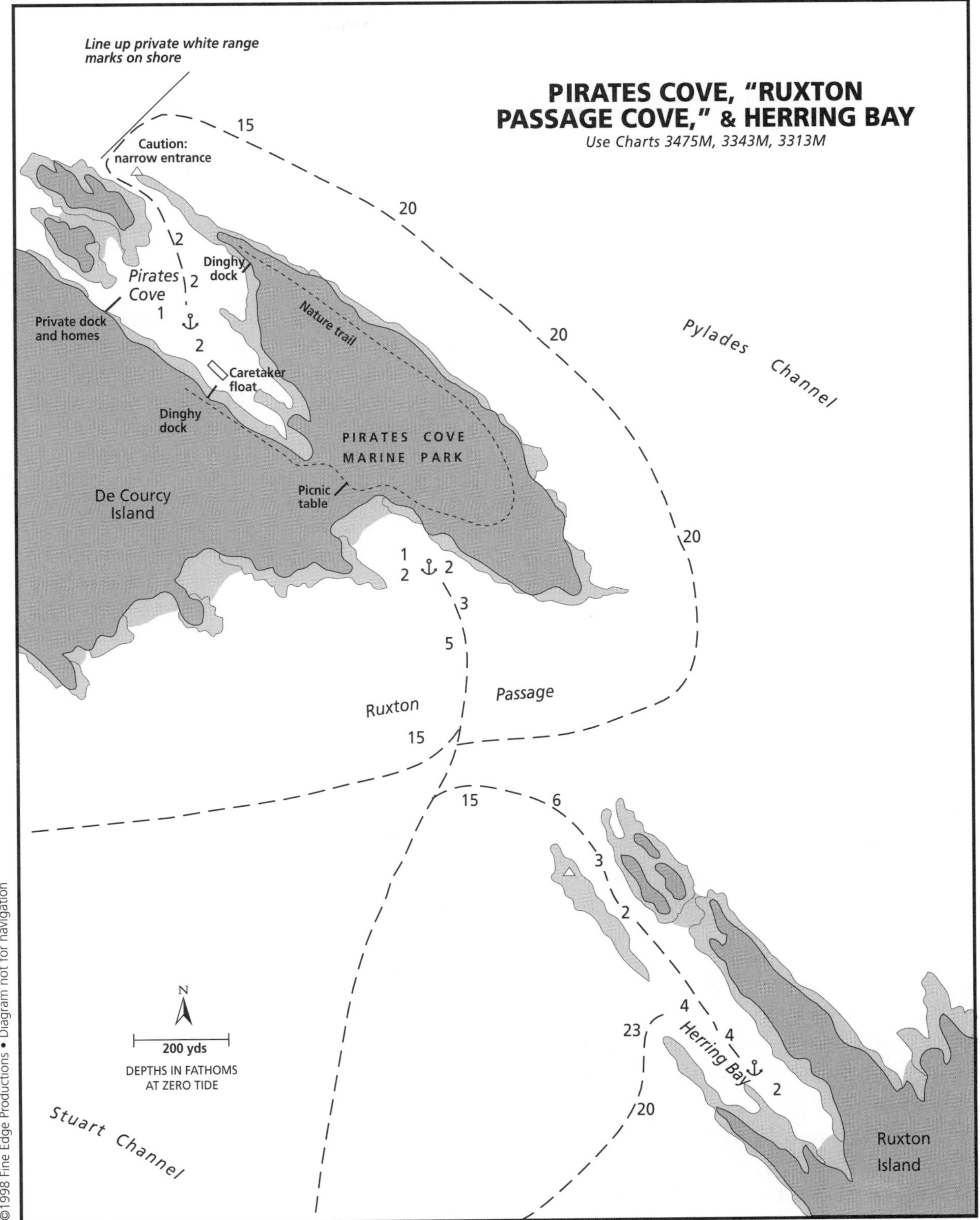

PIRATES COVE, "RUXTON PASSAGE COVE," & HERRING BAY
Use Charts 3475M, 3343M, 3313M
Line up private white range marks on shore
Caution: narrow entrance
15
20
2
Pirates Cove
Dinghy dock
Private dock and homes
1
2
Nature trail
Pylades Channel
Caretaker float
Dinghy dock
PIRATES COVE MARINE PARK
Picnic table
De Courcy Island
20
1
2
3
5
Ruxton
Passage
15
6
3
2
4
23
Herring Bay
20
Ruxton Island
200 yds
DEPTHS IN FATHOMS AT ZERO TIDE
Stuart Channel

"Ruxton Passage Cove" (De Courcy Island)

Ruxton Passage Cove, on the south end of De Courcy Island, is 0.75 mile northwest of Herring Bay.

Charts 3475 metric, 3343 metric, 3313 metric
Entrance: 49°05.48′ N, 123°43.37′ W (NAD 83)
Anchor: 49°05.56′ N, 123°43.43′ W (NAD 83)

> *The cove on the south side of the* [Pirates Cove Marine] *park is open and provides good anchorage only in west or NW weather. Fresh water is obtainable from a well onshore.* (p. 202, SCG, Vol. 1)

Ruxton Passage Cove is the cove off the small driftwood-choked beach along Ruxton Passage; it is just a short walk across the spit from Pirates Cove. The amount of driftwood on the beach is evidence of exposure to southeast gales meaning that the site should be used only in fair weather.

The north end of De Courcy Island can also be used as temporary anchorage when Pirates Cove is too crowded. *See:* Link Island Cove below.

Anne Vipond

Entrance to Pirates Cove

Anchor in 2 to 3 fathoms over a sand and gravel bottom with fair holding.

Pirates Cove Marine Park (De Courcy Island)

Pirates Cove Marine Park, on the east side of De Courcy Island, is 4.1 miles southeast of Dodd Narrows and 1.85 miles southwest of Gabriola Passage.

Charts 3475 metric, 3343 metric, 3313 metric
Entrance: 49°06.08′ N, 123°43.91′ W (NAD 83)
Anchor: 49°05.87′ N, 123°43.83′ W (NAD 83)

> *Pirates Cove lies on the NW side of a peninsula at the SE extremity of De Courcy Island. A drying reef, in the entrance of the cove, extends NW from the north end of this peninsula.*
>
> *Pirates Cove daybeacon, on the above-mentioned drying reef, consists of a concrete base surmounted by a mast displaying a port hand daymark.*
>
> *A starboard hand buoy, identified "U38", is close west of the above daybeacon. Pass between the beacon and buoy when entering Pirates Cove.*
>
> *A white line painted on a rock with a white cross on a pole above it serves as a range to clear the north end of the drying spit.*
>
> *Public dinghy floats are in the cove. Camping facilities and ring bolts for stern mooring are located along the shore of the peninsula on the east side of the cove. The nearest well for drinking water is on the shore of the cove at the south end of the peninsula; land at the south public float and follow the foot path leading south; it is about a 5 minute walk to the well.*
>
> *Anchorage in Pirates Cove is sheltered from all but north winds; good ground tackle is essential. If there are many small craft anchored in the cove be prepared for some to drag anchor if the wind turns to north.*
>
> *The NE shore of De Courcy Island, encumbered by rocks and shoals, has several small bays suitable for small craft. A small bight between De Courcy Island and Link Island offers temporary anchorage; it shoals to a depth of 3 feet (0.9 m).* (p. 203, SCG, Vol. 1)

Pirates Cove is one of the most popular marine parks in the Gulf Islands, and in summer it frequently has "wall-to-wall" boats. A seasonal host ranger stationed here can direct you to a space. However, if you show up in off-season, you'll probably have the cove to yourself. During crowded summer months, shore ties are used.

To enter Pirates Cove, stay well to the north until directly off the white "range" mark found on a tree on shore, then head in close to the range mark before turning carefully south across the shallow bar into the cove proper. Avoid the reef extending northwest from the daymark and pass between the daymark and red Buoy "U38."

Don Douglass

An off-season pirate ready to load his sea-chest

There are two dinghy docks in Pirates Cove; a nice trail system takes off above one of these docks, passes through lovely stands of arbutus, and leads to the tip of the eastern peninsula. A picnic area is located on the spit between Pirates Cove and Ruxton Pass Cove. The dock and islands at the northwest end of Pirates Cove are private.

Anchor in the center of the cove—or as directed by the park host—in 2 fathoms over a mud bottom with good holding.

"Link Island Cove" (Link and De Courcy Islands)

Link Island Cove is 1.3 miles northwest of Pirates Cove Marine Park, between Link and De Courcy islands.

Charts 3475 metric, 3343 metric, 3313 metric
Entrance: 49°06.83′ N, 123°45.28′ W (NAD 83)
Anchor: 49°06.77′ N, 123°45.38′ W (NAD 83)

> *A small bight between De Courcy Island and Link Island offers temporary anchorage; it shoals to a depth of 3 feet (0.9 m).* (p. 203, SCG, Vol. 1)

Quiet anchorage can be found in the small bight between Link and De Courcy islands. From this site, it is fun to explore the east side of De Courcy

Pirates Cove

De Courcy Island was named for Captain Michael De Courcy of Britain's Royal Navy who was stationed in local waters from 1859-61 in command of H.M.S. *Pylades*. However, the Englishman who gave De Courcy Island its fascinating history was Edward Arthur Wilson, who eventually became known as the notorious Brother Twelve—one of the 20th century's most fascinating cult leaders. A former sea captain, Wilson was a mysterious and charismatic man who could convince seemingly sensible people to donate large sums of money to his religious organization, the Aquarian Foundation, and to work like slaves at one of his colonies.

He built his headquarters at Cedar, north of Boat Harbour on Vancouver Island in 1927, before establishing a colony on De Courcy Island. With the help of his whip-wielding mistress named Madame Zee, he then turned the southern end of De Courcy into a secluded retreat. If any outsiders entered the harbor, they were driven out by Brother Twelve's curses and threats to ram them with his tugboat. After seven years of tyranny, his profitable cult collapsed as disgruntled disciples eventually rebelled and notified authorities of his activities. As the police closed in, Brother Twelve disappeared; he died a few years later in Switzerland. Mystery still surrounds his life and death, and the fate of his accumulated treasure, said to be 43 boxes of gold coins weighing close to half a ton, of which no trace was ever found.

Today, life is a lot more placid on De Courcy. Pirates Cove was turned into a marine park in 1966 and is now one of the most popular in the Gulf Islands. The park contains dinghy floats, some lovely trails on shore, and a beach area overlooking Ruxton Passage. —**AV**

by dinghy or kayak. A number of private homes are in the area.

Anchor in about 1 fathom over sand with fair holding.

Coal Mine Bay (Valdes Island)

Coal Mine Bay, located on the east shore of Valdes Island, is 0.83 mile southeast of Gabriola Passage.

Charts 3475 metric, 3343 metric, 3313 metric
Position: 49°06.94′ N, 123°42.50′ W (NAD 83)

> *Coal Mine Bay, 0.7 mile SE of Dibuxante Point, is a booming ground. Three mooring buoys, for log storage purposes, are in the bay.* (p. 204, SCG, Vol. 1)

You may be able to find temporary shelter from southeast gales tucked up close to shore in Coal Mine Bay. However, Degnen Bay and Wakes Cove in Gabriola Passage offer superior shelter and more swinging room

False Narrows

False Narrows, between Mudge and Gabriola islands, connects Pylades Channel to Percy Anchorage.

Charts 3475 metric, 3343 metric, 3313 metric
East entrance 49°07.43′ N, 123°45.58′ W (NAD 83)
West entrance: 49°08.21′ N, 123°47.61′ W (NAD 83)

> [False Narrows] *is suitable only for boats and small craft; local knowledge is required. The navigable channel, with depths of 3 to 5 feet (0.9 to 1.5 m), leads north of a long narrow drying ledge near the middle of the passage. During summer and autumn kelp grows profusely in the narrows and is an additional source of danger.*
>
> *Tidal streams through False Narrows, in the vicinity of the drying reef, run parallel with shore on both the flood and ebb. The flood sets NW and the ebb SE. At the east end of the narrows, at LW, the stream runs smoothly along the north shore of Mudge Island, and gradually extends over the whole narrows as the ride rises; on a falling tide the effect is reversed.*
>
> *Logbooms are often towed through False Narrows, usually southbound, with the first of the ebb; mariners intending to navigate the passage should be prepared to give them adequate clearance. Approaching False Narrows from Pylades Channel hold to the Mudge Island shore in order to avoid the drying area to the north which has a number of large boulders on it.*

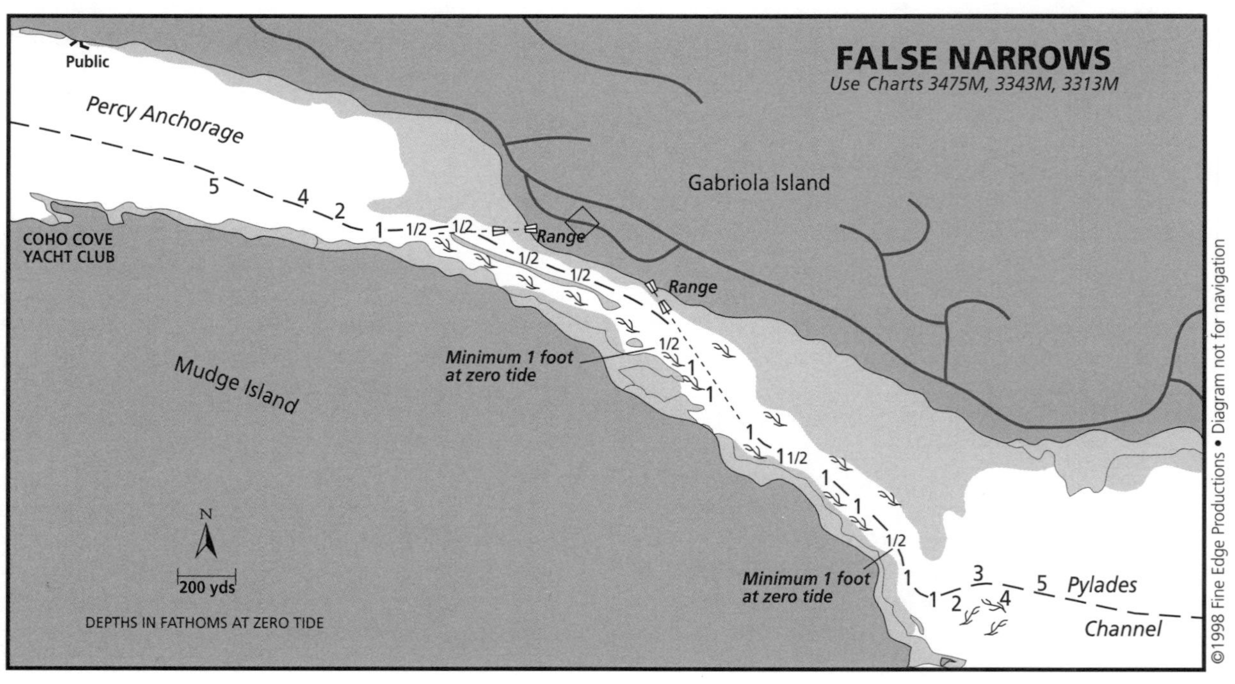

At the west end keep on the West Range until close to the Mudge Island shore in order to avoid the drying spit extending west from the West Range. (pp. 167, 169, SCG, Vol. 1; see also SD, p. 157)

False Narrows leads northwest along the north shore of Mudge Island from Pylades Channel to Percy Anchorage and Northumberland Channel. This shallow, intricate channel is entirely choked with kelp in late summer and should be attempted only by boaters who want a navigational challenge since it may take longer than the "straight-forward" transit of Dodd Narrows.

From west to east (southbound): Start from Percy Anchorage on the Mudge Island side, in line with the range markers (white with red center marks) located east of a housing complex on Gabriola Island. Do not let the ebb current carry you onto the mid-channel reef. The recommended route follows quite close to the north shore between the two ranges until the eastern range is directly behind.

We have found shallow spots of 1 or 2 feet at zero tide just west of the easternmost range and again at the east entrance, north of Link Island. There are large patches of bull kelp throughout the narrows, but the north-shore route is sometimes clear of kelp—except within the vicinity of the eastern ranges.

Anne Vipond

Gabriola Island public floats in Degnen Bay

The strength of the current in False Narrows is about half that of Dodd Narrows. Although False Narrows is used as a shortcut by local boats heading from Gabriola Passage to Nanaimo, such a slow, careful transit—with the additional anxieties involved—may not save much time or energy for visiting pleasure craft. In southeast gales, *Baidarka* has found False Narrows less choppy than Dodd Narrows.

Skippers of the small, shallow-draft logging boats that draw less than 3 feet have told us they regularly traverse False Narrows at low water. However, since the narrows are a challenge of navigational skills, and suited only to the intrepid, Dodd Narrows is the preferred passage to Northumberland Channel

Gabriola Passage

Gabriola Passage separates Valdes Island from Gabriola Island and connects the Strait of Georgia to Pylades Channel; it is 8.3 miles northwest of Porlier Pass.

Charts 3475 metric, 3343 metric, 3313 metric
West entrance (Gabriola Passage): 49°07.60′ N, 123°43.22′ W (NAD 83)
Southeast entrance (0.39 mile southeast of Breakwater Island): 49°07.20′ N, 123°40.62′ W (NAD 83)
Northeast entrance (0.5 mile east of Acorn Island): 49°09.37′ N, 123°40.10′ W (NAD 83)

Gabriola Passage . . . is narrow, intricate and has numerous dangers in its east approach. This combined with the velocity of the tidal currents does not recommend it for general navigation. It should be navigated at or near slack water by those familiar with local conditions. (p. 204, SCG, Vol. 1)

Caution: During summer months, the effects of the freshet from the Fraser River and the NW winds which blow strongly nearly every afternoon, cause rough conditions along the west portion of the Strait of Georgia. Crossing to the mainland or

travel along the east shores of Valdes and Gabriola Islands should be carried out early in the morning, but the most preferred time is late afternoon or early evening when the winds die away. Radio weather reports should be monitored . . .

The distance from Thrasher Rock to Cape Roger Curtis (Bowen Island), on the east side of the Strait of Georgia, is about 14 miles. This is the shortest practical crossing between the Gulf Islands and the lower mainland; it also avoids crossing the Traffic Separation Scheme used by merchant vessels bound for Vancouver Harbour. For the above reasons it is the route recommended for use by small craft. (p. 205, SCG, Vol. 1)

Gabriola Passage is the northeasternmost entrance from the Strait of Georgia to the protected waters of the Gulf Islands. It is best transited at or near slack water; even then turbulence can be significant during spring tides or during southeast gales. It can be entered from or exited directly into the Strait of Georgia southeast of Breakwater Island or from the northeast through the Flat Top Islands. Thrasher Rock and Gabriola Reefs, east of Flat Top Islands, usually marked by kelp, have caused many groundings.

On spring tides, there is a short section of highly turbulent and dangerous water at the east

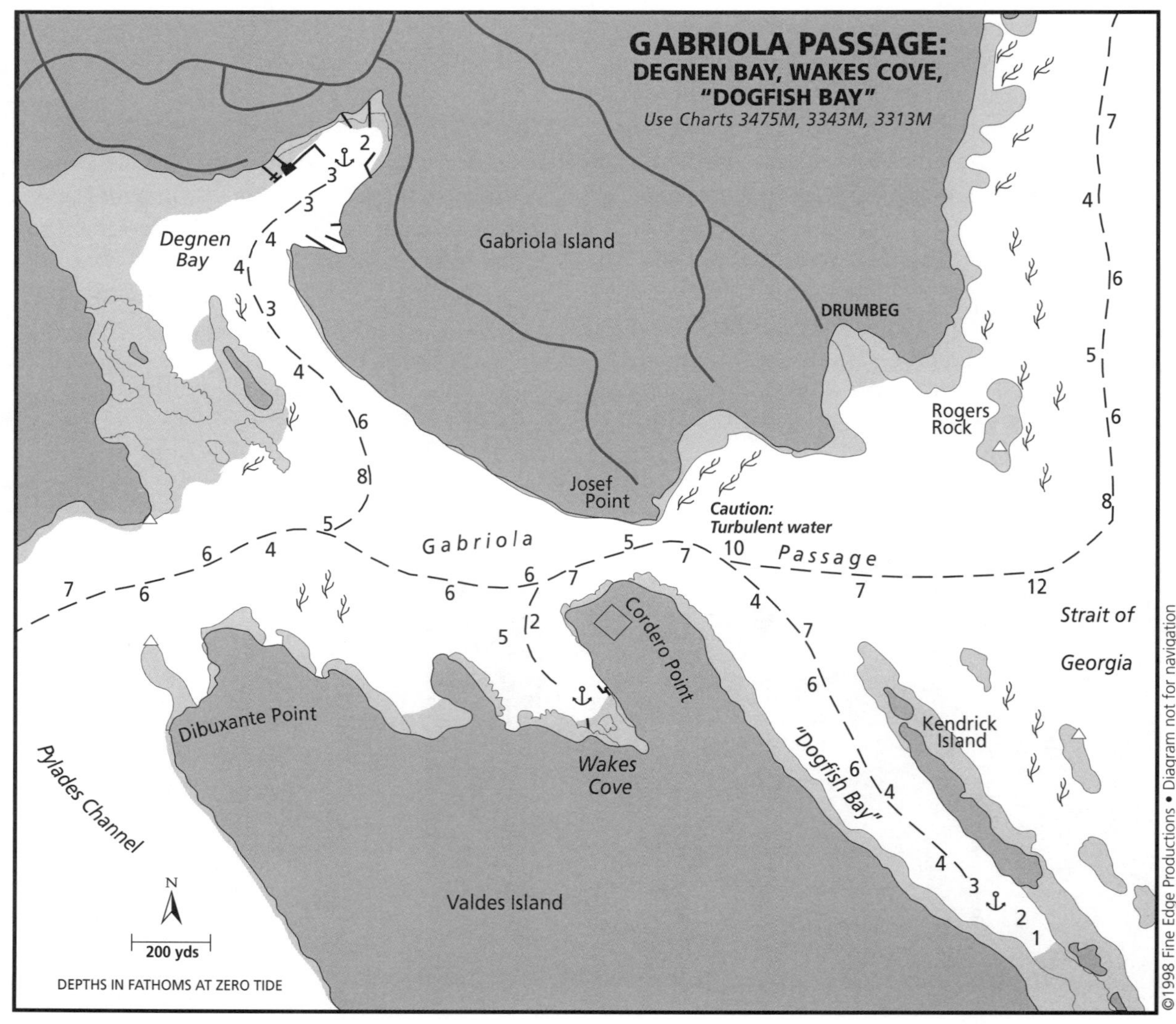

entrance of Gabriola Passage just north of Kendrick Island. When a stiff east wind is blowing on a spring flood tide, standing waves in the turbulent water can reach 2 meters in height and swamp a small boat. Degnen Bay and Wakes Cove provide good shelter to wait for optimum conditions when eastbound. Silva Bay and, to a lesser extent, Dogfish Bay provide shelter when westbound.

Drumbeg Provincial Park is on the north shore of Gabriola Passage at the east end of Gabriola Passage.

Anne Vipond

Degnen Bay, Gabriola Island

Degnen Bay (Gabriola Island)

Degnen Bay, on the north side of Gabriola Passage, is 2.3 miles northwest of Pirates Cove Marine Park.

Charts 3475 metric, 3343 metric, 3313 metric
Entrance: 49°07.85′ N, 123°42.61′ W (NAD 83)
Anchor: 49°08.24′ N, 123°42.66′ W (NAD 83)

> *Degnen Bay, on the north side of Gabriola Passage, is entered between a point on its west side, which is an Indian Reserve, and Josef Point, 0.6 mile east.*

> *Favour the east side when entering Degnen Bay; the shoal ledges around the islet are generally covered with kelp. Degnen Bay affords excellent shelter for small craft.* (p. 204, SCG, Vol. 1)

Degnen Bay is a beautifully-protected anchorage. However, since it is used by Gabriola residents for boat storage, it is crowded nearly year-round. A public float that accommodates about 30 boats is located on the north shore, but private floats

---

Degnen Bay

Degnen Bay was a one-man show back in 1862 when 30-year-old Irish immigrant, Robert Degnen, pre-empted 160 acres of waterfront property. He and his wife Jane, the daughter of a local chief, began farming the land and raising a family. To support their nine children, all of whom were born on the island, they worked hard plowing the fields with oxen, shooting local deer and pheasant, planting an apple orchard and keeping various farm animals which included sheep, pigs, chickens and a dairy cow. Degnen ferried their produce to the market in Nanaimo using a large dugout canoe which he loaded at a small wharf he had built in Degnen Bay. As his freight business increased, Degnen replaced the canoe with a steam launch, followed later by a gasoline launch.

Descanso Bay has become Gabriola's freight transportation hub because the car ferry from Nanaimo docks there, and so today Degnen Bay is busy instead with pleasure craft. Just a short walk from the government dock is one of the most accessible petroglyph sites in the Gulf Islands, located behind the United Church on South Road. These ancient rock carvings are a legacy of the complex and artistically accomplished civilizations that once thrived throughout the Pacific Northwest. The Gulf Islands lie within the territory of the Coast Salish, the southernmost group of natives inhabiting the Inside Passage when European explorers first ventured into these waters.

Petroglyphs are an ancient art form, possibly inspired by shamanism or perhaps serving a more practical purpose such as marking a territorial boundary. Those found in the Gulf Islands often portray mythical creatures embodying spiritual power. These rock carvings are difficult to date, and erosion has likely removed any that were carved thousands of years ago. However, many of the enduring examples are from prehistoric times. —**AV**

and mooring buoys take up much of the bay.

When entering the bay, favor the east shore—the low islet to port has a reef that extends quite a distance. This islet is a draw for birds and seals.

Anchorage, with limited swinging room, can be found mid-channel near the head of the bay. More swinging room can be found in the slightly less-sheltered west end of the bay. The petroglyph of a killer whale can be viewed at low tide near the head of the bay. From Degnen Bay it is a brisk 30-minute walk to Silva Bay.

Anchor in 2 fathoms over mud with good holding.

Wakes Cove (Valdes Island)

Wakes Cove is located on the south shore of Gabriola Passage, 0.7 mile southeast of Degnen Bay and 1.5 miles southwest of Silva Bay.

Charts 3475 metric, 3343 metric, 3313 metric
Entrance: 49°07.65′ N, 123°42.35′ W (NAD 83)
Anchor: 49°07.56′ N, 123°42.21′ W (NAD 83)

> *Wakes Cove, on the south side of Gabriola Passage, 0.4 mile east of Dibuxante Point, offers anchorage but is exposed to the NW. The floats in the cove are private.* (p. 205, SCG, Vol. 1)

Wakes Cove offers very good protection from east to southeast gales. It is open to the northwest but fetch is small. A 5-fathom shelf is located just west of the private float on the east shore.

Wakes Cove is out of the current stream and receives only slight eddy currents. It is, however, subject to the wake of larger traffic transiting Gabriola Passage.

Anchor in 1 to 2 fathoms over sand with fair-to-good holding.

Dogfish Bay (Kendrick Island)

Dogfish Bay lies between the north end of Valdes Island and Kendrick Island; it is 1.7 miles south of Silva Bay.

Charts 3475 metric, 3343 metric, 3313 metric
Entrance: 49°07.65′ N, 123°41.79′ W (NAD 83)
Anchor: 49°07.29′ N, 123°41.42′ W (NAD 83)

> *The three small islets SE of Cordero Point are wooded; the largest of these islets is Kendrick Island. The narrow bay, formed between these three islets and the east shore of Valdes Island, is known locally as Dogfish Bay; it provides a good sheltered anchorage and is regularly used by tugs with logbooms when awaiting tides or are weatherbound.*
>
> *The floats and mooring buoys of the West Vancouver Yacht Club lie on the west side of Kendrick Island.* (p. 205, SCG, Vol. 1)

Dogfish Bay, the local name for the anchorage on the south shore of Gabriola Passage, lies in the lee of Kendrick Island, 0.5 mile southeast of Cordero Point. It is a good place to await slack water in Gabriola Passage. Use caution on entering Dogfish Bay during spring tides or southeast gales since turbulent water and large standing waves northeast of Cordero Point are dangerous for small craft.

Enter Dogfish Bay from the north and anchor between Valdes and Kendrick islands, south of the West Vancouver Yacht Club floats and mooring buoys. In fair weather this is a good spot, but in a storm you should head for Degnen Bay or Wakes Cove. Shoal-draft boats can use the southern exit at high water by carefully crossing the drying section between the southernmost island and Valdes Island.

The rock face, north of the yacht club has names of boats that have anchored there.

Anchor in 4 to 5 fathoms over sand and small seaweed with very good holding.

Silva Bay (Gabriola Island)

Silva Bay, located on the eastern extremity of Gabriola Island, is 1.3 miles north of Gabriola Passage and 9.5 miles east of Nanaimo Harbour.

Charts 3475 metric, 3343 metric, 3313 metric
East entrance (0.1 mile west of Shipyard Rock): 49°09.20′ N, 123°41.34′ W (NAD 83)
Southeast dinghy entrance (south side of Sear Island): 49°08.58′, 123°41.29′ W (NAD 83)
North dinghy entrance (west of Carlos Island): 49°09.59′ N, 123°41.95′ W
Anchor: 49°09.05′ N, 123°41.78′ W (NAD 83)

> *Silva Bay, sheltered by Vance, Tugboat and Sear Islands, has three passages leading into it and is frequently used by small craft.*

The main entrance to Silva Bay is between Tugboat and Vance Islands. It is encumbered by a drying reef projecting north from Tugboat Island and Shipyard Rock in midchannel. The least depth through this channel, north of the reef, is 19 feet (5.9 m).

Silva Bay light, on Shipyard Rock, is exhibited at an elevation of 15 feet (4.6 m) from a white circular mast displaying a port hand daymark. Vessels entering the bay should pass this light on their port side.

The south entrance to Silva Bay leads between Sear and Gabriola Islands; it is about 100 feet (30 m) wide and has a least depth of 4 feet (1.2 m).

The north entrance to Silva Bay leads between Lily Island and Vance Island and is entered at its north end between Carlos Island and the shoals north of Lily Island. The least depth through this channel is 11 feet (3.6 m). (p. 215, SCG, Vol. 1)

Silva Bay is set in a maze of small, wooded islands which, as a whole, protect the bay in almost all weather. Good anchorage can be found in the center of the bay, and moorage for medium sized vessels is available through Silva Bay Boatel and Store (tel: 250-247-9351). Silva Bay Resort and Marina (tel: 250-247-8662) has excellent and complete facilities for pleasure boats,

Silva Bay

Silva Bay, for many Vancouver-area boaters, is the gateway to the Gulf Islands. Located just 25 miles from Vancouver, this sheltered bay is a popular entry point, lying as it does on the outside of the passes so boaters needn't worry about battling currents after crossing the Strait of Georgia. A Spanish explorer named Jose Narvaez was the first European to cruise past Silva Bay in the summer of 1791 when he sailed the strait in the schooner *Saturnina.* He charted the shoreline before returning to the expedition's commander, Francisco de Eliza, whose ship had remained anchored near the entrance to Puget Sound.

Narvaez named Gabriola Island when he sailed past its eastern end, but the sheltered bay which is today one of the busiest in the Gulf Islands—with marina facilities and plenty of room to anchor—was left unnamed. It became known as Silva Bay when a Portuguese settler and his native wife moved to Gabriola Island in 1883. John Silva came to the West Coast as a young seaman in 1852, jumped ship in Victoria, married a native woman named Louisa, and eventually moved to Village Bay on Mayne Island. Later, the Silva family moved to Gabriola after losing two of their ten children in drowning accidents in Active Pass. They took over the land adjacent to Silva Bay which had been abandoned by a Danish settler. John built himself a boat for fishing and, when hard times hit in the 1920s, they sold off parts of their property. The log church, a short walk up the road from Silva Bay Resort & Marina, was built in 1912 on land donated by the Silvas.

When moored in Silva Bay, it's pleasant to explore by dinghy the shoreline which includes Drumbeg Park, located about a mile south of the bay near the entrance to Gabriola Passage. —**AV**

Anne Vipond

The Bitter End, Silva Bay

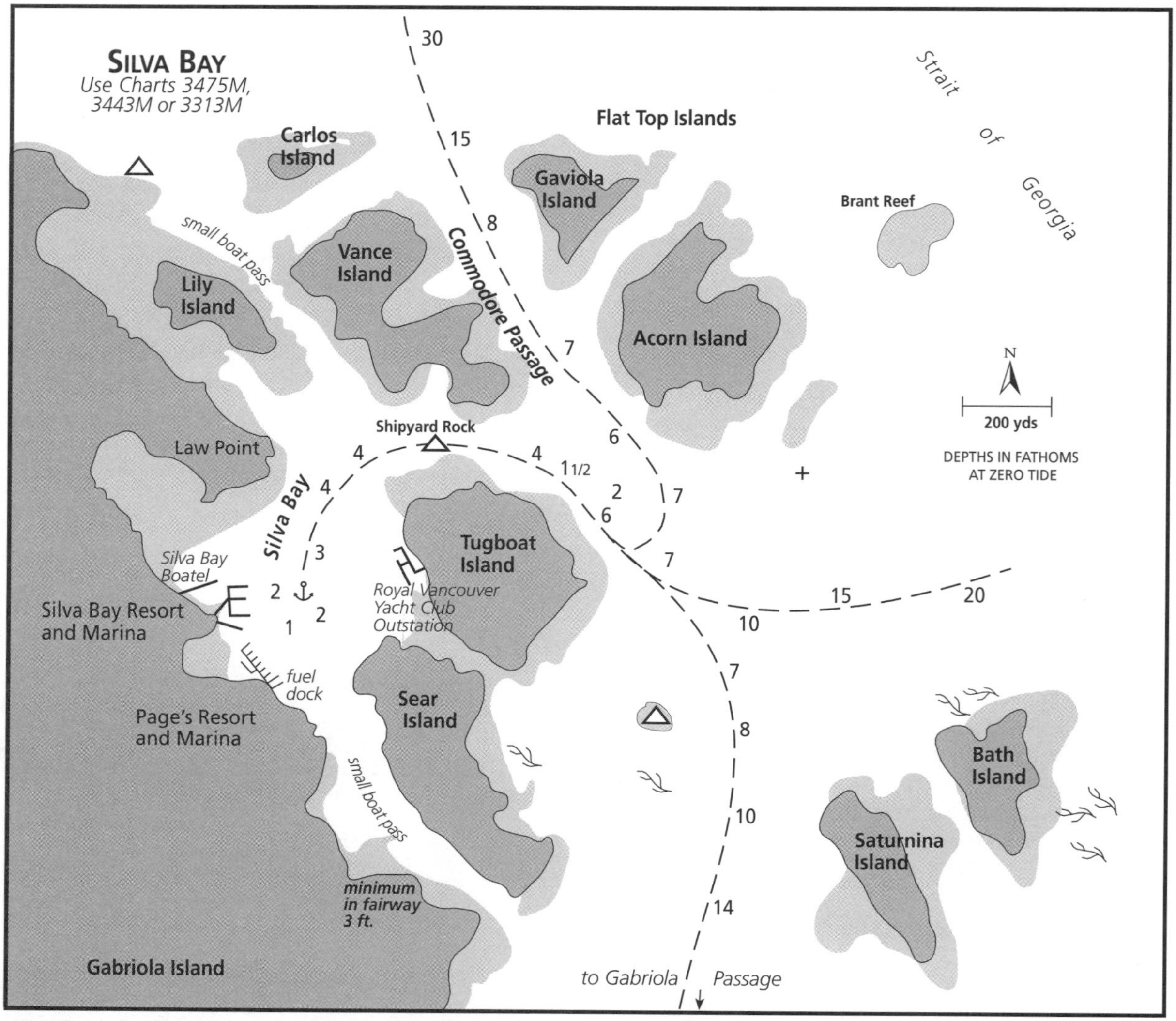

SILVA BAY
Use Charts 3475M, 3443M or 3313M

Carlos Island
Flat Top Islands
Strait of Georgia
Gaviola Island
Brant Reef
small boat pass
Vance Island
Commodore Passage
Lily Island
Acorn Island
200 yds
DEPTHS IN FATHOMS AT ZERO TIDE
Shipyard Rock
Law Point
Silva Bay
Tugboat Island
Silva Bay Boatel
Silva Bay Resort and Marina
Royal Vancouver Yacht Club Outstation
fuel dock
Sear Island
Page's Resort and Marina
small boat pass
Bath Island
Saturnina Island
minimum in fairway 3 ft.
Gabriola Island
to Gabriola Passage

which include a swimming pool and tennis courts for their guests. (During summer season, reservations are advised.) Page's Resort and Marina (tel: 250-247-8931) has full facilities, a dive shop and store. All three marinas are open year-round. The Royal Vancouver Yacht Club has a large outstation on Tugboat Island.

Vessels heading south in the Strait of Georgia that want to avoid Nanaimo and Dodd Narrows often enter sheltered waters via Silva Bay and Gabriola Passage.

To enter Silva Bay, the easiest route is to use Commodore Passage. Give Ship-

Anne Vipond

Silva Bay

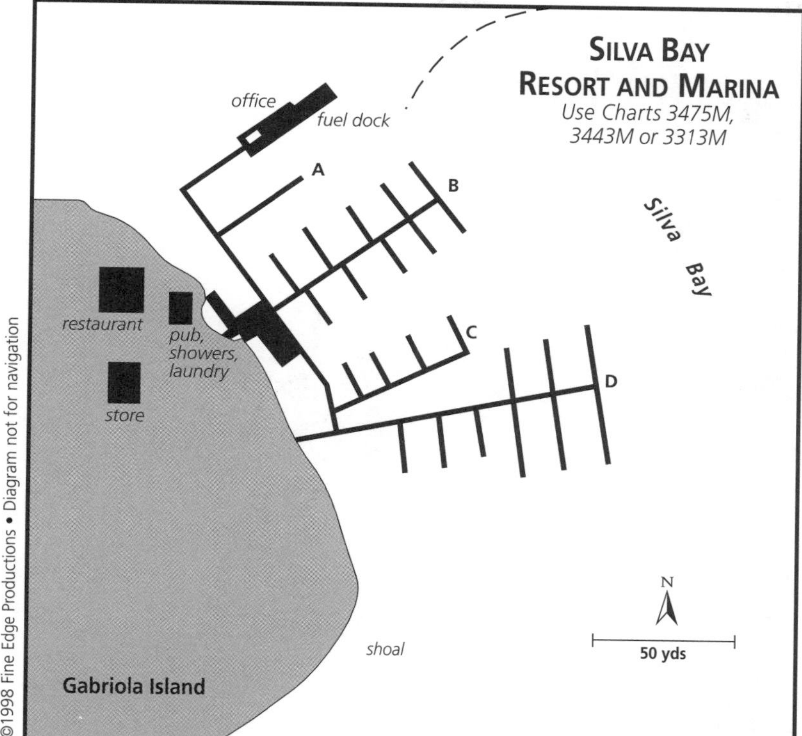

yard Rock due respect when passing through the entrance. Favor the north side of the entrance channel, until you pass west of can-Buoy "U39," then turn south.

Small craft can enter from the north between Lily and Vance islands. This passage, marked by Buoy "PA," can be used at all stages of the tide. However, it is very narrow with little turning room and reefs that extend from both islands. A small-boat entrance to the south of Silva Bay carries about 3 feet of water, and the fairway favors the Sear Island shore.

Anchorage can be found in the center of Silva Bay.

Anchor in 2 fathoms over a mud bottom with good holding.

Main entrance to Silva Bay

Flat Top Islands

The Flat Top Islands lie off the east end of Gabriola Island, 1.5 miles north of Gabriola Passage.

Charts 3475 metric, 3343 metric, 3313 metric
Position: 49°09.25′ N, 123°41.25′ W (NAD 83)

Flat Top Islands, north and west of Bath and Saturnina Islands, consist of several wooded islands lying close off the east extremity of Gabriola Island with passages between some of them. (p. 215, SCG, Vol. 1)

The Flat Top Islands are fun to explore by dinghy or kayak in fair weather when you are safely anchored in Silva Bay. This is a popular sportfishing area. Use caution around the reefs surrounding the islands and rocks.

Commodore Passage

Commodore Passage, the sheltered route through the Flat Top Islands, is east of Vance and Tugboat islands and west of Gaviola and Acorn islands.

Peter Fromm

Island silhouettes

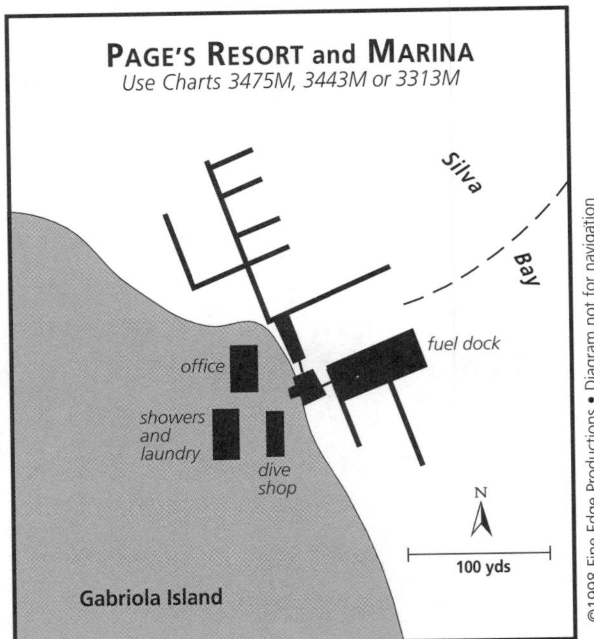

Charts 3475 metric, 3343 metric, 3313 metric
North entrance (0.13 miles northwest of Rowboat Point on Gaviola Island): 49°09.63′ N, 123°41.52′ W (NAD 83)
South entrance (0.17 mile south of Acorn Island): 49°09.12′ N, 123°41.02′ W (NAD 83)

> *Commodore Passage is entered at its SE end between Tugboat Island and Acorn Island. A reef, which dries 16 feet (4.8 m), lies 0.1 mile SE of Acorn Island; a rock awash lies close south of this reef.* (p. 215, SCG, Vol. 1)

Commodore Passage is a shortcut for entering or exiting Gabriola Passage and for heading north to the Strait of Georgia.

Gabriola Reefs

Gabriola Reefs lie east of Flat Top and Breakwater islands.

Charts 3475 metric, 3343 metric, 3313 metric

> *Gabriola Reefs, extending 1.5 miles SSW from Thrasher Rock, consist of drying and below-water rocks.* (p. 215, SCG, Vol. 1)

Gabriola Reefs are a long, curving series of reefs and rocks surrounded by kelp. The northeast and south ends are marked by buoys. The reefs have been the scene of many pleasure-craft disasters and must be avoided when entering and exiting Gabriola Passage

12

NORTHUMBERLAND CHANNEL TO NANAIMO AND DEPARTURE BAY

Once you have passed through Dodd Narrows and entered Northumberland Channel, signs of urban civilization increase. Log rafts nestled along the steep cliffs of Gabriola's west shore, the large MacMillan Bloedel Industrial complex along Vancouver Island, and the new ferry dock just south of Jack Point signal that your journey through the Gulf Islands has reached its northern terminus. The concentration of commercial and pleasure traffic requires alert helmsmanship.

If you prefer to anchor rather than head directly into Nanaimo Harbour, you can tuck into Descanso Bay on the northwest side of Gabriola Island; however, the anchorage is subject to wake. Noted for it many petroglyphs, Gabriola has striking formations of wave-carved sandstone; the Galiano (or Malaspina) Galleries just south of Malaspina Point are just one of many fine examples. The B.C. ferry dock in Descanso connects the island to Nanaimo. Taylor and Pilot Bays, part of Gabriola Sands Park, are closed to boat entry because of their bathing beaches.

Nanaimo Harbour west of Jack Point is well protected by the shallow bay off Nanaimo River to the south and by Protection Island on its east. Narrow McKay Channel leads directly into the harbor past the south end of Protection Island. Much of the bay south of a line west of Jack Point (49°10' N) dries at low water and many visiting boats have grounded here. You can avoid this area by favoring the Protection Island side of the channel.

Nanaimo is the transportation, supply, and repair center for the northern part of the Gulf Islands and home of the famous Nanaimo bars. Nanaimo is also a good place to drop off or pick up crew, or to leave your boat if you need to. The City of Nanaimo and its environs offer all the attractions of a big city. Visiting yachts are allowed to tie up at the public floats in Commercial Inlet for two hours at no cost, and moorage can be found here or at the several private facilities in Newcastle Island Passage.

Popular Newcastle Island Marine Park is located at the north end of Nanaimo Harbour in Mark Bay. In addition to excellent anchorage, the park facilities are readily accessible from the dinghy docks (limited moorage available) or by foot passenger ferry service; there are no cars on the island. Twelve miles of wooded trails, picnic grounds and lovely swimming beaches and campsites are included in the Park. The interesting grinding-stone quarry site is just north of the floats. Mallard Lake is a man-made lake, home to wood ducks, great blue herons, and beavers.

Newcastle Island Passage is the narrow channel which connects Nanaimo Harbour to Departure Bay. The passage has a strict no-wake speed limit; a large number of marine facilities are located along the Vancouver Island shore.

Departure Bay has a large ferry terminal and bathing beaches that preclude anchoring. The Pacific Biological Station, which monitors fish and shellfish, is located on the north shore.

Headed for town, Northumberland Channel

Northumberland Channel

Northumberland Channel, north of Dodd Narrows, lies between Gabriola and Vancouver islands.

Charts 3475 metric, 3458 metric, 3443 metric, 3313 metric
South entrance (Dodd Narrows): 49°08.28′ N, 123°49.09′ W (NAD 83)
East entrance (False Narrows): 49°08.21′ N, 123°47.61′ W (NAD 83)
North entrance: 49°10.23′ N, 123°53.13′ W (NAD 83)

> *Northumberland Channel leads NW from Dodd and False Narrows to Nanaimo Harbour and the Strait of Georgia. The channel is wide and deep with no off-lying dangers.* (p. 169, SCG, Vol. 1)

Northumberland Channel receives the bulk of vessel traffic bound for Nanaimo and small craft heading for the north coast of Vancouver Island; alert navigation is required in these water. The wake of passing vessels and low visibility in foggy weather can be problems. The channel has a large lumber mill operation on its south shore and a log-boom storage area off its Gabriola Island shore. Be on the lookout for logging tugs that shuttle back and forth across the channel. Boats entering Nanaimo Harbour at Jack Point should avoid submerged rocks near the point, as well as ferries and other traffic approaching from Gabriola Island.

The new high-speed ferry dock, 0.75 mile south of Jack Point, began operation in 1997.

Percy Anchorage, at the east end of Northumberland Channel, provides anchorage for boats waiting to transit Dodd or False narrows.

Percy Anchorage (Gabriola and Mudge Islands)

Percy Anchorage is 5.8 miles southeast of Nanaimo Harbour and 0.9 mile east of Dodd Narrows.

Charts 3475 metric, 3458 metric, 3443 metric, 3313 metric
West entrance: 49°08.37′ N, 123°48.29′ W (NAD 83)
East entrance (False Narrows): 49°08.21′ N, 123°47.61′ W (NAD 83)
Float (Gabriola Island shore): 49°08.53′ N, 123°48.29′ W (NAD 83
Anchor: 49°08.32′ N, 123°47.70′ W (NAD 83)

> *Percy Anchorage, at the east end of Northumberland Channel, is a convenient place to anchor to await slack water in Dodd and False Narrows.* (p. 169, SCG, Vol. 1)

Open and somewhat exposed, Percy Anchorage is used principally by large or commercial boats, but quiet shelter can be found close to shore at the head of the anchorage.

The small public float on Gabriola Island near Hoggan Lake is usually filled with local commercial and commuting boats.

Anchor in 3 to 5 fathoms over sand and gravel with fair-to-good holding and unlimited swinging room.

Coho Cove (Mudge Island)

Coho Cove is located on the north side of Mudge Island, 0.4 mile east of Dodd Narrows.

Charts 3458 metric, 3443 metric, 3313 metric
Position: 49°08.25′ N, 123°48.45′ W (NAD 83)

The Coho Cove Yacht Club maintains a small float between a natural breakwater on the north side of Coho Cove and a small rock breakwater on the west side. *Caution:* A submerged reef extends west of the point.

This tiny cove, which is too small for anchoring, is used by busy workboats. However, it's a good place to get up-to-date local information on False Narrows.

Descanso Bay (Gabriola Island)

Descanso Bay, on the northwest side of Gabriola Island, is 2.7 miles east of Nanaimo Harbour.

Charts 3458 metric, 3443 metric, 3313 metric
Entrance: 49°10.74′ N, 123°52.16′ W (NAD 83)
Anchor: 49°10.48′ N, 123°51.85′ W (NAD 83)

> *Descanso Bay, 1.3 miles NE of Jack Point, lies at the west end of Gabriola Island. In the north part of the bay there are drying ledges lying parallel to, and within 0.2 mile of the shore.*
>
> *A ferry landing is in the NE part of the bay. Frequent service to and from Nanaimo is maintained.* (p. 170, SCG, Vol. 1)

Good shelter from southeast weather can be found deep in the southern end of Descanso Bay. Due to frequent ferries and exposure to channel traffic, wakes are noticeable.

Anchor in 5 to 10 fathoms over an irregular bottom.

Taylor Bay (Gabriola Island)

Taylor Bay, on the northwest side of Gabriola Island immediately north of Malaspina Point, is 2.9 miles northeast of Nanaimo Harbour.

Charts 3458 metric, 3443 metric, 3313 metric
Position (Taylor Bay): 49°11.61′ N, 123°51.84′ W (NAD 83)

> *Taylor Bay . . .* [is] *in Gabriola Sands Provincial Park where picnic facilities and drinking water are available. To protect the safety of swimmers, craft of any kind are not permitted to enter these bays.* (p. 177, SCG, Vol. 1)

Gabriola Sands Park between Taylor and Pilot bays with its lovely swimming beaches is day-use only; facilities include toilets. During the summer when water temperatures rise, you will often see a dozen boats or more anchored in one to three fathoms, sand and mud bottom, avoiding the large shoal areas off the beach.

> SCG states that no boats are permitted in either Taylor or Pilot bays (see quotation above). According to the Park Superintendent, there are no anchoring restrictions for pleasure boats in either Taylor Bay or Pilot Bay; however caution is advised to protect swimmers.

Pilot Bay (Gabriola Island)

Pilot Bay, at the northwest corner of Gabriola Island immediately south of Tinson Point, is 3.5 miles northeast of Nanaimo Harbour.

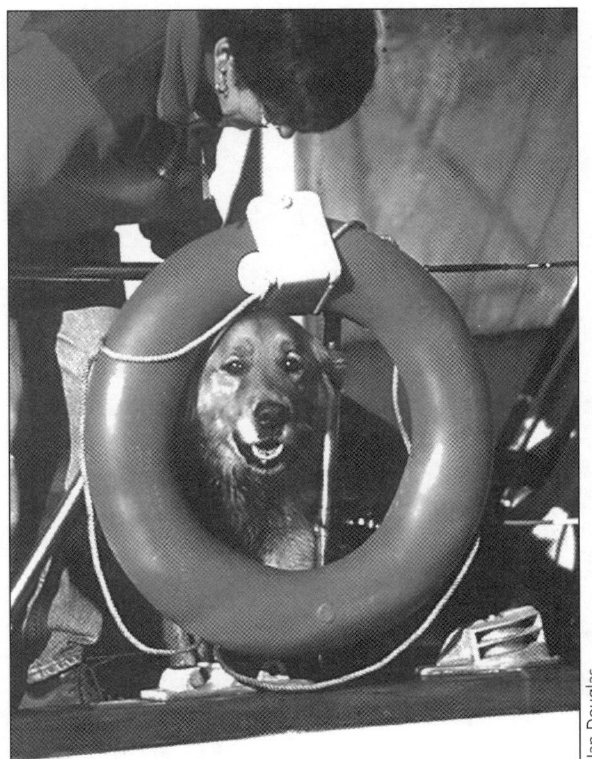

Ian Douglas

A sea dog

Don Douglass

Float plane taxi service

Charts 3458 metric, 3443 metric, 3313 metric
Position (Pilot Bay): 49°11.82′ N, 123°51.24′ W (NAD 83)

Clark Bay (Gabriola Island)

Clark Bay, on the north shore of Gabriola Island, is 0.9 mile east of Pilot Bay.

Charts 3458 metric, 3443 metric, 3313 metric
Position: 49°12.07′ N, 123°49.75′ W (NAD 83)

> *Clark Bay lies 0.45 mile SW of Orlebar Point.* (p. 177, SCG, Vol. 1)

Small craft can find temporary anchorage in Clark Bay with some shelter from southerly winds, but subject to wake from passing vessels.

Leboeuf Bay (Gabriola Island)

Leboeuf Bay is 0.9 mile southwest of Entrance Island.

Charts 3458 metric, 3443 metric, 3313 metric
Position: 49°11.66′ N, 123°48.96′ W (NAD 83)

> *Leboeuf Bay, close north of Lock Bay, has two islets in it which are joined to shore by a drying bank.*
>
> *Between Leboeuf Bay and Orlebar Point, drying and below-water rocks lie within 0.25 mile offshore.* (p. 216, SCG, Vol. 1)

Leboeuf Bay may provide anchorage from westerly winds; however, it is exposed to southeast winds. Avoid the reef and rock 0.3 mile southeast of Orlebar Point.

Lock Bay (Gabriola Island)

Lock Bay, on the northeast shore of Gabriola Island, is 1.25 miles southwest of Entrance Island.

Charts 3458 metric, 3443 metric, 3313 metric
Position: 49°11.27′ N, 123°49.00′ W (NAD 83)

> *Lock Bay, 0.8 mile south of Orlebar Point, is exposed and not recommended as an anchorage.* (p. 216, SCG, Vol. 1)

Lock Bay is encompassed by Sandwell Provincial Park. The bay is open to the east and southeast.

Approaches to Nanaimo Harbour

> *The approach to Nanaimo and its small craft facilities is not complicated. However, a sharp lookout should be kept for large cargo vessels, ferries and fishing vessels. A water aerodrome is east of the Customs float.* (p. 176, SCG, Vol. 1)

Fairway Channel

Fairway Channel lies between Gabriola Island on the south and Snake Island on the north.

Charts 3458 metric, 3443 metric, 3313 metric
Midchannel (0.75 mile northwest of Malaspina Point and 0.74 mile southeast of Snake Island): 49°12.20′ N, 123°52.92′ W (NAD 83)

> *Fairway Channel, between the NW part of Gabriola Island and Snake Island, has a navigable width of about 0.7 mile.* (p. 177, SCG, Vol. 1)

Fairway Channel is used by boats exiting Nanaimo Harbour or Departure Bay and heading for Vancouver.

Rainbow Channel

Rainbow Channel lies between Snake Island on the southeast and Five Fingers Island on the northwest.

Heading up-channel close-hauled

Nanaimo fishing float, Newcastle Island far left

Charts 3458 metric, 3443 metric, 3313 metric
Position (0.52 mile northeast of Snake Island, 1.1 miles east of Hudson Rock, and 0.9 mile southeast of Five Finger Islands): 49°13.55′ N, 123°53.64′ W (NAD 83)

> *Hudson Rocks consist of five islets and rocks, 3 to 39 feet (0.9 to 12 m) high, encircled by reefs.* (p. 177, SCG, Vol. 1)

Rainbow Channel is used by vessels leaving Nanaimo Harbour or Departure Bay bound for the Sunshine Coast on the north shore of the Strait of Georgia.

Horswell Channel

Horswell Channel lies between Hudson Rocks and Clarke Rock north of Horswell Rock.

Charts 3458 metric, 3443 metric, 3313 metric
Position (midchannel, 0.21 mile east of Clarke Rock): 49°13.52′ N, 123°56.15′ W (NAD 83)

> *Horswell Channel lies between Hudson Rocks and the coast of Vancouver Island. Clarke Rock, on the west side of Horswell Channel, is separated from Vancouver Island by a narrow channel in which there is foul ground.* (p. 177, SCG, Vol. 1)

Horswell Channel is used by vessels leaving Nanaimo Harbour or Departure Bay bound for the north coast of Vancouver Island.

Nanaimo Harbour Entrance

Charts 3457 metric, 3458 metric; 3313 metric

> *Nanaimo Harbour . . . has a large mud flat in its south part and is protected on its east and north sides by Protection Island and Newcastle Island. The harbour can be entered by small craft by way of McKay Channel, Newcastle Island Passage and the unnamed passage separating Newcastle and Protection Islands. This latter passage can only be used at or near HW.*
>
> *A ferry wharf, close NW of Gallows Point, is for*

Don Douglass

Nanaimo Inner Harbour, Commercial Inlet and waterfront

foot passengers only. A public float, for loading and unloading only, and launching ramp are alongside the ferry wharf. These facilities are protected by a breakwater.

A public float and ferry moorage are at Good Point. (pp. 170–171, SCG, Vol. 1)

Nanaimo Harbour, a major supply center for Gulf Island boats, offers complete yacht facilities. It is entered through McKay Channel on the south or Departure Bay on the north. Entry to the harbor should not be attempted between Newcastle and Protection islands.

McKay Channel

Charts 3457 metric, 3458 metric; 3313 metric
East entrance: 49°10.19′ N, 123°54.49′ W (NAD 83)
West entrance: 49°10.16′ N, 123°55.42′ W (NAD 83)

McKay Channel, south of Protection Island, is the channel most frequently used by large vessels; it is deep and without dangers. (pp. 170–171, SCG, Vol. 1)

McKay Channel, the busy south entrance to Nanaimo Harbour, has heavy traffic converging on the south side of Gallow Point off Protection Island. Avoid the large drying mud flat off the Nanaimo River outflow south of a line running through Jack Point.

Anne Vipond

Fishing fleet in Nanaimo Harbour

NANAIMO HARBOUR

Nanaimo Harbour (Vancouver Island)

Nanaimo Harbour, in the lee of Protection Island and on the south side of Newcastle Island, is 2.5 miles west of Gabriola Island. It is 33 miles southwest of Vancouver Harbour, 38 miles northwest of Sidney, and 63 miles northwest of Anacortes.

Charts 3457 metric, 3458 metric; 3313 metric
Floating breakwater: 49°10.20′ N, 123°55.95′ W (NAD 83)
Entrance (Commercial Inlet): 49°10.21′ N, 123°55.97′ W (NAD 83)
Fuel dock: 49°10.10′ N, 123°56.04′ W (NAD 83)

The city of Nanaimo, along the west side of the harbour. . . . The main industries are lumber, pulp, newsprint and fisheries. The city has a population of 49,029 (1986) . . . a full range of municipal services which include a hospital, shopping, centres and recreational facilities. Radio station

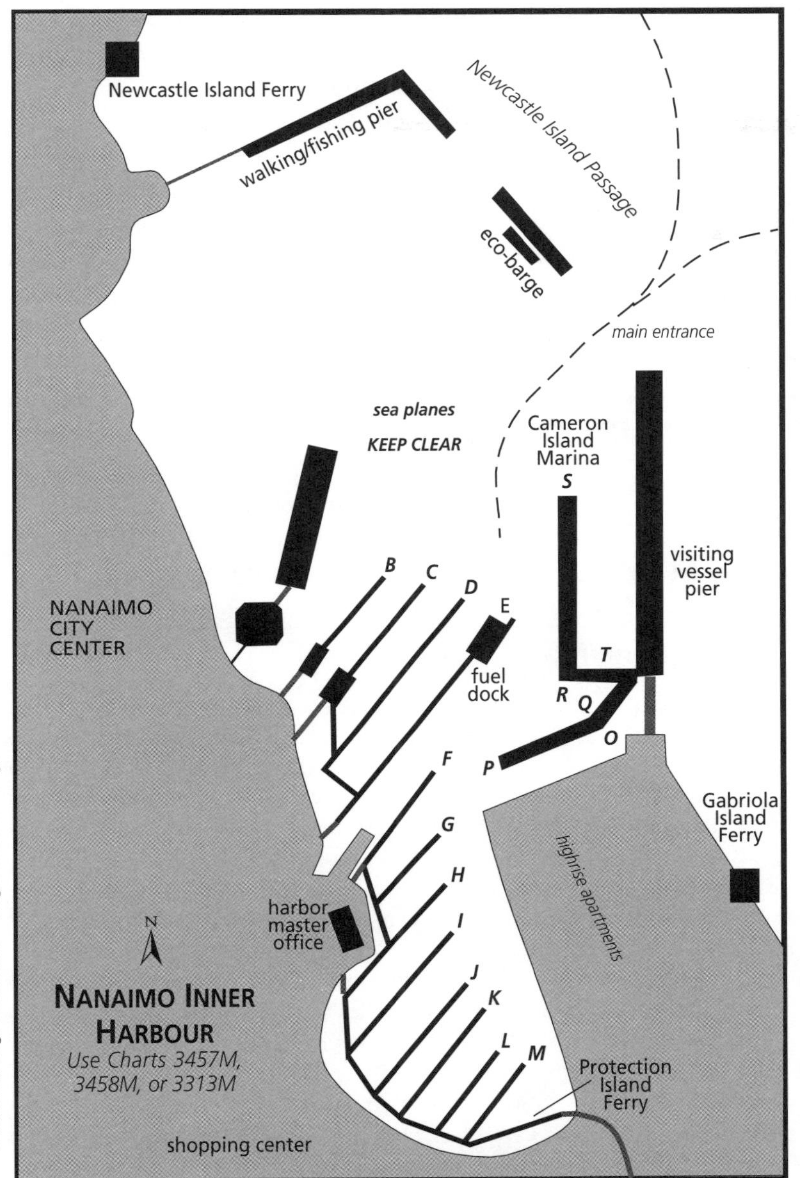

CHUB broadcasts on a frequency of 1570 kHz.

Anchorage berths in Nanaimo are assigned by the Harbour Master. (p. 156 SD)

Commercial Inlet, to the south of Beacon Rock, is a small craft basin; the floats are protected by a floating breakwater. (p. 171, SCG, Vol. 1)

In Commercial Inlet there are public floats for the use of small craft during summer months. Power and water are laid on the floats; toilets, showers, public telephones, garbage and used oil disposal facilities are available.

A fuel barge is located at the floats. A wharfinger is in charge of these floats. (pp. 175–176, SCG, Vol. 1)

Nanaimo Harbour has undergone a face lift. The waterfront has been redeveloped with attractive condominiums, green spaces, and small shops. The small-craft basin with public floats (Commercial Inlet) has a new floating breakwater with better protection from chop than formerly. The inlet is narrow and crowded. It is entered between Beacon Rock and the end of the new floating breakwater. Be alert for float planes and heavy traffic. There is a fuel float at the north end of Commercial Inlet.

Nanaimo is a designated Customs port of entry; convenient shopping and outfitting facilities are located within easy walking distance of the public floats. Harbour Park Mall, three blocks south of the floats, includes a supermarket, bakery, pharmacy, liquor, and laundromat (both self-serve and wash-and-fold).

Canadian charts can be purchased at the Dock Shop above the main floats or at Nanaimo Maps and Charts, 8 Church Street, three blocks from the floats. (For details, please see Sources of Information in the Appendix.)

The new floats, installed in 1994, have upgraded the boat basin, and moorage is now available for pleasure boats year-round. Water and power (15, 20 and 30 amp) are available, as are ice, public showers, laundry, and garbage disposal facilities. During summer months a second wharfinger is added to help with the increase in visiting boats. Advanced reservations for mooring at the visiting pier are recommended in

Don Douglass

Nanaimo Public Harbour

summer (tel: 250-755-1216 or 754-5053). To inquire about transient dock space (free for 2 to 3 hours), before you enter the harbor breakwater call the Wharfinger on Channel 67 for instructions.

The Petro Canada fuel dock has gas, diesel, stove oil, water, ice, and waste pump. Propane can be purchased at the Esso fuel dock, one mile north of the harbor.

Since space at the public floats is so limited in summer, we prefer to cross to Mark Bay and anchor off Newcastle Park.

[*Editor's note:* The Nanaimo Harbour Commission publishes an informative brochure for nautical visitors, "Your Guide to Port of Nanaimo's Boat Basin." To order a copy, contact Port of Nanaimo (tel: 250-753-4146; fax: 250-753-4899; email: info@nhc.ca).]

Nanaimo

The historic mining town of Nanaimo has undergone a transformation in recent years; its waterfront is now an attractive 2 1/2-mile network of public walkways, parks, restaurants and shops. Starting at the north end of Newcastle Island Channel where the Sealand Oceanarium & Market are located, this pedestrian-only promenade leads south past several marinas and chandleries to Maffeo Sutton Park and the Newcastle Island ferry dock. Nearby is a man-made tidal pool (Swy-A-Lana Lagoon), a fishing pier and playground. From here the walkway traces the waterfront to the Boat Basin where a white octagonal tower called The Bastion overlooks the harbor. Built by the Hudson's Bay Company in 1853 when coal deposits were discovered in the area, the arsenal's guns were never used to defend the surrounding settlement from native attack. Noon cannon-firing ceremonies now take place outside The Bastion, which contains artifacts and exhibits, and is open during summer months when it also serves as a Tourism Nanaimo Infocentre.

It's an easy walk up Bastion Street to the Old City Quarter where restored brick-and-stone buildings line Fitzwilliam, Wesley and Selby streets. These heritage buildings house an interesting selection of boutiques and outdoor cafes. A short distance south of The Bastion, a museum overlooks the harbor; its exhibits include a replica of a coal mine and an exhibit of downtown Nanaimo as it would have looked at the beginning of the 20th century. Originally called Colville Town by the white settlers who came from England and Scotland to work in the coal mines, the native name Nanaimo—meaning "big strong tribe" in reference to the area's five villages—was eventually adopted.

Just past the museum, near the southern end of the harborside walkway, is Harbour Park Mall with a range of stores that sell everything from food and liquor to specialty items. A few miles south of downtown, at the mouth of the Nanaimo River, is Petroglyph Provincial Park where visitors can view ancient rock carvings by the area's early natives.

Also south of downtown is the Bungy Zone Bridge and Park which opened in 1991. Since then, over 50,000 bungy jumpers have leaped from the center of the 140-foot bridge that spans the Nanaimo River.

Equally popular is Nanaimo's annual marine festival which includes the World Championship Bathtub Race, established in 1967 and held on the fourth Sunday of July. Competing vessels, which usually number about a hundred, "must contain a component which conforms to the general shape and design of an old-style roll edge bathtub" and contestants propel their craft with a 7.5 horsepower motor. An escort boat accompanies each "bathtub" on its trip across the Strait of Georgia to Vancouver. —**AV**

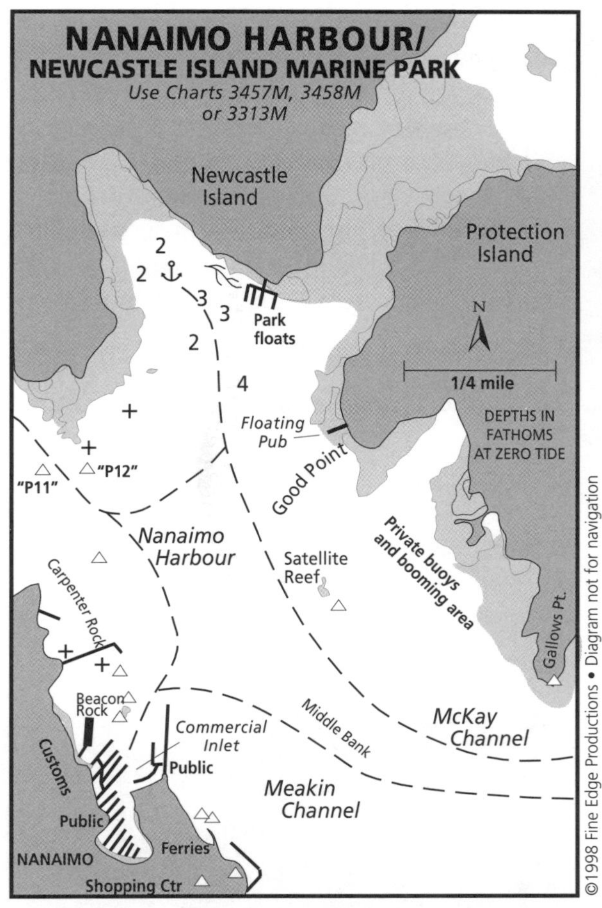

Mark Bay (Newcastle Island)

Mark Bay, on the south side of Newcastle Island in Nanaimo Harbour, is 0.75 mile north of Commercial Inlet.

Charts 3457 metric, 3458 metric; 3313 metric
Entrance: 49°10.75′ N, 123°55.85′ W (NAD 83)
Anchor: 49°10.82′ N, 123°55.89′ W (NAD 83)

Don Douglass

Mark Bay

Anne Vipond

Newcastle Island, squad of local Canada geese

> *Floats and mooring buoys are in Mark Bay, at the south end of the* [Newcastle] *island; picnic and camping facilities, a public telephone and drinking water are available.*
>
> *Anchorage can be obtained in Mark Bay in about 23 feet (7 m), mud bottom.*
>
> *The channel between Newcastle and Protection Islands, used only by small craft at or near HW, is unmarked except for a privately maintained beacon in its central part. A submarine cable and pipeline are laid across this passage.* (p. 174, SCG, Vol. 1)

Mark Bay, off the entrance to Newcastle Island Provincial Park, offers good protection in all weather and is a major yacht destination as well as a stop-over for boats heading north. From Nanaimo Harbour you can easily dinghy across to the Marine Park.

Anchor west of the public floats in 2 to 3 fathoms over sticky mud with very good holding.

Newcastle Island Marine Park (Newcastle Island)

Charts 3457 metric, 3458 metric; 3313 metric
Park floats and dinghy docks: 49°10.80′ N, 123°55.75′ W (NAD 83)
Dinghy Dock Pub floats (Good Point): 49°10.60′ N, 123°55.62′ W (NAD 83)

> *Newcastle Island Marine Park comprises the whole of Newcastle Island.* (p. 174, SCG, Vol. 1)

Newcastle Island Marine Park public floats are reserved for small boats and have a time limit; overnight moorage is available for a fee. In summer when space is at a premium, it's best to anchor offshore and take your dinghy to the floats.

On shore, you can visit a rock quarry site where old grinding stones are displayed or take a nice hike along one of the many park trails. The shallow, rocky slabs along the south and east sides of the island provide some of the warmest and most pleasant swimming in the Gulf Islands; to get away from the city drone, just hike around to the east side of Newcastle Island and sit looking out toward the Strait of Georgia—you'll forget all your worries!

During summer months, a small passenger ferry makes hourly runs between Newcastle Island and Nanaimo. Across (south) from Newcastle Island dock, Protection Island's popular floating pub—Dinghy Dock—is open from 1100 hours to 2300 hours in summer season. A small ferry runs hourly from Nanaimo Harbour directly to the pub.

Newcastle Island

Summer visitors to Newcastle Island used to arrive by steamship when the island was owned and operated as a resort by the Canadian Pacific Steamship Company. Today they arrive by passenger ferry from Nanaimo; it is the island's absence of vehicle access that makes it an ideal destination for pleasure boaters who tie up at the public floats or anchor nearby in Mark Bay. The entire island is park land and is home to blacktail deer, beavers, river otters, rabbits and raccoons, including some rare champagne-colored ones.

Groomed trails crisscross the island and it takes about two-and-a-half hours to hike right around the island. Maps are available at the Visitor Centre, a short walk from the floats where boaters who anchor out can tie their dinghies. Kanaka Bay, on the island's west side, offers good swimming with its sandy bottom and warm, shallow water. At the north end of the island, Giovando Lookout provides superb views overlooking the Strait of Georgia.

An exceptionally strong sandstone, used in many buildings on the west coast, was quarried on Newcastle Island from 1869 to 1932. Coal was also mined on the island, its name bestowed by British miners in honor of the famous coal town of northern England. Japanese settlers moved to the island in the early 1900s where they established a herring saltery and shipyard.

In 1931 the Canadian Pacific Steamship Company purchased the island and developed it as a resort for company picnics and Sunday outings. A dance pavilion (now the park's Visitor Centre) was built along with a tea house, picnic areas, change houses and a soccer field. An old ship was docked in Mark Bay to serve as a floating hotel and, until World War II, the ships arriving from Vancouver would bring as many as 1,500 people at a time. The City of Nanaimo acquired the island in 1955 and six years later it became a Provincial Marine Park.

A short dinghy ride takes you from Newcastle Island to neighboring Protection Island where a floating pub and shoreside store are located. Another pleasant excursion while at Newcastle Island is to take the small paddle-wheel passenger ferry to Nanaimo for shopping and eating. —**AV**

Anne Vipond

Newcastle Island Passage

Newcastle Island Passage, between Vancouver and Newcastle islands, leads from Nanaimo Harbour to Departure Bay.

Charts 3457 metric, 3458 metric, 3443 metric, 3313 metric
South entrance: 49°10.52′ N, 123°56.17′ W (NAD 83)
North entrance: 49°11.64′ N, 123°56.92′ W (NAD 83)

Newcastle Island Passage . . . leads north from the inner portion of Nanaimo Harbour to Departure Bay; it is used mainly by small vessels and recreational craft. The west shore of the passage has numerous wharves, marinas and fuel jetties.

A ferry provides transportation for foot passengers between Nanaimo and Newcastle Island during summer months. Small craft navigators are advised to keep clear of the ferry.

No vessel shall proceed at a speed greater than 5 kn in Newcastle Island Passage between Bate Point and Pimbury Point. (p. 171, SCG, Vol. 1)

An orange buoy, 0.1 mile SE of Bate Point, has a speed caution sign on it.

Oregon Rock, which dries 1 foot (0.2 m), lies on the west side of the fairway, 0.2 mile NW of Bate Point.

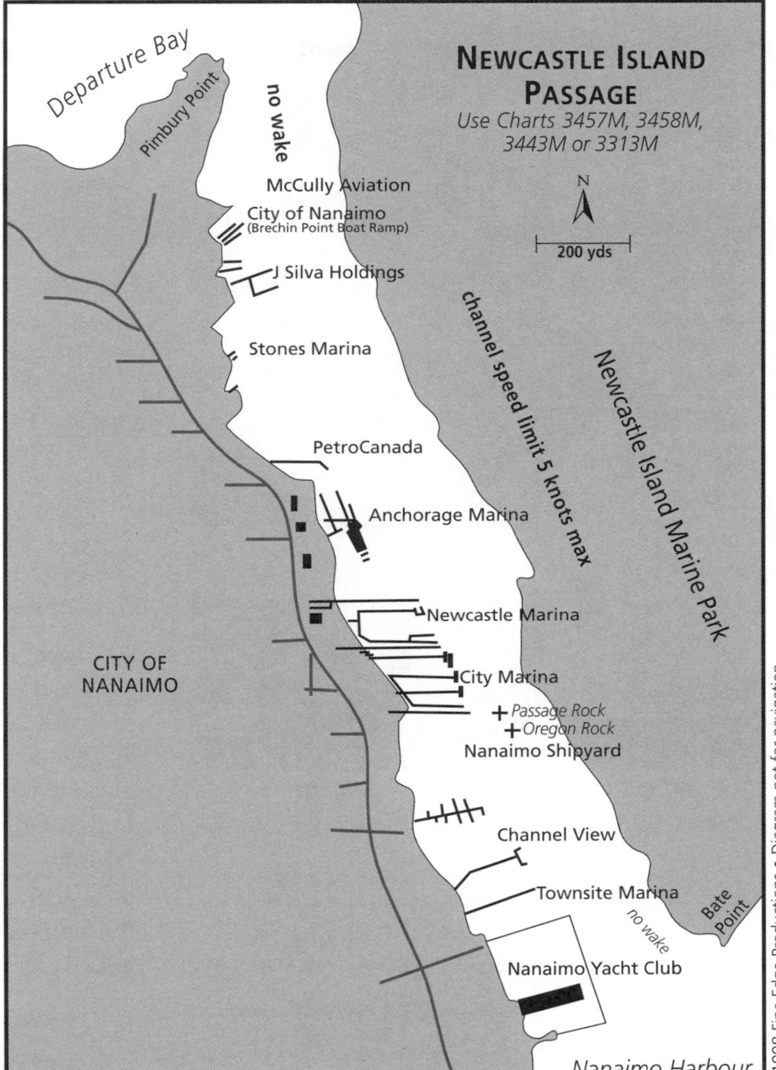

Newcastle Float

Ultra-light float plane at Newcastle Park

Anne Vipond

The Bastion overlooking Nanaimo Harbour

Passage Rock, with 1 foot (0.2 m) over it, lies about 300 feet (91 m) north of Oregon Rock.

A port hand buoy, identified "P13" marks Oregon Rock.

Passage Rock daybeacon, consisting of a 5-pile dolphin displaying a port hand daymark, marks Passage Rock.

Vessels should not pass between these markers as the channel lies on the east side, off the Newcastle Island shore. (p. 174, SCG, Vol. 1)

Newcastle Island Passage is narrow, shallow, and heavily used by local traffic and northbound pleasure craft. The channel skirts the city of Nanaimo and the many yacht facilities along its shore. A convenient fuel dock is located at the north entrance. A strict no-wake speed limit is enforced in Newcastle Passage to protect the numerous marinas and boat docks along the Vancouver Island shore. Avoid Passage Rock and Oregon Rock in midchannel.

Departure Bay (Vancouver Island)

Departure Bay is northwest of Newcastle Island.

Charts 3457 metric, 3458 metric, 3443 metric, 3313 metric
East entrance: 49°12.40′ N, 123°56.00′ W (NAD 83)
South entrance (Newcastle Island Passage): 49°11.64′ N, 123°56.92′ W (NAD 83)

Departure Bay . . . is entered between Horswell Bluff and Nares Point 0.6 mile south.

. . . It is well sheltered, however, few vessels anchor here due to a constant passage of ferries to and from the mainland causing large swells, which can be a problem to small craft. (p. 177, SCG, Vol. 1)

Anchorage is prohibited in the area north of Brandon Islands.

During summer months diving rafts, a water-ski raft and swimming area marker floats are moored off the west shore of Departure Bay. (p. 178, SCG, Vol. 1)

Although Departure Bay is well sheltered, no anchoring is permitted due to heavy ferry traffic and the public bathing beach. The large ferry terminal is located 0.25 mile west of Pimbury Point, and small craft should avoid this busy area. The east entrance to Departure Bay leads to Horswell, Rainbow and Fairway channels. Boats headed to the north coast usually exit through Horswell; those heading to the Sunshine Coast use Rainbow Channel; those heading to Vancouver use Fairway Channel.

Réanne Hemingway-Douglass

Sailing lesson at the Marine Park

Appendices and References

APPENDIX A
Documenting Local Knowledge

1. Coves, bays or bights which seem to offer full or limited protection from different weather conditions are identified and visited by the authors in *Baidarka*.
2. Routes are sketched and photographed.
3. Perusal of a possible anchor site is made with a dual-frequency recording echo sounder; major underwater obstacles are identified; depth and flatness of the bottom over the expected swinging area are checked; depths are then recorded on the sketches.
4. A sample test of the bottom is made by using a small "lunch hook" attached to light line and six feet of chain for maximum responsiveness and feel of the bottom.
5. The response of the anchor to the bottom is noted (i.e. soft or hard mud, sand, gravel, rocky, etc.; digging power, bounce, foul with kelp, pull out, etc.)
6. Additional line is let out to fully set the anchor.
7. A pull-down with the engine in reverse is made against the anchor to test holding power of the bottom.
8. Upon retrieving the anchor, we inspect the residue on its flukes to verify bottom material, as well as the type of grass, kelp, etc.
9. Discussions are held with local residents and fishermen about anchorages, names, etc., and their comments are noted on the sketches. In some cases rough drafts of the manuscript are sent to experts for review.
10. The information gathered from our tests or that submitted by local experts is consolidated and edited and becomes the local knowledge we have presented in our diagrams and text.

APPENDIX B
Sources for Fishing Regulations

San Juan Islands

Fishing licenses and regulations are available at most marinas and resorts. For current information on licensing requirements, fishing limits, etc., contact Fish and Wildlife Department (Washington State), Fish Management Program (tel: 360-902-2700; fax: 360-902-2183; website: www.wa.gov; address: 600 Capitol Way North, Olympia, WA 98501.

In addition, San Juan County has a bottom fish recovery program. For information, contact: Marine Resources Committee, 350 Court Street, Friday Harbor, WA 98250.

Gulf Islands

For current Canadian fishing regulations, request a free copy of *British Columbia Tidal Waters Sport Fishing Guide*, published by the Fisheries and Oceans and updated annually. Write to: Department of Fisheries and Oceans, 400-555 W. Hastings St., Vancouver, B.C. V6B 5G3 (tel: 604-666-0384; fax: 604-666-1847).

Toxic paralytic shellfish warnings, as well as local fishing closures and openings, are broadcast on VHF weather bands.

APPENDIX C
U.S. and Canadian Holidays

Holidays in the United States:
New Year's Day
Martin Luther King Jr. Day (3rd Monday in January)
President's Day (3rd Monday in February)
Easter Sunday
Memorial Day (last Monday in May)
Independence Day (July 4 or as designated)
Labor Day (1st Monday in September
Veteran's Day (November 11)
Thanksgiving Day (4th Thursday in November)
Christmas Day (December 25)

Holidays in British Columbia:
New Year's Day
Good Friday
Easter Monday
Queen's Birthday (by proclamation)
Canada Day (July 1)
Civic Holiday (1st Monday in August)
Labour Day (1st Monday in September)
Thanksgiving Day (by proclamation)
Remembrance Day (November 11)
Christmas Day
Boxing Day (1st working day after Christmas)

APPENDIX D
Short List of Flora and Fauna Found in the San Juan and Gulf Islands

Mammals
Dolphins
Porpoises: Dall and harbor
Seals, harbor
Sea lions: Steller, California
Sea otters
Whales: orcas (killer), gray, minke, humpback
Bears: black
Cougars (rare)
Deer: Black-tailed, mule
Rabbits
Raccoon
Skunk
Squirrels

Birds
More than 266 species of birds are found in the San Juan and Gulf islands. Some of the more common species found on or near the water are listed below.

Bittern, American
Cormorants: Brant, double-crested, pelagic
Coot, American
Ducks: (perching) wood; (dabbling) mallard, green-winged teal, northern pintail, blue-winged, northern shoveler, widgeons; canvas-backed, ring-necked, greater and lesser scaups; surf scoters, oldsquaw, harlequin, common and Barrow's goldeneye, bufflehead; ruddy
Egrets: cattle
Geese: Canada, Brant
Grebes: pied-billed, red-necked, eared, western
Gulls, jaegers and terns: numerous species
Herons: great blue
Loons: red-throated, common
Mergansers: hooded, common, red-breasted
Murres, murrelets, auks, puffins, guillemots
Pelicans: brown
Shorebirds: plovers, avocets, stilts, sandpipers, phalaropes
Eagles: bald, golden
Falcons: kestrel
Hawks: red-tailed, northern goshawk, rough-legged
Osprey
Owls: spotted, great horned, snowy, barn, screech, short-eared, sawhet
Turkey vulture
Crows and ravens
Jays: Steller
Killdeer
Kingfisher, belted
Woodpeckers: downy, pileated, red-breasted sapsucker, northern flicker

Trees
Alders: red, mountain, Sitka
Arbutus (Pacific madrone)
Birch: northwestern and western white
Dogwood
Evergreens: Douglas fir, western and red hemlock, western red cedar, dwarf juniper
Garry oak
Maple: broadleaf, vine

Shrubs
Berries: Blackberry, elderberry, currants, huckleberry, raspberry
Broom
Gorse
Hazel
Honeysuckle
Kinnikinnick
Manzanita
Mountain ash
Rhododendron
Salal
Salmonberry

APPENDIX E
Key VHF Radio Channels

Emergency
16—Calling and distress
06—Ship-to-ship safety
22A—Coast Guard working channel (B.C.)
Search & Rescue
B.C. tel: 800-742-1313;
US: call Coast Guard Seattle group

Weather Channels
WX-1—Seattle, Neah Bay, Comox
WX-2—Seattle, Saltspring Island
WX-3—Victoria, Vancouver
21 B—Vancouver, Victoria

Canadian Marinas & Yacht Clubs
68—South of Campbell River
73—North of Campbell River

Port Operations & Marinas
66—Puget Sound marinas
68—Southern B.C. & some San Juan Islands marinas
78 or 78A—used by many San Juan Islands marinas

Marine Telephone Operators
23—Vancouver
24—Everett
25—Port Angeles, Seattle, Vancouver
26—Bellingham
27—Victoria, Ganges
64—Ganges, Campbell River
85—West Vancouver, Bellingham
87—Whidbey I., Nanaimo
88—Vancouver

Ship-to-Ship
68, 69, 72, 78A

Vessel Traffic Services
11—Vancouver, Sector 1 (southern Strait of Georgia)
12—Vancouver, Sector 3 (Vancouver Hbr)
14—Seattle
71—Vancouver, Sector 4 (north of Strait of Georgia)
74—Vancouver, Sector 2 (Fraser River)
74—Tofino (west coast of Vancouver Island)

APPENDIX F
Cascadia Marine Trail Sites & Coordinates

Editor's Note: We include only those kayak sites covered in this book.

North Sound

Site	Latitude	Longitude
Cypress Head DNR	48°33.05' N	122°40.00' W
Deception Pass State Park	48°25.10' N	122°46.00' W
Lummi Island	48°39.50' N	122°37.85' W
Oak Bay County Park	48°01.54' N	122°43.60' W
Oak Harbor City Park	48°17.00' N	122°39.50' W
Pelican Beach DNR	48°36.00' N	122°42.10' W
Saddlebag Island	48°32.10' N	122°33.30' W
Strawberry Island DNR	48°33.70' N	122°44.05' W

San Juan Islands

Site	Latitude	Longitude
Blind Island State Park	48°35.05' N	122°56.20' W
Griffin Bay DNR	48°50.30' N	123°05.00' W
James Island	48°30.60' N	122°46.50' W
Jones Island	48°37.00' N	123°03.05' W
Obstruction Pass DNR	48°36.05' N	122°49.50' W
Point Doughty DNR	48°42.59' N	122°57.11' W
Posey Island State Park	48°37.10' N	123°10.00' W
Spencer Spit State Park	48°32.15' N	122°51.25' W
Stuart Island State Park	48°40.61' N	123°12.28' W

APPENDIX G
Sources of Charts, Books, & Information

Your ship's chandlery and nautical bookstore can supply you with nautical charts and books listed in the Bibliography, or contact:

Armchair Sailor
2110 Westlake Ave. North
Seattle, WA 98109
Tel: 800-875-0852, 206-283-0858;
fax: 206-285-1935

Compass Rose Nautical Books
9785 4th Street
Sidney, B.C. V8L 2Y9
Tel: 250-656-4674
Fax: 250-656-4760
email: compassrose@bc.sympatico.ca

Ecomarine Ocean Kayak Centre
1668 Duranleau Street
Vancouver, B.C. V6H 3S4
Canada
Tel: 604-689-7575; fax: 604-689-5926;
email: cladner@direct.ca

Eddyline Watersports Center
1019 Q Avenue
Anacortes, WA 98221
Tel: 360-299-2300

Tanners Books and Gifts
2436 Beacon Street
Sidney, B.C. V8L 4X3
Canada
Tel: 250-656-2345; fax: 250-656-0662

MARINE PARKS INFORMATION

For information on Marine Parks or to request a map, contact:

Provincial Marine Parks
Ministry of Environment, Lands & Parks
2nd Floor, 800 Johnson Street
Victoria, B.C. V84 1X4
Tel: 250-387-5002; fax: 250-387-5757

Washington State Parks Launch & Moorage Permit Program
Tel: 360-902-8608

APPENDIX H
Suggested Itineraries

San Juan Islands

Day 1 Blind bay (Shaw Island)
Spencer Spit (Lopez Island)
Day 2 West Sound (Orcas Island
Deer Harbor (Orcas Island)
Friday Harbor (San Juan Island)
Day 3 Roche Harbor (San Juan Island)
Day 4 Prevost Harbor (Stuart Island)
Reid Harbor (Stuart Island)
Day 5 Fossil Bay (Sucia Islands)
Echo Bay (Sucia Islands)
Day 6 Rosario Resort (Orcas Island)
Olga (Orcas Island)

Gulf Islands

Day 1 Victoria (Vancouver Island)
Oak Bay (Vancouver Island)
Day 2 Sidney (Vancouver Island)
Beaumont Marine Park (South Pender Island)
Day 3 Montague Harbour Marine Park (Galiano Island)
Winter Cove Marine Park (Saturna Island)
Day 4 Princess Cove (Wallace Island)
Day 5 Telegraph Harbour (Thetis Island)
Day 6 Pirates Cove Marine Park (De Courcey Island)
Day 7 Silva Bay (Gabriola Island)
Newcastle Marine Park (Newcastle Island)

Bibliography & References

Anderson, Hugo.*Secrets of Cruising the New Frontier, British Columbia Coast and Undiscovered Inlets.* Anacortes: Anderson Publishing Company, 1995.

Bailey, Jo, and Nyberg, Carl. *Gunkholing in the San Juan Islands* to be published in late 1998.

Blier, Richard K. *Island Adventures, An Outdoors Guide to Vancouver Island.* Victoria: Orca Book Publishers, 1989.

Calhoun, Bruce. *Cruising the San Juan Islands*, 2nd Edition. Bellevue, Washington: Weatherly Press, 1991.

Canadian Tide and Current Tables, Pacific Coast, Vols. 5 and 6 [issued annually]. Ottawa: Department of Fisheries and Oceans.

Chettleburgh, Peter. *An Explorer's Guide: Marine Parks of British Columbia.* Vancouver: Special Interest Publications, 1985.

Douglass, Don and Hemingway-Douglass, Réanne. *Exploring the North Coast of British Columbia, Cape Caution and Nakwakto Rapids to Dixon Entrance; includes the Queen Charlotte Islands.* Bishop, California: Fine Edge Productions, 1996.

_______. *Exploring the South Coast of British Columbia, Gulf Islands and Desolation Sound to Port Hardy & Blunden Harbour.* Bishop, California: Fine Edge Productions, 1996.

Fox, Duane. *The Marina Handbook, S.W. British Columbia Edition.* Nanaimo, British Columbia: Fox Pacific Marine Publications.

Fox, William T. *At the Sea's Edge.* New York: Prentice Hall Press, 1983.

Hill, Beth and Ray. *Indian Petroglyphs of the Pacific Northwest.* Saanichton, British Columbia: Hancock House Publishers Ltd., 1974.

Horn, Elizabeth L. *Coastal Wildflowers of the Pacific Northwest.* Missoula: Mountain Press Publishing Company, 1994.

Jones, Elaine. *The Northern Gulf Islands Explorer: The Outdoor Guide.* Vancouver/Toronto: Whitecap Books, 1991.

Kozloff, Eugene N. *Plants and Animals of the Pacific Northwest.* Seattle: University of Washington Press, 1976.

Kutz, David. *The Burgee: Premier Marina Guidebook,* 2nd Edition. Kingston, WA: Pierside Publishing, 1996.

Marine Weather Hazards Manual, a guide to local forecasts and conditions, 2nd Edition. Vancouver: Environment Canada, 1990.

Mueller, Marge and Ted. *The San Juan Islands, Afoot & Afloat,* 2nd Edition. Seattle: The Mountaineers, 1988.

Northwest Boat Travel, Anacortes: Anderson Publishing Company, published annually.

Obee, Bruce. *The Gulf Islands Explorer: The Outdoor Guide*: Vancouver/Toronto, Whitecap Books, Second Edition, 1990; Fourth Printing, 1994.

Pacific Coast, List of Lights, Buoys and Fog Signals. Canadian Coast Guard, Marine Navigation Services, 1992.

Renner, Jeff. *Northwest Marine Weather, from the Columbia River to Cape Scott.* Seattle: The Mountaineers, 1993.

Sailing Directions—British Columbia Coast (South Portion), Ottawa: Department of Fisheries and Oceans, Vol 1, Fifteenth Edition, 1990.

Small Craft Guide, British Columbia. Vol. 1, Seventh Edition. Sidney, B.C.: Department of Fisheries and Oceans, Institute of Ocean Sciences, 1989.

Small Fishing Vessel Safety Manual. Ottawa: Minister of Supply and Services, 1993.

Snively, Gloria. *Exploring the Seashore.* West Vancouver: Gordon Soules Book Publishers Ltd., 1978, sixth printing, 1985.

Stewart, Hilary. *Looking at Totem Poles.* Vancouver: Douglas & McIntyre, 1993.

Thomson, Richard E. *Oceanography of the British Columbia Coast.* Ottawa: Department of Fisheries and Oceans, Fisheries and Aquatic Sciences 56, 1981.

United States Coast Pilot 7, Pacific Coast, 31st Edition. Washington, D.C.: National Ocean Service, 1997.

Vassilopoulos, Peter. *Docks and Destinations: San Juan Islands to Port Hardy.* Vancouver: Seagraphic Publications, 1994.

Waggoner Cruising Guides. Edited by Robert Hale. Bellevue: Weatherly Press, published annually.

Wolferstan, Bill. *Gulf Islands, Cruising Guide to British Columbia,* Vol. 1. Vancouver: Whitecap Books.

Index

Please Note: Names in italics refer to sidebars

NAUTICAL TITLES FROM FINE EDGE PRODUCTIONS:

Exploring the San Juan and Gulf Islands

Cruising Paradise of the Pacific Northwest

by Don Douglass and Réanne Hemingway-Douglass

Contributions by Anne Vipond, Peter Fromm, and Warren Miller

The first publication to document all the anchor sites in the paradise of islands that straddles the U.S.-Canadian border, an area bounded by Deception Pass and Anacortes on the south, Nanaimo on the north, Victoria on the west, and Bellingham on the east. ISBN 0-938665-51-0

Exploring the South Coast of British Columbia Coast

Gulf Islands and Desolation Sound to Port Hardy and Blunden Harbour

by Don Douglass and Réanne Hemingway-Douglass

"Clearly the most thorough, best produced and most useful [guides] available . . . particularly well thought out and painstakingly researched." —*NW Yachting* ISBN 0-938665-44-8

Exploring the North Coast of British Columbia

Blunden Harbour to Dixon Entrance—Including the Queen Charlotte Islands

by Don Douglass and Réanne Hemingway-Douglass

Describes previously uncharted Spiller Channel and Griffin Passage, the stunning scenery of Nakwakto Rapids and Seymour Inlet, Fish Egg Inlet, Queens Sound, and Hakai Recreation Area. It helps you plot a course for the beautiful South Moresby Island of the Queen Charlottes, with its rare flora and fauna and historical sites of native Haida culture. ISBN 0-938665-45-6

Exploring the Inside Passage to Alaska

A Cruising Guide

by Don Douglass and Réanne Hemingway-Douglass

Almost completely protected, these waters give access to a pristine wilderness of breathtaking beauty—thousands of islands, deeply-cut fjords, tidewater glaciers and icebergs. ISBN 0-938665-33-2

Exploring Vancouver Island's West Coast

A Cruising Guide

by Don Douglass

With five great sounds, sixteen major inlets, and an abundance of spectacular wildlife, the largest island on the west coast of North America is a cruising paradise. ISBN 0-938665-33-2

FOR ALL NAUTICAL TITLES SEE WEB SITE: www.fineedge.com

GPS Instant Navigation

A Practical Guide from Basics to Advanced Techniques

by Kevin Monahan and Don Douglass

"If you want the greatest possible benefit from GPS, I strongly recommend this book. The illustrated techniques will save you time and clearly explain the system."
—John Neal, Bluewater sailor, *Mahina Tiare*

This book introduces the novice to the basics of instant navigation and carries him to advanced techniques of error reduction, electronic charting, and navigation software.
ISBN 0-938665-48-0

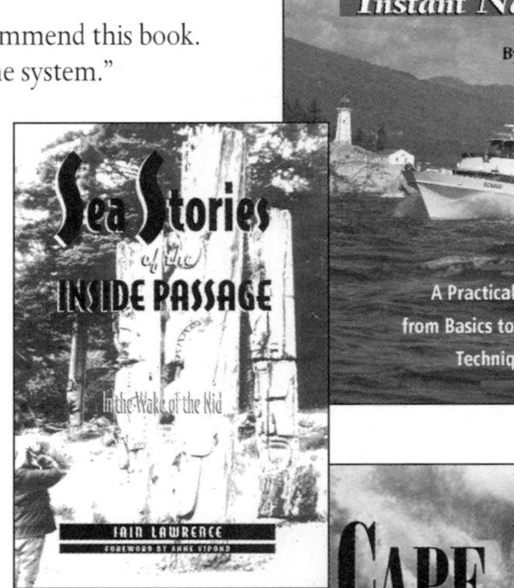

Sea Stories of the Inside Passage

by Iain Lawence

A collection of first-person experiences about cruising the North Coast; entertaining and insightful writing by the author of *Far-Away Places.* ISBN 0-938665-47-2

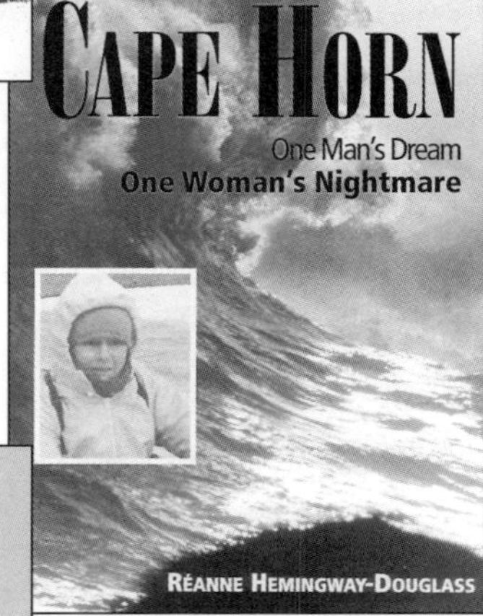

Cape Horn

One Man's Dream, One Woman's Nightmare

by Réanne Hemingway-Douglass

"This is the sea story to read if you read only one."
—McGraw Hill, International Marine Catalog

"The book grabbed me by the throat. . . . A true story about a couple in a ketch that pitchpoled on the edge of the Screaming 50s off southern Chile, the book, written by the wife, is easily the hairy-chested adventure yarn of the decade, if not the half-century."
—Peter H. Spectre, *Wooden Boat* ISBN 0-938665-29-4

Up the Lake with a Paddle

by Bill Van der Ven

Written by a local expert, this unique canoeing and kayaking guide covers the quiet waters of the Sierra Foothill Rivers and Reservoirs in the greater Sacramento area. Each paddle description features trip maps, route and hazard information, parking and observations on natural history."
ISBN 0-938665-54-5

Proven Cruising Routes for the Inside Passage to Alaska

by Don Douglass

3000 waypoints for routes, entrances, and anchoring, from Seattle to Glacier Bay. ISBN 0-938665-49-9

Trekka Round the World

by John Guzzwell

Long out-of-print, this international classic is the story of Guzzwell's circumnavigation on his 20-foot yawl *Trekka.* Includes previously unpublished photos and a foreword by America's renowned bluewater sailor-author Hal Roth. ISBN 0-938665-56-1

About the Authors

Don Douglass and Réanne Hemingway-Douglass have sailed from 60°N to 56°S latitude—Alaska to Cape Horn—logging more than 150,000 miles of offshore cruising over the past twenty-five years. They consider the Northwest as some of their favorite cruising grounds, and they spend summers exploring on their diesel trawler, *Baidarka.* The Douglasses have also kayaked extensively in the Northwest.

Don, who began exploring Northwest waters in 1949 as a boy, has crewed on the Inside Passage on everything from pleasure craft to commercial fishing boats and a Coast Guard icebreaker. He holds an engineering degree from Cal Poly University and an MBE from Claremont Graduate University. He is the author of *Exploring Vancouver Island's West Coast,* and with Réanne co-authored *Exploring the South Coast of British Columbia, Exploring the North Coast of British Columbia,* and the acclaimed *Exploring the Inside Passage to Alaska.* Articles by the Douglasses have appeared in *Pacific Yachting, Cruising World* and other outdoor magazines. Don is an honorary member of the International Association of Cape Horners.

Réanne Hemingway-Douglass, who holds a BA in French from Pomona College, attended the University of Grenoble, France, and Claremont Graduate University. A former French instructor, Réanne is now a full-time editor and writer. Her book, *Cape Horn: One Man's Dream, One Woman's Nightmare,* which describes their pitchpoling 800 miles northwest of Cape Horn and self-rescue in the seas and channels of Patagonia, will appear in both French and Italian translations in late 1998.

Authors at Ellerslie Falls

Anne Vipond, of Vancouver, B.C., is a writer-photographer, a regular contributor to *Pacific Yachting,* and author of the best-selling guidebook *Alaska by Cruise Ship.* Anne often collaborates with her husband and journalist William Kelly.

Peter Fromm, a resident of the San Juan Islands since 1975, is a professional photographer, journalist, and captain of whale-watching boats. He is the author of *Whale Tales: Human Interactions with Whales.*

Warren Miller, resident of the San Juan Islands, is known for his innumerable skiing and surfing films and his humorous books and syndicated newspaper columns.

Preliminary design for the next Fine Edge Productions Research Vessel

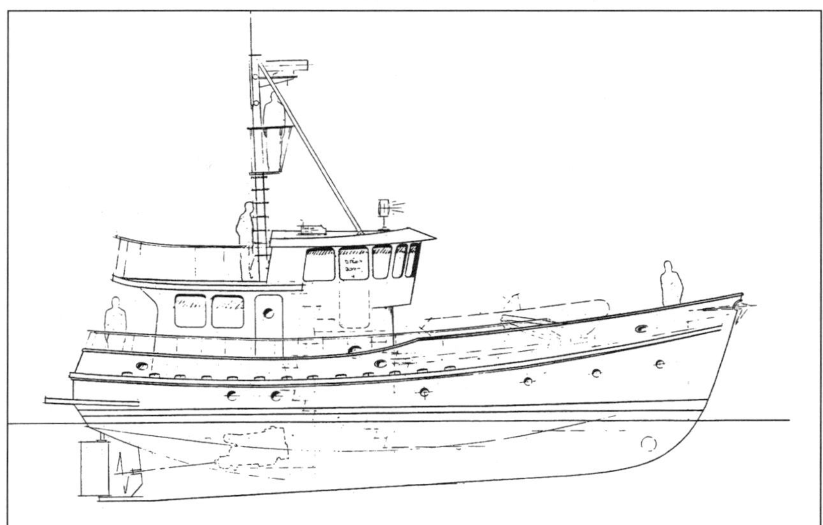

This future *Baidarka* by designer Scott Sprague follows the lines of a serious high-latitude trawler known for simplicity and safety. The design, which emphasizes superior comfort and reliability, is built for a couple who want to feel at home while exploring remote cruising grounds of the world. Sales information is available from publisher Don Douglass (tel: 760-387-2412 or visit Fine Edge web site at www.fineedge.com)

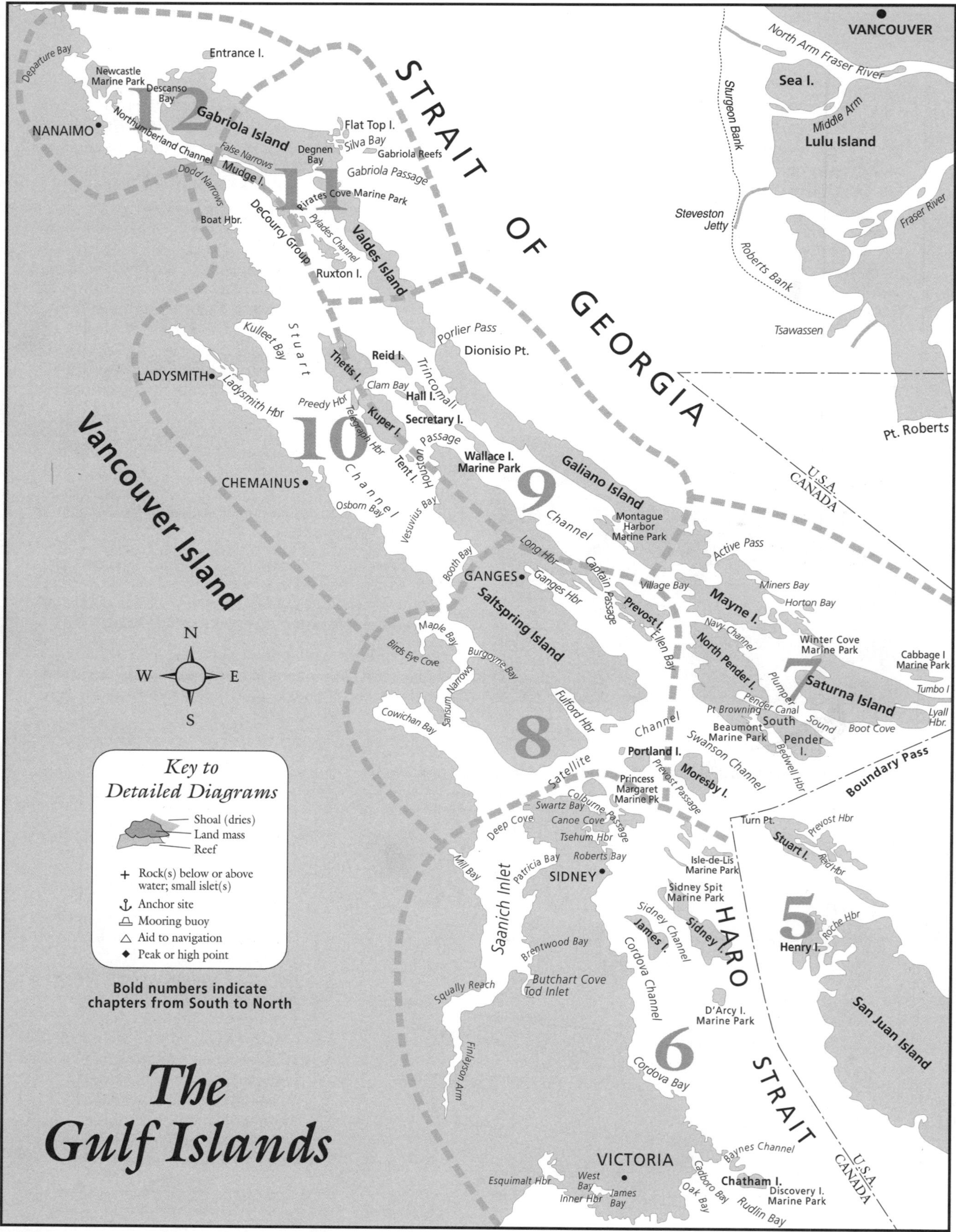
The Gulf Islands
STRAIT OF GEORGIA
VANCOUVER
North Arm Fraser River
Sea I.
Sturgeon Bank
Middle Arm
Lulu Island
Steveston Jetty
Fraser River
Roberts Bank
Tsawassen
Pt. Roberts
U.S.A.
CANADA
Departure Bay
Entrance I.
Newcastle Marine Park
Descanso Bay
NANAIMO
Gabriola Island
Northumberland Channel
False Narrows
Mudge I.
Dodd Narrows
Flat Top I.
Silva Bay
Degnen Bay
Gabriola Reefs
Gabriola Passage
Pirates Cove Marine Park
Boat Hbr.
DeCourcy Group
Pylades Channel
Valdes Island
Ruxton I.
Kulleet Bay
Stuart
Porlier Pass
Dionisio Pt.
LADYSMITH
Ladysmith Hbr
Thetis I.
Reid I.
Trincomali
Clam Bay
Hall I.
Preedy Hbr
Telegraph Hbr
Kuper I.
Secretary I.
Passage
Vancouver Island
CHEMAINUS
Channel
Osborn Bay
Tent I.
Houston
Vesuvius Bay
Wallace I. Marine Park
Galiano Island
Channel
Montague Harbor Marine Park
Active Pass
Long Hbr
Captain Passage
Booth Bay
GANGES
Ganges Hbr
Village Bay
Miners Bay
Horton Bay
Mayne I.
Prevost I.
Saltspring Island
Navy Channel
Ellen Bay
Winter Cove Marine Park
Cabbage I Marine Park
Maple Bay
Birds Eye Cove
Burgoyne Bay
North Pender I.
Plumper
Saturna Island
Tumbo I
Sansum Narrows
Fulford Hbr
Pt Browning
Pender Canal
Sound
Lyall Hbr.
Cowichan Bay
Channel
South Pender I.
Beaumont Marine Park
Boot Cove
Swanson Channel
Bedwell Hbr
Boundary Pass
Portland I.
Satellite
Prevost Passage
Moresby I.
Princess Margaret Marine Pk
Swartz Bay
Colburne Passage
Canoe Cove
Deep Cove
Tsehum Hbr
Turn Pt.
Prevost Hbr
Stuart I.
Reid Hbr
Mill Bay
Patricia Bay
Roberts Bay
Isle-de-Lis Marine Park
SIDNEY
Saanich Inlet
Sidney Spit Marine Park
Sidney Channel
James I.
Sidney I.
HARO
Henry I.
Roche Hbr
Brentwood Bay
Cordova Channel
Butchart Cove
Tod Inlet
Squally Reach
D'Arcy I. Marine Park
San Juan Island
Finlayson Arm
Cordova Bay
STRAIT
VICTORIA
Baynes Channel
Esquimalt Hbr
West Bay
Inner Hbr
James Bay
Cadboro Bay
Oak Bay
Chatham I.
Discovery I. Marine Park
Rudlin Bay
12
11
10
9
8
7
6
5
N
W
E
S
Key to Detailed Diagrams
Shoal (dries)
Land mass
Reef
+ Rock(s) below or above water; small islet(s)
Anchor site
Mooring buoy
Aid to navigation
Peak or high point
Bold numbers indicate chapters from South to North